National Identity and Social Cohesion in a Time of Geopolitical and Economic Tension: Australia – European Union – Slovenia

Robert Walters

National Identity and Social Cohesion in a Time of Geopolitical and Economic Tension: Australia – European Union – Slovenia

Springer

Robert Walters
Victoria University
Melbourne, VIC, Australia

ISBN 978-981-15-2163-8 ISBN 978-981-15-2164-5 (eBook)
https://doi.org/10.1007/978-981-15-2164-5

This Springer imprint is published by the registered company Springer Nature Singapore Pte Ltd.
The registered company address is: 152 Beach Road, #21-01/04 Gateway East, Singapore 189721, Singapore

This book is dedicated to my late father, Mr. Gordon Walters, and mother, Pam Walters, who have supported, inspired, and encouraged me to connect with my historical roots in Slovenia and Europe. My father had a profound impact on me as a child and throughout my teenage and early adult years. His guidance, wisdom, and mentoring provided the platform for me to always test, push, and better myself. Dad was more than a father; he was my best mate. Still to this day, I miss our weekly chats over coffee about cycling, cars, engineering, construction, and world affairs. Both Dad and Mum got me out of an orphanage in Melbourne, Australia, at age 5 after being there since 5 weeks old. Also, thanks to Mum's family specifically Heather and Janet whom I spent a lot of time with when younger.

Special thanks to my wife, Catherine Tan-Walters. Thanks also to my brother, Scott, and his family and to Marko Palajzer and his family for hosting me on many occasions while in Slovenia. A sincere thanks and gratitude to Dr. Robert Banagan and Dr. Stephen Theiler for the amazing work I did with them.

Foreword

Every nation-state has established its own national identity. Australia and Slovenia are no different. What is different is the fact that Slovenia is part of the European Union (EU), and their national identity is heavily influenced by the EU. The EU has established a supernational identity that is based on similar democratic values to that of Australia (human rights and the single market). The EU's identity, in part, is far reaching, and third countries such as Australia have looked to the EU for guidance and direction, particularly in regard to human rights law. Nonetheless, the EU, Australia, and Slovenia have been developing and continue to develop their respective identities, although they are quite different. A national and regional identity (of the EU) includes, but is not limited to, language, culture, religion, democracy and its institutions, and the rule of law. Identity is a contested concept and can invoke different responses and, in part, makes an important contribution to social cohesion. Part of a state's national identity is conferred through citizenship. This has been achieved by the state (including the EU) through their respective legislation framework, which includes citizenship, immigration, rights, and private international laws. These laws are used to reinforce, underpin, and strengthen identity and bring the community together. This book discusses the *public* and private aspects of citizenship. The public constitutes the state developing laws for citizenship, immigration, rights, and conflict of laws. The *private* constitutes those private activities undertaken by a citizen such as migrating from one state to another and engaging other citizens in marriage and divorce. The rights of citizens also constitute the private as it enables a citizen to protect themselves from other citizens and the state. A dichotomy that has emerged in the modern era is how states have a need to balance their economic and nationalist ambitions with laws that encourage immigration, citizenship, rights, and private activities. That is, the principles of these laws appear to be well settled. It is the national, regional, and international political overlay that challenges the way states develop these laws. Over the past century, these laws have been liberalized, although, as society changes, these laws have been tightened to strengthen the expression of national identity and social cohesion. A more pervasive dichotomy is the challenges states and the EU are likely to face in the future to retain and even strengthen their respective identities and social cohesion from continued geopolitical shocks, economic volatility, and environmental degradation. These alone pose some of the most complex political and policy issues facing all nation-states. However, the EU can be held up as a polity that has developed an identity and level of cohesion while allowing member states to retain their national identities. It has also been successful in holding back the rise of nationalism and nationalist practices up until the last decade. In other words, the very foundations of liberal democracy could be diluted from the impact of these challenges. The basic foundations of rights have, in part, already been diluted from the rise of terrorism, which is acceptable; however, the geopolitical differences pose a significant challenge in and of themselves. Therefore, this book confirms that citizenship is multidimensional and has been known to include and be used to define the legal status of a citizen. The multidimensional role citizenship has is complex both legally and politically. It is arguably used to strengthen a national or supernational identity. On the other hand, it is used as a tool to integrate and strengthen the social cohesion across a community. This is particularly important to multicultural societies. This book confirms there is currently no consensus of what citizenship and the respective laws that underpin it will look like in the future. However, it is safe to say that the legal principles of citizenship such as obtaining citizenship by birth, descent, or naturalization are unlikely to change anytime soon. Finally, this book aims to enrich the thinking and discussion in relation to the importance that citizenship, immigration, rights, and private laws play in the modern world, economically and socially. It also aims to reinforce the current liberal approach to the acceptance of multiculturalism across Australia, Europe, and Slovenia while considering the respective sovereign needs and Western democratic values to be upheld.

European Faculty of Law
Nova Gorica, Slovenia

Arne Mavčič,
Peter Jambrek
Marko Novak

Preface

It gives me great pleasure to introduce Robert Walters book *National Identity and Social Cohesion in a Time of Geopolitical and Economic Tension: Australia, European Union, Slovenia*, which is drawn from his doctoral thesis undertaken at Victoria University. He was my first doctoral student, and it is a privilege to share his journey. His Associate Supervisor was Professor, Dr. Arne Mavčič of the European Law School, Slovenia, and Robert successfully negotiated three legal systems and three supervisors on opposite sides of the globe. His second Associate Supervisor Professor, Dr. Bruno Zeller assisted in navigating the various different areas of law covered in his doctoral thesis. We have now welcomed him to the Faculty of the College of Law and Justice, Victoria University, Melbourne Australia.

The thesis was inspired by Robert himself holding Slovenian (European) and Australian citizenship. He also holds a long-term visitor pass of Singapore, and thus, he has a good understanding of the various citizenship and immigration laws across various jurisdictions. The combination of a significant Slovenian community in Australia and the emergence of an independent Slovenia in our adult lifetimes gave Robert the inspiration to compare these two very different countries, along with the European Union, that are grappling with their identity in a changing world.

Australia is a former British colony which federated in 1901, forged a new identity on the battlefields of the First World War, asserted its independence in 1942 under the threat of Japanese invasion, created its own citizenship in 1948, and only in 1986 severed all legal ties with Great Britain while continuing to share a Queen. Slovenia was colonized by the Romans and the Austrians, lumped in after the First World War with the Serbs and Croats in a state which was first a kingdom, then became Yugoslavia, and then the Republic of Yugoslavia, became a Republic in the Federal Republic of Yugoslavia, and then finally an independent republic in 1991. Slovenia immediately applied to join the European Union and was admitted in 2004.

Australia has lived through the transformation of the British Empire into the Commonwealth of Nations and changed its identity from being part of Britain to being part of Asia but retains its oddity as a Western, predominantly ethnic European country in Southeast Asia. Australia has been a country of immigration, receiving several million immigrants since 1945. Until the late 1960s, almost all of those immigrants were from Europe, including some thousands from Slovenia. In the last 50 years, the migration intake has been much more diverse. Slovenia by contrast has been a country of emigration with a large diaspora spread all around the world. Australia has wrestled with transformation from British to multicultural identity while also acknowledging its indigenous population, who only gained full citizenship in 1967. Slovenia has had an identity for many centuries but has only been a fully independent republic since 1991. In their different circumstances, it is not surprising that the two countries have rather different conceptions of citizenship. They also have very different approaches to immigration, rights protection, and private international law.

The EU has taken on some of the trappings of statehood, but the defeat of the Constitutional Treaty and subsequent resurgence of nationalism have caused it to take a step back. It has taken over many state functions but has not supplanted the member states in the hearts of its citizens. The author carefully and skillfully explores and compares the citizenship, immigration, rights protection, and private international law of the three jurisdictions and finds much that they can learn from each other. I congratulate him on his achievements and commend the book.

College of Law & Justice
Victoria University
Melbourne, VIC, Australia

Matt Harvey

Acknowledgement

Special thanks to Dr. Matt Harvey, Professor Dr. Arne Mavčič, and Professor Dr. Bruno Zeller for their guidance and direction and for reviewing several drafts of this work. Since completing this book and my PhD, Professor Zeller, Professor Trakman, and I have also published extensively in data protection law, along with international trade, finance, and arbitration law.

Thanks to Professor Mavčič for looking over and confirming the interpretation of the Slovenian and European components throughout this book. He has a remarkable legal and policy background that spans Eastern, Central, and Western Europe. He has written extensively on the Slovenian Constitution Law and was the Liaison Officer for Slovenia to the Commission for Democracy through Law (Venice Commission) under the Council of Europe between 1991 and 2009, the National Correspondent for Slovenia to the ACCPUF Paris (1998–2009), a Member of Slovenia to the EU Network of Experts for Human Rights (2002–2006) and of Slovenia of the EU FRALEX (from 2006), and a Fulbright Scholar. He continues to be engaged in practical, publication, and promotional activities in the fields of comparative constitutional review and human rights law and is associated with the European Faculty of Law and to the Faculty of Government and European Studies to the New University, Ljubljana, Slovenia.

Thanks to Professor Dr. Leon Trakman, University New South Wales, for taking the time to look over this book and identify gaps that needed to be addressed. He is a world authority in international trade, finance, data protection, and arbitration law. Our work with Professor Zeller continues today since meeting in 2016.

Thanks to Professor Kim Rubenstein, Faculty of Law, Australian National University, for assessing my thesis which was the basis for this book.

Contents

About the Author

Robert Walters is Lecturer of Law, Victoria University, Melbourne, Australia; Adjunct Professor in the European Faculty of Law, New University, Slovenia, Europe; and Member of the ASEAN Law Association Singapore, LAWASIA Australia, and United Nations Commission on International Trade Law Coordination Committee for Australia (UNCITRAL). For the past 3 years, he has presented papers to UNCITRAL throughout Asia and the Pacific. In 2019, he was appointed Member of the Asian Privacy (Data Protection) Scholars Network. Since completing his PhD, he now also specializes in data protection, artificial intelligence, technology (cybersecurity), and the law, along with international trade, finance, investment, and immigration/citizenship law with a particular emphasis on Australia, Asia-Pacific, Europe, and North America (APEC and ASEAN countries). He is admitted as an Australian Lawyer. Since 2016, he has been working closely with Professor Dr. Bruno Zeller, University Western Australia, and Professor Dr. Leon Trakman, University New South Wales, in areas of law and policy. He continues to work with Dr. Matt Harvey in this increasingly important area of citizenship, immigration, national identity, and social cohesion.

Abbreviations

AG	Advocate General
ASEAN	Association of Southeast Asian Nations
AU	Administrative Unit Slovenia
ECJ	European Court of Justice
ECoHR	European Court of Human Rights
ECFR	European Charter of Fundamental Rights 2000
EEC	Treaty Establishing the European Economic Community 1957
EU	European Union
FIRB	Foreign Investment Review Board Australia
IOM	International Organization for Migration
MS	Member States
NA	Slovenia National Assembly
OECD	Organisation for Economic Co-operation and Development
PIL	Private International Law
SC	Slovenian Constitution
SCC	Slovenian Constitutional Court
TEU	Treaties of the European Union
TFEU	Treaty on the Functioning of the European Union
TCN	Third Country National (noncitizen)
UNHCR	United Nations High Commissioner for Refugees
YU	Yugoslavia

Chapter 1
Australia, European Union and Slovenia

Abstract The concept of [national] identity and social cohesion are important political concepts to a state and supranational polity. They provide a sense of belonging and inclusiveness to citizens. This chapter will highlight that national identity, social coherence and citizenship are contested concepts, which have evolved over centuries. Today, citizenship provides a legal status. Secondly, citizenship affords a citizen with rights, duties and privileges. Thirdly, citizenship provides the collective of self-governance and to be active participants in the political community. The challenges facing national identity and social cohesion are multilayered and complex that can be directed by politics and to a lesser extent citizenship, immigration, rights and private international law. Moreover, citizenship is a form of identity (collective identity) and social membership that contributes to national identity in different ways. Citizenship has for centuries been used to develop and strengthen a national identity. That identity has enabled empires, communist, socialists, totalitarian, authoritarian and democratic rulers in the modern day nation state to build a level of cohesion and social engineering.

Keywords Citizenship · Immigration · National identity · Political community · Social cohesion

1.1 Introduction

The development, preservation and strengthening of the national identity and social cohesion in a time of the rise in geopolitical, economic, environment and security tensions, is complex and challenging. Since the rise of terrorism in the 2000s, there has been a rise in nationalist policy approaches that, have resulted in nation states strengthening their citizenship and immigration laws. The rise of geopolitical ten-

R. Walters, *National Identity and Social Cohesion in a Time of Geopolitical and Economic Tension: Australia – European Union – Slovenia*,
https://doi.org/10.1007/978-981-15-2164-5_1

sion across the world, is also resulting in nation states looking increasingly inward, and there has in some countries seen an increase in xenophobia behavior. The expansion in technology, degradation of the environment is also challenging national identity and social cohesion. However, this is nothing new. These policy drivers have been challenging the very notion of national identity for more than a century. The Australian Human Rights Commission expressed their concern in relation to the challenges facing social cohesion, in the contemporary period. They state that:

> We live in interesting times. We live in times when tolerance and harmony are becoming elusive, when intolerance and division are becoming the norm. In the United States, there have been calls for a wall to be built along the American border with Mexico, and having a ban on Muslims entering the country. In Britain, we've seen Brexit. Many of those voting for an exit from the European Union were motivated by a desire for Britain to reclaim its sovereignty on matters of immigration. There was a steep rise in hate crimes tied to the Brexit vote. In France, mayors from about 30 French towns along the sun-soaked Riviera have enforced a ban on the burkini. Many have said they will refuse to accept a recent ruling by the Council of State, France's highest administrative court, that held the ban to be unconstitutional. Elsewhere in Europe, social anxiety and cultural fear can be clearly detected. In Austria, there will be a re-run of its presidential election, which in May almost saw the far-right Freedom Party candidate Gerhart Holzinger claim victory. In Germany, for much of this year, the far-right Alternative for Germany party has been polling well above 15 per cent. In the Netherlands, Geert Wilders' Party for Freedom is leading the polls, and is pledging to ban all Islamic symbols and mosques. Across Scandinavia, anti-immigrant far-right parties have been growing in popularity, and are even partners in coalition governments. And, of course, we have seen far-right political organisations emerge, or re-emerge, here in Australia. During the past two years, protest movements targeting Islam have received significant media attention. Our parliament contains a number of senators who support a ban on Muslim immigration. These, then, are challenging times for liberal democracies. We are seeing social cohesion being tested across continents.[1]

The Organization for Economic Development (OECD), which takes a global view and have identified that while bringing opportunities and resources to fuel a more inclusive growth process, shifting wealth poses a series of challenges and risks for the cohesiveness of societies.[2] The OECD have predominantly taken an economic approach to future cohesion. First, the OECD identified that there are processes of shifting wealth and globalization have been accompanied by structural transformation in fast-growing economies with implications for social inclusion, social capital and social mobility. Second, they highlight that the shift in wealth has not necessarily been associated with sufficient employment creation, more formal jobs, or better gender outcomes. Third, the [re-]emergence of new growth poles has intensified both the pace of urbanization and South-South migration, which exacerbates the challenges that social cohesion faces in integrating immigrants. Furthermore, by threatening food security, both the steep increase in food prices observed in the 2000s and the large land-purchases occurring in many developing

---

[1]Australian Human Rights Commission, The Challenge of Social Cohesion (2016), https://www.humanrights.gov.au/about/news/speeches/challenge-social-cohesion

[2]Organisation for Economic Development, Perspective on Global Development 2012: Social Cohesion In A Shifting World, OECD Publishing. https://doi.org/10.1787/persp_glob_dev-2012-en

countries – as fast growing, land- scarce developing countries try to secure access to food – could also potentially compromise social cohesion.[3] The resulting effect from these challenges is the possible rise in migration, which will have a direct impact on citizenship and immigration law. It also challenges identity and cohesion, along with the possibility of putting pressure on private international law and rights.

Moreover, Christian Larsen in referring to the OECD expands on social coherence by highlighting the complex challenges faced by multiculturalism. He argues that similarity of mind is difficult and problematic to create in diverse multicultural and highly differentiated societies. However, a shared perception of unknown fellow citizens being trustworthy is highly relevant in order to make such societies work.[4] Larsen goes onto to say that a shared perception of fellow citizens being trustworthy is not easily achieved. Such "societal glue" is unlikely to be created by societies simply being wealthier. On the contrary, the increased economic inequality often attached to economic progress is likely to lower trust levels. Social trust in diverse multicultural and highly differentiated societies is dependent on collective political actions aiming at creating a coherent society; this is an ongoing nation building process.[5] Pivotal in this nation building process are a moderation of economic inequalities and the establishment of uncorrupt state institutions.[6] Social cohesion like identity, citizenship, immigration and rights is multilayered. They all challenge the state economically and socially. There is no better example as Larsen highlights with the rapid economic growth across Asia, which has lifted a large proportion of the world population out of severe poverty. This has also been the experience of economic development in India, Indonesia and other emerging countries.[7] However, the same process has pushed the issue of social integration to the forefront. Terms such as "inclusive economic growth" and "social inclusion" have in many countries reached the top of the political agenda. For instance, countries in Asia have launched the concept of a harmonious society.[8] The idea is to create a better balance than had been the case in the social development of some state. Larson goes onto say that most of the rich Western countries have also experienced a rapid increase in economic inequality. These economic developments have pushed the issue of social integration or social cohesion up the political agenda; but so has the general economic and cultural globalization, the flow of migrants across nation borders and the security concerns after 9/11.[9] This is also evident in most democratic states, as they continue to develop economic and social policies that marginalise the poor, weeks and those that are in the lower socio economic classes. However, apart from the geopolitical and security issues on the horizon, the world

---

[3] Ibid.

[4] Larsen, C, (2014) *Social cohesion: Definition, measurement and developments*, https://www.un.org/esa/socdev/egms/docs/2014/LarsenDevelopmentinsocialcohesion.pdf

[5] Ibid.

[6] Ibid.

[7] Ibid.

[8] Ibid.

[9] Ibid.

economy for more than a decade has been facing significant hurdles. This alone poses enormous challenges to identity and cohesion, as people from poorer nations want to relocate to wealthier states, to improve their economic situation. It places a lot of strain on state policy and legal frameworks that, support and include immigration, citizenship, rights and private international law.

These broader world and regional issues have not gone unnoticed in Australia, the EU and Slovenia. Both Australia and Slovenia, along with the EU continue to maintain a policy direction that goes along way to overcome those tensions that, are imposed on them by external forces. The development of any nation state, including Australia and Slovenia, including the broader EU territory have experienced significant geopolitical, economic and security tensions for more than a century. What sets Slovenia, the EU and Australia apart is their vastly different beginnings, location in the world, language and culture. The Slovene language can be traced over many centuries and is one of their most important elements of what defines a Slovene. The independent Slovenian state, which was established for the first time in 1991 was, in part, founded on its language.[10] Language is an important concept and forms an integral part of their national identity. On the one side, Slovenia has recognized the Slovene language as the official language of the state within the Slovene constitution. On the other side, English is the official language in Australia, although it is neither recognized in the constitution or in national legislation. The EU is made up of a multiple languages and cultures. For all of its complexities, the EU, in part, can be held up as being successful in building a sense of regional cohesion. It has established an identity that, is based on similar democratic principles to that of Australia and Slovenia. The identity of the EU cannot be underestimated. It is having far reaching impacts to third countries in the area of human rights. Australia is one third country that looks to the EU for guidance on human rights law, such as, data protection and privacy. However, the current status of cohesion in the EU, is currently under threat from member states wanting to leave, as a result of the rise in nationalist sentiment.

The question is how do these countries, along with the EU maintain and enhance social cohesion? This is a complex question, however citizenship and immigration, rights and private international law – do have a role, although varied. This book addresses some of these tensions, and poses a way forward, albeit a limited one, due to the many other policy and legal elements that need to be considered by a nation state to strengthen social coherence through the laws discussed in this book.

Notwithstanding the above, further questions arise as to what contribution citizenship, immigration, rights and other private laws make to a national identity? Furthermore, how can these legal concepts be reconciled with the development and current day national identity? Arguably, the concept of nation state, national identity, citizenship, immigration, human rights and private laws have evolved over many centuries. National identity provides citizens with a shared identity. This shared identity, can come in many different forms. For instance, it has been shaped by the rule of law. It is also influenced **by** culture, which in turn is shaped by

[10] Rupel, D, (2003) *Between National and European Identity: A view from Slovenia*, Cambridge Review of International Affairs, Vol *16*, No 2.

literature, religion, values, heritage, location, geography, maps, a national flag, sport, commerce, national anthem, amongst many other policy drivers.

Citizenship plays a different role to that of national identity. One could be mistaken for thinking that citizenship is standalone and has very little to do with national identity. Citizenship is bound up with the nation state and is often thought of in national terms.[11] Linda Bosniak believes that citizenship provides the basis for social integration and cohesion. Bosniak highlights that citizenship is the formal legal relationship between the individual and polity (nation state), and invokes the collective identity of the national community. This has been reinforced by Kim Rubenstien who, in the Australian context has argued that citizenship is an important component of, and too, identity and cohesion. The collective identity is a component of national identity, which goes some way to providing a level of cohesion.

Arguably, everyone has a national identity whether they like it or not.[12] However, this is contestable, particularly for those people that have no citizenship of any country and are declared stateless. Even people having no citizenship may identify with a community or tribe. They may also have a [national] identity that, is not officially recognized by the international community. Indigenous Australians can identify with a local tribe and community, along with national and state identity (e.g. Australia and the state of Victoria). People from different ethnic backgrounds that have Australian citizenship might identify as being both Australian and their country of origin (e.g. Slovenian). The same can be said in the former Yugoslavia where people in the Slovenian Republic may identify as being Slovenian or Yugoslav or both. Societies such as Australia, today, have evolved into an amalgam of ethnic groups, which have core values such as democracy, language, the rule of law, a fair go, but culturally it is very diverse. To a lesser extent, Slovenia is also diverse and made up of different ethnic groups. However, most of the ethnic groups that make up Slovenia today have come from surrounding territories such as Italy, Croatia, Austria, Republics of the former Yugoslavia and the Rom people.

As the nation state and national identity began to evolve, so too did citizenship. Citizenship began to take on a greater role by providing continuity when rulers over territory changed. The French Revolution had a profound influence on the development of citizenship, identity and to a lesser extent social cohesion. It also provided rulers and states with a tool to assist in unifying the population within a defined territory, since the Roman Empire. The concept itself has encouraged citizens to be active participants by promoting participatory democracy, focusing on the integration of foreigners. This is certainly true of the Australian, EU and to a lesser extent the Slovenian story. It wasn't until the decade of 2000s that Australia, the EU and Slovenia's policy approach would intersect and have to deal with similar international and regional security threats (terrorism), which resulted in legislative reform. At the same time, Slovenia was also preparing for membership to the European

[11] Bosniak, L, (2000) Citizenship Denationalised (The State of Citizenship Symposium), *Indiana Journal of Global Legal Studies*, Vol 7: Iss 2, 449.

[12] Bechhofer, F., McCrone, D, (2009) *National Identity, Nationalism and Constitutional Change*, Palgrave MacMillan, 1–5.

Union. More recently, Australia has begun extending citizenship to regulate the activities of its citizens-when abroad, such as stripping dual citizens of their Australian citizenship.

Today citizenship is more than a legal status. It is a bundle of rights that are provided by the state and international law. Apart from citizenship being acquired by birth and descent, it may also be acquired by naturalization. Therefore, migration is a pathway to citizenship. Migration is a complex area of law and this book explores a number of the visas and permits available for a noncitizen to enter either state. These include, business unification, education, humanitarian (refugees and asylum), and permanent residence. However, the added complexity in the case of Slovenia, is that their national immigration laws are directed by the EU. In other words, the EU's immigration law(s) and policy have to be implemented by all member states. The resulting effect is the requirement for Slovenia to transpose the immigration law of the EU into national immigration law.

Moreover, Slovenia has been required to incorporate the European Schengen Borders Code, Schengen Convention and associated regulations, directives and decisions into national law. Slovenian's upon membership to the European Union were able to move freely throughout other member states. However, for Australian's they would be considered third country nations and restrictions currently apply for entry and stay. That is, unless an Australian citizen has dual citizenship of Australia and Slovenia. In this case they are also afforded the same movement rights throughout the EU. Moreover, an Australian citizen only holding single citizenship of Australia, once they arrive in an EU member state they can also travel throughout the EU unimpeded. The difference is that, the dual Slovenia and Australian citizen will be able to stay longer than the normal 90-day period. It is argued that Slovenia in its early beginnings and an independent nation state did not welcome non Slovenes. Even so, as Slovenia became ever closer to the EU, they would have to adopt the more liberal European migration policy, however, and at the same time establish strong border controls. Slovenia has been an external border of the EU for more than a decade. Nevertheless, with Croatia recently becoming a member of the EU, the external border of the EU will shift away from Slovenia's southern border to Croatia, southern eastern and western borders.

Australia, on the other hand, and having a very different beginning has developed its own story. It is argued that Australia could look to the EU and Slovenia to modernise and update its visa framework. Australia, the EU and Slovenia's visa and permit frameworks are remarkably different. Slovenia has three permits whereas Australia has more than 100. Australia and Slovenia have established bilateral agreements to assist their respective citizens when present in either state (for social security and health care). Consideration could be given by both countries to extending the framework of bilateral agreements. The proposed development of the EU-Australian Free Trade Agreement may also be an opportunity for the respective states to expand strengthen their respective economic ties.

A further element to this book is the laws that govern the private activities of individuals in the globalized world. It is well understood that the mass movement of people across international borders has resulted in citizens engaging in private activities such as marriage, divorce, paternity, child maintenance, parental responsibility, international adoption, matrimonial property [immovable and common assets], inheritance and superannuation. Private international law helps facilitate transnational activities. This book will confirm that citizenship is not the deciding factor when determining the choice of laws in private international law. Exploring this later in the book provides a more complete picture of the laws affecting migration and the daily lives of citizens in a globalized and regionalized world.

Moreover, as society and nation states have matured so has their approach to their citizens also being citizens of another state. Dual citizenship has gone some way to establishing a more global or regional concept of citizenship. It has, largely, by accident gone along way to breaking down barriers of entry, exit and stay in countries that have accepted this liberal approach. Dual citizenship has assisted states in retaining a connection with those citizens who are mobile and resident in other nation states. In other words, dual citizenship assists the diaspora who are for a number of reasons residing in other countries, to retain their individual and collective relationship and formal network with the state. The diaspora of Slovenia and Australia are both vast and varied, being scattered across many countries. They contribute economically and socially to the state of origin and state of destination through the transfer of knowledge, skills, investment and trade. Their role in the polity cannot be underestimated. For instance, the Slovenian diaspora in Australia, along with the Slovene diaspora in Argentina and the United States have played crucial a role in the development of the modern day citizenship laws of Slovenia. Following independence, the Slovenian diaspora in these states lobbied Slovenian politicians to change the citizenship laws to ensure second, third and fourth generation Slovenians could obtain citizenship. Australia's diaspora in foreign countries is less developed but could include the source countries of many of its immigrants. Therefore, one aspect of the future of citizenship lies in the way states engage and maintain an ongoing connection with their citizens no matter where they have migrated to across the world. Doing so, strengthens a state's identity and cohesion, by exerting its values to other countries throughout the world.

However, and on the backdrop of the above, determining what the future holds for citizenship will be complex and a continuing evolving story. That is, as society changes and shifts, the subtle geopolitical challenges facing all nation states (e.g. the rise of Asia, nationalism and BREXT), could have enormous ramifications for the future of citizenship and more so for immigration. It can also challenge the vary nature and expression of rights, which has become an important feature of the EU, Slovenia and Australia. Therefore, strengthening the concept of citizenship for the future should require a state to have a modern day constitution that adequately reflects national identity, citizenship and the rights and freedoms afforded to its citizens. Slovenia can be used as an example of how a state has had the opportunity to develop a modern day legal framework that includes a constitution. This could assist Australia as its constitution was developed more than a century ago, and could be considered as outdated.

The comparative study of Slovenia, the European Union and Australia's respective citizenship, migration, rights and private international law (legislation) is stand alone. While, often not thought of as a likely comparison, it is argued that in the face of how society is shifting, the rise of nationalism and the ongoing impact of economic volatility and immigration, states are looking at ways to hold their citizens closer. The recent 2019 EU elections is a good example of how there has been a shift to a more nationalist approach to the political discourse. This shift could have far reaching implications for the future of citizenship, rights and particularly immigration. Thus, this book will demonstrate how three separate but distinct identities now exist in Australia, Slovenia and the EU. It will also highlight that while they are distinct identities, they are largely based on similar Western democratic principles. However, Slovenia even as part of the wider EU community still retain and continue to work towards strengthening their national identity. This is what sets them apart from other member states of the EU, and they should continue to be encourage to promote and exert their identity, within and outside the EU.

1.2 Methodology, Limitation and Structure

Comparing the laws and policy of Australia, the EU and Slovenia requires analysis of complex legal concepts, principles and jurisprudence. Comparative law is used as a means of effecting sameness and suppressing differences in the law.[13] Comparative legal research is the practice of comparing legal norms, case law, legal jurisprudence and legislation from different states and legal families. A comparative study of law from three different jurisdictions can be used to effect change and strengthen the law. Therefore, in adopting Peter de Cruz's methodology of comparative legal research provides the platform for understanding the subtle, but, significant difference between two legal families. de Cruz methodology considers the linguistic and terminological problems; cultural differences between legal systems; and the tendency to put one's own interpretation on legal concepts.[14]

Slovenia, along with the EU has adopted the civil law as the basis of its legal system, while Australia has inherited the common law legal system from its colonial origins. William Tetley[15] identifies 13 differences between legal families that include the order of jurisprudence and doctrine (their function and style). For instance, the doctrine of *stare decisis* under common law compels lower courts to follow decisions of higher courts, whereas, under civil law, the doctrine is unknown as judges only have the "authority of reason".[16] Furthermore, the drafting of legislation, which is applicable to this book, is somewhat different. That is, under civil law the

[13] Valentine Palmer, V, (2004) From Lerotholi to Lando: Some Examples of Comparative Law Methodology, *Global Jurist Frontiers*, Vol *4*, 12–24.

[14] de Cruz, P, (1991) *Comparative Law in a Changing World*, Cavendish Publishing Limited, 213.

[15] Tetley W, QC, (1999) *Mixed jurisdiction: common law vs civil law (codified and uncodified) (Part1)*, Unif. L. Rev, 591–617.

[16] Ibid.

legislation consists of codes and statutes that are concise.[17] The interpretation of legislation is undertaken differently between the legal codes. On the one side, the doctrine of jurisprudence constante[18] is important when discussing and comparing rules established by the judiciary, as the rules evolve in civil law. On the other side, the interpretation of common law legislation is objectively construed according to certain rules.[19] The interpretation of civil law legislation is often ambiguous to and applying it can require understanding the intention of the legislature by examining the entire legislation. The legislative analysis also includes international treaties and conventions, international case law and legislation of the European Union (conventions, treaties, regulations, directives and decisions).

The structure of the book has been deliberately based on time periods beginning in the first millennium BC to 2018. In other words, the analysis is also structured in time periods. This has enabled the evolution of citizenship and immigration law to be articulated clearly, while capturing the transition and developments of the respective identities of Australia, EU and Slovenia. In addition, and where possible, themes have been identified and discussed within the time periods. For instance, there has been significant political, social and economic events that have occurred, which have made a significant influence and contribution to national identity, citizenship and immigration. This provides clear points of reference where either state has been influenced by a significant geopolitical, economic, social or national political event. There is overlap in the discussion and analysis between 1990 and 1991 due to Slovenia becoming an independent state and establishing a new legal framework over those 2 years. It must be noted that the referencing due to referring to Slovenia, Yugoslav, European, Australia, International and law from when Slovenia was ruled by Empires and monarchs, has been duplicated, to ensure the reader understands the source.

This book offers a deliberate focus on the legislation and policy that was developed from 1990 following the fall of the former Yugoslav state, and the creation of an independent Republic of Slovenia. The comparative approach was selected to identify improvements for both states, including the EU, in order to maintain and enhance the ongoing adaptability of citizenship and immigration law in these jurisdictions. However, this book has its limitations. For example, due to the breadth of legislation including reports and case law analyzed: it was decided to only focus on those key elements of the law that directly relate to citizenship (obtained by birth, descent and naturalization) in the context of their role as a pathway to citizenship. Furthermore, due to the large number of visa types available for a person to enter Australia, this research only discusses the common visas used (business [skilled], family, education and humanitarian).

[17] Ibid.

[18] Dennis, J, (1993) *The John Tucker Lecture in Civil Law: Interpretation and application of the civil code and the evaluation of judicial precedent*, Louisiana Law Review, 54:1.

[19] Ibid.

The discussion in relation to human rights can be vast and therefore, any discussion only identifies and compares the rights afforded to Slovenian citizens by the European Convention for the Protection of Human Rights and Fundamental Freedoms 1950, the European Charter of Fundamental Rights 2000, the Slovenian constitution (SC) and compare the rights expressed in these legal instruments with the Australian constitution (AC), and national laws. The book does not discuss how the rights expressed in the law have been implemented, but it reinforces the point that these laws go some way to strengthening social cohesion. The book only briefly highlights the suppression of rights in the former Yugoslavia, even though the constitution, post WWII had adopted many of the rights expressed by the 1948 Declaration of Human Rights. The introduction of private international law (PIL) has been limited to its effect on citizenship rights, and is an important legal component of citizenship in the contemporary world, as people continue to be transient across international borders.

Moreover, a further question arises as to what extent does the private side of citizenship play in the modern day states of Slovenia and Australia. Karen Knop[20] observes that most scholars when discussing citizenship usually begin with the state being able to protect its sovereignty and choose its citizens and not the private side of citizenship.[21] The private side of citizenship is where a person has citizenship of either Australia or Slovenia, or both and what rights that person is afforded in either state. This book demonstrates how human rights operate in the private sphere (horizontally) between citizens and the public sphere (vertically).[22] That is, rights are used by the citizen to protect themselves from each other (horizontal) and from the state (vertical). In the case of Slovenia, they have had to shift their values from their past socialist system to embrace the EU's human rights values and transpose the human rights legal framework of the EU into national law.

The book has been written through the lens of an Australian having an historical connection to Slovenia. The views expressed in this book, could be viewed quite differently to those individuals based in Slovenia, Europe or elsewhere. It does not purport to influence or project the political discourse of leading scholars and others writing about Slovenia and the former Yugoslavia. The positive discussion in relation to the development of the Slovene and European identity and cohesion of its people, is viewed as a result of comparing it, and them, with Australia. In other words, there is much to be celebrated in Australia, Europe and Slovenia from their respective beginnings, even though parts of history tell us, it was not all smooth sailing.

[20] Karen Knop, *The Private Side of Citizenship,* Proceedings of the Annual Meeting, American Society of International Law, Vol. 101, 2007, 94–97.

[21] Ibid.

[22] Willem Maas, *Multilevel Citizenship*, University of Pennsylvania Press, 2013, 200–202.

1.2.1 Chapters

This book has 12 chapters. Each chapter is stand alone and discusses citizenship, immigration, rights and private international law. Chapter 1 introduces the structure of the book and outlines the methodology and limitations of the research. Chapter 2 also provides a 'Literature Review' of the nation state, national identity and citizenship. In the case of Slovenia, any laws they choose to borrow from Australia would need to be assessed against the laws of the EU. Chapter 3 traces the historical developments of citizenship, constitutions and national identity of Slovenia to 1990. In the context of Slovenia, the book begins by tracing habitation of the current day Slovene territory to 32,000 BC. The study then moves to Slovenia during the 1700s when it was under the rule of the Habsburg Monarchy, to Yugoslavia through to Slovenia finally obtaining independence and forming a state of its own for the first time in history. There is a year overlap between Chaps 2 and 3 from 1990 to 1991 because of the independence of Slovenia.

Chapter 4 discusses the historical beginnings of Australia from the late 1800s when it was still an out-post of the British Empire. Importantly, citizenship was being written about during the 1700 and 1800s, however, there appears to have been little scholarly work undertaken until the mid 1900s. Chapter 5, begins the discussion in regards to citizenship by exclusion and statelessness. During the early period of independence, Slovenia found itself excluding many former Yugoslav citizens that had emigrated to Slovenia for various reason. This chapter also traces the development of citizenship from 1990 to 2018. It is an important jump off point, because 1990 was the time when Slovenia became a new state. It was having to undertake a massive law reform program. Chapter 6 discusses the current day citizenship laws of both states. Chapter 7 deals with the evolution of European citizenship, and how it shaped not only member states, but also Slovenia's future direction. It also highlights some of the tangible impacts this had on Slovenes.

Chapter 8, also becomes important part of the book, because it examines the supranational and constitutional rights of each jurisdiction. These rights have gone a long way for each jurisdiction to exert its identity and a level of cohesion. Rights in the EU are very important and placed as one of the highest level policy pillars when developing law. A pathway to citizenship is through immigration and Chap. 9 compared the respective laws and policy. Chapter 9 only deals with economic and family migration. Chapter 10 deals with international protection (refugees). Globalization has enables citizens from states to interact and engage with other citizens with ease. Chapter 11 explores the role of citizenship in private international law, between Slovenia and Australia. It does not deal with EU law. Finally, Chap. 12 identifies some of the most pressing issues facing national identity and social cohesion. This chapter will provide a pathway forward, and points to the other chapters for the respective jurisdictions to consider reforming their laws, when and if needed to retain their identity, and strengthen cohesion.

1.3 Conclusion

This chapter has introduced the book. Chapter 1 has briefly highlighted to the complexity and challenges faced by governments in building and retaining identity and social cohesion in a time of geopolitical and economic tension. The book will compare the citizenship, immigration, rights and private international laws, that underpin nation and supranational identity and social cohesion. The laws, while well settled over a long period of time, do make a valuable contribution to the identity and cohesion of a state. In their own way, they provide governments with tools to direct their citizenry, bridge multicultural divides, and exert their identity to the people and the world. While there is no silver bullet to resolving all issues related to identity and cohesion, they are as a collective, political, yet, they can be used successfully by states and their people to ensure people retain certainty and a level of belonging.

References

Bechhofer, F., & McCrone, D. (2009). *National Identity, nationalism and constitutional change* (pp. 1–5). London: Palgrave Macmillan.

de Cruz, P. (1991). *Comparative law in a changing world* (p. 213). London: Cavendish Publishing Limited.

Dennis, J. (1993). The John Tucker lecture in civil law: Interpretation and application of the civil code and the evaluation of judicial precedent. *Louisiana Law Review, 54*, 1.

Knop, K. (2007). The private side of citizenship. In *Proceedings of the annual meeting, American Society of International Law*, Vol. 101, pp. 94–97.

Maas, W. (2013). *Multilevel citizenship* (pp. 200–202). Philadelphia: University of Pennsylvania Press.

Rupel, D. (2003). Between national and European identity: A view from Slovenia. *Cambridge Review of International Affairs, 16*(2), 207–208.

Tetley, W. (1999). QC, Mixed jurisdiction: common law vs civil law (codified and uncodified) (Part 1). *Uniform Law Review, 23*, 591–617.

Chapter 2
The Nation State, National Identity and Citizenship

Abstract The nation state, national identity and citizenship can be best described as separate and distinct legal concepts. While these concepts are standalone, they do, in part, support and underpin each other. In other words, they go hand in hand, and provide the basis for providing a platform for the inhabitants of a state – to identify as being, or, belonging to a state. Moreover, in the case of Slovenes they have the opportunity to also identify themselves as being part of broader Europe (the European union). On the backdrop of the above, the theoretical understandings of the nation state, national identity and citizenship is divided into three parts. The first section discusses the development of the nation state and national identity. Secondly, the literature review traces the evolution of citizenship and its linkages to the nation state and national identity. The third element identifies how citizenship and nationality are recognized in national and international law, although there are subtle differences between the two. The literature review adopts the position of Linda Bosniak, who is the leading scholar in this area to identify the link between citizenship, the nation state and national identity. In addition to Linda Bosniak, the literature also reinforces and adopts Kim Rubenstein's position that citizenship has evolved into a legal status. It is this legal status that is not only multilayered but provides a level of social cohesion.

Keywords Citizenship · Classical · Liberal · Liberal democratic · National identity · Postnational · Republic

2.1 [The] Nation State and National Identity

The nation state and national identity are highly political, fluid and separate concepts, however, they reinforce each other. The nation state and the national identity, and their respective subjective meanings have drawn a lot of attention from scholars

R. Walters, *National Identity and Social Cohesion in a Time of Geopolitical and Economic Tension: Australia – European Union – Slovenia*,
https://doi.org/10.1007/978-981-15-2164-5_2

in many disciplines such as law, psychology[1] and social sciences.[2] Psychological citizenship constitutes the identification with a national community that is inclusive of the modern day concept of citizenship (equality, rights and responsibilities, values, history and culture). Apart from a person having nationality of one or more states, in an imagined world that is globalised, but divided into nations, individuals in most circumstances have citizenship of a state (except those people that are stateless). National identity is a basis for an individual's personal identification with their citizenship, whether single or multiple. A person having dual citizenship, could identify themselves as being a citizen of the country they were born, but also, inheriting the citizenship and identity of the country they have acquired their second citizenship. The nation state can be best described as a legal fiction[3] that is based on the present and the past.[4] The nation state is, by its nature, a modern institution that emerged from kingdoms and empires – from the idea of allegiance to a person, to allegiance to one's fellow people.

National identity in the contemporary world remains strong, even in the face of constant geopolitical, economic and environmental change and volatility. Even with this volatility states, particularly the EU has established a comprehensive legal framework that provides citizens with a level or rights and responsibilities. Slovenia and Australia, have also established a level of equal rights for all citizens to access, no matter what race, color or ethnic background a person might be. However, in practice the application of rights has been very different in both Slovenia and Australia. Throughout Slovenia, former Yugoslav citizens were denied the right to citizenship, and in Australia it is well documented the discriminatory practices that have impacted the indigenous community. Both Australia and to a lesser extent Slovenia have experienced race based national identity. Race based national identity is nothing new and was present more than 100 years ago when Britain asserted its authority when colonizing Australia.[5] The aborigines were described as black settlements, and perceived as a threat to the nation. On the other hand, many former citizens of Yugoslavia residing on the territory of current day Slovenia, upon independence experienced varying levels of race based identity-discrimination and exclusion.

---

[1] Sindic, D, (2011) *Psychological Citizenship and National Identity*, Institute of Social Sciences, University of Lisbon, Portugal, 204–215. Mark Nolan and Kim Rubenstein, K, (2009) *Citizenship and Identity in Diverse Societies*, Humanities Research, Vol XV. No 1. 29.

[2] Sheppard, J, (2015) *Australian Attitudes Towards National Identity: Citizenship, Immigration and Tradition*, Australian Centre for Applied Social Research Methods, ANU College of Arts and Social Sciences, Report No 18. 1–15.

[3] Douglas Howland and Louise White, *The State of Sovereignty: Territories, Laws, Populations*, Indiana University Press, 2009, 182.

[4] Renan, E, (2007) 'Qu' est-ce qu' une nations' Paris, Calmann-Levy, 1826, in Jiri Pribán, *Legal Symbolism, On Law, Time and European Identity*, Ashgate Publishing Limited, 80.

[5] Gilroy, P, (1987) *There Ain't No Place in Union Jack: The Cultural Politics of Race and Nation*, Chicago: University of Chicago Press, 45.

Nationality can be best described as the imagined community while citizenship is a political construct from people's relationship to a state.[6] Nationality is expressed in the 1948 Universal Declaration of Human Rights[7] whereby it is stated that no person shall be arbitrarily deprived of nationality or denied the right to change nationality.[8] Additionally, the (Hague) Convention on Certain Questions Relating to the Conflict of Nationality Law[9] states that it is for each state to determine under its own law who its nationals[10] will be. It is argued that both nationality and citizenship provide a citizen with an identity to a state. Nationality is reflected in international law whereas citizenship is provided for by national law. For instance, a person refers to themselves as an Australian, who belongs to Australia (the state that provides the legal status to the citizen).

The Treaty of Westphalia in 1648 paved the way for what can be seen today as the pillars of the modern day nation state.[11] Westphalia rejected the idea that an Emperor had universal authority, establishing concepts of territorial sovereignty and a national consciousness (interest).[12] Westphalia also represented the critical developments from colonization to decolonization; the establishment of national, regional and international institutions to the rise of global markets and global civil society.[13] However, by its very title, it is argued that this is predominantly related to the West. That is, Western democratic states, even though it has gone some way to defining the territory of all states around the world. Moreover, the rise of the nation state established a common identity that incorporated ethnicity, historical ancestry, language and culture.[14] The impact of Westphalia for the Slovene's would arrive three centuries later. Up until 1990, the modern day Slovenian[territory] was part of a socialist federal state, kingdom and ruled by monarchs and empires. For Australia, it was not a nation state when colonized, and was only fully realized in 1901. Today they, along with the EU are grounded in Western democratic principles and legal framework, however, this is fragile. The political divergence and economic inequalities around the world, along with the rise and change in political powers are challenging the very notion of democracy.

On the backdrop of Westphalia and the development of the nation state, what emerged was identities of these states. Today, these identities are referred to as a

---

[6] Jamieson, L, (2002) Theories *Identity, Nationality and Citizenship: Implications for European Citizenship Identity,* Department of Sociology, University of Edinburgh, Sociology 34, 10–12.

[7] Article 15, Universal Declaration of Human Rights, 1948.

[8] Ibid.

[9] Hague Convention on Certain Questions Relating to the Conflict of Nationality Law of League of Nations, of 13 April 1930, League of Nations, Treaty Series, vol. 179, 89, No. 4137.

[10] Ibid, article 1.

[11] Falk, R, (2002) *Revisiting Westphalia, Discovering Post-Westphalia,* The journal of Ethics, 312.

[12] Gallaher, C., Dahlam, C., Giltmartin, M., Mountz, A., Shirlow, P, (2009) *Key Concepts in Political Geography*, SAGE Publications, 69.

[13] Ibid.

[14] Gordon Finlayson, J, (2005) Habermas: *A very short introduction*, Oxford University Press, 2005, 120–125.

national identity. National identity can be complex to describe, however, it is often thought of as being multidimensional,[15] contestable, fluid in nature and a political concept. National identity is both identified within and beyond the state. Other states and their citizens identify other states from their identity. For instance, people from Europe know where Australia is located in the world. However, they may not know what the identity is. Thus, national identity can be confirmed by several sources. It can be determined by democracy, communism (authoritarianism-totalitorism) or other some form of governance, such as, local cultural centric homogeny, within a free trade environment. Furthermore, citizens identify with the rights afforded to citizens, particularly the freedom of speech and association. However, and in part that, this is a myth even Western democracies. These rights are controlled through the legal framework. Thus, national identity can be confusing, but, generally people can identify with several elements of the political discourse to identify the state. While it is largely limited to a defined border, it can be exerted beyond its borders. Yet, this is not new. The Greeks and Romans were exerting their identities across the world – through many different ways for a long period of time. This type of activity is being played out today from the West to the East and from North to South.

Anthony Smith[16] argues that national identity not only includes citizenship (immigration) but also history, community, territory, values, traditions and patria. The idea of patria, is not new, and is a community of laws and institutions that regulate society with a single political will.[17] The community of laws include those laws that regulate citizenship and immigration, as they are developed by state institutions under the political will of that state, and its people. Smith further highlights how community laws also extend to civil and legal rights, political rights and duties, and socio-economic rights. He further points out how the modern day nation state signifies a cultural and political bond that unites a political community who share an historical culture and homeland.[18] By adopting the position taken by Smith, a state's national identity has been constructed over time, in the consensual sphere of everyday interactions but also through a state's institutions. However, it is not limited to this single approach. It is much broader than a states' current day institutions, and has been captures by the experiences that have been lived by the people within a territory that, in some cases spans centuries.

Nevertheless, by doing so, what has emerged is that the state influences and is able to manage, develop and strengthen its national identity. It is argued that citizenship is just one component-concept that enables a state to manage its national identity. Furthermore, as a single concept, citizenship arguably underpins the idea that people are able to relate to a national identity. In addition to this, people that migrate

---

[15] Smith, A, (1992) *National Identity and the Idea of European Unity*, International Affairs, 55–76.

[16] Smith, A, (2011) *National Identity*, University of Nevada Press, 9–11. Smith cites the work undertaken by Federick Meinecke.

[17] Ibid.

[18] Ibid, 14–15.

do so for various reasons, and on reason could be as a result of the cultural and legal identity of the state. Therefore, immigration when coupled with citizenship, further underpins the notion that the state has a level of identity based on these concepts. It is argued therefore that the citizenship along with immigration [law] have evolved in the EU, Australia and Slovenia, and today, play an important role in reinforcing and strengthening their respective identities. In achieving this, it will be demonstrated how both of these legal concepts include and exclude people from the reception jurisdictions. More importantly, national identity has also shaped citizenship. This is particularly evident in more recent times, the political discourse has slowly transitioned to a nationalist approach, and states are beginning to implement laws that control their citizen's activities outside the state.

However, in defining or attempting to establish a national or supranational identity, comparable concepts emerge. For instance, the EU, Slovenia and Australia have a defined territory, lengthy history, and their own core values and traditions, although vastly different. Comparatively, Australia being an island has been easier to define its territory, even though it includes an economic zone that extends 200 nautical miles offshore. Slovenia on the other hand only began defining its current day territory when the Republics were formed under the former Yugoslavia. Benedict Anderson argues that national identity is the imagined community that even in the smallest nations such as Slovenia, fellow members would not get to meet ever other community members. In reality, this is true due to the size of the territory, what people do on a daily basis and the extent or size of a states population. Anderson goes further and highlights that villages are always connected to others whom they have never seen.[19] Thus, the imagined nation (community) today is limited. Australia and Slovenia and to a lesser extent the EU do not restrict their people from transcending national boundaries. However, it must be noted that under the current immigration and citizenship legal framework, without the correct documentation, citizens are limited in their movement, in and out of, and across national borders. The exception is for Slovene citizens who are free to move anywhere within the Union. Therefore, it is argued that the imagined community, to some degree, has been broken down significantly by the introduction of technology, particularly the internet. It has enabled citizens who would not otherwise engage with each other, to do so. Yet, both Australia and Slovenia along with the EU have imagined, at different times, the community they wanted to develop. For Australia, this was white until the government accepted people from other nation states that were different ethnically and religiously. Slovenia, on the other hand have imagined themselves upon independence as purely Slovene, which saw many former Yugoslav citizens excluded from this community. For the EU, it has largely been a peace project that arose out of WWII and developed into a single economic market that, has required human rights to be considered at every turn, and today is a central pillar of EU law. More

[19] Benedict, A, (1991) *Imagined Communities: Reactions On The Origin and Spread of Nationalism*, London: Version, 7–8.

importantly, the development of the EU has, arguably, been successful in pushing back on nationalist ideology and practice.

National identity on the one hand, can be described as the crucial bond between the citizen and the state.[20] It can also be used to enhance social cohesions amongst citizens of the state. The state is continuously faced with legitimizing itself to the citizens of the state.[21] On the other hand, defining national identity can never be singular, as the state is redefined or in some cases such as Slovenia, re-invented, such that identity will continue to evolve. Even for Australia, as it continues to promote multiculturalism in the modern era, its identity can be very difficult to pin down. Therefore, in the context of this book, the EU's, Slovenia and Australia's identities have evolved and continue to evolve. National identity also involves inclusion, exclusion and discrimination.[22] These concepts and principles can be seen in the citizenship and immigration laws of these jurisdictions. In other words, the EU, Slovenia and Australia have and continue to include and exclude people from obtaining citizenship. Their respective immigration laws also have a formidable role by including and excluding people from entering their respective territories and taking out citizenship. Foreigners must meet certain residency requirements, know the states language and values before applying for citizenship. These restrictive measures all contribute to national identity. Additionally, it is argued that Australia similar to Slovenia and the EU has inherited, and continues, to identify as Christian even though the people may not attend church and see Islam as alien. This is not to say that either jurisdiction does not allow or embrace those people who have this backgrounds. In reality, it is quite the contrary, because in Australia alone has a large population of people who are Islam.

More importantly, it is argued that national identity is used as a tool to protect and unite[23] the people (citizens and residents).[24] Uniting the people and building social cohesion in a defined territory is an important part of national identity (e.g. political community, history, territory, patria, language, citizenship, common values and traditions).[25] Arguably, it is a "condition in which a mass of people have made the same identification with national symbols".[26] It enables the state to assert its values, culture and law, to the people, so as the people either embrace or otherwise the identity of that state. A further and just as important to national identity, the

[20] Minter, J, (2011) *National Identity and Immigration: The Cases of Israel and Australia*, Queensland Law Student Review, Vol 4, No 1, 1–10.

[21] Bechhofer, F., McCrone, D, (2009) *National Identity, Nationalism and Constitutional Change*, Palgrave MacMillan, 1–5.

[22] Ibid, 15.

[23] Habermas, J (1994) *Citizenship and National Identity*, in Bart Van Steenbergen, the Condition of Citizenship, SAGE Publications, 19–20.

[24] Guibernau, M., Smith, A, (2004) *'On nations and national identity: a critical assessment'*, Nations and Nationalism 10 (1/2), 133.

[25] Ibid.

[26] Bloom, W, (1990) *Personal Identity, National Identity and International Relations*, Cambridge University Press, 52.

concept itself assists the state to deliver a standard cultural message to the entire population of a state.[27] This becomes fundamentally important for the citizenry to by into the values, culture and rule of law of that state. The benefit to that state is, a level of social cohesion amongst the people. On the other hand, the benefit to the individual is, an identity with a state and/or a supranational polity. That is, a person identifying themselves to be an Australian, or, Slovenia, or both, or a citizen of the EU. It could also result in a person identifying themselves as all three.

On the backdrop of national identity, citizenship and, and to a lesser extent immigration contributes to uniting the people by providing the sense or feeling of being a citizen. Human rights and private international law also go some way to reinforcing the national identity. It also has a role to play in social coherence of a state. Yet, national identity is underpinned by a number of other policy areas, that include but not limited to; economic growth and productivity, economic development (international trade and finance) along with current and future technologies. With the fourth industrial revolution just around the corner, wide scale use of robotics and artificial intelligence, are going to change how citizens work and undertake their daily lives. What impact this will have on national identity and social cohesion in not known. It could however challenge the laws discussed in this book.

Linda Bosniak argues that in practice citizenship helps to shape the citizenry sentiment, which has independent sources in society and culture.[28] Today citizenship is an important part of national identity, which goes some way to providing a sense of solidarity and a patriotism amongst the citizens.[29] However, this becomes problematic in multicultural societies such as Australia, where people often maintain a greater allegiance to their ethnic group than they do to the nation state itself.[30] Bosniak highlights, even though ethnic groups have a presumed national identity, it is still within the boundaries of the state. The territory of a state contributes to national identity, as this represents the territory where citizenship is regulated and provided. Even so, the core values such as culture, rule of law and democracy provide potential for a single point of common identity.

Yet, put another way, Ernest Renan argues that citizens and residents conduct a daily 'plebiscite', choosing whether to affirm their cultural heritage.[31] The idea of a daily plebiscite followed the defeat of France by Prussia in 1870 to 1871, whereby the rights of the inhabitants of Alsace-Lorraine were attached without their consent to the emerging German Empire, which took control to decide their destiny through

---

[27] Jamieson, L, (2002) *Theorising Identity, Nationality and Citizenship: Implications for European Citizenship Identity,* Department of Sociology, University of Edinburgh, Sociologia 34, 6.

[28] Bosniak, L, (2000) *Citizenship Denationalised (The State of Citizenship Symposium),* Indiana Journal of Global Legal Studies, Vol 7: Iss 2, 447.

[29] Ibid.

[30] Flahive, E, *National Identity in Crisis: The Politics of Constructing National Identity and Mandatory Detention of Asylum-Seekers in Australia and Japan,* https://sydney.edu.au/law/anjel/documents/ZJapanR/ZJapanR23/ZJapanR23_13_Flahive.pdf, accessed 2 August 2016.

[31] Renan, E, (2012) What is a Nation? ('Qu' est-ce qu' une nations') in Bernard Yack, *Nationalism and Moral Psychology of Community*, The University of Chicago Press, 29–30

the expression of their collective will.[32] The collective will can be in the form of culture. The culture of a national community (citizens and residents) can be best described as a rational attachment to freely chosen principles that has been affirmed by culture, history,[33] and the law. It is the culture and history of Slovenia, the EU and Australia that has played an important role in the development and evolution of their respective identities. For Slovenes today being part of the European Union they have assumed a wider identity of the European community. One component of this wider identity has been the automatic acquisition of European citizenship, which has provided them a wider set of rights and responsibilities. However, it is argued that European citizenship does not in itself provide a supranational identity, and has not weakened member state's national identity. It has provided a greater sense of integration and social cohesion of member states citizens across the European Union.

Today, national identity along with the nation state and citizenship has been challenged. The rise in transnational engagement has allowed people to develop transnational identities. This is no more evident in Australia and Slovenia that allow their citizens to obtain citizenship of another state. Australia and Slovenia also allow their citizens to migrate to other states. Migration, allows people to adopt other values and identities in states, other than their own state of origin. It is asserted that these people blend their own personal identity, with that of the state they are located possibly picking the best elements of each state's identity, which they practice. Therefore, and as Linda Bosniak argues, this trans-border identity is not confined within the borders of a single state.[34] Elements of this can be seen in Australia's multicultural or blended identity.[35]

Culture, as a sociological concept is diverse and varied across the world. Like citizenship, culture can mean different things to different people. Felicita Medved argues that culture is an important part of national identity, and is distinctive and associated with an individual language and social environment.[36] Culture has a small, but an important role to play in social cohesion.

Nonetheless, culture is the totality of a society's distinctive ideas, beliefs, values and language.[37] The Slovene language, for many centuries has been the single common concept that has enabled a level of continuity to the Slovene people when developing a Slovene identity. This has been reaffirmed by Tomaž Deželan who argues that the Slovene language has been an important part of what it means to be

[32] Weil, P, (2001) *From conditional to secured and sovereign: The new strategic link between the citizen and the nation-state in a globalised world*, I-CON, Vol. 9 No. 3–4, 2011, 615–635.

[33] Yack, B, (2012) *Nationalism and Moral Psychology of Community*, The University of Chicago Press, 29–30.

[34] Bosniak, L, (2000) *Citizenship Denationalised (The State of Citizenship Symposium)*, Indiana Journal of Global Legal Studies, Vol 7: Iss 2, 447.

[35] Crock, M, (2007) *Defining Strangers: Human Rights, Immigrants and the Foundations for a Just Society*, Melbourne University Laws Review, Vol 31, 1050–1070.

[36] Felicita Medved, *Nationality, Citizenship and Integration, A European Perspective*, Council of Europe, 2001, 2–24.

[37] Serrat, O, (2008) *Culture Theory*, Knowledge Solutions, Asian Development Bank, 1–3.

Slovenian and the development of Slovenia as a nation state.[38] For Australia, the English language is an important part of what it means to be Australian,[39] however, it could be argued that it does not distinguish who is Australian in the same way the Slovenian language has been able to achieve. Moreover, a distinction between Slovenia and Australia is through language. The English language in Australia has not been codified in the same way as the Slovenian language has been in Slovenia. However, the English language is universal, whereas the Slovenian language is not and is largely confined to the territory of modern day Slovenia.

Citizens have an assumed identity (consciousness) where they belong to a state. The state establishes an identity to set itself apart from other nation states. A nation state's power is articulated through the laws that have been granted to its subjects [citizens].[40] Jurgen Habermas argues that national identity is formed under constitutional patriotism, and a common set of constitutional principles such as fundamental rights and democratic institutions that bind the community.[41] The nation state and its identity is defined by a national consciousness,[42] which is facilitated by political activation of the citizen.[43] This book will demonstrate that Slovenia has through history and citizenship developed a strong attachment to an identity that is Slovenian. That is, the territory of modern day Slovenia, the Slovenian language, the national flag and national colors of the state, food and traditional dress form part of the modern day Slovene identity. This is also the case for the EU, as they have a flag, however, there is no single language or an anthem. Australia on the other hand has a very different identity. It could be argued that the identity of Australia and what it means to be Australian has not been cohesively identified and is difficult to define.

Moreover, national identity in some states has been difficult to quantify. Mary Crock argues that there continues to be confusion about what the Australian identity is.[44] Thus, the Australian identity can be found and is based on similar democratic and other principles to that of Slovenia such as the national colors, the national flag, language, citizenship and the rule of law. Arguably, the current day Australian identity includes, but is not limited to, multiculturalism, tolerance, a strong political institutional framework that forms part of a liberal democracy, and the celebration of national

---

38 Deželan, T, (2011) *Citizenship in Slovenia: the regime of nationalising or a Europeanising state?* CITSE Working Paper Series, The University Edinburg, 2–30.

39 Sheppard, J, (2015) *Australian Attitudes Towards National Identity: Citizenship, Immigration and Tradition*, Australian Centre for Applied Social Research Methods, ANU College of Arts and Social Sciences, Report No 18. 1–15.

40 Minter, J, (2011) *National Identity and Immigration: The Cases of Israel and Australia*, Queensland Law Student Review, Vol 4, No 1, 1–9.

41 Habermas, J, (1994) *Struggles for recognition in the democratic constitutional state*, in Amy Guttman, Multiculturalism: Examining the politics of recognition, Princeton University Press.

42 Habermas, J, (1996) *The European Nation State. Its achievements and limitations. On the Past and Future of Sovereignty and Citizenship*, Ratio Juris, 125–137.

43 Ibid.

44 Crock, M, (2007) *Defining Strangers: Human Rights, Immigrants and the Foundations for a Just Society*, Melbourne University Laws Review, Vol 31, 1054–1056.

days and sport. Multiculturalism is arguably a corner stone of Australian society that, is made up of an amalgam of ethnic groups that make up Australia, and to a lesser extent Slovenia's population. However, and to a large extent, the identity of what it means to be Australian is liely to vary, depending who is being asked e question. What is quantifiable, in the Australian conext is that, a national identity does exist, and in both states citizenship along with immigration contribute to that identity.

2.2 Citizenship

The contemporary understanding of citizenship has been heavily influenced by classical traditions of Western,[45] postcolonial[46] denationalized (liberal) thought.[47] On the backdrop of this, the meaning of citizenship is highly contested, and the term has a broad range of uses. Citizenship has been difficult to define and is considered one of the oldest institutions in Western political thought and practice. It is not one of the easiest concepts to grasp, as a single comprehensive thought.[48] Yet, the policy and law that supports this concept is arguably complex and wide ranging. It covers many areas of law and society. The evolution of citizenship has evolved as nation states have evolved. Citizenship in the modern day straddles the boundary of law and politics,[49] sociology[50] and psychology.[51]

2.2.1 Classical Citizenship

The classical traditions of citizenship date back to ancient civilization of the fourth and fifth centuries BC in Athens and Rome, and from the third century B.C. to the first A.D. Citizenship theory in the sixteenth and seventeenth century focused on the

[45] Pocock, J, (1995) *The Ideal of the Citizen Since Classical Times*, in Robnald Beiner, *Theorising Citizenship,* State University of New York Press, 30–50.

[46] Ray, A, (2008) *Post Colonial Theory and Law: A critical Introduction*, Adelaide Law Review, Vol 29: No ½, 315–325. Postcolonial thought is relevant to citizenship and this study as it presents how for example the law either included or excluded people from citizenship, when territorial rule changed. In postcolonial though, it is essential that a state create an identity to ensure there is a stable society.

[47] Bosniak, L, (2000) *Citizenship Denationalised (The State of Citizenship Symposium),* Indiana Journal of Global Legal Studies, Vol. 7: Iss 2. This presents how citizenship has been affected by regionalisation and globalisation.

[48] Resenberg, P, (1992) *Citizenship in the Western Tradition, Chapel Hill and London*: The University of North Carolina Press, xvi.

[49] Rubenstein, K, (2002) *Australian Citizenship Law in Context*, Lawbook Co, 2002.

[50] Turner, B, (1990) *Outline of a Theory of Citizenship,* Sociology, Vol. 24, 190–2010.

[51] Sindic, D, (2015) *Psychological citizenship and national identity,* Journal of Community and Applied Social Psychology.

social contract between the citizen and the state. Postcolonial thought followed the developments of citizenship up until World War Two. Moreover, citizenship informs the contemporary notion that citizenship transcends the boundary of the nation state. Australia had been colonized by the British and inherited the democracy and law. The current day territory of Slovenia had also been colonized over many centuries by Slovenes, however the people have been ruled by various rulers. Slovenia and Australia has seen the development of their respective citizenship laws across these three periods.

Aristotle defined this activity as the *polis* which represented the community of citizens that were organized by a constitution.[52] Aristotle refereed to citizens as those who rule, and are ruled by individuals, which allowed them take part in the deliberative or judicial administration of society. Shafir explains that the "citizen Greek *polites* or Latin *civis* has been defined as the Greek polis or the Roman *republica*."[53] To participate in politics citizenship was inherited from Rome and the conception of citizenship was defined in terms of judicial status. Citizenship became part of the law as opposed to the function (s) undertaken by an individual.[54] John Pocock reinforces this point and argues that citizenship has been inherited from both the Greeks (a collective of self-rule) during antiquity and the Romans (legal status).[55] Throughout antiquity and the middle-ages citizenship was associated with townships and as Max Weber points out a class concept.[56] Shafir further highlights that citizenship changed three times during antiquity Greek *polis*, to the Roman law, to where citizens are now part of the modern times of nation states. Slovenes were part of the Roman Empire. Australia was not.

2.2.2 Liberalism and Republicanism Citizenship

Throughout the 1600s and 1700s philosophers such as Thomas Hobbes, John Locke,[57] Jean-Jacques Rousseau[58] and Immanuel Kant[59] began writing about citizenship and all espoused the social contract [theory]. The social contract theory

---

[52] Miller, F, *The State and Community In Aristotle's Politics*, Bowling Green State University, pp. 1–9, http://www.reasonpapers.com/pdf/01/rp_1_5.pdf

[53] Shafir, G, (1998) *The citizenship Debates*, University of Minnesota Press, 31.

[54] Isin, E, (1997) *Who is the new citizen? Towards a Genealogy*, Citizenship Studies, 115–131.

[55] Pocock, J, (1998) *The Ideal of Citizenship since Classical Times*, 20–50.

[56] Weber, M, (1998) *Citizenship in Ancient and Medieval Cities*, in Gershon Shafir, *The citizenship Debates*, University of Minnesota Press, 43–49.

[57] Olynyk, S, (2010) *Convenient Fictions: A comparison and Critical Analysis of Hobbes and Locke's Social Contract Theories*, The Western Australian Jurist, Vol. 1, 132–140.

[58] Desmond Nbete, A, (2012) *The Social Contract Theory: A Model for Restructuring a True Nigerian Nation-State*, International Journal of Humanities and Social Science, Vol. 2 No. 15, 267–270.

[59] Ibid.

establishes society as a collective having a set of equal rights.[60] Locke's notion of society is based on voluntary agreements that are not political. A political society formed by individuals representing their families also theoretically came together under the State of Nature and agreed to give power to their government.[61] An important point made by Locke is that the government is formed by its people (the citizens) who have established laws to protect themselves, people and property; including the protection of people from the state.[62] Locke through his work has influenced Europe's ideologies by separating public and private (rights, freedoms and protections). That is, citizens act as part of society and for themselves (the private), and by coming together to form communities delegating some of their power to government (the public). Governments make the laws in order to create societal norms and protect the citizenry.

Jean-Jacques Rousseau[63] takes the position that the social contract provides equality as society develops, and thus no single individual has a right to govern others. However, that authority is generated by agreements or covenants.[64] Within the modern day states of Slovenia and Australia the social contract is well entrenched through the acceptance of the rule of law. This is arguably also a central pillar of the EU. The legal frameworks of both states protect their citizens and ensure equality across society, even though in practice this is not always evident. Rousseau further points out that, citizenship is an "attachment to a political community that has a set of traditions and customs".[65] However, this was not the case for women. He concluded that women's rights were restricted and administered by their husbands.[66] Not only would Rousseau be criticized for this position today, Mary Wollstonecraft[67] criticized him for advocating that women should be educated in the same manner as men. In applying the natural law of man to women Wollstonecraft promoted the idea that women have the right to educate themselves and participate in society equal to that of men. The challenges for women were immense, not only had the law reduced their acceptance and participation in society, but scholars such as Rousseau were writing to ensure women retained second place behind man.

Yet, Karl Marx highlighted that the state stands in the same opposition to civil society and overcomes it in the same way as religion overcomes restrictions of the profane world. Man in civil society is a profane being.[68] Marx drew the distinction

---

[60] Social Contract Theory: *Internet Encyclopedia of Philosophy, A Peer-Reviewed Academic Resource*, www.iep.utm.edu/soc-cont/print

[61] Ibid.

[62] Locke, J, (1998) *Two Treatises of Government*, edited by Peter Laslett, Cambridge, United Kingdom: Cambridge University Press, 93–122.

[63] Ibid.

[64] Ibid.

[65] Heater, D, (2004) *A Brief History of Citizenship*, Edinburg University Press, 67–72.

[66] Jean-Jacquues Rousseau's philosophy on gender 1762, in Sirkkuy Hellsten, Anne Maria Holli, Krassimira Daskalova, Palgrave McMillan, (2005) 14–16.

[67] Wollstonecraft, M, (2000) *Vindication of the Rights of Women*, 1792, University of Oregon.

[68] Marx, K, (1963) *On the Question of the Jewish Community*, T.B Bottomore, McGraw-Hill.

of man (citizen) being part of not only a political community but a much broader part of society as a whole.[69] This new membership ensured there was equality before the law and the legal right to private property while enhancing political participation by the citizens.[70] Nonetheless, throughout the period of colonization, law played a major role in shaping colonies. Those territories ruled by empires had law imposed upon them. Australia and current day Slovenia were not excluded. Australia was colonized through acquisition and settlement, which automatically saw British law being applied.[71] Slovenia on the other hand had been colonized by conquest and cession. Marx endorsed European legal superiority and promoted the idea of 'mankind' that saw predictive laws[72] being established to govern larger areas of territory that the modern state has become.

The resulting effect of the rise of the modern day state has seen a change in territorial boundaries, rulers and the law. At different periods, the change in law has created the subaltern.[73] This is particularly the case when the British colonized Australia and the indigenous aboriginal people were viewed as the 'other'. Ninety years later, in the Slovenian context, the 'other' were the former Yugoslav citizens. The 'other' being those inhabitants on a territory that had been excluded by the citizenship laws. Linda Bosniak argues the 'other' is the 'alien' or noncitizen. Today, a non-citizen has the ability to reside on the territory of a state long term, under permanent residence. They have assumed many of the rights a citizen has. However, there has been a subtle shift that is taking place particularly in Australia and to a lesser extent in Europe (Slovenia included), where long term residents are being removed.

2.2.3 Liberal Democratic Citizenship

The twentieth century saw a renewed interest in citizenship. Thomas Marshall wrote the book *Citizenship and Social Class and Other Essays*, which would become one of the most influential studies into citizenship. Marshall saw citizenship that formed part of the interrelated processes of nation building and the emergence of commercial and industrial society. Furthermore, Marshall also aligned citizenship with the construction of a national consciousness. The national consciousness is part of national identity where citizens feel they belong to a nation state. Marshall's account of citizenship was modelled on Britain, which reflected the modern day democratic

---

[69] Ibid.

[70] Brubaker, R, (1989) *The French Revolution and Invention of Citizenship*, French Politics and Society, Vol 7, No 3, 30–49.

[71] Blackstone, W, (2001) *Commentaries on the Laws of England*, Vol 1. 2001, 107.

[72] Kelly, D, (1990) *The Human: Social Thought in the Western Legal Tradition*, Harvard University Press, 263–268.

[73] Spivak, G, (1994) *Can the Subaltern Speak?* in Patrick Williams and Lara Chrisman, Colonial Discourse and Post-Colonial Theory: A Reader, Hertfordshire: Harvester Wheatsheaf, 93.

(welfare) state. Marshall aligned citizenship to social class and categorized a citizen as having three sets of rights that included political, civic and social.[74] In the context of the Slovene people the rights outlined by Marshall can be traced from the Habsburg Empire, Kingdom of Serbs, Croats and Slovenes, Social Federal Republic of Yugoslavia, through to independence. The same can be said for the citizens of Australia, even though it has been over a much smaller time frame than the Slovenes. Human rights have evolved over many centuries, and today Slovene citizens have been afforded national, supranational and international rights, which Marshall would describe as an egalitarian society.[75] For Australian citizens however they haven't been afforded supranational rights. In the eyes of Marshall, gaining social equality is the final step in developing citizenship.[76] The rights based model has shaped political and social thought about citizenship during the post-war period. However, Marshall was writing at a time when western democratic states were expanding their welfare protections for their citizens.

Nonetheless, it can be argued that citizenship is the 'right' to have rights[77] (civil and political)[78] which is absolute and guaranteed. However, the rights afforded are limited by fellow citizens and the boundary of the state. Arguably, this is an aspirational proposition, because in practice there are more than 12 million people that have no citizenship of any state in the world. More than 600,000 of these people are located across Europe.[79] Citizenship has also been described as providing something that all citizens have in common no matter what their race, religion, color, political persuasion or gender.[80] Therefore, the law has been developed to apply to everyone in the same way.[81] Citizenship[82] has been discussed by the political elite and community when particular events have taken place, whether locally or globally. In other words, as states become increasingly multicultural, social equality ensures stability and goes some way to unifying the citizenry. In the post war period citizenship was largely viewed in terms of possession of rights,[83] from the development and rise of human rights law.

---

[74] Marshall, T, (1950) *Citizenship and Social Class and Other Essays*, Cambridge University Press.

[75] Ibid.

[76] Ibid.

[77] Arendt, H, (1951) *The Origins of Totalitarianism*, Harcourt, Brace and Company. New York, 266–298, in Daniel Tabb, Statelessness and Columbia: Hanna Ardent and the Failure of Human Rights, 2006, 40–52.

[78] Marshall, T, (1950) *Citizenship and Social Class and Other Essays*, Cambridge University Press, 1950.

[79] Statelessness, European Network on Statelessness, Everyone has the right to nationality, http://www.statelessness.eu

[80] Lister, R, (1997) *Feminist Perspectives*, Macmillan: Basingstoke, 190–196.

[81] Young, I, (1989) *Polity and Group Difference: A Critique of the Ideal of Universal Citizenship*, Ethics, Vol. 99, No 2. 205.

[82] Kymlicka, K., Norman, W, (1994) *Return of the Citizen: A Survey of Recent Work on Citizenship Theory,* Ethics.

[83] Ibid.

Following WWII, decolonization resulted in the emergence of newly independent nation states.[84] They would assume political independence, which resulted in centralized system of government and control. There was a shift from the former colonies, in the primary loyalty of a citizen from family, community or religious ties, to the nation state.[85] The postcolonial period saw the rise of identity as fundamental to constructing the state. Even though there was a continued push to the hegemonic position that state's held by excluding outsiders, this began to change. Engagement of new ethnic and political identities were embraced by states. In the early period post WW II Australia began to open its doors to foreigners, however, this was restricted to those from central, eastern and western Europe. Australia was not as welcoming to people from other regions such as Asia or Africa. Nonetheless, this would change over time. Slovenians along with many other European ethnic groups began arriving in Australia to assist in building the nation. Largely, Australia was a destination country, whereas people were leaving Slovenia and Europe. Post WW II was an important stage in the development of the early EU identity. A number of countries formed the Benelux Union to unite the communities with a single economic focus. As it will be demonstrated, the EU has evolved significantly since then, and today they have what can be best described as a level of identity in its own right.

Nevertheless, Jean Bethke Elstain understands the importance of participatory politics by the citizens. Elstain differentiates between the state and politics by emphasizing the importance of society as a whole for the common good.[86] Elshtan also favors this form of citizenship as it establishes a national identity, while maintaining relationships with other states. By focusing on the national identity, Elshtain[87] argues that citizens will contribute to a global citizenship because of the awareness of inequalities between states. Moreover, Matthew Gibney points out that by opening global borders would take away the legal role that citizenship has in regulating the movement of people.[88] The concept of a global citizenship[89] in its extreme sense could allow any individual to move and take up residence anywhere they wish without any monitoring from an institution or state. In other words, every person of every state has a single citizenship that operates across all states. This is arguably an aspirational concept, as the institutional framework is not established to accommodate or even administer a global citizenship. As an extreme form of citizenship, it would not benefit states in maintaining their national identity, sovereignty, culture and heritage. Arguably, it would dilute a state's ability to retain its ability to provide a sense of belonging, and in turn, it would have a significant impact to the identity

[84] Ray, A, (2008) *Post Colonial Theory and Law: A critical Introduction*, Adelaide Law Review, 315–325.

[85] Ibid, 334.

[86] Bethke Elshtain, J (1987) *Women and War*, United States of America: Basic Books, 250–265.

[87] Ibid.

[88] Gibney, M, (2009) *Statelessness: Statelessness and the right to citizenship*, Refugee Studies Centre, University of Oxford, 51–52.

[89] Barber, B, (1984) *Strong Democracy*, University of California Press, 118–225.

of a state. However, and conversely, done under a tight set of international, national constitutions and laws, this could be achieved, in the same way that can be seen in the European Union. What this could achieve is; minimizing or even seeing statelessness fully extinguished.

From the early developments in citizenship, it can be seen that a citizen becomes a member of a nation. Jurgen Habermas argues that the concept of citizenship has been used as a policy principle by nation states such as Slovenia and Australia to build the "nation state."[90] There is no better example than post WWII. Since then, states such as Australia have welcomed foreigners from across the world to assist in building the nation. Slovenia on the other hand, did not welcome others to build the independent new state. Rather, Slovenia relied solely on Slovenes. This is not to say they would be viewed differently under the Habermas model, it rather points to how Slovenes and Slovenia wanting to establish their own identity, separate and distinct from their past rulers. Nonetheless, under the former Yugoslavia, Habermas' conception of citizenship underpinning the building of the state was evident, although in a slightly different form. Rather than large scale immigration, emigration throughout the territory was popular amongst Yugoslav citizens. They did so, to enhance their economic position. Nevertheless, what Habermas is saying is that there are two theoretical concepts in relation to citizenship, one communitarian and the other individualist. The first concept is based on people's individual rights and equability before the law, and secondly, the citizen being part of a community. Barrington describes a citizen as an official member of the state,[91] who participates in nation building process. Ronald Beiner expands the notion of citizenship as a membership that, establishes a national identity and provides obligations that give effect to legal bonds of a community.[92] The position taken by Beiner has similarities to that of Linda Bosniak. This position is further reinforced by Kymlicka and Norman[93] who argue that citizenship describes is an identity that forms part of the nation state.

As the 1990s emerged scholars began to think of citizenship as forming part of the political collective. Yasemin Soysal took the view that citizenship was no longer part of the national political collective.[94] Soysal advocates that the concept of post-national citizenship has been on the rise, with the increased acceptance by states to allow their citizens to hold more than one citizenship. Dual or multiple citizenship comes with its own challenges. Having more than one citizenship allows a person to move with ease between two states. On the one hand, at the state level, governments grapple with the idea of dual or multiple citizenship because they are implementing

[90] Habermas, J, (1998) *The Inclusion of the Other: Studies in Political Theory*, 110–115.

[91] Barrington, L, (1995) *Nation, States and Citizens: An Explanation of the Citizenship Policies in Estonia and Lithuania*, Review of Central Eastern European Law, 103–150.

[92] Beiner, R, (1998) *Citizenship and Nationalism: Is Canada a Real Country*? In K Slawner and M E Denhim, Citizenship after Liberlism, Peter Lang Publishing, 185.

[93] Kymlicka, K., Norman, W, (1994) *Return of the Citizen: A Survey of Recent Work on Citizenship Theory*, Ethics.

[94] Soysal, Y, (1997) *Changing Parameters of Citizenship and Claims-Making: Organised Islam in European Public Spheres*, Theory and Society, Vol 26, No 4, 509–513.

liberal reforms to allow for this. This is particularly the case for those countries that have not embraced liberal democracy, in the same way as the West. On the other hand, governments continue to make it harder for non-citizens to become citizens by developing complex and sometimes cumbersome immigration laws. This is certainly evident in Australia. Arguably, Soysal's basis for citizenship is the notion of universal personhood as opposed to a citizen belonging to a single nation.[95] She takes the position that following the postwar era, the world has witnessed an increasing recasting of (national) citizenship rights as human (or personhood) rights. Rights that were once associated with belonging in a national community have become increasingly abstract and legitimated at the transnational level, within a larger framework of human rights.

Soysal's argument can be found in international law. In other words, and since globalisation and agreements between nations have indirectly resulted in the rights of citizens going far beyond the nation state they are in.[96] This evolution supports the argument that citizenship can no longer be considered at the state level. It must also be considered in the private sphere, because the body of law now straddling the boundary of nation states enable the citizen to engage in private activities with ease, compared to a century ago. Furthermore, Soysal's position also extends to non-citizens (those holding a visa or permit), that are also players within the international sphere (as private citizens of a state). For instance, the guest worker (a person from a third country) program across the European Union provide these people with certain rights. However, and while the law crosses the territory of nation states, the state has retained its ability to choose who its citizens will be. The state, provides citizenship and allows its citizens to be regional and global, transcending national boundaries. Similar exists in Australia where a foreigner can obtain a short term visa to work and reside in the state. In Australia this person certainly is not afforded the same level of rights as a permanent resident or citizen.

More recently, it has been argued that postnational citizenship, dual citizenship should be characterized as multinational.[97] Arguably, the position taken by Linda Bosniak reinforces the modern times with which nation states have opened their doors to many different ethnic groups. Whether citizenship is described as postnational or multicultural, the concept performs the same function. Thus, European citizenship represents a combination of these scholar's positions such as Bosniak and Soysal. For instance, a citizen of Slovenia may be resident in France, and they are afforded the same European rights as a French citizen. However, European citizenship poses a challenge to this hegemonic concept of national citizenship".[98]

---

[95] Soysal, Y, (1994) *Limits of Citizenship: Mirgrant and Postnational Membership in Europe*, Chicago University Press, 1–15.

[96] Ibid, 140–145.

[97] Bosniak, L, (2000) *Citizenship Denationalised (The State of Citizenship Symposium)*, Indiana Journal of Global Legal Studies, Vol 7: Iss 2, 463.

[98] Shore, C, (2000) *Building Europe: The Cultural Politics of European Integration*. London and New York, Routledge, 72.

Issever and Rummelili argue that European citizenship[99] does not bring a solution to the dichotomy of the nation-state citizenship.[100] From a theoretical perspective European citizenship does not clearly distinguish between citizens and foreigners. It renders third country nationals (such as Australians) as others and creates categories of Europeans versus non-Europeans.[101] European member states, while transferring some of their sovereignty to the European Union, have and continue to struggle, but, have retained much of their sovereignty in the area of citizenship law. Citizenship[102] has been identified as being the cosmopolitan (multicultural and multinational).[103] Multicultural citizenship is evident in both states.[104] However, both states have adopted restrictive measures (language and testing) to protect their national identities.

Citizenship provides a sense of belonging within and with a state.[105] Citizenship enables a citizens to be an active participant within the state and beyond.[106] It has been used in areas such as participation and governance within a state or territory, rights and duties, identities (both national and at an individual level). Thus, it is argued that citizenship can be differentiated between individuals to mean different things. The evolution of citizenship has seen the concept play an important role in building a nation, and assist a nation to formulate an identity.

In the contemporary world, citizenship law straddles the boundary of public and private law.[107] Scholars have identified citizenship to include, but not limited to, the

---

[99] Issever, E., Bahar Rumelili, B, (2009) *European Citizenship and Third Country Nationals: A Comparative Analysis of Germany and Britain*, INTL 533, 1.

[100] Ibid.

[101] Maas, W, (2008) *Migrants, States, and EU Citizenship's Unfulfilled Promise*, Citizenship Studies, 583–596.

[102] Linklater, A, (1998) *Cosmopolitan Citizenship*, Citizenship Studies, Vol. 2, No. 1, 26.

[103] Salmond, J, (1902) *Citizenship and Allegiance, Nationality in English Law*, The Law Quarterly Review.

[104] Castles, S, (2005) *Migration and Community Formation Under Conditions of Globalisation*, International Migration Review, 1143–1166.

[105] Werbner, P., Yuval-Davis, N, (2002) *Women and the New Discourse of Citizenship*, Zed Books, London, 1999, 2, in Lyn Jamieson, *Theorising Identity, Nationality and Citizenship: Implications for European Citizenship Identity'*, Soliologia 34, 14–15.

[106] Medved, F, *EUDO Citizenship Observatory, Country Report: Slovenia*, 2013, 20–27, http://eudocitizenship.eu/admin/?p=file&appl=countryProfiles&f=2013-24-Slovenia.pdf

[107] Weil, P, (2001) *Access to Citizenship: A comparison of twenty five nationality laws*, in Thomas Aleinikoff and Douglas Klusmeyer, Citizenship Today: Global Perspectives and Practices, Carnegies Endowment for International Peas, Washington DC, 17–35.

social contract,[108] political[109] community or participation,[110] social equality,[111] being inclusive (active) and enables full participation in public life and the law.[112] These all contribute to social cohesion, in some form. Furthermore, social cohesion straddles the public and private. On the one hand the state establishes law (s) and policy programs to build social cohesions. On the other hand, citizens by participating in the state and embracing its values actively contribute to society being cohesive.

Moreover, it has also been argued that citizenship is exclusive,[113] a desirable activity,[114] including a civic virtue[115] and universal,[116] which all represent citizenship in the modern state. Therefore, the multilayered approach to citizenship has been described in many different forms, over a long period that, can be best described as being settled, however, under constant evolution. Moreover, citizens often do not think of citizenship under a complex framework and multilayered approach such as this, but rather, how citizenship allows them to do certain things within and outside their state of origin. On the one side, citizens of both states are active participants in the polity, and the laws allow their citizens to transcend international borders. Determining citizenship is the public element associated with the sovereign state. On the other side, the private law determines the way the national law regulates an individual's daily activities. These activities extend to rights in general such as property, travel (migration), marriage, divorce, inheritance amongst others.[117] The citizenship law and policy of both Australia and to a lesser extent Slovenia are closely intertwined with the respective states immigration laws. In the modern era they cannot be decoupled.

---

[108] Olynyk, S, (2010) *Convenient Fictions: A comparison and Critical Analysis of Hobbes and Locke's Social Contract Theories*, The Western Australian Jurist, Vol. 1, 132–140. Alubabari Desmond Nbete, *The Social Contract Theory: A Model for Restructuring a True Nigerian Nation-State*, International Journal of Humanities and Social Science, Vol. 2 No. 15, 2012, 267–270.

[109] Cohen, J, (1999) "Changing Paradigms of Citizenship and the Exclusiveness of the Demos", **International Sociology**, 14 (3): 245–268. Joseph Carens, J. H., 1987, "Aliens and Citizens: The Case for Open Borders", *The Review of Politics*, 1987, 49 (2): 252–273. Joseph Carens, 2000, *Culture, Citizenship, and Community. A Contextual Exploration of Justice as Evenhandedness*, Oxford: Oxford University Press, 2000.

[110] Brubaker, R, (1989) *The French Revolution and Invention of Citizenship*, French Politics and Society, Vol 7, No 3, 30–49. Karl Marx, *On the Question of the Jewish Community*, T.B Bottomore, McGraw-Hill 1963. Lister, R, (1997) *Feminist Perspectives*, Macmillan: Basingstoke, 196.

[111] Marshall, T, (1950) *Citizenship and Social Class and Other Essays*, Cambridge University Press. John Rawls, *A Theory of Justice*, Harvard University Press, 1971, 3–5.

[112] Young, I, (1989) *Polity and Group Difference: A Critique of the Ideal of Universal Citizenship*, Ethics, Vol. 99, No 2. 250–270.

[113] Zorn, J, (2004) *The Politics of Exclusion Citizenship, Human Rights and the Erased in Slovenia*, UDK, 1–7.

[114] Kymlicka., W, Norman, W, (1994) *Return of the Citizen: A Survey of Recent Work on Citizenship Theory*, 104, Ethics, 351–354.

[115] Ibid.

[116] Young, I, (1989) *Polity and Group Difference: A Critique of the Ideal of Universal Citizenship*, Ethics, Vol. 99, No 2, 250–270.

[117] Ibid.

Nevertheless, there has been a struggle regarding citizenship beyond the nation state, because citizenship is a core concept in the current day political vocabulary.[118] Linda Bosniak denotes citizenship in four ways. Firstly, the legal classification or legal status. Secondly, the enjoyment of rights and privileges. Thirdly, the collective of self-governance and be active participants in the political community. Fourthly, citizenship is the form of identity (collective identity) and social membership. It is argued that this collective identity is a component of national identity. Therefore, citizenship is the broad right to lead a private life.[119] The private, as Bosniak argues, is where the citizen and citizenship is transnational. Today, with the emergence of regionalization and globalization citizens of both states can conduct their private activities that transcend the respective borders. Karen Knop argues citizenship in the private sphere is triggered by travel and cross border engagements between citizens from different states.[120] The private act of a citizens constitutes an individual's ability to decide to marry, divorce, purchase property and have a family. The state does not intervene in a citizen's private activities, other than providing the legal framework to enable this cross border private engagement. Moreover, citizens are afforded human rights, which also constitutes the private. Human rights operate in the private sphere (horizontally) between citizens and the public sphere (vertically).[121] That is, rights are used by the citizen to protect themselves from each other and from the state. The citizen has the right to participate in politics, public affairs, reside in the state, marry and can choose to serve in the military. The citizen as part of their private activities can be employed or establish a business, and has a duty to pay taxes.

However, citizenship also stands at the boundary of national and international law.[122] Human rights law is one example where citizens of Australia and Slovenia enjoy rights, protections and freedoms not only within the state but also outside the state. Citizenship today also includes the diaspora, or invisible citizenry located in other states.[123] Citizenship has also been described as being symbolic when compared to those individuals that are permanent or long term residents.[124] It is the

---

[118] Bosniak, L, (2006) *The Citizen and the Alien: Dilemmas of Contemporary Membership,* Princetown University Press, 18–19.

[119] Lund Black, C, (1969) *Structure and Relationship in Constitutional Law*, Ox bo Press, in Linda Bosniak, *Citizenship Denationalised (The State of Citizenship Symposium),* Indiana Journal of Global Legal Studies, Vol 7: Iss 2, 2000, 447.

[120] Knop, K, (2008) *Citizenship Public and Private*, Law and Contemporary Problems, Vol. 71:309, 309–340.

[121] Maas, W, (2013) *Multilevel Citizenship*, University of Pennsylvania Press, 200–202.

[122] Ibid.

[123] Beine, M., Docquier, F., Ozden, C, (2009) *Diasporas*, University of Luxembourg, Journal of Development Economics. Stine Neerup, *Diasporas in the Commonwealth, Focus on diasporas in the Commonwealth*, Institute for the Study of Global Movements, Monash University, Vol 6 No 1, 2009.

[124] Betts, K., Birrell, B, (2007) *Making Australian Citizenship Mean More*, People and Place, Vol 15, No 1, 44–55.

migrant's own decision[125] to move from one country to another, and take out citizenship of the destination country. It will be highlighted that migration constitutes economic, humanitarian or family reunification. It is argued that citizenship is the private, and involves the private activities of citizens across international borders such as marriage.[126] These principles all have a place in assisting a state to develop and retain national identity. Citizenship is bound up with the nation state and is often thought of in national terms.[127] Furthermore, citizenship in national terms is how the state regulates citizenship,[128] through national laws.[129] It remains largely a national enterprise, with the European Union citizenship being an exception.[130] This is an important observation because Slovenia today is a member of the European Union. The European Union does not regulate citizenship, but rather, provides citizens of member states with equal rights. Nonetheless, today citizenship can be best described as the legal status of a person to a nation state.[131] It connects an individual to a state.[132] Citizenship is bound up with the nation state and is often thought of in national terms.[133] The state regulates citizenship[134] through national laws.[135]

---

[125] Tabor, A., Milfont, T, (2011) *Migration change model: Exploring the process of migration on a psychological level*, International; Journal of Intercultural Relations, 818–820.

[126] Knop, K, (2007) *The Private Side of Citizenship*, Proceedings of the Annual Meeting, American Society of International Law, Vol. 101.

[127] Bosniak, L, (2000) *Citizenship Denationalised (The State of Citizenship Symposium)*, Indiana Journal of Global Legal Studies, Vol 7: Iss 2, 2000, 449. Kim Rubenstein, Daniel Adler, *International Citizenship: The Future of Nationality in a Globalised World*, Indiana Journal of Global Legal Studies, Vol. 7: Iss. 2, 2000, 521.

[128] Irving, H, (2008) *Still Call Australian Home: The Constitution and the Citizen's Right of Abode*, Sydney Law Review, Vol 30: 133.

[129] Crock, M., Berg, L, (2011) *Immigration Refugees and Forced Migration Law, Policy and Practice in Australia*, The Federation Press, 17–20.

[130] Above, n 86, 463.

[131] Kymlicka, K., Norman, W, (1994) *Return of the Citizen: A Survey of Recent Work on Citizenship Theory*, Ethics.

[132] Rubenstein, K., Adler, D, (2000) *International Citizenship: The Future of Nationality in a Globalised World*, Indiana Journal of Global Legal Studies, Vol. 7: Iss. 2, 521.

[133] Bosniak, L, (2000) *Citizenship Denationalised (The State of Citizenship Symposium)*, Indiana Journal of Global Legal Studies, Vol 7: Iss 2, 449.

[134] Irving, H, (2008) *Still Call Australian Home: The Constitution and the Citizen's Right of Abode*, Sydney Law Review, Vol 30: 133.

[135] Crock, M., Berg, L, (2011) *Immigration Refugees and Forced Migration Law, Policy and Practice in Australia*, The Federation Press, 17–20.

2.2.4 Legal Status

Citizenship has been confirmed by both Linda Bosniak along with Kim Rubenstein that citizenship is a legal status.[136] At the time of writing this book, more than 18 million people have Australian citizenship.[137] In addition, Australia's population was 24 million.[138] On the other hand, Slovenia has more than 1.9 million people holding citizenship out of 2.07 million in total population.[139] It must be noted that Slovenia is much smaller in population and territory than Australia. Today, both Australian and Slovenian citizenship laws are based on the principle of *iu sanguinis* and *ius soli.*[140] Thus, it is argued that citizenship law in Slovenia and Australia contributes to national identity and provides individuals with a sense of nationality.

2.2.5 Citizenship and Nationality

Nationality is synonymous with public international law. However, citizenship is national. Kim Rubenstein[141] states that "conceptually and linguistically the terms emphasize two different aspects of the same notion.....nationality stresses the international,[142] while citizenship is the national".[143] Federich Nottebohm, who was born in Germany and received citizenship by naturalization from Liechtenstein in 1939, later lived and undertook business in Guatemala,[144] but frequently returned to Germany to visit family, and in 1941 the United States (US) froze his assets which were located in the US. In 1943, he was arrested in Guatemala and deported to the US, where he was held until 1946 as an enemy.[145] Liechtenstein would take Guatemala to the ICJ, where the court found that Nottebohm's Liechtenstein nationality was effective.[146] The court repeatedly referred to nationality rather than citizenship. Additionally, the reference to nationality by the court in international matters

---

136 Rubenstein, K, (2011) *Australian Citizenship Law in Context*, Lawbook Co, 2002.

137 Australian Bureau of Statistics, Census, https://www.censusdata.abs.gov.au/webapi/jsf/selectTopic.xhtml

138 Ibid.

139 Slovenia Statistics Office, Republic of Slovenia, Population data, http://pxweb.stat.si/pxweb/Dialog/Saveshow.asp

140 Kogovsek, N, (2007) *The Principle of Iussanguinis (blood descent)*, The Peace Institute, 1–15.

141 Rubenstein, K, (2004) *Globalisation and Citizenship and Nationality*, The University of Melbourne, Faculty of Law, Legal Studies, Research Paper No.69, 1–29.

142 Ibid.

143 Weis, P, (1979) *Nationality and Statelessness in International Law*, Hyperion, Connecticut, 2–7.

144 *Liechtenstein v Guatamela*, International Court of Justice, 1955, ICJ 4, in Kim Rubenstein, *Globalisation and Citizenship and Nationality*, The University of Melbourne, Faculty of Law, Legal Studies, Research Paper No.69, 2004, 18.

145 Ibid.

146 Ibid.

reinforces the point that citizenship is used nationally and nationality is used internationally.

European law has defined nationality to mean (1) "the legal bond between a person and a states and does not indicate a person's ethnic origin[147] and, (2) multiple nationality is also defined as a person having the simultaneous possession of two or more nationalities.[148] Kay Hailbronner believes that European citizenship is having an impact on nationality because of the expanded rights associated with the supranational polity citizenship.[149] Citizenship of the European Union was first established in the Maastricht Treaty 1992, 'that every person holding nationality of a MS is a citizen of the European Union'.[150] This in itself could be somewhat confusing to the lay person. In *Micheletti*[151] the Advocate General argued that possession of nationality of a member state is the only prerequisite which an individual must satisfy in order to be able to exercise their rights. There is a general theme in most European Union case law that either nationality or citizenship is used depending on the legal matter. Later in *Carlos Garcia Avello v Etat Belge,*[152] the Advocate General referred to nationality rather than citizenship of a member state, in relation to discrimination. The Federal Court of Australia described the concept of nationality when referring to the application by a person for a protection visas. Weinberg J in the Federal Court of Australia stated[153] that the term nationality lacks precision. It is generally used to signify the legal connection between an individual and a state.

Notwithstanding the above, the European University Institute has focused on what and how the terms are used by MS and other countries outside of the EU. The European Union Democracy Observatory is consistent with scholars and also points out that 'nationality' is part of public international law, while citizenship is part of national domestic law.[154] EUDO explain that in Croatia, Serbia and Bosnia and Herzegovina "citizenship is known as *državljanstvo* which is a neutral term designating a person's link to the state".[155] While nationality (*nacionalnost or, narodnost - people*) "refers to an individual's ethnic background".[156] That said, EUDO[157]

---

[147] Article 2, European Convention on Nationality, Strasbourg, 6.XI 1997.

[148] Ibid.

[149] Hailbronner, K, (2006) *Nationality in public international law and European law*, in R Baubock, E Ersholl, K Groenendijik and H Waldrauch, Acquisition and Loss of Nationality: Policies and Trends in 15 European States, Amsterdam University Press, 70–79.

[150] Article 8 Maastricht Treaty 1992.

[151] Case C-369/90 Mario *Vincente Micheletti and others v Dlehacion del Gobierno en Cantabria* (1992) ECR I-4239.

[152] Case C-148/02 *Carlos Garcia Avello v Etat Belge* (2003) ECR I-11613.

[153] *VSAB v MIMA* (2006) FCA 239, 48.

[154] European University Institute, European Union Democracy Observatory, *Citizenship or Nationality*, www.eudo-citizenship.eu

[155] Ibid.

[156] Ibid.

[157] EUDO Observatory on citizenship, *Citizenship or Nationality*, European University Institute, http://eudo-citizenship.eu/databases/citizenship-glossary/terminology

outlines the complexity and differences of how European languages apply both terms within national law. Across the European Union both terms have been used, broadly linking the state and citizen though rights, responsibilities, culture and historical community. *Državljanstvo* (citizenship) is the legal bond between citizen and state. However, the English translation of *državljanstov* refers to both nationality and citizenship.[158]

The legislative translation of 'citizenship' is commonly used however nationality has been used when translating decisions into English.[159] Furthermore, *narodnost* when translated into English is also nationality, indicating the quality of belonging (narod, nation as a cultural, ethnic and historic community).[160] *Narodnost* is also used when referring to autochthonous minority communities such as Italians and Hungarians, and the term *nacionalnost* is a synonym for *državljansto* that indicates a tie to a certain ethnic or cultural group. The application of nationality in the United Kingdom is a wider term than citizenship, and similar to Australia both terms are interchangeable. It was not until the *British Nationality Act 1981* introduced the term 'British citizen'. British citizenship is identified with a citizen having a passport while nationality is referred to by a citizen as their identity or ethnicity. The word citizenship can be readily found in the national laws of Slovenia and Australia. Citizenship and nationality can be easily discerned. Citizenship is synonymous with national law. Nationality is commonly used in international law, and confirms the legal status of an individual and to what state or states they belong.

2.3 Conclusion

The concept of national identity and citizenship meet very different needs of the state. Yet they reinforce each other. The collective nature of these two political concepts, and in the case of citizenship being a legal concept, play an important role in providing a level of social cohesion.

National identity has become synonymous with how a nation state projects itself to the world through language, culture, values amongst other things. National identity belongs to no single person, but rather, the state. National identity provides citizens with a sense of belonging. This shared identity is in the form of language, culture, origin and having an emotional bond with the nation. A national identity is also shaped by the rule of law ([constitution and national laws] citizenship, immigration, rights, and private laws). Culture also forms part of a state's identity and is shaped by literature, religion, values, heritage, location, geography, maps, a national flag and national anthem.

---

[158] Ibid.

[159] Ibid.

[160] Ibid.

Arguably, citizenship is multi-dimensional. The concept allows a state to provide a sense of belonging to its populations. The state by providing for citizenship also uses it to underpin national identity, by establishing a collective through what it means to be a legal member of the state. It has been used in areas such as participation and governance within a state or territory, rights and duties, identities (both national and at an individual level). The evolution of citizenship has seen the concept play an important role in building a nation, and assist a nation to formulate an identity.

Citizenship is used by states to include and exclude, through immigration law and policy. By using citizenship to exclude individual from society poses many challenges because in some cases the state may force people to become stateless. It affords citizens with rights and responsibilities, and enables them to engage with other citizens under the PIL framework. On the one hand, it has been used to strengthen nationalism. On the other hand, it has been used to integrate and strengthen social cohesion of different ethnic groups. Citizenship provides the individual the right to have rights, participate in the polity along with the ability to be transnational. As a legal status, citizenship in Australia can be summarized as more than 18 million and Slovenia having 1.9 million people who hold citizenship.

References

Arendt, H. (1951). The origins of totalitarianism. In D. Tabb (Ed.), *Statelessness and Columbia: Hanna Ardent and the failure of human rights* (pp. 266–298). New York: Harcourt, Brace and Company. 2006, 40–52.

Barber, B. (1984). *Strong democracy* (pp. 118–225). Chicago: University of California Press.

Barrington, L. (1995). Nation, states and citizens: An explanation of the citizenship policies in Estonia and Lithuania. *Review of Central Eastern European Law, 21*, 103–150.

Bechhofer, F., & McCrone, D. (2009). *National Identity, nationalism and constitutional change* (pp. 1–5). London: Palgrave Macmillan.

Beiner, R. (1998). Citizenship and nationalism: Is Canada a real country? In K. Slawner & M. E. Denhim (Eds.), *Citizenship after Liberlism* (Vol. 185). New York: Peter Lang Publishing.

Benedict, A. (1991). *Imagined communities: Reactions on the origin and spread of nationalism* (pp. 7–8). London: Version.

Betts, K., & Birrell, B. (2007). Making Australian citizenship mean more. *People and Place, 15*(1), 44–55.

Blackstone, W. (2001). In W. Morrison (Ed.), *Commentaries on the Laws of England* (Vol. 1, p. 107). London: Cavendish Publishing.

Bloom, W. (1990). *Personal identity, national identity and international relations* (p. 52). Cambridge: Cambridge University Press.

Bosniak, L. (2000). Citizenship denationalised (the state of citizenship symposium). *Indiana Journal of Global Legal Studies, 7*(2), 447.

Brubaker, R. (1989). The French revolution and invention of citizenship. *French Politics and Society, 7*(3), 30–49.

Carens, J. (1987). Aliens and citizens: The case for open borders. *The Review of Politics, 49*(2), 252–273.

Carens, J. (2000). *Culture, citizenship, and community. A contextual exploration of justice as evenhandedness*. Oxford: Oxford University Press.

Castles, S. (2005). Migration and community formation under conditions of globalisation. *International Migration Review*, 1143–1166.
Cohen, J. (1999). Changing paradigms of citizenship and the exclusiveness of the demos. *International Sociology, 14*(3), 245–268.
Crock, M. (2007). Defining strangers: Human rights, immigrants and the foundations for a just society. *Melbourne University Laws Review, 31*, 1050–1070.
Crock, M., & Berg, L. (2011). *Immigration refugees and forced migration law, policy and practice in Australia* (pp. 17–20). Sydney: The Federation Press.
Desmond Nbete, A. (2012). The social contract theory: A model for restructuring a true Nigerian nation-state. *International Journal of Humanities and Social Science, 2*(15), 267–270.
Deželan, T. (2011). *Citizenship in Slovenia: the regime of nationalising or a Europeanising state?* (CITSE Working Paper Series, The University Edinburg, pp. 2–30).
Elshtain, J. B. (1987). *Women and war* (pp. 250–265). New York: Basic Books.
Falk, R. (2002). Revisiting Westphalia, discovering post-Westphalia. *The Journal of Ethics, 312*.
Finlayson, J. G. (2005). *Habermas: A very short introduction* (pp. 120–125). Oxford: Oxford University Press.
Gallaher, C., Dahlam, C., Giltmartin, M., Mountz, A., & Shirlow, P. (2009). *Key concepts in political geography* (p. 69). London: SAGE Publications.
Gibney, M. (2009). *Statelessness: Statelessness and the right to citizenship, refugee studies Centre* (pp. 51–52). Oxford: University of Oxford.
Gilroy, P. (1987). *There Ain't no place in union Jack: The cultural politics of race and nation* (p. 45). Chicago: University of Chicago Press.
Guibernau, M., & Smith, A. (2004). On nations and national identity: A critical assessment. *Nations and Nationalism, 10*(1/2), 133.
Habermas, J. (1994a). Citizenship and National Identity. In B. Van Steenbergen (Ed.), *The condition of citizenship* (pp. 19–20). London: SAGE Publications.
Habermas, J. (1994b). Struggles for recognition in the democratic constitutional state. In A. Guttman (Ed.), *Multiculturalism: Examining the politics of recognition* (p. 1994). Princeton: Princeton University Press.
Habermas, J. (1996). The European nation state. Its achievements and limitations. On the past and future of sovereignty and citizenship. *Ratio Juris, 9*, 125–137.
Habermas, J. (1998). *The inclusion of the other: Studies in political theory* (pp. 110–115). Cambridge, MA: MIT Press.
Hailbronner, K. (2006). Nationality in public international law and European law. In R. Baubock, E. Ersholl, K. Groenendijik, & H. Waldrauch (Eds.), *Acquisition and loss of nationality: Policies and trends in 15 European states* (pp. 70–79). Amsterdam: University Press.
Heater, D. (2004). *A brief history of citizenship* (pp. 67–72). Edinburgh: Edinburg University Press.
Howland, D., & White, L. (2009). *The state of sovereignty: Territories, Laws, populations* (p. 182). Bloomington: Indiana University Press.
Irving, H. (2008). Still call Australian home: The constitution and the Citizen's right of abode. *Sydney Law Review, 30*, 13.
Isin, I. (1997). Who is the new citizen? Towards a genealogy. *Citizenship Studies, 27*, 115–131.
Issever, E., & Rumelili, B. (2009). European citizenship and third country nationals: A comparative analysis of Germany and Britain. *INTL, 533*, 1.
Jamieson, L. (2002). Theorising identity, nationality and citizenship: Implications for European citizenship identity, department of sociology. *University of Edinburgh, Sociologia, 34*, 6.
Kelly, D. (1990). *The human: Social thought in the Western legal tradition* (pp. 263–268). Cambridge, MA: Harvard University Press.
Knop, K. (2007). The private side of citizenship. *Proceedings of the Annual Meeting, American Society of International Law, 101*, 99–102.
Knop, K. (2008). Citizenship public and private. *Law and Contemporary Problems, 71*(309), 309–340.

Kymlicka, W., & Norman, W. (1994). Return of the citizen: A survey of recent work on citizenship theory. *Ethics, 104*(2), 352–381.
Linklater, A. (1998). Cosmopolitan citizenship. *Citizenship Studies, 2*(1), 26.
Lister, R. (1997). *Feminist perspectives* (pp. 190–196). Basingstoke: Macmillan.
Locke, J. (1998). In P. Laslett (Ed.), *Two treatises of government* (pp. 93–122). Cambridge: Cambridge University Press.
Maas, W. (2008). Migrants, states, and EU Citizenship's unfulfilled promise. *Citizenship Studies, 12*, 583–596.
Marshall, T. (1950). *Citizenship and social class and other essays*. New York: Cambridge University Press.
Marx, K. (1963). In T. B. Bottomore (Ed.), *On the question of the Jewish community*. New York: McGraw-Hill.
Medved, F. (2001). *Nationality, citizenship and integration, A European perspective* (pp. 2–24). Council of Europe.
Minter, J. (2011). National Identity and immigration: The cases of Israel and Australia. *Queensland Law Student Review, 4*(1), 1–10.
Neza Kogovsek, N. (2007). *The principle of Iussanguinis (blood descent)* (pp. 1–15). Ljubljana: The Peace Institute.
Nolan, M., & Rubenstein, K. (2009). Citizenship and identity in diverse societies. *Humanities Research, XV*(1), 29.
Olynyk, S. (2010). Convenient fictions: A comparison and critical analysis of Hobbes and Locke's social contract theories. *The Western Australian Jurist, 1*, 132–140.
Pocock, J. (1995). The ideal of the citizen since classical times. In R. Beiner (Ed.), *Theorising citizenship* (pp. 30–50). New York: State University of New York Press.
Rawls, J. (1971). *A theory of justice* (pp. 3–5). Cambridge, MA: Harvard University Press.
Ray, A. (2008). Post colonial theory and law: A critical introduction. *Adelaide Law Review, 29*, 315–325.
Renan, E. (2007). 'Qu' est-ce qu' une nations' Paris, Calmann-Levy, 1826. In J. Přibáň (Ed.), *Legal symbolism, on law, time and European identity* (p. 80). Farmham: Ashgate Publishing Limited.
Resenberg, R. (1992). *Citizenship in the Western tradition* (p. xvi). Chapel Hill: The University of North Carolina Press.
Rousseau, J. (2005). In S. Hellsten, A. M. Holli, & K. Daskalova (Eds.), *Philosophy on gender 1762* (pp. 14–16). Palgrave McMillan: London.
Rubenstein, K. (2002). *Australian citizenship law in context*. Sydney: Lawbook Co.
Rubenstein, K. (2004). *Globalisation and citizenship and nationality* (The University of Melbourne, Faculty of Law, Legal Studies, Research Paper No.69, pp. 1–29).
Rubenstein, K., & Adler, D. (2000). International citizenship: The future of nationality in a globalised world. *Indiana Journal of Global Legal Studies, 7*(2), 521.
Salmond, J, (1902). Citizenship and allegiance. Nationality in English Law. *The Law Quarterly Review*.
Serrat, O. (2008). *Culture theory, knowledge solutions* (pp. 1–3). Manila: Asian Development Bank.
Shafir, G. (1998). *The citizenship debates* (p. 31). Minneapolis: University of Minnesota Press.
Sheppard, J. (2015a). *Australian attitudes towards national identity: Citizenship, immigration and tradition*. Australian Centre for Applied Social Research Methods, ANU College of Arts and Social Sciences, Report No 18. 1–15.
Sheppard, J, (2015b) *Australian attitudes towards national identity: Citizenship, immigration and tradition*. Australian Centre for Applied Social Research Methods, ANU College of Arts and Social Sciences, Report No 18. 2015, 1–15.
Shore, C. (2000). *Building Europe: The cultural politics of European integration* (p. 72). London: Routledge.

Sindic, D. (2015). Psychological citizenship and national identity. *Journal of Community and Applied Social Psychology, 24*(2), 100–110.

Smith, A. (1995). National Identity and the idea of European Unity. *International Affairs, 1992*, 55–76.

Smith, A. (2011). *National identity* (pp. 9–11). London: University of Nevada Press. Smith cites the work undertaken by Federick Meinecke.

Soysal, Y. (1994). *Limits of citizenship: Mirgrant and postnational membership in Europe* (pp. 1–15). Chicago: Chicago University Press.

Soysal, Y. (1997). Changing parameters of citizenship and claims-making: Organised Islam in European public spheres. *Theory and Society, 26*(4), 509–513.

Spivak, G. (1990). *Can the subaltern speak? In Patrick Williams and Lara Chrisman, colonial discourse and post-colonial theory: A reader* (p. 93). Hertfordshire: Harvester Wheatsheaf.

Tabor, A., & Milfont, T. (2011). Migration change model: Exploring the process of migration on a psychological level. *International Journal of Intercultural Relations, 35*, 818–820.

Turner, B. (1990). Outline of a theory of citizenship. *Sociology, 24*, 190–2010.

Weber, M. (1998). Citizenship in ancient and medieval cities. In G. Shafir (Ed.), *The citizenship debates* (pp. 43–49). Minneapolis: University of Minnesota Press.

Weil, P. (2001). Access to citizenship: A comparison of twenty five nationality laws. In T. Aleinikoff & D. Klusmeyer (Eds.), *Citizenship today: Global perspectives and practices* (pp. 17–35). Washington, DC: Carnegies Endowment for International Peas.

Weil, P. (2011). From conditional to secured and sovereign: The new strategic link between the citizen and the nation-state in a globalised world. *I-CON, 9*(3–4), 615–635.

Weis, P. (1979). *Nationality and statelessness in international law* (pp. 2–7). Connecticut: Hyperion.

Werbner, P., & Yuval-Davis, N. (2002). *Women and the new discourse of citizenship*. London: Zed Books. 1999, 2, in Lyn Jamieson, Theorising Identity, Nationality and Citizenship: Implications for European Citizenship Identity', Soliologia 34, 14-15.

Wollstonecraft, M. (2000). *Vindication of the rights of women, 1792*. Oregon: University of.

Yack, B. (2012). *Nationalism and moral psychology of community* (pp. 29–30). Chicago: The University of Chicago Press.

Young, I. (1989). Polity and group difference: A critique of the ideal of universal citizenship. *Ethics, 99*(2), 205.

Chapter 3
The Slovenian National Identity and Citizenship

Abstract This chapter traces the evolution of the theory and practice of citizenship, and to a lesser extent immigration, in Slovenia. It does not discuss the evolution of citizenship or the identity of the EU. The French and United States (American) Revolutions had a significant influence on the historical development of citizenship law. More importantly, and in part, Slovenia's beginnings will be traced from when the territory of modern day Slovenia was part of the Holy Roman Empire.

Citizenship has evolved from occupation of a territory to excluding people from being a citizen. Citizenship has also been a choice for individual resident in a territory. The disintegration of empires and kingdoms shaped citizenship, and exclusionary approaches were adopted to restrict people from being a citizen or resident. One of the most important roles citizenship has played over the past two centuries has been its ability to provide a level of certainty to individuals as rulers and borders change. Arguably, the two world wars had a significant impact on citizenship. The resulting effect of WWII alone saw the outward migration from Europe and Slovenia, whereby Australia was considered a destination state. Finally, it will highlight how, from the early developments of the nation state to the modern day, citizenship transitioned from allegiance to a legal status.

Keywords American Revolution · Citizenship · French Revolution · Immigration · World War I [WWI] · World War II [WWII]

3.1 Slovenes [Early Period]

Evidence of the occupation of the current day Slovenian territory dates to the Mesolithic (Neanderthals) period, from which a human cranium has been found.[1] According to Peter Štih et al., inhabitants were known to have occupied caves in the

[1] Luthar, O, (2008) *The Land Between: A History of Slovenia*, Peter Lang International Academic Publishers, 10–13. Peter Štih, Vasko Simoniti, Peter Vodopivec, Slovene History, Society-Politics-Culture, Besedilni podatki, Ljubljana: Inštitut za novejšo zgodovino: Sistory, 2008.

R. Walters, *National Identity and Social Cohesion in a Time of Geopolitical and Economic Tension: Australia – European Union – Slovenia*,
https://doi.org/10.1007/978-981-15-2164-5_3

eastern Savinja Alps around 32,000 BC.[2] By the end of the first millennium BC, the Celts began to exert their presence and control over much of the current day Slovene territory.[3] The Celts had brought with them religion, culture, technologies (swords and tools for daily survival) and language.[4] During this early period, it was established that Slovenes were and are today a mix of Old Slavic descent with the majority of genetics deriving from Europe (the Balkans and the Ukraine).[5]

As democracy emerged in Greece, the early beginnings of citizenship began to take shape. The Pericles' Citizenship law of 451–50 BC of Athens required both parents to be citizens and to share in the city.[6] Citizenship represented membership of the *polis,*[7] which was organized by a constitution.[8] However, during the early Roman times[9] the concept of citizenship was defined in terms of a judicial status, whereby, it became part of the law as opposed to the function (s) undertaken by an individual.[10] These early beginnings saw the development of the foundations of citizenship as a legal status. However, national border, at the time, were porous and largely the concept of citizenship was tied to local communities. John Pocock argues aspects of modern citizenship were inherited from both the Greeks (a collective of self-rule) and the Romans (legal status).[11] Slovenians were part of the Holy Roman Empire. Slovenes found themselves being drawn into the cultural life of the German princes, within the jurisdiction of the Roman Church.[12] This was an important influence on the early developments of the national character of Slovenians,[13] because they were part of the Frankish Empire, which became the Holy Roman Empire where the people inherited Roman Christianity.[14] Even today, Slovenes continue to embrace these early beginnings, particularly the Roman Catholicism.

---

[2] Štih, P, (2008) Vasko Simoniti, Peter Vodopivec, *Slovene History, Society-Politics-Culture*, Besedilni podatki, Ljubljana: Inštitut za novejšo zgodovino: Sistory, 9.

[3] Luthar, O, (2008) *The Land Between: A History of Slovenia*, Peter Lang International Academic Publishers, 32–33.

[4] Ibid.

[5] Škulj, J, *Genetske raziskave in njihov pomen za preučevanje Venetov*, Hindu Institute of Learning Canada, http://www.korenine.si/zborniki/zbornik02/skulj02.htm

[6] Patterson, C, (1981) *Pericles Citizenship Law* of 451–50 BC, 1981, 1–8, in Kim Rubenstein, *Citizenship in Australia: Unscrambling its Meaning,* Melbourne University Law Review, 1995, 504–508.

[7] Shafir, G, (1998) *The citizenship Debates*, University of Minnesota Press, 31.

[8] Miller, F, *The State and Community In Aristotle's Politics*, Bowling Green State University, 1–9, http://www.reasonpapers.com/pdf/01/rp_1_5.pdf

[9] Aristotle, *Politics* (ed Sir Ernest Barker, 1946), 134, in Kim Rubenstein, *Citizenship in Australia: Unscrambling its Meaning,* Melbourne University Law Review, 1995, 504–508.

[10] Isin, E, (1997) *Who is the new citizen? Towards a Genealogy*, Citizenship Studies, 115–131.

[11] Pocock, J, (1992) *The Ideal of Citizenship since Classical Times*, Queen's Quarterly, Vol.99, No. 1, 10–50.

[12] Singleton, F, (1989) *A Short History of the Yugoslav People's*, Cambridge University Press, 15.

[13] Ibid.

[14] Črnič, A., Komel, M., Smerke, M., Šabec, K., Vovk, T, (2013) *Religious Pluralisation in Slovenia,* Teorija in Praksa, let. 50, 1/205–229.

Nonetheless, and more importantly, the Slovene language is arguably the single identifying feature that can be traced over many centuries. The Slovene language can be found in the Freising Manuscripts (*Brižinski spomeniki*).[15] They are a record of the Slovene language that was spoken in a much larger territory than modern day Slovenia, and included most of the present day Austrian states of Carinthia and Styria.[16] The Slovenian language was also spoken in East Tyrol, South Tyrol, and some areas of Upper and Lower Austria.[17] Moreover, rare writings have been located that date back to 1227 and the Carinthia region, referring to written text that had been prepared by Styrian Ulrich von Liechtenstein. von Liechtenstein who upon his arrival in Carinthia would be greeted in Slovenian.[18] Slovenian phrases were also used in poetry written by Oswald von Wolkenstein during the thirteenth and fourteenth centuries.[19] Later, Primož Trubar published the first two books in Slovenian the *Katekizem* and *Abecednik*.[20] His influence in the development of the Slovene identity was recognized when Slovenia became an independent state, whereby he appears on the 10 Tolar banknote together with some fragments of his writings.[21] Such was his determination to espouse the Slovene language and identity, he translated the New and Old Testament psalms into Slovene.[22]

One of Trubar's protégés Jurij Dalmatin translated the entire Bible into Slovene (from 1547 to 1589).[23] More importantly, the works and teachings of Trubar brought to life the Slovenian language, which was the catalyst for spreading the language across Europe, even though, it has largely remained quite limited to the territory of modern day Slovenia. Although, it is commonly used in the border regions of Italy, Austria, Croatia and Hungary. It is also recognizable more broadly across the modern day states that made up the former Yugoslavia. Trubar was a great advocate for establishing schools so local people could receive an education in their native Slovene language. Nonetheless, as the European continent began to take shape, the next big influence in relation to citizenship, the nation states and the rule of law would be the American and French Revolutions.

---

[15] Ibid.

[16] Ibid.

[17] Kreacic, G., Grafenauer, B, (2000) *Karantanija: izbrane razprave in članki*, Zavod Republike Slovenije za šolstvo, Ljubljana, Slovenska matica.

[18] Ibid.

[19] Ibid, 160.

[20] Resnik-Planinc, T, (2013) *Development and present situation of Slovene didactics of geography*, Annales Universitatis Paedagogcae Cracovensis, 113.

[21] Slovenian Fact, *Famous Slovenians*, http://www.un.int/slovenia/famous.html

[22] Črnič, A., Komel, M., Smerke, M., Šabec, K., Vovk, T, (2013) *Religious Pluralisation in Slovenia,* Teorija in Praksa, let. 50, 1/205–229.

[23] Luthar, O, (2008) *The Land Between: A History of Slovenia*, Peter Lang International Academic Publishers, 225–240.

3.1.1 American Revolution

Arguably, as nation states began to evolve and take shape, the elites began to consider how its inhabitants would be formally recognised. The influence of the Greek and roman developments of the law, particularly with respect to citizenship can be found in these revolutions. Firstly, the American Revolution provided for the allegiance of the people to the state, through voluntary citizenship.[24] This new found legal status has contributed to the way citizenship has been developed as a concept by nation states ever since. In 1779, the state of Virginia established a statute describing 'citizens as all those born within the state or who had resided within the state for at least 2 years (at the time the statute was passed)'.[25] Obtaining citizenship by naturalization or relinquishing citizenship could be undertaken by attending a local court and taking an oath.[26] The 13th 14th and15th amendments to the United States constitution would make American citizenship a national status of rights that would be protected by the national courts but these were not made until after the civil war.[27]

Comparatively however, citizenship between America and Britain were different. The social organization of life in America was defined and protected by the common law, as it was in Britain.[28] However, allegiance (for British subjects) was based on natural obligations.[29] That is, subjects looked up to a master (King) and were considered to be their servants, even though they were afforded shared liberties.[30] Citizens possess a right to sovereignty and were granted protection from other citizens and the state.[31] According to John Salmond citizenship was an association of members incorporated by a body politic, and citizens were bound to one another.[32] Citizens under the English common law were not bound to one another, but bound to a common superior, owing an allegiance to the Crown.[33] Frederick Pollock and Federic Maitland reaffirmed the position of the court in the *Calvin*[34] case that determined those individuals who were not born in the territory were aliens and not

[24] Gundersen, J, (1987) *Independence, Citizenship, and the American Revolution*, Chicago Journals, The University of Chicago Press, 60–77.

[25] Ibid, 62.

[26] Ibid.

[27] Bradburn, D, (2010) *The Problem of Citizenship in the American Revolution, Binghampton University*, State University of New York, Blackwell Publishing, 1096–1099.

[28] Ibid.

[29] Ibid.

[30] Ibid. Price, P, (2013) *Natural Law and Birthright Citizenship in Calvin's Case (1608)*, Yale Journal of Law and the Humanities, Vol 9. 73–80.

[31] Ibid.

[32] Salmond, J, (1902) *Citizenship and Allegiance, Nationality in English Law*, The Law Quarterly Review, 50–54.

[33] Ibid.

[34] *Calvin Case* [1572] Eng.R. 384.

subjects of the King. Pollock and Maitland stated that in the history of the English common law, defining the subject included:

> As regards to the definition of two great classes of men which have to be distinguished from each other, the main rule is very simple. The place of birth is all important, a child within any territory that is subject to the king of England is a natural-born subject of the king of England and is no alien of England. On the other hand, with some exceptions, every child born elsewhere is an alien, no matter the nationality of his parents.[35]

The importance of the position taken by the court is arguably one of setting the legal and policy citizenship discourse across the UK and established the basis for citizenship, when Australia was later colonized by the British Empire. Arguably, the principle of citizenship by birth right, that is, being born on the territory of a states exists in most, if not all national citizenship laws today. Nonetheless, in the context of the former British Empire, allegiance dominated the legal status of citizenship, rather than a codified form of citizenship that, can be seen today. Furthermore, allegiance was absolute and permanent whereby the individual was provided protection in return for duties of fealty.[36] Allegiance to the monarchy emerged with the establishment of the Church of England in the sixteenth century.[37] Therefore, citizens during the early period can be described as a collective of people who possess a level of sovereignty while subjects were under the power of another.[38] The American Revolution was important to the development of citizenship, providing a legal status to the inhabitants of the new republic and developing a sense of what it is to be American. Not long before the American Revolution Australia was claimed for the British crown by James Cook. Australia was inhabited by Aboriginal people and was yet to be fully colonised by the British. As such the laws of Britain did not apply to Australia. Slovenia on the other hand was part of the Austrian-Hungarian Empire, and they would be directly influenced by the French Revolution.

3.1.2 French Revolution

Arguably, the next major influence on the theory and practice of citizenship and the evolution of the national identity was the French Revolution beginning in 1789. A year earlier in 1788, the First Fleet arrived in Australia[39] and the beginnings of

---

[35] Maitland, F., Pollock, F, (1968) *The History of English Law before the Time of Edwards I*, vol. 2, Liberty Fund, 1898, 458.

[36] Salmond, J, (1902) *Citizenship and Allegiance, Nationality in English Law*, The Law Quarterly Review, 50–54.

[37] Sawyer, C., Wray, H, (2014) *Country Report: United Kingdom*, EUDO Citizenship Observatory, European University Institute, 7.

[38] Bradburn, D, (2010) *The Problem of Citizenship in the American Revolution, Binghampton University*, State University of New York, Blackwell Publishing, 1096–1099.

[39] Richards, R, (1987) *Transported to New South Wales: medical convicts 1788–1850*, British Medical Journal, Vol 295, 1609.

British rule would see British law slowly introduced across the Australian territory. As discussed later in this chapter, Australia would be colonised as a whole by the British, bringing with them their laws, identity and culture.

Nevertheless, the French Revolution included; "a bourgeois, democratic, national and bureaucratic, and state strengthening revolution".[40] The French Revolution built on the idea of the nation state and national citizenship by introducing legislation that would differentiate between a French citizen and a foreigner, by affording them different sets of rights.[41] More importantly, the medieval, seigniorial rights, local privileges, municipal monopolies and provincial constitutions were all swept away by the French Revolution, which allowed the nation state to form.[42] On the backdrop of this change, the democratic revolution expanded to include political rights. However, political rights were only afforded to citizens of France. French citizenship was finally codified.[43]

It arguably expanded on the 1648 Peace of Westphalia, because states had evolved into a territory with defined borders. This boad well for the concept of citizenship and immigration. The merging states were able to assert more control over the people within the territory and aliens wanting to enter the territory by determining who were theirs. The beginnings of citizenship having a legal status could be seen from this period. Nevertheless, citizenship could be obtained by a person who was born in France; where at least one of the parents was French and was domiciled in France.[44] The principle of acquiring citizenship through birth on the territory and having one parent being French still exists today. The early developments of legal principles that underpin citizenship had also begun to take hold, which has stood the test of time and form part of citizenship law today.

The next major influence on the development of citizenship came in 1789. The Declaration of the Rights of Man and Citizen in 1789 reinforced the rights of the citizen and man within the French territory. Even though there was limited reference to the citizen, Article 6 provided that 'every citizen has a right to participate personally, or through his representative, in its foundation', and that all citizens were equal in the eyes of the law.[45] It should be noted that the Declaration reinforced the notion of the position that no one individual could exercise any authority which had not been afforded to them by the nation state.[46] The resulting effect, provided greater inclusion of the people and no longer providing sole power to a single individual.

---

[40] Brubaker, R, (1989) *The French Revolution and Invention of Citizenship*, French Politics and Society, Vol 7, No 3, 30–49. Jurgen Habermas, *Citizenship and National Identity*, in Steenberghen Bart Van, the Condition of Citizenship, SAGE Publications, 1994, 20–22.

[41] Ibid.

[42] Ibid.

[43] French Civil Code 1803, in Marie-Claire Foblets, Zeynep Tanasmayan, *Country Report: Belgium*, EUDO Citizenship Observatory, European University Institute, 2010, 2.

[44] Ibid.

[45] Declaration of the Rights of Man and Citizen, National Assembly of France August 261,789, http://www1.curriculum.edu.au/ddunits/downloads/pdf/dec_of_rights.pdf

[46] Ibid, article 3.

The rights extended to protecting an individual's liberty, property, security and resistance from oppression.[47] More importantly, the rights afforded to citizens by the 1789 Declaration have been the basis for the rights afforded to citizens by states and the international community in the modern day. For instance, the right to free communication and opinion in accordance with Article 1, continues today in the legal frameworks of Slovenia, the EU and Australia, and is considered an important democratic value.

The rights established in this early period was the beginning of states steering their citizens to behave according to the values of the state. The natural rights and freedoms had no limits other than those determined by the law.[48] That is, not only rights law, but the law in general has been used by states as a demographic tool to control and develop society. Furthermore, this saw the beginnings of the rights taking a greater role in the daily lives of citizens. Citizens were afforded protection not only against the state but also against other citizens.

Rogers Brubaker summarizes the French Revolution as levelling the legal distinction inside the nation state and providing a common substance of civil equality for all citizens.[49] National citizenship had been strengthened, which provided the basis for modern nationalism.[50] The 1804 French Civil Code was introduced[51] and went some way to define who a French citizen was. It also allowed the state to determine who was not a citizen.[52] Both the American and French Revolutions along with the Haitian Revolution[53] and Spanish Revolution all dealt with the transition of the inhabitants of the territory from subjects to citizens.[54] The nation state and democracy are two concepts that emerged from the French Revolution that can still be seen today in current day laws regarding citizenship.[55] The influence that these events had across Europe and other states cannot be underestimated. The laws of modern day nation states including Slovenia and Australia have evolved and adopted many of the principles pertaining to citizenship, deriving from these events. In other words, the acquisition for the first time of citizenship which gained a legal status. However, that legal status was limited and did not fully extend to women. It is well

---

[47] Ibid, article 2.

[48] Ibid, article 4.

[49] Brubaker, R (1989) *The French Revolution and Invention of Citizenship*, French Politics and Society, Vol 7, No 3, 30–49.

[50] Ibid.

[51] Bertossi, C., Hajjat, A, (2013) *Country Report: France*, EUDO Citizenship Observatory, European University Institute, 1–2.

[52] Ibid.

[53] opkin, J *A concise History of the Haitian Revolution*, Blackwell Publishing, 2012, 170–180.

[54] Ghachem, M, (2003) *Slavery and Citizenship in the Age of the American Revolutions*, Historical Reflections, Vol 29. No 1, 2003, 10–15.

[55] Habermas, J, (1994) *Citizenship and National Identity*, in Steenberghen Bart Van, the Condition of Citizenship, SAGE Publications, 1994, 20–22. Jurgen Habermas, *The Inclusion of the Other: Studies in Political Theory*, Edited by Ciaran Cronin and Pablo De Greiff, Translated by Carian Cronin, Cambridge: MIT Press, 1998, 130–135.

understood that in the early period women did not enjoy the same rights as men. However, it is out of scope to explore the evolution of womens rights in this book.

3.1.3 1800–1848

From the mid 1800s to the break-up of the Habsburg Monarchy, the Slovenes continued their struggle to be formally recognised. Between 1813 and 1888, the Klagenfurt Priest, Andrej Einspieler worked towards creating a United Slovenia and recognition of Slovenian autonomy within the inner provinces of Austria. However, there was little support for the idea.[56] Citizenship of the Slovenian population, at the time, was regulated by the 1811 Austrian Code.[57] Citizenship could be obtained by birth[58] or for a female foreigner marrying an Austrian citizen.[59] Citizenship could also be obtained by accepting employment in the Public Service, provided there was an uninterrupted period of residence of 10 years. Additionally, those individuals that lost their citizenship could have it reinstated by the Imperial Majesty.[60] What can be seen from this early period is the development of legal principles and concepts that continue to be present in the modern day laws of citizenship. That is, the principle of residency and loss of citizenship emerged into the legal framework. Today, modern states have retained the residency principle as part of a person wanting to acquire citizenship by naturalisation. Additionally, Slovenia and Australia allow for the loss of, and reinstatement of citizenship.

3.1.4 1848–1900

The March Revolution in 1848 (known as the Spring of Nations) resulted in Slovenes demanding unification of all territories into one unit under the Austrian emperor.[61] Otherwise referred to as the revolutions of 1848 in the German states, broke out in many European countries. They were a series of loosely coordinated protests and

[56] Štih, P., Simoniti, V., Vodopivec, P, (2008) *Slovene History, Society-Politics-Culture*, Besedilni podatki, Ljubljana: Inštitut za novejšo zgodovino: Sistory, 296.

[57] Medved, F, *EUDO Citizenship Observatory Country Report Slovenia,* European University Institute, Robert Schuman Centre for Advanced Studies, 2010, 5–30.

[58] Section 28 Austrian Civil Code 1811, Great Britain, Report of the Royal Commission for Inquiring into the Laws of Naturalisation and Allegiance: An account of British and Foreign Laws, and of the Diplomatic Correspondence, Reports from Foreign States, and other Papers, 1896, 2–30.

[59] Decree of the Imperial Chancery, 23 February 1833, No. 2.569.

[60] Ibid, article 29.

[61] Klemenčič, M., Žagar, M, (2004) *Ethnic Diversity within Nations, The Former Yugoslavia's Diverse Peoples*: A Reference Sourcebook, 49.

rebellions in the states of the German Confederation, including the Austrian Empire. The revolutions, which stressed pan-Germanism, demonstrated popular discontent with the traditional, largely autocratic political structure of the 39 independent states of the Confederation that inherited the German territory of the former Holy Roman Empire. The resulting effect saw the rise of the middle class seeking improvements to working and daily life conditions. However, they would have to contend with higher forces and many liberals were forced in exile, making their way to the United States. Moreover, and similar to the French in 1789, the Frankfurt Parliament throughout the late spring of 1848, gave a very great deal of its attention to questions of basic constitutional law. Citizenship was front and center of this debate, endeavouring to frame a *Grundrecht* or "Declaration of the Fundamental Rights of the German People." From this movement, it can be seen how continental Europe had begun to take major steps forward in establishing citizenship as a formal legal; concept of the state. Since then, the law of Germany has not influenced Europe, but also can be found in the modern day Slovene legal framework.

On the backdrop of the events taking place from the March Spring, Slovene nationalism would evolve and be strengthened by peasants' who signed petitions between 1848 and 1849. The were seeking to unite Slovenes.[62] Josip Mursec and other scholars petitioned and prepared a memorandum for the Slovene nationality and language to be formally recognized.[63] Matija Majar (a Carinthian, Slovenian Catholic priest) would attempt to establish a Kingdom for Slovenes [Slovenian: Združena Slovenija] in their own right - in 1848.[64] However, a Kingdom was not successfully proclaimed. In his attempt, Majar[65] wrote:

'What We Slovenians, Demand':

1. *Slovenians must unite and have a general local assembly.*
2. *The Slovenian language in the Slovenian region must have the same rights as German has in German regions and Italian in Italian regions.*
3. *Slovenians are free to introduce the Slovenian language to all institutions, universities and secondary schools whenever they choose.*
4. *Each civil servant must learn the Slovenian language before being appointed to a civil institution in Slovenian regions.*
5. *In each high school in Slovenia, Slovenian language teachers must understand all Slavic dialects.*
6. *Slovenes do not want to be in the German alliance, they are loyal to their emperor and constitutional government. Any alliance with the Germans (outside Austria) would obviously hurt us, they would dominate us with the German language and culture, take over our cities, then our castles and finally our fields and vineyards, as this has already happened in some area.*[66]

---

[62] Ibid.

[63] Klemenčič, M., Žagar, M, (2004) *Ethnic Diversity within Nations, The Former Yugoslavia's Diverse Peoples*: A Reference Sourcebook.

[64] Ibid.

[65] Vasiljevna Čurkina, I, (2011) *Matija Majar Ziljski, Enlightener, Politician, Scholar*, Traditiones, 40/2, 9–26.

[66] Ibid.

The importance of the words used by Majar cannot be underestimated. Majar was demanding the Slovenian language be used across all areas of life. It reinforces the earlier point that language as part of an identity, to some people (s) and states is a principal policy and legal concept. It plays a similar role to that of citizenship by creating a sense of belonging, commonality and continuity amongst the people. More importantly, [Iskra] Čurkina in referring to Janko Pleterski argues that Majar's activities and writing (s) played a major role in the further development of the Slovenian national movement.[67] Arguably, this went further also expanding the identity fo the Slovene's to what can be seen today, the Slovene national identity. Between 1869 and 1871, Matjaž Klemenčič and Mitja Žagar bother argue that the demands for a United Slovenia were reaffirmed when the taborsko gibanje occurred (English: mass meetings movement), through which the modern Slovenian national consciousness began to spread to peasants and townspeople.[68]

Throughout this period there were subtle, at the time, but significant advances of the Slovene identity. The first newspapers in Slovene began appearing in Ljubljana in about 1848. In the same year Fran Milkošič published a manifesto in the Slovene newspaper *Novice*. During the same period "Zdravljica" (English: A Toast), a poem was written by a Slovene poet France Prešeren, in Slovenian. The poem would become one of the fundamental elements of the current day Slovenian identity. It was later adopted as the national anthem in the 1980s and is referred to in article 6 of the current day Slovenian constitution. Furthermore, its importance to the Slovenian state and national identity ensured the national anthem was codified following independence by the Act Regulating the Coat-of-Arms, Flag and Anthem of the Republic of Slovenia of the Slovenian Nation.[69]

The push for the Slovene language be formally recognized was gathering pace, and in 1849, the Austrian Civil Code was translated into Slovenian by the government. It was backed by an order to the local provinces to translate provincial laws into the provincial languages (including Slovenian).[70] Australia at the time was being colonised and the first Slovenian arrived to Australia[71] in 1855 along with many other immigrants from Europe including from the United Kingdom, France, Italy, Germany, Poland and Hungary. This was an important moment for Australia and Slovenia. Australia and Slovenia saw the beginnings of a long standing relationship that can still be seen today.

Because of the separation of the Austrian and Hungarian territories, there were separate laws in the Hungarian territory that, specifically dealt with citizenship. The

---

[67] Ibid.

[68] Klemenčič, M., Žagar, M, (2004) *Ethnic Diversity within Nations, The Former Yugoslavia's Diverse Peoples*: A Reference Sourcebook, 49.

[69] Official Gazette of the Republic of Slovenia, 67/1994.

[70] Štih, P., Simoniti, V., Vodopivec, P, (2008) *Slovene History, Society-Politics-Culture*, Besedilni podatki, Ljubljana: Inštitut za novejšo zgodovino: Sistory, 287.

[71] Immigration from Slovenia, http://museumvictoria.com.au/origins/history.aspx?pid=54

Hungarian nationality laws of 1868 provided equal rights to its people,[72] which were part of the creation of the separate Hungarian crown. People who did not speak or use Magyar were granted the right to use their mother tongue in special circumstances such as in the courts, books, texts and lectures at the National University. However, the nationality laws were limited, and did not extend to the regions of Slavonia (Croatia) and Dalmatia.[73] Rainer Bauböck and Dilek Cinar argue that in 1867 when Hungary gained autonomy of their citizenship legislation, citizens within the Austrian part of the empire were treated as foreigners.[74] During the same period, Slovenian academia and cultural life became closely entwined with national politics. The academic associations of Germans and Slovenians worked together to promote Slovenian culture.[75] This was reinforced with The Society of Hermagoras working in Klagenfurt which had 25,000 members, which released books and educational material.[76]

Despite Slovenes being present in both the Austrian and Hungarian sections of the empire, those Slovenians residing in the Hungarian sector were subject to the Hungarian Nationality Law of December 1879. These laws outlined how a person could become a citizen of the territory. Similar to the Austrian Code, individuals could obtain citizenship by descent, legitimisation, marriage and naturalisation.[77] Legitimisation was quite progressive for the time allowing citizenship to be obtained by a Hungarian's illegitimate children born to an alien woman.[78] However, the provision did not extend to women who were Hungarian citizens. Citizenship by descent[79] could only be obtained following 10 years of continuous residence in the territory. However, a notable difference between the two territories was the acceptance of dual citizenship under the Hungarian territory. Dual citizenship was not permitted under Austrian law. Importantly, the citizenship laws under Habsburg rule continued through to the formation of the Kingdom of Serbs, Croats and Slovenes.

Prior to World War I (WW I) being declared, the rulers within the Austro-Hungarian Empire were concerned about issues surrounding the Balkan region, particularly in the area occupied by the Bosnians.[80] What followed was the assassination

---

[72] Viator, S., *Racial Problems in Hungary*, Hungary Law on Nationalities 1868, http://www.oocities.org/gogastransylvania/Seton-Watson/Appendice03.htm

[73] Ibid.

[74] Bauböck, R., Cinar, D, (2011) *Nationality law and Naturalisation in Austria*, (draft) 1–12.

[75] Štih, P., Simoniti, V., Vodopivec, P, (2008) *Slovene History, Society-Politics-Culture, Besedilni podatki*, Ljubljana: Inštitut za novejšo zgodovino: Sistory, 296.

[76] Ibid.

[77] Floumoy, R., Hudson, M, (1930) *A Collection of nationality laws of various countries*, as contained in Constitutions, Statutes and Treaties, Carnegie Endowerment for International Peace, 337–344.

[78] Ibid, legitimation Article 4, citizenship is acquired by a Hungarian citizen's illegitimate children born by an alien woman through legitimation.

[79] von Hirschhausen, U, (2009) *From imperial inclusion to national exclusion: citizenship in the Habsburg monarchy and in Austria 1867–1923*, European Review of History, 551–573.

[80] Ibid.

of Archduke Franz Ferdinand on 28 June 1914 [who was], the heir to the Austrian throne. The assassination resulted in a diplomatic crisis and as a result the fighting began.[81] The resulting effect saw Russia came to the defence of Serbia and Germany began to invade its neighbours Belgium and Luxembourg.[82] WWI broke out across the territory of continental Europe and lasted for 5 years.

3.1.5 World War I (WW I)

WW I had such a profound impact across Europe, not only to the population.[83] WW I began in July 1914 and concluded in November 1919. What followed was that the Austrian-Hungarian, German and Ottoman Empires all disintegrated while the internal borders of Europe would be redrawn. During WW I the Slovenians aligned themselves with the South Slavs who spoke a similar language, and in "1915 the Yugoslav Committee was founded in Paris".[84] The Australian territory was not impacted from the war, however many Australians would find themselves across Europe assisting the Allied Forces. According to Ben Bagwell, the Slovenes and Croats, by joining the South Slav alliance would be granted greater autonomy in the new Kingdom.[85] The committee was represented by Slovenes, Croats and Serbs who advised the Allied Forces in relation to those people who inhabited the Austrian-Hungarian territory and how to establish an autonomous state.[86] William Bartlett argues the committee's work was unsuccessful and the Entente Powers (the Allies) had already reached agreement in Italy, where Italy inherited parts of Dalmatia.[87] As the war progressed Slovenes[88] found themselves being drawn closer to aligning with the South Slavs.

What followed was the establishment of the May Declaration in 1917. It demanded the unification of the Slovenes, Croats and Serbs (three peoples) residing under Habsburg rule to be under a single constitutional entity.[89] Two months later in July 1917, the Corfu Conference and Declaration led to the formation and unification of the Kingdom of Serbs, Croats and Slovenes.[90] Importantly, the Corfu Declaration was

---

[81] Ibid.

[82] Ibid.

[83] Williamson, S, (1988) *The Origins of World War I, The Journal of Interdisciplinary History*, Vol. 18, No. 4, 795–818.

[84] von Hirschhausen, U, (2009) *From imperial inclusion to national exclusion: citizenship in the Habsburg monarchy and in Austria 1867–1923*, European Review of History, 2009, 551–573.

[85] Ben Bagwell, *Yugoslavian Constitutional Questions: Self-Determination and Secession of Member Republics*, 21, Georgia. J. Int'l & Comp. L., 1991, 489–499.

[86] Mavčič, A *The Slovenian Constitutional Review*, www.concourts.net, 2009, 10.

[87] Bartlett, W, (2003) *Croatia between Europe and the Balkans*, Routledge, 13.

[88] Meier, V, (1999) *Yugoslavia: A History of its Demise*, Routledge, 53.

[89] Mavčič, A *The Slovenian Constitutional Review*, www.concourts.net, 2009, 10.

[90] Frucht, R, (2005) *Eastern Europe: an introduction to the people, land, and culture*, Library of Congress in Publication data, 420–430.

considered to be a legal agreement between the Yugoslav Committee and the Ravai Serbian Government, attempting to be a final settlement on the political form, function and organization of the new Kingdom.[91] This was an important time for Slovene's. While they may not have fully accepted the idea of aligning themselves with the South Slavs, at the time, it appears to have been a direction of least resistance.

The first Vidovdan (St Vitis Day) constitution declared the temporary royal dictatorship of the new Kingdom of Serbs, Croats and Slovenes, and centralized administration to Belgrade.[92] However, the Slovene territory had been divided into two districts of Ljubljana and Maribor.[93] The declaration allowed for the Kingdom to be formed under a constitution in October 1918.[94] A year later, the Kingdom of Serbs, Croats and Slovenes (renamed the Kingdom of Yugoslavia 1918) was finalized in 1919. The resulting effect was positive for Slovenes. On the one side, the Slovene territory began to take shape with the borders being drawn between Italy, Austria, Hungary and Croatia.[95] On the other side, the southern border of Slovenia with Croatia was an internal administrative border of Yugoslavia. By defining the external borders with Italy and Austria in 1918, resulted in a wider acceptance of the Slovene identity, even though it was now part of a new Kingdom. Nevertheless, the Slovenes would for the first time have a defined territory of their own, albeit, as it continued to evolve and take shape as their interrogating into the new Kingdom continued for the next few decades. As WWI continued, the political elites began to look at how to formally bring the territories and peoples together, which resulted in the Treaty of Versailles being established.

3.1.6 Treaties of Versailles and Germain

In 1919 Treaty of Versailles was signed and implemented. The Treaty was an important step to ending the war between Germany and the Allied Forces. Even though the fighting did not stop across Europe in 1919, the road to peace for the people of Europe and those people who occupied the modern day Slovene territories had begun. The League of Nations was established in June 1919. The official languages of the League of Nations were English, French and Spanish.[96] More importantly, the League of Nations played a major role in promoting international cooperation, peace and security across Europe. The road to international co-operation would assist in promoting transnational activities such as trade, transport and finance.

---

[91] Sotirovič, V, (2014) *The 1917 Corfu Declaration*, The South Journal, Vol. 33. No 1, 2–6.

[92] Gow, J., Carmichael, C, (2001) *Slovenia and Slovenes: A Small State and the New Europe*, C. Hurst & Co, 35.

[93] Ibid.

[94] Mavčič, A *The Slovenian Constitutional Review*, www.concourts.net, 2009, 10.

[95] Radan, P, (2002) *The Breakup of Yugoslavia and International Law*, Routledge, 137–145.

[96] Mavčič, A *The Slovenian Constitutional Review*, www.concourts.net, 2009, 10.

Despite the short history of the League of Nations, it would not prevent the rise of Nazism.

In the same year, the peace treaties of St Germain in 1919, declared the Austrian Hungarian Empire to be dissolved. Article 70 provided that every person possessing the right of citizenship in the territory of the Austro-Hungarian Monarchy shall obtain exclusion of Austrian nationality.[97] Article 76 went further stating that persons who acquired the rights to citizenship after 1 January 1910 did not acquire nationality without a permit from the state of Serbs, Croats and Slovenes.

The Treaty of Trianon came a year later in 1920, and provided citizenship through succession, ensuring continuity throughout the region, and defined the Hungarian borders. Individuals having the right to citizenship under the Austro-Hungarian monarch, could opt for either citizenship of either Austria, Italy, Poland, Romania or the Kingdom of Serbs, Croats and Slovenes.[98] Citizenship had begun expanding its role confirming the legal status of citizens within a territory, but also provided continuity of that legal status in the transition from one ruler to another and the changing territorial boundaries of empires and kingdoms. The continuity, provided by the law, would also allow the rulers over the territory to impart the identity of the Empire or Kingdom to the new rulers. It also enables people to retain their citizenship. It further strengthened the sense of belonging and certainty for the people, even though their rulers would impose a different form of governance over the territory.

3.1.7 Kingdom of Serbs, Croats and Slovenes

The Kingdom of Serbs, Croats and Slovenes would mark a new beginning for the Slovene people. However, they would not rid themselves of the Austrian – Hungarian monarch totally. The citizenship laws of the Habsburg period were carried over to the Kingdom of Serbs, Croats and Slovenes.[99] Furthermore, the Austrian Civil Code 1811would remain in place until the 1946 Yugoslav constitution had been implemented. According to Andre Liebich "individuals having citizenship in the former Austro-Hungary territory could choose to have either citizenship of the state, or, citizenship of the state where the population predominantly was of the same race and spoke the same language.[100] Providing that flexibility of choice may have favored

---

[97] Article 70 Treaty of Peace between the Allied and Associated Powers and Australia: Protocol, Declaration and Special Declaration (St. Germain-en-Laye, 10 September 1919) Australian Treaty Series 1920 No.3.

[98] Ibid, article 80.

[99] Rava, N *Country Report: Serbia*, European University Institute, EUDO Citizenship Observatory, (2010), 3.

[100] Article 64, Treaty of Trianon and Article 80 Treaty of Saint Germain, in Andre Liebech, Altneulander or the vicissitudes of citizenship in the new EU states, Working Paper Series 5, Osterreichische, Akademie der, Wissenschaften, Commission for Migration and Integration Research, 2005, 2–21.

Slovenes, by enabling individuals with a common language to remain together. This recognition of the common Slovenian language would contribute to the formation of a wider community of Slovenians. As the community and population grew, the Slovenian language would be used by more people within the Kingdom and within other neighboring states, which ensured it became increasingly recognized.

In 1911, there was an attempt by the Lower House of the Austrian Parliament to pass legislation that would allow women's participation in political associations. The legislation would not pass.[101] It wasn't until after WWII when women's rights in Yugoslavia would be expanded and they again would have a greater role in the political discourse of the kingdom. Some 10 years later the 1921 constitution of the Kingdom of Serbs, Croats and Slovenes stated 'all citizens were equal'[102] in an attempt to unify the people. The constitution reinforced the administrative districts (*oblasti*) as the basis of political, economic and administrative units within Yugoslavia.[103] However, it wasn't until 1928 that the citizenship laws[104] were approved and legislation was introduced into the Kingdom.[105] These new laws were based on the principle of *ius sanguinis*.[106] Medved reinforces this point and argues that the 1928 citizenship laws went some way to unifying the people and developing a single Yugoslav identity.[107] The citizenship laws also confirmed the legal status or people under the newly formed kingdom. However, a single Yugoslav identity would never be realised. King Alexander proclaimed personal rule over the Yugoslav territory on 6 January 1929.[108] The name of the Kingdom would be changed to the Kingdom of Yugoslavia in 1929.

The decade of the 1930s saw the further political destabilization throughout the Kingdom. King Alexander's rule came to an end in September 1931, with the introduction of the unitarist Constitution of the Kingdom of Yugoslavia.[109] There was considerable restructuring of the districts, which were reduced from 33 to 9 provinces. Ljubljana (the capital of modern day Slovenia) and the Slovene territory came under the province of *Dravska*.[110] In 1934, King Alexander was assassinated by

---

[101] Ibid.

[102] Shoup, P, (1963) *Yugoslavia's National Minorities Under Communism,* Slavic Review, 65.

[103] 1921 Constitution of the Kingdom of Serbs, Croats and Slovenes, in Peter Radan, *The Breakup of Yugoslavia and International Law*, Routledge, 2002, 137–145.

[104] 1928 Citizenship Act, in Felicita Medved, *Country Report: Slovenia*, University Institute, EUDO Citizenship Observatory, 2010, 2.

[105] Zakon o državljanstvu kraljevine S. H. S. z 21. 9. 1928, *Uradni list ljubljanske in mariborske oblasti z dne* 19. 11. 1928, št. 109

[106] 1928 Citizenship Act, in Felicita Medved, *Country Report: Slovenia*, University Institute, EUDO Citizenship Observatory, 2013, 1–5.

[107] Ibid.

[108] Radan, P, (2002) *The Breakup of Yugoslavia and International Law*, Routledge, 137–145.

[109] Ibid.

[110] Ibid.

Croatian and Macedonian revolutionaries[111] and the Regency Council was installed. This Council would be headed by the King's cousin Prince Paul.[112] The Regency Council was, at the time, considered to be a mock parliamentary system maintaining central power that continued until 1941,[113] when the Yugoslav territory was invaded by the Axis. The Draft Decree of the Banovina Slovenia in August 1939 (drafted on the basis of the Decree of the Banovina Hrvartska) had incorporated some elements of the constitution.[114] In August 1939, a quasi federal system in Yugoslavia was introduced that saw the creation of the Croatian *banovina*.[115] Peter Radan argues that at the time, Slovenes supported the establishment of the Croatian *banovina* in the hope they (the Slovenes) would also be granted a *banovina*.[116] However, this did not occur. Should the *banovina* been granted at the time, it could be argued that it would have further enhanced the Slovene identity and further strengthened their move towards independence. Not long after this period, Europe again would descend into war.

3.1.8 1939–1945

WWII began in 1939, and again Europe and its inhabitants would be subject to war and conflict until 1945. Slovenes would be particularly impacted by the German (including Italian and Hungarian) invasion. Many Slovenes would leave the territory and migrate to other countries within and outside of Europe. This included countries such as Austria, Italy, Germany, Switzerland, Australia, Argentina and the United States. The Axis Powers created an Independent State of Croatia in 1941, which saw the Serbs persecuted.[117] Across Yugoslavia including the Slovene territory, national and religious tension emerged between Croats and Serbs, which escalated into further conflict. According to Irina Ognyanova the war became increasingly nationalistic and within Croatia Ustasha's nationalism reached its highest and most extreme.[118] The Ustasha was an organization made up of Croatian nationalists and their oath demanded independence - 'I swear to fight in the Ustasha army for a free

[111] Djokic, D, (2010) *National Mobilisation in the Kingdom of Yugoslavia*, in Dejan Djokic and Jker-Lindsaym, New Perspective on Yugoslavia: Key Issues and Controversies, London and New York: Routedge.

[112] Singleton, F, (1989) *A Short History of the Yugoslav Peoples*, Cambridge University Press, 145.

[113] Ibid.

[114] Radan, P, (2002) *The Breakup of Yugoslavia and International Law*, Routledge, 137–145.

[115] Ibid.

[116] Ibid.

[117] Ognyanova, I, (2000) *Nationalism and National Policy in Independent State of Croatia* (1941–1945), in Topics in Feminism, History and Philosophy, IWM Junior Visiting Fellows Conferences, Vol. 6, edited by Rogers, Dorothy, Joshua Wheeler, Marina Zavacka and Shawna Casebier. Vienne: IWM 2000.

[118] Ibid.

Independent Croatian State'.[119] Even though the Ustasha assumed power that was created by the Germans, an independent state did not succeed and Croatia would again become part of Yugoslavia. Despite the support from the Allied Forces in the defence of the Yugoslav territory, there continued to be internal power struggles between the Četnick and Partisans.

The Partisans led by Josip Broz Tito would prevail. Tito would inherit the leadership. He would bring a flexible leadership style to the territory and worked hard to ensure the different ethnic groups that resided throughout Yugoslavia were considered equal. Tito's influence cannot be underestimated. As a leader he was not only able to make a valuable contribution to uniting the Yugoslav people, but he also managed to ensure there would be very little conflict throughout the territory, while he remained leader. This stability would be good for Slovenians in continuing to quietly pursue their position within Yugoslavia. However, it is argued that while to the outside world it appeared there was a period of stability within Yugoslavia, however, this was far from the truth. Slovenes would become under the rule of totalitarianism. This did not pose well for the Slovenes, as their rights would be diluted. Slovenians were progressive and considered economically advantaged having access to central and western Europe.

Between 9142 and 1945, a lot was happening across the European continent. Apart from the war, several committees had been formed to provide a basis for the future governance of the territory and its people. Beginning in September 1941, the first Slovenian Parliament (Committee of National Liberation) was established. Its principal role was to represent the whole nation and was considered to be a crucial step towards independent sovereignty.[120] A year later in 1942, the first session of the Antifascist Council of the People's Liberation of Yugoslavia (AVNOJ), an ostensibly multi-party 'partisan Parliament' organized by the Communist Party of Yugoslavia - declared itself the legitimate representative of the Yugoslav Peoples.[121] A further year on in October 1943, in Kočevje, the next iteration of the Slovenian National Liberation Committee was formed, which adopted a declaration incorporating Slovenia into federal Yugoslavia, on the basis of self-determination.[122] The following year, in February 1944, the "Council" and the National Committee of the Liberation Front was established, and the first Slovenian Government was constituted on 5 May 1945 in Ajdovščina.[123] Zoran Polič became the first Slovenian Minister for Interior and in June of the same year the government would invite all

---

[119] Ibid.

[120] Ferš, D, (2003) *From Security and Intelligence Service to Slovene Intelligence and Security Agency*, Slovenian Intelligence and Security Agency, National Security and the Future, 1–2 (3), 61–65.

[121] Radan, R, (2002) *The Breakup of Yugoslavia and International Law*, Routledge, 137–145.

[122] Prunk, J., Šavli, J *Slovenian in light of Parliamentary Tradition*, 2008, http://imss.dz-rs.si/imis/6eb718f995c33fb7ce4f.pdf

[123] Ibid.

former state employees to report to their former employment.[124] Due to the war, most of the government services ceased and many employees would defend Yugoslav (and Slovenian) interests.

Nonetheless, and on the backdrop of the war, the 1928 citizenship legislation of the former Kingdom of Serbs, Croats and Slovenes was used as the basis of forming the citizenship laws of Yugoslavia from 1945 to 1989.[125] Doing so, ensured that the citizenship law continued to define the legal status of people within the territory and provided continuity of the people within the state. Arguably, there were attempts to ensure that the inhabitants would not become stateless. However, during the war, between 1941 to 1945 German and Hungarian citizenship law applied to the territories, as a result of their occupation.[126] Thus many Slovenes, depending on where they were located, were considered either German or Hungarian citizens. This had a significant impact on the development of the single Yugoslav identity. Arguably, it halted any further progress of the Slovene identity, and most likely set it back decades. The separation of the citizenship laws resembled the legal framework for citizenship in the former Austrian Hungarian Empire, where there were separate laws for the Austrian and Hungarian territories. German and Hungarian influence had rained over the Slovenian territory during the war. The resulting effect was Slovenians found themselves having to become citizens of a foreign occupying power. Again, the Slovenes found themselves being reluctantly ruled, occupied and citizens of an occupying force. Nonetheless, the resilience of the Slovene people would be tested that, arguably placed them in a good position following the war both economically and socially. The resulting impact to the Slovene's saw them assume, even for a brief period, an identity that, was imposed on them. Notably though, the German and Hungarian national identity are very different in many ways to that of the Slovene identity. An obvious example, is the Slovenian language, to that of Hungarian and German.

WWII began in 1939, and again Europe and its inhabitants would be subject to war and conflict until 1945. Slovenes would be particularly impacted by the German (including Italian and Hungarian) invasion. Many Slovenes would leave the territory and migrate to other countries within and outside of Europe. This included countries such as Austria, Italy, Germany, Switzerland, Australia, Argentina and the United States. The Axis Powers created an Independent State of Croatia in 1941, which saw the Serbs persecuted.[127] Across Yugoslavia including

[124] Pogorevc, M *Director General of the Police*, The Slovene Police, http://www.policija.si/eng/images/stories/Publications/book_slovene-police.pdf

[125] Prunk, J., Šavli, J *Slovenian in light of Parliamentary Tradition*, 2008, http://imss.dz-rs.si/imis/6eb718f995c33fb7ce4f.pdf

[126] Bauböck, R, (2009) Bernard Perching and Viebke Sievers, *Citizenship Policies in the New Europe*, Expanded and Updated Edition, Amsterdam University Press, 330–350.

[127] Ognyanova, I, (2000) *Nationalism and National Policy in Independent State of Croatia* (1941–1945), in Topics in Feminism, History and Philosophy, IWM Junior Visiting Fellows Conferences, Vol. 6, edited by Rogers, Dorothy, Joshua Wheeler, Marina Zavacka and Shawna Casebier. Vienne: IWM 2000.

the Slovene territory, national and religious tension emerged between Croats and Serbs, which escalated into further conflict. According to Irina Ognyanova the war became increasingly nationalistic and within Croatia Ustasha's nationalism reached its highest and most extreme.[128] The Ustasha was an organization made up of Croatian nationalists and their oath demanded independence - 'I swear to fight in the Ustasha army for a free Independent Croatian State'.[129] Even though the Ustasha assumed power that was created by the Germans, an independent state did not succeed and Croatia would again become part of Yugoslavia. Despite the support from the Allied Forces in the defence of the Yugoslav territory, there continued to be internal power struggles between the Četnick and Partisans.

The Partisans led by Josip Broz Tito would prevail. Tito would inherit the leadership. He would bring a flexible leadership style to the territory and worked hard to ensure the different ethnic groups that resided throughout Yugoslavia were considered equal. Tito's influence cannot be underestimated. As a leader he was not only able to make a valuable contribution to uniting the Yugoslav people, but he also managed to ensure there would be very little conflict throughout the territory, while he remained leader. This stability would be good for Slovenians in continuing to quietly pursue their position within Yugoslavia. However, it is argued that while to the outside world it appeared there was a period of stability within Yugoslavia, thus was far from the truth. Slovenes would become under the rule of totalitarianism. This not pose well for the Slovenes, as their rights would be diluted. Slovenians were progressive and considered economically advantaged having access to central and western Europe.

Between 9142 and 1945, a lot was happening across the European continent. Apart from the war, several committees had been formed to provide a basis for the future governance of the territory and its people. Beginning in September 1941, the first Slovenian Parliament (Committee of National Liberation) was established. Its principal role was to represent the whole nation and was considered to be a crucial step towards independent sovereignty.[130] A year later in 1942, the first session of the Antifascist Council of the People's Liberation of Yugoslavia (AVNOJ), an ostensibly multi-party 'partisan Parliament' organized by the Communist Party of Yugoslavia - declared itself the legitimate representative of the Yugoslav Peoples.[131] A further year on in October 1943, in Kočevje, the next iteration of the Slovenian National Liberation Committee was formed, which adopted a declaration incorporating Slovenia into federal Yugoslavia, on the basis of self-determination.[132] The following year, in February 1944, the "Council" and the National Committee of the

---

[128] Ibid.

[129] Ibid.

[130] Ferš, D, (2003) *From Security and Intelligence Service to Slovene Intelligence and Security Agency*, Slovenian Intelligence and Security Agency, National Security and the Future, 1–2 (3), 61–65.

[131] Radan, R, (2002) *The Breakup of Yugoslavia and International Law*, Routledge, 137–145.

[132] Prunk, J., Šavli, J *Slovenian in light of Parliamentary Tradition*, 2008, http://imss.dz-rs.si/imis/6eb718f995c33fb7ce4f.pdf

Liberation Front was established, and the first Slovenian Government was constituted on 5 May 1945 in Ajdovščina.[133] Zoran Polič became the first Slovenian Minister for Interior and in June of the same year the government would invite all former state employees to report to their former employment.[134] Due to the war, most of the government services ceased and many employees would defend Yugoslav (and Slovenian) interests.

Nonetheless, and on the backdrop of the war, the 1928 citizenship legislation of the former Kingdom of Serbs, Croats and Slovenes was used as the basis of forming the citizenship laws of Yugoslavia from 1945 to 1989.[135] Doing so, ensured that the citizenship law continued to define the legal status of people within the territory and provided continuity of the people within the state. Arguably, there were attempts to ensure that the inhabitants would not become stateless. However, during the war, between 1941 to 1945 German and Hungarian citizenship law applied to the territories, as a result of their occupation.[136] Thus many Slovenes, depending on where they were located, were considered either German or Hungarian citizens. This had a significant impact on the development of the single Yugoslav identity. Arguably, it halted any further progress of the Slovene identity, and most likely set it back decades. The separation of the citizenship laws resembled the legal framework for citizenship in the former Austrian Hungarian Empire, where there were separate laws for the Austrian and Hungarian territories. German and Hungarian influence had rained over the Slovenian territory during the war. The resulting effect was Slovenians found themselves having to become citizens of a foreign occupying power. Again, the Slovenes found themselves being reluctantly ruled, occupied and citizens of an occupying force. Nonetheless, the resilience of the Slovene people would be tested that, arguably placed them in a good position following the war both economically and socially. The resulting impact to the Slovene's saw them assume, even for a brief period, an identity that, was imposed on them. Notably though, the German and Hungarian national identity are very different in many ways to that of the Slovene identity. An obvious example, is the Slovenian language, to that of Hungarian and German.

At the conclusion of WWII, the law on citizenship for the Democratic Federal Republic of Yugoslavia[137] was adopted on 23 August 1945.[138] The new laws stated that a citizen of the state was considered to be all those people who on the 6th of

---

[133] Ibid.

[134] Pogorevc, M *Director General of the Police*, The Slovene Police, http://www.policija.si/eng/images/stories/Publications/book_slovene-police.pdf

[135] Prunk, J., Šavli, J *Slovenian in light of Parliamentary Tradition*, 2008, http://imss.dz-rs.si/imis/6eb718f995c33fb7ce4f.pdf

[136] Bauböck, R, (2009) Bernard Perching and Viebke Sievers, *Citizenship Policies in the New Europe*, Expanded and Updated Edition, Amsterdam University Press, 330–350.

[137] From 10/8–1945 to 29/11–1945: based on the agreement of Tito-Šubašić signed on 16 June, 1944, the delegates of the third session of Anti-Fascist Council in Belgrade 10 August 1945 announced a new country as the Democratic Federal Yugoslavia (DFJ).

[138] Zakon o državljanstvu DFJ, Official Gazette DFJ, No. 64/1945.

April 1941 had been domiciled in one of the previous Yugoslavian municipalities. They provided a level of ongoing continuity and unification of the citizenry across the territory. The constitution of the Yugoslav Federation of 1946 (named the Federal Peoples' Republic of Yugoslavia) was modelled on Stalin's Soviet constitutions,[139] and strongly emphasized a federal system of governance. Furthermore, the 1946 constitution[140] provided for the six Republics, which included Slovenia, Croatia, Serbia, Macedonia, Montenegro as well as Bosnia and Herzegovina.[141] Article 1 stated that the Federative People's Republic of Yugoslavia is a federal people's State, Republican in form, a community of peoples equal in rights who, on the basis of the right to self-determination, including the right of separation, have expressed their will to live to together in a federative State.[142] Arguably, the inclusion of this provision (and the words 'right to self-determinate and right of separation') was a pivotal moment in the history for Slovenes and Slovenia. Whether by accident or by design, it provided Slovenia and other Yugoslav Republics with the first steps towards independence. The 1945 citizenship legislation also introduced the concept of dual citizenship that allowed for citizenship at both the Federal and Republic level. However, citizenship at the Republic level had no legal effect. Yet, what it did do was form the basis for citizenship when Slovenia would separate from Yugoslavia.

3.1.9 1946–1950

The 1946 Constitution of Yugoslavia was an important unifying law. It stated that all republican citizenships across the entire territory of Yugoslavia were equal in status.[143] In other words, Article 2 of the citizenship act stated that citizenship excluded any other citizenship and there was no ability for any person to have dual citizenship. A Slovene could have Republic and Federal citizenship; however, they were not entitled to have citizenship of another state such as Australia. This limitation had very little effect to the overall development of the Slovene identity, other than, the people and the state no embracing what would become a more liberal approach to citizenship. Furthermore, the 1946 constitution provided the basis for the rights and duties of its citizens. Most notable, was the introduction of Article 21 that ensured

139 Haug Hilde, K, (2012) *Creating a Socialist Yugoslavia: Tito, Communist Leadership and National*, I.B. Tauris, London, Chapter 4.

140 Constitution of the Federative People's Republic of Yugoslavia, Official Gazette of the Federative People's Republic of Yugoslavia 1946.

141 Article 12, The Constitution of the Republic of Slovenia, Official Gazette Republic of Slovenia Nos. 33/91-I, 42/97, 66/2000, 24/03, 69/04, 68/06, and 47/13.

142 Article 1, Constitution of Yugoslavia 1946, in Ben Bagwell, Yugoslavian *Constitutional Questions: Self-Determination and Secession of Member Republics*, 21, Georgia. J. Int'l & Comp. L., 1991, 489–499.

143 Ustava FLRJ, Official Gazette FLRJ, No. 10/46. Citizenship Act of the Peoples Republic of Slovenia, Official Gazette of the Democratic Republic of Yugoslavia 64/1945.

there was equality before the law of all citizens (men and women) no matter what race or nationality. It also provided for a number of fundamental rights that can be seen today. For instance, Yugoslav citizens were afforded the right to elect and be elected, along with equal rights for women, the right to education, and the freedom of conscience. They were also afforded the religion, the protection of the family, and the freedom of speech, association and assembly.[144] Arguably, it could be considered progressive law for its time. These rights went some way to unifying the citizens of Yugoslavia. However, they fell short of creating a single Yugoslav identity. Furthermore, as part of the modern day legal framework of the European Union and Slovenia, these rights form part of the national identity of Slovenia.

More importantly, for Slovenia, the people's right to self-determination[145] was reinforced within the 1946 constitution. Article 1 was reinforced by articles 2 and 10 of the constitution of the People's Republic of Slovenia 1947. In other words, while there was a federal constitution for the whole of Yugoslavia, the Slovenian Republic had its own constitution that resembled in large part the federal constitution. This was arguably a pivotal step towards Slovenian independence in 1990. The Slovenian constitution of 1947 ensured the organization of Slovenia as a Constituent Republic of the Yugoslav Federation, would be based on the principles of unity of power, democratic centralism and double responsibility.[146] The acceptance and introduction of the concept of democratic centralism, arguably, assisted the Slovene elites, at the time to argue for greater alignment to Western Europe. It was a subtle shift from socialist principles of governance to the acceptance that democratic principles would by just as important. The resulting effect saw the government being responsible the administration of the state, however the power was with the People's Assembly and its Presidium.[147] A speech by Tito himself in 1948 highlighted the importance oi unity. He stated:

> The truth is that it is, at best, disloyal and unobjective behavior towards our party and the country. The result of a terrible blunder. Now the whole issue has been blown up to monstrous proportions: in order to destroy the respect enjoyed by our party and its leaders and to strip the Yugoslav nations of their glory in their heroic struggle, in order to trample under foot all the great things our peoples have achieved by the tremendous sacrifices and by the rivers of blood they have shed, in order to destroy the unity of our party, which is the guarantor for the successful building of Socialism in our country and the creation of a happier life for our people.[148]

The call for building socialism, was a profound statement and arguably lead to a more authoritarian form of governance to be established over the territory and people. The resulting effect saw the rise of Yugoslav communist rule. Up until 1948, Slovenes had experienced new rule, territorial change and two world wars. For a

---

[144] Haug Hilde, K, (2012) *Creating a Socialist Yugoslavia: Tito, Communist Leadership and National*, I.B. Tauris, London, Chapter 4.

[145] Mavčič, A *The Slovenian Constitutional Review*, www.concourts.net, 2009, 10.

[146] Ibid.

[147] Ibid.

[148] Henry, C, (1970). *The Essential Tito*. St. Martin's Press, 69.

short period, their push towards unification within Yugoslavia and the advancement of their identity had been placed on hold due to German occupation. The impact to the Slovenian territory and Slovenes was vast and varied. There was significant civilian casualties and property throughout the territory was damaged, particularly those having a religious connection such as churches. Nonetheless, Slovenes quickly assumed greater autonomy within the constitutional framework of Yugoslavia. WW II also had a major impact on Australia, with the bombing of Darwin by the Japanese and submarines in Sydney Harbour. However, as discussed later in this chapter, Australian citizens were in theatres located throughout Europe to assist the Allied forces. As WWII drew to a close the international community came together and began to work through a process of ensuring such a bloody conflict would not occur again. The United Nations would be established, and Australia took a leading role in the creation of the organization.

The resilience of the Slovene people is nothing short of remarkable. By the end of WWII they had experienced had gone through all three types of totalitarian regime in the twentieth century: Fascism, Nazism, and Communism.[149] Hančič and Podbersič are of the view that the west of present Slovenia, which in 1920 with the Treaty of Rapallo became part of the Kingdom of Italy, was the first region confronted with the first totalitarian system – Fascism. Italian Fascism denied any national rights to Slovenes (also, Istrian Croats) and tried to Italianize them. The nationally conscious Slovenes, above all priests and educated people were exiled and moved towards interior of Italy.[150] However, the Primorska region or Venezia Giulia, was inhabited by Italians from others parts of the country. Fascist terror increased more and more, year by year, and flourished between 1941–1943, when Italy occupied part of post-war Slovenia (the Drava Province) the so-called Ljubljana region (Notranjska, Dolenjska, Ljubljana). The authors go onto say that the next totalitarian regime which affected the Slovenes was German National Socialism. This influenced a Slovene minority in Carinthia, which found itself within the borders of the Third Reich in March 1938 after the "Anschluss". Educated Slovenes, particularly Slovene priests, were the most affected.[151] When the Germans attacked Yugoslavia and occupied a large region of the post-war Slovene territory, the circumstances aggravated. (Gorenjska, Styria, part of Carinthia). In these areas they immediately undertook rigorous denationalizing measures, which included not only the deportation of educated Slovenes, but also of a major part of the Slovene population from various regions. Then these areas were populated by the German population. By the end of 1941, the Nazis and the Italian fascist authorities jointly achieved the migration of the Germans from Kočevje area and colonized them to the region of the Sava and Sotla rivers; the Slovene population had already been removed. This ethnic cleaning of Kočevsko was completed after the war by the Slovene-Yugoslav

[149] Hančič, M., Podbersič, R, *Totalitarianism Regimes In Slovenia In the 20th Century*, http://www.crce.org.uk/lessons/Articles/eu_hearing.pdf

[150] Ibid.

[151] Ibid.

communist authority.[152] Arguably, this had a significant impact not only the development of any Yugoslav identity, but, set the Slovene identity back significantly. The migration outwards would have also had a significant on cohesion amongst the Slovene people, and in part, diluted their identity, during this period.

Hančič and Podbersič further argue that the third and longest totalitarian system in Slovenia was Communism. Its beginnings go back to before WWII, however, it's crucial influence became stronger after the occupation of Slovenia in the middle of 1941, when it started a communist revolution under the pretense of liberation struggle against the occupation. This is shown in the monopolization of the resistance movement and the liquidation of political opponents even in time of war. On account of this, it is hard to distinguish precisely between the liberation struggle and the communist revolution even today, because both occurred simultaneously.[153] Although there were differences in individual Slovene regions: civil war and revolution took place mainly in the Italian Ljubljana region, while in the northern, regions occupied by Germans and Hungarians the so-called second phase of the revolution occurred, which during wartime had been set aside, even though it had showed signs of "ideological" struggle or communist revolution.[154]

The suppression of basic human rights was enormous, particularly racism, which also extended to the right of freedom of expression, and particularly freedom of the press. Similar to the Communist regimes in Eastern Europe, the Communist regime in Yugoslavia did regard the freedom of expression as important and took a number of measures to suppress this right, particularly towards journalists.[155] The Yugoslav and Slovene Communist Union controlled all aspects of public life with the help of institutes, so-called "social-political suitability", which enabled privileges and discrimination regarding the views of the world or political beliefs and activity.[156]

More pervasively, the authors highlight how the Third Reich was established on racially organized and legitimized society, where the "perfect" Germans should be united in the people's community and where legislative implementation against "inferior" nations would be justified. They argue that the foundation of National Socialism was racism. The laws which regulating this were the so-called "Nuremberg Laws", which deprived Jews and Roma/Sinti of German citizenship. During the war they were exterminated in massive numbers. Other nations, particularly the Slavs, were also considered inferior people.

Moreover, post WWII Slovenia experienced two forms of communism. Hančič and Podbersič are of the view that there were two phases in the worst Communist repression after the war. First, there was the bloody battle with the Home Guard and other members of armed anti- communist and partly collaborationist units, the elimination of some most exposed anti-communists and bigger entrepreneurs

[152] Ibid.

[153] Ibid.

[154] Ibid.

[155] Ibid.

[156] Ibid.

(for example, culturist Narte Velikonja, industrialist Josip Benko) on Slovene territory.[157] Thus, in autumn 1945 there were more than 3500 Germans from Lower Styria and Prekmurje in prison or camps; 7400–9000 *folksdolčerjev* and Slovenes who acted for the Germans in the war, but were deported between 1945–1946 by the Slovene and Yugoslav authorities.[158] Then follows the period from August 1945 until the middle of the 50s, when terror weakened.

The Slovenia Consttitional Court in *Ustavno Sodisce RS: UeI-109/10, 2011* reinforced the notion that under Tito, the people were ruled under the notion of totalitarianism and confirmed that it had:

> annulled a decision by the Ljubljana Municipality, which wanted to name a road under construction after the Josip Broz Tito. In the judgment, the Court mentioned "Tito's symbolic meaning" associated with "the post-war totalitarian communist regime", and affirmed that "Tito symbolizes the totalitarian regime". In addition, the Slovenian Court also designated the entire period "totalitarian", with no substantive or temporal reservations.[159]

However, the Church would come under considerable pressure from the communist elites. Tamara Griesser Pečar believes that following World War Two, the communist regime applied tremendous pressure on the Roman Catholic Church. Until that "people's regime" finally collapsed in 1990–1991, the Catholic Church was its internal enemy number one, because it remained the only organization that was not controlled by the communist party, and had great influence on the population. First the regime tried to eliminate the Church as it did the political opposition, but when it recognized how deeply Catholic Church was rooted in the population, it changed tactics.[160] Second, it tried to discredit Church representatives in the eyes of the faithful using all possible means, regardless of how morally dubious they were. Pečar was of the view that the communist government regarded religion as a symbol of a reactionary past.

The war would finally conclude and the international community would come together, under the leadership of the ally forces to plan a way forward, to ensure such atrocities would not occur in the future. The United Nations promoted and implemented co-operation amongst states and kingdoms to ensure there was no repeat of the bloody conflict that had raged across Europe. The United Nations would quickly work to ensure citizen's rights of nation states were protected and in 1948 the Declaration of Human Rights was created. The declaration, while not binding law was a first step towards states taking into consideration the broader rights of its citizens and people of the world. Importantly, many of the provisions of the 1948 Declaration were expressed in the 1946 Yugoslav constitution. Doing so assisted the state to further unify and integrate the different ethnic groups. Since

---

[157] Ibid.

[158] Ibid.

[159] Flere, S., Klanjsek, R., *Was Tito's Yugoslavia totalitarian?, Communist and Post-Communist Studies* (2014), https://doi.org/10.1016/j.postcomstud.2014.04.009 *Ustavno Sodisce RS: UeI-109/10, 2011*

[160] Tamara Griesser Pečar, The Roman Catholic church in Slovenia Under Three Totalitarian Regimes, http://www.crce.org.uk/lessons/Articles/eu_hearing.pdf

1948, there has been a significant increase in international law attempting to protect the rights of citizens and people of all nation states.[161] However, while Yugoslavia would look to the international community in the adoption of human rights, in practice, the picture on the ground would be very different.

Following WWII, the European Community began to take a greater role in cooperation amongst states with the European Coal and Steel Community being introduced. The founding members included Belgium, France, Germany, Italy, Luxembourg and the Netherlands. Post WWII there were three waves that had an impact on a states' citizenship policies and law. The first was the 'struggle for decolonization between 1948 and 1965. The second phase[162] saw the struggle against racial segregation and discrimination and the third phase was the struggle of multiculturalism and the rights of minorities.

The Cold War began in 1947 and continued through to the 1990s, which saw the rise of the civil rights movement. However, the Cold War period can be best described as Yugoslavia wanting to have a foot in each camp. In other words, Yugoslavia while adopting and copying Soviet (communist) policies, and relying on economic assistance from the East, economic assistance from the West would not be excluded.[163] Even with sustained pressure from the Soviets in their attempt to create a satellite Soviet territory in Yugoslavia, the West intervened and provided economic support to Yugoslavia. The action by the West to support a communist country changed the perception of the Cold War bloc, and Yugoslavia began to change its policy direction. The new direction enabled Yugoslavia to separate themselves from the Soviets.[164] The Belgrade Declaration in 1955 was an important time for Yugoslavs, which formalized the Soviet acceptance of Yugoslavia's independence.[165] This was important to Yugoslavia's ongoing unification and push towards establishing an identity that all citizens and Republics would accept. However, this was not successful because of the push by each of the Republics to gain more autonomy over their internal affairs.

The federal structure[166] was fundamental to the governance of Yugoslavia and the establishment of the six Republics[167] (including the autonomous provinces of Vojvodina and Kosovo-Metohija within the Republic of Serbia).[168] This was important to Slovenians. The establishment of the Slovenian Republic cannot be underestimated. The role it would play when Slovenia would eventually break away from

[161] Ibid.

[162] Kymlicka, W, (2012) *Multiculturalism: Success, Failure, and the Future*, Migration Policy Institute, 6.

[163] Batovič, A, (2009) *The Balkans in Turmoil-Croatian Spring and the Yugoslav Position Between the Cold War Blocs 1965–1971*, London School of Economics, Cold War Studies Programme, 1–10.

[164] Ibid.

[165] Ibid.

[166] Radan, P, (2002) *The Breakup of Yugoslavia and International Law*, Routledge, 137–145.

[167] Ibid.

[168] Ibid.

Yugoslavia was profound. Yugoslavia was highly centralized under the rule of Tito. The federal structure of Yugoslavia had many similarities to the federal structure that Australia had established, with a central government along with State and Territory governments that had autonomy to govern their respective territories. On the one hand there was significant disparity in the level of economic development between the Republics. Slovenia, for example was considered the most economically advanced Republics. While at the lower end of economic development was Macedonia and Kosovo. By the end of the 1980s and the disintegration of Yugoslavia, Slovenia would be even more economically advanced that the other Republics.

3.1.10 1950–1960

Following the aftermath of WWII, new citizenship laws were introduced by the Republics of Yugoslavia. In 1950, Slovenia (part of Yugoslavia) adopted the citizenship laws for the People's Republic of Slovenia. Republican citizenship[169] was valid from 21 June 1950 to 8 April 1965. Article 1 stated that a citizen of the Slovene Republic is a person who at the same time is a citizen of Yugoslavia.[170] The adoption of Republican citizenship would later provide continuity for Slovenia and its people when developing its citizenship laws at the time of independence, in 1990. Furthermore, the Republican citizenship enabled a legal status to be developed that defined what it meant to be Slovenian.

Slovenians would continue to reside in Austria and due to the many changes in borders where they were located, those who remained in the Austrian territory became a minority. Nevertheless, the Slovenians were assured equal rights in accordance with article 19 of the Basic Law of Austria (*Staatsgrundgesetz)* that stated:

> (1) All the ethnic entities of the empire enjoy equal rights, and each ethnic entity has an inviolable right to the preservation and fostering of its nationality and language.[171]
> (2) The state recognises the equal rights of all current languages in schools, administration and public life.[172]

However, in practice Austria continued to deny Slovenes living on its territory the use of their rights such as, the use of language in offices, schools, on topographical tables of towns and villages. It was not until the Australian Federal Constitutional

[169] Official Gazette LRS, No. 20/50.

[170] Ibid, Article 2 provided that a citizen of another Yugoslav republic could be an honorary citizen of the Slovenian Republic. Articles 4 and 5 allowed citizenship to be obtained where a child who's both parents or, one of the parents was a Slovene citizen. Article 7 enabled citizenship by birth on the territory of Slovenia, or, found and both of the parents were unknown or couldn't be known up until 14 years of age.

[171] Council of Europe, *Report by the Republic of Austria pursuant to Article 25 paragraph 1 of the Framework Convention for the Protection of National Minorities*, 2000, 5–14.

[172] Ibid.

Court ordered that relevant local communities to remedy the violations.[173] The Austrian Independence Treaty re-established Austria as a sovereign state, and was signed on May 15, 1955. The Treaty came into force on July 27, 1955.[174] Article 7 ensured the minority rights of Slovenes and Croats were protected.

The Slovene minority in Italy (Slovene: *Slovenska manjšina v Italiji*), also known as the Slovenes in Italy (Slovene: *Slovenci v Italiji*) would also enjoy special protection. The vast majority of members of the Slovenian ethnic minority resided in Trieste, Goriza and Udine. The Slovene minority in Italy enjoyed legal protection of its collective rights, guaranteed by the Italian constitution and international treaties (London Memorandum 1954). The London Memorandum of 1954[175] regulated the conduct of the inhabitants comprising the Free Territory of Trieste. The Slovene minorities located throughout the Province of Friuli Venezia were protected[176] under article 5 of the Peace Treaty, as well as article 3 of the Statute of the Province of Friuli Venezia Giulia following its approval in 1963.[177] Moreover, Slovenes were gradually being recognized by laws of other states outside of Yugoslavia. On this backdrop, the recognition would be important to the ongoing development of the Slovenian identity.

3.1.11 1960–1975

The 1960s saw Yugoslavia rise to an internationally recognized independent state. However, the new state struggled to establish a single identity. The citizenship laws were playing an active role in strengthening the collective social cohesion. The 1963 Yugoslav constitution expanded the concept to further decentralize the self-managed society.[178] The country was renamed again to the Socialist Federal Republic of Yugoslavia. A year later, the Yugoslav Citizenship Act was passed in 1964.[179] Section 2 of that Act provided that Republic (Slovenian) citizenship could only be

---

[173] Austrian Constitutional Court VfSlg 16,404/2001 and 17,733/2005, pertained to the use of the Slovenian language in local schools.

[174] State Treaty for the Re-establishment of an Independent and Democratic Austria, 1955, http://www.cvce.eu/content/publication/1999/3/2/5c586461-7528-4a74-92c3-d3eba73c2d7d/publishable_en.pdf

[175] United States of America, United Kingdom of Great Britain and Northern Ireland, Italy and Yugoslavia, Memorandum of Understanding Regarding the Free Territory of Trieste, singed 1954, Treaty Series, No. 3297, vol 49 and 50.

[176] The Constitution of the Italian Republic 1948, Official Gazette, December 27, 1947, no. 298.

[177] Autonomous Region of Friuli Venezia Giulia, Association of European Border Regions, http://www.aebr.eu/pdf/fmanager/Regionen/F/Friuli_Venezia_Giulia/Fact_sheet_Friuli_Ven_Giulia_EN.pdf

[178] Autonomous Region of Friuli Venezia Giulia, Association of European Border Regions, http://www.aebr.eu/pdf/fmanager/Regionen/F/Friuli_Venezia_Giulia/Fact_sheet_Friuli_Ven_Giulia_EN.pdf

[179] Zakon o jugoslovanskem državljanstvu – Official Gazette of the SFRY, No. 38/64 of 1964.

held by a Yugoslav citizen,[180] thus retaining the primacy of federal citizenship. Loss of Yugoslav citizenship automatically resulted in the loss of Republic citizenship. At that time, there was a strong official preference towards Yugoslav citizenship as opposed to Republican citizenship. It is argued that the citizenship laws went someway to strengthening the sense of solidarity of all citizens across the Yugoslav territory. However, this was at the same time when the Republics had assumed more autonomy. The federal laws certainly played a role in providing a sense of who and who was not Yugoslav. For example, when travelling abroad it was the Yugoslav citizenship that allowed a person to obtain a Yugoslav passport.

During this period, the Republic of Slovenia and Republic of Croatia demanded greater control over their economic resources.[181] The fall of Aleksandar Rankovič who was Vice President of Yugoslavia, would be seen by Slovenian and Croatian reformers as an opportunity to strengthen their respective nationalist sentiments. However, Tito would view this as a potential threat to the wider unification and social cohesion of Yugoslavia and intervened to suppress any further growth in nationalism.[182] This was a complex period for Yugoslavia. On the one hand, Tito was continuing to develop a common culture amongst the Yugoslavs that would lead to a shared identity.[183] On the other hand, the reformers within Republics were steering the nationalist argument towards greater autonomy and possibly independence.

The 1968 constitutional reforms[184] saw the provinces of Kosovo and Vojvodina being granted greater autonomy[185] (redefining the six Republics and two Socialist autonomous provinces).[186] Three years later, the constitutional amendments of 1971 came into effect in 1974 and saw the number of the presidency reduced from 23 to 9 members. Originally there were three members from each of the Republics, which would be reduced to one. The two members from Kosovo and Vojvodina would also become one. In the same year, the Federal constitutional amendments provided wider powers to the Federal Chamber of Nationalities and the Republics.[187]

As part of the constitutional amendments of 1974, the Chamber of Republics and Provinces was formed. The main function of the Chamber was to provide [other] nationalities with an equal level playing field, as the Serbians dominated most of the governance bodies that had been established under the constitution. All citizens were considered equal before the law and enjoyed equal rights in accordance with article 21. More importantly, the 1974 amendments decentralized society by providing the six Republics and two autonomous provinces with more control over internal

[180] By the Constitution of 1963 the State was renamed as the Socialist Federal Republic of Yugoslavia (SFRJ), Official Gazette SRS, No. 10/63.

[181] Peter Radan, *The Breakup of Yugoslavia and International Law*, Routledge, 2002, 137–145.

[182] Ibid.

[183] Marshall, T, (1965) *Class, Citizenship and Social Development*, New York, Anchor, 101–103.

[184] Mavčič, A *The Slovenian Constitutional Review*, www.concourts.net, 2009, 10.

[185] Cohen, L., Dragovič-Soso, J, (2008) *State Collapse in South-Eastern Europe: New Perspectives on Yugoslavia*, Purdue University Press, 101–103.

[186] Ibid.

[187] Ibid.

affairs.[188] A collective presidency was set up to ensure the Federative state would continue following the death of Josip Broz Tito.[189] However, and as noted by Tierney sophisticated institutional framework established by Tito had not gone unnoticed. Theoretically, decentralized powers were in fact highly centralized and oppressive.[190] The Communist Party was extremely dominant and the Army gradually assumed a lot more control over the people. More importantly, human rights were routinely suppressed and economic inequality reigned across the territory.

Throughout the 1970s, European countries began thinking about and discussing the idea of a European citizenship. At the 1972 meeting of the Heads of Government of the European Communities wider integration and the concept of European citizenship were discussed.[191] This is an important point because the beginnings of a wider citizenship for the region was being considered to further unify the citizens of Europe. Two years later in 1975, the European Commission released a report 'Towards European Citizenship'considering the political rights to be afforded to citizens of the European Communities such as the right to vote and participate in elections.[192] These early ideas of what European citizenship would become important to Slovenia and Slovenians following the break-up of Yugoslavia and their membership to the European Union. However, at the time, the developments by the European Community while having little direct impact on Slovenia and Yugoslavia as a whole, they were beginning to prosper from the economic development of its northen and western neighbours. Most notably, people from within Slovenia and Yugoslavia would be eyeing off the progressive policy moves in western and central Europe. The resulting effect would see Slovene, at least economically begin to aligning themselves closer to Europe. This was also understood by the inhabitants of the southern Republics of Yugoslavia that, saw large number emigrate to the Slovene Republic to enhance their economic prospects.

---

188 Bagwell, B, (1991) *Yugoslavian Constitutional Questions: Self-Determination and Secession of Member Republics*, 21, Georgia. J. Int'l & Comp. L., 489–499.

189 Ibid.

190 Tierney, S, (2000) *Accommodating national Identity: New Approaches in International and Domestic Law*, Kluwer international Law.

191 Meeting of the Heads of State or Government ARIS, The First Summit Conference of the Enlarged Community (II), Resolution of the European Parliament on the Results Reproduced from the Bulletin of the European Communities, No. 11, 1972.

192 Commission of the European Communities, Towards European Citizenship, COM (75) 321, July 1975.

3.1.12 1975–1980

Notwithstanding the developments in Europe, between 1975 to 1980 a subtle transition of Yugoslavia from a state had begun. They were grappling economically and diplomatically with its neighbors. The legal arrangement concerning the territory and borders of Yugoslavia had not been finalized with Italy. Subsequently, the Treaty of Osimo was signed on 10 November 1975[193] by the Socialist Federal Republic of Yugoslavia and the Italian Republic in Osimo, Italy and became effective on 11 October 1977. Article 3 provided that nationality of persons who on 10 June 1940 were Italian nationals and had their permanent residence in the territory would become citizens in the territory they resided, with the option of being able to move to either the Italian or Yugoslav territory.[194] Article 8 stated Italy was obliged to ensure the Slovene minority had the same protections as provided by the London Memorandum. The memorandum handed civil administration of Zone A to Italy and of Zone B to Yugoslavia. On the backdrop of these new arrangements, the Slovene language had been fully recognized in many of the municipalities where the Slovenian minority resided. It is argued that this would have suited the Slovenes and enabled the Slovenian identity to be retained, if not strengthened it. In other words, Slovenes were not forced to adopt or use Italian or any other language.

Apart from defining the territory and protecting the Slovenian language, Slovenians and Italians residing in either Yugoslavia (later Slovenia) or Italy were afforded legislative rights.[195] Similarly, the Rába Slovenes who spoke a different dialect (*Prekmurje*) to the other Slovenians across modern day Slovenia and are located within modern day Hungary had also assumed protection under the Hungarian law. When there had been changes to the border (s), at least on paper, those individuals that had been affected by the change assumed a level of legal rights and protections.[196] Today, many of the minority rights still exist in these border area, but they do vary between the states, both in practice and their respective legislative frameworks. More importantly, the border regions and governance of theme preserved elements of the Slovene identity, both in practice and within the law.

Notwithstanding the above, the 1976 citizenship laws maintained continuity of Yugoslav citizenship, however a provision was inserted into Article 22 to ensure disputes between Federal and Republic citizenship could be resolved.[197] It is argued that Yugoslavia by inserting this provision within the law reinforced the earlier

---

[193] Italy and Yugoslavia Treaty on the delimitation of the frontier for the part not indicated as such in the Peace Treaty of 10 February 1947, Signed in Osimo, Ancona, 10 November 1975, No. 24848, United Nations Treaty Series, 1987.

[194] Ibid.

[195] Marinac, B., Mavčič, A, (2004) *Pravni položaj slovenske manjšine v Sloveniji: magistrsko delo*, Brdo pri Kraju.

[196] Grča, T., Mavčič, A, (2007) *The situation of the Hungarian minority in Slovenia with an emphasis on the Lendava region and Slovenian in Hungary*: Kranj.

[197] Council of Europe, *Citizenship and state succession: proceedings*, Unidem seminar, European Democracy through law, 1998, 195–200. Official Gazette SFRY 58/76.

position that Federal law provided the legal status of citizens within the territory, while Republican citizenship law remained symbolic. However, as history demonstrates, that symbolic act would be a very useful part of the law between 1989 and 1990, and the move towards independence.

The legal norms allowed the status of a child to be recognized by Republic law of which the parents were citizens. Importantly, the laws allowed the parents who might have been a Republican citizen of Slovenia and Serbia to choose the child's Republican citizenship.[198] In 1977, new laws were introduced[199] that were adopted across Yugoslavia and provided the Republic with the right to begin to choose their citizens. However, the federal laws still prevailed. At the federal level the legislation enabled citizenship to be obtained in a similar manner, but expanded on the naturalization requirements by allowing Yugoslavia to choose who could become a citizen, even if he or she did not fulfil all of the conditions.[200] The new structure of citizenship which was provided by article 274 of the constitution created the situation where a citizen of one Republic who was on the territory of another Republic, had the same rights and obligations of a citizen of that Republic.[201] However, the next decade would see Yugoslavia go through further turmoil. During the past 70 years, Slovenes new nothing but content change of rulers and systems of governance, however, through all of that they maintained a level of citizenship. Even so, citizenship through this period did not come without its challenges. The most challenging time for the Slovene people would have been throughout the period of Nazi occupation. While they assumed another form of citizenship, arguably it significantly impacted on their collective development, autonomy and identity.

3.1.13 1980–1990 [Death of Josip Broz Tito]

The decade of 1980 to 1990 would emerge as the most testing for Yugoslavia. It ultimately resulted in the disintegration of the Yugoslav experiment. Arguably, the death of the president of the former Yugoslavia Josip Broz Tito[202] in 1980, resulted in the state would never recovering. However, history would describe Tito as a totalitarian leader, who suppressed human rights. Slavenka Drakulic argues that it was Tito's leadership that left the country in significant debt. Drakulic further argues that he was responsible for the massacre of ward prisoners Bleiburg and forced labour camps such as Goli Otok for political prisoners.[203] Upon Tito's death the policy of

[198] Ibid.

[199] Law on Citizenship, Official Gazette Socialist Republic of Slovenia, No. 23/76.

[200] Article 9, Law of Citizenship 1976, Social Federal Republic of Jugoslavia 58/76.

[201] Štiks, I, (2010) *A Laboratory of Citizenship: Shifting Conceptions of Citizenship in Yugoslavia and its Successor States*, University of Edinburgh, School of Law.

[202] Olivia Hinerfield, *The Rise and Fall of Yugoslavia, Modern European History*, Portland State University, 2013, 1–12.

[203] Drakulic, S, (1996) *Café Europa: Life After Communism*, Hachette Digital.

'polycentrism' collapsed due to ineffective leadership, and with a greater focus on economic policy, division amongst leaders from across Yugoslavia and the Republics emerged.[204] According to Olivia Hinerfield, there was a lack of clear direction by the leaders, and eventually the economy collapsed.[205] The state reverted to a collective presidency, which was headed by Milka Planinc.[206] Milka Planic, a woman whose heritage was Croatian and Serbian commenced her political career in 1959. The acceptance of a woman as a leader would have been viewed as a positive step for the acceptance of women in political life, within communist regimes, but also in western democratic society [states].

Notwithstanding the above events, Slovenia was quietly working in the background, sharpening its nationalist knife. In the same years as the death of Tito, the first *Nova revija* (English: New magazine) was published in the Republic. This was a small but important step in raising the nationalist profile and identity of Slovenes and went onto play an important role in influencing the process of Slovene nationalism throughout the decade. The economic situation continued to decline and in 1984 the United States issued a National Security Directive seeking to topple communist nations. This policy response form the West did not bode well for socialism, and was designed to force Europe to participate in a market-oriented economy.[207] Furthermore, the West established trade barriers that halted the economic growth of the Yugoslav economy, forcing the government to obtain loans from the International Monetary Fund. By 1985 the net foreign debt of Yugoslavia had been estimated at more than $18 billion [US].[208] The political trust of the population reached its lowest point, creating an unprecedented crisis of legitimacy for political institutions and leaders.[209] Furthermore, the changes imposed by the 1974 constitution were designed to restructure the performance of the economy, however they were never realized.[210] A year later, in 1986, the Slovenian national program had begun and in 1987 the concept of the constitutional program was prepared by Slovene intellectuals.[211]

The year of 1988 was 2 years out from the disintegration of Yugoslavia. Leading up to 1988, the economy was in steep decline. Due to the IMF intervention there were up to 18 laws that were passed to restructure the governance arrangements of labour and industry that, would have allowed for privatization. However, this would not be realized and the IMF proposal was never implemented. In the same year, the

[204] Ibid.

[205] Ibid.

[206] Ibid.

[207] Ibid.

[208] Jambrek, P, (2014) *Nation's Transitions, Social and Legal Issues of Slovenia's Transitions 1945–2015,* Graduate School of Government and European Studies, Brdo pri Kranju and European Faculty of Law, Nova Gorica, Slovenia, 37.

[209] Ibid.

[210] Ibid.

[211] Ibid.

'Theses for the Slovene constitution was released to the public,[212] which was prepared by the Constitutional Commission of the Slovene Writers Association and the Working Group for Constitutional Development. The 'Theses' (otherwise known as the Writers Constitution) was an important document outlining the constitutional text but more importantly was one of the steps to democracy. The Theses disregarded the socialist provisions of the former Yugoslavia and Slovenian Republic constitutions. Furthermore, it directed the state to decide how it would establish associations with other states. Slovenia was defined as a state based on sovereignty, a nation of all people who have the right to Slovenian citizenship, in accordance with the law.[213] Importantly, by expressing the steps towards democracy and the rule of laws as foundational principles for the establishment of the new independent Slovenian state. This was an expression of Slovenia's identity that would be used to set itself apart from other Yugoslav Republics.

Slobodan Milošević emerged in the 1980s and by 1987 he had placed himself in a position to lead the Serbian's and declared Serbia to be Communist by name and nationalist by choice. Milošević would begin exerting his nationalist tendencies across the territory. By the end of the Yugoslav experiment, Slovenia was the most advanced economically, and the censure had strengthened its grip on the states' politics in Belgrade. This would have a significant impact on the Yugoslav population. Worker strikes had trebled over the decade in a united front from the peoples from across the Yugoslav state had formed. However, the united front would be [politically] turned into the happenings of the people, which resulted in different ethnic groups turning against each other. What followed was the 1989 May Declaration of Slovenia demanded independence and the creation of a new Slovenian state. Moreover, Milošević had gained enough influence in Montenegro, Vojvodina and Kosovo to control half of the territory of Yugoslavia. However, such was the discontent that the Albanian majority in Kosovo rose up in opposition to the transition of power. For all of its [Yugoslavia] complexities, and even at the conclusion of Yugoslavia, it is asserted that citizenship went part way to uniting the people. More importantly, citizenship could not construct a single identity on its own due to the disunity amongst the Republics and the economic decline of the state.

Towards the end of the 1980s there was fundamental changes occurring across Europe, particularly in socialist states. The rise of nationalism swept across central, south eastern and eastern Europe. The Berlin Wall would fall in 1989, which eventually saw the unification of East and West Germany. Additionally, the Soviet Union began to breakup. At the same time Yugoslavia was beginning to disintegrate. The citizenship laws of East and West Germany were independent of each other between

---

[212] Ibid. 259.

[213] Pavčnik, M, (2009) *Constitutionis, Glosses on the Writers' Constitution upon the Occasion of its 20th Anniversary*, Ljubljana, Vol. 63, 125, Nos. 11–12, 567–580. Peter Jambrek, *Nation's Transitions, Social and Legal Issues od Slovenia's Transitions 1945–2015,* Graduate School of Government and European Studies, Brdo pri Kranju and European Faculty of Law, Nova Gorica, Slovenia, 2014, 260.

1967 and 1990.[214] Following the unification of Germany on 3 October 1990, the citizenship laws of East Germany were abolished.[215] However, as a result of immigration into the territory, those individuals who were long term residents were only afforded limited political rights.[216] The German Constitutional Court ruled that this was unconstitutional and stated that the basic concept of democracy does not permit disassociation of political rights.[217] Interestingly, the unification of Germany and the introduction of a single citizenship was to some degree used to exclude individuals from fully participating in the newly formed political community. Today, all German's enjoy a single citizenship and political rights. The unification of Germany had similarities to Yugoslavia, whereby, Germany had a single citizenship for the entire state. They had begun to use citizenship to unify the East and West of former German states, into a single unified Germany. Throughout the collapse of socialism, there is no doubt that citizenship as a policy tool and legal concept played more than a single role of providing people with a sense of belonging. It provided a sense of unity and more importantly provided a level of continuity from changes in rulers, and from socialism to democracy.

As the former Soviet Union disintegrated between 1989 and 1991, the nationalist movement within Estonia, Lithuania, Latvia and other Republics emerged, seeking independence. These historical events was not only swift but the impact it had on citizens of the former Republics[218] within and outside of Russia would be enormous. The structure and formation of citizenship within the former Soviet Union and its 15 Republics resembled the same structure to that of Yugoslavia.[219] Each of the Republics had their own citizenship laws, however they had very little legal basis. At least on paper Soviet citizenship appeared inclusive and allowed foreigners to apply for citizenship. However, dual citizenship was prohibited.[220] More importantly, the breakup had a profound impact on the people who previously had access to the right of residence, citizenship and property as a result of emigrating within the Soviet territory. Many people found themselves without citizenship or any rights in the new territories, and were effectively stateless.[221]

---

[214] Hailbronner, K, (2012) *Country Report: Germany*, EUDO Citizenship Observatory, European Union Institute, 2012, 1–4.

[215] Ibid.

[216] Ibid.

[217] Federal Constitutional Court, vol. 83, p. 37, 59. in Kay Hailbronner, *Country Report: Germany*, EUDO Citizenship Observatory, European Union Institute, 2012, 1–4.

[218] The 15 Republics included Armenia, Azerbaijan, Belarus, Estonia, Georgia, Kazakhstan, Kyrgystan, Latvia, Lithuania, Moldova, Russia, Tajikistan, Turkmenistan, Ukraine and Uzbekistan.

[219] Shushanik Makaryan, Trends *in Citizenship Policies of the 15 Former Soviet Union Republics: Conforming the World Culture or Following National Identity?* Washington State University, 2006, 1–10.

[220] Ibid.

[221] Tishkov, V., Zayinchkovskay, Z., Vitkovskaya, G, (2005) *Migration in the countries of the former Soviet Union*, A paper prepared for Policy Analysis and Research Programme of the Global Commission on International Migration, 5–15.

The resulting impact to citizens across the Soviet Union would later be resembled in the breakup of Yugoslavia, where citizens lost citizenship and many of their rights. Furthermore, the breakup of the Soviet Union clearly demonstrated that socialism had collapsed across Europe. Some but not all of the Republics that left the Soviet bloc would today be part of the European Union (Estonia, Lithuania, Latvia). The collapse of the Soviet Union had no effect on Australian citizenship. However, with the decline in the standard of living across Russia, Australia had to expand its export trade to other regions.[222]

The Yugoslav experiment is, and was, an example of how the pressures of international, regional and societal expectations coupled with mounting foreign debt went along way to erode the social fabric of the state. The resulting effect was a rapid acceleration of declining living standards, condition of weak state authority and intrastate tensions which lead to conflict. Moreover, the innovation of Yugoslav "Self-Management" doctrine once considered a benchmark in creative economic reform. However, it proved to be a major contributing factor in the fall of Yugoslavia.

Nonetheless, up until this period and the fall of Yugoslavia, the history of Slovenes is quite remarkable for such a small population, which had been repeatedly denied their right to form an independent state of their own, following several attempts. Arguably, those failed attempts only galvanized the Slovenians and made them more determined to raise and promote themselves and their identity to Europe and the world. Following the WW I Slovenians changed their master from the Habsburg Empire to Yugoslavia which was ruled by a Serbian King.[223] According to Peter Jambrek, Slovenes were never asked to become subjects of the Austrian Kaiser, or the Serbian King, or of a Communist Party Boss.[224] The fate of the entire people was decided by political factions of the nation, foreign occupation, mass violence and institutional decay.[225] This is an important point made by Jambrek, and it is argued that history had not favored the Slovenian people. There was the continued oppression of Slovenians and the Slovene identity by rulers and political allegiances. The censure continued to force the economically advanced states to subsidize the less performing Republics. However, all this did not deter the Slovenes, and they continued to push forward enhancing and strengthening their identity and place in Europe and the former Yugoslavia.

Notwithstanding the above, the story of the former Yugoslavia is nothing short of complex and unique. Yugoslavia had experimented in nearly all forms of governance and government, however, it still failed to resolve differences between ethnic groups and nationalist ideology. Yugoslavia had been a monarchy, a republic, multiparty and one party state, centralized, regionalized to decentralized, a federal state,

---

222 Bradshaw, M, (2001) *The Russian Far East and Pacific Asia: Unfulfilled Potential*, Routledge, Chapter 14.

223 Jambrek, P, (2014) *Nation's Transitions, Social and Legal Issues of Slovenia's Transitions 1945–2015,* Graduate School of Government and European Studies, Brdo pri Kranju and European Faculty of Law, Nova Gorica, Slovenia, 244–245.

224 Ibid.

225 Ibid.

ruled by civilian and military elites (totalitarianism). Yugoslavia had also experienced dominant private and state owned companies. Moreover, Yugoslavia had been made up by eight major ethnic groups that included Slovenes, Croats, Hungarians, Serbs, Montenegrins, Macedonians, Bosnians, Austrians and Albanians. Linguistically and religiously they were very different. However, the 'elites in former Yugoslavia never opted for the obvious choice to allow the nations driven into and uneasy cohabitation to freely express their will in a democratic procedure of self-determination'.[226] Had this been realized, this book might be discussing a single Yugoslav identity and citizenship, immigration, rights and private international laws, from a very different perspective. The people experienced first-hand the dichotomy of totalitarianism rule. One the one hand they were afforded extensive set rights under the Yugoslav constitution. On the other hand, any rights were suppressed enormously. The church was under considerable pressure, there was significant constraints placed in the press to publish. However, throughout the occupation of the Slovene territory by the Germans, Slovenes would have many of their rights suppressed. This was not a good period for the Slovene people. Alternatively, had Slovenia gained independence and a state of their own before 1990, their identity today - while based on similar principles of language and culture, the historical narrative would be very different. Nevertheless, throughout all of this volatility, Slovenes had been working hard to retain and strengthen as minorities within the border villages and towns of Austria.

3.1.14 Minority in Austria

[While at least on paper] the Slovene minority located in other neighboring territories outside of Yugoslavia were afforded legal rights, however this was far from the case in practice. During the 1980s the rights of the Slovene minority was tested in the Austrian Constitutional Court. The court held in Marianne Pasterk-Reisinger that article 7 of the State Treaty of Vienna recognized that the Slovene language would be official in the judicial districts of Carinthia, Styria and Burgenland,[227] and that the language was protected by extension to members of minority and other social groups. The court went on to rule that it may be justified or even require more favorable treatment of minorities,[228] so as to protect small minority communities within the Austrian territory. It demonstrates that from region to region the actual implementation of rights on the ground varied greatly. Furthermore, it wasn't until the courts or government intervened that the Slovene minorities would be afforded the same treatment as local Austrian citizens. This highlighted that not only was the

[226] Ibid.

[227] Article 7 State Treaty of Vienna, for the Re-establishment of an Independent and Democratic Austria, Federal Law Gazette No. 152/1955, in Marianne Pasterk-Reisinger, *Constitutional Developments in Austria*, State Treaty of Vienna, 2008, 131.

[228] Austrian Constitutional Court, Judgment 28 June 1983, VfSlg. 9744/1983.

language an important part of a Slovenes' own identity, it highlighted that Slovenians as a people were being accepted and recognized for their identity.[229] The next phase of the Slovene identity, was arguably the most profound it its history.

3.1.15 Towards Independence

In 1990, the Slovenian elites had worked towards full independence during the final years of Yugoslavia. The rise of Serbian nationalism and centralization of power towards Belgrade had begun to undo the previous 40 years of work of continuing to decentralize and provide more autonomy to the Republics. Slovenia only made up 8% of Yugoslavia's total population but provided one-third of Yugoslavia's exports and funded 20% of the overall federal budget.[230] Republics were beginning to lean further towards Europe as the economic gap between the two regions was ever widening. Following the termination of autonomy to Kosovo, Vojvodina and Montenegro by Serbia, other Republics became increasingly concerned with the approach taken by Serbian and its nationalist ideals.[231] One of the most important moments came at the January meeting of the Yugoslav Congress (Kongress), whereby the Serbs attempted to suppress the defiance by the Slovenes. However, the Slovenes found an ally in Croatia. Part way through this meeting the Slovenes would leave, followed by the Croats. Yugoslavia was all be finished. Nonetheless, the Slovenes were also on the pathway to establish democracy, the rule of law and the respect for human rights.[232] That goal was expressed by Peter Jambrek (the United Slovene Opposition) in a letter to the United States Undersecretary and the United States Embassy in Belgrade, stating:

> *[t]he objective of the Declaration of Slovene Self-determination is to undertake democratic reforms which began in January 1990 and the need to find a new regulatory formula for coexistence of Yugoslav nations, encouraged by the profound political changes in Eastern Europe, and inspired by the new thinking about a future European Confederation, the Slovene democratic and oppositional parties joined into the Slovene United Opposition to promote by peaceful means the democracy and independence of the Slovene people. The political objective of the Slovene United Opposition is to secure free and honest election resulting in a representative and legitimate parliament, hold a plebiscite to allow Slovenes to freely express there will and decide on the political future and hold a referendum to let*

[229] Beiner, R, (1998) *Citizenship and Nationalism: Is Canada a Real Country*? In K Slawner and M E Denhim, Citizenship after Liberalism, Peter Lang Publishing, 185.

[230] Bagwell, B, (1991) *Yugoslavian Constitutional Questions: Self-Determination and Secession of Member Republics*, 21, Georgia. J. Int'l & Comp. L., 489–499.

[231] Matija Rojec, M., Silva-Jauregui, C, (2004) *Slovenia: From Yugoslavia to the European Union*, The World Bank, 5–15.

[232] Jambrek, P, (2014) *Nation's Transitions, Social and Legal Issues of Slovenia's Transitions 1945–2015*, Graduate School of Government and European Studies, Brdo pri Kranju and European Faculty of Law, Nova Gorica, Slovenia, 19–22.

> *the Slovene nation determine the nature of its state in the form of a new constitution. For Slovenes, democracy and national independence are inseparable.*[233]

The importance of this correspondence was a clear demonstration that Slovenians were looking to self-determinate and become independent from Yugoslavia and the other Republics. Furthermore, and while there was an attempt to coexist with other Yugoslav Republics, Slovenians were pushing their credentials and identity to establish a new democratic state, which other Republics had not yet expressed. The importance of the expression by Slovenians to adopt democracy cannot be underestimated as separating themselves from their socialist past. It is argued that adopting democracy itself was one of the most important principles Slovenians saw as a way to finally get their independence. Once independence had been achieved, it was the Slovenian language and territory that would be used to define its citizens.

The Constitutional Court did not escape the transition from socialism to democracy. The election cycle for judges coincided with the timing of transition to independence. As it turned out, five of the nine posts of the Constitutional Court became available in 1990. The filling of these positions were delayed due to the transition phase Slovenia was undertaking and the distrust that had formed when transitioning from communist rule to a parliamentary democracy.[234] Subsequently, the Constitutional Court was not in session from April to October in 1990. In April of the same year there were elections held, which resulted in the defeat of the Communists, Socialists, and Liberal Democrats (the Socialist Youth Organisation).[235] What followed was the formation of a coalition of parties that were made up of prominent Slovenian intellectuals, politicians and the Farmers Union, who formed government.[236] The Catholic Church also played a major role having influence across Slovenia. There were contributions to the Slovenian National Program, also known as *Nova revija* 57, or, 57th edition of *Nova revija* which was a special issue of the Slovenian opposition (intellectual) journal.[237] It contained 16 articles by non-Communist and anti-Communist dissidents in the Slovenian Republic, outlining the possibilities and conditions for Slovenia to achieve independence.

[233] Ibid, 248–251.

[234] Ibid, 328.

[235] Ibid.

[236] Ibid.

[237] Ibid, 5.

3.2 Independence

The newly independent Slovenia was granted the opportunity to establish a modern day constitution. In 1990, the Draft Slovenian Constitution[238] was published and the Declaration of Sovereignty of the Republic of Slovenia was proclaimed.[239] The Slovenian Assembly passed the constitutional amendments XCVI–XCVIII in 1990, which invalidated all constitutional laws of the Socialist Federal Republic of Yugoslavia (that were not in conformity with the Slovenian Constitution).[240] On 25 June 1990, the Basic Constitutional Charter was promulgated and Sovereignty of the Republic of Slovenia was established. The people of Slovenia decided they no longer wanted to be part of Yugoslavia which was expressed in the Statement of Good Intentions on 6 December 1990[241] [that stated]:

> *Through the will expressed in the plebiscite by the Slovene nation, the Italian and Hungarian ethnic communities and all other voters in the Republic of Slovenia, Slovenia may finally and actually become a sovereign, democratic and social state based on the rule of law.*[242]

The next legislative step was the implementation of 'The Plebiscite on the Sovereignty and Independence of the Republic of Slovenia Act on 6 December 1990.[243] Article 4 determined that '[t]he decision adopted at the plebiscite that the Republic of Slovenia become a sovereign and independent state bound the Assembly of the Republic of Slovenia to adopt within 6 months from the date of the declaration of the decision the constitutional and other acts and actions necessary for the Republic to take over the exercise of the sovereign rights transferred to the bodies of the Socialist Federal Republic of Yugoslavia regarding the legal succession of the Socialist Federal Republic of Yugoslavia and the future regulation of mutual relations on the basis of principles of international law, which includes the proposal of a treaty on a confederation'.[244] This legislative step towards independence was important by ensuring the transition was as efficient as possible, with the resulting legal acts having the power of law on the constitutional territory of the Republic of Slovenia, binding all state parties. The step was also important in establishing the

[238] Jambrek, P, (2014) *Nation's Transitions, Social and Legal Issues of Slovenia's Transitions 1945–2015*, Graduate School of Government and European Studies, Brdo pri Kranju and European Faculty of Law, Nova Gorica, Slovenia, 5.

[239] Ibid, Official Gazette of the SFRY, 41/1991.

[240] Ibid.

[241] Mag. Kogovsek, N., Pignoni, R, *Erased People of Slovenia*, Peace Institute Report on Discriminatory Practices in Slovenia concerning Legal Statuses of Citizens of the Former Republics of Yugoslavia, http://www.europarl.europa.eu/hearings/20070626/libe/pignoni_en.pdf

[242] Ibid.

[243] The Plebiscite on the Sovereignty and Independence of the Republic of Slovenia Act, Official Gazette of the Republic of Slovenia, No 44, 6 December 1990. in Peter Jambrek, *Nation's Transitions, Social and Legal Issues od Slovenia's Transitions 1945–2015*, Graduate School of Government and European Studies, Brdo pri Kranju and European Faculty of Law, Nova Gorica, Slovenia, 2014, 257.

[244] Ibid.

first phase of authority for the new Slovenia to begin to operate as an independent state.

The Slovenian Republic was founded on 23 December 1990, following the plebiscite, which continued to reinforce the notion of independence and the establishment of a democratic state.

A year later, in 1991, the Slovenian parliament passed the independence amendments, providing the basis for the new sovereign state to conduct internal and international affairs.[245] On 20 November 1991 the Denationalization Act[246] came into effect to assist the newly independent Slovenia in managing the transition of property owned and occupied under the former Yugoslavia to the new Slovene state. The process for handing back property under the denationalisation law varied from the process and practice of the European Court of Human Rights in Strasbourg.[247] On the one hand, the national law allowed a person to make an application for the return of the property and was subject to administrative decision.[248] On the other hand, the European Court of Human Rights (ECoHR) process enabled an individual to initiate a court proceeding for compensation. However, this could only be achieved when the person has fully exhausted all legal avenues in Slovenia.

On 23 December 1991 the constitution of the Republic of Slovenia was adopted. The Slovenian constitution served to reinforce the state's new found independence and more importantly establish a Slovenian identity. The constitution states that 'citizenship is regulated by the law'.[249] The constitutional amendment[250] of XCI–XCV was an important step towards the new democratic Slovenia, because it deleted the term "socialist" from the Republic's name. The amendment also established the freedom to found political organizations and provided these organizations with equal rights.[251] The constitution justified the independent process by the constitutional doctrine to self-determinate.[252]

The Slovenian state was in a rapid phase of transition to implement new laws, democratic values and principles, along with transitioning the people from socialism to democracy and a market based economy. At the same time, the new state was establishing its own identity and defining its citizens. The Slovenian constitution recognised Slovenia as an independent nation state and provided its citizens with

[245] Ibid.

[246] Official Gazette of the Republic of Slovenia 27/1991.

[247] Ibid.

[248] Ibid, 358.

[249] Article 12, The Constitution of the Republic of Slovenia, Official Gazette Republic of Slovenia Nos. 33/91-I, 42/97, 66/2000, 24/03, 69/04, 68/06, and 47/13.

[250] Arne Mavčič, *Modern Constitutionalism and the Slovenian Constitution of 1991*, The Analysis and International Department, Constitutional Court of the Republic of Slovenia, 2006, 1–21.

[251] Ibid.

[252] Jambrek, P, (2014) *Nation's Transitions, Social and Legal Issues of Slovenia's Transitions 1945–2015,* Graduate School of Government and European Studies, Brdo pri Kranju and European Faculty of Law, Nova Gorica, Slovenia, 278.

rights, freedoms and protections, with the supreme power vested in the people.[253] Citizens exercise this power directly and indirectly through the legislature that adopts and implements national laws. These laws include but are not limited to the public and private side of citizenship. Therefore, the power can be considered as a two-way street, from the top down and bottom up. The national laws of Slovenia must conform to international and European law.[254] This is a notable difference between Slovenia and Australia. Australia is not constitutionally, politically or legally obliged to implement the law of a supranational polity. Furthermore, the Slovenian constitution stated that citizenship of Slovenia is to be regulated by law.[255] Article 6 describes the Coat-of-Arms that is in the form of a shield, and in the middle of the shield there is the outline of the highest mountain peak in Slovenia, Mount Triglav. It is argued that the new constitution was a statement to the people, the state, Europe and the world of its new found independence. There was hardly a mention of Slovenia's historical past, rather focusing on the future state. The preamble particularly emphasized the importance of fundamental rights and freedoms, and the fundamental and permanent rights of the Slovene nation to self-determinate. Thus, the drafters of the constitution were focused on statehood and establishing for the first time an independent identity of its own.

However, some commentators have suggested the right to self-determinate and secede by Slovenia from Yugoslavia was unconstitutional.[256] The 1963 and 1974 constitution of Yugoslavia stated that the right to self-determinate belonged to Yugoslavia. Richard Iglar argues that Article 203 precluded the use of constitutionally-granted rights that threatened the existence of the state, and Article 244, guaranteed Yugoslavia territorial integrity. Yet, Articles 5 and 283 provided the ability for Yugoslavia's borders to be changed. According to Iglar the Presidency contended that Slovenia before seceding was required to explore options to restore relations with other Republics and that a process of constitutional reform must be implemented in a democratic way. Nevertheless, the federal government did acknowledge that the constitution provided the right to secede, however, Slovenia should have convinced and negotiated a pathway to independence with the rest of Yugoslavia.[257]

Despite the relatively smooth road to independence, Slovenes and the Slovenian territory experienced the beginnings of the wider conflict that engulfed the former Yugoslav Republics from 1991 to 1999. What is often referred to as the 10 day war (Slovene: *destdnevna vojna*) began on 27 June and concluded on 7 July 1991 in

---

[253] Article 3, The Constitution of the Republic of Slovenia, Official Gazette Republic of Slovenia Nos. 33/91-I, 42/97, 66/2000, 24/03, 69/04, 68/06, and 47/13.

[254] Ibid, articles 8 and 153.

[255] Article 5, Official Gazette of the Republic of Slovenia 27/1991.

[256] Igar, R, (1992) *The Constitutional Crisis in Yugoslavia and the International Law of Self-Determination: Slovenia's and Croatia's Right to Secede*, 15 B.C. Int'l &Comp.L.Rev.213, 213–418.

[257] Ibid.

Slovenia.[258] Slovenia was the victor in this short conflict and with the signing of the Brioni Accord[259] both Slovenia and Croatia agreed to independence. As Slovenia became an independent state, there were many legal and policy issues running concurrently. This was no more evident when Slovenia was grappling with determining who and who was not Slovenian under the new citizenship arrangements, but also providing its new citizens and others with rights and protections.

The transition of Slovenia from a socialist Republic to a new independent democratic state was a significant shift for the state and its people and the Slovenian identity. In contrast, Australia retained a close connection with Britain and did not have to transition from a socialist to a democratic system of governance. The institutional arrangements in place for Australia, originated in Britain. Similar democratic institutional arrangements weren't in place in Slovenia, even though they had begun developing institutions throughout 1989 and 1990. Apart from the potential constitutional issues, Slovenia during the transition phase found itself having to transition its economy from state owned enterprises to a market based economy. The privatization of land and other building assets was a gradual process that saw the Catholic Church regain many of the assets it had lost 40 years prior to independence.[260] Slovenia reinstated the Catholic Church to its former standing in the region. However, this democratization and opening the economy to a free market did have its drawbacks. It displaced a number of Slovenes who had access to government property, and in some cases it forced those citizens out of the capital.

3.3 Symbols of Statehood

The national flag of Slovenia retained the colours of white, blue and red[261] similar to the former Yugoslavia. However, the blue is a slightly lighter shade. Most of the former Yugoslav Republics have also adopted similar colours of red, white and blue that represent their national flags, with the exception of Macedonia which has adopted red and yellow. Australia's national flag is also red, white and blue. The national flag of a state represents and is a symbol of a state's identity. According to Dimitrij Rupel[262] the Slovenian nation state was founded on linguistic affiliation. That is, the Slovene language that was one of the most important policy principles of continuity of establishing the new state and its people (citizens). Another important

---

[258] Brändström, A., Malesic, M, (2004) *Crisis Management in Slovenia: Comparative Perspectives*, Eslanders Gotab, Stockholm, 58–61.

[259] Van Vooren, B., Blockmans, S., Wouters, J, (2013) *The EU's Role in Global Governance: The Legal Dimension*, Oford University Press, 115.

[260] Petra Ramet, S, (1993) *Slovenia's Road to Democracy*, Europe Asia Studies 45.5, 1993, 887.

[261] Uradni List, Republic of Slovenia, October 1994, http://www.uradni-list.si/_pdf/1994/Ur/u1994067.pdf

[262] Dimitrij Rupel, *Between National and European Identity: A view from Slovenia,* Cambridge Review of International Affairs, Vol 16, No 2, 2003.

component of the new Slovene identity was the introduction of the modern day national anthem. The Slovenian national anthem was created to reflect the historical past and the conflicts the Slovene people and its lands have experienced over the past century. The national anthem of Slovenia also seeks to reinforce the idea that Slovenia wants to be friends with its neighbors and no longer foes:

> *'God's blessing on all nations, Who long and work for that bright day, When o'er earth's habitations', No war, no strife shall hold its sway, Who long to see, That all men free, No more foes, but neighbors be.*[263]

The national anthem reflects a further symbol of peace. In expressing its indemnity to the world, it also reflects the volatile and turbulent past Slovenes had experienced for nearly a century. It also went some way to demonstrate to the European community that the people's by wanting peace, also wanted to back in Europe.

3.4 Conclusion

Modern day Slovenia had been under the rule of the Roman Empire, the Habsburg Monarchy, the Austrian Empire, the Austro-Hungarian Empire, the Kingdom of Serbs, Croats and Slovenes (later renamed the Kingdom of Yugoslavia), Democratic Federal Yugoslavia, to the Federal People's Republic of Yugoslavia. The Federal People's Republic of Yugoslavia would later become the Socialist Federal Republic of Yugoslavia and in 1990 the Republic of Slovenia was born. Throughout this long history, citizenship had evolved by adopting exclusionary and inclusionary measures. More importantly, for Slovenes, the various rulers over the territory had bought with it elements of socialism to modern day democracy.

The territory of current Slovenia between 1800 and 1900 had been ruled by the Habsburg's and later came under the Austro-Hungarian Empire. A combination of Austrian and Hungarian law used to regulate citizenship, and afford rights to citizens, depending on where the individual resided (Austrian section or Hungarian section). Slovenian nationalism had gained momentum and the language would be used across the territory. The Slovene language, at least on paper, received formal recognition and could be used in book and lecture. Importantly, the Australian and Hungarian citizenship laws would be used as the basis to provide continuity of the inhabitants, in the respective regions when the Empire collapsed.

On 27 August 1991, the European Community and its member states convened a meeting on the Peace in Yugoslavia. However, initially the European Community appeared to have taken a hands-off approach towards the conflict. Germany had decided to recognize Slovenia and Croatia and supported independence, and thus pressured the European Community to also take an interest. According to Anuradha

[263] Protocol of the Republic of Slovenia, Republic of Slovenia, http://www.protokol.gov.si/en/useful_information/national_insignia/text_of_the_slovenian_national_anthem_in_different_languages/

Chenoy the Germans had urged the European Community (later the European Union) to broker a ceasefire.

The European Commission attempted to keep Yugoslavia together. This resulted in Germany falling in behind the European Commission.[264] There were many Croatians who were resident in Germany, and consequently Germany recognized these historical links. With continued pressure from Germany on the European Commission, following the Maastricht negotiations, the European Community eventually supported Slovenia and Croatia, and the protection of the people.[265] As the world and Europe had not fully recognized Slovenia as a state upon independence, this placed the people and the territory in a precarious legal position between 1990 and 1991. In other words, they had fully separated from Yugoslavia, established a constitution and, were working towards establishing the institutional arrangements required to run a state. However, they had not been recognized legally by any other states. This legal recognition would have wider ramifications as other states and their citizens would have been concerned about the stability within the state and surrounding region to undertake business and other social engagements.

The European Commission would conclude a total of 13 opinions on the separation of Yugoslavia, focusing on the application of international law.[266] The Commission noted that there are well established principles in the Vienna Conventions on the Succession of States 1978 and 1983 that provide guidance for state succession. The Commission also noted that the succession of states should be based on core principles that include complying with international law, agreement, the protection of fundamental rights of peoples and minorities, and the principles of equality of rights and duties between states.[267]

The national identity of the Slovenian people from the time of the Holy Roman Empire ruling over the lands to the end of Yugoslavia can be considered a complex road towards independence. The lands of Slovenia have experienced two world wars, internal conflicts and been ruled by empires, monarchs, socialist, communists and totalitarian regimes. Throughout all of that, the Slovenian people managed to strengthen who they were as a people and their identity. The citizenship law throughout this period no longer had a single dimension of confirming the legal status of a citizen within a state. Rather, citizenship began to transform and take on a multidimensional role that, took into consideration immigration, rights and PIL. The multidimensional application of citizenship included continuity for the people from one ruler to the next, unification of citizens within a defined territory, and confirmed the legal status of citizenship. The laws, along with the Slovene language and culture have been pivotal in establishing a string level of cohesion across society. Slovenia has continued to use the citizenship laws to enhance and strengthen its identity. The

---

[264] Chenoy, A, (1996) *The European Union and the Breakup of Yugoslavia*, International Studies, Sages, 33, 4, 442–446.

[265] Ibid.

[266] Craven, M, (1996) *The European Community Arbitration Commission on Yugoslavia*, University Leicester, 60–80.

[267] Ibid.

same can be said of Australia, but Australia has taken a very different path in the development of its national identity and citizenship laws. The next chapter traces the development of Australia and its national identity.

References

Bagwell, B. (1991). Yugoslavian constitutional questions: Self-determination and secession of member republics. *Georgia Journal of International and Comparative Law, 21*, 489–499.

Bartlett, W. (2003). *Croatia between Europe and the Balkans* (p. 13). London: Routledge.

Batovič, A. (2009). *The Balkans in Turmoil-Croatian spring and the Yugoslav position between the cold war blocs 1965–1971* (pp. 1–10). London: London School of Economics, Cold War Studies Programme.

Bertossi, C., & Hajjat, A. (2013). *Country report: France* (pp. 1–2). France: EUDO Citizenship Observatory, European University Institute.

Bradburn, D. (2010). *The problem of citizenship in the American Revolution, Binghamton University* (pp. 1096–1099). New York: State University of New York/Blackwell Publishing.

Bradshaw, M. (2001). *The Russian Far East and Pacific Asia: Unfulfilled potential*. London: Routledge. Chapter 14.

Brändström, A., & Malesic, M. (2004). *Crisis management in Slovenia: Comparative perspectives* (pp. 58–61). Stockholm: Eslanders Gotab.

Beiner, R. (1995). Citizenship and nationalism: Is Canada a real country? In K. Slawner & M. E. Denhim (Eds.), *Citizenship after liberalism* (p. 185). New York: Peter Lang Publishing.

Bauböck, R., Perching, B., & Sievers, V. (2009). *Citizenship policies in the new Europe* (Expanded and Updated ed., pp. 330–350). Amsterdam: University Press.

Brubaker, R. (1989). The French Revolution and invention of citizenship. *French Politics and Society, 7*(3), 30–49.

Cohen, L., & Dragovič-Soso, J. (2008). *State collapse in South-Eastern Europe: New perspectives on Yugoslavia* (pp. 101–103). West Lafayette: Purdue University Press.

Chenoy, A. (1996). The European Union and the breakup of Yugoslavia. *International Studies, Sages, 33*(4), 442–446.

Craven, M. (1996). *The European Community Arbitration Commission on Yugoslavia* (pp. 60–80). Leicester: University Leicester.

Črnič, A., Komel, M., Smerke, M., Šabec, K., & Vovk, T. (2013). Religious pluralisation in Slovenia. *Teorija in Praksa let, 50*, 205–229.

Drakulic, S, (1996) *Café Europa: Life after communism*. Hachette Digital.

Djokic, D. (2010). National Mobilisation in the kingdom of Yugoslavia. In D. Djokic & Jker-Lindsaym (Eds.), *New perspective on Yugoslavia: Key issues and controversies*. London: Routedge.

Elshtain, J. B. (1987). *Women and war* (pp. 250–265). New York: Basic Books.

Ferš, D. (2003). From security and intelligence service to Slovene Intelligence and Security Agency. *Slovenian Intelligence and Security Agency, National Security and the Future, 1–2*(3), 61–65.

Floumoy, R., & Hudson, M. (1930). *A collection of nationality laws of various countries, as contained in constitutions, statutes and treaties* (pp. 337–344). New York: Carnegie Endowerment for International Peace.

Frucht, R. (2005). *Eastern Europe: An introduction to the people, land, and culture* (pp. 420–430). Santa Barbara: Library of Congress in Publication data.

Ghachem, M. (2003). Slavery and citizenship in the age of the American revolutions. *Historical Reflections, 29*(1), 10–15.

Gow, J., & Carmichael, C. (2001). *Slovenia and Slovenes: A small state and the new Europe* (p. 35). London: C. Hurst & Co.

Grča, T., & Mavčič, A. (2007). *The situation of the Hungarian minority in Slovenia with an emphasis on the Lendava region and Slovenian in Hungary*. Kranj.

Gundersen, J. (1987). *Independence, citizenship, and the American Revolution* (pp. 60–77). Chicago: The University of Chicago Press.

Habermas, J. (1994). Citizenship and National Identity. In B. Van Steenberghen (Ed.), *The condition of citizenship* (pp. 20–22). London: SAGE Publications.

Habermas, J. (1998). *The inclusion of the other: Studies in political theory* (C. Cronin & P. De Greiff, Ed., C. Cronin, Trans., pp. 130–135). Cambridge: MIT Press.

Hailbronner, K. (2012). *Country report: Germany* (pp. 1–4). Italy: EUDO Citizenship Observatory, European Union Institute.

Haug Hilde, K. (2012). *Creating a socialist Yugoslavia: Tito, communist leadership and national*. London: I.B. Tauris. Chapter 4.

Henry, C. (1970). *The essential Tito* (p. 69). New York: St. Martin's Press.

Hinerfield, O. (2013). *The rise and fall of Yugoslavia, modern European history* (pp. 1–12). Oregon: Portland State University.

Igar, R. (1992). The Constitutional Crisis in Yugoslavia and the International Law of Self-Determination: Slovenia's and Croatia's Right to Secede, 15 B.C. *International and Comparative Law Review, 213*, 213–418.

Isin, E. (1997). Who is the new citizen? Towards a genealogy. *Citizenship Studies, 1*, 115–131.

Jambrek, P. (2014). *Nation's transitions, social and legal issues of Slovenia's transitions 1945–2015* (p. 37). Nova Gorica: Graduate School of Government and European Studies, Brdo pri Kranju and European Faculty of Law.

Klemenčič, M. & Žagar, M. (2004). *Ethnic diversity within nations, the former Yugoslavia's diverse peoples: A Reference Sourcebook*, 49.

Kreacic, G., & Grafenauer, B. (2000). *Karantanija: izbrane razprave in članki*. Ljubljana: Zavod Republike Slovenije za šolstvo.

Kymlicka, W., & Norman, W. (1994). Return of the citizen: A recent work on citizenship theory. *Survey Article, 104*, 352–381.

Kymlicka, W. (2012). *Multiculturalism: Success, failure, and the future* (p. 6). Washington, DC: Migration Policy Institute.

Luthar, O. (2008). *The land between: A history of Slovenia* (pp. 32–33). New York: Peter Lang International Academic Publishers.

Maitland, F. & Pollock, F. (1898). (reprinted 1968), *The history of English Law before the time of Edwards I*, vol. 2, Liberty Fund, 458.

Makaryan, S. (2006). *Trends in citizenship policies of the 15 former Soviet Union republics: Conforming the world culture or following National Identity?* (pp. 1–10). Washington, DC: Washington State University.

Marinac, B. & Mavčič, A. (2004) *Pravni položaj slovenske manjšine v Sloveniji: magistrsko delo*. Brdo pri Kraju.

Marshall, T. (1965). *Class, citizenship and social development* (pp. 101–103). New York: Anchor.

Mavčič, A. (2006). *Modern constitutionalism and the Slovenian constitution of 1991* (pp. 1–21). Slovenia: The Analysis and International Department, Constitutional Court of the Republic of Slovenia.

Meier, V. (1999). *Yugoslavia: A history of its demise* (p. 53). London: Routledge.

Ognyanova, I. (2000). *Nationalism and National Policy in Independent State of Croatia* (1941–1945). In D. Rogers, J. Wheeler, M. Zavacka, & S. Casebier (Eds.), *Topics in feminism, history and philosophy, IWM junior visiting fellows conferences* (Vol. 6). Vienne: IWM.

Patterson, C. (1995). *Pericles Citizenship Law* of 451-50 BC, 1981, 1-8. In K. Rubenstein (Ed.), *Citizenship in Australia: Unscrambling its meaning* (pp. 504–508). Melbourne: Melbourne University Law Review.

Resnik-Planinc, T, (2013) *Development and present situation of Slovene didactics of geography*. Annales Universitatis Paedagogcae Cracovensis, 113.
Pavčnik, M., & Constitutionis, M. (2009). Glosses on the writers' constitution upon the occasion of its 20th anniversary. *Ljubljana, 63, 125*(11–12), 567–580.
Pocock, J. (1992). The ideal of citizenship since classical times. *Queen's Quarterly, 99*(1), 10–50.
Popkin, J. (2012). *A concise history of the Haitian revolution* (pp. 170–180). Malden: Blackwell Publishing.
Price, P. (2013). Natural law and birthright citizenship in Calvin's case (1608). *Yale Journal of Law and the Humanities, 9*, 73–80.
Petra Ramet, S. (1993). Slovenia's road to democracy. *Europe Asia Studies, 45*(5), 887.
Radan, P. (2002). *The breakup of Yugoslavia and international law* (pp. 137–145). New York: Routledge.
Rava, N. (2010). *Country report: Serbia* (p. 3). Florence: European University Institute, EUDO Citizenship Observatory.
Richards, D. (1987). Transported to New South Wales: Medical convicts 1788–1850. *British Medical Journal, 295*, 1609.
Rupel, D. (2003). Between national and European identity: A view from Slovenia. *Cambridge Review of International Affairs, 16*(2).
Matija Rojec, M., & Silva-Jauregui, C. (2004). *Slovenia: From Yugoslavia to the European Union* (pp. 5–15). Washington, DC: The World Bank.
Shafir, G. (1998). *The citizenship debates* (p. 31). Minneapolis: University of Minnesota Press.
Shoup, P. (1963). Yugoslavia's national minorities under communism. *Slavic Review, 22*, 65.
Štih, P., Simoniti, V., & Vodopivec, P. (2008). *Slovene history, society-politics-culture*. Ljubljana: Inštitut za novejšo zgodovino: Sistory. Besedilni podatki.
Štiks, I. (2010). *A laboratory of citizenship: Shifting conceptions of citizenship in Yugoslavia and its successor states*. University of Edinburgh, School of Law, 2010/12.
Salmond, J. (1902). Citizenship and allegiance, nationality in English law. *The Law Quarterly Review, XVIII*, 50–54.
Sawyer, C., & Helena Wray, H. (2014). *Country report: United Kingdom* (p. 7). Florence: EUDO Citizenship Observatory, European University Institute.
Singleton, F. (1989). *A short history of the Yugoslav People's* (p. 15). Cambridge: Cambridge Cambridge University Press.
Sotirovič, V. (2014). The 1917 Corfu declaration. *The South Journal, 33*(1–2), 2–6.
Teierney, S. (2000). *Accommodating national identity: New approaches in international and domestic law*. Boston: Kluwer international Law.
Van Vooren, B., Blockmans, S., & Wouters, J. (2013). *The EU's role in global governance: The legal dimension* (p. 115). Oxford: Oford University Press.
Vasiljevna Čurkina, I. (2011). Matija Majar Ziljski, Enlightener, Politician, Scholar. *Traditiones, 40*(2), 9–26.
von Hirschhausen, U. (2009). From imperial inclusion to national exclusion: Citizenship in the Habsburg monarchy and in Austria 1867-1923. *European Review of History, 16*, 551–573.
Williamson, S. (1998). The origins of World War I. *The Journal of Interdisciplinary History, 18*(4), 795–818.

Chapter 4
The Australian Identity and Citizenship

Abstract Australia history and beginning is very different to that of Slovenia and the EU. Australia has been occupied by the Indigenous Aboriginal peoples for centuries. However, the treatment of the Indigenous community can be best described in the modern period as barbaric and quite shocking. They were excluded from all forms of the polity and society. They were dispersed across the entire continent. Upon Federation their plight got no better, when the White Australia policy was invoked. This chapter traces some of the issues the Aboriginal people faced. Since then, Australia has abolished its White policy, at least on paper, and today Australia is an amalgam of different ethnic and religious groups. National identity and social cohesion has not been smooth. The national identity has, at times, been difficult to define and locate. It has been challenged, along with cohesion. Both have been highly politicised over the past two decades with the rise of nationalist thought and politics. It has galvanised Australia to strengthen its identity. More importantly, government(s) have begun to recognise the Aboriginal people, even though they continue to be excluded from many areas of the law and policy. In 1948–1949, the first citizenship laws were introduced, and ever since there has been reform to strengthen the laws in response to regional and international events. They support multicultural Australia today, immigration, rights, PIL, identity and social cohesion.

Keywords Australia · Aboriginal people · Citizenship · Dual citizenship · Language · Migration · National days WWI · WWII

4.1 Introduction

Australia is an island continent, unlike Slovenia which borders Italy, Austria, Hungary and Croatia. Australia has had a very different beginning to Slovenia. It is well recorded that Australia has been occupied for many millennia by the Aboriginal peoples. It was relatively recent in historical terms that Australia was occupied by European settlers and democratically governed. Australia's national identity has

R. Walters, *National Identity and Social Cohesion in a Time of Geopolitical and Economic Tension: Australia – European Union – Slovenia*,
https://doi.org/10.1007/978-981-15-2164-5_4

been influenced by the indigenous inhabitants and then initially by the first British arrivals in the late1700s. James Cook mapped the east coast of Australia and landed at Botany Bay in present day Sydney in 1770.[1] However, the first Europeans (Spanish, Dutch and possibly Portuguese) had visited Australia by the seventeenth century.[2] The First Fleet arrived in Sydney Cove in 1788[3] and brought with it British culture, way of life, food, farming techniques, trade, governance and political structure as well as the English language.

In 1816 Governor Macquarie had made a martial-law style proclamation, banning aboriginal meetings, the carrying of weapons (including those used for hunting, abolished their own system of punishment and reconciliation, and entitled settlers and military troops to use Force of Arms on armed aboriginal people or unarmed groups of six or more. The suppression of their rights to function as a community had enormous impact to their identity.

In *R v Lowe* (1827) Supreme Court of NSW Forbes CJ and Stephen J decided that aboriginal people in conflict with Europeans were subject to British justice and intervention but a different approach was taken in relation to criminal matters between Aboriginals. The resulting effect saw three key decisions made by the Supreme Court of NSW on these issues. Later in *R v Ballard or Barrett*[4] it was held an Aboriginal person could not be prosecuted for the murder of another aboriginal person due to lack of jurisdiction. Some 7 years later, *in R v Murrell [1836]* aboriginal defendant's counsel argued that the court had no jurisdiction to try him (in line with the decision in Ballard) but court completely rejected its previous line of argument). Yet, in *R v Bonjon (Unreported, Supreme Court of New South Wales, Willis J, 20 September 1841),* it was reported that the shooting murder at Geelong between two separate aboriginal groups. Bonjon's lawyer argued that occupation did not give the Crown authority over indigenous inhabitants unless there was a treaty or agreement between them and they chose to come under English law. Again, there was a type of 'no jurisdiction' argument. Furthermore, there appeared to be some recognition of their own systems and customs. However, that would be as far as it went. More pervasively, Richard O'Connor, the then government leader in the Senate, argued that such a blanket exclusion:

> would be a monstrous thing, an unheard of piece of savagery on our part, to treat the aboriginals, whose land we were occupying, in such a manner as to deprive them absolutely of any right to vote in their own country, simply on the ground of their colour, and because they were aboriginals.[5]

---

[1] Department of Environment, Australian Government, http://www.environment.gov.au/cgi-bin/ahdb/search.pl?mode=place_detail;place_id=105812

[2] Scott, E, (1916) *A Short History of Australia*, The University of Melbourne, 3–91, www.ebooksoneverything.com

[3] Richards, D, (1987) *Transported to New South Wales: medical convicts 1788–1850*, British Medical Journal, Vol 295, 1609.

[4] [1829] NSW Sup Crt 26.

[5] Chesterman, J, Galligan, B. (1997) *Citizens Without Rights: Aborigines and Australian Citizenship*, Cambridge: Cambridge University Press. Chesterman, J, Galligan, B, (1999) *Defining Australian Citizenship: Selected Documents*, Melbourne: University of Melbourne Press.

Clearly, O'Connor was highlighting a wider issue for Australia, and its development of its early identity. Moreover, O'Conner was calling for a level of cohesion amongst the early settlers and the indigenous community. As history highlights, O'Connor's call was never taken into consideration. O'Connor was defeated and the Indigenous community would remain excluded until 1962. The voting exclusion set the pattern for exclusion of Aboriginal natives from many basic citizenship rights and entitlements: for example, in denying maternity benefits and invalid and old age pensions. This concluded with the 1967 referendum. However, since then, practices have continued to be implemented that have excluded them from being full participants in the polity. As highlighted in an earlier chapter the Indigenous community through High Court rulings and governments, particularly the Australian Labor Party have made a concerted effort to recognise this community. Nonetheless, the impact on social cohesion, and national identity has been enormous. That is, and arguably, it is well understood in other countries around the world, the lack of recognition the Aboriginal people have had and continue to have in Australia.

Galligan believes that the Australian constitution itself was largely procedural, the national purpose it would serve was establishing a liberal democratic nation composed of Australians who shared British ancestry (English, Scottish, Irish, and Welsh), common social and political values, aspirations, and traditions.[6] For Galligan, in referring to Helen Irvin, argues that the federation of Australia achieved "A nation, but not yet a nation-state." Australia was "both a post- colonial nation and a peculiarly Australian nation," "domestically sovereign, culturally distinctive, but still tied in community, language and law to the nation from which it had sprung."[7]

In New South Wales there was law in 1828 that allowed the Governor to grant letters, which was the first act of naturalization.[8] An important observation to make in Australia's history and identity was the application of the British legal system and the establishment of the doctrine *terra nullius*. The New South Wales court[9] stated that the inhabitants of the Australian territory were subject to the laws of England. It was later confirmed by the Australian High Court that upon colonization Australia was not a sovereign nation and that *terra nullius* did not apply, as the territory was inhabited by indigenous Aboriginal people.[10] The *Australian Constitutions Act 1842* provided for the New South Wales Colony to be divided into separate colonies. Two years later the *Australian Constitutions Act 1844* would define the colony and provide the Governor and Legislative Council the power to repeal, vary or alter legislation.[11]

---

[6] Galligan, B. (2017) *Australian Citizenship in a Changing Nation and World*, https://link-springer-com.wallaby.vu.edu.au:4433/content/pdf/10.1007%2F978-3-319-53529-6_4.pdf

[7] Ibid.

[8] Ibid.

[9] *R v Tommy* [1827] NSW SupC70.

[10] *Mabo v Queensland* [2] (1992) 175 CLR 1, *Co v Commonwealth* (1979) HCA 68.

[11] Australian Heritage, http://www.heritageaustralia.com.au/articles/features/4576-a-nation-subdivided

Between 1851 and 1890 mining for gold became so popular that it had attracted people from many different countries. The first Slovene was recorded as arriving in Australia in 1855.[12] This was the beginning of a long standing relationship between Australia and Slovenes that continues today. During the same period, all colonies agreed to restrict the entrance of Asian, particularly Chinese into the territory. By 1859 it was estimated there were more than 42,000 Chinese people in Victoria.[13] The *Chinese Immigrants Statute 1865 (Vic)* and later *The Chinese Act 1881 (Vic)*, imposed a tax on individuals arriving in Australia, and restricted the number of immigrants to one per 100 tonnes of goods on an individual shipping vessel. Even though there was no formal multicultural policy established, many immigrants from around the world had arrived in Australia to be part of the gold rush, from the United Kingdom, the Americas, France, Italy, Germany, Poland, Hungary and China.[14]

The colonies were granted the right to self-govern with the implementation of the *Australian Constitutions Act* (No. 2) 1850.[15] Section 35 enabled Legislative Councils to be established within the colonies, whereby members could be elected and conduct elections.[16] Importantly, the Act recognised the institution of parliamentary democracy in Australia, which ever since has been a fundamental and core value of Australia's identity. The Aboriginal people had their own customs, culture, languages and community governance structures. However, they were not adopted by the new arrivals who imposed their own system of governance and law upon the indigenous people.

Discussing the laws of each of the individual colonies is outside the scope of this research due to the breadth and depth of the law. However, the following section briefly discusses those laws of the State of Victoria. The first Victorian Parliament was elected in accordance with the 1855 *Constitutional Act*.[17] [Zelman] Cowen highlights that the laws constituted a Legislative Council and created the district of Port Phillip from the Murray River to the Murrumbidgee at its northern boundary. Section 1 of the *Constitutional Act 1855* provided the authority for the Victorian legislature to make laws, which regulated the behavior of its citizens, however the citizens remained British subjects under the law of Britain.

In 1865 the *Colonial Laws Validity Act*[18] was enacted to remove any inconsistency between the colonies and Britain. The British Parliament retained the power to make laws for each of the colonies. The *Colonial Laws Validity Act 1865* provided the Governor with the power to grant a letter of naturalisation of residence

[12] Immigration from Slovenia, http://museumvictoria.com.au/origins/history.aspx?pid=54

[13] Kim Rubenstein, K, (2002) *Ausralian Citizenship Law in Context*, 27.

[14] Immigration from Slovenia, http://museumvictoria.com.au/origins/history.aspx?pid=54

[15] *Australian Constitutions Act (No.2) 1850* (UK), http://ozcase.library.qut.edu.au/qhlc/documents/qr_cons_australian_1850_13-14_Vic_c59.pdf

[16] Ibid.

[17] Cowen, Z, (1957) *A Historical Survey of the Victorian Constitution*, 1856 to 1956, Melbourne University Law Review, vol 1, 1–5.

[18] *Colonial Laws Validity Act 1865*, http://caid.ca/ColLawValAct1865.pdf

and take the oath of allegiance to the British Crown to inhabitants.[19] To obtain naturalisation the individual was to verify on oath; stating their name, age, birthplace, occupation and length of residence in the colony.[20] Individuals who were resident in Victoria and had been naturalised in the United Kingdom or another British colony were able to be naturalised by the Governor, provided a certificate was presented confirming their naturalisation in the other colony.[21] Following the passage of the *Naturalisation Act 1870*, British women who married alien men lost their status as British subject on the legislative assumption that their allegiance to the Crown ceased.[22] This reinforced the earlier exclusive developments in citizenship where the women would continue to follow the husband.

In 1891, constitutional conventions were adopted based on those of the United Kingdom, the United States, Canada and Switzerland.[23] The delegates were informed that there is to be a double citizenship to be conferred by the constitution on every citizen of these states and the nation. However, this was never realized. The Constitutional Bill of 1891 bought together the colonies as a federated state. Nonetheless, the first legislation, the *Naturalisation Act 1897* was introduced, which provided for the recognition of naturalisation throughout the Australasian territories. In the same year the *Aboriginal Protection and Restriction of the Sale of Opium Act 1897* was introduced in Queensland, and were the first Aboriginal protection legislation in Queensland and Australia. It ushered in the long ear of protection and segregation during the Aborigines and Torres Strait Islanders lost their legal status as British citizens and became wards of the state.[24] The power provided by the law enabled aboriginal people to be removed and placed on a reserve.[25] This was a difficult period for the aboriginal people as they would witness their own culture and identity being diluted by the new settlers.

---

[19] Great Britain, Report of the Royal Commission for Inquiring into the Laws of Naturalisation and Allegiance: An account of British and Foreign Laws, and of the Diplomatic Correspondence, Reports from Foreign States, and other Papers, 1896, 12–15.

[20] Ibid.

[21] Ibid.

[22] Irving, H, (2008) *Still Call Australia Home: The Constitution and the Citizen's Right of Abode*, Sydney Law Review, Vol 30: 133, 2008 135.

[23] Barton, 379–381, *Official report of the National Australasian Convention debates, Adelaide, 22nd March to 5 May, 1897, Parliament of Victoria*. Frank McGrath, *The Intentions of the Framers of the Commonwealth of Australia Constitution in the Context of the Debates at the Australasian Federation Conference of 1890*, and the Australasian Federal Conventions of 1891 and 1897–8, Doctor of Philosophy, 2000, 6.

[24] Reynolds, H, (2003) *Race relations in northern Queensland*, Townsville, James Cook University, 20–24. *Aboriginal Protection and Restriction of the Sale of Opium Act 1897* http://www.foundingdocs.gov.au/resources/transcripts/qld5_doc_1897.pdf

[25] Ibid.

During the debates dual citizenship[26] was a consideration for Australia. The idea was to have citizenship at both the State and Federal level. However, there was no discussion as to how this would operate.[27] Sir Richard Baker stated:

> [T]here must be dual citizenship. In a Federation the people are citizens of two different nationalities, if I may so express myself. They are citizens of the States and also of the Federation. Both the States and Federal Governments act directly on them.[28]

During the 1898 Melbourne Convention, the treatment of people from one state who were present in another state was discussed to ensure they would be equal. The resulting affect saw the current day sections 51 and 117 form part of Australia's constitution, allowing the commonwealth to legislate in certain areas. Today, the commonwealth has responsibility for citizenship and migration. Additionally, the opposition to ensuring equality highlighted the different understandings of the meaning of citizenship, and its omission from the constitution.[29] Thus, citizenship was to be defined as a franchise. A citizen is one who is entitled to immunities of citizenship. The notion of excluding other races was also raised during the debates, whereby James Howe argued that the first duty is to ourselves and to make Australia a home for Australians and the British. The reference to the British reinforced the connection and influence the Empire had over the Australian territory. Even though the Empire had exerted a lot of influence throughout the territory, the beginnings of an Australian identity could be seen. At the convention debates the drafted noted that 'A state shall not make or enforce any law abridging any privilege or immunity of citizens from other states of the commonwealth'.[30] Political rights were also raised as the only rights associated with citizenship which were derived from the English law.

In 1900, the inhabitants (British subjects) voted[31] in favor of a constitution that would see the formation of the Australian federative state. However, while citizenship was not included into the constitution, the topic was raised and considered during the drafting of the constitutional conventions.[32] Further, there was a proposal put forward to define a 'citizen of the Commonwealth' to include: the citizens of each state and all other persons owing allegiance to the Queen, and residing in any

[26] *Official report of the National Australasian Convention debates, Adelaide, 22nd March to 5 May, 1897, Parliament of Victoria.*

[27] *Official Record of the Debates of the Australasian Federal Conventions*, Melbourne 1898, 673–675. http://parlinfo.aph.gov.au/parlInfo/search/summary/summary

[28] Sir Richard Baker, 99–101, *Official report of the National Australasian Convention debates*, Adelaide, 22nd March to 5 May, 1897, Parliament of Victoria.

[29] Rubenstein, K, (2002) *Australian Citizenship Law in Context*, Lawbook Co, 24–35.

[30] Ibid.

[31] Gibb, D, (1982) *National identity and consciousness: commentary and documents*, Melbourne, Victoria.

[32] John Quick and Robert Garran, *Annotated Constitution of the Australian Commonwealth*, 1901, in Kim Rubenstein, *Citizenship in Australia: Unscrambling its Meaning*, Melbourne University Law Review, 1995, 504–508.

territory of the Commonwealth shall, be citizens of the Commonwealth.[33] However, neither proposal was accepted. The debate considered discrimination between the states, and how to deal with the Chinese and Indian residents. This also failed. Had this been realized, citizenship would have gained formal recognition in the national law of Australia at the time of federation.

The *Commonwealth of Australia Act* was passed by the British Parliament in July 1900 and on 9 July was given Royal Assent by Queen Victoria,[34] taking effect on 1 January 1901. Comparatively, Australia and Slovenia had been ruled by an Empire. However, Slovenian citizens had their legal status grounded within the territory they resided. Australian citizens during the same time were considered subjects of Britain and more importantly, their legal status rested in Britain and not the territory they were located.

4.1.1 1900–1948

In 1901, Australia was federated and the first Australia constitution came into effect. Australia at federation was at a significant advantage to that of Slovenia. Australia did not have to separate its legal framework and institutions from another state. Australia inherited its legal framework and institutions from Britain. Citizenship was not recognised in the constitution and citizens remained defined as British subjects. Mary Crock highlights the lack of recognition of citizenship in the constitution dates back to its development and preparation at federation.[35] Crock further argues that the silence in the constitution created ongoing uncertainties about who Australians (the citizens) think they are, and what citizenship should mean.[36] This along with the other citizenship measures Australia adopted in the early period of Federation was indicative of the racial approach taken by Australia's "White Australian Policy". This exclusionary approach would go onto dominate the citizenship landscape for decades.

The Australian High Court argued that 'citizenship is a concept that is not constitutionally necessary'.[37] This is an important point because the lack of recognition of citizenship in the constitution allowed the British Empire to strengthen its rule over the territory and exert its identity, rather than, a new identity being forged. Conversely, it could also be said that an Australian identity began to develop despite lacking a distinct citizenship. The resulting effect was a limited national identity. Furthermore, the people of the states of Victoria, New South Wales, South Australia,

[33] Ibid.

[34] Irving, H, (1997) *To Constitute a Nation: A Cultural History of Australia's Constitution*, Cambridge University Press, Melbourne.

[35] Crock, M, (2007) *Defining Strangers: Human Rights, Immigrants and the Foundations of a Just Society*, Melbourne Law Review 39, 1–14.

[36] Ibid.

[37] *Chu Kheng Lim v MILGEA* (1992) 176 CLR 1, 54.

Queensland, Tasmania and Western Australia agreed to unite to become a united Federal Commonwealth under the Crown of the United Kingdom.[38] Australia was a collection of six self-governing colonies. However, the constitution does not mention the two Territories, the Australian Capital Territory (where the capital of Australia, Canberra is located) and the Northern Territory because they did not exist at federation.

The *Immigration Restriction Act 1901* came into effect to regulate immigration into the Australian territory. Immigration is a pathway to citizenship. The early immigration law required a migrant to take a dictation test to assess their command of the English language. Immigrants who failed the test could be deported.[39] The dictation test was used as an exclusionary tool that reinforced the 'White Australia Policy', where a person was required to write without errors 50 words in a European language.[40] Not only was it a tool to manage convicts, it was also a tool to reinforce the White Australia Policy and discriminate on racial ground, where a person did not complete the language test. Moreover, if the person failed the test, or was convicted of any crime of violence, they could be deported.[41] In the early period following federation, the policy was that convicts were not to be sent back to Britain.[42] Today, deportation has become part of the state's ability to manage non-citizens.

Helen Irving highlights the conceptual difference between a British subject and Australian British subject.[43] The 1901 Act served Australia's 'white' citizenship policy, even though many colored people were born throughout the British Empire.[44] British subjects born India or Hong Kong, for example, would be able to travel freely amongst the colonies. Arguably, this placed Australia in an uncomfortable position. On the one hand, the British government opposed immigration restrictions based on race and color as they were discriminatory. On the other hand, a British subject was, in principle, able to move quite freely amongst colonies. Therefore, Australia established the 1901 Act to minimize the entry of people of non-whites.

Australia was in a building phase and ethnicity was the principal policy approach for colonization and citizenship. Alfred Deakin made the point that the Bill was an expression of the national manhood, the national character, and the national future.[45] Deakin was expressing the beginnings of the Australian identity making reference

---

[38] Preamble, Australian Constitution, 1900.

[39] *Immigration Act 1901*, section 5.

[40] Above, n 482.

[41] Crock, M., Berg, L, (2011) *Immigration, Refugees and Forced Migration, Law, Policy and Practice in Australia*, The Federation Press, 521.

[42] Ibid.

[43] Irving, H, (1997) *To Constitute a Nation: A Cultural History of Australia's Constitution*, Cambridge University Press, Melbourne, 144.

[44] Ibid.

[45] Australia, House of Representatives, *Parliamentary Debates* (12 September 1901), 4804 (Alfred Deakin, Attorney-General), in Kim Rubenstein, *Australian Citizenship Law in Context*, Lawbook Co, 2002, 52.

to the national character and future, and the importance migration law would have in contributing to the identity.

The constitution was constructed gender neutral and provides the right to vote[46] amongst others. The expressed constitutional rights were afforded to both women and men. It is argued that even though the common law 'doctrine of coverture' was still very relevant as part of society, the constitution would begin to provide the opportunity for greater participation of women. The introduction of the *Commonwealth Franchise Act 1902*, extended the rights of women to vote in Australia, however indigenous people were excluded.[47] Section 51 (xxvi) provided the Commonwealth with the ability to make laws relating to the people of any race, other than aborigines in any state. This was yet another exclusionary measure for the indigenous community. Furthermore, section 127 of the constitution excluded aboriginal people from being counted in the census.[48]

In 1903, Australia introduced the *Naturalisation Act* detailing how immigrants could obtain the rights of a British subject.[49] Importantly, the legislation reinforced the British law that women would assume the rights and privileges of their husband.[50] The indigenous populations of Asia, Africa and the Pacific Islands, except New Zealand, were excluded from naturalisation.[51] At the time aborigines were considered to be British subjects by birth and therefore, they were not required to be naturalised.[52] However, this did not allow them to fully embrace the Australian way. In fact, their experience of membership of the Australian community did not enhance their standing.[53] Even though they had formal status, it has been well documented that aboriginal people were excluded from many areas of daily life.

The *Australian States Constitutions Act 1907* enabled the British Government to disallow legislation passed by colonial parliaments. Britain would still retain a lot of control over the governance of the territory, transferring its identity. In 1908, Issacs J in *Potter* stated the ultimate fact to be reached as a test whether a given person is an immigrant or not, is whether he is or is not at that time a constituent party to the community known as the Australian people.[54] Nationality and domicile are not the tests'.[55] The test is understanding and practicing the norms of society on a daily basis. The court went onto say that 'A person born in Australia, and by reason of that

[46] Rubenstein, K, (2000) *Citizenship and the Centenary-Inclusion and Exclusion in 20th Century Australia*, Melbourne Law Review, 576.

[47] *Commonwealth Franchise Act 1902, ss 3 & 41.*

[48] Mercer, D, (2003) *Citizen Minus?: Indigenous Australian and the Citizenship Question*, Citizenship Studies, Vol. 7, No. 4, 424–430.

[49] Klapor, M., Coombs, M., Bohm, C*Australian citizenship: a chronology of major developments in policy and law*, Parliament of Australia, www.citizenship.gov.au/_pdf/cit_chron_policy_law.pdf

[50] *Naturalisation Act 1903*, s9.

[51] Rubenstein, K, (2002) *Australian Citizenship Law in Context*, Lawbook Co, 52–53.

[52] Ibid.

[53] Ibid.

[54] *Potter v Minahan* (1908) 7 CLR 277.

[55] Ibid.

fact a British subject owing allegiance to the Empire, becomes by reason of the same fact a member of the Australian community and is entitled to the rights and benefits which membership of the community involves'.[56] However, Issacs J stated that he did not accept that birth in Australia concluded that someone was a member of the community.[57] This is an important observation because it could be argued that Issac's position was squarely directed at those aboriginal people who were born on the territory. Arguably, the judiciary did not accept the aboriginal people as being members of the broader community.

The commencement of WWI saw Australia send troops to the front line in Europe. The Australian and New Zealand Army Corps (ANZACs) was born, along with the notion of mate-ship that entrenched a spirit of solidarity and heroism.[58] This was a defining moment in the history and development of the national identity, which was summarised as:

> [t]he price of nationhood must be made in blood and tears....Before the Anzacs astonished the watching nations, our sentiment was flabby and sprawling character. We were Australian in name and had a flag but we had been taught by our politicians not to trust ourselves, in tail of the great Empire....Anzac Day has changed that. The Australian flag has been bought from the garret and has been hoisted on a lofty tower in full sight of the people. No matter how the war may end – and it can only end one way – we are at last a nation, with one heart, one soul, and one thrilling aspiration.[59]

The legacy of the ANZACs continues today to be an important part of the spirit and identity of Australia. Additionally, the landing of Australian troops in Gallipoli and the impact that this event had on the soldiers at the time has been etched in history and is celebrated annually, not only in Australia but also Turkey.[60] Women also played a vital role during the war serving as medical nurses. Comparatively, Australia was not invaded during WWI, unlike the current day Slovenian territory. The inhabitants of Australia were not displaced like many Slovenians. For Australia, not only the historical but also the more recent involvement of the Australian military around the world has formed part of the national identity. The importance of the military to the state is also reflected in a national holiday being declared annually (discussed later in this chapter).

The 1918, Imperial War Conference was held in London and attempted to resolve the functions of Governments across the Commonwealth, including Australia. There was a clear recognition from London that it was time for Australia to have complete control over the composition of its population by means of restricting immigration.[61] The *1920 Nationality Act* (Cth) was based on the *British Nationality*

---

[56] Ibid, O'Connor J, 305.

[57] Ibid, 308.

[58] Kuhn, R, (2004) *Class and struggle in Australia seminar series*, Australian National University, October, 2004, 8.

[59] Crowley, F, (1973) *Modern Australia* in Documents: 1901–1939, Wren Publishing, 1973, Vol 1, 250–255.

[60] Ibid.

[61] Arthur Berriedale Keith, Speeches and Documents on the British Dominions, 1879–1944.

and Status of Aliens Act 1914 which recognized the uniform naturalization certificate within any of the countries of the British Empire.[62]

Kim Rubenstein makes the point that in 1914, a British common code was introduced, which was intended to the implemented throughout the dominions and mirror the *British Nationality and Status of Aliens Act 1914*.[63] Australia was involved in its development, however it was not introduced until 1920 when the *Naturalisation Act 1903* was repealed and the *Nationality Act 1920* was introduced.[64] The legislation introduced a definition of a natural born British subject (s) who was a person born within or outside His Majesties dominions. This included a person who was born on a British ship, residing within His Majesty's dominions for a period of 5 years; of good character and having the intention to serve the Crown. Elements of these principles such as residency, born on a ship and of good character remain in Australia's current day citizenship laws. However, the indigenous people suffered greatly from the incursion and colonization by the British and had an uncertain status.

One of the most important changes to the law in relation to the indigenous peoples came with the introduction of the 1920 Nationality Act, which removed the exclusionary provisions related to them.[65] However, exclusionary provisions were retained in section 10 that enabled a person to be categorized as having a disability. A disability at that time included someone who was a married woman, a minor lunatic or idiot. Therefore, while it appeared exclusion of indigenous people had been removed, section 10 could still be used to exclude anyone.

The 1920s were also an important phase of the law and the recognition of women. Women were British subjects; however, this came in three forms 1). foreign born women, 2). Australian-born women and 3). non-married women.[66] The situation for foreign-born wives of people naturalized in Australia subsequent to marriage, the wife acquired British subject status provided the husband had naturalized between 1 January 1921 and 31 March 1937. The wife did not obtain British subject status where the husband had acquired naturalization between 1 April 1937 and 25 January 1949. This also applied if the husband had been naturalized before 1 January 1921, and it was questionable as to whether the wife (may or may not) acquired the status of British subject. Women born on the territory of Australia automatically obtained British subject status by birth or naturalization. However, that status could be lost where the person was naturalized in a foreign state, were declared alienage, or been revoked by the Minister and by marriage to an alien.

---

[62] Rick Kuhn, *Class and struggle in Australia seminar series*, Australian National University, October, 2004, 8.

[63] Rubenstein, K, (2002) *Australian Citizenship Law in Context*, Lawbook Co, 53. The Act was amended with similar titled Acts of 1922 (No 24); 1925 (No 10); 1930 (No 9); 1936 (No 62) and 1946 (No 9 and 28).

[64] Ibid.

[65] Ibid.

[66] Ibid, 55–57.

In 1921, the first woman[67] was elected to an Australian Parliament, the Western Australian Legislative Assembly in Perth. The broader recognition of women in Australian citizenship had begun, along with their ability to have a greater role in the political process. The 1929 Imperial Conference noted the beginnings of a broader multidimensional approach that nationality provided, stating:

> [that] 'nationality as a term comes with varying connotations. In one sense it is used to indicate a common consciousness based on race, language, traditions, other ties and interests. .....Nationality has existed in the older communities of the Commonwealth and is a connexion between with a State and Government. With the constitutional developments within the British Commonwealth of nations, the terms 'national, 'nationhood', and nationality', in connexion with each member, have come into common use.[68]

The reference to common consciousness based on race, language and traditions are principles that connect to nationality, and provide an understanding of the national identity that Australia has been built on. It is argued that the foundations of Australia's modern day identity have been shaped by inheriting the legal system Imperial Britain. More importantly nationality (citizenship), language and constitutional law have shaped and continued to shape and underpin the national identity of Australia and Slovenia.

Internationally, the Convention on Certain Questions Relating to the Conflict of Nationality Law was established in 1930,[69] with Australia ratifying the convention in 1937. Article 1 states that it is for each state to determine under its own law who its nationals are. This principle being more than 80 years old remains important to the international community. Today the European Union, Slovenia and other member states have maintained the right to choose their nationals. When Slovenia was part of the former Yugoslavia, the state chose who its citizens would be.

The *Statute of Westminster* in 1931, would replace the 1865 *Colonial Laws Validity Act*[70] but it continued to apply to the States until the *Australia Act of 1986* came into effect. The *Statute of Westminster* enabled the state to develop its own legislation. The importance of relations between Britain and Australia was also reflected in the establishment of a Trade Agreement in 1932 to secure Australian goods.[71] This agreement would be important to Australia's continued connection to Britain, even though it had little relevance to citizenship. In 1936, the *Nationality Act 1920* was amended to provide greater recognition of women. Section 6 allowed women to regain their British subject status, having lost it on their marriage to an

---

[67] McCann, J., Wilson, J, (2012) *Representation of Women in Australian Parliaments*, Parliament of Australia, Department of Parliamentary Services, 12.

[68] Report of the Conference on the Operation of Dominion Legislation and Merchant Shipping Legislation 1929, in Arthur Berriedale Keith, Speeches and Documents on the British Dominions, 1879–1944.

[69] Convention on Certain Questions Relating to the Conflict of Nationality Law was established in 1930, http://eudo-citizenship.eu/InternationalDB.pdf

[70] *Colonial Laws Validity Act* 1865, https://www.legislation.qld.gov.au/ColoniLwsValA1865_01_.pdf

[71] United Kingdom and Australia Trade Agreement Act 1932 (No. 57, 1932).

alien, if their husband naturalized and the women had the opportunity to make the declarations of naturalization once the husband had naturalized.[72]

The state of Queensland introduced the *Aboriginal Preservation and Protection Act 1939*, did little to provide equality for indigenous Australians in Queensland. The Act reinforced that Aborigines could be segregated and isolated from participation in mainstream society and concentrated in reserves and missions. The Act provided extensive power whereby children could be relocated without their parents. Even though the legislation was limited to Queensland, it is argued Australia continued to invoke its discriminatory behavior towards all people that were not white. This identity of 'whiteness' worked in its favor as Australia was continuing to implement British law over the territory. Furthermore, it restricted the rights of these people to be full and active citizens. On the one hand, the Australian Constitution had been established, with rights that were afforded to all British subjects, including aboriginal people. However, as this example highlights, states were impending their own laws to further discriminate and restrict the rights of aboriginal people.

As stated earlier, WWII had such an impact on Europe, and the current day Slovenia and Australia would not be spared. The then Prime Minister of Australia, Robert Gordon Menzies announced to the nation that as a consequence of Germany invading Poland, Britain had declared war and as such, Australia was at war.[73] The Prime Minister was defining national identity and linking it to the historical connection to Britain. In 1942, as the war spread to South East Asia, British and Australian forces would come together to defend Singapore. WWII saw the development of a new global community where modern nationhood established human rights.[74] The large number of men that left Australia for Europe resulted in women having to take on much of the role of men at home. Women would become part of the manufacturing industry while still maintaining a household. They would also serve in the medical core providing medical assistance to the armed forces.[75]

In 1944, Western Australia established the *Native (Citizenship Rights) Act*, which provided indigenous people with the right to apply for citizenship. However, the requirement was quite strict and the individual had to demonstrate they could speak English and of good character for a period of 2 years. The legislation was a step forward for the indigenous community, however, it was still subject to the powers within the Australian Constitution.[76] According to John Chesterman, successful application who obtained the certificate of citizenship were deemed as no longer being a native aboriginal, and therefore, they were excluded from other racially discriminatory legislation.[77] During the time in which the legislation was operational,

---

[72] Rubenstein, K, (2002) *Australian Citizenship Law in Context*, Lawbook Co, 57.

[73] Crowley, F, (1973) *Modern Australia in Documents: 1901–1939*, Wren Publishing, Vol 1, 1–4.

[74] Kepple, L, (2009) *Jewish Immigrants in Australia Before, During and After WWII*, The Monitor.

[75] Ibid.

[76] *Native (Citizenship Rights) Act* 1944 (WA), section 2.

[77] Chesterman, J, (2005) *Civil Rights: How Indigenous Australians won formal Equality*, University of Queensland Press, 126.

1615 certificates were issued from more than 2000 applicants.[78] However, there were more than 1500 people were protected from the legislation but had not received their certificate of citizenship, were in no man's land, as they were not entitled to any of the benefits that state citizenship had attributed.[79] Broadly this state-based form of citizenship resembled the former Yugoslav citizenship, where each of the Republics had established citizenship, although it was federal citizenship that prevailed.

This was the first formal recognition of the indigenous people in Australia, however the legislation expired in 1971. In 1945, the Department of Immigration was established to assist Australia in managing its postwar reconstruction and large-scale immigration program.[80] Since then the department has had oversight and administrative responsibility on behalf of the government for all immigration and citizenship programs including deportation, detention, passports and naturalisation. As the war ceased, Australia adopted a new vision for assimilation, which saw the traditional race-based immigration policies (White Australia) becoming outdated.

Australia began to industrialize and major infrastructure projects was developed, which required migrants from other states to converge on Australia as the local population was not large enough. The policy of the Australian Government was becoming more flexible towards accommodating other nationalities, which saw the beginnings of the transition to multicultural Australia. Following WWII, many displaced people from across Europe including Yugoslavia (Slovenia) found themselves making their way to Australia to take up permanent residence and citizenship.[81] Citizenship in the early period of Australia was a term of popular usage by the press and debates about political entitlements.[82] Citizenship entailed commitment, belonging and contribution to Australian society. However, Rubenstein argues the courts appeared to look at citizenship as an administrative concept. This would be used to develop the policy for establishing Australian citizenship in 1948. Even in this early period citizenship had become more than a legal status. Nation states had begun using citizenship to provide its inhabitants with a sense of who they were – Australians.

From colonization through to 1948, citizenship across the Australian territory remained under the laws of the British and all inhabitants retained the status of British subjects. Allegiance was the central in the first 48 years, since federation. The policies towards aliens during this period was that citizenship status provided

---

[78] Ibid.

[79] Ibid.

[80] Ferguson, L., Gardner, W, (2004) Fostering *Australian Citizenship in a Changing World*, in Glenn Patmore, Gary Jungwirth, The Vocal Citizen, Fitzroy Vic, 163.

[81] Australian Government, Department of Immigration and Border Protection, More than 65 year of postwar Migration, https://www.immi.gov.au/media/fact-sheets/04fifty.htm

[82] Helen Irving, '*Citizenship before 1949*' in Kim Rubenstein (ed), *Individual, Community, Nation: 50 Years of Australian Citizenship*, 2000, 10, in Kim Rubenstein, *Australian Citizenship Law in Context*, Lawbook Co, 2002, 47.

an accurate guide to the political allegiance. There was a clear distinction between British subjects and aliens. At common law, an individual's legal status was determined by allegiance to the monarch, either by birth or naturalization.[83] Up until this point citizenship had been considered defacto administrative, which operated during a period of necessity to distinguish between British subjects who were permanent residents and belonged to the Commonwealth, and those British subjects who were visitors and did not reside in Australia long enough to be regarded as belonging.[84]

Moreover, as Rubenstein notes, there were three forms of membership (1) those British subject permanently residing in Australia, (2) those British subject temporarily in Australia, and (3) those people who were not British subjects (aliens). The foundations of citizenship in Australia had begun to developed, where a person was born on the territory or naturalized they became a British subject. There was a clear desire to preserve the identity and historical links to the British. However, in 1948 this would change. Citizenship and the national identity would begin to transition from its historical past, to what can be defined as an independent Australian identity that was and continues to be underpinned by citizenship, immigration, rights and private international laws.

4.1.2 1948–1980

The first citizenship laws of Australia in 1948 were an opportunity for the state to develop its own identity.[85] Additionally, the laws provided the ability for the state to develop their own treaties and define with absolute precision who the individuals that belong to the state will be. Not only did these first laws assist in developing the national identity, the citizenship laws also provided continuity to existing British subjects. Furthermore, the new act enabled women to make their own choice so far as their national status was concerned. Moreover, the new citizenship laws confirmed the legal status of what it meant to be an Australian citizen, including Aboriginal and Torres Strait Islander people, within the Australian territory. This reinforced the early developments of the concept of citizenship by Locke and Rousseau where laws define the legal status of the inhabitants of a territory. Slovenians at the time remained under the rule of Yugoslavia.

[83] Pryles, M, (1981) *Australian citizenship law*, Sydney: Law Book Co.

[84] Dutton, D, *Citizenship in Australia: A guide to Commonwealth Government Records*, 1999, in Kim Rubenstein, *The vulnerability of dual citizenship: The impact of the recent changes to the Australian Citizenship Act (2007) on the place of citizenship in Australia today*, Australian National University, Law Council of Australia conference, 4 March 2016.

[85] Australia, Nationality and Citizenship Bill 1948, Explanatory Memorandum, Department of Immigration, 2.

The legislation underpinned Australia's immigration program and strengthened the nation building exercise.[86] In the words of the first Minister of Immigration, Arthur Calwell, Australia was to 'populate or perish'.[87] Lord Tweedsmuir stated that the real basis of the legislation was that would provide recognition to a separate identity. He was referring to a separate identity to that of Britain.[88] By fully recognizing the individual identity of each community while preserving the common nationality possessed by all, will prove to be a unifying factor between the communities that make up the commonwealth. Importantly, the legislation was an expression of Australia's identity (common bond, rights, unification, sharing democratic beliefs and upholding the law). This also saw the beginnings of a greater acceptance of multiculturalism that began to enrich the national identity with the introduction of many different ethnic and religious groups. The creation of Australian citizenship in no way lessens the advantages and privileges which British subjects who may not be Australian citizens enjoy in Australia.[89] In a similar fashion this bill, by fully and properly recognizing the individual identity of each Commonwealth community and at the same time preserving the status of a common nationality possessed by all these people, will prove a binding and unifying factor between the various communities comprising the British Commonwealth.

The commonwealth chose to have exclusively regulate for immigration and citizenship under section 52 of the *1948 Citizenship Act*, whereby the Act shall apply to the exclusion of any provisions, providing for Australian citizenship of any law of a State.[90] The new legislation did not regulate the activity of aliens entering the Australian territory. The Act came into effect on 26 January 1949. Up until this point, the status of British subject was shared with various commonwealth countries. It is asserted that the former status of British subject resembles the supranational citizenship afforded by the European Union, today. However, Australians would retain the status of British subject, and it wasn't until 1987 that this status would be replaced fully by Australian citizenship. The Act enabled a person to obtain citizenship by birth, descent, adoption and resumption. A comprehensive discussion related to each of these principles is outside the scope of this book between 1948 to 1990. Citizenship by registration was also allowed where the Minister could grant a certificate of Australian citizenship to a person, for example, an Irish citizen, or the person resided in Australia or New Guinea for not less than 5 years. The person was also required to be of good character and have a knowledge of the English language. These criteria still exist today.

[86] Arthur Calwell, Parliamentary Debates, House of Representatives, Second Reading Speech of the Nationality and Citizenship Bill, 1948, 1060–1065.

[87] Ibid.

[88] Nationality and Citizenship Bill, 1948, Second Reading Speech, House of Representatives, 30 September 1948.

[89] Arthur Calwell, Parliamentary Debates, House of Representatives, Second Reading Speech of the Nationality and Citizenship Bill, 1948, 1060–1065.

[90] Rubenstein, K, (2002) *Australian Citizenship Law in Context*, Lawbook Co, 65.

Postnational or multinational citizenship (dual citizenship) was not accepted and section 17 of the Act specified that any Australian citizen who acquired citizenship of another country would cease being an Australian citizen. The restrictive approach by Australia and Slovenia towards dual citizenship existed until the decade of 2000. Nevertheless, Australia would allow a restricted form of dual citizenship to be held from 1986 to 2002, where it was fully realized. Dual citizenship and the principles for acquiring citizenship exist in Australian law today.

The changing policy of welcoming other ethnic groups was important for the next phase in Australia's growth, while maintaining its historical links to Britain. This was affirmed by the Minister for Immigration Harold Holt in 1950 who stated:

> we attach importance to ensuring British immigration is first and foremost in order to retain as much as reasonably can the present balance of our population. This is a British community, and we want to keep it a British community living under British standards and by the methods and ideals of British parliamentary democracy.[91]

This was a clear message to the community that the foundation of the Australian identity has been derived from the British. It is argued that the British standards, ideals and parliamentary democracy have been and continue to be an important part of the current day Australian identity expressed by the constitution, citizenship, immigration and private international laws. Harold Holt reiterated the importance of the historical links to Britain stating that Australia had an opportunity to make a nation with basically British characteristics but with a distinctly Australian tradition.[92] What Holt was arguing was that Australia's traditional 'white' and Christian beliefs had originated in Britain and remained fundamental to Australia's developing identity.

WWII concluded and Australia strengthened its legislation towards deporting non-citizens. The *Alien Deportation Act 1948* provided the government with power to deport a non-citizen on grounds of 'bad character and conduct. A Commissioner was established to provide advice on deportations. The *Migration Act 1958* would be introduced and effectively adopted the deportation principles of the *Alien Deportation Act 1948.* British subjects were absorbed into the community and immune from deportation. However, this was not the case for other non-citizens (immigrants) that were not British subjects or Irish nationals. At the time 'aliens' could be deported at any time, whereas 'immigrants' could only be deported on the basis of offences or conduct which occurred within the first 5 years of their entry onto the territory. Thus, immigrants appeared to be immune from deportation following the five-year period elapsing. This was an extension of 2 years that previously existed under the 1901 immigration laws.[93]

---

[91] NAA: A438/1, 1950/7/217, Address to the Australian Citizenship Convention by the Minister for Immigration the Honourable Harold Holt, 1950.

[92] NAA: A445/1, 146/3/3A, Opening Address of Immigration Minister Harold Holt to Citizenship Convention, 1952, 1.

[93] Crock, M., Berg, L, (2011) *Immigration, Refugees and Forced Migration, Law, Policy and Practice in Australia*, The Federation Press, 523.

The *Migration Act 1958* removed the dictation test. This was important transition in Australia's policy direction, because Australia was taking a far more liberal approach to migration by removing obstacles for new entrants. However, the dictation test would be replaced with the visa systems, which has grown into a comprehensive framework today. Thus, on the one hand Australia was removing obstacles for entry and stay, while on the other hand the visa system provided greater accountability for the person entering the territory.

By 1960, the United Nations recognized that the historical colonial systems such as the British Empire were outdated and no longer relevant to the modern area. This led to the formation of the 1960 Declaration on the Granting of Independence to Colonial Countries and Peoples.[94] Small steps had been taken by the government to consider the indigenous peoples during the 1960s. The *Commonwealth Electoral Act 1962* was introduced to allow aboriginal people to enroll and vote as electors of the Commonwealth.[95]

In 1967, the laws were amended to allow those individuals who had served in the Australian armed forces to obtain citizenship, provided they had served for a minimum of 3 months. The state wanted to recognize those people (non-citizens) who had assisted Australia and its Allies in a number of conflicts around the world. Australia was demonstrating to the world that it was a country that recognized those people who believed in and practiced the values of the state. The Act stated that a person would not be an Australian citizen, at birth, if that person's father at the time of the birth was not an Australian citizen themselves. Additionally, if the father was not ordinarily resident in Australia, or the father was an enemy alien and the birth occurred in a place occupied by an enemy force. In the same year, there was a national referendum on whether section 51(xxvi) and 127 should be amended to include aboriginal people. Consequently, the *Constitution Alterations (Aboriginals Act 1967* was passed to give effect to the outcome of the referendum. The Australian constitution was amended[96] and section 51 now ensure laws can be made for all Australian people. Section 127, now takes into account the aboriginal people as part of the entire population of Australia. Before the constitutional change, the indigenous people had their rights restricted to the extent that it impacted on their community way of life. They were not able to vote, marry whoever they chose, and in some cases their movements were restricted. Additionally, their right to own property was restricted, and in many cases they were paid far less than white people when undertaking the same employment.

Australia was yet to realize and establish a common culture or social equality that was inclusive of aboriginal people, something that Marshall[97] would have been concerned with. It is argued this, while small steps, was Australia beginning to

---

[94] Declaration on the Granting of Independence to Colonial Countries and Peoples, GA Res 1514 (XV), UN GAOR, 15th session, 947th plen, mtg, UN Doc A/4684 (1961).

[95] *Commonwealth Electoral Act, No. 31, 1962.*

[96] Constitutional Recognition of Indigenous Australians, *Discussion paper*, Law Council of Australia, 2001.

[97] Marshall, T, (1965) *Class, Citizenship and Social Development*, New York, Anchor, 101–103.

include indigenous people into the national identity. Australia was starting to be more inclusive and by amending the constitution it is argued that it went some way to unifying the citizenry. It was a step to building greater social cohesion.

Two years on, and the *Citizenship Act 1969* required a person to be able to read, write, speak and understand English.[98] Section 5 of the principal act was amended to define an alien as a person who does not have the status of a British Subject and is not an Irish citizen or a protected person.[99] The inclusion provided clarity as to who was not an alien. The legislation also clarified that when a person was born outside the Australian territory to an Australian citizen, they could obtain citizenship by descent.[100]

Between 1970 and December 1973 there was an additional form of acquisition of citizenship introduced into the legal framework, which included obtaining citizenship by notification. However, this was restricted to only those people who were British subjects in countries such as the United Kingdom and Colonies of Canada, New Zealand, the Union of South Africa, Newfoundland, India, Pakistan, Southern Rhodesia and Ceylon.[101] In 1973, the Australian Government undertook further amendments to the law. The Minister could grant a certificate to a person who qualified as an Australian citizen. A certificate was only granted where the person was of full age, capable of understanding the application, resided in Australia or New Guinea for 1 year. In addition a certificate would be granted when the individual was resident in the territory for no less than 2 years during eight, of good character and had a knowledge of the English language.[102] Additionally, the person must have a knowledge of the responsibilities and privileges that are afforded by having Australian citizenship.

More importantly, the Act no longer gave preferential treatment to British subjects wanting to naturalize in Australia. They were required to meet the same criteria as every other alien. At the same time, the Australian Government was also promoting multiculturalism describing Australia as a 'family of a nation'.[103] In 1974, Australia had introduced a further category to enable a person to acquire citizenship – by grant.[104] This new category represented the continuing shift in Australia's view of restricting the existing discriminatory that favored British subjects to acquire citizenship. Australia, was opening its doors to other ethnic groups and the law represented the multicultural direction the country was heading. This slow and subtle transition by Australia would arguably enhance the state's ability to not only

---

[98] *Citizenship Act 1969*, Section 10.

[99] Ibid, *Citizenship Act 1969.*

[100] Ibid, 7, section 11.

[101] Rubenstein, K, (2002) *Australian Citizenship Law in Context*, Lawbook Co, 102–103.

[102] *Citizenship Act 1973*, section 14.

[103] Al Grassby, *Second Reading Speech: Australian Citizenship Bill 1973*, House of Representatives, Debates, 11 April 1973, 1312.

[104] Rubenstein, K, (2002) *Australian Citizenship Law in Context*, Lawbook Co, 102–103.

increase the population, but also, ensure integration and social cohesion of the different ethnic populations.

4.1.3 Dual Citizenship

Dual citizenship would become part of the wider discussion on citizenship in Australia in the 1970s and 1980s. It is arguably, a more liberal though and concept of citizenship. It allows people to have a binding to another state. In 1976, dual citizenship was reviewed by the Joint Committee on Foreign Affairs and Defence.[105] The committee supported the idea that every person should only have one nationality and not two. Later in 1982, dual citizenship became a topic of interest again, and found its way onto the national agenda on multiculturalism.[106] However, dual citizenship was not accepted by the government, and the citizenship laws retained the status quo.

4.1.4 National Symbols

Australia's national anthem reflects the historical connection to the British Empire and does not form part of the Australian constitution. Arguably, it is an important component of national identity. The national anthem of Australia describes the vast island continent that is surrounded by sea and has vast areas of soil that houses the natural wealth of the state.[107] The National Anthem, *Advance Australian Fair*, was adopted through a plebiscite in 1977, and includes the lyrics:

> Australian all let us rejoice, for we are young and free, we've golden soil and wealth for toil, our home is girt by sea, our land abounds in nature's gifts, of beauty rich and rare, in history's page, let every stage, advance Australia Fair. In joyful strains then let us sing advance Australia Fair.
>
> Beneath our radiant Southern Cross, we'll toil with hearts and hands, to make this Commonwealth of ours, renowned of all the lands, for those who've come across the seas, we've boundless plains to share, with courage let us all combine, to advance Australia Fair, in joyful strains then let us sing advance Australia Fair.[108]

When compared with Slovenia's national anthem, the Australian national anthem makes no reference to the individual struggle of the people or state as a result of war or conflict with regional neighbors. Legally, a national anthem has no influence on

---

[105] Joint Committee on Foreign Affairs and Defence, *Dual Nationality*, Report, 1976, 8.

[106] Department of Immigration and Ethnic Affairs, *National Consultation on Multiculturalism and Citizenship*, Report, 1982, 28.

[107] Australian National Anthem, https://www.itsanhonour.gov.au/symbols/docs/anthem_words.pdf

[108] Ibid.

the acquisition or lose of citizenship in either Slovenia or Australia. However, the national anthem of a state does contribute to the national identity and goes some way to uniting the people (citizens), in the same way that citizenship does.

In the same year Sir Garfield Barwick argued that Australia and even the courts in Australia had been inherited from the British Empire. Barwick argued that '[t]here had not been a substantial reason to resort to the Privy Council from the colonists and [b]y the time federation was in discussion amongst the colonists, the Supreme Courts...had attained in general a reputation for sound administration'.[109] There had been no requirement for the colonialists to refer to the Privy Council located in Britain, the Supreme Court had been established in each of the colonies and was modelled on the British system. Thus, reinforcing the historical connection to the British and the ongoing push by the state to ensure this was also reflected in the law.

4.1.5 1980–1990

In 1981, the United Kingdom established and implemented the *British Nationality Act*. It was seen by the Australian High Court of Australia as a critical point in the relationship between Britain and Australia. The Australian High Court in *Pochi*[110] determined that the allegiance which Australians owed to Her Majesty is owed not as British subject but as subject of the Queen of Australia. Three years later, in 1984, the Australian legislation was changed again to include a more liberal approach and make it easier to obtain citizenship. The amendments removed discriminatory aspects in relation to sex, marital status and nationality. However, the language requirements were changed from adequate to basic and, applicants over the age of 50 were exempted from the language requirement.[111] The definition of British subjects was removed from the definitions within the *Australian Citizenship Act 1948*. Arguably, the resulting effect from this legislative reform was a strengthening in the new Australian national identity by affirming that citizenship of Australia had finally broken away from its historical roots. Australian citizenship had been based on a social rather than a territorial concept due to the indigenous Australians who were grouped together with migrants and subject to exclusion and deprivation.[112]

Mary Crock and Laurie Berg highlight that this was a 'double irony for the first Australian peoples, because Australian citizenship should have been solely base on *jus soli*, as the original and true native Australians who had a connection to the

[109] Sir Garfield Barwick, (1977) '*The State of the Australian Judicature*', Australian Law Journal, 481–2.

[110] *Pochi v MacPhee (1982) 151 CLR 101, 109–110.*

[111] Australian citizenship: a chronology of major developments in policy and law, http://www.aph.gov.au/About_Parliament/Parliamentary_Departments/Parliamentary_Library

[112] Crock, M., Berg, L, (2011) *Immigration Refugees and Forced Migration, Law, Policy and Practice in Australia*, The Federation Press, 19.

land'.[113] The aboriginal people also had their own customs, culture and law. Therefore, it could be argued they had their own identity, even though any identity may have varied depending on the tribe its location. Thus over time there has been an erosion of their identity, as they have been absorbed into the Australian system, including citizenship. This is a part of Australia's culture and story that has been suppressed over many decades. However, as the citizens of the state continue to learn more and the oppressive actions and behavior of the state towards these people, there continues to be a slow shift and acceptance that the wrongs need to be addressed.

Throughout the 1980s, the Australian Government changed its course on migration policy and allowed greater diversity of people into the country, particularly from South East Asia. The former [Bob] Hawke government in 1983 described the national identity of Australia as being multicultural and the country needing to embrace the cultural diversity that Australia had become.[114] However, this acceptance of Asians into the state did not come without criticism. Michael Barnes[115] argues that the global conditions and government policy at the time began to threaten the Anglo-Celtic identity of Australia. This resulted in the state reverting back to its constructed past and links to the British. Australia was having to balance the retention of its national identity with the nationalist program of building the state.

In the same year the *Migration Amendment Act 1983* was introduced and retained the idea that there continued to be a meaningful distinction between a non-citizen and alien. However, deporting permanent residents convicted of offences became an issue and the Australian High Court in *Pochi* highlighted the extraordinary power afforded to the parliament to legislate with respect to aliens under section 51 (19) of the constitution.[116] The court accepted that immigrants would escape the reach of the legislature by being absorbed into the community, and thus by passing the 'immigration power'. However, the 'aliens' power was held to apply to all persons who did not have the status of Australian citizen.[117]

Thus, in 1983 the migration laws were amended and concessions that were previously afforded to British subjects and Irish nationals were abolished and deportation was extended to all permanent residents. The new section 12 allowed the Minister to issue a deportation order where a person had been convicted of an offence within a period of less than 10 years. The timeframe was extended again, from the previous position in 1948 of 5 years and 1901 3 years. Thus, the possibility for immunity from deportation continued to be extended by the government. Additionally, the ability for a permanent resident to enter and exit the country was relatively free after

113 Ibid.

114 Michael Barnes, M, (2004) *Anglo-Celtic Australians Perspective of Multiculturalism*, Macquarie University, 1–20.

115 Ibid.

116 Crock, M., Berg, L, (2011) *Immigration, Refugees and Forced Migration, Law, Policy and Practice in Australia*, The Federation Press, 524–525. *Pochi v Macphee* (1982) 151 CLR 101.

117 Ibid.

the first 2 years of residence, provided the individual did not remain outside of the country for more than 5 years.[118]

The amendments to the citizenship laws in 1986 marked another shift in policy approach, with the acceptance that some people may hold dual citizenship. However, this was very limited and only applied to this individuals that were wanting to renounce their citizenship. Removing the requirement for a person to renounce their citizenship allowed migrants from countries that allowed for dual citizenship to retain their original citizenship.

A year later on 1 May 1987 marked an important period in Australian citizenship law. The definition of British subject and alien were finally removed by the *Australian Citizenship Amendments Act 1984*. Kim Rubenstein highlights the change to the definition was particularly important to British subjects who did not become an Australian citizen and were subject to deportation.[119]Australian citizenship was exclusive for the first time, even though Australia continued to retain close ties with Britain. The removal of British subject was also viewed as removing discrimination against migrants who were not British. By 1987, Australia's acceptance of migrants from various other countries was well underway. The White Australia Policy was no longer formally relevant to Australia.

Despite the 1948 citizenship laws being in place for 40 years, the 1988 Constitutional Commission[120] recommended that section 51 of the constitution be amended to provide for citizenship. The citizens of Australia had, by this time, been afforded a legal status in the state for four decades. The proposal would have provided the Australian Parliament with the express power to make laws with respect to nationality and citizenship. Had the proposal been implemented, it would have further reinforced the legal status of citizenship in Australia and contributed to strengthening the national identity.

In 1989, was an important year for citizenship. For the first time, the Year of Citizenship was declared by the government.[121] A letter was sent to every household in Australia encouraging those eligible to apply for citizenship. The program resulted in more than 130,000 people taking out citizenship between 1989 and 1990.[122] Despite Australia recognizing the growth in multiculturalism, the policy of citizenship began to also focus on unification, cohesion and integration. As a program the Year of Citizenship benefited both the citizen and state by enhancing the sense of belonging of an individual to the state and what it means to be either Slovenian or Australian.

---

[118] Ibid.

[119] Rubenstein, K, (2002) *Australian Citizenship Law in Context*, Lawbook Co, 81.

[120] Constitutional Commission, *Final Report of the Constitutional Commission*, 1998, vol 1, 4.176–4.199.

[121] National Archives Australia, http://www.naa.gov.au/collection/explore/cabinet/by-year/1988-89/background.aspx

[122] Ibid.

Citizenship encourages inclusion and full participation in public life and the law.[123] Citizenship includes the rules and laws that are blind to any one individual or group (community) within a state.[124] States throughout the nineteenth century largely focused on defining and unifying its citizens. A study undertaken of the Australian, German and Swedish national identities confirmed what it means to be Australian, and what is important to Australians. It included being born in the territory; having resided (citizens and migrants) for most of the individual's life in the territory; able to speak the English language; having citizenship; respecting and understanding the laws and institutions.[125] The study reinforced the notion that language and a sense of feeling or belonging to a state by a person having citizenship of that state, is part of what it means to be a member of a community. Thus, while Australia's multicultural community consists of many different ethnic groups that speak many different languages, citizenship and the English language are two very important common principles that people identify with as being part of Australia. The national identity of Australia while having its historical connection to Britain has become a blended national identity.[126] However, that blended identity is made up of an amalgam of ethnic groups.

From 1970 when the former Prime Minister Gough Whitlam recognised China through to 1990 when consecutive national governments enhanced that engagement with Asian countries,[127] the establishment of the Asia Pacific Economic Co-operation (APEC) forum and the Association of South East Nations Regional Forum, saw Australia move ever closer to Asia. However, Australia like many other nations including Slovenia within Yugoslavia, was having to juggle different policy issues. On one hand, Australia was continuing to develop its national identity and maintaining its historical connection to Britain. On the other hand, Australia was opening its doors to migrants and economically establishing closer ties with Asia. Therefore, the complexity and issues a state has to grapple with in developing, establishing, protecting and enhancing a national identity cannot be underestimated. In the context of this book, citizenship, immigration, constitutional rights and private laws all contribute to national identity. Without these laws a state's identity would be weakened and in some cases it would be difficult for a state to assert what and who it represents.

---

[123] Young, I, (1989) *Polity and Group Difference: A Critique of the Ideal of Universal Citizenship*, Ethics, Vol. 99, No 2. 250–270.

[124] Ibid.

[125] Hjerm, M, (1998) *National identity: a comparison of Sweden, Germany and Australia*, Journal of Ethnic and Migration Studies, Vol 24 No. 3: 452–462.

[126] Nolan, M., Rubenstein, K, (2009) *Citizenship and Identity in Diverse Societies*, Humanities Research, Vol XV. No 1. 29.

[127] Beeson, M, (2001) *Australia and Asia: The Years of Living Aimlessly*, in Daljit Sing, Anthony Smith Southeast Asian Affairs, Singapore: Institute for Southeast Asian Studies, 44–55.

4.2 Language

Language is an important part of a nation state and citizen's identity. Languages have been grouped into language trees by Dario Benedetto, Emanuel Caglioti and Vittorio Loreto[128] who present the phylogenetic like tree constructed on about 50 different versions of the Universal Declaration of Human Rights, and its interpretation. The authors in outlining the language tree use the Fitch-Margoliash method of realistic entropy between linguistic groups that consists of Romance, Celtic, Germanic, Ugro-Finnic, Slavic and Baltic branches. Slovenian for example falls within the Slavic languages.[129]

Within the Slavic branch, all of the main languages spoken in the former Yugoslav Republics are represented i.e. Croatian, Serbian, Bosnian, Montenegrin and Macedonian.[130] In a study undertaken by David Bennett in relation to the differences between Slovene and Serbo-Croatian text (up to 14,000 words long), it was concluded that the major difference between the languages is the word order.[131] That is, the order of words differ. A similar study was undertaken by Benjamins which determined that the textual comparison between the two languages is the position of the finite main verb.[132] In 52 of the 54 cases examined the finite verb in Slovene was in the second position, whereas, in Serbo-Croatian it came later.[133] However, it must be noted that the Serbo-Croatian language was artificially constructed under the creation of Socialist Yugoslavia after WWII. In fact, Serbian and Croatian are two distinctly separate languages that exist today as separate languages, even though they are similar. English[134] which is from the Germanic group is the official language of Australia and is very different to the Slovenian language. With the arrival of many different ethnic groups into Australia, the English language has taken on some different, but not officially recognised dialects. However, it must be noted that a full examination and comparison of the Slovene and Australian languages is outside the scope of this research.

---

[128] Benedetto, D., Caglioti, E., Loreto, V, (2002) *Language Trees and Zipping*, Physical Review Letters, Vol 88, La Sapienza University, Mathematics Department, Rome Italy, 1–5.

[129] Ibid.

[130] Ibid.

[131] Bennett, D, (1996) *Towards an Explanation of Word-Order Differences between Slovene and Serbo-Croat*, The Slavonic and East European Review, Vol. 64. No. 1, 1–20.

[132] Benjamins, J, (2000) *Functional Approaches to Language, Culture and Cognition*, Library of Congress Cataloging in Publication Data, 448.

[133] Ibid.

[134] Short, D, (2003) *History of the English Language*,, http://www.danshort.com/ie/timeline.htm

4.3 National Days

The national identity is also reinforced by a state regulating its national (official) days, allowing their citizens to recognize and appreciate the importance of the achievements and progress of the state and its citizens. For Slovenes, the Slovenian Statehood Day (Slovene: *Dan državnosti*) is a holiday that occurs annually on 25 June to commemorate the country's formal declaration of independence from Yugoslavia in 1991. Although the formal declaration of independence did not occur until 26 June 1991, Statehood Day is considered to be 25 June, as this was the date on which Slovenia became independent. Slovenia's declaration saw the commencement of the 10 day war with Yugoslavia, which was defeated by the Slovenes. Slovenia's Independence and Unity Day is another important national day, which is celebrated annually on 26 December to mark the official proclamation of the results of the plebiscite in which 88.5% of all Slovenian voters were in favor of Slovenia becoming a sovereign independent state in 1990. Australia's most important days include the 26th of January (Australia Day), 25th of April (Australia and New Zealand Army Corps – ANZAC Day) and Queen's Birthday[135] celebrating the historical connection to the British Empire. Along with the other national holidays such as Christmas Day, Boxing Day and Easter, all reflect the Judeo-Christian heritage.[136] Similar religious days are also celebrated in Slovenia. The national days of both states reflect their historical beginnings.

4.4 Religion

Religion, while having no bearing on the acquisition or loss of citizenship has played an important role in the identity of Slovenians, the Slovenian state, and the development of Australia. Slovenes have been influenced by the Roman Catholic Church for centuries, dating back to the Frankish (Carolingan) Empire and Roman Empire[137] right through to contemporary Slovenia. Slovenians and the current day Slovenian territory was on the front line of the border of Orthodoxy and close to the frontier of the Ottoman Empire, to its south. Slovenia, unlike Serbia, was never ruled by the Ottoman Empire. The Hungarians and Italians while also Catholics, had their own distinct culture. Even so, in modern day Slovenia there are a mix of religions that include Roman Catholicism, Eastern Orthodox and Islam, with Roman Catholicism still being predominant. A recent study confirmed that 38% of the

---

[135] Australian Government, Special dates and events, http://www.australia.gov.au/about-australia/special-dates-and-events

[136] Farida Fozdar, *The importance of Christianity in Australian national identity construction*, Institute for Citizenship and Globalisation, Deakin University, 2009, 14–15.

[137] Črnič, A., Komel, M., Smerke, M., Šabec K., Vovk, T, (2013) *Religious Pluralisation in Slovenia,* Teorija in Praksa, let. 50, 205–229.

people residing in the capital of Slovenia, Ljubljana province, are Roman Catholic, 8% follow other Christian denominations.[138] The Orthodox domination accounted for 7.3% of the 8%, with 4.8% of the total population being Muslim.[139]

Australia on the other hand, has its religious roots in its Anglo Saxon heritage and Christianity (Catholicism, and Protestantism). The Indigenous [Aboriginals] had their own religious traditions. However, since Australia opened its doors to immigrants from across the world, Christianity is still the majority amongst many other religions such as Islam and Buddhism, amongst other faiths. Today about 60% of the population in Australia are Christian (Catholic, Anglican, Baptist, Uniting Church, Lutheran, Orthodox).[140] The remaining 40% of the population are practitioners of Islamic, Buddhist, Hinduism, Sikhism and Judaism faiths. Religion has helped shaped the values and identity of both states.[141] Thus, in Australia the religious diversity has prevented a single religion from being dominant and has given effect to secularism. The role of religion in national or supranational identity is complex. It is well understood that the EU is predominantly Christian. It also plays a subtle role in cohesion of a society. It achieves this by providing a sense of sameness. That sameness allows people to come together and believe and practice similar values and behaviours. It has historically, in the British Empire, Roman and Greek times been used to influence the understanding of the law.

4.5 Conclusion

The historical paths of Slovenia and Australia have been very different but share some similar features. Australia's relationship with Slovenia began in 1855, with the first Slovenian arriving on the Australian territory. Australia had been occupied by indigenous aboriginal people, and settled by the British Empire who imposed their governance and legal framework over the people and the territory. Australian citizenship had evolved from the British Empire and allegiance to the King, and later to a single legal status of the country in 1948. The commencement of the twentieth century saw the collapse of Austrian-Hungarian Empire and the internal borders of Europe were redrawn, and the Federation of Australia was established. The border regions of current day Slovenia with Austria, Italy and Hungary were being shaped. Individuals could choose whether they wanted to remain a citizen in Austria or take out citizenship of the Kingdom. This choice suited those who wanted to align themselves on linguistics.

---

[138] Ibid.

[139] Ibid.

[140] Australian Bureau of Statistics, 2011 Census, 2012–2013, http://www.abs.gov.au/ausstats/abs@.nsf/lookup/2071.0main+features902012-2013

[141] Ibid.

Federation of Australia occurred in 1901, and the inhabitants were defined as British subjects. However, Australia had adopted a very restrictive policy that excluded anyone that was not deemed to be white. Not only did the immigration laws require persons to undertake a dictation test, the constitution was silent on citizenship. Australia had excluded the indigenous people from citizenship, the polity and community. The discriminatory approach taken in Australia during the early years, assisted in the British retaining and strengthening their influence across the territory. World War One commenced and a new Kingdom was born. The Kingdom of Serbs Croats and Slovenes would form, and in 1928 the new citizenship laws were introduced to unify the citizens. The early period was good for women being included into the political discourse, however this lasted a decade and they found themselves again excluded from political participation.

World War Two had a profound impact to the world. Australia was not immune. However, in n 1948, the first citizenship laws of Australia were implemented that assisted the state to establish its own identity but also define who its citizen would be. Since then, consecutive Australian Governments have changed its policy direction from that of White Australia to multiculturalism. The influx of many different ethnic groups has contributed to shaping national identity. That identity, while retaining its historical roots from Britain has what could be argued as transitioning to an amalgam of cultural mixes that define Australia. The Migration Act 1958 was introduced that began to change how migration was managed. A visa system was established, and non-citizens would have to have a visa to enter the country. British subjects and Irish nationals would be absorbed into the migration laws, ensuring all non-citizens were equal according to the law. They along with other non-citizens' resident in the state could be deported upon conviction of a criminal activity. The most notable change was the increased timeframe imposed by the government since 1901, which applied 3 years' residence, and in1948 this was increased to 5 years. By 1983, a 10-year timeframe was imposed on residency before immunity from deportation could be applied. The resulting effect to national identity was that the state was asserting its values, by demonstrating to the country, its citizens and citizens from other states that it was less tolerant towards individuals that have been convicted of a criminal activity.

In 1950, Australia began implementing a mass migration program that saw many people arrive from Europe. The citizenship law, apart from providing a legal status was welcoming of people wanting to take out citizenship. The previous policy of White Australia had all but gone, and different ethnic groups began to arrive from Asia. However, the indigenous Aboriginal peoples remained excluded. In 1967, the Australian constitution was amended to recognize these people. Upon the death of Josip Broz Tito the longtime leader of Yugoslavia, the state went into economic, social and political decline. Towards the end of the 1980s, Slovenia and Croatia began the process of separating from Yugoslavia. By 1986, Australia was embracing migrants from across the world to participate in building the nation, and accepted the fact that some citizens would hold dual citizenship. A defining moment for Australia was in 1987 when finally, the term British subject was removed from the legislation.

The collapse of socialism across Europe would see the collapse of Yugoslavia in the late 1980s. In 1989, the Year of Citizenship was declared in Australia, which went some way to promoting citizenship to residents who did not have citizenship. A similar policy approach of implementing the 'Year of Citizenship' could be undertaken by both Slovenia and Australia every decade or every 5 years to encourage individuals that are long-term residents (permanent residents) to take out citizenship.

Up until 1990, citizenship in both jurisdictions has been used to define the legal status of a citizen and unify citizens within a state. Coupled with immigration, rights and PIL, the laws have made a contribution to cohesion and identity of both states, and the EU. The citizenship laws had been used to ensure continuity of inhabitants within a state or territory, and contributed to developing national identity. Citizenship had transformed from allegiance to a master, to a legal status. However, a notable difference between the two states was that Australia had gone from being very restrictive at federation, to opening its doors and embracing multiculturalism. Slovenia upon independence had followed a similar path to Australia's early period of being very restrictive. During this period, the EU was further developing its single market concept and developing a citizenship framework of its own. The restrictive approach adopted by both states was important in the early period for establishing a national identity because, it allowed the state to clearly define and determine who and who was not going to be part of the state. Being part of the state would allow those individuals to participate in, and contribute to national identity, by implementing the values and laws of the state.

References

Beeson, M. (2001). Australia and Asia: The years of living aimlessly. In D. Sing & A. Smith (Eds.), *Southeast Asian affairs* (pp. 44–55). Singapore: Institute for Southeast Asian Studies.

Benedetto, D. (2002). Language trees and zipping. In E. Caglioti & V. Loreto (Eds.), *Physical review letters* (Vol. 88, pp. 1–5). Rome: La Sapienza University, Mathematics Department.

Chesterman, J. (2005). *Civil rights: How indigenous Australians won formal equality* (p. 126). St. Lucia: University of Queensland Press.

Crock, M. (2007). Defining strangers: Human rights, immigrants and the foundations of a just society. *Melbourne Law Review, 39*, 1–14.

Crock, M., & Berg, L. (2011). *Immigration, refugees and forced migration, law, policy and practice in Australia* (p. 521). Leichhardt: The Federation Press.

Crowley, F, (1973) *Modern Australia* in documents: 1901–1939, Melbourne Wren Publishing, 1, 250–255.

Gibb, D. (1982). *National identity and consciousness: commentary and documents*, Melbourne, VIC.

Hjerm, M. (1998). National identity: A comparison of Sweden, Germany and Australia. *Journal of Ethnic and Migration Studies, 24*(3), 452–462.

Irving, H. (1997). *To constitute a nation: A cultural history of Australia's constitution*. Melbourne: Cambridge University Press.

Irving, I. (2008). Still call Australia home: The constitution and the Citizen's right of abode. *Sydney Law Review, 30*(133), 135.

Kepple, K. (2009). Jewish immigrants in Australia before, during and after WWII, *The Monitor*.
Kuhn, R. (2004, October 8). *Class and struggle in Australia seminar series*. Australian National University.
Marshall, T. (1965). *Class, citizenship and social development* (pp. 101–103). New York: Anchor.
Mercer, D. (2003). Citizen minus?: Indigenous Australian and the citizenship question. *Citizenship Studies, 7*(4), 424–430.
Michael Barnes, B. (2004). *Anglo-Celtic Australians perspective of multiculturalism* (pp. 1–20). Sydney: Macquarie University.
Nolan, M., & Rubenstein, K. (2009). Citizenship and identity in diverse societies. *Humanities Research, XV*(1), 29.
Pryles, M. (1981). *Australian citizenship law*. Sydney: Law Book Co.
Richards, D. (1987). Transported to New South Wales: Medical convicts 1788–1850. *British Medical Journal, 295*, 1609.
Rubenstein, K. (1995). Citizenship in Australia: Unscrambling its meaning. *Melbourne University Law Review, 28*, 504–508.
Rubenstein, K. (2000). Citizenship and the centenary-inclusion and exclusion in 20th century Australia. *Melbourne Law Review, 24*, 576.
Rubenstein, K. (2002). *Australian citizenship law in context* (p. 50). Sydney: Lawbook Co.
Young, I. (1989). Polity and group difference: A critique of the ideal of universal citizenship. *Ethics, 99*(2), 250–270.
Zelman Cowen, Z. (2007). A historical survey of the Victorian Constitution, 1856 to 1956. *Melbourne University Law Review, 1*(1957), 1–5.

Chapter 5
Citizenship & Exclusion [Statelessness]

Abstract Citizenship can be obtained by birth, descent or naturalisation. This chapter discusses the development in citizenship law of both Australia and Slovenia. The comparative discussion will be undertaken in four parts. The first will commence in 1990 and conclude in 2000. The second will be between 200 and 2005 when Slovenia moved closer to membership of the European Union. Thirdly, there were considerable developments in citizenship law that will be discussed from 2005 to 2010. Fourthly, the citizenship laws and expression of the national identity continued to be strengthened between 2010 and 2018, although differently. Moreover, the world would see the rise of terrorism and states would react by adopting restrictive measures into their citizenship laws. The chapter will demonstrate how the citizenship laws of both states would have a significant role in reaffirming, enhancing and strengthening national identity. This chapter will identify themes where both states amended their respective citizenship laws as a result of world, regional or national events. This chapter will also highlight patterns that have been adopted by both states and used to make changes in the laws. For instance, this chapter will explore whether national and international events have had an impact on Slovenia and Australia's approach to reforming their citizenship laws.

Keywords Australia · Citizenship testing · Exclusion · Naturalization · Slovenia · Statelessness · State succession · Yugoslavia

5.1 Introduction

During the early period of independence, Slovenia was having to grapple with many different economic and social challenges. In establishing a new democratic state, Slovenia had to undertake and enormous restructuring and reform program that included, but not limited to ensuring continuity of its people and economy. Furthermore, it was also fending off criticism and conflict from former Yugoslavian Republics. Citizenship at the time was socially complex for former Yugoslav citi-

R. Walters, *National Identity and Social Cohesion in a Time of Geopolitical and Economic Tension: Australia – European Union – Slovenia*,
https://doi.org/10.1007/978-981-15-2164-5_5

zens. Citizens from the former Yugoslavia who had not registered as permanent residents of the new Slovene Republic were required to apply for Slovenian citizenship. Subsequently, many people did not register and found themselves without citizenship of any state (stateless).[1] While considered by many as a process of exclusion, which resembled Australia's approach to the Aboriginal people, analyzing this issue through the lense of identity and social cohesions, it can be seen how Slovenia was making a statement regarding its identity.

At the time of the Yugoslavian breaking up, it was thought that the Slovenian territory was populated with about 90% Slovenes and the remaining 10% of the population was made up of Croats, Serbians, Bosnians and others.[2] Many of the 10% of people who were not Slovene, had only found themselves resident in Slovenia, because under the former Yugoslav state, citizens were able to freely move and reside anywhere. According to Neza Salamon at the time of Yugoslavia's break up there were approximately 200,000 people residing in the Slovenian territory that were from other Yugoslav Republics, and it was confirmed that 170,000 people did obtain Slovene citizenship upon application.[3] Yelka Zorn estimates that there were 18,305 people that were erased from the residency register. The ratio of men to women being excluded was estimated at 58% and 42% respectively.[4] Even though there was a choice and the ability for people to apply for citizenship, Janja Zitnik argues many people did not know or in some cases chose not to apply.[5] This lack of knowledge and failure of the then government to adequately inform people of the new citizenship laws was problematic. Had the government implemented a comprehensive program to ensure everyone had knowledge of and understood the new citizenship laws, the result may have been very different.

The new citizenship laws came under increasing scrutiny by lawyers, government and legal scholars. Throughout the 1990s the case of the erased would be in and out of the Slovenian Constitutional Court on a number of occasions. The first case was heard in 1992. The Slovenian Constitutional Court held that article 28 should be repealed in accordance with article 25 of the constitution to ensure everyone has the right of appeal against decisions of the state including local authorities.[6] The court focused on the discretionary nature the authorities had in determining who would and who would not obtain citizenship in the new independent Slovenia. The discretionary power under article 41, afforded to the Ministry of Internal Affairs

[1] Australian Bureau of Statistics, 2011 Census, 2012–2013, http://www.abs.gov.au/ausstats/abs@.nsf/lookup/2071.0main+features902012-2013

[2] Lak, M, (1992) *The Involvement of the European Community in the Yugoslav Crisis during 1991*, Yearbook of European Studies 5, 175–185.

[3] Kogovšek Salamon, N, (2001) *Still Waiting: The Erased People of Slovenia*, in Building and Open Society in Western Balkans, Open Society Foundations, 27–29.

[4] Impact to women from being erased, statistics www.mirvni-institut.si8/izbrisani/en/statistics

[5] Žitnik, J, (2004) *Immigrants in Slovenia: Integration Aspects*, Scientific Research Centre of the Slovenian Academy of Sciences and Arts, Institute of Emigration Studies, Ljubljana.

[6] U-I-98/91, Constitutional Court, Official Gazette of the Republic of Slovenia, No, 1/91-I, 30/90-I and 38/92.

was considered a problem enabling officers to make decisions at their own discretion.[7]

Article 41 of the Nationality Law required that persons deprived of nationality of Slovenia and of the Federative People's Republic of Yugoslavia in accordance with the Act on Depriving Un-commissioned Officers and Officers of Former Yugoslav Army Who are not Willing to Return to their Fatherland, Members of Military Formations Having Collaborated with Occupational Forces and Having Fled Abroad, and the Persons Fleeing Abroad after the Liberation, of Nationality[8] and their children may acquire the nationality of the Republic of Slovenia if, within 2 years from the passing of this Law. The second section of the said article specified that the nationality of the Republic of Slovenia may be acquired by Slovenian emigrants who have ceased to be citizens of the former Republic of Slovenia and the Federative People's Republic of Yugoslavia due to their absence. Decisions concerning the acquisition of nationality according to the first and second sections of Article 41 of this Law shall be made by competent administrative authorities of internal affairs of the Republic of Slovenia (Article 42 of the Law) on the basis of their 'free discretion'. It was this free discretion that posed the greatest problem. There was no clear oversight of individual decisions at the local level. The Slovenian Constitutional Court ruled[9] that articles 41 should be repealed, and argued that this did not conform with article 120 of the Constitution.[10]

Article 120 of the Slovenian constitution ensures the protection of rights of citizens is guaranteed against the actions and decisions of administrative bodies and their representatives. Thus, citizens are protected by the constitution from individual decision making within government institutions. Such was the importance of the infringement of individuals rights that the Slovenian Constitutional Court in the same case, also referred to article 8 of the 1948 Declaration of Human Rights and article 13 of the European Convention on Human Rights (even though at the time Slovenia was not a signatory to the European Convention) that there is a right of remedy where it is found that a person has had their rights violated. With Slovenia moving closer to the European Union, the Slovenian Constitutional Court also noted that providing 'the necessary law was important to ensure the provisions of the Nationality Law be amended to meet international and European Union standards.[11] However, the discretionary power remained.

As discussed earlier in this book, when Slovenia was part of Yugoslavia, effectively people had two levels of citizenship, one by the individual Republic such as Slovenia, Serbia or Croatia, as well as having Federal citizenship of Yugoslavia. Republic citizenship did not come with any legal status. Yugoslav citizenship was

[7] U-I-69/92 Nationality Law, Slovenian Constitutional, Official Gazette of the Republic of Slovenia, no. 61/92.

[8] Official Gazette of the Republic of Slovenia 86/46.

[9] U-I-69//92-03, Official Gazette of the Republic of Slovenia, 61/1992.

[10] Ibid.

[11] Ibid.

considered the legal citizenship and was internationally recognised by other states. The newly formed Slovene government used the earlier Republican legal framework to its advantage in creating the new Slovenian state. That is, allowing those that had citizenship of the former Republican level to obtain citizenship in the new Slovenia. In 1994, the Slovenian National Assembly established the Act on the Regulation of the Status of Citizens of Other Successor States to the Former Social Federal Republic of Yugoslavia that would allow those former citizens of Yugoslavia who had been removed by the register of permanent residence, to obtain a valid residence permit.[12] More importantly, the Court noted that by adopting the above mentioned Act, had in fact established the unconstitutionality of the statutory regulation as it did not recognise 'permanent residence' retroactively to those citizens of the former Yugoslavia.

The National Assembly was given a six-month time-limit to remedy the anomaly, however this was not achieved. During 1994, the Slovenian Constitutional Court established the unconstitutionality of the statutory regulation in relation to the legal status of citizens of other Republics from the former Yugoslavia, who were removed from the register of permanent residence, and annulled the 3 month waiting period.[13] The Court asserted that:

> by treating former Yugoslav citizens within Slovenia unequal in comparison to other aliens who were considered citizens of other states, caused those individuals to find themselves in a situation of legal uncertainty, which was inconsistent with article 2 of the Slovenian constitution (the state is governed by the rule of law).[14]

The other issue discussed by the court was the Act and the legal certainty in relation to the words 'actual presence' in the Republic of Slovenia". It was established that the Act was not clear enough, and was considered to be an undefined legal notion. Therefore, even with the implementation of the new legislation in 2002, the erased issue had not been dealt with in the eyes of some, who continued challenging the state.

In 1999, the Slovenian Constitutional Court would again revisit the erased issue and considered the acquisition of citizenship in accordance article 40.[15] The court ruled there was a statutory problem that required the third paragraph of article 40 to be repealed.[16] That is, applicants for citizenship would need to meet the public order test. The court also ruled that the legislature did not have any basis to impose the public interest test because it was considered, it would, outweigh the protected trust in law. When the new citizenship laws of Slovenia came into force on 25 June 1991, the contentious article 40.3, allowed an application to be rejected where that individual was deemed to be threat to public order, security or defense of the State. It appears that Slovenia could have used the public order test very broadly and rejected

[12] U-I-246/02, Official Gazette of the Republic of Slovenia 36/2003.

[13] U-I-248/94, Official Gazette of the Republic of Slovenia 14/99.

[14] Ibid.

[15] U-I-89/99, Official Gazette of the Republic of Slovenia 59/99.

[16] Ibid.

citizenship applications by people who may not have necessarily been a threat to the state, but may have been involved in the early and wider Yugoslav conflict. However, the issue of the erased would remain unresolved. In U-II-1/10, the Slovenian Constitutional Court decided that:

> unconstitutional consequences would occur due to the rejection of the Act on the amendments and modifications of the Act on the Regulation of the Status of Citizens Other Successor States to the Former Social Federal Republic of Yugoslavia at a referendum.[17]

There was a push by government to take the laws to a referendum. The Act on the Regulation of the Status of Citizens Other Successor States to the Former Social Federal Republic of Yugoslavia, established a remedy for the violations of human rights towards the erased people. Human rights violations had become the principal argument for the protection of the erased people against the state.

The constitutional rights of the erased people had been violated, and those rights were extensive. They included the protection of human personality and dignity; the right to equal protection of rights; the prohibition of torture; the protection of personal liberty; freedom of movement; the right to personal dignity and safety and protection of family integrity", as a result of the individuals becoming stateless.[18] These rights can be found in the Slovenian Constitution and form an important part of Slovenia's modern day transition from a socialist Republic to a democratic state. Furthermore, these rights noted by Jelka Zorn are a fundamental part of the long standing European Rights framework that began in 1950 with the introduction of the European Convention for the Protection of Human Rights and Fundamental Freedoms.

In 2010, the European Court of Human Rights (ECoHR) got involved as a result of individuals making an application to the court under article 34 of the Convention for the Protection of Human Rights and Fundamental Freedoms 1950. The ECoHR found in favour of *Kuric*[19] ruling that:

> the Slovenian government had failed to issue residency permits and amend the legislation. In 2012, the ECoHR would further consider the case of *Kuric*,[20] and ruled Slovenia had violated articles 8, 13 and 14 of the 1950 ECoHR.

It wasn't until 2014 that the Grand Chamber of the ECoHR made the final judgment in relation to the 'Erased' by awarding €250,000 to human rights protestors (the group who applied to the court) who lost their permanent residence upon Slovenia becoming independent.[21] It is worth noting that the decision of the ECoHR is final and there is no appeals process for either party. Finally, it took nearly 15 years for

---

[17] U-II-1/10–26, Official Gazette of the Republic of Slovenia. No. 50/2010.

[18] Zorn, J, (2004) *The Politics of Exclusion Citizenship, Human Rights and the Erased in Slovenia*, UDK, 1–7.

[19] *Kurić and Others v. Slovenia*, European Court of Human Rights, *26,828/06*.

[20] Ibid.

[21] Council of Europe, Human Rights Europe, http://www.humanrightseurope.org/2014/03/slovenia-erased-people-human-rights-protest-leads-to-e250000-award

the 'Erased' issue to be resolved, and it wasn't until the European Court of Human Rights got involved that the matter was finalised.

5.1.1 Australia

Statelessness in the Australian context has not been evident in the same way as in Slovenia. The indigenous people had occupied the Australian territory long before colonisation. However, the indigenous people were not considered to be stateless even prior to being recognised as citizens (British subjects) in 1949. During this transition from a British subject to an Australian citizen, there were no records of people becoming stateless, because people did not have to apply for citizenship upon the 1948 Act being implemented. It is worth noting that during this period neither the United Nations Convention Relating to the Status of Refugees 1951 and the 1954 Convention Relating the Status of Statelessness had been implemented. These legal instruments had been in place for more than 40 years when the former Yugoslavia broke up.

The potential for statelessness to have occurred in Australia was when New Guinea became independent, and Australia relinquished sovereign rights over the territory. In 1975, the Papua New Guinea Independence Act and the Papua New Guinea Independence (Australian Citizenship) Regulations were introduced. On 16 September of the same year, a person who was an Australian citizen that was born in and resident of Papua and New Guinea, ceased to be an Australian citizen and automatically took up citizenship of Papua New Guinea.[22] There are no records that indicate any person became stateless through this transitional process. Today section 16, 19G and 21 of the Australian Citizenship Act 2007, provides that any person is eligible to apply for citizenship where they have been declared as such.

In August 2005, the Australian High Court[23] decided Ame who was born in the former Australian territory of Papua was facing deportation from Australia due to overstaying his visa. It was argued that Ame was born an Australian citizen and continued to retain that status, allowing him to reside in the current day territory of Australia. However, the High Court determined that people born in Papua were never full Australian citizens, and that nationality ceased to exist when Papua and New Guinea became independent in 1975. The High Court ruled that people such as Ame had no right of entry to Australia without a current visa and were not deemed to be Australia citizens. Therefore, these people could be removed from the territory. In an earlier case in the Australian Full Federal Court it was held that:

---

[22] Regulation 4, Papua New Guinea Independence (Australian Citizenship) Regulation 1975, A person who immediately before independence day, was an Australian citizen within the meaning of the Act and on independence day becomes a citizen of the independent state of Papua and New Guinea ceases on that day to be an Australian citizen.

[23] *Re Minister for Immigration and Multicultural and Indigenous Affairs; Exparte Ame* [2005] HCA 36.

> a person born as an Australian citizen in Papua in 1970 had not been absorbed into the Australian community, never having resided in the territory, and remained an immigrant under Australian law with no automatic right of entry onto mainland Australia.[24]

Even though these cases did not determine these people as stateless, it did show how people from Papua were viewed by the courts in Australia. Today, Slovenia is a partner to the United Nations Convention relating to the Status of Stateless Persons of 1954.[25] Australia is also a signatory and has ratified both international conventions in relation to stateless persons. The United Nations Convention Relating to the Status of Refugees 1951 and the 1954 Convention Relating the Status of Statelessness[26] are fundamental to ensuring every person has citizenship of at least one nation.

From the early beginnings of citizenship many centuries ago statelessness was not even a consideration. People were either citizens or subjects of an empire or kingdom. It wasn't until the conclusion of WWII that citizenship became important internationally and laws were developed to minimise the occurrence of when a person would find themselves without citizenship of any state. However, even with strong national laws in place, should there be a change in rulers within both Slovenia and Australia in the future, there is no guarantee[27] that statelessness would not occur.

5.1.2 State Succession

State succession is complex. It involves the process of when a state no longer exists, and the laws of that state are no longer applicable. Paul Weis like many other scholars is of the opinion that when a state ceases to exist, so do the nationals of that state.[28] However, Weis goes on to say that in many circumstances it is difficult to determine when exactly a state ceases and a new state commences. The international legal principles for state succession can be found in the 1978 Vienna

[24] *Minister for Immigration and Multicultural Affairs v Walsh* [2002] FCAFC 205 AS [16]–[17].

[25] Akt o notifikaciji nasledstva glede konvencij organizacije združenih narodov in konvencij, sprejetih v mednarodni agenciji za atomsko energijo, Official Gazette of the Republic of Slovenia, No. 35/92. Official Gazette FLRY, MP, No. 17/67. Article 4, Constitutional Law Implementing the Basic Constitutional Charter on the Sovereignty and Independence of the Republic of Slovenia, Official Gazette of the Republic of Slovenia, No. 1/91-I. The Conventions are also included into the Act notifying succession to conventions of the United Nations and conventions adopted by the International Atomic Energy Agency, Official Gazette of the Republic of Slovenia, No. 9/92.

[26] Carol Batchelor, *Statelessness and the Problem of Resolving Nationality Status*, International Journal of Refugee Law, 1998, 238–249.

[27] *Australian Citizenship Act 2007*, sections 3, 16, 19.

[28] Paul Weis, *Nationality ad Statelessness in International Law*, Sijthoff & Noordhoff, 1979, 135–140.

Convention on Succession states in relation to treaties, and the 1983 Vienna Convention on Succession of States in respect of State property, archives and debt.[29]

The provisions of international treaties that dealt with nationality can be found in the peace treaties following the First World War.[30] Following WW I, the territorial boundaries of a number of states changed and as a consequence the issue of nationality had to be resolved in the succession states. Kay Hailbronner notes that the rules surrounding the acquisition and loss of nationality upon territorial changes are some of the most complex at international public law.[31] Chapter VI, article 18 of the European Convention on Nationality refers to 'State Succession and Nationality', outlining the principles that states should consider when forming a new state. Article 18 states that in matter of nationality in cases of State succession, each State Party concerned shall respect the principles of the rule of law, the rules concerning human rights and the principles contained in articles 4 and 5 of the Convention. Furthermore, article 18 stated that in deciding to grant or allow retention of nationality in cases of State Succession, each State Party concerned shall take account of the genuine and effective link of the person concerned with the state and the habitual residence of the person at the time of state succession. However, this convention was established post 1990 and was not relevant to the Yugoslav breakup.

In 1996, the ILC developed 'draft' articles and a Declaration setting out the rules that deal with 'nationality of persons in relation to state succession'. The International Law Commission has attempted to expand these rules by obliging successor states to ensure nationality is granted to all people that are residing permanently within the new territory.

State succession and citizenship for the Slovene people can be traced back to end of the Austro-Hungarian Empire in 1918. The 1919 Saint-Germain Treaty and the Trianon Treaty were concluded following the breakup of the Austro Hungarian Monarchy. The treaties stated that:

> every person possessing the rights of citizenship in territory which formed part of the territories of the former Austro-Hungarian Monarchy were entitled to nationality of State exercising sovereignty over the territory.[32]

That is, everybody having citizenship and domicile within the territory was automatically entitled to citizenship under the State of the new territory. A similar approach could have been taken during the breakup of Yugoslavia, which may have prevented the potential for people to become stateless. The next section traces the legislative reform that has been undertaken by both states from 1990 to 2015.

---

[29] Articles 1 I, Is(a), 16, 24(1), Vienna Convention on succession of States in respect of Treaties, 1978, No. 33356, Articles 12, 14(2), IS(I)(a), 18, Vienna Convention on Succession of States in Respect of State Property, Archives and Debts 1983, https://treaties.un.org

[30] Hailbronner, K, (2006) *Nationality in public international law and European law*, in R. Bauböck, E. Ersboll, K. Groenendijk and H. Waldrauch, *Acquisition and Loss of Nationality: Policies and trends in 15 European countries,* Amsterdam: Amsterdam University Press, 49.

[31] Ibid, 60–70.

[32] Section VI, Article 70, Clauses Relating to Nationality, Saint-Germaine Treaty 1919, http://www.dipublico.com.ar/instrumentos/145.html

5.2 Part One

5.2.1 Slovenia

In 1991, article 40 was amended, which extended the restrictive policy approach taken by the government to exclude individuals from citizenship. As discussed above, the amendment allowed a person's application to be rejected if that person was considered to pose a threat to public order and security of the state. This also extended to those non-citizens that had committed a criminal offence directed against the state.[33] Article 40 of the original citizenship laws stated that:

> any citizen of another Yugoslav Republic who was on the day of the Plebiscite on the independence and sovereignty of the Republic of Slovenia, dated 23 December 1990, a registered permanent resident in the Republic of Slovenia, and who actually resides in the country, may acquire Slovenian citizenship, if he or she submits an application to the internal affairs administration body of the municipality where he or she is a permanent resident, within six months from the date of this Act coming into force.[34]

The public order test was decisive in excluding former Yugoslav citizens. As pointed out earlier, the Slovenian Constitutional Court had ruled extensively on article 40, which will be discussed later in this chapter. In the same year, Slovenia finally adopted the Aliens Act,[35] which regulated immigration, which imposed conditions on non-citizens, on how they could enter and stay in the country. One feature of these new laws was the implementation of a permit system that required non-citizens to have before entering the Slovenian territory. The Aliens Act also provided the legal framework for refugees to enter and stay.

A year later in 1992, article 13 was amended to allow individuals to obtain Slovene citizenship by naturalisation. However, this was restricted to those persons of Slovenian descent (having at least one parent who is Slovene) if their Slovenian citizenship had ceased as a result of release, renunciation or deprivation because they had not acquired Slovenian citizenship due to historical circumstances.[36] This reinforced Slovenia's sovereign right to choose its citizens, but also strengthened the links of the state with Slovenes that were located abroad.

1993 was an important year for Slovenia. Even though Slovenia's membership to the European Union was a decade away, the European Court of Human Rights underwent reform. The number of judges were increased to 29, with Slovenia being

---

[33] Article 40, Zakon o spremembi in dopolnitvi zakona o državljanstvu Republike Slovenije (ZDRS-A), Official Gazette of the Republic of Slovenia, No. 30/1991–1.

[34] U-I-89/99, Official Gazette of the Republic of Slovenia, No. 59/99.

[35] Alien Act, Official Gazette of the Republic of Slovenia, No. 1/1991. These laws were not valid from 1999.

[36] Article 13a, Zakon o spremembi in dopolnitvi zakona o o državljanstvu Republike Slovenije (ZDRS-A), Official Gazette of the Republic of Slovenia, No. 38/1992. Command declaring Law amending and supplementing the Law on Citizenship of the Republic of Slovenia.

represented by Dr. Peter Jambrek.[37] In May 1993, Slovenia joined the European Council. This was a good sign for Slovenia that they had been accepted by the European Community as embracing democracy and making a speedy transition from former socialism. Chapter four discusses in depth the transition from independence to membership of the European Union by Slovenia and the impact this had on Slovenian citizens.

5.2.1.1 Australia

Throughout the 1990s, there was a renewed interest in the national identity.[38] The concept of citizenship as a legal status had been entrenched into the state's legal framework for more than 40 years. Forty years on from Thomas Marshall writing about citizenship, scholars began to take a lot of interest in the concept throughout the 1990s. Citizenship was expanding and considered a desirable activity,[39] including a civic virtue[40] and universal.[41] Immigration had become an important part of citizenship and the wider economic and population policy of Australia.

In 1992, the Australian Government introduced major amendments to the *Migration Act 1958* which resulted in the immigration program and visa framework being codified. The changes also resulted in strengthening the national interest by placing visas requirements on all non-citizens entering the state.[42] Migration is considered a pathway to citizenship. Chapter five discusses migration and the visa framework in more depth, to demonstrate the differences between both states. The visa framework becomes important because non-citizens require a visa or permit to legally enter Australia or Slovenia, stay and apply for citizenship.

The migration laws were changed to abandon deportation of permanent residents. This was replaced with the ability for visas to be cancelled on the grounds of character and conduct.[43] The newly included provision allows the Minister to refuse to grant a visa or entry permit to a person, or may cancel a valid visa entry permit.[44] Thus, upon cancellation of a visa or permit the person was effectively an illegal

[37] Jambrek, P, (2014) *Nation's Transitions, Social and Legal Issues of Slovenia's Transitions 1945–2015,* Graduate School of Government and European Studies, Brdo pri Kranju and European Faculty of Law, Nova Gorica, Slovenia, 301.

[38] Rubenstein, K, (1995) *Citizenship in Australia: Unscrambling its Meaning*, Melbourne University Law Review, Vol 20, 504–505.

[39] Kymlicka, W., Norman, W, (1994) *Return of the Citizen: A Survey of Recent Work on Citizenship Theory*, 104, Ethics, 351–354.

[40] Ibid.

[41] Young, I, (1989) *Polity and Group Difference: A Critique of the Ideal of Universal Citizenship*, Ethics, Vol. 99, No 2, 1989, 250–270.

[42] Second Reading Speech: Migration Reform Bill 1992, House of Representatives, 2620.

[43] Crock, M., Berg, L, (2011) *Immigration, Refugees and Forced Migration, Law, Policy and Practice in Australia*, The Federation Press, 526.

[44] *Migration Act 1958,* s180A.

migrant and could no longer stay on the territory. However, the non-citizen had the ability to appeal the decision on grounds of merit.

Indigenous Australians

The plight and exclusion of the indigenous people in Australia has been well documented.[45] Upon colonisation by the British, these people lost their right to the land and its resources. It wasn't until 1992 when the Australian High Court[46] recognised the impact that the colonisation of the continent had to the indigenous community. This is an important observation in the discussion of the Australian national identity. The Australian High Court ruled that:

> Aboriginal and Torres Strait Islander peoples have the right to the land, and that those rights existed before the British arrived.[47]

In the same year, the Prime Minister Paul Keating as part of his speech in relation to the Year of the World's Indigenous People recognised the importance of indigenous music, art and dance being recognised in the community and the benefits of enriching the national life and identity of Australia, from their contribution.[48] As a result, the Australian Government introduced the *Native Title Act 1993* (the Act). This was an important step forward for Australia and the recognition of the aboriginal people. However, constitutional recognition still eluded them. The Act[49] also recognised the past injustices that had been attributed to the Aboriginal and Torres Strait islander people, providing them with full recognition of the role they have played in the development of Australia. It is asserted that the 1993 Act was a major step forward for the Australian people and Australia in recognising and understanding its past. As discussed later in 2012, the plight of indigenous people in relation to citizenship would be raised by the United Nations.

In 1993, the *Australian 1948 Citizenship Act* had some minor inclusion to sections 15, 41, 46A and 53, whereby, the words of "the oath or affirmation of allegiance" was replaced with the words "a pledge of commitment".[50] The pledge of commitment would remove all reference to 'God', 'allegiance' and 'Her Majesty Elizabeth the Second, Queen of Australia'.[51] The pledge of commitment aimed to

---

[45] Irving, H, (1997) *To Constitute a Nation: A Cultural History of Australia's Constitution*, Cambridge University Press, 100.

[46] *Mabo and others v Queensland* (No 2) (1992) 175, CLR 1.

[47] Ibid.

[48] Redfern Speech (Year for the World's Indigenous People), Prime Minister Paul Keating, 1992, https://antar.org.au/sites/default/files/paul_keating_speech_transcript.pdf

[49] *Native Title Act 1993*, Preamble.

[50] Australian Citizenship Amendment Bill 1993, The Parliament of the Commonwealth of Australia, Senate, Explanatory Memorandum, No. 933576 X, http://www.austlii.edu.au/au/legis/cth/bill_em/acab1993344/memo_0.pdf

[51] *Australia Citizenship 1973*, sections 15 & 26A.

strengthen the beliefs upheld by the Australian state, the rule of law and reinforced the Australian identity. The introduction of the Pledge came about as a commitment by the Australian Labor Party to emphasise the importance of the core values and character of Australia which was designed to unify the citizens of the country.[52] The Preamble was also introduced which took effect in 1994, and states[53]:

> Australian citizenship represents formal membership of the community of the Commonwealth of Australia; and Australian citizenship is a common bond, involving reciprocal rights and obligations, uniting all Australians, while respecting their diversity; and
>
> Persons granted Australian citizenship enjoy these rights and undertake to accept these obligations by pledging loyalty to Australia and its people, and by sharing their democratic beliefs, and by respecting their rights and liberties, and upholding and obeying the laws of Australia.

The Preamble represents the core principles of what citizenship means to Australia. Moreover, the reference to common bond, rights, democratic beliefs, respecting rights and liberties as well as upholding the law, all reflect different elements of how citizenship contributes to national identity. Australia is a democratic state that has provided rights and obligations to all its citizens through the law. However, the Act did not define citizenship. In 1994, a Joint Standing Committee identified eight ways to enhance citizenship.[54] Most notable was encouraging citizens to be active and participate in Australian life. A national citizenship week and awards was introduced to promote the idea of citizenship, what it means to be Australian and enhance the understanding of Australian values.[55] The Australian values originated from its historical past and connection to Britain, and was considered an important part of the ongoing identity of the state. It is argued that by raising the awareness and promoting citizenship to the broader community enables the state to reinforce what it means to be Australian. Thus, in turn, raising the awareness of Australian identity.

5.2.1.2 Slovenia

The citizenship laws of Slovenia would undergo further reform in 1994. Article 10, of the Law on Amendments and Supplements to the Law on Citizenship of the Republic of Slovenia[56] minimised the occurrence of those individuals that could

---

[52] Australian Citizenship Amendment Act 1993. 16. Australian Labor Party, Advancing a Multicultural Australia, Immigration and Ethnic Affairs Policy, 1993 federal election. 17. Senate, Debates, 29 September 1993, 1439

[53] Rubenstein, K, (2002) *Citizenship Law in Context*, Lawbook Co, 75.

[54] The Parliament of the Commonwealth of Australia, Joint Standing Committee on Migration, Australians All Enhancing Australian Citizenship, Australian Government Publishing Services, 1994.

[55] Ibid.

[56] Official Gazette of the Republic of Slovenia 25/1994.

become stateless (particularly those individuals from the former Yugoslavia). However, this provision was introduced to provide a basis for allowing some, not all people, who were part of the former Yugoslavia, and resident in Slovenia, an avenue to continue to stay in Slovenia. This was however on the condition that the applicant no longer had citizenship of their former Republic such as Serbia or Croatia.

In the same year, 'The Slovene May Declaration'on Independence was released and reinforced the earlier 1989 May Declaration. The declaration demanded national independence, democracy, a multiparty parliamentary system and an economy based on the modern welfare state.[57] The public statement reminded Slovenians what they had already achieved in establishing independence by adopting a constitution of a sovereign state, based on democratic principles, the rule of law and protection of human rights. Paragraph 4 of article 3 was included to read:

> if the person is a frequent offender is prosecuted ex officio and offences against public order, 4 if the person despite the call by the competent authority refuses to meet with the Constitution and statutory duties of a citizen of the Republic of Slovenia.

A new paragraph 3 was included to read as follows:

> It is considered that a person has the nationality of a foreign country if the foreign national's travel document or, if exercised military duty under the regulations of that country or, if employed in a state body or in the armed forces of a foreign country.

This reflects strongly Slovenia's national identity because it is confirming who is a national of a foreign country and not a Slovene citizen. Furthermore, in article 8, a new second paragraph was inserted that read: 'In order to obtain citizenship a child over 14 years requires his consent'. These minor changes were a small but important expression of national identity, because Slovenia was reinforcing its public order test where individuals had committed a crime against the state.

National Interest

Article 12 focused on the 'national interest' whereby emigrants and their descendants to the third generation could obtain citizenship of Slovenia. However, the individual had, had to have resided continuously in the territory of Slovenia for at least 1 year. Those individuals that had been married to a Slovene citizen for 2 years, could also apply for citizenship. The second paragraph of article 13 was amended and stated:

> The existence of the grounds referred to in the preceding paragraph on the basis of the opinion of the competent bodies previously found Government of the Republic of Slovenia, which at the same time be required to meet one or more of the conditions referred to in paragraph 10.

---

[57] Jambrek, P, (2014) *Nation's Transitions, Social and Legal Issues of Slovenia's Transitions 1945–2015*, Graduate School of Government and European Studies, Brdo pri Kranju and European Faculty of Law, Nova Gorica, Slovenia, 262.

The change was to allow the administrators of the law to make a decision on whether the applicant had met the other exclusive requirements, in order to obtain citizenship. The third paragraph of article 14 was replaced with a new paragraph that read:

> A child who has no parents, or whose parents have lost their parental rights or their ability from birth and living in Slovenia can obtain citizenship of the Republic of Slovenia at the request of the administrator who is a citizen of the Republic and with whom the child lives, if for the benefit of the child to the granting of citizenship to the consent of a state administrative body responsible for social welfare.

The article was an important inclusion to ensure children do not become stateless. In article 16, the first paragraph was replaced with a new paragraph that read:

> The decision to set aside even if the person has been admitted to citizenship of the Republic of Slovenia on the basis of assurances from foreign countries to who the foreign citizenship has been terminated if the citizenship of the Republic of Slovenia if within the period specified in the decision on admission to citizenship of the Republic of Slovenia does not submit evidence that it has closed its previous citizenship.

The inclusion was to ensure that Slovenian citizenship was exclusively Slovene and ensured a person could not have dual citizenship.

A new article 28 was introduced outlining a criterion for determining the 'national interest of the Republic of Slovenia'. Article 10 requires that a person must be 18 years of age, have or obtain release from current citizenship be living in Slovenia for 10 years and have a guaranteed income. The person must have a good knowledge of the Slovene language and be able to prove they have not been in prison or sentenced for crimes in Slovenia. It is argued that the single common denominator that separates Slovenes from other is their language. Hence, the importance that has been placed on language in citizenship law. These exclusionary measures reinforced the Slovenian position that they were in a building phase and wanted to ensure people understood the Slovenian values and national identity.

The introduction of article 39 would represent a significant policy shift by allowing a person to be a citizen of the state if they had been a resident in the Slovene Republic on 23 December 1990 at independence. This is an important observation in which Slovenia began to recognise in law those individuals from the former Yugoslavia, who were Yugoslav citizens. However, evidence must have been provided by the person proving they were actually resident in Slovenia at the time the state became independent.

A new article 41 was inserted to allow a person between 18 and 23 years of age to obtain citizenship by descent. However, this article would need to be read in conjunction with article 10. Article 10, the first sentence was amended to ensure those applying for naturalisation also met the national interest test. Article 10 paragraph 5 was also amended to require an active command of the Slovenian language in written and oral form and to be demonstrated by taking a test. A further inclusion to article 10 required a person seeking citizenship by naturalisation to not have any outstanding tax liabilities. Obtaining citizenship by descent can be viewed as Slovenia wanting to make a connection with those Slovene residing in other states.

It is argued that due to the small population inside and outside of Slovenia, the state was wanting to expand its citizenry.

5.2.1.3 European Union

The European Union would implement the European Convention on Nationality 1997 (ECN).[58] Apart from the ECN establishing a set of consistent principles for the acquisition and loss of citizenship across member states, there was greater recognition of women. Article 4 states that neither marriage nor the dissolution of a marriage between a national of a state party and alien, nor the change of nationality by one of the spouses during marriage, shall automatically affect nationality of the other spouse. Furthermore, article 5 protected individuals (race, colour and sex) from discrimination. There was a continued push towards citizenship and rights equality for women. The ECN also addressed the issue of statelessness and state succession to provide the basis for the transition by states and ensure the inhabitants within the territory would retain their nationality based on habitual residence.[59] Importantly, and while the ECN was established long after the fall of Yugoslavia, it reinforced the importance of nationality as a human right and the need to minimise the occurrences of people becoming stateless. However, even today the full principles of the ECN have not been fully realised or used by the European community to ensure, when there is a change in rule, people retain citizenship of the territory in which they reside.

5.2.1.4 Australia

The citizenship laws received minor changes as a result of amendments to the Migration and Family Law legislation.[60] The national identity was summarised in 1995 by the Prime Minister Paul Keating as:

> all Australians must accept the basic principles of Australian society including the constitution and the rule of law, parliamentary democracy, freedom of speech and religion, English as the national language, equality of the sexes and the right of every Australian to express his or her views and values.[61]

Keating was not only reaching out to multicultural Australia but more importantly reinforcing the historical identity of Australia and what it means to be an

---

[58] European Convention on Nationality, 6XI.1997.

[59] Articles 18 & 19, European Convention on Nationality, Strasbourg, 6.XI.1997.

[60] *Migration Reform Act 1992, Family Law Reform (Consequential Amendments) Act 1995, Statue Law Revision Act 1996, Federal Magistrates (Consequential Amendments) Act 1999, Criminal Code Amendment (Theft, Fraud, Bribery and Related Offences) Act 2000.*

[61] Paul Keating, Opening Address, Global Cultural Diversity Conference, Sydney, Australia, 1995, 23, www.immi.gov.au/media/publications/multicultural/confer/speech

Australian. The reference to the English language, rights, the constitution and rule of law have and continue to be fundamental pillars of the Australian identity.

A year later in 1996, there was a change of government in Australia, and John Howard would be elected as Prime Minister. The government denounced racial intolerance as being incompatible with the kind of society Australia wanted to be.[62] Pauline Hanson would enter the political stage through her 'One Nation Party', and attempted to exploit the xenophobia elements of the Australian community and political discourse. Xenophobia behavior was specifically directed toward the Asian population.[63] It is argued that the xenophobia behavior would have had an impact on national identity. On the one hand, national identity would have been expressing the old days of 'white' Australia. On the other hand, the government was wanting national identity to express unification of multi-ethnic groups. Thus, there were elements of the community that would have been in a dichotomy as to what national identity stood for. This was a tough period for the government having to grapple with large numbers of migrants entering the state along with building social cohesion.

Nonetheless, the Prime Minister John Howard, rather than agree, praised the tolerance of the community towards the many different ethnic and religious groups that make up the Australian citizenry.[64] The Australian Government stated that the country remained confused about its identity and concluded that citizenship is fragile by having no constitutional recognition.[65] McHugh J of the High Court of Australia had also argued that Australia is in need of a statutory Bill of Rights.[66] Rather than a Bill of Rights, it is proposed that Australia reform its constitution to resemble Slovenia's modern day constitution because a constitution provides greater legal certainty than national legislation. The High Court of Australia also stated there was a growing sense of national independence and identity given to the consideration of citizenship.[67] Thus, as citizenship and the national identity have evolved, national courts have also come to understand the importance of both concepts to the state. Moreover, the statements made by the Australian Government reinforced the amalgam of identities that had and continues to form part of the Australian society.

By 1998, the *Migration Legislation Amendment (Strengthening of Provisions relating to Character and Conduct) Act* was introduced to strengthen the powers of the Immigration Minister to cancel or refuse to grant a visa, and remove a non-citizen on grounds of criminality and bad conduct.[68] The changes altered the

---

[62] Motion from the then Prime Minister on this matter; Racial Tolerance, Parliament of Australia, House of Representatives, Official Hansard 30 October 1996, in Australian Citizenship Council, Australian Citizenship for a New Century, 2000, Commonwealth of Australia, 18.

[63] Ibid.

[64] Ibid.

[65] Ibid.

[66] *Al- Kateb* [2004] HCA 37; (2004) 219 CLR 562.

[67] *DJL v Central Authority* [2000] HCA 17; 201 CLR 226; 170 ALR 659; 74 ALJR 706, 135.

[68] Crock, M., Berg, L, (2011) *Immigration, Refugees and Forced Migration, Law, Policy and Practice in Australia*, The Federation Press, 527.

individual's ability to access independent merits review, and the role of the Australian Administration Tribunal, which had jurisdiction in reviewing matters of visa cancellations.[69] Effectively the Minister could override the decision of the tribunal. The Minister could also provide a written direction to an individual, and reversed the onus of proof to the person to prove they are of good character. The resulting effect was the bar had been raised for migrants having to comply with the deeming provisions.

By the end of the 1999, Slovenia had been independent for nearly a decade. The people and territory had transitioned from socialism to democracy. The state implemented new citizenship laws that were nationalist in their approach welcoming Slovenians but excluding former Yugoslav citizens from the other Republics. Slovenia was moving ever closer to Europe and preparing itself for accession to the European Union. Economically, Slovenia had also transitioned to a market based economy that was integrated with Western and Central Europe. Australia continued to take in large numbers of immigrants from across the world. The economy had been shifting from agriculture to mining and the next decade would see huge wealth and exports from Australia to South East Asia and China. Thus, reinforcing an earlier point in chapter two that Australia had for the past 25 years moved ever closer economically to Asia.

5.2.2 2000–2005

The most notable change to citizenship law during this five-year period was the introduction and acceptance of dual citizenship by both Australia and Slovenia, although quite differently. It is argued that by adopting this postnational approach, both states would allow their citizens to have a greater participation in an ever increasingly globalised world.

The *Australian Citizenship Legislation Amendment Bill of 2001* made a number of amendments to the *Australian Citizenship Act 1948*.[70] For Australia, 2001 was an important year as it marked 100 years of Federation, and it was nearly 50 years since the first citizenship laws had been introduced. The Australian Citizenship Council identified 64 recommendations to strengthen the country's national identity.[71] In response, the Australian Government released a report "*Australian Citizenship*

---

[69] Ibid.

[70] Australian Citizenship Legislation Amendment Bill 2001, The Parliament of the Commonwealth of Australia, House of Representatives, Explanatory Memorandum (Circulated by authority of the Minister for Immigration and Multicultural Affairs, The Hon Phillip Ruddock MP), http://www.comlaw.gov.au/Details/C2004B01003/Explanatory%20Memorandum/Text

[71] Australian Citizenship Council, Australian Citizenship for a New Century: February 2000, Ausinfo, Canberra, 2000.

Our Common Bond", in 2001.[72] Despite the Australian Government agreeing with the Council's view that citizenship law is important to the state and citizens, the government found that there was no need to change the laws.

The Australian Government held that citizenship is an important concept that 'unifies' society, bringing citizens closer together.[73] This was reaffirmed when the Prime Minister John Howard, stated that 'there is something special about being an Australian'. That Australian spirit; that capacity; that mateship allows us to pull together in times of challenge and times of adversity is something that is very special. The things that unite us are infinitely greater and more enduring than the things that divide us'.[74] Clearly there was an attempt by government to further unify the amalgam of ethnic groups that make up the Australian society. Furthermore, the government was addressing the people and directing them to embrace and practice the values of the state.

Further minor amendments were undertaken, even though they did not directly reflect strengthening or enhancing national identity. However, it is important to outline these amendments to provide a complete understanding of the legislative change undertaken by the state. Section 5 was changed to clarify what it meant by the Australian reserve force; the Naval Reserve, Army Reserve and Air Force Reserve, and their predecessors. Paragraph 10B (1)(a) of the section omitted the number '18' which was substituted '25'. The following paragraph was also inserted (1A): 'if the relevant person referred to in subsection (1) has attained the age of 18 years, the name of the relevant person must not be registered for the purposes of this section unless the Minister is satisfied that the relevant person is of good character'. Section 13(3) had (3A) inserted to provide that (1)(d) and (e) do not apply in relation to (a) a person who has completed full-time service as a member of an Australian reserve force for a period of, or for periods amounting in the aggregate to, not less than 6 months; or (b) a person who (i) has been discharged from service as a member of an Australian reserve force before completing full time service as such a member for a period of, or for periods amounting in the aggregate to, 6 months; and (ii) was so discharged while undertaking unfit for service or further service; (iii) was so discharged while undertaking full-time service as a member of the reserve force; and (iv) became medically unfit for service because of the person's service as a member of the reserve force. Even though, these changes had little effect on national identity, it is argued they reinforced the point that Australia considers military as an important part of national identity.

Section 13(9A) was established to provide that the Minister may have the discretion on application in accordance with the approved form, grant a certificate of Australian citizenship to a child if:

---

[72] Australian Government, *Australian Citizenship....A Common Bond*, Government Response to the Report of the Australian Citizenship Council, 2001, http://www.citizenship.gov.au/_pdf/0501report.pdf

[73] Ibid.

[74] John Howard Election Speech, Sydney, 10 November 2001, http://pmtranscripts.dpmc.gov.au/browse.php

(a) the child was under 16 at the time of the application; and (b) the application is set out in the same document as an application made under subsection (1) by a responsible parent of the child for the grant of a certificate of Australian citizenship to the responsible parent.

Section 13(9C) (9D) described the forms to be used as an application for citizenship. The application form assists a non-citizen to apply for citizenship. The application form is a formal government document. Section 13(9E) (a) and (b) a child under the age of 16 can be granted citizenship and a responsible parent of the child is an Australian citizen.

Section 13(11) Omitted 'or (9)', substitute, (9), (9B) or (9E), and, omit 'or include the name of the person in a certificate of Australian citizenship under subsection (10)'. Section 13(11)(a), (b) and (c) at the end of the paragraphs add the word 'or'. These minor changes had no direct impact to enhancing or diluting national identity. After paragraph 13(11)(c) the following was inserted (ca) if the person is a serious repeat offender in relation to a sentence of imprisonment (within the meaning of subsection (11A)-during the period of 10 years after the end of any period during which the person has been confined in a prison in Australia because of the imposition on the person of that sentence. Section13(11)(d) after the words 'from serving', inserted the words 'the whole or'. Additionally, omit 'the whole or part of the remainder of that sentence', substitute, 'the whole of that sentence, or the whole or part of that sentence of the remainder of that sentence, as the case requires'. Also the word 'or' was added to s13(11)(e) After 'from serving', insert 'the whole or', and, add 'or'. Furthermore, subsection (11)(ca)(a) highlighted that:

> a serious prison sentence was imposed on a person; and (b) the person was confined in a prison in Australia because of the imposition of that sentence; and (c) another serious prison sentence was imposed on the person in relation to an offence committed by the person at a time after the person ceased to be confined in prison because of the imposition of the sentence mentioned in paragraph (a), serious prison sentence means (d) a sentence of imprisonment for life; or (e) a sentence of imprisonment for a period of not less than 12 months.

The restrictive approach Australia adopted reinforced its policy approach of welcoming new arrivals provided they are of good character and have not been convicted of criminal offences. It is argued that Australia through its citizenship laws is asserting national identity by ensuring only those who become citizens do not have a criminal background that could harm the state.

Section 14A(2) was changed to omit 'or for periods that in total, exceed', substitute 'that exceeds, or for periods that in total exceed' and the following was inserted;

> 14B Revocation of grant of certificate of Australian citizenship before conferral of citizenship. 14C Deferral of conferral of Australian citizenship.

Within section 15, 15(4) was repealed and at the end of section 15 add (6) A person to whom a certificate of Australian citizenship has been granted under subsection (13)(9B) is an Australian citizen on and after: (a) the day on which the responsible parent mentioned in that subsection becomes an Australian citizen under section 15, or (b) if the certificate is granted after the responsible parent becomes an Australian citizen under section 15 the day on which the certificate is granted. Subsection (7) was clarified to include

> A person to whom a certificate of Australian citizenship has been granted under subsection 13(9E) is an Australian citizen on and after the day on which the certificate is granted.

It is argued the Australian citizenship formalizes the process of becoming a full citizen of the state. Furthermore, the citizenship certificate provides a greater sense of belonging and individual identity of the person, connecting them to the state. This was a positive outcome for national identity because the person should better understand what it means to be Australian.

5.2.2.1 Dual Citizenship

It was not until 2002[75] that cosmopolitan, multinational or postnational (dual) citizenship would be fully effective in Australia. Throughout the eighteenth, nineteenth and twentieth century states imposed a strong sense of nationalism and the territorial competition resulting in dual citizenship being viewed as undesirable.[76] For Andrew Linklater[77] the cosmopolitan resembles postnational citizenship and obliges all human beings to extend hospitality to strangers as fellow citizens of a universal state of humanity.[78] Furthermore, postnational citizenship extends the concept of citizenship and no longer restricts it to a single state.

With section 17 being amended, consequential amendments were necessary to s23 and subsequently s23B to enable a person to resume their Australian citizenship.[79] Additional amendments detailed in the table below included strengthening aspects of the integrity of Australian citizenship to sections 21, 23 and 52, that provided clarity around the application of the law and other minor drafting errors. Section 21(1) inserted that:

> a person who was convicted of an offence pertaining to people smuggling in accordance with section 232A, 233 or 233A of the *Migration Act 1958*, and is sentenced to imprisonment for a period of not less than 12 months, the person may be liable to deprivation of citizenship. Section 23AA(1)(e) the word 'and' was an addition along with (f) that the person is of good character. 23AB was inserted to provide that a 'Person may resume citizenship lost under section 18'. Section 23D(3)(a)(i) Omitted the number 18 which was substituted by the number 25.

---

[75] Australian Citizenship Legislation Amendment Bill 2002, House of Representatives, Information and Research Services, No. 782001–02.

[76] Sassen, S, (2002) *The Repositioning of Citizenship: Emergent Subjects and Spaces for Politics*, Berkley Journal of Sociology, vol 6, 1–10.

[77] Linklater, A, (1998) *Cosmopolitan Citizenship*, Citizenship Studies, Vol. 2, No. 1, 26.

[78] Ibid.

[79] Australian Government, *Australian Citizenship....A Common Bond*, Government Response to the Report of the Australian Citizenship Council, 2001, http://www.citizenship.gov.au/_pdf/0501report.pdf

Section 52A(1) following the word 'review of' insert 'the following decisions'. Section 52A(1)(a) at the conclusion of this paragraph the following was inserted (ab) decisions of the Minister under section 14B revoking the grant of a certificate. That is, the Minister has the ability to issue or revoke a certificate of citizenship. Section 52A(1)(e) Omitted '(2)' and substitute 'under subsection 23AA(2)'. Section 52A(1)(e) omitted 'and' and further inserted (ea) decisions of the Minister under subsection 23AB(3) refusing to register a declaration or under subsection 23AB(3) refusing to include the name of a child in a declaration. Even though these minor changes did not directly reflect strengthening national identity, the amendments provide a complete understanding of the legislative change undertaken by Australia.

5.2.2.2 Slovenia

By 2002, there were a number of minor amendments made to the citizenship laws of Slovenia. Slovenia would again reaffirm its identity by ensuring individuals had a command of the Slovenian language.[80] This restrictive policy approach reinforced Deželan's theory of nationhood where language is to be protected,[81] and that the Slovenian language is part of the national identity. The language requirement was considered fulfilled if a person had either completed primary school, secondary school, a certificate of education to VI or VII, degree, college or university studies.[82] Article 2 had a small change to the first where number 23 was replaced with the number 36. The importance of the Slovene language cannot be underestimated. It has been used to identify who is Slovene and who is not for more than a century. Comparatively, Slovenia has placed a higher value on language to that of Australia.

Article 3 also had minor changes. The 10 paragraph of article 3 the word 'application' and the words 'and the alien status' were included. The 4th paragraph included the words 'provided that the apartment and'. Paragraph 5 was amended to include '5 the command of the Slovenian language for everyday communication needs, attested by a certificate of successful completion of the exam of Slovene at the basic level'. The 7th paragraph the word 'failure' replaced the word prohibition'. The 9th paragraph the word 'obligation' full stop is replaced by a semicolon. A new 10th paragraph was added: 'to make a statement that the acquisition of citizenship of the Republic of Slovenia agrees with the legislation of the Republic of Slovenia'. The existing 5th paragraph became the 7th paragraph and was amended to read 'It is considered that the condition of the first paragraph of this Article shall be satisfied if the conditions are for deletion are from the conviction from criminal records'. Similarly, in article 11, the first paragraph the number '7', the word 'and'

[80] Promulgation of amendments to the Law on Citizenship of the Republic of Slovenia (ZDRS-D), 2002, Official Gazette of the Republic of Slovenia 96/127.

[81] Deželan, T, (2011) *Citizenship in Slovenia: the regime of nationalising or Europeanising state*, Working Paper, 2011/16, The University of Edinburg, 2–13.

[82] Promulgation of amendments to the Law on Citizenship of the Republic of Slovenia (ZDRS-D), 2002, Official Gazette of the Republic of Slovenia 96/127.

was replaced with a comma and the number '8' was added to the comma and the numbers '9' and '10' were also included. Even though these small changes did not contribute to national identity, they were important to the overall legislative framework, which clarified punctuation and sentence structure.

Article 12 would enable the acquisition of citizenship by those who had lost their citizenship of Slovenia as a result of being denied citizenship. People could now apply for, and obtain citizenship provided they had resided in the Slovene territory for a minimum of 6 months.[83] The importance of language to Slovenia was no more evident than during the transition period and establishment of independence and a new constitution. New fifth, sixth, seventh and eighth paragraphs were added, which read as follows: 'to provide the authorities with the discretion for granting citizenship to a refugee or stateless person'. Firstly, this enable the state to fulfil its commitment under international law towards refugees and ensuring people do not remain stateless. However, it appears to have taken Slovenia more than a decade after independence to fully commit to the idea that they should protect people from statelessness, according to the law. The 1st paragraph of article 13 was amended to read:

> Slovenian citizenship can be acquired by naturalization if the individual provides a benefit to the country such as scientific, economic, cultural, national, or similar reasons provided that actually lived in Slovenia continuously for at least one year prior to the application and the alien status and qualifies under the Aliens Act.

It is argued Slovenia while welcoming foreigners wanted to ensure they make a valuable contribution to the state. Moreover, new paragraph was inserted and stated: 'The person referred to in the preceding paragraph, which claims the benefit of the country for national reasons, need not comply with the requirement of actual residence in Slovenia'. The 3rd paragraph, the word Slovenia comma was replaced by a dot, and the remainder of the text is deleted. Not all of the above changesdirectly relate to national identity. These minor changes provide a complete understanding of the legislative change undertaken by the state. Slovenia was only 12 years old and scholars had taken an interest in the state, its size and its people.

5.2.2.3 Slovenia's Smallness

The size of Slovenia both geographically and its population are well understood. In 2002, Milan Brglez and Zlatko Šabič highlighted several studies had been undertaken of Slovenia's identity.[84] What makes Slovenia stand out from other countries is its size both geographically and its population. They noted that the idea of Slovenia's size was not an important factor to inhibiting Slovenia in creating its

[83] Ibid.

[84] Brglez, M., Šabič, Z, (2002) *The national identity of post-communist small states in the process of accession to the European Union: the case of Slovenia*: Faculty of Social Sciences, University of Ljubljana, 2–18.

identity.[85] Slovenia has one of the smallest populations when compared to many states in Europe. Thus in the eyes of Slovenes, they are potentially vulnerable due to the status of their 'smallness'.[86] The status of 'smallness' as an independent variable[87] affecting the Slovenian national identity appears pertinent.[88]

Many scholars begin a discussion of Slovenia's viability in the international arena by presupposing Slovenia's smallness[89] In the context of Slovenia's size within the European community, Luxembourg has a quarter of the population about 509,000 in an area of approximately 2586 square kilometers.[90] Malta is another state that has a smaller population of about 409,000 with a land mass of just 316 square kilometers.[91] Arguably, Slovenia's smallness should not be viewed as inhibiting its long term viability. Slovenia's national identity is defined, in part, by its smallness, geographical location and population size. However, this smallness must not be confused with the place Slovenes and Slovenia have in the European Union and the rest of the world. Slovenes and Slovenia has a remarkable story to tell the world. In the same way, Australia has a great story to tell with its beginning and now place in Asia and the world.

With Slovenia being 2 years out from becoming a full member of the European Union in 2004, the state was well down the road to conforming to the principles of European Union law. There was a collective effort to harmonize the national laws to ensure consistency with the European Convention on Nationality 1997 (ECN). Citizenship by naturalization was to a certain extent becoming more liberal in accordance with article 14, whereby children who were under the age of 18, could acquire citizenship provided their parents had citizenship of the state.[92] Additionally, further changes were made to article 14. The second paragraph at the end the words 'continuously for at least 1 year prior to the application and the alien status'. A new third and fourth paragraph provided a child born in the Slovene Republic could obtain citizenship if requested by one of the parents who has received citizenship by naturalization. This also extends to a person under the age of 18, provided the parent has acquired citizenship by naturalization. The words 'a state administrative body responsible for social security' was replaced by 'the ministry responsible for family

---

[85] Ibid.

[86] Brinar, I., Bučar, B, (1994) *Slovenian foreign policy*. Civil Society, Political Society, Democracy. Ljubljana, Slovenian Political Science Association, 425–447.

[87] Fierke, K, (1996) *Multiple identities, interfacing games: the social construction of western action in Bosnia*. European Journal of International Relations, 467–497.

[88] Ibid.

[89] Svetličič, M, (1997) *Small States: New Challenges and Opportunities*: Development and International Cooperation, 24–25. in Zlatko Šabič, Charles Bukowski, Small States in the Post-Cold War World: Slovenia and NATO Enlargement, PRAEGER, 2002.

[90] Central Intelligence Agency, Country Comparisons to the World, https://www.cia.gov/library/publications/the-world-factbook/fields/2119.html

[91] Ibid.

[92] Promulgation of amendments to the Law on Citizenship of the Republic of Slovenia (ZDRS-D), 2002, Official Gazette of the Republic of Slovenia 96/127.

and social affairs', in the 5th paragraph. However, Slovenia had not ratified this convention. Even today, Slovenia has not ratified the ECN. Slovenia should ratify this convention. The importance of the ECN, is it provides the framework for all member states of the European Union a consistent approach to regulating citizenship. It does not take away any further sovereign right of member states to continue to regulate citizenship at the national level.

5.2.2.4 Dual Citizenship

Slovenia began expanding its direction to encourage individuals who could provide scientific, economic or a cultural benefit to the state, with a pathway to citizenship. However, the pre-condition was that the individual must have resided in Slovenia continuously for at least one year. A year later, in 2003, the Slovenian Law on Citizenship would be amended again allowing an individual to obtain dual citizenship. Slovene citizens would finally be allowed to become part of the broader regional and global world. The European Union encouraged member state to accept dual citizenship as part of their citizenship laws. This change was one of the most liberal changes Slovenia undertook since independence.[93] However, dual citizenship is restricted and has been exclusively reserved to those individuals who can demonstrate a connection to Slovenia. Today, across European member states, Australia and most other western democratic states dual citizenship has become the norm, and has expanded to multiple citizenship.[94] Dual citizenship in itself is multidimensional and serves to allow a state to maintain a connection with their citizens. Dual citizenship allows the individual to be more global gaining access to other regions of the world where they would not otherwise be able to do, with ease. This saw Slovenia beginning to embrace the postnational concept of citizenship. Some argue that the introduction of dual citizenship devalues national citizenship.[95] However, it is argued that it is an inevitable part of the evolution and expansion of citizenship in a globalized world that states have had to embrace the idea that their citizens can be citizens of another state. That is, as states begin to open up and allow their citizens to participate across the world, eventually other states follow.

The introduction of dual citizenship was seen by the Slovenes as continuing down the road to membership and meeting the requirements of the European Union leading up to membership in 2004.[96] From a unification perspective the state was wanting to provide a pathway (for those Slovenians abroad that had a connection

[93] Law on the Citizenship of the Republic of Slovenia, Official Gazette (ZDRS-OCT1) 7/2003.

[94] Rubenstein, K., Adler, D, (2000) *International Citizenship: The Future of Nationality in a Globalised World*, Indiana Journal of Global Studies, 519–548.

[95] Spiro, P, (1997) *Dual Nationality and the Meaning of Citizenship*, Emory Law Journal, 46–50.

[96] Medved, F, *Unified Slovenian Nation: Slovenian Citizenship Policy towards Slovenians Abroad*, InGyõzõ Cholnoky, Zoltán Kántor, András Ludányi and Eszter Herner-Kovács, Minority Studies Special issue Trends and Directions of Kin-State Policies in Europe and Across the Globe, Lucidus Kiadó, 2014, 153–184.

with the state) to citizenship. There was a minor change to article 5 allowing an application for citizenship to be submitted with a Slovenian Embassy abroad.[97] The fifth paragraph, second sentence of article 10 was changed to read 'evidence of compliance with this requirement, the alleged cause of failure for the test shall be carried out by experts'. The legislation determined that a person residing in Slovenia, is only when that person is physically present on the territory. Additionally, it would also require a person to determine where the center of their interests would be (this would be assessed on the basis of that person's professional, economic, social and other ties, which indicate that the person and the Republic of Slovenia have a close and lasting connection). Article 13 was amended to allow the Ministry of Interior to have determination and jurisdiction on decisions of citizenship.[98] Moreover, article 27 set out the requirements for submitting an application of loss of citizenship, and a minor change was inserted to clarify the notification statement where the application may be submitted to either an Embassy abroad or the local Administrative Unit within Slovenia.[99] The changes largely focused on ensuring appropriate administrations of the laws by officials. It is argued that the laws for administering citizenship also contribute to national identity because all official must do so in a consistent approach as possible. The state cannot have an official in Maribor administer the laws differently to an official in Koper.

This was an interesting period, here Slovenia was embroiled in multiple court actions from former Yugoslav citizens being excluded from citizenship and made stateless. The dichotomy, or conflicting messages from Slovenia cannot be more stark. On the one hand they were further liberalizing their legal framework. On the other hand, they continued to exert the homogenous indemnity. The remaining minor amendments of 2002 focused on numbers and word changes. They do not directly relate to national identity, but they provide a complete understanding of the legislative change undertaken. The requirement for an individual to demonstrate they can provide a benefit to the state. Article 15, number '40' deleted the word 'or' and the number '41'. The 1st paragraph in article 16 the words 'set aside the decision of the words 'within three years after it is delivered'.The 2nd paragraph in article 18 the words 'a state administrative body responsible for defense matter' were replaced by 'the ministry responsible for defense matter'. In 22 article, the third paragraph, the words "a state administrative body responsible for social security" is replaced by "the ministry responsible for family and social affairs". In paragraph 27 of article 32 the words "a state administrative body responsible for internal affairs" was replaced by "the ministry responsible for internal affairs". Additionally, the words "a state administrative body competent for internal affairs" was replaced by "the Ministry of the Interior." The first paragraph of article 35, the words' internal

---

[97] Law on the Citizenship of the Republic of Slovenia, Official Gazette (ZDRS-OCT1) 7/2003. Article 12 replaced the word two with the word three.

[98] Ibid.

[99] Ibid, after the first paragraph, the second paragraph is added to read as follows: Statement of the notification referred to in the preceding paragraph may be filed with the embassy of the Republic of Slovenia abroad or in the administrative unit.

affairs bodies "shall be replaced with the word" police". In the second paragraph of article 36 the words 'internal affairs bodies was replaced with the word 'police'. In both article 37 and 44 the words 'administrative unit' replaced the words 'the interior competent authority of the municipality'. The number 40 was deleted the word 'and' as well as the number 41, in article 42. Article 43 the word 'competent administrative unit' replaced the words 'competent municipal body'. In article 46, the phrase 'a republican administrative body responsible for internal affairs' was replaced with 'The Minister of the Interior'. These changes had no effect on national identity, but clarified important provisions in the legislation to ensure the law was current and effective. The changes reflect the minor changes for the state to competently administer the citizenship laws of the state.

5.3 Part Two

5.3.1 2004–2018

Despite Slovenia becoming a member of the European Union in 2004, there was no requirement to amend its citizenship laws. Slovenia, had a lot to contend with since independence. The accession process for membership to the European Union had been running throughout the 1990s. Consequently, Slovenia was required to undertake a comprehensive law reform program across all policy areas that included, but not limited to, agriculture, environment, health, education, transport, financial and banking. Since the fall of Yugoslavia, Slovenians had experienced three separate currencies': the Yugoslav Dinar, Slovenian Tolar and the Euro.

The Prime Minister Janez Janša reinforced to Slovenian citizens (at home and abroad) Slovenia's past, its national identity and independence even though they were part of the European Union. He stated in celebrating Independence Day:

> Slovenia's autonomy was built over the course of centuries. The past was marked by Carantania, the Freising Monuments, the peasant uprisings, Trubar, the United Slovenia project, the national resistance against Fascism and Nazism, and the opposition to communism. Slovenia fought for religious freedom and resisted the attempts to denationalise literature classes in schools. The decision 14 years ago to independence was done so in the most democratic manner, through a plebiscite in which the whole of Slovenia's population expressed support for its establishment. The fall of the Berlin Wall was symbolic and a real milestone which enabled tectonic political and geostrategic shifts in Europe and the world at large. It ended the cold war and a year later on 1990 the parliamentary party and leadership of DEMOS, headed by Dr Jože Pučnick, seized the initiative of Dr Peter Jambrek and formulated a proposal for holding a referendum on an independent Slovenia...governed by the rule of law. Today Slovenes live in a time aspired to and predicted with such clairvoyance by our greatest poet France Prešeen in his poem Zdravljica, which became the national anthem. Since the time these words were written, the Slovene nation has undergone great and bloody trials. It has had to defend its origin, its land and its freedom in three wars, before its dream came true......[3]

The importance of this speech marked not only the historical connection of the development in the Slovenian identity over many centuries but also highlights the elements that form the current day Slovenian identity. The reference to Carantania, the Freising Monuments, the peasant uprisings, Trubar, the United Slovenia project go back well before Yugoslavia and independence in 1990. The speech acknowledged in the same way that Australia does, that, Slovenian's involvement in war and conflict did not go unrecognised, and what it means to be Slovene. It was beginning to form part of the national identity narrative. Importantly, the speech emphasises that by embracing democracy, the rule of law, the national anthem including national days all form part of what it means to be a Slovenian. Additionally, the speech noted the Slovenians at home and abroad (the diaspora) are both important to the identity of the state. The reference to Dr. Jože Pučnick and Dr. Peter Jambrek was a clear acknowledgement of the important work these two people have contributed to the formation of the current day national identity of Slovenia.

In the same year Slovenia adopted the Implementation of the Principle of Equal Treatment Act 2004[100] which coincided with membership to the European Union, and was the umbrella act in the field of non-discrimination. The legislation prohibits direct and indirect discrimination, harassment and victimisation. Apart from these principles being European Union norms, they would play a significant role in further protecting and enhancing the political participation of women in Slovenian political life. The economies of both Slovenia and Australia had done well from 2000 to 2004. Slovenia upon joining the European Union, subsequently inherited citizenship, immigration, rights and private international law of the Union. Both states continued to strengthen and retain their historical connection of the national identity while allowing their citizens to participate regionally and globally. However, the world was experiencing a different phase of conflict, there was a shift from the traditional notion of war between states to the rise of individuals taking action against citizens of other states. Terrorism was on the rise and Slovenia and Australia responded by strengthening their citizenship and immigration laws. This approach would continue through to 2018.

5.3.2 2005–2008

5.3.2.1 National Security

In 2005, the Australian citizenship laws would be amended again. The changes were a national security response to the terrorist events that occurred globally between 2000 and 2004. In 2002, Australia and Australians were directly affected by bombings that occurred in Bali, Indonesia, with many Australian lives lost. As a result, there was a significant security response by the Australian Government. The citizenship law was amended to require the collection, use and storage of personal

[100] Principle of Equal Treatment Act 2004, Official Gazette of the Republic of Slovenia 50/2004.

identifiers.[101] This was reaffirmed by the Prime Minister John Howard who announced the need to strengthen the state's terrorism laws and extend the waiting period for citizenship.[102] Australia took a cautious and restrictive approach that included measures to ensure a person applying for citizenship had basic knowledge of the English language, and increased the residential qualifying period from 2 years in the previous 5 years, to 3 years. It is argued that the government was expressing to its citizens, future citizens and immigrants that the English language was an important part of the state's identity. Additionally, the reference to Australia's values was an attempt to not only unite the people but also send a message to the amalgam of ethnic groups within Australia and abroad that the state has embraced certain values that must be adhered too. These values include, but not limited to, pulling together through adversity and mateship, along with its historical connection with Britain.

5.3.2.2 Multiculturalism

Domestically, Australia was grappling with multiculturalism. There were riots in Sydney which spread to other parts of the country, with people expressing their displeasure at the perception of some ethnic groups in the community not conforming to the Australian way. The distinction was made between people born in the country to those who were not (*'we grew here you flew here and go home'*). This attitude by some had seen the rise of xenophobic behavior creeping into the community.[103] Apart from identifying the lack of understanding from all sectors of the community in relation to the different cultural mix that makes up the Australian society, what stood out was the complex position government policy had taken. For instance, for more than 50 years Australia continued to open its doors to migrants, but at the same time hold onto its identity and historical connection to Britain. This balance will only continue in Australia as it allows large numbers of immigrants to enter and reside in the country annually.

More importantly, xenophobic behavior and race violence is not limited to Australia and has also been present across Europe and in smaller pockets of Slovenia. Xenophobic behavior in Slovenia has largely occurred in the workplace in the form of discrimination.[104] At a political level, it was played out towards the

---

[101] *Australian Citizenship Bill 2005 (Transitionals and Consequentials)*, Parliament of Australia, Department of Parliamentary Services, 2005, Nos 72–72, 1–19.

[102] Ann Palmer, Rosemary Bell, Angus Martin, Patrick O'Neill and Peter Prince, *Australian Citizenship Bill 2005 Australian Citizenship (Transitionals and Consequentials) Bill 2005,* Law and Bills Digest Section, Parliament of Australia, Department of Parliamentary Services, 2005, http://www.aph.gov.au/binaries/library/pubs/bd/2005-06/06bd072.pdf

[103] Due, C., Damien Rigs, D, (2008) *We Grew Here You Flew Here: Claims to Home in the Cronulla Riots*,, Colloquy text theory critique, Monash University, 1–5.

[104] European Union, Report on Racism and Xenophobia in Member States, European Union Agency for Fundamental Rights, 2007.

erasure peoples, through the courts and publicly. However, this may change with the huge influx of refugees into Slovenia and Europe in 2015 as a result of the Syrian conflict. The impact to 'other ethnic' groups have to national identity cannot be underestimated. Australia's traditional 'white' policy officially lasted for more than 50 years. However, with the increased acceptance of other nationalities, the national identity could be argued today, as being blended.

5.3.2.3 Adoption

Adoption, enables couples to establish a family, which is a right under European Union law. International adoption adds to the citizenry, and enables people from other countries and cultures to become an Australian citizen. Therefore, changes were made to take into account citizenship of people who were adopted in accordance with the Hague Convention on Intercountry Adoption.[105]

By 2006, the *Transitionals and Consequentials Bill 2006* largely applied amendments to other commonwealth legislation in Australia such as the *Australian Passports Act 2005 and Administrative Appeals Tribunal Act 1975* amongst others, to recognise the enactment of the *Australian Citizenship Act 2006.*[106] In an Australian Day address the Prime Minister stated:

> nations experience different levels of cultural diversity while having a dominant cultural pattern running through the. In the case of Australia, that dominant cultural pattern comprises of Judeo-Christian ethics, the progressive spirit of enlightenment and institutions and values of British political culture.[107]

Importantly, Australia while continually developing a national identity of its own, there was, and continues to be, a concerted effort to maintain and strengthen the historical values and political culture that had been inherited from Britain. Not only has this been reflected in the national policy discourse of the Australian Government since federation, but it is also reflected in the constitution and national laws of citizenship and immigration.

---

[105] Supplementary Explanatory Memorandum, House of Representatives, http://www.austlii.edu.au/au/legis/cth/bill_em/acacb2005598/memo_1.html

[106] Australian Citizenship (Transitionals and Consequentials) Bill 2006, House of Representatives, The Parliament of the Commonwealth of Australia. Other legislation amended included *Age Discrimination Act 2004, Air Navigation Act 1920, Australian Security Intelligence Organisation Act 1979, Migration Act 1958Commonwealth Electoral Act 1918 Commonwealth Serum Laboratories Act 1916, Consular Privileges and Immunities Act 1972, Crimes Act 1914, Criminal Code Act 1995, Diplomatic Privileges and Immunities Act 1967, Electronic Transactions Act 1999.*

[107] John Howard, *A Sense of Balance: the Australian Achievement in 2006*, Australia Day Address to the National Press Club, the Great Hall, Parliament House Canberra, 2006.

5.3.2.4 Slovenia

There were no major policy inclusions or exclusion for the citizenship laws of Slovenia in 2006.[108] In the same year a working group was established to identify changes to the naturalisation and clarify record keeping requirements.[109] Further minor amendments were undertaken, even though they did not directly reflect strengthening or enhancing national identity. However, it is important to outline these amendments to provide a complete understanding of the legislative change undertaken by the state. Article 4, paragraph 6 included 'that was not sentenced to a term of imprisonment of more than 3 months, or that he has not been given a suspended sentence of imprisonment with a probation longer than a year'. The 2nd point in the 4th paragraph was amended to read 'if the person has successfully completed a state approved program of secondary education in the Republic of Slovenia. The 4th point the dot was replaced by a semicolon, and the following was added 'if the person has completed primary or secondary school with Slovene language as instruction in areas inhabited by indigenous members of the Slovenian minority in neighboring countries'. The 5th paragraph, second sentence added the text to read 'evidence of compliance with this requirement, the alleged actual state of incapacity to perform the examination is carried out by experts. Costs incurred due to the implementation of this evidence, the burden of the person'. The minor changes to costs was to ensure the state would not be liable. The change for completion of primary school, was to ensure the person understood the Slovene language. Today, as it was upon independence Slovenia continues to value the language as one of its single most principles to retain its national identity.

5.3.2.5 Naturalisation

Natualisation is a pathway to citizenship in both states. By a state requiring a person to meet the requirements of their naturalisation process, it is the state expressing national identity. Article 11 guaranteed that a person who had applied for citizenship by naturalisation would do so, provided they had met the requirements set out in article 10. That is, the individual would need to be 18 years old and have been residing in Slovenia for 10 years (and 5 years prior to the submission of the application must be continuous). Additionally, the person was required to have a command of the Slovenian language, posed no security threat to the state and fulfilled their tax obligations.[110] Slovenia was imposing restrictive measures that excluded people from automatically obtaining citizenship. This policy approach strengthened Slovenia's national identity by ensuring individuals had a longer stay on the terri-

---

[108] Law on the Citizenship of the Republic of Slovenia, Official Gazette (ZDRS-D) 127/2006.

[109] Felicita Medved, EUDO Citizenship Observatory, *Country Report: Slovenia*, 2013, 20–27, http://eudo-citizenship.eu/admin/?p=file&appl=countryProfiles&f=2013-24-Slovenia.pdf

[110] Law on the Citizenship of the Republic of Slovenia, Official Gazette (ZDRS-D) 127/2006.

tory, which translated to a better understanding of what it meant to be Slovenian. Article 11, 1st paragraph added a new second, third and fourth paragraphs to include 'Against the assurance of the preceding paragraph may be filed'.

Before deciding on the naturalisation of an alien who submit proof of eligibility of 2 the first paragraph of 10 of the Act, the competent authority shall re-examine the conditions of 6 and 8 the first paragraph of 10 of the Act. If the customer does not meet the conditions set out in the preceding paragraph, the application may be rejected. The 1st paragraph of article 12 was amended to read the competent authority may, if it is in line with the national interests, at the discretion adopt the citizenship of the Republic of Slovenia, Slovenian emigrants and their descendants to the fourth generation in a straight line, if you reside in the Republic of Slovenia for at least one year. The 3rd paragraph amended the word 'two' and replaced this with the word 'three', and at the conclusion of the paragraph the following was inserted 'it is considered that the continuous residence requirement is satisfied, even if the person is not physically present in the territory of the Republic of Slovenia for reasons which on its part or on the side of the spouses are not considered terminating the stay'. In the fourth paragraph the words 'condition of 2, 10 points Article 'the words' and the condition of continuous residence in the preceding paragraph'. Articles 27a, 27B, 27c, 27d, all relate to an application being submitted for citizenship and the administrative processes of how and where that application can be submitted (whether abroad or to an Administrative Unit). Additionally, 27B provided that a decision made by the administrative unit can be reviewed by the Ministry of Interior. It is argued, in part, the changes strengthened national identity by clarifying the conditions in relation to naturalisation.

5.3.2.6 Central Registry

Slovenia had established a central registry to record citizenship applications. The registry enabled the state to monitor the numbers of citizenship from the time of independence. Article 30 was changed to require personal information in relation to an individual's citizenship to be collected by central registry. This includes the identity number, gender, permanent or temporary residence status, occupation, schooling, citizenship by naturalisation name and date of birth. Additionally, article 31changes related to information on citizenship for citizens of the Republic of Slovenia is collected and further processed in the base register in accordance with the purpose of collection and further processing of personal data in the base register under the provisions of the law governing the register. Article 37, the amendments related to the keeping of records by the Ministry of Interior and Administrative Unit in relation to citizenship obtained by naturalisation, or on the basis of international treaties. Article 41, the number 23 was replaced with the number 36. Article 43, the words 'birth'was replaced with the words 'the register', the word 'Registers' but by 'regulating the entry in the register'. Article 44, the emended article related to the issuing of a certificate of citizenship by the state no matter where the person was resident. The changes continued to focus on unifying Slovenes[111] that could demonstrate an active link to the Republic by being part of an association or a Slovenian language school.

5.3.2.7 National Council of the Republic of Slovenia

In 2007, the National Council of the Republic of Slovenia which represents local interests lobbied for the citizenship laws to be changed. The National Council is the representative body for professional and local interests and articles 91 to 101 of the Slovenian Constitution outlines the Council composition, power, election, decision making, immunity and rules of procedure. The National Council, consisting of 40 members includes the upper chamber of the parliament who represents the social, economic, professional, local and territorial interests of the state.[112] The Council was established to neutralize political parties involved in the legislative process in the National Assembly.[113] The rules and procedures established by the National Council assigns matters and decides on jurisdictional disputes between the National Council Commission.[114] As a result, article13a was finally repealed,[115] which allowed an individual over the age of 18 to obtain citizenship by naturalisation. However, this was on the condition that the individual was of Slovenian origin, having one parent who was Slovene. Additionally, the parent must have had their citizenship renounced, dismissed or was no longer valid due to historical circumstances such as the breakup of the former Yugoslavia.[116] The proposal was as a result of discussions at the National Assembly's Committee of Interior Affairs, Public Administration and Justice from the Slovenian diaspora in Argentina, Australia, Brazil and Canada. The diaspora put forward the amendment, which was promised by Slovene politicians.[117] The important contribution the diaspora community has played in strengthening the Slovenian identity cannot be underestimated. It reinforces the notion that individuals who had most likely migrated from the former Yugoslavia as a result of WW II wanted to retain a connection with the homeland.

---

[111] Official Gazette of the Republic of Slovenia, No. 45/2010.

[112] Ibid.

[113] Ibid.

[114] Štrus, D, (2009) *Poslovnik Državega sveta s komentarjem,* The National Council of State, Slovenia.

[115] Law on the Citizenship of the Republic of Slovenia, Official Gazette (ZDRS-OCT2) 24/2007.

[116] Ibid, the Government of the Republic of Slovenia shall preliminarily state their opinion on the acquisition of citizenship of the Republic of Slovenia pursuant to the preceding paragraph.

[117] Medved, F EUDO Citizenship Observatory, *Country Report: Slovenia*, 2013, 20–27, http://eudo-citizenship.eu/admin/?p=file&appl=countryProfiles&f=2013-24-Slovenia.pdf

5.3.2.8 Citizenship Testing

In 2006 the Australian Government released a discussion paper, Australian Citizenship: Much more than a ceremony, which sought community view on whether citizenship testing should be implemented. The paper emphasised the importance of citizenship as being the single most unifying principle that lies at the heart of the national identity.[118] Citizenship testing was identified as a way to promote the values of Australia and what it means to be Australian. The test consists of 20 multiple-choice questions drawn randomly from a pool of confidential questions that focused on the responsibilities and privileges of Australian citizenship.[119] The policy approach also linked testing to assist immigrants to integrate into the Australian community. This was done by expanding the knowledge and values of Australia and its identity.[120] Integration was considered to be easier where a person has an understanding of their responsibilities and the privileges that are afforded to them by having Australian citizenship. Furthermore, it is argued testing is also exclusionary because those who do not pass the test are potentially excluded from citizenship. Subsequently, the *Australian Citizenship Amendment (Citizenship Testing) Bill 2007* was introduced. Section 19 was changed to require an applicant in order to meet the eligibility requirements in s21(2) must have successfully completed a citizenship test. Section 21 of the Act was amended to reflect and ensure an individual successfully completes the citizenship test before submitting an application. A pass mark of 50% was required to determine whether the individual had successfully completed the test. This inclusion ensured the individual had a basic understanding of the English language.[121] Section 23A was a new subsection that was introduced to enable the Minister to approve in writing the citizenship test. Subsection 40(1) was replaced and extended the power in section 40 to also apply to a person who has sought to sit a test approved in a determination under new section 23A. Technical and consequential amendments were made to ss40 (3) by omitting 'paragraph (1)(b)' & (4) omitted 'paragraph (1)(c) which was substituted with paragraph (1)(e). New subsection 46(1A) provided that the fee prescribed by the regulations for applications made under section 21 of the Act, in relation to persons who have sat a test or tests approved in a determination under new section 23A. This new section allows for some or all of the costs of a person sitting a test or tests to be recovered. New subsection 53(2) provides that the Minister's power to delegate any of the Minister's powers or functions under the Act or regulations made under the Act does not apply to the Minister's function under new subsection 23A(1) to

[118] Australian Government, *Citizenship: Much more than a ceremony*, discussion paper considering the merits of introducing a formal citizenship test, 2006, 2–5.

[119] Kevin Andrews, *Second Reading Speech*, Minister for Immigration and Citizenship, Australian Citizenship Amendment (Citizenship Testing) Bill 2007, House of Representatives, Debates, 30 May 2007, 2–3.

[120] Australian Citizenship Amendment (Citizenship Testing) Bill 2007, Explanatory Memorandum, House of Representatives, the Parliament of the Australian Commonwealth of Australia, 1–6.

[121] Ibid.

approve a test by written determination for the purposes of subsection 21(2A). These changes are administrative and allow the government to effectively manage the test. The test is seen as an important part of what it means to become and Australian citizen. The test enables the person to understand the values and identity of Australia.

The introduction of the citizenship test has in the eyes of Stephen Castles *etal* undermined the Australian policy of multiculturalism.[122] However, and arguably, citizenship testing has become and important part of Australia expressing a small part of its identity. That is, it requires a person to engage with and understand a small component of what it means to be Australia, and therefore, could be seen to strengthen multiculturalism overall. It allows a person from a different ethnic background to not only be aware of their own ethnic values but also Australia's. This can only benefit all. Australia has embraced an amalgam of ethnic groups that form part of Australian society. The diversity that Australia had become was summed up as a nation where 45% of the population had been born overseas, with more than 300 languages spoken from 230 different countries.[123] The Prime Minister, John Howard stated:

> citizenship provides an opportunity for people to maximise their participation in society and to make a commitment to Australia's common values, which includes the respect of the freedom and dignity of the individual, our support for democracy and commitment to the rule of law.[124]

In reinforcing the Australian position towards national identity, the Minister for Immigration Kevin Andrews stated:

> [t]he material which will form the basis of the citizenship test will highlight the common values we share, as well as something of our history and our background.[125]

The changes to the citizenship law made it more difficult for individuals to obtain citizenship in Australia. It is my view that the Prime Minister and Minister for Immigration and Citizenship were also sending a clear message and reference to Australia's historical past that includes the connection to Britain, but also the multicultural society Australia had become. Moreover, by the end of 2007 similar themes and approaches taken by Australia and Slovenia in the development of their citizenship laws had emerged. The states are different and their identities are different, but language, legal status, unification, integration, participation by men and women had all formed part of citizenship law. More importantly, the most notable

[122] Castles, S., Vasta, E., Ozkul, D, (2012) *The Internal Dynamics of Migration Processes and their Consequences for Australian Government Migration Policies*, Working Paper for the Department of Immigration and Citizenship, University of Sydney, 1–16.

[123] Laurie Ferguson, *Diversity of Australia's People*, Media Release, Parliament House, 26 November 2008, www.minister.immi.gov.au/parlsec/media/mesia-release/2008

[124] Nolan, M., Rubenstein, K, (2009) *Citizenship and Identity in Diverse Societies,* Humanities Research, Vol XV. No 1. 29.

[125] Kevin Andrews, Minister for Immigration and Citizenship, Second Reading Speech, Debates, House of Representatives, 30 May 2007, 3.

difference had been Slovenia putting the past socialist system behind them and embracing democracy. Additionally, Slovenians were now part of the European Union. Australia, however, had begun to think about expanding its citizenship.

5.3.3 2008–2013

With an election looming in 2008, the ongoing debate surrounding citizenship in Slovenia continued. Felicita Medved noted that there was a shift in political debate regarding citizenship. Up until 2008, the debate focused on the erased people. But in 2008 the debate shifted to include active citizenship.[126] Active citizenship promotes participatory democracy by focusing on the integration of foreigners.[127] The political discourse began focusing on the greater inclusion and cohesion of the states citizenry and newcomers. Additionally, there was also a need to continue strengthening and reinforcing the collective identity of what it means to be Slovenian.[128] Thus, it is argued that 2008 was the start of Slovenia shifting its approach to citizenship, from consolidating the legal status of Slovenians within the new state, to integrating and being more accepting of foreigners.

2008 was also an important milestone for Slovenia. They held the European Union presidency[129] and continued the process of integration by meeting the requirements of the European community.[130] Slovenia's return to Europe had been smooth when compared to other the former Yugoslav Republics.[131] Croatia for example, only became a member of the European Union in 2013. None of the other former Yugoslav Republics are close to becoming full members today. Croatia finalised its accession negotiations on 30 June 2011, and signed the Treaty of Accession in Brussels on 9 December 2011. This was followed by approval in the national referendum on 22 January 2012. Croatia completed the ratification process on 4 April 2012. Entry into force and accession of Croatia to the European Union took effect on 1 July 2013.

---

[126] Medved, F EUDO Citizenship Observatory, *Country Report: Slovenia*, 2013, 20–27, http://eudo-citizenship.eu/admin/?p=file&appl=countryProfiles&f=2013-24-Slovenia.pdf

[127] Ibid.

[128] Ibid.

[129] European Parliament, Slovenia takes over EU presidency: prime minister addresses European Parliament, http://www.europarl.europa.eu/sides/getDoc.do?pub

[130] Jaks, J, (2010) *EU enlargement and current adaptation challenges*, Central European Journal of International and Security Studies, 125–134.

[131] Juncos, A, (2005) *The EU's post-conflict Intervention in Bosnia and Herzegovina: (re) Integrating the Balkans and (re) Inventing the EU?* South East European Politics.

5.3.3.1 Australia

In today's globalised world countries are wanting to hold their citizenry closer to the state.[132] This was no more evident than in Australia when in 2009 the Australian Government established a committee to review the Australian citizenship test. The aim of the review was to assist government in examining the content and operation of the test as well as ensuring effective pathways were in place for foreigners to become an Australian citizen.[133] The review found that the test was intimidating and discriminatory and needed to be rewritten in basic English.[134] It is argued that with the various different ethnic groups arriving in, and resident in Australia the ability for new migrants to fully understand English may never be realised. This is because upon arrival most seek out their respective community groups and put simply may never need to converse in English. However, it is argued that Australia continues to use English as its working language and is part of the fabric of the modern day Australian identity.

The changes introduced a requirement for those applying for citizenship to sit the test within a specified period of time. A citizenship course was introduced to provide applicants with a chance to understand the test and types of questions asked. To obtain citizenship by conferral an applicant must be under the age of 18.[135] The changes to s19 removed the word 'permanent' to ensure consistency with ss21(3)(d) and 21(3) in relation to physical and mental incapacity. It required a person to take a test and have a basic knowledge of the English language. Section 19G also included consequential changes to s21. The purpose of the new subsection 21(2A) was to remove the 'requirement that a person must sit and successfully complete a citizenship test before making an application' and require the person to sit the test within a certain period of time. Section 21(3B) was also inserted to account for those individuals incapable of understanding the contents of an application, as a result of trauma received outside of Australia. Section 26 (1)(ba)[136] was amended to provide an exemption to sit the citizenship test and make a pledge for those individuals that had suffered from torture, trauma, a mental or physical incapacity. A fee

[132] Bechhofer, F., McCrone, D, (2009), *National Identity, Nationalism and Constitutional Change*, Palgrave McMillan, 1–10.

[133] Commonwealth of Australia, *Moving Forward Improving Pathways to citizenship: A Report by the Australian Citizenship Test Review Committee*, 2008, http://www.citizenship.gov.au/_pdf/moving-forward-report.pdf

[134] Ibid.

[135] Australian Citizenship Amendment (Citizenship Test Review and Other Measures) Bill 2009, Explanatory Memorandum, The Parliament of the Commonwealth of Australia, Senate, 2008–2009, 1–3.

[136] Section 26(1)(ba), Australian Citizenship Amendment (Citizenship Test Review and Other Measures) Bill 2009, Explanatory Memorandum, The Parliament of the Commonwealth of Australia, Senate, 2008–2009.

was now required to be paid by the individual sitting the test.[137] These changes were largely administrative.

Citizenship in Australia had turned 60 in 2009. It was an opportunity for all Australians, whether citizens by birth or by choice, to understand the role Australian citizenship plays in building a strong harmonious and unified nation.[138] The approach taken by government was not to impede or jeopardise those individuals that were physically or mentally incapacitated from becoming an Australian citizen. Political participation[139] at the highest levels of government in Australia would be recongised and be a momentous moment for women. Both the Australian Prime Minister and Australian Governor-General would be both women (Julia Gillard and Quentin Bryce). Slovenia had not had a woman as prime minister of the state since independence. A year later, in 2010, the Prime Minister Kevin Rudd expressed the importance of the ANZACs as part of the identity of the country. Rudd stated:

> All nations are shaped by their memories and their stories, by their triumphs, tragedies, myths and legends. For Australia, our identity has been etched deeply by what we call ANZAC and nearly a century on, ANZAC has occupied a sacred place in the nation's soul, and shapes what we do in the world.[140]

The importance of this speech reinforced the notion that in Australia the military plays and important role in shaping, maintaining and strengthening the national identity. Even though the speech had nothing to do with citizenship, the words 'shaped by their history' were not only directed at the ANZAC history but also the ongoing history of Australia before, during and after federation. This is an area of difference between Slovenia and Australia. Slovenia does not appear to attach the same level of an identity and value to its current or past military. The only reference to military appears at the time of breaking away from the former Yugoslavia, when Slovenia won the ten-day war.

5.3.3.2 Defence

Niether the *Australian Citizenship Amendment (Defence Service Requirement) Bill 2012* and *Australian Citizenship Amendment (Defence Families) Bill 2012* had any impact on citizenship. In summary, there was no major policy inclusions as a result of these Bills other than minor changes or words in s21 and substituting s23 respectively.[141] Sections 21(2)(c), 21(3)(c) and 21(4)(d) omitted 'has completed relevant

---

[137] Section 46 (1A) Australian Citizenship Amendment (Citizenship Test Review and Other Measures) Bill 2009, Explanatory Memorandum, The Parliament of the Commonwealth of Australia, Senate, 2008–2009.

[138] Chris Evans, *Australia Celebrates Australian Citizenship Day*, Minister for Immigration and Citizenship, 2009, www.minister.immi.gov.au/media/media-release/2009

[139] Lister, R, (1997) *Feminist Perspectives*, Macmillan: Basingstoke, 196.

[140] Anzac Day 2010 National Ceremony Commemorative Address, Kevin Rudd, Prime Minister of Australia.

[141] Australian Citizenship Amendment (Defence Service Requirement) Bill 2012.

defence service' to include 'satisfies the defence service requirements'. Further amendments were included to the Australian laws in 2013. The recognition of defence in national identity is Australia dates back to the First World War.

5.3.3.3 Ministerial Discretion

Following vigorous lobbying from Cricket Australia, whereby there was political intervention (a Minister) to allow a former asylum seeker to obtain citizenship and represent Australia in cricket.[142] The change resulted in the legislation being strengthened in relation to individuals engaged in employment that is beneficial to Australia. Section 22A(9) allows an individual to become an Australian citizen where at the discretion of the Minister in accordance with s22A(1) where there is an administrative error in the assessment of an application for citizenship. Section 24(2) was changed to avoid the split in decision making in relation to an application for citizenship between the Minister and the Minister's delegate.[143] The common thread of Australia's national identity has been summarised as a 'common commitment to Australian civic values of democracy, the rule of law, respect for the rights of individual men and women and a deep intuitive sense of a fair go'.[144] Arguably, Australia and Australian's typically being sports lovers had little concern over the political interference on this occasion. However, had the asylum seeker was not a good sports person that had the necessary skills and talent to represent the country, the outcome would most likely have been very different.

5.3.3.4 Birth Certificate

The United Nations in 2012 criticised Australia for its implementation of the Convention on the Rights of the Child.[145] Citizenship can be acquired by birth in the territory of a state and arguably represents the private side of citizenship. The registration of a birth provides the individual with a certificate.[146] The birth certificate enables a citizen to be fully active within the community and state. For instance, to obtain a passport and travel abroad, the individual must be able to produce their

[142] Glenday, J *Fawad Ahmed asylum case: Spin-bowler 'got special treatment' in borderline citizenship case*, 2014, http://www.abc.net.au/news/2014-01-30/documents-suggest-fawad-ahmed-asylum-case-was-borderline/5225808

[143] Australian Citizenship (Special Residence Requirements) Bill 2013, Explanatory Memorandum. The Parliament of the Commonwealth of Australia, House of Representatives, 2013.

[144] Malcom Turnbull, *My Australia: How it has Changed*, Australian Financial Review, 2013.

[145] Article 7, 8, 13–17, 19 and 37, Convention on the Rights of the Child 1989, Treaty Series, vol. 1577, p. 3. United National CRC/C.AUS/CO/4, General 28, August 2012.

[146] Birth, deaths and marriages, Victoria Australia, http://www.bdm.vic.gov.au/home/births/register+a+birth. Birth Registration Slovenia, https://e-uprava.gov.si/e-uprava/en/zivljenjskeSituacijeStran.euprava?dogodek.id=12594

birth certificate. The same applies to gaining full access to a bank and other government services. Therefore, this restrictive measure has been identified by the United Nations as impacting on the citizenship of these people. It is argued that those individuals who do not receive registration of birth are only partly receiving citizenship of the state. They are not full citizens and able to fully participate in the community, even though their parents might be. Since the report was tabled the Governments of each of the States has undertaken their own review.

In Victoria, a state of Australia, there were a number of recommendations to improve the registration and availability of birth registrations and certificates for aboriginal people. Nevertheless, this is another example of the lack of recognition and effort by consecutive governments across Australia towards the aboriginal people. This issue is a very important component of active citizenship and full participation of these people within the community. The lack of registration affects the daily lives of individuals. It is argued that such a restriction does not allow a citizen to be a full and active participant in the community. It is also argued this is discriminatory in nature, and restricts people's full access to basic rights and participation in society beyond the border of the nation state. State, Territory and Australian governments should undertake a review of this practice every 5 years. A similar review was undertaken recently in Slovenia and found there were no cases of births not being registered.[147] Historically, there appears to have been issues with the Rom people in Slovenia, however in more recent times this group of people have also registered all births. It is argued a citizen can only be a full and active citizen when they are able to participate in the community. Any element of the law or government practice that excludes active citizenship, dilutes citizenship and in turn national identity. The exclusion of citizens this way further highlights the discriminatory measures states will take against certain groups in the community.

5.3.4 2013–2018

5.3.4.1 European Member States [Buying Citizenship]

By 2013 the traditional means of obtaining citizenship by birth, descent or naturalisation had begun to be tested. Emerging from Europe, in November 2013, Malta offered citizenship at a price €650,000.00.[148] A month later in December 2013, the Maltese government increased the price to €1,150,000 million and required investment in real estate and government bonds. The Maltese government settled on an 'Individual Investor Programme' that requires a person to make a contribution to the government's national development and social fund, of €650,000 for the application, €25,000 for a spouse and minors, and

---

[147] Ending Childhood Statelessness: A Study on Slovenia, Working Paper 08/15, European Network on Statelessness, 2015, 18–19.

[148] Shachar, A Bauböck, R, (2014) *Should citizenship be for sale?* European University Institute, European Union Democracy Observatory on Citizenship, 1–20.

€50,000 for a person over 55 years old. The individual must also purchase €150,000 of government approved securities.[149] In exchange, the person obtains citizenship and a passport (enabling them to also become a European citizen). This is a highly debatable area of citizenship law and policy and it did not come without criticism. The Vice President of the European Commission Viviane Reding stated in 2014 that citizenship should not be up for sale.[150] In her view citizenship should only be issued to a person where there is a genuine link or genuine connection to the country in question.[151] My view supports the European Commission and suggests that allowing states to put a price on citizenship will exclude many who do not have the financial resources to pay such a high price.

The problem with member states going it alone and implementing these types of programs, is that by default they are affording these people the same rights as other European citizens. For instance, a person could buy their way into Malta and move freely[152] along with their family anywhere throughout the Union. Furthermore, the precedent being set for other nations across the world could potentially result in further dividing citizens of a state and nations. The balance between economic advancement of the state and citizenship needs to be measured against the long term impact of such a program to the nation state and its citizens. Conversely, those who invest in the state have a positive impact by providing economic opportunity to the citizens and residents. Australian states have also established similar investment (visas) schemes that enable a person to effectively buy citizenship.

5.3.4.2 Slovenia

In 2013 and 2014, Slovenia did not undertake any legislative change in relation to citizenship. However, another milestone had been reached in Slovenia with the appointment of Alenka Bratušek as the first female Prime Minister of Slovenia, since independence. Her term extended from 20 March 2013 to 18 September 2014. At the conclusion of Alenka Bratušek's reign of Prime Minister, Miroslav Cerar was elected to the position. On Independence and Unity Day 2014, Cerar asserted the importance of the national identity, stating:

> that one of the brightest eras in Slovenia's history was at the time of independence, where the people were proud of the national identity and joyful in self-determination and establishing a new state. Slovenians decided to establish a democratic country and the

[149] Malta Individual Investor Programme, http://malta-citizenship.info/individual-investor-program-faq.html#IIP-GRP

[150] Reding, V *Plenary Session debate of the European Parliament on 'EU citizenship for sale'*, Strasbourg European Parliament Plenary, 15 January 2014, *http://www.europarl.europa.eu/plenary/en/newgsasearch.html*

[151] Ibid.

[152] Article 21, Treaty on the Functioning of the European Union, Official Journal of the European Union C 326.

expressed will of the citizens was the political, legal and moral foundation of independence.[153]

Importantly, the speech referenced the national identity of the state and its citizens to their historical past, in the same way as Australia continues to do so with Britain. Slovenia makes the connection to its independence. Independence marked the transition from socialism to democracy, something which Slovenians had been pushing for in the lead up to 1990 and 1991.

5.3.4.3 Citizens Abroad

In 2014, Australia began to look more broadly at regulating the activities of citizens and residents abroad, from a security perspective. It is argued that the postnational concept of citizenship has been expanded by Australia with the introduction of the *Counter Terrorism Legislation Amendment [Foreign Fighters] Bill 2014* into the Australian Parliament. Furthermore, the state has also extended the notion of what its citizens should be from historically shaping their behavior through rights law and policy to understanding and living the national identity. Thus, the role citizenship now has within a state has gone beyond a legal status of inclusion and exclusion, to a demographic tool that shapes the way citizens are to think about the state and the broader community.

Australia had taken the concept one step further to regulating the activities of its citizens when abroad. The new laws prevent a person from travelling to areas that have been declared by the Australian Government as areas where citizens or permanent residents cannot attend due to the presence of terrorist organizations.[154] Even though the new legislation does not revoke or cancel a person's citizenship or residence status, they may lose their right to travel outside, or, re-enter Australia in the future. The new law also creates an offence for those who advocate and promote terrorism. This approach demonstrates that government is expanding the field of regulation to activities of its citizens while abroad. Slovenia has not established similar laws to regulate its citizen's movements abroad in the same way as Australia.

---

[153] Speech by the Prime Minister Cerar on the occasion of Independence and Unity Day: 'Slovenia must wake up and start building', http://www.kpv.gov.si/nc/en/press_centre/news/article/252/7604/

[154] Counter-Terrorism Legislation Amendment (Foreign Fighters) Bill 2014, Second Reading Speech, 24 September 2014, Senator George Brandis Commonwealth of Australia Parliamentary Debates.

5.3.4.4 Australia's Attitude Towards National Identity

Jill Sheppard released a report on the 'Australia's Attitude Towards National Identity' that identified the ability to speak English as an important to what it means to be Australian.[155] It identified that language plays an important role in national identity. Shepard also stated that other measures of what it meant to be Australian included citizenship, respect for political institutions and the law. The report reinforces the overall argument presented throughout the book that citizenship underpins, contributes to and strengthens national identity.

5.3.4.5 Terrorism

The rise of terrorism saw governments including Australia respond in a number of ways. In May 2015, the Australian Government has been debating whether citizenship should be renounced if the person can be linked to terrorist activities.[156] There are members of government that want to apply this proposal to those who hold single citizenship of Australia.[157] Other members of the Australian Government want the proposal to only apply to those people holding dual citizenship.[158] The new proposals have ignited constitutional debate within the Australian Government Solicitors Office. On 12 June 2015, the Solicitor General declared the proposed new laws (bill) unconstitutional, because the new powers would be provided directly to the discretion of the minister and declare a person guilty without having judicial review.[159] Only 5 days later on 17 June 2015, a senior member of the Cabinet of the Australian Government stated that the proposed changes to the citizenship laws should not be supported if they erode the rule of law or contravene the separation of powers doctrine within the constitution.[160] The ministerial discretion that may be provided as a result of the changes to citizenship have been viewed as going too far,

---

[155] Sheppard, J, (2015) Australian A*ttitudes Towards National Identity: Citizenship, Immigration and Tradition*, Australian Centre for Applied Social Research Methods, ANU College of Arts and Social Sciences, Report No 18. 1–15.

[156] Sydney Morning Herald Sun, Cabinet revolt over Tony Abbott and Peter Dutton plan to strip Australians of citizenship, http://www.smh.com.au/federal-politics/political-news/cabinet-revolt-over-tony-abbott-and-peter-dutton-plan-to-strip-australians-of-citizenship-20150526-gh9q8y.html

[157] James Massola, The Age Newspaper, *Citizenship Compromise*, 2 June 2015, page 8.

[158] Dual-national Jihadis risk Australian citizenship, SBS Television, http://www.sbs.com.au/news/article/2015/05/21/dual-national-jihadis-risk-australian-citizenship

[159] Abbott Government hits legal hurdle over bid to strip suspected terrorists of citizenship, http://www.msn.com/en-au/news/australia/abbott-government-hits-legal-hurdle-over-bid-to-strip-suspected-terrorists-of-citizenship/ar-BBl1tnv?ocid=SKY2DHP

[160] Malcolm Turnbull breaks ranks on citizenship, declaring constitution cannot be compromised, http://www.msn.com/en-au/news/australia/malcolm-turnbull-breaks-ranks-on-citizenship-declaring-constitution-cannot-be-compromised/ar-BBlcEwt?ocid=SKY2DHP

without a conviction recorded against the person who may be stripped of their citizenship.[161]

On 25 June 2015, the *Australian Citizenship Amendment (Allegiance to Australia) Bill 2015*[162] was introduced into the Australian Parliament for the first time. The Bill introduces three ways that a citizen of Australia can have their citizenship renounced.[163] These include where the person acts inconsistently with their allegiance to Australia by engaging in specified terrorist-related conduct, or where the individual fights for or is in the service of a declared terrorist organization, and where the individual is convicted of a terrorist offence.

The proposed amendments are only designed to capture those individuals who hold dual citizenship. Furthermore, the Bill links the offences to the Commonwealth Criminal Code, whereby the Minister can make a decision to renounce citizenship on the grounds of public interest. In this circumstance it would involve those engaged in terrorist activities, providing or receiving training, directing terrorist activities, recruitment of individuals to undertake terrorist activities, and financing and engaging in foreign incursions.[164]

On 24 July 2015, the Commonwealth Ombudsman, Colin Neave, entered the public debate stating that the proposal to strip dual citizens of their Australian citizenship is a legal fiction and could result in people being detained long term.[165] Neave is concerned that the Bill does not outline or clearly define what standard an official would use to make a judgment as to what constituted conduct that (the) (person's conduct) was (in fact) likened to terrorist activities (planning, operation or assistance).[166] The criticism from these laws were no only limited to within government. Kim Rubenstein argues that using citizenship to deal with this issue is inappropriate and would create division among Australians.[167] Therefore, citizenship is a 'secure status that affirms a sense of national cohesion and inclusion.[168] This is an important point because, similar to European and Slovenian citizenship, citizenship in Australia has also evolved to bring the community together. Australia does not need laws that divide citizens, but rather, laws that continue to unify the citizenry. Slovenia has not presented similar legislative controls on its citizens to the Slovenian Parliament. Slovenia should consider adopting a similar approach to Australia.

[161] Ibid.

[162] Irving, I., Thwaites, R, (2015) *Australian Citizenship Amendment (Allegiance to Australia) Bill 2015 (Cth).* Public Law Review, 143–149.

[163] Australian Citizenship Amendment (Allegiance To Australia) Bill 2015, The Parliament of the Commonwealth of Australia, House of Representatives, Explanatory Memorandum, 2015, 2.

[164] Ibid.

[165] Hasham, N, (July 2015) *Citizenship strip plan rests on legal fiction*, The Age, 4.

[166] Ibid.

[167] Yaxley, L *Citizenship expert, Kim Rubenstein, questions PM's claim potential terrorists given 'benefit of the doubt'*, The World Today, http://www.abc.net.au/news/2015-02-17/expert-questions-tony-abbotts-citizenship-security-claims/6129248

[168] Ibid.

In 2017, introduced a raft of changes to the citizenship laws that would require increasing the residence requirement to a minimum of 4 years' permanent residence, with no more than 1 year spent outside Australia. While not going back 100 years to a dictation test, one of the proposal is to require a person to successfully complete a separate English language test. The government's position is that applicants will need to demonstrate English language listening, speaking, reading and writing skills. They also want to strengthen the Australian values statement to include reference to allegiance to Australia and require applicants to undertake to integrate into and contribute to the Australian community. The test would be further strengthened by including Australian values, privileges and responsibilities.

Moreover, the current pledge would be extended to aged 16 years and over for all streams of citizenship including citizenship by descent, adoption and resumption. The aim was to enhance social cohesion throughout the Australian community, and assist in integrated newcomers. However, as at January 2019, these proposals had not been approved by the federal parliament. Throughout 2017, citizenship became a political football once again, when it was found that a number of politicians who were elected to the Australian parliament had dual citizenship. A number of politicians were referred to the Australian High Court for review. The Australian High Court[169] ruled and reinforced that section 44 of the Australian constitution is clear and requires those who are elected to the Australian Parliament, not to be dual citizens. However, this had little impact on multiculturalism and social cohesion in Australia. Rather, the case indirectly reinforced Australia as inheriting its legal system from the British, and that the 1901 constitution provides the foundation and identity of what Australia's society is today.

5.4 Conclusion & Similarities

There are many similarities between Slovenia and Australia in the ongoing development of the respective national identities and citizenship laws. The multidimensional approach taken by both states has seen citizenship rise beyond a mere legal status, to be used as a tool for unification, integration, social cohesion, political participation, rights, maintaining a connection (registration and certification) with a state, postnational, civic virtue, universal, and a state directing the citizens to embrace its values. This chapter has confirmed the legislative changes untaken by

[169] High Court of Australia 27 October 2017 in the matter of Questions Referred to the Court of Disputed Returns Pursuant To Section 372 of the Commonwealth Electoral Act 1918 (Cth), Concerning Senator The Hon Matthew Canavan, Mr. Scott Ludlam, Ms. Larissa Waters, Senator Malcolm Roberts, The Hon Barnaby Joyce MP, Senator The Hon Fiona Nash and Senator nick Xenophon [2017] HCA 45

both states has been inclusive, exclusive, postnational, economic, multicultural and Ministerial.

The exclusive has seen both states require a knowledge of the language. In the case of Australia this have been through citizenship testing. In Slovenia, to be an active citizen one must be able to converse (verbally and in writing) in Slovene. More importantly, this extended to also include restricting dual citizenship to those individuals that can prove a direct line of ascendants to Slovenia through family. Slovenia has not fully liberalized its dual citizenship laws in the same way as Australia. The exclusive approach adopted by Slovenia denying former Yugoslav citizens resident in Slovenia at the time of its break up, citizenship. Today, Australia has taken the principle of exclusiveness to a new level. Australia not only excludes non-citizens, but where it is proved its own citizens are a threat to national security they may lose their citizenship.

Australia and Slovenia have both adopted a postnational or multinational (liberal) policy approach to dual citizenship, although differently. The acceptance of dual citizenship appeared to be a balancing act for both states in a time when security was high on the agenda of government. The states were tightening their respective citizenship laws, at the same time loosening them to allow their citizens to participate, with ease, globally.

Both Slovenia and Australia undertook reforms of their respective migration programs, at the same time as reforming their citizenship laws. It is also argued that migration and dual citizenship constitutes the inclusive. Interestingly, Ministerial intervention formed part of the legislative reforms in both Australia and Slovenia. In Slovenia this extended to the management and continual exclusion of former Yugoslav citizens. At the same time, they were considering and meeting the needs of its diaspora located in other countries. Yet, in Australia an inclusionary approach was adopted to allow the person to represent the country in sport.

Arguably, the development and reform program undertaken by both states has been complex and there has been a need to balance a number of different and competing policy agendas. Nonetheless, what can be confirmed is that the reform programs have to some extent not only contributed to national identity, but also, the legislative changes have reinforced nationalist political agendas. In some cases the amendments did not directly relate to national identity, however, it was important that they be discussed to highlight the extent of legislative change.

However, it must be noted that both states were, in the beginning of the 1990s largely developing their respective citizenship laws for very different reasons. Slovenia, was emerging into full independence. They arguably wanted to exert their identity in whatever they could. They did so by excluding many for Yugoslav citizens from Slovenian citizenship. Slovenia was also working towards membership of the EU. This is something Australia has never had to consider. Although, as the 2000s emerged both states laws began to converge, due to the rise in national security threats. Nonetheless, and even though both states were implementing restrictive legal and policy approaches to citizenship, they were also liberalizing their respective laws. Thus, it is argued that the balancing act citizenship law has within the political discourse is highly complex, cutting across various national policies. Moreover, it can be demonstrated that the law reform programs certainly pushed for a more cohesive society. The next section compares the current day citizenship laws of Slovenia and Australia.

References

Batchelor, C. (1998). Statelessness and the problem of resolving nationality status. *International Journal of Refugee Law, 10*, 238–249.

Brglez, M., & Šabič, Z. (2002). *The national identity of post-communist small states in the process of accession to the European Union: The case of Slovenia* (pp. 2–18). Ljubljana: Faculty of Social Sciences, University of Ljubljana.

Brinar, I., & Bučar, B. (1994). *Slovenian foreign policy. Civil society, political society, democracy* (pp. 425–447). Ljubljana: Slovenian Political Science Association.

Castles, S., Vasta, E., & Ozkul, D. (2012). *The internal dynamics of migration processes and their consequences for Australian government migration policies* (Working Paper for the Department of Immigration and Citizenship, University of Sydney, pp. 1–16).

Due, C., & Rigs, D. (2008). *We grew Here you flew here: Claims to home in the Cronulla riots, colloquy text theory critique* (pp. 1–5). Melbourne: Monash University.

Fierke, K. (1996). Multiple identities, interfacing games: The social construction of western action in Bosnia. *European Journal of International Relations, 2*, 467–497.

Hailbronner, K. (2006). Nationality in public international law and European law. In R. Bauböck, E. Ersboll, K. Groenendijk, & H. Waldrauch (Eds.), *Acquisition and loss of nationality: Policies and trends in 15 European countries* (p. 49). Amsterdam University Press: Amsterdam.

Irving, H., & Thwaites, R. (2015). Australian citizenship amendment (Allegiance to Australia) bill 2015 (Cth). *Public Law Review, 26*, 143–149.

Jambrek, P. (2014). *Nation's transitions, social and legal issues of Slovenia's transitions 1945–2015* (p. 301). Nova Gorica: Graduate School of Government and European Studies, Brdo pri Kranju and European Faculty of Law.

Kogovšek Salamon, N. (2001). Still waiting: The erased people of Slovenia. In *Building and Open Society in Western Balkans* (pp. 27–29). New York: Open Society Foundations.

Lak, M. (1992). The involvement of the European Community in the Yugoslav crisis during 1991. *Yearbook of European Studies, 5*(1992), 175–185.

Linklater, A. (1998). Cosmopolitan citizenship. *Citizenship Studies, 2*(1), 26.

Lister, R. (1997). *Feminist perspectives* (p. 196). Basingstoke: Macmillan.

Medved, F. (2014). Unified Slovenian nation: Slovenian citizenship policy towards Slovenians abroad. In G. Cholnoky, Z. Kántor, A. Ludányi, & E. Herner-Kovács (Eds.), *Minority studies special issue trends and directions of kin-state policies in Europe and across the globe* (pp. 153–184). Budapest: Lucidus Kiadó.

Nolan, M., & Rubenstein, K. (2009). Citizenship and identity in diverse societies. *Humanities Research, XV*(1), 29.

Rubenstein, K. (2002). *Citizenship law in context* (p. 75). Sydney: Lawbook Co.

Sassen, S. (2002). The repositioning of citizenship: Emergent subjects and spaces for politics. *Berkley Journal of Sociology, 6*, 1–10.

Shachar, A., & Bauböck, R. (2014). *Should citizenship be for sale?* (pp. 1–20). Italy: European University Institute, European Union Democracy Observatory on Citizenship.

Spiro, P. (1997). Dual nationality and the meaning of citizenship. *Emory Law Journal, 46*, 1411–1485.

Svetličič, M. (1997). Small states: New challenges and opportunities: Development and International Cooperation. In Z. Šabič & C. Bukowski (Eds.), *Small states in the post-cold war world: Slovenia and NATO enlargement* (pp. 24–25). Westport: PRAEGER, 2002.

Weis, P. (1979). *Nationality ad statelessness in international law* (pp. 135–140). Leiden: Sijthoff & Noordhoff.

Žitnik, J. (2004). *Immigrants in Slovenia: Integration aspects*. Ljubljana: Scientific Research Centre of the Slovenian Academy of Sciences and Arts, Institute of Emigration Studies.

Zorn, J. (2004). *The politics of exclusion citizenship, human rights and the erased in Slovenia* (pp. 1–7). Ljubljana: UDK.

Chapter 6
Current Day Citizenship Law [2018–2019]

Abstract This chapter identifies the differences between the current day citizenship laws of Slovenia and Australia. While they are grounded in the same concepts and principles, such as, the citizenship by birth, descent and naturalization, it will be demonstrated how the respective laws do differ. It is argued that their role within each state while achieving a similar outcome, they have, and continue to play a different role within each state. For Slovenia, they provide a pathway to European citizenship. They also reinforce and strengthen the national identity, along with ensuing their current citizenry is cohesive. The laws also largely deter people who cannot show a direct connection to Slovenia, from entering and obtaining citizenship of the state. This approach is vastly different to Australia. Australia, being a multicultural society have established a legal framework for citizenship that largely supports their ongoing nation building program, through immigration. It could be argued that Australia's approach of not requiring a person to show an historical connection to the state, takes a more liberal approach to citizenship policy and law. The French and American Revolutions, to some degree, began to codify elements of citizenship. Since then Slovenia and Australia have experienced different forms of citizenship that, have largely been based on birth, descent and naturalization. What has changed is the process by which a person can obtain citizenship, particularly by naturalization.

Keywords Australia · Birth · Conferral · Descent · Oath naturalization · Pledge · Slovenia

6.1 Introduction

The *Australian Citizenship Act 2007* (ACA) is the principal legislative instrument in Australia that provides for the acquisition and loss of citizenship. The *Australian Citizenship Regulations 2007* were also implemented in the same year, however, the regulations will not form part of this research because they support the administration

R. Walters, *National Identity and Social Cohesion in a Time of Geopolitical and Economic Tension: Australia – European Union – Slovenia*,
https://doi.org/10.1007/978-981-15-2164-5_6

of the principal Act. Justice Mary Gaudron of the High Court of Australia[1] stated that citizenship is a concept that is entirely statutory and falls within the citizenship legislation.[2] In Te and Dang, this was also confirmed in relation to aliens entering Australia, whereby the process for naturalization is statutory based.[3]

Slovenian citizenship is regulated by the Law on Citizenship (LC).[4] Not only did the new citizenship laws of Slovenia provide an opportunity for the state to unify its citizens, Slovenia was able to for the first time legally define who its citizens would be. Australia on the other had confirmed the legal status of its citizens in 1948, and was already moving towards expanding its laws to include the civic virtues and postnational concepts. The Slovenian Constitutional Court noted that Slovenia is required to regulate citizenship because their population is one of the constitutive elements[5] of their national identities. Citizenship of the new Slovenia was an opportunity to define an independent national identity,[6] in a similar way that Australia's first citizenship laws were established in 1948. Today, both states citizenship laws are based on both *ius soli and ius sanguinis*. The citizenship act of Australia states that the parliament recognizes that Australian citizenship represents full and formal membership of the community of the Commonwealth of Australia, and Australian citizenship is a common bond, involving reciprocal rights and obligations, uniting all Australians, while respecting their diversity.[7] Additionally, the preamble outlines the policy approach for citizenship that has been approved by the Australian Parliament, particularly to those individuals who apply to obtain citizenship in the country. Thus, a person applying for citizenship has certain obligations such as pledging their loyalty to Australia, sharing its values and beliefs; respecting rights and liberties, and obeying the laws of the country.[8] These principles form part of the

[1] *Chu Kheng Lim v Minister for Immigration, Local Government and Ethnic Affairs* (1992) CLR 1, 54.

[2] *Re Minister for Immigration and Multicultural and Indigigenous Affairs; Ex parte* Ame [2005] HCA 35, Justice Kirby noted that citizenship is no more than a statutory status. *Shaw v Minister for Immigration and Multicultural* Affairs (2004) ALR 168. *Re Patterson; Ex parte Taylor* (2001) 207 CLR 391.

[3] *Te and Dang* (2002) 212 CLR 170, 180, 188, 194.

[4] Law on Citizenship, Official Gazette of the Republic of Slovenia, No. 30.91.

[5] U-I-89/99, Official Gazette of the Republic of Slovenia, No. 59/99 and OdIUS VIII, 147.

[6] Medved, f, (2014) *Unified Slovenian Nation: Slovenian Citizenship Policy towards Slovenians Abroad,* in Gyõzõ Cholnoky, Zoltán Kántor, András Ludányi and Eszter Herner-Kovács, Minority Studies Special issue Trends and Directions of Kin-State Policies in Europe and Across the Globe, Lucidus Kiadó, 153–184.

[7] Preamble, *Australian Citizenship Act 2007*, Sections 1, 2, 2A and 3 of the ACA were structural elements of the legislation that explain the commencement dates for particular provisions and the legislation commenced on the day of Royal Assent, on 15 March 2007. The summary in s2A explains where a person can locate the relevant provisions in the ACA as well as citizenship by conferral that is common for those people on permanent residency visas to gain citizenship in Australia. Additionally, s3 defines up to 29 words such as Australia and permanent resident that have been defined for the purposes of the legislation, outside of the traditional definition of the same word with a dictionary.

[8] Ibid.

Australian national identity. On the other hand, the Slovenian legislation does not have a preamble and has no reference to policy (rights and obligations) for people wanting to be a member of the Slovenian state.[9] Slovenia could expand its legislation to provide a preamble similar to Australia. The citizenship laws of Australia and Slovenia are gender neutral and do not separate women from men, unlike the early citizenship laws and doctrines of the British common law and French civil law.

6.2 Birth and Descent

The current laws as they relate to acquiring citizenship by birth and descent can be traced back to the French Revolution[10] for which citizenship could be obtained by a person who was born in France; and at least one of the parents was French. The acquisition of citizenship by birth automatically confirms the legal status of the person and connects them to either Slovenia or Australia.

An individual can obtain citizenship at birth provided the person is born in the territory to a parent that is an Australian citizen. This also includes a parent who is a permanent resident at the time of the birth, or where the person has been a resident for 10 years.[11] Citizenship will not be granted where a parent is an enemy alien and the place of birth was under the occupation by an enemy.[12] Interestingly, the ACA does not define 'enemy' or 'enemy alien', and furthermore, the Slovene legislation does not discuss a similar approach to enemy aliens.[13] Comparatively, Australia recognises that citizenship cannot be granted twice.[14] The Slovenian law does not.

In Slovenia both of the child's parents must be citizens at the time of the birth, or one of the parents is a citizen, and the child was born on the territory.[15] If one of the parents is a citizen of the Republic and the other parent is unknown, or, of unknown citizenship, or the child was born in a foreign country,[16] they can acquire citizenship in Slovenia. This reinforces Locke's position that 'family is a natural social unit and parents possess dominion over their children' and, a child when born is no subject of any country or government'.[17] Additionally, there may be situations where a

[9] Article 1, Citizenship Act of the Republic of Slovenia 2007, Official Gazette of the Republic of Slovenia 24/2007.

[10] Brubaker, R (1989) *The French Revolution and the Invention of Citizenship*, French Politics and Society, vol 7, No 3, 30–32.

[11] *Australian Citizenship Act 2007*, section 12.

[12] Ibid, s12 (b).

[13] Ibid, s12 (d).

[14] Ibid, s12 (c).

[15] Article 4, Citizenship Act of the Republic of Slovenia 2007, Official Gazette 24/2007.

[16] Ibid, article 4.

[17] Schuck, P., Smith, R, (1996) *Citizenship without Consent*, The Social Contract, Yale Law School, 2.

person will be born outside of a state, on a ship or an aircraft.[18] Australian law allows a person to obtain citizenship in this situation.[19] Article 5 of the Slovenian law provides that a child born abroad where one of the parents has Slovenian citizenship[20] can obtain citizenship. It could be argued that the use of the term 'origin' in article 4 could apply to a person being born on an aircraft. In accordance with article 4 (3), provided one of the parents is a Slovene citizen at the time of the birth and the individual was born in a foreign country, they are entitled to citizenship by origin. Ships[21] and aircraft[22] are considered to be the territory of the nation state they are registered in. The Slovenia legislation is not clear and may cause confusion to individuals that do not understand the law. Therefore, it would be beneficial for Slovenia to tighten this section to include reference to ships and aircraft.

In the contemporary world, children are being conceived and by artificial conception. Arguably, Australia has recognised the importance of this conception by ensuring the citizenship laws cater for this technology. Doing so demonstrates that many elements of Australia's citizenship laws have evolved as society and technology have similarly evolved. Under the provisions of s8 of the ACA, a child that has been born as a result of artificial conception with the consent of the husband provided the child is not the biological child of the husband can obtain citizenship. The child must be created with the consent of the husband or defacto partner. The ACA is silent on whether this would apply to a single mother. However, s60B of the *Family Law Act 1975* considers both parents having a meaningful involvement in a child's life as an important factor when artificial conception is involved. Slovenian citizenship law is silent on artificial conception. Article 4 allows a person to obtain citizenship where one parent is a Slovene citizen. Slovenia could include a similar provision to Australia to ensure there is clarity in situations that involve a child who has been artificially conceived being able to obtain citizenship.

The acquisition of citizenship at birth is a process within itself. On paper the individual automatically gains citizenship of the state. However, if born on the territory in Australia to a parent who is neither a citizen of permanent resident, the individual does not automatically assume Australian citizenship. The person must be registered and provide evidence in the form of a birth certificate that details of the birth and the day on which the birth occurred. As discussed above, the importance of a person obtaining registration and a birth certificate enables them to fully participate in the community (the private side of citizenship). If this process is not undertaken, it is argued the person is being excluded from full participation in society and does not have full citizenship of the state.

---

[18] *Australian Citizenship Act 2007*, s7.

[19] Ibid, s7 (a).

[20] Article 5, Law of Citizenship, Official Gazette of the Republic of Slovenia 24/2007.

[21] Article 91 & 92, United Nations Convention on the Law of the Sea 1982.

[22] Annex 7, Convention on International Civil Aviation 1944. Article 77 of the convention permits joint operating organizations, 'Common Mark Registered Authority" and "International Operating Agency" to enable an aircraft of international operating agencies to be registered other than on a national basis.

Citizenship by descent (by blood) is a powerful mode for acquiring citizenship of a state when a person's parent or parents are residing in another state. Citizenship by descent can be obtained under Slovenian and Australian citizenship law. However, the conditions that apply within the respective state's citizenship laws vary. It is not necessary for the person to be born in the territory of either state to obtain citizenship in this manner. A person born to an Australia citizen while in France can obtain citizenship of Australia. At least one parent must be an Australian citizen.[23] This was confirmed by the Federal Court of Australia in 2010.[24] The court in referring to section 16(2) of the ACA stated that the reference to parent in this section was a reference to the child's parent who is an Australian citizen.[25] The Minister has the power to refuse the application where a person is unable to prove their identity, and where the individual poses a risk to national security.[26] The person must be 18 years of age, of good character and is not a national or a citizen of another state, at the time of application.[27] The ACA is silent on the level of descent that applies.

In Slovenia obtaining citizenship by descent, extends to the fourth generation and must be in direct descent.[28] In other words, there must be a clear line of descent from the child to the parent, grandparent and great grandparent. It could be argued that Slovenia continues to allow the nation state to build and retain its identity over the longer term, by ensuring the state is connected to Slovenians regardless of what state in which they reside. This could apply to those people that have permanently migrated to other states and their grandchildren want to become an Australian citizen. Importantly, the legislation is gender neutral and does not discern between male and female in either state. Thus, as the law has evolved the recognition and equality of women in citizenship law has also evolved to ensure there is no segregation of either sex. The Australian Citizenship Act 2007 does not describe a generational principle. Australia should amend the Act and borrow from Slovenia to include a similar provision. Such an inclusion would assist those individuals born to former Australian citizens, now residing in other states to obtain Australian citizenship. This could be an opportunity for Australia to expand its diaspora.

---

[23] *Citizenship Act Australia 2007*, s15A.

[24] *Hudson v Minister for Immigration and Citizenship* [2010] FCAFC 119–130.

[25] Ibid, s16, (2) (a).

[26] *Citizenship Act Australia 2007*, s17.

[27] Ibid, s16 (2), note that where the parent was an Australian citizen under this subdivision AA, or section 10B, 10C or 11 of the old Act at the time, the parent has been present in Australia for a period of 2 years, or, the person is not a national or a citizen of any country at the time of application.

[28] Article 12, Citizenship Act of the Republic of Slovenia 2007, Official Gazette 24/2007.

6.3 Abandoned or Found Children

The protection of children is not only a parental responsibility but in cases where the child, at birth is abandoned or found, the state has a role to ensure that the child belongs to a state. Section 14 of the ACA allows citizenship to be granted where a child has been abandoned in Australia. This may occur whether the individual has parents that are or are not citizens of the state. However, the legislation states that "unless and until the contrary is proved".[29] That is, the commonwealth department responsible for citizenship has the burden to prove otherwise and could be in the form of a birth certificate from another country.[30] Where it is found that the child's parents cannot be located, and they are declared stateless, an application for citizenship can be made under s21(8) of the ACA. However, abandonment in Australia is restricted to post 2007. The Federal Court of Australia concluded that s14 of the ACA 2007 applied only to a child who was found abandoned prior to 1 July 2007.[31] This was recently reaffirmed by the Federal Court of Australia in *SZRTN*,[32] whereby the person was deemed not to be abandoned where the individual was born outside of Australia in 1981 and arrived in the state in 1987 in the company of a parent. Within months of arrival the individual was abandoned by the parent and resided with a relative. Slovenia recognises that a child could be 'found on the territory' to have unknown parents. In this situation the individual is entitled to acquire citizenship.[33] Comparatively, the legislation of both states provide a mechanism for the state to manage situations where a child has been abandoned or found in the territory, and the parents are not known. Arguably, this not only protects the child but also ensures the child does not become stateless.

6.4 Conferral

Immigration is a pathway to citizenship and is discussed in chapter five. In a globalised world individuals are moving from one state to another to better their lives or experience a new culture and surroundings. Migration not only allows citizens to be naturalised in another state, but also, engage with other citizens across international borders in personal activities such as marriage. The rules of naturalisation between Slovenia and Australia vary. The current process for obtaining citizenship by naturalisation is to enter the state on a valid visa or permit, meet the necessary residency conditions and make an application for citizenship. This can also extends

[29] *Australian Citizenship Act 2007*, s14.

[30] *Nicky v Minister for Immigration and Border Protection* [2015] FCA 174 at 38.

[31] Ibid, 25.

[32] *SZRTN v Minister for Immigration and Border Protection* [2015] FCAFC 110.

[33] Article 9, Citizenship Act of the Republic of Slovenia, Official Gazette of the Republic of Slovenia 24/2007.

to a person who has previously been in Australia and held a valid visa before leaving the territory.[34]

To obtain citizenship in Australia, an individual must be 18 years of age; be a permanent resident and possess a basic knowledge of the English language. The individual must be able to understand the responsibilities and privileges that come with being an Australian citizen. This is an important point where the state appears to be directing new citizens to meet certain expectations in understanding the Australian identity. The individual must also be of good character and be likely to reside in the Australian territory or continue a close association with Australia.[35] The person must also meet the residency requirements.[36] During the residency period, the person must not have at any stage been in the Australian territory unlawfully.[37] Section 23 of the ACA is another general requirement whereby an individual can obtain citizenship on completion of 3 months service in the armed forces, or 6 months in either the Navy, Army or Air Force reserves.[38] This further reinforces the level of respect given to people by the people and government of those who contribute to the military. The military has a significant role in Australia's history and the current day national identity. The above conditions also relate to those individuals that are applying for citizenship that have a permanent physical or mental illness. However, there is no requirement to undertake duties in either of the armed forces.[39]

A person who is aged 60 or over and has a hearing, speech or sight impairment is also eligible to become an Australian citizen, although certain specific condition apply.[40] The individual must be of good character, be 18 years age and born outside the Australian territory.[41] Citizenship will not be granted where one of the parents is not an Australian citizen. Additionally, citizenship will not be granted where the person holds dual citizenship and is not of good character. An individual who was born in Papua before 16 September 1975 and one parent was an Australian citizen at the time of birth, will be granted citizenship. A person who has been determined stateless can become an Australian citizen.[42] In Slovenia, article 10[43] provides that an individual can apply for Slovene citizenship by naturalization.

[34] *Australian Citizenship Act 2007*, s5. Australia has described what constitutes permanent residency, to also include special category visas, which are issued for humanitarian reasons, and those individuals who are present in Norfolk Island, or, the Cocos Islands.

[35] Ibid, s21 (2).

[36] Ibid, s22.

[37] Ibid, s22 (1) (b).

[38] Ibid, s23.

[39] Ibid, s21 (3).

[40] Ibid, s21 (4).

[41] Ibis, s 21.

[42] Ibid, s21 (8).

[43] Article 10, Law on Citizenship of the Republic of Slovenia, Official Gazette of the Republic of Slovenia 24/2007.

Comparatively, Slovenia's requirements go further than Australia whereby the person must be18 years of age,[44] have release from their current citizenship or can prove that such a release will be granted if the individual acquires citizenship of Slovenia.[45] The individual must have resided in the Slovene territory for a period of 10 years, and five of those years must have been continuous.[46] Furthermore, the person must prove they have a permanent source of income that is of an amount to sustain themselves while in Slovenia.[47] This could be in the form of income derived while working in Slovenia or income and investments they bring with them to Slovenia. Similar to the character test in Australia, the person can apply for citizenship provided they have not been sentenced in the state where they currently reside (origin), or sentenced while present in Slovenia to a prison term no longer than 1 year.[48] The requirement to have knowledge of the Slovenian language reinforces the Slovenia's long held position that language is what sets Slovenes apart from others. However, there are exemptions. It is considered that an individual will have met this requirement where they have (1) completed primary school within the Republic; (2) completed a state approved program of secondary education in Slovenia; (3) the person has completed level VI or VII certificate education; (4) the individual is over the Age of 60; and (5) the person has completed primary or secondary school in Slovene.[49]

6.5 Oath and Pledge

Both states require prospective citizens to undertake the oath[50] or pledge.[51] They reinforce the need for new citizens to understand what it means to become and Australian or Slovenian. Apart from an expression of national identity, they also go some-way to exerting a level of cohesion.

The Slovenian oath is:

> loyalty, gives my new homeland, the Republic of Slovenia and the oath I undertake to respect the freedom of a democratic constitutional order of the Republic of Slovenia, values and principles of freedom and democracy, and that I as a citizen of the Republic of Slovenia to meet its duties and obligations. I swear that I will work and support the operation against the free and democratic constitutional order or the existence of the Republic of Slovenia and unlawfully will not undermine the authorities of the Republic of Slovenia or representative bodies. I swear that I will support the operation against the interest of the Republic of Slovenia with the use of violence or acts preparatory to the use of violence.

[44] Ibid, article 10 (1).

[45] Ibid, article 10 (2).

[46] Ibid, article 10 (3).

[47] Ibid, article 10 (4).

[48] Ibid, article 10.

[49] Ibid, article 10 (10).

[50] Ibid, article 10(10),

[51] Ibid, schedule 1.

The Australian pledge is:

> From this time forward, under God, I pledge my loyalty to Australia and its people, whose democratic beliefs I share, whose rights and liberties I respect, and whose laws I will uphold and obey. From this time forward, I pledge my loyalty to Australia and its people whose democratic beliefs I share, whose rights and liberties I respect, and whose laws I will uphold and obey.

However, in Australia there are exemptions for those under the age of 16, those who are physically or mentally incapacitated and do not understand the nature of the pledge or those who demonstrate a lack of command of the English language.[52] A pledge cannot be made before the Minister has approved the individual's application to become a citizen. The person taking the pledge can delay it for up to 12 months where the person has been charged under Australian law, or in the event that the individual holds a valid visa under the *Migration Act 1958* (and that visa has been cancelled).[53] Furthermore, the oath of Slovenia and the pledge of Australia refer to the democratic principles that uphold both states. The oath and pledge reinforce the obligations of a citizen towards the respective state. It is argued that by requiring citizens to understand and uphold the principles of the oath and pledge, both states are directing future citizens to participate in and embrace their values. Additionally, it enables new citizens to understand an element of a state's national identity. Despite the current approach taken by both states, the 'oath' and 'pledge' could be expanded to include further reference to the respective states national identities. This could include recognizing dual citizenship, and the need to continue to maintain their loyalty to the state whether abroad or in the territory. In addition, greater emphasis could be placed on an individual's rights and obligations to the state. For example, an outline of the rights, freedoms and protections could be included in both the Slovenian 'oath' and the Australian 'pledge'. This would go some way to reinforce to prospective citizens that Slovenia and Australia of how the state wants them to behave (upholding and implementing fundamental elements of a democratic society) and strengthening their belonging to the state.

6.6 Citizenship Test

Citizenship testing can be highly political. It can also be sued by a state to develop cohesion, by expressing our values of what makes up its overall identity. A person must take a Slovenian language test, both written and oral[54] (having a working knowledge of the language). Although, the test[55] in Australia is not on the person's

[52] *Citizenship Act Australia 2007*, s26.

[53] Ibid.

[54] Article 10, Citizenship Act 2007, of the Republic of Slovenia, Official Gazette 24/2007.

[55] *Australian Citizenship Act 2007*, s23A.

ability or level of comprehension of the English language.[56] However, in order to undertake the test the person needs to have a basic understanding of the English language. The test consists of about 20 questions that cover the following topics: Australia and its people; the state and territory boundaries, indigenous people, traditional symbols, the coat of arms, national flowers and the national colors of green and gold. The test also covers Australia's democratic beliefs, rights and liberties (citizen's freedoms such as freedom of speech, religious and association). There is also the requirement for a new citizen to have knowledge of the Australian:

> state and government and the law, including the Australian constitution, Head of State, and parliamentary structure (three levels of government: commonwealth state and local) and the courts.[57]

Individuals must have a pass rate of no less than 75%. The test[58] demonstrates Australia's commitment to ensuring the national identity is accepted and understood by newcomers. Some of the questions include:

> What happened in Australia on 1 January 1901(?): What is the name of the legal document that sets out the rules for the government of Australia; What is a referendum; Which arm of government has the power to interpret and apply laws; Which of these is a role of the Governor-General; Which of these statements about state governments is correct; What is the name given to the party or coalition of parties with the second largest number of members in the House of Representatives.

The test provides the opportunity for the individual applying for citizenship to better understand the values and identity of the state. It is argued that citizenship testing has seen a dramatic shift in Australia to the earlier migration laws of 1900s where there was a dictation test. On the one hand Australia is expressing to new citizens that you must understand and know the identity of the state. On the other hand, Australia is still welcoming large numbers of migrants on to the territory. However, today, there are large numbers of individuals holding permanent residency in both states, which has developed into a key feature of both Australia and Slovenia's legal

---

[56] Regulation 1.15B, 1.15C, 1.15D, 1.15E, 1.15EA, *Migration Regulations 1994,* outlining the different levels of English that includes; vocational English, competent English, proficient English, concessional English, superior English.

[57] Department of Immigration and Citizenship, Practice Test, http://www.citizenship.gov.au/learn/cit_test/_pdf/practice-questions.pdf

[58] Australian Government, Australian Citizenship – Our Common Bond, 2009, 5. The following test questions include; which of these is an example of freedom of speech. Which of these statements about government in Australia is correct. Which of these is an example of equality in Australia. Which of these is a responsibility of Australian citizens aged 18 years or over. Which of these statements about passports is correct. Which of these statements about voting in Australian elections is correct. What happened in Australia on 1 January 1901. What is the name of the legal document that sets out the rules for the government of Australia. What is a referendum. Which arm of government has the power to interpret and apply laws. Which of these is a role of the Governor-General. Which of these statements about state governments is correct. What is the name given to the party or coalition of parties with the second largest number of members in the House of Representatives. What is the name of a proposal to make a law in parliament. Who maintains peace and order in Australia. http://www.citizenship.gov.au/learn/cit_test/_pdf/practice-questions.pdf

framework. Testing (language, history and culture), could be imposed on permanent residence every 5 years. This has a double benefit. It could encourage people to take out citizenship, and also provides a mechanism for the state to push the nationalist agenda and get people to better understand national identity.

6.7 Adoption

Naturalisation can also be obtained by a person through adoption, in accordance with the Hague Convention on Intercountry Adoption 1993. Both Australia and Slovenia have ratified this convention in 1998 and 2002 respectively. The convention ensures states establish institutional arrangements so that intercountry adoption is undertaken with the interest and wellbeing of the child being foremost. Article 4 of the Slovenian citizenship laws provide that the state of origin has determined the child can be adopted[59] and that the child is able to be placed with parents.[60] Additionally, the child will be authorized to enter the state and reside permanently within the territory.[61] In accordance with section 13 of the ACA, citizenship can be obtained where the individual has been adopted by two people and only one of those people is an Australian citizen or a permanent resident.[62] This form of acquiring citizenship, confirms the legal status of an individual to the state. The process of naturalization such as testing, language proficiency and length of stay all contribute to national identity. The process provides the individual with a better understanding of the state and its core values, and in turn provides that individual with a sense of belonging. More importantly, the above naturalization requirements are a reflection of the high value placed on acquiring citizenship by the respective states.

[59] Article 4, Hague Convention on Intercountry Adoption 1993, Hague Conference on Private International Law, Proceedings of the Seventeenth Session (1993), Tome II, Adoption – co-operation (ISBN 903990728 X), 695. Australia signed, ratified and was entered into force in 1998. Slovenia signed, ratified and was entered into force 2002.

[60] Ibid, article 5.

[61] Ibid.

[62] *Australian Citizenship Act 2007*, s13.

6.8 Dual Citizenship

Dual citizenship has increasingly gained acceptance[63] from nation states across the world. Joachim Blatter argues dual citizenship creates innovation,[64] through the transfer and mobility of citizens, values, culture and heritage from one state to another. It is arguably a liberal form of citizenship. In Australia dual citizenship had been subject to review by government in 1976 and 1982.[65] However, it did not gain full acceptance in Australia until 2002 and a year later in 2003 Slovenia.

Dual citizenship expands the notion of postnational citizenship, allowing a person to transcend international borders and participate in more than one state. Dual citizenship enables a state to maintain a connection with their citizens while abroad.[66] However, dual citizenship has been seen to challenge the nation state.[67] Historically, single citizenship has assisted states for centuries to maintain control of the territory and its inhabitants.[68] A Slovenian citizen can have citizenship of another state.[69] Dual citizenship in Slovenia is restricted.[70] A foreigner who does not have any connection with Slovenia, cannot obtain Slovene citizenship. Therefore, dual citizenship along with single citizenship and immigration is inclusive and exclusive.

Apart from states outside of Slovenia and Australia allowing their citizens to obtain citizenship of another state, Slovenia with its current restrictive approach is rather exclusive. Dual citizenship can increase naturalisation rates,[71] and thereby allows a state to expand its citizenry. However, many scholars oppose dual citizenship as demonstrating a lack of loyalty, resulting in a lack of integration within a state and a reduced sense of national identity. On the other hand, it could be argued that dual citizenship provides the opportunity for skills, knowledge and capacity to be transferred between Slovenia and Australia, thus enhancing national identity. Furthermore, dual citizenship confirms the legal status of the person by two states. In the following subsection, some of the benefits that a dual Slovenian and Australian citizen can enjoy have been identified.

---

[63] Rubenstein, K., Maquire, N, (2011) *Citizenship and the boundaries of the Constitution*, Social Science Research, Legal Scholarship Network, The Australian National University, Law Research Paper, No. 11–15, 143–153.

[64] JBlatter, J, (2011) *Dual citizenship and theories of Democracy*, Citizenship Studies, Institute of Political Science, University of Lucerne Switzerland, 769–798.

[65] Rubenstein, K, (2002) *Australian Citizenship Law in Context*, Lawbook Co, 141.

[66] Rubenstein, K, (2007) *Chair of the Citizenship Council*, The Australian National University, 80.

[67] Morjt Howard, M, (2005) *Variation in Dual Citizenship Policies- in the Countries of the EU*, International Migration Review, Vol 39. No 3, 697.

[68] Ibid.

[69] Article 2, Citizenship Act 2007 of the Republic of Slovenia, Official Gazette 24/2007.

[70] Ibid, article 10(3).

[71] Faist, T., Gerdes, J, (2008) *Dual Citizenship in an Age of Mobility*, Migration Policy Institute, 3–20.

6.9 Entry to the EU, Slovenia and Australia

A dual citizen of Slovenia and Australia is entitled to hold a passport of both states. This allows an individual to enter Australia or Slovenia including anywhere in the European Union. For instance, a dual citizen entering Slovenia using their Slovene passport, wherever they first enter the European Union (this could be Germany), obtains immigration clearance and can stay and move freely for as long as they choose, subject to European Union and Slovene national law. However, where the dual citizen only uses their Australian passport entering the European Union and Slovenia (whether as a tourist or other visa type) they will be subject to the restrictions of a non-citizen.

6.10 Voting and Standing for Elections

A dual citizen of Slovenia and Australia is eligible to vote in Australian elections, however, under section 44(i) of the Australian Constitution, an individual is not eligible to stand for election in the national parliament (men and women). In *Sykes v Cleary*[72] the Australian High Court held that those individuals of foreign birth having acquired Australian citizenship and severed links with their country of birth, but having not renounced their foreign nationality would not be eligible under section 44(i) of the constitution to stand for election in the national parliament. Conversely, a Slovenian citizen is eligible to have residence in another member state as well as the right to vote and stand for elections in that member state.[73] Council Directive 94/80/EC, outlines the arrangements for European Union citizens that are residing in another member state of which they are not a citizen, enabling them to stand as a candidate in municipal elections.[74] A dual citizen could also vote and stand as a candidate in Municipal and European Parliament elections.[75] The European Court of Justice ruled that while a member state could restrict the right to vote and stand in the European Parliament elections, the principle of equal treatment applies and thus a person may stand for election.[76] Nevertheless, this is restricted to elections at

[72] *Sykes v Cleary* [1992] HCA 32; (1992) ALR 577; (1992) 66 ALJR 577 (9 July 1992),

[73] Article 20 (2), Treaty of the European Union, Official Journal of the European Union C 326/57.

[74] Council Directive 94/80/EC, laying down detailed arrangements for the exercise of the right to vote and to stand as a candidate in municipal elections by citizens of the Union residing in a Member State of which they are not a national, Official Journal of the European Communities, L 368/38.

[75] Article 22 Treaty on the Functioning of the European Union, Official Journal of the European Union C 83/47. Every citizen of the Union residing in a Member State of which he is not a national shall have the right to vote and to stand as a candidate at municipal elections in the Member State in which he resides, under the same conditions as nationals of that State.

[76] Case – 300/04 *Eman and Sevinger v College van burgemeester en wethouders van Den Haag* [2006] ECR I - 8055

the municipal level (local government units) and not national elections.[77] Therefore, an Australian Slovenian dual citizen could stand for local municipal elections in another member state outside of Slovenia.[78] While in theory there may be an opportunity for a dual citizen to stand for election to the European Parliament, in practice this may never be achieved unless the individual is actually resident in the European Union.

6.11 Employment (Civil Service)

A dual citizen is allowed to seek employment in either state. However, it is a little more difficult in practice for an Australian wanting employment in Slovenia, as they would need to be able to converse (read and write) in the Slovene language. It may be easier for a Slovene to gain employment in Australia because English is used across Europe and in Slovenia. The rules on employment in the national civil (public) service are controlled by legislation. In Australia a dual citizen would be able to obtain employment in the Victorian and other State public service sectors including local government. In Slovenia, a dual citizen would be eligible for employment within local municipalities. It is usually determined that these employment positions, unlike the national level, do not engage in, or, undertake duties that are in the national interest. However, to be eligible for employment within the Australian commonwealth civil service there is a requirement for a person to be an Australian citizen.[79] There are exemptions depending on the government department (agency).[80] Furthermore, prospective employees must undertake a probation period, security, character and health clearance, and provide formal qualifications.[81] According to the Slovenian Civil Servant Act, any appointment is on the condition of having citizenship of the Republic and subject to similar security and character testing as required in Australia.[82]

[77] Article 2, Council Directive 94/80/EC, laying down detailed arrangements for the exercise of the right to vote and to stand as a candidate in municipal elections by citizens of the Union residing in Member States of which they are not nationals, Official Journal of the European Communities, L 368/38.

[78] Article 7, *National Assembly Elections Act 1992*, Official Gazette of the Republic of Slovenia, 44/92.

[79] *Public Service Act 1999*, s22 (8).

[80] Ibid, s22 (8).

[81] Ibid, s22 (6).

[82] Article 88, *Civil Servant Act*, Official Gazette No. 020–05/98–20/8, 2002.

6.12 Loss of Citizenship

Gerard René de Groot and Maarten Vink[83] argue that an important part of citizenship law is where an individual loses their citizenship. This not only allows a state to protect its national interest and identity, but also, protect its citizens.[84] The loss of citizenship allows a state to continue to reinforce its sovereign right to choose who its citizens will and will not be. More importantly, the principle of loss of citizenship poses difficulties for states, particularly where an individual who loses their citizenship and may become stateless. In Slovenia, an individual can lose their citizenship by remission, renouncement, deprivation or international agreement. In Australia, the loss of citizenship is different and has been described as renunciation and revocation where it is proved that a person has served in the armed forces of an enemy country.[85]

Renouncing Australian citizenship can be decided by the Minister provided the individual is over the age of 18[86] and must be a national of another nation state to ensure the person does not become stateless.[87] The renouncement of citizenship cannot be undertaken unless the person can be identified or where the application was submitted in war time, provided Australia is a participant.[88] Furthermore, the Minister may not approve the renouncement of citizenship where it has been determined it is not in the best interest of Australia. The Minister cannot approve renouncing of citizenship unless the person is a citizen of another state, or will become a citizen of another state upon cessation of Australian citizenship.[89] This is to avoid situations where the person may become stateless. A person can independently decide to renounce their citizenship in Australia. The Minister cannot approve the person becoming a citizen again during the 12 months from the day the citizenship ceases.[90] A person's citizenship may cease where the individual is a citizen of a foreign country and serves in the armed forces of that country in war with Australia.[91] In Slovenia a person will be considered a foreign national where they have undertaken foreign military service or are employed in a State agency.[92] While there is no guidance on what is in Australia's best interest, this would be a policy decision for government that would consider economic, security or social issues.

---

[83] René de Groot, G., Vink, M, *Loss of Citizenship*, EUDO Citizenship Policy Brief No. 3, Maastricht University and University College Dublin, http://eudocitizenship.eu/docs/policy_brief_loss.pdf

[84] Ibid.

[85] *Australian Citizenship Act 2007*, s33 and 34.

[86] Ibid, s33 (3) (a).

[87] Ibid, s33 (3) (b).

[88] Ibid, s33 (5).

[89] Ibid, s33 (7).

[90] Ibid, s24 (7).

[91] Ibid, s35.

[92] Ibid, article 26 (4).

6.13 Revoke

Both Australia and Slovenia have the ability to revoke - or in the case of Slovenia - force the loss of citizenship. Revoking (the term used) Australian citizenship can be undertaken by the government in situations where the individual has obtained Australian citizenship either by descent or is a person adopted under the Hague Convention for Intercountry Adoption.[93] In summary, revocation of citizenship in Australia will occur when a person has committed an offence and been convicted against national or foreign law.[94] This involves those offences that have been determined serious enough that the individual has been sentenced to death or long term imprisonment.

Citizenship may also be revoked where that person has been convicted of the offence of providing false and misleading information when applying,[95] or, providing false and misleading information and documents to the Commonwealth.[96] On the other hand, in Slovenia an adult citizen who was born and living in another nation state, provided they have citizenship of another state. Also the person up to 25 years of age can renounce their citizenship[97] that is, the individual can renounce their own citizenship in Slovenia. This has little bearing on national identity.

Section 34(6) of the ACA provides the Minister with the power to revoke citizenship where the individual has committed fraud related offences under the *Migration Act 1958*.[98] That is, where an individual has provided false or misleading information to obtain an entry visa, or, uses a visa contrary to the law, such as, providing the visa to another person to assist with entry and stay in Australia. There is also a significant emphasis placed on third party fraud for various offences under *the Commonwealth Criminal Code Act 1995*[99] that relates to crimes such as conspiracy, bribery, corruption, and forgery.[100] The loss of citizenship can also occur where it has been determined that the person is part of an organization whose activities are in contravention with the provisions of the constitution.[101] Additionally, if a person is a member of a foreign intelligence service, that is determined to be detrimental to the Slovene state, the person can lose their citizenship.[102] This also applies in Australia, although citizenship would be revoked.

---

[93] *Australian Citizenship Act 2007*, s34.

[94] Ibid, s34 (1) (2) (5).

[95] Ibid, s50.

[96] *Commonwealth Criminal Code Act 1995*, s137.1 or 137.2,

[97] Article 25, Citizenship Act 2007, of the Republic of Slovenia, Official Gazette 24/2007.

[98] *Migration Act 1958*, s234, 236, 243, s236.

[99] *Commonwealth Crimes Act 1914*, s19B, Discharge of offenders without proceeding to conviction.

[100] *Australian Citizenship Act 2007*, s34(8), refers to the Criminal Code Act 1995.

[101] Article 26, Citizenship Act 2007, of the Republic of Slovenia, Official Gazette 24/2007.

[102] Ibid, article 26 (4).

The Australian legislation goes into more detail by describing what illegal activities such as bribery, fraud, providing false and misleading information and documents, or, migration related fraud that will constitute loss of citizenship. In the case of Slovenia, the loss of citizenship can occur when the person resides in another nation state and has taken out citizenship of that state, with the individual having the option of withdrawing their citizenship. This is another example of the citizenship laws expressing a component of national identity by ensuring the state has the ability to remove and decline citizenship where a person has been convicted of criminal offences.

The loss of Slovene citizenship can also occur where the child has been granted citizenship as a result of being found in the territory, at the request of the parents provided the child is over 18 years of age and the parents are foreign nationals.[103] A person may also have their citizenship released (dismissed).[104] The criteria for what constitutes the 'national interest' in article 28 must be read in conjunction with articles 10 (3)[105](4)[106](8),[107] 12 (citizenship by naturalization) and 13 (citizenship by descent). Refusing an application for citizenship applies where the person has incurred debt or is subject to criminal proceedings. This test ensures that the person does not pass the burden of debt to the state and also requires that the person has fulfilled their obligations under the judicial system, which would be a deterrent of others to not undertake the same or similar conduct. Release from citizenship can be cancelled within 1 year of being notified of the cessation in accordance with article 21.[108] Dismissal of citizenship commences on the date the decisions has been made and served.[109]

A parent of a child can request release of citizenship of that child provided they are under 18 years of age, but only applies to the parent who has custody or with whom the child resides.[110] However, where the other parent may not agree with the release of citizenship, consent is required from the Ministry of Labour, Family, Social Affairs and Equal Opportunities. Release is not necessary where the other parent's residence cannot be determined.[111] For instance, with the international adoption of a Slovene child that has full citizenship, the individual may obtain release of Slovene citizenship, provided they do not become stateless.[112] Article 24 requires a child who is over 14 years of age to obtain consent. This age limit requirement is something the ACA does not provide.

[103] Ibid, article 9.

[104] Ibid, article 18.

[105] Reside in Slovenia for 10 years with the last 5 continuous.

[106] Funds provided that can sustain the individual whilst in Slovenia.

[107] Poses no threat to public order, security or national defence.

[108] Ibid, article 21.

[109] Ibid, article 20.

[110] Ibid, article 22.

[111] Ibid, article 22.

[112] Ibid, article 23.

6.14 Resuming Citizenship

The resumption[113] of citizenship has many benefits to the individual, state and national identity. The state benefits from having former citizens returning and resuming their citizenship by contributing economically and socially. A person applying for resumption of citizenship in Australia will need to meet the national security requirements.[114] Slovenia's citizenship laws do not provide for resumption of citizenship, although an individual could resume their citizenship in accordance with the naturalization requirement in article 10. It could be argued that Slovenia should amend their citizenship laws to clear up any confusion that might exist in the law.

6.15 Other Provisions

An examination of the administration of citizenship laws is outside the scope of this research. However, the following sections largely relate to national security and good character. For example, section 6A of the ACA provides for issues of national security, whereby the government through the Attorney General can determine what constitutes a national security offence.[115] Furthermore, there is consideration of a person in psychiatric care and subject to the good character test (the criminal history of the person).[116] National security has become important to a state's identity by not only protecting the state but also its citizens. In Australia this includes the personal identifying features of a person such as fingerprints or handprints, the height and weight of the person and a photograph of the persons face and shoulders, a scan of the eyes and the person's signature.[117] These requirements in Slovenian can be found in the Aliens Act.[118] The final provisions are outside the scope of this research and relate to records, storage and collections of data in Slovenia.[119]

---

[113] *Australian Citizenship Act 2007*, s29.

[114] Ibid, s30.

[115] *Crimes Act 1914*.

[116] 2.11, Australian Citizenship Instructions, May 2012, www.citizenship.gov.au

[117] *Australian Citizenship Act 2007*, s10.

[118] Article 119, Law on International Protection Slovenia, Official Gazette of the Republic of Slovenia 2011/11

[119] Ibid, article 41.

6.16 Citizens Abroad

Diasporas constitute the invisible nation that resides outside of their state of origin.[120] The diaspora can consist of citizens who are resident in another state or dual citizens resident in another state other than the state they hold citizenship. Individuals that form a diaspora have migrated from their home country to another. Diasporas are important to the state of origin and the state of destination, and are considered an extension of the nation state.[121] They make a valuable contribution to trade, investment and the transfer of knowledge and skills.[122]

Slovenia has established the Act Regulating the Relations Between the Republic of Slovenia and Slovenes Abroad,[123] which has been used to unify Slovene that are located abroad.[124] The legislation is predominantly targeted at those Slovenes (the diaspora) located in those minority communities in the border locations of Austria, Italy, Hungary and Croatia. The legislation defines those Slovenes that do not necessarily have citizenship of Slovenia but are of Slovene origin. This Act allows Slovenes to participate in organizations outside of Slovenia. According to Felicita Medved, there has been political debate as to whether Slovenia should continue its efforts with the engagement of the diaspora. In 2013, there was a proposal for the Office of Slovenes Abroad to be moved to the Ministry of Culture, which would have resulted in the Ministry for Slovenes Abroad being abolished.[125] However, it was the Slovene diaspora that placed enough pressure on the Slovene government to shelve the proposal.[126] The diaspora saw this as a significant step backwards in Slovenia engaging its people that do not reside in the state. Nevertheless, it is argued that this Act should be extended to include those Slovenes that are located in third countries such as Australia. Australia could investigate the opportunity of establishing similar legislation, particularly to engage those diasporas located in the European Union and Association of South East Asian Nations (ASEAN) member states.

[120] Beine, M., Docquier, F., Ozden, C, (2009) *Diasporas*, University of Luxembourg, Journal of Development Economics, 1–12.

[121] Koopmans, R., Statham, P, *How national citizenship shapes transnationalism: A comparison analysis of migrant claims-making in Germany*, Great Britain and the Netherlands, WPTC-01-10, 1–5.

[122] Newland, K., Plazza, S, (2013) *What we know about Diasporas and Economic Development*, Migration Policy Institute, No 5.

[123] Act Regulating the Relations Between the Republic of Slovenia and Slovenes Abroad, Official Gazette of the Republic of Slovenia No. 43/2006.

[124] Medved, F *Unified Slovenian Nation: Slovenian Citizenship Policy towards Slovenians Abroad*, InGyõzõ Cholnoky, Zoltán Kántor, András Ludányi and Eszter Herner-Kovács, Minority Studies Special issue Trends and Directions of Kin-State Policies in Europe and Across the Globe, Lucidus Kiadó, 2014, pp. 153–184.

[125] Ibid.

[126] Ibid.

Stine Neerup argues that "in order to create benefits for all parties involved in the migration process, the diaspora needs to be taken seriously".[127] For example, the Slovene diaspora in Australia has been estimated at approximately 25,000.[128] Diasporas have had a role in shaping nation states such as Slovenia and its independence.[129] Throughout the 1980's Slovenes made a concerted effort to establish closer ties with Austria.[130] With proponents and opponents in Austria for Slovenia's independence, the diaspora kept the pressure on the decision makers and government. By the late 1980s they had supported the Slovenes as their good neighbours.[131] The National Council of Slovenes called on Austria to assist in diplomatic discussions with the European Union. The Slovene diaspora in Italy also took up the cause, and at the time Italy held the European Presidency, thus having direct access to Brussels. This line of communication proved to be very positive for the Slovenes. Furthermore, the Slovenian World Congress conducted protests in Italy and offered its support for the Slovene diaspora's across Europe.[132]

Engaging the diaspora is seen as an important part of expanding national identity. It is argued that by ensuring the diaspora is engaged, provides continuity and a connection and with their state of origin. Upon their return the diaspora can enrich the citizenry with new ideas and thought. Even while the diaspora is abroad, their connection to their state of origin also enables them to pass on knowledge, which can be used by other citizens to enrich the state. Half of all Australian diaspora are resident in the European Union.[133] A smaller diaspora community is located throughout ASEAN member states such as Singapore.[134] Australia can gain from Australian citizens working and living in other nation states.[135] Both states could do more to engage their respective diasporas. Arguably, the future of citizenship will in part involve the ability of states to engage and maintain their connection with their citizens who reside abroad.

[127] Neerup, S, (2009) *Diasporas in the Commonwealth, Focus on diasporas in the Commonwealth*, Institute for the Study of Global Movements, Monash University, Vol 6. No 1, 5. http://www.globalmovements.monash.edu.au/publications/documents/atgissues/Volume.pdf

[128] Klemenčič. M., Harris, M, (2009) *European migrants, diaspora and indigenous ethnic minorities*, Pisa: Plus-Pisa University Press, 56–78. Note the data used appears to have come from 1994, Cebulj Sajko, Settling Slovenes in Australia, Slovenian Emigration, 256.

[129] Radeljić, B, (2013) *Diaspora impact on European Community policy-making*, Ex-Yugoslavia as a case study, in Ulrike Ziemer and Sean Roberts, *East European Diasporas,* Migration, and Cosmopolitanism, Routledge, 43–57.

[130] Ibid.

[131] Ibid.

[132] Ibid.

[133] Hugo, G., Rudd, D., Harris, K, (2003) *Australia's Diaspora: Its size, Nature and Policy Implications*, Committee for Economic Development of Australia, 9–13

[134] Ibid.

[135] Ibid.

6.17 European Union Observatory on Democracy

Thus far this book has focused on comparing the laws of Slovenia and Australia. ever, the laws of the European Union also have to be considered, in the context of Slovenia now being a full member of the Union. Nevertheless, the European Union Observatory on Democracy (EUDO) undertakes important work to better understand citizenship law across European member states. Slovenia is represented on EUDO. The work has also extended to reviewing the citizenship laws (legal norms and modes of acquisition, loss of citizenship and protection against statelessness).[136] The EUDO's work also ensures that member states consider the impact their citizenship laws have on other member states and their respective citizens.[137] Due to the breadth and depth of work undertaken by EUDO, this section focuses on the laws relating to the loss of citizenship.

The EUDO has identified that the loss of citizenship laws varies across member states. Even so, the variables constitute the false information or fraud when a person was applying for citizenship. This also included information regarding the status of the individual's permanent residence abroad, retaining a foreign citizenship, foreign military service, loss of citizenship by parents, and employment in a foreign public service. Additionally, there were variables with the loss of citizenship by a spouse or registered partner, acquisition of foreign citizenship, and information pertaining to criminal offences.[138] The EUDO could consider Australia as being a partner, which would provide further enrichment to the discussion of citizenship.

6.18 Conclusion

Chapter six has confirmed that the citizenship laws of Slovenia and Australia have, and continue to contribute to their respective national identities. Postnational citizenship was embraced by both states. Both states introduced dual citizenship, although to varying degrees. Slovenia decided to restrict dual citizenship to those who could demonstrate a connection with the state. Slovenia has taken a greater interest in its diaspora introducing the Act Regulating the Relations Between the Republic of Slovenia and Slovenes Abroad. Australia hasn't considered its diaspora in the same way as Slovenia, implementing legislation.

---

[136] The consortium consists of the European University Institute, Florence, Italy. University College Dublin, Dublin Ireland, University of Edinburgh, Edinburgh, Scotland, Maastricht University, Maastricht, Netherlands, Migration Policy Group, Brussels, Belgium. http://eudo-citizenship.eu

[137] Ibid.

[138] René Groot, G., Vink, M, (2010) *Loss of Citizenship: Trends and Regulations in Europe*, EUDO Citizenship Observatory, Robert Schuman Centre for Advanced Studies, European University Institute, 4.

The decade of 2000 to 2010 was very busy for Slovenia, they were preparing for accession to the European Union and in 2004 obtained full membership. Australia was one of the first countries outside of the European Union to recognised their independence. Moreover, their new found membership obliged Slovenia to implement European law. The resulting effect was major amendments to the Aliens Act. All Slovenian citizens automatically assumed European citizenship. The concept of a person being able to buy their citizenship emerged in Malta and other nation states. However, it has been argued that this form of citizenship is on the one hand inclusive (for the wealthy) and exclusive for those people who do not have the financial resources to purchase citizenship.

Comparatively, both states have introduced and expanded the concept of citizenship, which has contributed to their respective national identities. The laws have also directed new citizens to whom the state wants them to be. There has been a balancing act by both states, implementing liberal reforms to allow for dual citizenship. Slovenia were developing laws to reach out to their diaspora and descendants of Slovenes residing in other states. On the other hand, there has been a significant shift by both states increasingly making harder for non-citizens to obtain citizenship. Slovenia and Australia have ensured the language used within citizenship law is gender neutral, not separating male and female within the law on citizenship. On the other hand, Australia began to extend the postnational concept of citizenship further by beginning to regulate the activities of its citizens while abroad.

This chapter has highlighted the multidimensional role citizenship has become today is a legal status. Citizenship is an important component of a state's national security, immigration, multicultural, economic, and population policies. More broadly the citizenship reform undertaken by both states, while different, has been undertaken in the national interest. In the case of Slovenia, they have had to undertake their reform program, post 2004, on the backdrop of being a member of the EU club. More importantly, this chapter has confirmed that the principles and concepts of citizenship (birth, descent and naturalization) are well grounded in the law and policy of the respective states. These are unlikely to change anytime soon, however states respond by establishing different threshold requirements to be met, in order, to obtain citizenship by descent or naturalization.

References

Beine, M., Docquier F., & Ozden, C. (2009). Diasporas, University of Luxembourg. *Journal of Development Economics*, 1–12.

Blatter, J. (2011). *Dual citizenship and theories of democracy, citizenship studies* (pp. 769–798). Lucerne: Institute of Political Science, University of Lucerne.

Brubaker, R. (1989). The French revolution and the invention of citizenship. *French Politics and Society, 7*(3), 30–32.

Faist, T., & Gerdes, J. (2008). *Dual citizenship in an age of mobility* (pp. 3–20). Washington, DC: Migration Policy Institute.

Hugo, G., Rudd, D., & Harris, K. (2003). *Australia's diaspora: Its size, nature and policy implications* (pp. 9–13). Melbourne: Committee for Economic Development of Australia.

Klemenčič, M., & Harris, M. (2009). *European migrants, diaspora and indigenous ethnic minorities* (pp. 56–78). Pisa: Plus-Pisa University Press.

Koopmans, R., & Statham, P. (2001). *How national citizenship shapes transnationalism: A comparison analysis of migrant claims-making in Germany, Great Britain* (WPTC-01-10, pp. 1–5).

Medved, F. (2014). Unified Slovenian nation: Slovenian citizenship policy towards Slovenians abroad. In G. Cholnoky, Z. Kántor, A. Ludányi, & E. Herner-Kovács (Eds.), *Minority studies special issue trends and directions of kin-state policies in Europe and across the globe* (pp. 153–184). Budapest: Lucidus Kiadó.

Morjt Howard, M. (2005). Variation in dual citizenship policies- in the countries of the EU. *International Migration Review, 39*(3), 697.

Neerup, S. (2009). *Diasporas in the commonwealth, focus on diasporas in the commonwealth*. Institute for the Study of Global Movements, Monash University, Vol. 6(1), 5.

Newland, K., & Plazza, S. (2013). *What we know about diasporas and economic development* (Migration Policy Institute, No 5). Washington, DC: Migration Policy Institute.

Radeljić, B. (2013). Diaspora impact on European Community policy-making, Ex-Yugoslavia as a case study. In U. Ziemer & S. Roberts (Eds.), *East European diasporas, migration, and cosmopolitanism* (pp. 43–57). New York: Routledge.

Rubenstein, K. (2002). *Australian citizenship law in context* (p. 141). Sydney: Lawbook Co.

Rubenstein, K. (2007). *Chair of the citizenship council* (p. 80). Melbourne: The Australian National University.

Rubenstein, K., & Lenagh-Maquire, N. (2011). *Citizenship and the boundaries of the constitution* (Social Science Research, Legal Scholarship Network, The Australian National University, Law Research Paper), Vol. 11–15, pp. 143–153.

Schuck, P., & Smith, R. (1996). *Citizenship without consent* (p. 2). New Haven: The Social Contract, Yale Law School.

Chapter 7
European Citizenship

Abstract European citizenship has to be one of the most significant changes to citizenship law and policy since WWII. It is the only supranational citizenship in the world. This chapter explores what it means for Slovenians to be part of the European Union. Slovenia became a member to the European Union (EU) in 2004. As a result, they inherited European Law and became European citizens. It begins by tracing the steps of what is known as European citizenship today, from 1957 and the implementation of the European Coal and Steel Community through to the 2007 Treaty of Lisbon. The Maastricht Treaty provides a legal status of European Union citizenship, although different from member states national law. It is argued that the EU through its legal, institutional, judicial, economic and social framework, has to some level established an identity. However, it is not what people would otherwise consider as a national identity. This chapter traces the steps Slovenia has taken on the path to joining the European Union in 2004. The most significant change for all Slovenians was the ability to move freely throughout the European Union. Slovenia would also find itself having to apply the European Union norms of equality between men and women. Equality is a component of modern democracy and national identity. Equality, or otherwise referred to as discrimination, is a fundamental principle of the European Union.

Keywords Accession · Convention · European citizenship · Treaty

7.1 Introduction

European citizenship has risen out of the European peace project, enhancing the single market and human rights of citizens, of member states. Arguably, EU citizenship has provided a level of social coherence. It has not developed a level of supranational identity as the national identity of member states, but, its own identity, can be best described as being strong. People, whether citizens of the EU or not can identify with the EU, its values and legal framework. The EU, has today, developed a comprehensive legal framework that cuts across every area of society (economic,

R. Walters, *National Identity and Social Cohesion in a Time of Geopolitical and Economic Tension: Australia – European Union – Slovenia*,
https://doi.org/10.1007/978-981-15-2164-5_7

social and environmental). One of the drawbacks with the EU framework, is that it provides several exemptions and allows member states to leave. That is, some countries are not part of the EU, but are part of the EEA and their citizens do enjoy some of the rights afforded to EU citizens. Moreover, a member state, can at any time leave the EU. This, arguably, has significant ramifications economically and socially for citizens of the EU and member states. However, it is out of scope to discuss this issue, or BREXIT.

Notwithstanding the above, Karen Knop argues citizenship has branched out from individual rights.[1] Rights are afforded to all citizens who have citizenship of a state, and are gender blind. Kate Nash reaffirms this stance, arguing that human rights and citizenship have long been entwined.[2] A constitution can exclude[3] individuals who do not adhere to the values of the state. Put another way, the expressed and implied rights of a constitution is what Kymlicka would describe as a state directing its citizens to engage in society and embrace the values and expected behaviors of the state. This forms part of a state's identity, and in today's modern world where states have become multi-ethnic rights assist a state in building an inclusive identity.[4] Human rights have been and are currently used to unify and integrate citizens within a states and across national boundaries. However, by states directing their current and future citizens a certain way could be considered as suppressing multiculturalism. Nonetheless, to some extent whether by accident or by design this would occur. Even so, within states such as Slovenia and to a lesser extent Australia laws have been established to recognise, unify and integrate the amalgam of ethnic groups.

Human rights are a reflection of a modern day states democratic values. Human rights can be found in international, supernational and national law. Rights have and continue to be used by states to contribute to their national identity. With the requirement for Slovenia to transpose European law into their national law, Slovenian citizens found themselves gradually becoming part of the European internal (single) market. The chapter compares the constitutional and legislative rights afforded to citizens of Australia and Slovenia. The chapter argues that Slovenia had the opportunity in 1990 to establish a new constitution, whereas Australia's constitution is more than 100 years old (established in 1901). It will also be argued that Australia's constitution is in need of reform. This chapter will identify areas that Slovenia and Australia could take into consideration and use them to change their respective laws in the area of human rights.

---

[1] Knop, K, (2008) *Citizenship Public and Private*, Law and Contemporary Problems, Vol. 71:309, 309–340.

[2] Nash, K, (2009) *Between Citizenship and Human Rights*, Goldsmiths University of London, Volume 43(6), 1067–1083.

[3] Bruce Ackerman, *Reviving Democratic Citizenship*, 2011, http://www.ssc.wisc.edu/~wright/ASA/Ackerman%20Real%20Utopia%20Essay%2D%2D%20Democratic%20Citizenship.pdf

[4] O'neil, C., Watts, T, (2015) *Two Future: Australia at a Critical Moment*, The Text Publishing Swann House, 200–205.

7.2 Slovenia and the European Union

Slovenes would, upon Slovenia becoming a member of the European Union (EU), assume citizenship of the Union.[5] This has brought with it additional rights and responsibilities. The EU has been one of the most complex modern political projects ever undertaken, and has been portrayed as a symbol of unity.[6] This unity has resulted in the shared sovereignty and unity.[7] The unity developed by the EU is no more evident than the rights and responsibilities that have been afforded to all citizens of all Member States. These rights and responsibilities afforded to Slovene citizens with their new found acceptance into the European Union are consistent with being a membership of a political community.[8]

The initial steps to establishing common rights and responsibilities for citizens of the EU can be found in the 1951 Treaty establishing the European Coal and Steel Community (ECSC)[9] which expired in 2002. Apart from building a closer community, the beginnings of the recognition of women can also be found in the ECSC, which promoted the idea of equal pay for equal work.[10] On paper there was no separation of men and women, thus is could be argued the principle of equal pay for equal work applied to both. However, in practice this may have been very different. The principal objective was to unite countries and their people and encourage cooperation. In 1957, the Treaty of Rome, significantly extended the ECSC and introduced the right of "free movement of persons and services".[11] Citizens from Iceland, Lichtenstein and Norway who make up the European Economic Area have also been included and are able to freely work and reside in other EU member states (MS).

In 1968, Council Regulation 1612/68 was introduced to distinguish between free movement and mobility of labour. Free movement constituted the right of a worker and their family to move, reside and work across the EU. However, mobility of labour extended to the worker being guaranteed the possibility of improving their living and working conditions and promoting their social advancement.[12]

[5] Article 20, Treaty on the Functioning of the European Union, Official Journal of the European Union 2012/C 326/01, Volume 55, 26 October 2012, Citizenship of the Union is hereby established. Every person holding the nationality of a Member State shall be a citizen of the Union. Citizenship of the Union shall be additional to and not replace national citizenship.

[6] Walters, R., Bohnic, E, (2015) *Constitutional citizenship, integration and dual citizenship among ASEAN member states*, DIGNITAS Državljanstvo, integracija in pravo nepremičnin, 83–102.

[7] Ibid.

[8] Weil, P, (2001) *Access to Citizenship: A Comparison of Twenty-Five Nationality Laws,* in Citizenship Today" Global Perspectives and Practices, T Alexander Alienikoff and Douglas Klusmeyer, Carnegies Endowment for International Peace, 15–40.

[9] Treaty establishing the European Coal and Steel Community 1951 http://www.consilium.europa.eu/uedocs/cmsUpload/Community.pdf

[10] Ibid, article 119.

[11] Article 3 and Title III, The Treaty of Rome, 25 March 1957, http://ec.europa.eu/economy_finance/emu_history/documents/treaties/rometreaty2.pdf

[12] Council Regulation 1612/68, on freedom of movement of workers within the Community, Official Journal of the European Communities L 257/2.

Furthermore, the abolition of restrictions on movement and residence within the community for workers and their families was enhanced with the introduction of Council Directive 68/360/EEC that enables citizens to leave their territory to undertake activities (employment) in a territory of another member state.[13] However, the European Union in 1970 recognised that many citizens once they had moved to another state may want to move permanently, and introduced law enabling this to occur.[14] For example, at the time when this legislation was implemented, a German citizen who moved to take up employment in France generally had the same working rights[15] as a French citizen (which included conditions of work, tax and social security).

7.2.1 Schengen

The next major change to the European legal framework was the introduction of the Schengen Agreement (SA), signed in 1985.[16] The SA gave effect to the principle of free movement through the abolition of internal frontiers and the introduction of common conditions for the entry of third country nationals into (Schengen Zone of the European Union) MS. In 1986, the Single European Act (SEA) was implemented.[17] The SEA reinforced the 'internal market' concept by allowing EU citizens to move, reside and work freely across the European Union, ensuring the area was without any internal frontiers.[18] Moreover, the SEA also played a major role in establishing economic and social cohesion across member states by reducing the differences in the level of development across the region, and between MS. Furthermore, the SEA was a step forward in closing that gap. By closing the gap, the intention was for citizens across the European Union to become equal (economically and socially) encouraging unification and integration. However, to achieve full equality, unification and integration remains a work in progress.

---

[13] Ibid, article 2.

[14] Regulation (EEC) 1251/70, on the right of workers to remain in the territory of a Member State after having been employed in that State, Official Journal of the European Communities L 142/24.

[15] Council Regulation 312/76, amending the provisions relating to the trade union rights of workers contained in Regulation (EEC) 1612/68 on freedom of movement for workers within the community, Official Journal of the European Union L 039.

[16] Schengen Area and Cooperation, http://eur-lex.europa.eu/legal-content/EN/TXT/HTML/?uri=URISERV:l33020&from=EN

[17] Single European Act 1986, Official Journal of the European Communities L 169.

[18] Ibid, section II, Article13 EEC Treaty, Article 8a. http://www.eurotreaties.com/singleeuropeanact.pdf

7.2.2 European Citizenship

In 1992, the Maastricht Treaty (MT), was signed.[19] The MT created the EU itself, and also created European Union citizenship.[20] It is asserted that the MT confirmed the legal status of Union citizen. Even so, the new found legal status was very different to the legal status of a citizen under the national law of member states. European citizenship is not citizenship in the traditional sense of state based citizenship because the European Union does not register individuals in the same way as member states do. The responsibility for registering and choosing citizens remains with member states. The MT also provided the basis to progress towards a single EU immigration and asylum framework through the new pillar of Co-operation in Justice and Home Affairs.[21]

Citizenship of the Union was not only developed to enhance and advance the single market concept, it has also been used as a tool to further unify and integrate the European Union and its citizens. Seyla Benhabib argues that national citizenship is being devalued and is in decline because of the rise and impact of globalisation and regionalisation.[22] Richard Falk highlights that traditional citizenship is being challenged by trans-national political and social evolution.[23] Globalisation and regionalisation progressively breaks down barriers and borders, and over time this could extend to citizenship.[24] Furthermore, opening global borders takes away the legal role that citizenship has in regulating the movement of people.[25] There is no better example than the European Union and its member states. Member states have retained their individual state identities and responsibility for choosing their citizens while allowing their citizens to be part of the European community. However, European citizenship provides citizens of all member states with a consistent set of rights and freedoms.

The single European currency was also established by the MT and came into effect in 1999. The roll out of the currency would have negative impacts for Slovenes travelling abroad to other EU MS before Slovenia was a full member of the Union. For instance, the new single currency would be one of the most significant and

[19] Article A, Maastricht Treaty 1992, Official Journal of the European Union C 191,

[20] Ibid, article 8, states citizenship of the Union is hereby established. Every person holding the nationality of a Member State shall be a citizen of the Union. 2. Citizens of the Union shall enjoy the rights conferred by this Treaty and shall be subject to the duties imposed thereby, http://www.eurotreaties.com/maastrichtec.pdf

[21] Ibid, article B.

[22] Benhabib, S, (2004) *The Rights of Others: Aliens, Residents, and Citizens*, Cambridge University Press, 110–118.

[23] Faslk, R, (1994) *The Making of Global Citizenship in the Condition of Citizenship*, edited by Bart van Steenbergen, Sage Publications, 127–140.

[24] Brodie, J, (2004) *Introduction: globalisation and citizenship beyond the nation state*, Citizenship Studies, 323–331.

[25] Gibney, M, (2009) *Statelessness: Statelessness and the right to citizenship*, Refugee Studies Centre, University of Oxford, 51–52.

tangible changes Slovene citizens would experience along with the dismantling of its borders with Austria, Italy and Hungary, when the state became a member of the Union. European citizenship provides rights to all citizens within their state of citizenship but in the same way as residence restricts full access to all rights, Union citizenship is also limited. Long term third country national's resident in the Union have similar rights to long term residents in Australia. They are entitled to education, welfare benefits such as retirement pensions, recognition of qualifications, freedom of association and assembly, residence and movement. In both states their political rights are restricted.

Moreover, a Union citizen not resident in their state of origin can vote and stand for election in another member state. A third country national such as an Australian citizen cannot vote or stand for election in Slovenia. Likewise, a Slovenian citizen resident in Australia cannot vote or stand for elections. Thus, the difference in rights afforded to residents and citizens are subtle but are very important to full active citizenship and participation in the political community. Human rights are afforded to all citizens who have citizenship of a state and in the case of Slovenia, also part of the supernational polity. Human rights and citizenship have long been entwined[26] and assist states and supernational polity to build an inclusive society. That inclusiveness at a state level contributes to a common sense of belonging and equality that forms part of national identity.

The Treaty of Amsterdam (AT) 1997 followed the MT, and provided greater recognition of European Union citizenship, immigration, asylum and the inclusion of references to refugees. The AT would also provide greater economic and social activity through the single currency that can be seen today in Slovenia, with the Euro being the only currency used by most EU member states (MS). However, not all MS of the European Union such as the United Kingdom have adopted the Euro as their currency. The AT also marked a new stage for the European Union by bringing the peoples of Europe closer together, and ensuring the decisions made by European Union included a greater dialogue and involvement of all citizens. This included greater participation by citizens in the affairs of the European Union. Citizens could use their language (Spanish, French, German etc.) when communicating with those institutions. The reference to the people or citizens was gender blind ensuring that men and women were equal in the law.

Apart from reinforcing the earlier principle of equal pay[27] for all that had been established by the ECSC in 1957, the AT promoted gender equality across all activities in the Community. This included political participation and policy development in the areas of trade, education, health, agriculture and transport. There was a greater focus on strengthening the protection of rights and interests of all nationals (women and men) of MS through the introduction of citizenship.[28] Article 1 confirmed the

[26] Nash, K, (2009) *Between Citizenship and Human Rights*, Goldsmiths University of London, Volume 43(6), 1067–1083.

[27] Article 137 and 141, Amsterdam Treaty, Official Journal of the European Union C 340.

[28] Ibid, article 1 & B.

importance of fundamental rights that were defined in the 1961 European Social Charter and the 1989 Community Charter of the Fundamental Social Rights of Workers. These legal instruments expressed the same rights of work, conditions, collective bargaining, remuneration, health and safety and training that would apply across the Union.

In reinforcing these earlier rights afforded to citizens, the AT affirmed that the European Union had been founded on key democratic principles that include the right to liberty, respect for human rights and fundamental freedom, the rule of law. Additionally, the AT guaranteed the protection of those rights established by the 1950 European Convention for the Protection of Human Rights and Fundamental Freedoms.[29] These principles can be also found in the constitution of Slovenia today.

The (TN) followed the AT in 2001.[30] It had little to say on citizenship and immigration (asylum and refugees) other than reinforcing the goal of harmonisation and co-operation among EU MS, through a single institutional legal and policy framework. The main point of the TN was to prepare the EU for the accession of the Central and East European countries such as Slovenia, and it reinforced the right to move and reside freely within the territory of any MS'.[31] It was also notable for the adoption of the European Charter of Fundamental Rights 2000, but on a political rather than legally binding basis. However as discussed later in this chapter, the 2000 European Charter of Fundamental Rights would later become an important and binding legal document on all European Member States.

Three years later, in 2004, the European Council approved the Constitutional Treaty (CT),[32] which was signed by the then 25 MS. On 1 February 2005, the Slovenian Parliament ratified the CT.[33] However, the constitution was rejected by the citizens of France and the Netherlands. After the failure of the Constitutional Treaty, the Lisbon Treaty (LT) was signed in late 2007. The LT was initially rejected by the voters of Ireland, the only MS to hold a referendum on the establishment of this European Union Treaty, however the Irish people subsequently approved the LT at the second referendum.[34] The LT came into effect in 2009, incorporating many of the principles of the Constitutional Treaty. Article 2 of the LT outlines the common values for MS of the European Union that are based on pluralism,[35] and aims to create a closer union whereby decisions are inclusive of all citizens.[36] Arguably, this encourages citizens to take a greater role in developing and deciding where the EU should head in the future.

---

[29] Ibid, Article 6.

[30] Treaty of Nice 2001, Official Journal of the European Union C 80/1.

[31] Ibid, article 18,

[32] Treaty establishing the Constitution for Europe, Official Journal of the European Union C 310.

[33] Act ratifying the Treaty on the Constitution for Europe and the Final Act, Official Gazette Republic of Slovenia, No. 1/2005.

[34] Miller, V, (2009) *The Treaty of Lisbon after the second referendum,* Research Paper 09/75, House of Commons.

[35] Article 2, Treaty of Lisbon, Official Journal of the European Union, C 83/171, 2010.

[36] Ibid, article 1.

More importantly, the treaty formally recognised and guaranteed rights to citizens, including reference to the European Union Charter of Fundamental Rights of 2000, as well as referring to the 1950 European Convention for the Protection of Human Rights and Fundamental Freedoms.[37] That guarantee extended to all citizens of the community and did not separate men from women. Moreover, the rights framework established by the EU promotes and protects political citizenship, allowing women to have a greater say and participation in the political discourse of the Union. The Slovenian Constitutional Court in U-I-109/10[38] ruled that the European Union Charter of Fundamental Rights became binding law, protecting the rights of all citizens of the Union, including Slovenians. The treaty also created a common immigration and asylum policy[39] that focused on border checks,[40] subsidiary and temporary protection and migration flows. Additionally, conditions of entry and residence, rights of non-citizens and the protection of individuals subject to people trafficking and illegal immigration were introduced.[41] Furthermore, the LT, rather than making reference to the 'people' as it did when discussing the role of the European Parliament, now refers to the 'citizens'.[42] The LT provides an 'identity clause' that builds on the express duty to respect national identities that was introduced by the Maastricht Treaty.[43]

The citizen's initiative was also introduced to provide greater participation in European Union affairs by all citizens and transcend member states borders. Article 11 requires that no less than one million citizens can petition the European Commission to submit a policy proposal on behalf of the citizens to the European Union (for a policy change that could include economic, social or the protection of the environment). However, for Slovenia, meeting this requirement could be problematic due its population only being approximately two million. Article 11 is better suited to the larger states such as the United Kingdom, France and Germany. To build a more inclusive European Union, particularly for the smaller member states such as Slovenia, there should be a threshold included in this provision to allow those states with a population of less than ten million to be able to submit a policy proposal provided there are between 250,000 and 300,000 citizens who form part of that submission.

---

[37] Ibid, article 6.

[38] Official Gazette of the Republic of Slovenia 78/2011.

[39] Chapter 2, Consolidated Versions of the Treaty of the European Union and the Treaty on the Functioning of the European Union, Official Journal of the European Union, 2010.

[40] Ibid.

[41] Ibid.

[42] Article 10, Treaty of Lisbon, Official Journal of the European Union, C 83/171, 2010.

[43] Article 4 (2) of the TEU, provided by the LT, ensures the European Union respects MS national identities by recognising a states identity as an inherent part of the political and constitutional structure of the country.

Issever and Rummelili[44] note that "European citizenship does not bring a solution to the dichotomy of the nation-state citizenship[45] between citizens and foreigners, "but rather, replaces it with a new one that renders third country nationals (non-citizens) as others and creates categories of Europeans versus non-Europeans".[46] Moro argues that for European citizenship to be fully effective it must eventually replace MS citizenship, to ultimately validate the supernational state.[47] A single European citizenship and identity where member states' citizenship no longer exists is a long way off. Member States would have to concede more of their sovereignty to the European Union, which is very unlikely in the short term. However, and while a single citizenship or European identity has not yet been realised, progress towards a coherent and a more inclusive society has certainly taken shape over the past 50 years. The establishment of European Law; the European Union, the European Commission, the European Bank and European Parliament along with other European institutions is what John Rawls would define as an ordered society. This is where 'everyone accepts and knows that the others accept the same principles of justice and that the basic social institutions generally satisfy and are generally known to satisfy these principles'.[48] The same can be said of Australia and Slovenia, which have established a well ordered society through strong institutions that protect, guide, direct and enhance participation of their respective citizens, within and outside the state.

It could be argued that the European Union has not been particularly successful in creating a European identity. However, it is argued that a level of an identity has been established. On the one side, citizenship has to some level provided a sense of what it means to be European, as people know they can easily move throughout the Union. The EU has a common policy and law on immigration, human rights and private international laws. On the other side, the ability for member states to collaborate on trade and human rights and ensure they are able to bargain with other nation states as a collective – does provide the basis for a level of EU identity. On the backdrop of this, with the EU establishing laws that influence third countries to adopt similar, is the EU and its member states exerting a collective identity to the world. A good example of this is the implementation of the General Data Protection Regulation in 2018,[49] whereby, these data protection law has not only influenced but forced third countries to adopt similar legal principles. The GDPR, is based on one

[44] Issever, E., Rumelili, B (2009), *European Citizenship and Third Country Nationals: A Comparative Analysis of Germany and Britain*, INTL 533, 1.

[45] Ibid.

[46] Maas, W, (2008) *Migrants, States, and EU Citizenship's Unfulfilled Promise*, Citizenship Studies, 583–596.

[47] Moro, G, (2001) *The Lab of European Citizenship: democratic deficit, governance approach and non-standard citizenship*, International Institute of Sociology Congress, 2–11.

[48] Rawls, J, (2005) *A Theory of Justice*, Oxford University Press, 4–6.

[49] General Data Protection Regulation (EU) 2016/679, on the protection of natural persons with regard to the processing of personal data and on the free movement of such data, and repealing Directive 95/46/EC.

of the most important principles and values of the EU-Human Rights. There are many other examples where the EU has extend their collective identity, and this is no more evident than with the development and establishment of Free Trade Agreements. Although, it is outside the scope of this book to examine various examples where the EU has established a level of identity.

Nonetheless, and however, people have European Union citizenship, but they still feel like MS citizens first, and European citizens second (if at all). For Slovenes this was evidenced in the 2010 research project undertaken by the European Commission (the Flash Eurobarometer) which surveyed European citizens on how familiar they were with their understanding of European Union citizenship and the rights they possess. The report found that 79% of European Union citizens interviewed had minimal understanding and familiarity of the term "citizen of the European Union".[50] About 22% of people surveyed had not even heard of the term. For Slovenia, having been a member for 6 years, only 49% were familiar with and understood what a European citizen means. Only 36% being familiar, but, not sure of its meaning of EU citizenship, and a mere 15% never having heard of the term.[51] Further work is needed by Slovenia to promote European Union citizenship and the benefits this has afforded its citizens.

The European Union had an opportunity, but failed to strengthen the identity with the proposed constitution. The major reform from the introduction of the LT was establishing a single legal framework that would remove the three pillars (1) European Communities, (2) Common Foreign and Security Policy, (3) Police and Judicial Co-operation in Criminal Matters) by merging the first and the third pillar. One of the outcomes was improved controls over the number of third country nationals entering member states. Article 79 (5) allows for MS to maintain their control on the numbers of non-citizens (third country nationals) seeking to work (employed or self-employed) in their respective territories. Arguably, the above pillars go some way for the Union to exert a level of identity to the world.

Member states are required to transpose European Union legislation, legal principles and norms from treaties, conventions, regulations and directives into their respective legislation. The European Union develops and implements legislation in the areas of immigration, citizenship, rights and international protection. Article 288 reinforces the position of the European Union that regulations are binding in their entirety on MS. Directives are also binding, but left to MS on how they implement them. Decisions of the European Union will be binding on those to whom the decision is addressed and recommendations including opinions remain without any binding force. Article 289 of the LT is important, outlining the ordinary legislative procedure (otherwise known as the Co-decision procedure) and consists of joint adoption by the European Parliament and the European Council. This procedure is defined in Article 294.

[50] European Commission, *Flash Eurobarometer European Union Citizenship; Analytical Report*, 2010, 7.

[51] Ibid, 8.

Despite the European Parliament and European Council having the initiative to prepare Union legislation, MS do have the ability under article 289 of the LT to also put forward a legislative proposal. There are specific powers provided that allow, on behalf of Member States, the European Union competence to legislate and adopt binding acts, and for MS to implement those legal instruments.[52] *Furthermore, the European Parliament has established the Rules of Procedure.*[53] *Rule 36 is particularly important to the citizens of the* European Union, *in which the 2000 Charter of Fundamental Rights and Freedoms should be considered as part of all activities undertaken by the Union.*[54] *Articles 37 and 37a ensure that any legislative act proposed, is verified as to its legal basis in accordance with article 290 of the Treaty on the Functioning of the European Union (TFEU). Where a new act or amendments are proposed, a resolution must be adopted pursuant to article 225 of the TFEU. The legislation can go through three readings before it is adopted.* However, this can only occur on the recommendation of the European Central Bank or the Court of Justice of the European Union.

The Slovenian National Assembly (NA) has responsibility for the adoption of a constitutional act amending the Constitution and national laws[55] that at the time and continuing today can be undertaken by referendum or the general business of government.[56] That is, the draft laws are adopted by the NA[57] and sent to either the President of the NA, National Council or at least 5000 voters,[58] for the laws to be accepted an implemented. The legislation must contain the reason for its adoption, a presentation of the harmonisation in regards to European Union law and a presentation of the legislation in the legal system of a minimum of three other MS.[59] The proposal must be accompanied by a presentation of the same EU law and how it has been adopted in (three other) EU MS. Slovenia's road to accession saw the state adopt and transpose EU law into its national legislative framework. EU citizenship along with national citizenship is multidimensional.

Citizenship of the Union has been used to enhance the single market concept, while integrating and unifying member states and their citizens. Furthermore, Union citizenship has also confirmed the legal status of who is a citizen of the EU and who is not. It must be noted that EU citizenship has very little direct influence on Slovenia's national identity. This identity while limited, when coupled with other elements of the law, institutions, and policy of the EU goes some way to establishing

---

[52] Article 2 (1), Lisbon Treaty, Official Journal of the European Union, C 83/171, 2010.

[53] European Parliament, Rules of Procedure, Chapter 1, 2012, 29–65.

[54] Article 2, 6 (2) and (3), Treaty of the European Union, Official Journal of the European Union C 83/19.

[55] Article 107, Rules and Procedure of the National Assembly, Official Gazette of the Republic of Slovenia No. 64/07.

[56] Ibid, article 108.

[57] Ibid, article 113.

[58] Ibid, article 114.

[59] Article 115, Rules and Procedure of the National Assembly, Official Gazette of the Republic of Slovenia No. 64/07.

a level of indentity across the Union. Moreover, this identity of the EU and its law directly influences Slovenia's identity. There is a requirement for Slovenia to adopt the democratic principles and law of the EU. Thus, Slovenia's identity has adopted the values of the EU, along with its laws pertaining to human rights, amongst others.

7.3 Slovenia's Road to Accession

Relations with the European Union began on conclusion of the Cooperation Agreement by the Former Socialist Republic of Yugoslavia in 1980. In 1993 Slovenia began to consider the rights and obligation of the agreement.[60] On 15 January 1992, not long after independence the European Community, which was the forerunner of today's European Union formally, recognised Slovenia as an independent state. Slovenia was also recognised by the international community, becoming the 176th member of the United Nations.[61] Australia was one of the first countries outside Europe, along with Canada, to recognise Slovenia's independence on 16 January 1992.[62] However, the European Union would be divided over the breakup of the former YU. For example, Germany provided support for Slovenia and Croatia in developing and becoming independent states, unlike France and the United Kingdom.[63] The German motivation was to stop the expansion of Serbian nationalism that was spreading across the territory. The United Kingdom did not favor Slovenia breaking away from Yugoslavia (YU), and perceived the problem did not lie in the expansion of Serbian nationalism but rather with all the Republics of the former YU. The European Union saw Slovenia and Croatia as a threat to peace across Southeast Europe, and were of the view that the YU communist government and federal army stood for European stability.[64] Marolov argues that the European Union feared other states and territories would follow the same path, and conflict would once again spread across Europe.

The diaspora community of Slovenia played a part in the former Republic's move towards independence. James Gow and Cathie Carmichael note that the Slovene World Congress of 1990 sought a common goal of independence establishing links with its diplomatic community abroad, including Slovene- Australians and particularly those Slovenes located in the neighbouring states of Austria, Italy and

---

[60] European Parliament, Briefing No 9, Slovenia and the Enlargement of the European Union, www.europa.eu/enlargement/breifings/9a3_en.htm

[61] Ministry of Foreign Affairs, Twenty Years of Slovenia's International Recognition, Republic of Slovenia, http://www.mzz.gov.si/en/twenty_years_of_slovenias_international_recognition

[62] Ibid.

[63] Marolov, D, (2012) *The Policy of the USA and EU towards the Disintegration of Yugoslavia*, Goce Delcev University, Strip, Republic of Macedonia, International Journal of Social Science Tomorrow, Vol 1, No.2, 2–5.

[64] Ibid.

Hungary.[65] What emerged was a diaspora community that got involved by influencing the diplomatic community of the benefit and need for Slovenia to become an independent state. One of those benefits was its geographic position to Europe providing easy access to the East and Southern European countries. Increasingly for states such as Slovenia the diaspora community has played and continues to play, a critical role in the politics and identity of the state.

Not long after independence, Slovenia would commence the process of EU accession. There was a formal process and the EU required all future MS to meet certain economic, social and environmental criteria set out in the Amsterdam Treaty,[66] and the Copenhagen European Council[67] as well as Madrid European Council. The Madrid principles are important, requiring not only that EU law be transposed into national legislation, but also that EU law be implemented by MS. Following the signing of the European Agreement in 1996, Slovenia submitted an application for full membership of the Union. In July 1997 the agreement was ratified by the Slovenian National Assembly following an amendment to article 68 of the Slovenian constitution. This was based on the Constitutional Court's opinion[68] and enabled a 4 year transition period for non-citizens to own real-estate within the Republic. Slovenia implemented the *acquis communautaire*, which began in 1998. The European Commission began negotiations with Slovenia and by 1999 the European Parliament announced that progress towards accession was on track, meeting the necessary economic criteria and implementation of the *acquis communautaire*.[69]

By 2000, Slovenia was required to have implemented major economic reforms including privatisation of banks and other institutions (telecommunications and pensions), to ensure there was a free market. This process would also see the demise of any legacy of the former YU socialist arrangements. By the end of 2002, Slovenia had adopted up to 1000 pieces of European legislation, into the national legislative framework. This included 288 parliamentary acts, 272 governmental regulations, and 784 ministerial regulations as part of the National Programme for the Adoption of the Acquis (NPAA).[70] However, this only accounted for 67% of the NPAA being fulfilled, and being 2 years away from full membership, Slovenia still had considerable work to do.

---

[65] Gow, J., Carmichael, C, (2000) *Slovenia and the Slovenes: A Small State and the New Europe*, London: Hurst & Co.

[66] Article 6 (1), upon application the principles of liberty, democracy, respect of human rights and fundamental freedoms and the rule of law apply.

[67] Copenhagen European Council required stability of a nation states institutions guaranteeing democracy, rule of law, human rights and respect of minorities, the existence of a functioning market economy able to cope with market forces of the Union as well as the ability to take on obligations of membership, economic, economic and monetary.

[68] Paragraph 2, Article 160 Slovenian Constitution and article 70 Constitutional Court Act, Official Gazette of the Republic of Slovenia 64/07, Official Gazette of the Republic of Slovenia 40/97.

[69] Regular Report, From the Commission on Slovenia's Progress Towards Accession, 1999, 71, http://ec.europa.eu/enlargement/archives/pdf/key_documents/1999/slovenia_en.pdf

[70] Republic of Slovenia, *Amendments to the Republic of Slovenia's National Programme for the Adoption of the Acquis*, 2002, 1.

The Slovenian constitution was amended to include article 3a (3) that provided legal effect for Slovenia to adopt European Union legislation and have representation to European institutions. The constitutional doctrine of the right to self-determination allows Slovenia to be a member of the European Union, but also allows the state to exit upon agreement from the European Union. However, there have been many positive benefits from integrating Slovenia into the Union such as securing further progress towards democracy, social justice, freedom and the basic rights of the Slovene citizens.[71] The introduction of this provision also allowed for the automatic transfer of parts of the Slovene sovereignty to the EU. The ECJ developed legal doctrine that is the cornerstone of the interpretation and implementation of EU legislation such as *direct effect*,[72] *legal certainty*,[73] *proportionality*,[74] *conflict of laws*,[75] *and supremacy*.[76] These principles have a significant role to play in linking European

[71] Jambrek, P, (2014) *Nation's Transitions, Social and Legal Issues of Slovenia's Transitions 1945–2015*, Graduate School of Government and European Studies, Brdo pri Kranju and European Faculty of Law, Nova Gorica, Slovenia, 279.

[72] Direct effect has been fundamental to the ECJ in establishing a basis for giving effect to article 288 of Lisbon Treaty (article 249 of the EC Treaty) that states a regulation shall have general application, shall be binding in its entirety and directly applicable to Member States of the European Union.

[73] Legal certainty is closely aligned with the many European Union legal principles and doctrines such as the doctrine of *acte clair* pertaining to languages used across the European Union, and requires the law to be clear and accurate. Legal certainty has also been well established under article 2 of the Slovenian Constitution.

[74] Article 5, Consolidated Version of the Treaty of the European Union, Official Journal of the European Union, 2008. The principle was nevertheless present in former Yugoslavia, the Slovenian Internal Affairs Act 1980, forming part of Slovenian penal law, and in 1994 was included in the Penal Procedure Act Official Gazette RS, No 28/80. In Australia proportionality has been recognised in relation to sections 92 and 117 of the Constitution (express and implied freedoms). *In Minister for Resources v Dover Fisheries Pty Ltd* (1993) 43 FCR 565, the Federal Court stated; the concept of proportionality' as a criterion for assessment of validity in constitutional and administrative law appears to have entered the stream of common law from Europe and in particular, from the jurisprudence of the Court of Justices and the European Communities, including the European Court of Human Rights".

[75] Conflict of laws exists between the European Union and member states and in Australia between the commonwealth and states. Case 224/97 *Erich Ciola v Land Vorarlberg* [1999], Second Chamber, ECR I-257/8, stated that community law takes precedence over national law. In the Australian context, the executive power of the commonwealth is provided by section 61, and s51 of the Constitution, providing the Commonwealth the necessary powers to legislate and control such things as trade and commerce with other countries, taxation, external affairs and the immigration and entry of aliens, amongst others.

[76] The doctrine of supremacy, Case *6/64 Flaminio Costa v ENEL* [1964] ECR 585, CMLR 585, 593, and the court stated EU law is supreme to MS constitutions, and the doctrine also applies to any present and future European Union law. The principle is found in article 3 of the Slovenian Constitution. Section 75 of the Australian Constitution provides exclusive jurisdiction of High Court in matters that arise under any treaty provided that Australia is a signatory and ratified the legal instrument. Furthermore, sections 51 (ii), 92, 99 and 117 of the constitution effectively provides that Australia is a stand alone country that is made up of states and territories, and national law takes precedence over state and territory law.

Union and MS national laws that regulate the activities of citizens (immigration, rights and private international law). Similar legal principles exist in Australia's common law system, where national legislation interacts with state and territory law. In *Minister for Resources v Dover Fisheries Pty Ltd*,[77] the Federal Court stated; the concept of proportionality' as a criterion for assessment of validity in constitutional and administrative law. Section 51 and 52 of the Australian constitution provide the.

Commonwealth with exclusive right to legislate for certain areas such as immigration. Section 109 provides that a valid law of the Commonwealth which is inconsistent with a State based law, the Commonwealth law prevails. Section 75 provides exclusive jurisdiction of High Court in matters that arise under any treaty provided that Australia is a signatory and ratified the legal instrument. The Commonwealth applies the principle of supremacy when it comes to the adoption of international law. Furthermore, sections 92, 99 and 117 effectively provides that Australia is a stand-alone country that is made up of states and territories, and national law takes precedence over state and territory law.

The Accession Treaty 2004 was established to assist states in their transition in joining the EU including Czech Republic, Republic of Estonia, Republic of Cyprus, Republic of Latvia, Republic of Lithuania, Republic of Hungary, Republic of Malta, Republic of Poland, Slovak Republic and Republic of Slovenia. Article 53 of the Treaty stated that upon accession, the new MS shall be considered as being addressees of directives and decisions within the meaning of article 249 of the EC Treaty and Article 161 of the Euratom Treaty[78] (Treaty establishing the European Atomic Energy Community). Along with other MS, Slovenia was now required to adopt EU law, which has had an impact on all Slovene citizens, including the free movement of goods and free movement for persons.[79] However, despite full membership of the EU there were restrictions placed on Slovenes working in certain states, as discussed later in this chapter. Having this new found freedom to move and reside in other MS saw a rise in emigration of Slovenes abroad totaling 8269 in 2004, up from 5876 in 2003.[80] In 2002 7269 Slovenes moved abroad.[81] The statistics do not state whether this movement was to other European Union MS, or other countries outside of Europe.[82] Finally, the 2003 Slovenian referendum for membership to the EU concluded that 89% of the voters, voted in favour of European Union membership. On 16 April 2003, Slovenia signed the Accession treaties in Athens, Greece.[83] Slovenia and its citizens finally became a member of the EU on 1 May 2004.

---

[77] (1993) 43 FCR 565.

[78] Title II Applicability of the Acts of the Institutions, Official Journal of the European Union, 2003, L 236.

[79] Article 53, Official Journal L 236, Slovenia's Accession to the European Union, 2003.

[80] Migration changes and total increase, 2004, Statistical Office of the Republic of Slovenia, http://www.stat.si/eng/novice_poglej.asp?ID=705

[81] Ibid.

[82] Ibid.

[83] Facts about Slovenia, Slovenia a Member of the EU by 1 May 2004, http://www.ukom.gov.si/fileadmin/ukom.gov.si/pageuploads/dokumenti/Publikacije/european-union.pdf

7.3.1 Impact to Slovenes from European Union Accession

Arguably, the most notable immediate impacts on the citizens included the transition from the Slovene currency (the Tolar) to the Euro. The legal steps to adopting the Euro began on 28 June 2004 with Slovenia entering the ERM II (exchange rate mechanism).[84] The adoption of the Euro currency was undertaken incrementally with the exchange rate mechanism to ensure stability between the currencies in 2004. It was not until 2006 that prices for goods and services began to be displayed in both currencies. The European Commission and European Central Bank at a meeting in the Economic and Financial Affairs Council approved Slovenia fully adopting the Euro on 11 July 2006. On 1 January 2007, the Slovene Tolar ceased to be used as a currency in Slovenia. The Euro is now the principal currency used by Slovenians in Slovenia and across the European Union.

Slovenians were no longer inhibited by border crossings when travelling to other EU MS. They would also be afforded access to European institutions such as the European Central Bank, European Parliament, European Commission, the European Court of Human Rights and the European Court of Justice. The freedoms afforded to Slovene citizens included the freedom to move, work, establish a business, study or provide services also enabled Slovenes to gain access to other markets across the European Union. The mutual recognition process established by the EU, resulted for example, in a diploma obtained in Slovenia being recognized in other EU MS. One of the most significant changes was the requirement to allow foreigners from other EU MS to purchase property in Slovenia. The 1997 Constitutional Court[85] observed that the Article 68 was changed to enable aliens to acquire property in Slovenia.[86]

Prior to 1997 the Slovenian Constitution went some way to enabling aliens to acquire property, however this was subject to the national laws.[87] No longer was Slovenian property an exclusive right for Slovenians as it was under the former Yugoslavia. Slovenians were able to get full access to employment only in the United Kingdom, Ireland and Sweden. It was not until 2011, that all restrictions would be lifted allowing Slovene citizens to work without a permit anywhere across the European Union.[88] Even so, there was no impact where a Slovene national was already working in a MS at the time of accession. However, the person needed to

---

[84] Slovenia joins the Euro area, European Commission, http://ec.europa.eu/economy_finance/articles/euro/slovenia_joins_the_euro_area_en.htm

[85] Slovenian Constitutional Court, Official Gazette of the Republic of Slovenia No. 42/97.

[86] Jambrek, P, Professor Graduate School of Government and European Affairs Substitute member, Venice Commission, Strasbourg 2009. http://www.venice.coe.int/webforms/documents/default.aspx?pdffile=CDL-JU(2009)034-e

[87] Ibid.

[88] Regulation (ECC) No 1612/68, reinforces the right of freedom of movement for workers within the Community, Official Journal of the European Union, L 257.

have been working in that MS for a period of 12 months or longer. Article 1 through to 6 of Regulation 1612/68, applied for 7 years following accession, restricting access by Slovenes to other MS labour markets where that MS determined there could be a threat to their own citizens.

It was on 30 March 2008 that Slovenia finally released the control of its air borders. As a result, Slovenia would then be subject to the European Union common visa system and Schengen Information System (SIS), a data base used by MS to track people entering and exiting the European Union. A Slovene citizen who had left Slovenia and the EU would, upon re-entry only had to produce their Slovene passport once, whether the individual arrived from Serbia or Switzerland.

Despite the long road to EU membership, in 2015, Slovenia's acceptance, accession, and membership to the European Union can be described as a great success following the breakup of the former YU. The only other former YU Republic to gain membership of the European Union is Croatia, in 2013. Joining the European Union and implementing European Union law has provided Slovene citizens with an expanded set of rights. The next section compares how Slovenia has reflected the rights afforded by the European Charter of Fundamental Rights 2000 in the Slovene constitution and compares those rights with Australia's constitution and national laws. The provisions of the 1950 European Convention on Human Rights and accompanying provisions of Protocol and Protocols No 4, No 6, No 7, No 12 and No 13, are also referenced where applicable. It must be noted that the 1950 European Convention on Human Rights, has been the basis for the further development of rights in the European Union and its legal framework. As stated earlier in this chapter, the European Union and its law directly influences Slovenia's identity. There is a requirement for Slovenia to adopt the democratic principles and law of the European Union. Thus, Slovenia's identity has adopted the values of the European Union, along with its laws pertaining to human rights.

7.4 Conclusion

European citizenship arguable has provided the opportunity for the collective Union to direct its citizens to embrace and practice the democratic principles of the Union. Therefore, it has been demonstrated that the EU has to some degree established an identity. This identity is different to what is described as a national identity, but forms part of the supranational polity that this Union has become. European citizenship has established a legal status confirming who is and who is not a citizen of the European Union, even though member states retain the sovereign right to choose who will be a citizen of the EU. It has been used to enhance the single (economic) market concept, while integrating and unifying member states and their citizens.

Arguably EU citizenship to be one of the most significant changes to citizenship law and policy since WWII. It is the only supranational citizenship in the world. It is very different to the federal citizenship of Australia and the United States, as they have total responsibility for citizenship – at the federal level. In 2004, Slovenia gained membership of the European Union. This provided Slovenes with new found rights and freedoms for all its citizens. European citizenship along with national citizenship is also multidimensional. Despite this, this chapter has traced the steps of what is known as European citizenship today, from 1957 and the implementation of the European Coal and Steel Community through to the 2007 Treaty of Lisbon. European citizenship has not meant that member states have had to relinquish their sovereign right to choose who will and who will not be a citizen of their state. The EU and its institutions do not register citizens in the same manner as member states under nation laws. As a result of EU citizenship and the integration of member states has made a strong contribution to EU identity and social cohesion of 28 member states.

References

Benhabib, S. (2004). *The rights of others: Aliens, residents, and citizens* (pp. 110–118). Cambridge: Cambridge University Press.

Brodie, J. (2004). Introduction: Globalisation and citizenship beyond the nation state. *Citizenship Studies, 8*, 323–331.

Faslk, R. (1994). In B. van Steenbergen (Ed.), *The making of global citizenship in the condition of citizenship* (pp. 127–140). London: Sage.

Gibney, M. (2009). *Statelessness: Statelessness and the right to citizenship* (pp. 51–52). Oxford: Refugee Studies Centre, University of Oxford.

Gow, J., & Carmichael, C. (2000). *Slovenia and the Slovenes: A small state and the new Europe*. London: Hurst & Co.

Issever, E., & Rumelili, B. (2009). European citizenship and third country nationals: A comparative analysis of Germany and Britain. *INTL, 533*, 1.

Jambrek, P. (2014). *Nation's transitions, social and legal issues of Slovenia's transitions 1945–2015* (p. 279). Nova Gorica: Graduate School of Government and European Studies, Brdo pri Kranju and European Faculty of Law.

Knop, K. (2008). Citizenship public and private. *Law and Contemporary Problems, 71*(309), 309–340.

Maas, W. (2008). Migrants, states, and EU citizenship's unfulfilled promise. *Citizenship Studies, 12*, 583–596.

Marolov, D. (2012). The Policy of the USA and EU towards the disintegration of Yugoslavia. *Goce Delcev University, Strip, Republic of Macedonia, International Journal of Social Science Tomorrow, 1*(2), 2–5.

Moro, G. (2001). *The Lab of European Citizenship: Democratic deficit, governance approach and non-standard citizenship*. International Institute of Sociology Congress, pp. 2–11.

Nash, K. (2009a). Between citizenship and human rights. *Goldsmiths University of London, 43*(6), 1067–1083.

Nash, K. (2009b). Between citizenship and human rights. *Goldsmiths University of London, 43*(6), 1067–1083.

O'Neil, C., & Watts, T. (2015). *Two future: Australia at a critical moment* (pp. 200–205). Melbourne: The Text Publishing Swann House.

Rawls, J. (2005). *A theory of justice* (pp. 4–6). Oxford: Oxford University Press.

Walters, R., & Bohnic, E. (2015). *Constitutional citizenship, integration and dual citizenship among ASEAN member states* (pp. 83–102). Slovenia: DIGNITAS Državljanstvo, integracija in pravo nepremičnin.

Weil, P. (2001). Access to citizenship: A comparison of twenty-five nationality Laws. In T. A. Alienikoff & D. Klusmeyer (Eds.), *Citizenship today: Global perspectives and practices* (pp. 15–40). Washington, DC: Carnegies Endowment for International Peace.

Chapter 8
Human Rights, Identity and Social Cohesion

Abstract Human rights are an important part of a state's identity. They are fundamental democratic principles that have been embraced by the EU, Slovenia and Australia. More importantly, they make a significant contribution to social cohesion. This chapter has been divided into two parts. Part one highlights compares the constitutional rights of Slovenia and Australia. Part two compares the extent of rights reflected in the 1950 European Convention on Human Rights and Fundamental Freedoms (ECFF) and more recently the European Charter of Fundamental Rights (ECFR) 2000, and the national laws of Australia and Slovenia. This chapter does not highlight any constitutional changes that have been established after 2017. Notwithstanding the above, the rights established by the EU, are in my view the most comprehensive legal framework for rights, anywhere in the world. They have been developing now for more than 70 years, particularly following WW II. Since then, the rise of human rights has largely focused on equality, aspects of privacy, civil and political rights. However, today, with technology at the forefront of the economy, privacy over the Internet has, arguably, become one of the most challenging areas of emerging law and policy to regulate and manage. It has the ability to undermine the identity of a jurisdiction and disrupt social cohesion. Yet, applied in the right way, it can enhance identity and cohesion. Therefore, this chapter also demonstrates how privacy over the Internet is becoming a formidable challenge for the EU, Slovenia and Australia.

Keywords Constitution · Data protection · Freedoms · Human right · Privacy · Social cohesion

R. Walters, *National Identity and Social Cohesion in a Time of Geopolitical and Economic Tension: Australia – European Union – Slovenia*,
https://doi.org/10.1007/978-981-15-2164-5_8

8.1 Part One: Introduction

A constitution is a state's basic legal document that has been designed to endure over a longer period than national legislation.[1] Helen Irving argues the constitution distributes power to government to make laws,[2] to protect the rights and freedoms of its citizens. The constitution provides legal certainty and can endure changes in society and the wider world. The population (citizens) of a state is one of the constitutive elements of nationalism and statehood and is supported by a state establishing citizenship laws[3] and a constitution.

The Australian High Court has referred to the constitution of Australia[4] as being the foundation of the state,[5] which provides the state with the highest legislative power.[6] According to Gary Jacobsohn, a state's constitution is more than a written document.[7] A constitution outlines the fundamental norms and principles of the states' society that blend the state's identity with its values and culture.[8] The values and culture include the expressed constitutional rights of a state that forms part of the overall national identity. Comparatively, the expressed constitutional rights of Slovenia and Australia are different. Slovenia, having what could be argued is a modern day constitution has explicitly expressed the rights and freedoms afforded to its citizens and non-citizens.

The Australian constitution[9] has express and implied rights. The express rights have been limited to the right to vote,[10] with the right to trial by jury being another expressed right.[11] However, this is restricted to where there is a trial by indictment.[12]

[1] Novak, M, (2010) *Three Models of Balancing (in Constitutional Review)*, Ratio Juris, Vol. 1. 101–112. The Constitution of the Republic of Slovenia, Official Gazette Republic of Slovenia No. 33/91-I, 42/97, 66/2000, 24/03, 69/04, 68/06, and 47/13. Slovenia on the other hand has been able to amend its constitution seven times since independence, with the most recent occurring in 2013. These changes are outside the scope of this research.

[2] Helen Irving, *Australia's Constitutional Identity: A conundrum for the 21st Century*. in Not known (Eds.), *Unity and diversity: a national conversation*: Barton lectures, Australia: ABC Books, 2001, 194–221.

[3] U-I- 89/99, Official Gazette of the Republic of Slovenia, No. 59/99.

[4] Australia referendum requirements set out in section 128. Since the Australian constitution was established there has been 44 referendums to change the constitution, and only 8 referendums have been successful.

[5] *Wik Peoples v Queensland* (1996) 187 CLR 1 at 182.

[6] *R v Secretary of State for the Home Department; Ex parte PieRson* [1998] AC 539 at 587.

[7] Jacobsohn, G, (2012) *Constitutional Identity*, Harvard University Press, Vol. 21 No.3, 132–134.

[8] Ibid.

[9] Harvey, M, (2001) *Australia and the European Union: Some Similar Constitutional Dilemmas*, DeakinLaw Review, 312.

[10] Australian Constitution 1900, s 41. *R v Pearson; Exparte Sipka* (1983) 152 CLR 254. *Kingsville v The Queen* (1985) 159 CLR 264. *Cheatle v The Queen* (1993) 177 CLR 541.

[11] Australian Constitution 1900, s 80.

[12] *R v Bernasconi* (1915) 19 CLR 629.

Freedom of religion can be found in section 116 of the Australian constitution[13] and applies to any religion and religious observance.[14] The Australian constitution differs from the Slovenian constitution in the area of citizenship. The Slovenian constitution specifies that citizenship is regulated by the law.[15] Australia's does not. Furthermore, the Australian Commonwealth Parliament has the power to make laws with respect to the acquisition of property, medical or dental services, the High Court's jurisdiction to control the executive, guaranteeing that trade and commerce amongst states is free, and the imposition of discrimination.[16]

George Williams and David Hume argue that there is an expanded list of rights and protections where the Commonwealth is prohibited from discriminating between states. These include; protecting public servants that have been transferred from the state to the Commonwealth and prohibiting the Commonwealth from preferencing one state over another in trade and commerce. Additionally, the Commonwealth is prohibited from abridging the right of a state or the residents of a state to the reasonable use of water. Changing the constitution cannot be undertaken without the consent of the electors.[17] The 'implied' rights and freedoms can be summarized as the freedom of political communication,[18] the freedom of movement, association and speech.[19] Even though these rights and freedoms have not been explicitly expressed in the Australian constitution, the High Court of Australia has ruled that these rights do exist. Frank Bechhofer and David McCrone[20] argue a state's constitution contributes to its identity, and modernizing a constitution will enhance that state's identity and strengthen nationalism.[21] A constitution can be used by a state to direct its citizens to engage in society and embrace the values and expected behaviors of the state. Constitutions can set out the rights and obligations afforded to citizens, and assist a state in building an inclusive identity.[22]

---

[13] Constitution of Australia 1900, s116.

[14] *Adelaide Company of Jehovah's Witness Inc v Commonwealth* (1943) 67 CLR 116.

[15] Article 12, Slovenian Constitution, Official Gazette of the Republic of Slovenia, 33/91, 42/97, 66/2000 and 24/03, 68/06 and 47/2013.

[16] Williams, G., Hume, D, (2013) Human Rights under the Australian Constitution, Oxford University Press, 112–113. Constitution of Australia 1901, s51(xxxi), 51(xxiiiA), 75(v), 92.

[17] Australian Constitution, ss84, 99, 100, 128.

[18] *Kruger v Commonwealth* (Stolen Generation Case) (1997) 190 CLR 1.

[19] *Australian Capital Television v Commonwealth* (1992) 177 CLR 212.

[20] Frank Bechhofer and David McCrone, *National Identity, Nationalism and Constitutional Change*, Palgrave Mcmillan, 2009, http://www.institute-of-governance.org/__data/assets/pdf_file/0011/35939/chap1_intro.pdf

[21] Ibid.

[22] O'neil, C., Watts, T, (2015) *Two Future: Australia at a Critical Moment*, The Text Publishing Swann House, 200–205.

The Slovenian constitution[23] distinguishes between two groups to whom the rights apply. The first group applies to everyone[24] (including citizens and residents in the territory) and the second group only applies to Slovene citizens.[25] Australia's constitution does not provide the same distinction. The rights of the citizen and non-citizen are a man-made 'construct'. Since the establishment of the 1948 Universal Declaration on Human Rights, nation states have improved their regulatory frameworks that ensure their citizens are afforded expressed rights and freedoms. Both Slovenia and Australia have ratified the 1948 Universal Declaration on Human Rights. Since 1948 there have been a number of legal instruments established to promote and protect all people of the world, such as the International Convention on the Elimination of all Forms of Racial Discrimination 1965 and International Covenant on Civil and Political Rights 1966.[26] These international legal instruments have all assisted in shaping the European Union, Slovenian and Australian law.

The European Union considers human rights as one of the principal policy objectives to the ongoing integration and unification of MS and their citizens. This has been achieved along with the extensive European legal framework, with the implementation of the 1950 European Convention on Human Rights and Fundamental Freedoms (ECFF)[27] and more recently the European Charter of Fundamental Rights (ECFR) 2000. The importance of the ECFR cannot be underestimated. Arguably, it has become one of the most important rights based legal documents that applies across the EU. Today, it is binding law[28] on all 28 member states of the European Union. However, it must be noted that the 1950 ECFF is also binding law and was established by the Council of Europe which has a much broader membership than the European Union. For instance, the Council of Europe has 47 members that includes states such as Russia Armenia, Azerbaijan, Georgia, Serbia, Albania, Andora, Montenegro, Macedonia, Bosnia and Herzegovina, Switzerland, Moldova,

---

[23] Mavčič, A, (2008) *Constitutional Values in Practice with a Special Reference to the Slovenian System outline*, The Analysis and International Cooperation Department, Constitutional Court of the Republic of Slovenia, 1–18.

[24] Part II, Slovenian Constitution, Official Gazette of the Republic of Slovenia, No. 33/91-I, 42/97, 66/2000, 24/03, 69/04, 68/06, and 47/13.

[25] Ibid.

[26] International Legal Instruments include; International Covenant on Economic, Social and Cultural Rights 1966, adopted by UN General Assembly resolution 2200A (XXI), 16 December 1966, entry into force 3 January 1976, Treaty Series, vol. 993, p. 3. Convention on the Elimination of All Forms of Discrimination Against Women, adopted by UN General Assembly resolution 34/180 18 December 1979, entry into force 3 September 1981, Treaty Series, vol. 1249, 13.

[27] Act ratifying the Convention on Human Rights and Fundamental Freedoms as amended by Protocols Nos. 3, 5 and 8 and amended by Protocol No. 2 and its Protocols Nos. 1, 4, 6, 7, 9, 10 and 11, Zakon o ratifikaciji Konvencije o varstvu človekovih in temeljnih svoboščin, spremenjene s protokoli št. 3, 5 in 8 ter dopolnjene s protokolom št. 2, ter njenih protokolov št. 1, 4, 6, 7, 9, 10 in 11, Official Gazette Republic of Slovenia Treaties, MP, No. 7/94

[28] Article 6, Lisbon Treaty 2009, Official Journal of the European Union, C83/389, 2; contains the Charter of Fundamental Rights of the European Union, and has the same legal value as the Treaties.

Ukraine, Monaco, Iceland, Norway, San Marino, Liechtenstein and Turkey who are not members of the European Union.

Many of the principles found in the 2000 ECFR originated from the 1950 ECRFF. This is an important point because the earlier decisions of the European Court of Human Rights (ECoHR) located in Strasbourg relied on the principles laid out in the 1950 Convention. Over a 50-year period not only has the European Union and Slovenia relied on the decisions of the ECoHR, Australia has also referred to and borrowed from Europe in this very important area of law. In *Dietrich*[29] the High Court of Australia referred to the European Court of Human Rights and article 6 of the ECR&FF when determining what constituted the right to a fair trial. The court noted the 1950 European Convention for the Protection of Human Rights contains basic minimal rights for an accused to have adequate time to facilitate the preparation of their defense. Justice Michael Kirby[30] highlights that there have been many occasions where the Australian courts have looked to the European Court of Human Rights in Strasbourg for reference and guidance in relation to human rights (free speech, the right to fair trial), migration law and family law. By Australia looking to the EU for guidance on human rights law and jurisprudence, is another example of where the EU's limited identity is transcending international borders.

The Court of Justice of the European Union is the highest level court, and the Council of Europe has the European Court of Human Rights. Australia should not only borrow from Slovenia but also continue to borrow from the European Union and European Council in this important area of law. Australia should establish an independent Human Rights Court. Doing so, will provide greater cohesion and legal certainty in periods of heightened geopolitical tension. It will also ensure that the framework of democratic rights and values will not be restricted from the possible dilution of Western democracy.

However, for Slovenia the implementation of human rights has not been as smooth as the transition from socialism to democracy. The ECoHR has convicted Slovenia on 275 occasions for violations of human rights.[31] Even though the majority of violations were related to the inefficient judiciary (length of proceedings and right of remedy), other areas where breaches were recorded include, the lack of effective investigation and inhumane or degrading treatment. Furthermore, the right to liberty and security, non-enforcement, respect for private and family life, discrimination and protection of property were identified as areas Slovenia had not fully upheld. This is an area for improvement for Slovenia. The benefit for Australia is that the state and its institutions and judiciary do not have the same oversight or scrutiny as Slovenia does with a supranational polity – the European Union.

The European Charter of Fundamental Rights 2000 consists of seven chapters that include dignity, freedoms, equality, solidarity, citizen's rights, justices and

[29] *Dietrich v R* [1992] HCA 57; (1992) 177 CLR 292.

[30] The Hon Justice Michael Kirby AC CMG, Australia's Growing Debt to the European Court of Human Rights, The Seventh FIAT JUSTICIA Lecture, Monash University, Faculty of Law 2008.

[31] European Court of Human Rights, http://www.echr.coe.int/Documents/Stats_violation_1959_2013_ENG.pdf

general provisions.[32] The Slovenian constitution has expressed certain rights that are more relevant at the national level. Apart from the minimal rights expressed in the Australian constitution, the state has largely relied on the judiciary and legislation including:

- Australian Human Rights Commission Act 1986;
- Age Discrimination Act 2004;
- Disability Discrimination Act 1975; and
- Sex Discrimination Act 1984.[33]

The Australian Capital Territory and State of Victoria have both established the *Human Rights Act 2004* and the *Charter for Human Rights Act 2006* respectively. Australia, by establishing rights and freedoms within legislation, enables the parliament at any time to amend or change the nature, meaning or context of what a right or freedom is, and, how it can be applied. According to Zimmermann the effectiveness of human rights legislation is dependent on the socio-political context in which it operates.[34] That is, the social and political climate will in part determine how and when human rights will be enacted to protect citizens. Nonetheless, Australia has given effect to a large body of international human rights law that includes:

- The *Racial Discrimination Act 1975* implementing the International Convention on the Elimination of All Forms of Racial Discrimination (1966);
- *Sex Discrimination Act 1984* – implementing the Convention on the Elimination of All Forms of Discrimination Against Women (1979);
- *Disability Discrimination Act 1992*, implementing elements of the ILO Convention Concerning Discrimination in Respect of Employment and Occupation (1958); and
- *Human Rights and Equal Opportunity Commission Act 1986*, establishing a national human rights body for the purposes of law reform, education, intervention in court proceedings and investigations.

Slovenia has also given effect to the above international legal instruments through article eight of the Slovenian Constitution. This also includes those international conventions and treaties that have been ratified and published. Similarly, section 51(xxix) of the Australian constitution provides the power for the Australian Government to legislate in relation to those issues such as implementing international treaties and conventions on human rights into Australian law. It is argued that the Australian framework doesn't provide the same level of legal certainty as Slovenia. Interestingly, the expansion of rights at an international and regional level (in the case of Europe) has impacted on and influenced states and citizenship in four ways. Firstly, the rise of rights has been used by states and incorporated into national

---

[32] Charter of Fundamental Rights 2000, Official Journal of the European Communities 2007 C 364/13.

[33] Williams, G., Hume, D, (2013) *Human Rights under the Australian Constitution*, Oxford University Press, 14–15.

[34] Zimmermann, A (2006) *What is wrong with a Charter of Rights?* Orig Law Rev., Vol 1, 29

law (constitutionalized or national legislation), which has resulted in an expansion of civil and political rights afforded to citizens. Secondly, many of these rights allow citizens to challenge the state. Thirdly, rights allow states to establish values and behaviors that they expect their citizens to follow. Fourthly, and more importantly it could be argued that institutionalizing rights beyond the state has heightened the tension between globalization and the nation state. In other words, the state no longer has total control over the rights of its citizens. Citizens can choose to exercise their rights in the international arena, when they have exhausted all channels with the state.

Today, citizens after exhausting their national legal remedies can seek representation to international institutions such as the United Nations. For Slovenians, they have an advantage whereby after exhausting their legal remedies at a national level, they can go directly to the European Union, European Commission, European Parliament or the European Court of Human Rights. Therefore, it could be argued that on the one hand states are using citizenship and rights to enhance their national identities, but on the other hand the national identity and citizenship is being diluted by the institutional framework that lies beyond the state. More importantly, and without providing a detailed comparison, the basis of rights that Slovenian and Australian citizens have been afforded can be found in the Declaration of the Rights of Man and Citizen 1789. This reinforces the earlier point that the American and French Revolutions have had a significant influence on the development of citizenship, the nation state, national identity and shaping how citizens are to conduct themselves in everyday life.

8.2 National Communities

Apart from Slovenia ensuring continuity of Slovenians upon independence, the ethnic communities of Italy and Hungary were also afforded the same recognition. Dating back to the 1963 Republic of Slovenia and its former constitution, Italian and Hungarian ethnic groups were guaranteed equal rights for the use of their language, education and media.[35] As such, the Slovenian constitution upon independence upgraded the level of protection for the Italian and Hungarian communities. Most notable was the recognition that the people were no longer considered minorities but rather had a status of being part of a national community. Raising the status of these minorities to national communities strengthened their participation in the state by allowing them to vote and stand for election. This has similarities with an individual having the status of citizenship or residence. Residence status does not allow a person to vote or stand for election. Thus, article 65 of the Slovenian consti-

[35] Lipott, S, (2013) *The Hungarian National Minority in Slovenia: Assessment of Protection and Integration after the EU Accession*, Romanian Journal of European Affairs, Vol. 13, No. 3, 65–70.

tution provides special rights for those Italian and Hungarian national communities[36] residing in Slovene territory, and for those individuals determined to be part of the Rom community.[37]

The autochthonous Italian and Hungarian national communities[38] (and their members) are guaranteed the right to use their national symbols freely and, preserve their identity. These national communities also have the right to establish organizations and develop economic, cultural, scientific and research activities. It must be noted that the national communities of Hungary and Italy are afforded quite different rights and freedoms to that of the Rom community under national laws. However, a comparison is not required as part of this research. Additionally, these national communities have the right to education and schooling in their own languages.[39] Article 61 of the Slovenian constitution provides a broader right for individuals resident in Slovenia to express their affiliation with their own nation and national community. Arne Mavčič argues this was a deliberate inclusion by the constitutional drafters to protect individuals from the former Yugoslav Republics. Arguably, the constitutional recognition of the Rom and national communities is an important component of continued unification and integration of these people within Slovenia. It can be argued within Australia that national minorities are protected by national discrimination laws. However, Australia has continued to exclude one national minority – the indigenous community, and it is time they are recognized in the constitution.

8.2.1 Discrimination

Article 63 of the Slovenian Constitution prohibits incitement to national, racial, religious or other discrimination as well as inflaming national, racial religious or other hatred and intolerance.[40] This discrimination extends to protecting the rights

---

[36] Article 64 and 65 of the Slovenian Constitution, Official Gazette of the Republic of Slovenia, 33/91, 42/97, 66/2000 and 24/03, 68/06 and 47/2013.

[37] It is estimated the Roma people have been residing in Slovenia since the fifteenth century, and today they reside in the regions of Prekmurje, Dolenjska and Gorenjska, which has seen them come from the Hungarian, Croatian and Austrian regions, http://www.mnz.gov.si/en/minorities/roma_community/. Arne Mavčič, Slovenia, *International encyclopedia of laws*, Constitutional law, suppl. 27, 28. The Hague; London; Boston; Kluwer Law International, 1998, 44, 302, 250–258.

[38] U-I-267/09-11-2-2010, Official Gazette of the Republic of Slovenia 14/2010, U-I-176/08-7-10-2010, Official Gazette of the Republic of Slovenia 84/2010, U-I-416/98-22-3-2001, Official Gazette of the Republic of Slovenia 28/01.

[39] Mavčič, A, (1998) *Slovenia, International encyclopedia of laws*, Constitutional law, suppl. 27, 28. The Hague; London; Boston; Kluwer Law International, 44, 302, 250–258.

[40] Mavčič, A (2008) *Constitutional Values in Practice with a Special Reference to the Slovenian System outline*, The Analysis and International Cooperation Department, Constitutional Court of the Republic of Slovenia, 2008, 1–18.

of national communities of Hungarians and Italians. Furthermore, article 300 of the Penal Code of the Republic of Slovenia determines the nature of 'stirring up Ethnic, Racial or Religious Hatred, Strife or Intolerance as a criminal offence'.[41] Moreover, Slovenia in accordance with the EU[42] has implemented the *Principle of Equal Treatment Act 2004 and Equal Opportunities for Women and Men Act of 2002* that determines a common ground for the assurance of equal rights of everyone. Australia should consider making special recognition of indigenous Australians.

Comparatively, Australia could do a lot more to reduce the level of discrimination towards the indigenous peoples. Indigenous land rights have been established through the *Native Title Act 1993* (Cth) and respective state and territory laws such as the 1994 *Native Title (South Australia) Act*, these and other rights such as discrimination can be reviewed and changed at any time. Since implementing the national 1993 Native Title legislation governments have significantly reduced the rights to land by the indigenous aboriginal peoples.[43] However, this book does not have the scope to discuss those changes. The Australian constitution provides provision for the race power under sect. 51(xxvi), which goes some way to protecting the indigenous peoples of Australia from discrimination. The debate over racial discrimination led the current national government in 2014 to propose repealing s18 of the *Racial Discrimination Act 1975*. Section 18 makes it unlawful for any person to offend, insult, humiliate or intimidate a person on racial or ethnic grounds. Repealing such a law would take Australia backwards in relation to the progress the state has made towards multiculturalism and closing the gap with indigenous Australian's. This proposal has, to date, been shelved, however it could be on the agenda in the future. However, due to the negative public reaction to the proposal, the Australian Government backed down on 6 August 2014 and the changes were not going ahead at the time of writing.[44] The plight and story of the First Australians (Aboriginal Peoples), in my view, is one area of policy that Australia cannot be proud of. The policy discourse towards this group continues to pose many challenges, politically. They continue to be excluded, and it was only in 2019 Election that Australia saw its first Aboriginal Minister. The states of Victoria and Queensland are possible working towards establishing a Treaty with the local indigenous peoples. However, the content and form of these Treaties, if realized, will be extremely important.

---

[41] Ibid.

[42] Council Directive 2000/43/EC, established equal treatment between persons irrespective of their racial, or, ethnic o'rigin for all citizens of all Member States.

[43] Brennan, S, (2003) *Native Title in the High Court of Australia a decade after Mabo*, Tobin Centre of Public Law, Faculty of Law, University of New South Wales, 14 PLR 209, 209–201.

[44] The Australian Financial Review, 6 August 2014, 6.

8.3 Temporary Suspension and Detention

With the onset of war or a state of emergency, the Slovenian constitution can be restricted or temporarily suspended.[45] However, it must be noted there are certain basic rights that cannot be suspended even in the case of war, such as the right to life and prohibition against torture. The European Charter of Fundamental Rights and Australian constitution provides no similar provision. Suspending the European Charter of Fundamental Rights in war time, particularly if the conflict is within the borders of the EU, would significantly reduce the protection of member states citizens

8.4 Part Two: Rights and Freedoms

This section discusses the rights and freedoms afforded to citizens of modern day Europe, Slovenia and Australia. The basic rights afforded to individuals under the Slovenian constitution include: equality before the law[46]; the exercise and limitation of rights[47]; the temporary suspension or restrictions of rights[48]; equality in the protection of rights[49]; and due process of the law.[50] The most important provisions of the Slovenian constitution includes the protection of human rights against possible repressive state interventions against abuse of power[51]; and the protection of economic, social and cultural rights.[52]

Another important element of the Slovenian constitution is the reference to the Slovenian language, which has been recognized as the official national language (article 11). This has been reinforced by article 4 of the Slovenian constitution, which enshrines the language policy to also include the legal basis for its use.[53] Australia's constitution does not officially recognized the English language. The Slovenian language has also been reinforced by article 5 requiring its use by state bodies, local communities, public servants and public authorities. An individual who is employed as a professional, by government or the holder of a public

[45] Slovenian Constitution, Official Gazette of the Republic of Slovenia, No. 33/91-I, 42/97, 66/2000, 24/03, 69/04, 68/06, and 47/13.

[46] Article 14, The Constitution of the Republic of Slovenia, Official Gazette Republic of Slovenia No. 33/91-I, 42/97, 66/2000, 24/03, 69/04, 68/06, and 47/13.

[47] Ibid, article 15.

[48] Ibid, article 16.

[49] Ibid, article 22.

[50] Ibid, article 23.

[51] Ibid, articles 16, 17, 18–31, 34–38.

[52] Ibid, Part II.

[53] Article 4, Slovenian Constitution, Official Gazette of the Republic of Slovenia, Nos. 33/91, 42/97, 66/2000, 24/03, 69/04, 68/06, 47/13.

authorizations must have a working knowledge of Slovenian.[54] The public use of the Slovenian language has been reinforced by articles 91 and 107 of the constitution.

The Act to Exercise of Public Interest in Culture was implemented in 2002 to promote the public interest of the Slovene culture. Article 6 relates to the national identity, whereby, cultural events should be announced, advertised and explained using the Slovene language. Additionally, article 6 goes onto say that films should also be played in Slovenian or Slovenian subtitles used.[55] Furthermore, the Public Use of the Slovene Language Act[56] was established to reinforce that Slovene is the official language of the Republic. It is used in spoken and written communication in all areas of public life, unless when the constitution states, such as, allowing Italian and Hungarian to be used as official languages. To enhance Australia's identity, Australia should investigate whether to recognize English as the official language in the constitution, in the same way as Slovenia. This is a complex area of public policy and such a proposal would need to be weighed up against the formal recognition of indigenous aboriginal languages that exist throughout Australia. Nevertheless, Slovenia has reaffirmed the importance of language to the state and its national identity by codifying its language.

The part compares the rights expressed within the Convention for the Protection of Human Rights and Fundamental Freedoms1950, the European Charter of Fundamental Rights 2000, the Slovenian constitution (SC) and the Australian constitution (AC), and national laws. However, the next section only confirms whether the right (s) has been recognized within the legal framework of Slovenia and Australia. There is no comparison of how the jurisdictions have applied or implemented the right (s). To compare the implementation of these rights is outside the scope of this book.

The structure follows the format of the 2000 European Charter of Fundamental Rights including (1) Dignity, (2) Freedoms, (3) Equality, (4) Solidarity, (5) Citizens (Political) Rights and (6) Justice. It is argued that all the principles discussed below have a role in expressing part of Slovenia and Australia modern day identity. That is, being both democratic states both Slovenia and Australia have afforded rights, protections and freedoms to their respective citizens. Moreover, it is these concepts and principles the reinforce the supranational identity of the EU. While their contribution is limited as individual concepts, as a collective, it is argued that these concepts and principles play a major role in developing the Union's identity. This is because, they find their way into other areas of the law, which then force third countries to either adopt or consider as part of their legal framework (s).

[54] Ibid, article 7.

[55] Article 6, Act to Exercise of Public Interest in Culture, Official Gazette of the Republic of Slovenia 96/2002.

[56] Public Use of the Slovene Language Act, Official Gazette of the Republic of Slovenia, Nos. 96/2004 and 91/2008.

8.4.1 Dignity

The concept of dignity is fundamental to all citizens and non-citizens.[57] Dignity[58] includes the right to life,[59] integrity of the person,[60] freedom from torture[61] slavery[62] and forced labour.[63] Jack Donnelly argues that 'dignity' is something that comes with being human and makes an individual worthy or deserving of respect.[64] The European Union respects human dignity as a fundamental human right.[65] The ECJ has recognized human dignity as being a general principle that is compatible with community law.[66] The ECoHR in *Guduz v Tukey*[67] ruled that 'dignity of all human beings (citizens and non-citizens) constitutes the foundations of a democratic and pluralistic society'. The Slovenian constitution ensures human dignity is considered and respected in criminal proceedings.[68] The Slovenian Constitutional Court ruled that human dignity is a fundamental part of human rights that are the legal-ethical essence of the constitutions of democratic states.[69] The Australian High Court has a similar position to that of the Slovenian Constitutional Court where it stated that "a human right may be subject to the law only to such reasonable limits as can be demonstrably justified in a free and democratic society based on human dignity".[70] The Australian constitution makes no express reference to the legal concept.

[57] Vienna Declaration 1993 World Human Rights Conference, http://www.ohchr.org/en/professionalinterest/pages/vienna.aspx

[58] Article 1, Charter of Fundamental Rights of the European Union, 2000, Official Journal of the European, (2007/C 303/01).

[59] Ibid, article 2.

[60] Ibid, article 3.

[61] Article 3, Convention for the Protection of Human Rights and Fundamental Freedoms, Council of Europe, Rome, 4.XI. 1950.

[62] Article 4, Convention for the Protection of Human Rights and Fundamental Freedoms, Council of Europe, Rome, 4.XI. 1950.

[63] Article 5, Charter of Fundamental Rights of the European Union, 2000, Official Journal of the European, (2007/C 303/01).

[64] Donelly, J, (2009) *Human Dignity and Human Rights*, Geneva Academy of International Humanitarian Law and Human Rights in the framework of the Swiss Initiative to Commemorate the 60th Anniversary of the Universal Declaration of Human Rights, University of Denver, 2009, 10. Dignity was initially established in article 1 of the 1948 Declaration, that is, 'all human beings are born free and equal in dignity and rights'.

[65] Article 2 and 21 (1), Treaty on the European Union, Official Journal of the European Union, C 83/28.

[66] Case – 36/02, *OMEGA* [2004] (First Chamber), 23.

[67] 35071/97 *Gunduz v Turkey* (2003) (2004-Final) ECHR, 40, www.global.asc.upenn.edu/fileLibrary/.../20_mcgonagle_reading7.d....

[68] Article 21, The Constitution of the Republic of Slovenia, Official Gazette Republic of Slovenia No. 33/91-I, 42/97, 66/2000, 24/03, 69/04, 68/06, and 47/13.

[69] Slovenian Constitutional Court, U-I-109/10, Official Gazette of the Republic of Slovenia 78/2011.

[70] *Momcilovic v The Queen* 92,011) HCA 34, 165.

However, the state of Victoria, in Australia, is an example of where human dignity has been provided by the *Charter for Human Rights and Responsibilities Act 2006*. The Australian High Court[71] stated the validity of state based legislation in protecting human rights, provide that human rights such as dignity, equality and freedom are part of a free and democratic society. The majority ruled that the Charter was valid and compatible to human rights. However, the Charter is only applicable in the state of Victoria and no other state or territory of Australia.

The right[72] to life[73] is a controversial policy issue concerning, for example, abortion. While not expressed in either the SC or AC, article 17 of the SC states that human life is inviolable. The birth of a child will add to the citizenry of a state. However, in some circumstances the birth may not occur and a parent or parents could decide to abort the pregnancy. Apart from the moral and ethical issues surrounding abortion, opponents to abortion could argue that doing so denies an individual the right to a life. In circumstances such as this, a medical practitioner may have the 'right to conscientious objection'.[74] The woman must be informed of the right to refuse a procedure of abortion.[75] Importantly, abortion has and continues to be a decisive issues in the community.

The integrity of the person (both physical and mental) has been included as part of the European Charter of Fundamental Rights 2000, to provide a broad right to minimize the potential of physical or mental torture, or degrading treatment of citizens.[76] While different in approach, the SC in accordance with article 35 guarantees the protection of every Slovene citizens' physical and mental integrity. In Australia, the legal principle is associated with those citizens who have a disability, and has been implied by the *Disability Discrimination Act 1992 (Cth)*. The legislation was established to protect citizens that may have a mental or physical disability and enables those citizens to have access to education, employment and public facilities in the same way as other citizens in the community. Discrimination is closely associated with other rights and freedoms, particularly equality.

---

[71] *Momcilovic v The Queen* [2011] HCA 34.

[72] Council Regulation 1352/2011 concerning the trade in certain goods which could be used for capital punishment, torture or other cruel, inhuman or degrading treatment or punishment, Official Journal of the European Union C 28/1. Charter of Fundamental Freedoms of the European Union, Official Journal of the European Union, C83/393.

[73] Article 2, Convention for the Protection of Human Rights and Fundamental Freedoms, Council of Europe, Rome, 4.XI. 1950.

[74] Article 10.2, Charter of Fundamental Freedoms of the European Union, Official Journal of the European Union, C83/393. *Abortion Law Reform Act 2008* (Vic), Australia, s8. Article 56 Health Services Act, Official Gazette of the Republic of Slovenia 23/05, 14/13.

[75] *Abortion Law Reform Act 2008* (Vic), Australia, s8.

[76] Council Directive 2011/36/EU preventing and combating trafficking in human beings, Official Journal of the European Union L 101/. Council Directive 2010/45/EU standards of quality and safety of human organs intended for transplantation, Official Journal of the European Union L 207. Council Directive 98/44/EC protection of biotechnological inventions, Official Journal of the European Union L 213. Council Directive 2006/17/EC standards of quality and safety for the donation, procurement of human tissue and cells, Official Journal of the European Union L 38/40.

Torture[77] can be found in article 5 of the 1948 Declaration on Human Rights, and article 7 of the United Nations Convention on Civil and Political Rights 1966. While not expressed in the AC, the Australian Government has ensured the protection against torture is covered under the Commonwealth *Criminal Code Act 1995*.[78] For example, the treatment by public officials of citizens such as being detained for terrorism related offences within the Criminal Code. The second is the approach taken within the *Crimes (Torture) Act 1998* that prohibits acts of torture outside Australia where a person has committed the act in their capacity while acting as a public official on behalf of the state. This could apply to military personnel who are representing the state in conflict zones and may be engaged in detaining citizens from other states on foreign soil. This protects those individuals representing Australia in an official capacity while located in another state. In *Sadiq Shek Elmi v Australia*, it was considered Elmi would be subjected to torture if returned to Somalia.[79] Australia and Slovenia have obligations under international law not to return refugees to a country where the person could be subject to torture. Both states have a legislative framework that allows non-citizens to be granted a visa or permit under the international protection. In doing so, both states, to varying degrees, meet their international obligations under the Refugee Convention 1951 and 1967 Protocol and the respective national laws (*Migration Act 1958 and Law on International Protection 2011*).[80] These protections also apply to a person in detention as an asylum, ensuring a non-citizen is not returned to their state of origin where it is proved they could be subject to torture or inhumane treatment.[81]

Slavery[82] is generally associated with human trafficking (illegal migration).[83] Freedom from slavery is one of the oldest protections that has been recognized by the international community, dating back to the 1885 Berlin Treaty and the 1926

[77] Article 4, Charter of Fundamental Rights of the European Union 2000, Article 18, The Constitution of the Republic of Slovenia, Official Gazette Republic of Slovenia No. 33/91-I, 42/97, 66/2000, 24/03, 69/04, 68/06, and 47/13.

[78] Division 274 Criminal Code Act 1995 defines what constitutes torture in accordance with the 1984 Convention Against Torture and Other Cruel, Inhuman or Degrading Treatment or Punishment, section 22 Extradition Act 1988, and other legislation.

[79] *Sadiq Shek Elmi v Australia* Communication No 120/1998, CT/C/22/D/120/1998, 6.9–7.

[80] Migration Act 1958, s 36. Articles 27 & 28, Law on International Protection, Official Gazette of the Republic of Slovenia 2011/11.

[81] *Cruz Varas and Others v Sweeden* (Application no. 15576/89), HCHR, Judgment Strasbourg, 1991.

[82] Article 8, International Covenant on Civil and Political Rights 1976, adopted by the UN General Assembly resolution 2200A (XXII) 16 December 1966, entry into force on 23 March 1976, Treaty Series, vol. 999, p 171 and vol. 1057, p. 4077.

[83] Article 67 and article 79 Treaty on the Functioning of the European Union, Official Journal of the European Union, C83/49. Council Directive 2002/90/EC defining the facilitation of unauthorised entry, transit and residence, Official Journal of the European Communities, L 328/17. Council Directive 2004/80 EC relating to compensation to crime victims, Official Journal of the European Union L 261/15. Council Directive 2004/81/EC residence permit issued to third-country nationals who are victims of trafficking in human beings who have been subject to illegal immigration, official Journal of the European Union L 261.

International Convention to Suppress the Slave Trade and Slavery. Rather than establish slavery as a constitutional right or protection, Slovenia[84] and Australia[85] have criminalized the legal principle. Slovenia and Australia have been consistent in the application of slavery. The European Court of Human Rights in *Siliadan*, ruled that it is incumbent on states to adopt criminal law provisions in relation to slavery.[86] The High Court of Australia stated that the definition of slavery is based on the definition of the 1926 Slavery Convention.[87] Forced migration (trafficking and smuggling) is also an issue for both states and can result in a person being subject to slavery. Australia continues to grapple with smuggling of people through South East Asia, particularly from Sri Lanka, Myanmar, Pakistan, Afghanistan and other central Asian countries through Malaysia and Indonesia. The European Union is facing similar issues on a much larger scale with people illegally arriving from North Africa and Eastern Europe and the Middle East. Article 5 of the European Charter of Fundamental Rights ensures there is protection for victims and individuals that are subject to trafficking. The European Union has also reaffirmed its commitment to protecting people from trafficking by establishing minimum rules for defining offences and sanctions across MS.[88] In *Tang*,[89] the Australian High Court looked to the European Court of Human Rights for further guidance on the protection from modern day slavery, stating that slavery today includes those that become domestic workers and mail order brides.

8.4.2 Freedoms

Freedoms are an important part of a citizen and non-citizens ability to participate in society.[90] Those freedoms include liberty and security,[91] private and family life,[92] protection of personal data, marriage and family, conscious thought and religion.[93]

---

[84] Articles 101–102, Slovenian Criminal Code Act, Official Gazette of the Republic of Slovenia 1/2008.

[85] Divisions 270, *Commonwealth Criminal Code Act 1995*. Section 245AH of the *Migration Act 1958*.

[86] *Siliadin v France*, European Court of Human Rights, No. 73316/01, 2005, 89.

[87] *The Queen v Tang* (2008) HCA 39, Order, 33.

[88] Council Directive 2011/36/EU on preventing and combating trafficking in human beings and protecting its victims, and replacing Council Framework Decision 2002/269/JHA, Official Journal of the European Union L 101/1.

[89] *The Queen v Tang* [2008] HCA 39

[90] Marshall, T, (1950) *Citizenship and Social Class and Other Essays*, Cambridge University Press.

[91] Article 5, Convention for the Protection of Human Rights and Fundamental Freedoms, Council of Europe, Rome, 4.XI. 1950.

[92] Ibid, article 8

[93] Ibid, article 9.

Moreover, the freedom of expression,[94] information, assembly and association,[95] arts and science, and the right to education[96] are fundamental rights of the European Union. The right to engage in work of one's choosing, conduct of business and the right to property provide citizens with choice. The right to asylum and protection against expulsion or extradition have been identified as important freedoms to ensure people are not arbitrarily returned to a state where they may face torture or persecution.

8.4.2.1 Liberty and Security

States have to balance security (state and community), the rule and implementation of the law, including the rights of the person when incarcerating individuals. The Australian High Court argued 'the right to personal liberty is the most elementary and important of all common law rights.[97] The right has no Australian constitutional recognition. In *C v Australia*[98] the Human Rights Committee found Australia would be in violation of articles 7 and 9 of the 1966 ICCPR where the detainee was in detention for an extended period that the individual had developed a psychiatric illness, and, that deportation to the country of origin (Iran) would not allow the person to obtain effective treatment. Thus, and while being an illegal immigrant, the individual would remain protected from deportation, but also, demonstrated the complexities and impacts detention can have on individual's personal liberties. Even so, a person who is detained when illegally entering either state, is not guaranteed citizenship upon release. Article 6 of the European Charter of Fundamental Rights 2000, states that everybody has the right to liberty and security, including citizens and non-citizens. Article 19 of the Slovenian constitution allows the state to restrict liberties under national legislation. However, where personal liberty has been restricted the citizen is to be informed by the state.[99] The European Union has implemented Council Directive 2003/9/EC for the detention of asylum seekers, to ensure their liberties are protected whilst in detention.[100] Personal liberty also extends to criminal law and procedure such as the detention and imprisonment of a

---

[94] Ibid, article 10.

[95] Ibid, article 11.

[96] Article 2, Protocol, Paris, 20.III, 1952, Convention for the Protection of Human Rights and Fundamental Freedoms, Council of Europe, Rome, 4.XI. 1950.

[97] *Williams v The Queen* (1987) HCA 36; 161 CLR 278, 292.

[98] *C v Australia,* Human Rights Committee, Communication No. 900/1999, 2002. CCPR/C/76/D/900/1999.

[99] Article 19(3), The Constitution of the Republic of Slovenia, Official Gazette Republic of Slovenia No. 33/91-I, 42/97, 66/2000, 24/03, 69/04, 68/06, and 47/13.

[100] Council Directive 2003/9/EC, laying down minimum standards for the reception of asylum seekers, article 2(k) detention shall mean confinement of an asylum seeker by a Member State within a particular place, where the applicant is deprived of his or her freedom of movement, Official Journal of the European Union L31/18.

citizen and non-citizen. That is, a citizen who has been sentenced to life in prison without the possibility of ever being released is contrary to article 1 of the European Charter of Fundamental Rights 2000.

In *Vasileva v Denmark* the ECoHR concluded the right to liberty should be narrowly interpreted to ensure no one is arbitrarily deprived of their liberty.[101] Moreover, article 9 of the ICCPR states that 'everyone has the right of life, liberty and security'. With ever increasing border restrictions placed on immigration across Europe and Australia, the detainment and detention of non-citizens who have enter the jurisdictions illegally is a complex for authorities. On the one hand authorities are protecting the external Schengen borders of the European Union and subsequently protecting the citizens of European Union member states. On the other hand, authorities must respect the rights of illegal entrants. Australia is also faced with similar issues.

8.4.2.2 Private and Family Life

The respect for private and family life is a fundament right in the European Union,[102] and international law.[103] This right is neither expressed in the SC or AC. The European Court of Human Rights in *Kurić*[104] ruled that Slovenia had violated the right to private or family life when the state did not grant citizenship or residence to individuals who were no longer considered citizens of Slovenia at the time of the breakup of the former Yugoslavia. Australia has not dealt with the same exclusionary measures as Slovenia did when the 1948 citizenship laws were introduced. The Federal Court of Australia in discussing the importance of this right referred to the European Convention for the Protection of Human Rights and Fundamental Freedoms 1950 for guidance in relation to a visa being issued under the Australian *Migration Act 1958*.[105] This highlights another example where Australia is looking to the European Union and the European Council for guidance and assistance in human rights based law. The broad reach of the above legal principle could imply that the protection comes without interference from government. However, the right

---

[101] *Vasileva v Denmark*, Application No. 52792/99, 25 September 2003, ECoHR, 32–33.

[102] Regulation 1179/2011 Official Journal of the European Union OJL 301. Additionally, Regulation 996/2010 on the investigation and prevention of accidents and incidents in civil aviation, Official Journal of the European Union L 295. Council Directive 2011/98/EU a single procedure for a single permit for third country nationals to reside and work in the territory of a member state, Official Journal of the European Union L 343. Council Directive 2002/58/EC concerning the processing of personal data and the protection of privacy in the electronic communications sector, Official Journal of the European Union L 201.

[103] Article 4 (3), Council Directive 2003/86/EC on the right of family reunification, Official Journal of the European Union 251/12.

[104] *Kurić and Others v Slovenia, Application no. 26828/06.*

[105] *MZ RAJ v Minister for Immigration and Multicultural and Indigenous Affairs* (2004) FCA 1261, 28–29.

could be infringed by the state in situations where there is a public interest threat or prevention of criminal activity.

8.4.2.3 Protection of Personal Data

The protection of personal data, otherwise known as data protection, which is closely associated with the right to privacy, has emerged as one of the most important policy and legal issues of the EU in recent times. It has become one of the most significant challenges of the modern erea. Data protection has been viewed differently. For instance, Walters, Trackman and Zeller argue that the data protection laws of the EU and Australia are different, inconsistent and fragmented.[106] The authors argue that data protection is a tool of privacy over the Internet, and consistent with other areas of EU policy, it is, arguably viewed as a fundamental right, while having to balance the emerging technology economy in the trade in personal data.

Article 29.2 of the 1948 Declaration of Human Rights states that 'in the exercise of his rights and freedoms, everyone shall be subject only to such limitations as are determined by law solely for securing due recognition and respect of rights and freedoms in a democratic society'.[107] The 1966 ICCPR is more specific and states that 'no one shall be subject to unlawful interference with his privacy, family, home, correspondence or reputation'.[108] Furthermore, the Lisbon Treaty,[109] has reinforced article 8 of the European Charter of Fundamental Rights 2000 and article 38 of the SC that the protection of personal data is a fundamental right to an individual's privacy. This was also reaffirmed by the Slovenian Constitutional Court in 1992.[110] The European Union has implemented specific European Union legislation to also ensure there is a consistent approach taken by all member states in processing personal data.[111] In Australia, the protection of personal data falls within privacy laws such as the commonwealth *Privacy Act 1988*. The Australian High Court stated, the origin of this right can be found in article 17[112] of the ICCPR.[113] The protection of personal data can extend to health, defence, and other areas of regulated activities of government, business and individuals. The *Privacy Act 1988 (Cth)* does not define privacy but rather specifies the many different principles of where privacy in Australia can apply. Personal information has been defined to mean information or

---

[106] Walters, R., Trakman, L., Bruno, Z, (2019) *Data Protection A Comparative Analysis of Asia-Pacific and European Approaches*, Springer.

[107] Article 29.2, Declaration of Human Rights 1948.

[108] Article 17, International Covenant on Civil and Political Rights, Treaty series, vol. 999, p. 171.

[109] Article 39, Lisbon Treaty, Official Journal of the European Union C 36.

[110] U-I-115/92, Official Gazette of the RS, No. 3/93. Article 38 of the constitution ensure the right to the protection of personal data.

[111] Council Directive 95/46/EC on the protection of individuals with regards to the processing of personal data and the free movement of such data, Official Journal of the European Union 281/31.

[112] Article 17 (1) and (2) International Convention on Civil and Political Rights 1966.

[113] *Australian Broadcasting Corporation v Lenah Game Meats Pty Ltd* (2001) 208 CLR 199.

opinion that can identify an individual. Additionally this applies where that information or opinion is true or not and is recorded in a material form.[114] International legal instruments have provided a wider interpretation of protecting personal data and privacy. Data protection and privacy is an excellent example of how the EU have exerted their limited identity not only on member states, but also, third countries. Walters, Trakman and Zeller are of the view that the EU has had a profound impact on data protection law across the world.[115] The EU, through the way in which they have drafted their respective laws have effectively dragged other nation states into adopting similar laws. Even those countries that have not adopted specific data protection laws, are, and have been looking to the EU for guidance. The GDPR, which came into effect in 2018, has influenced the development of many countries data protection laws, but also forced countries to adopt and apply similar laws, so as they can maintain a relationship with the EU, particularly in the private sector. At the 2019 G20 Leader conference in Japan, the leaders highlighted the challenges, concerns, and the need for national and international law to be respected to ensure personal data and privacy over the Internet is protected.

8.4.2.4 Marriage and Family

The right to marry and have a family is protected across the European Union,[116] and ensures that families can reunite with their children and spouse.[117] The SC expresses the right to marriage[118] however there is no mention that this is solely heterosexual or includes transsexual relationships. The ECoHR has confirmed the right to marriage exists in accordance with article 12 of the 1950 European Convention of Human Rights and Fundamental Freedoms,[119] and under the national laws of member states. This is another demonstration where member states have retained the sovereign right to determine what their respective citizens can and cannot do. The Slovenian Constitutional Court in 2015 attempted to adopt the Act Amending the Marriage and Family Relations Act.[120] The court ruled that the 2015 legislation had not been declared or published in accordance with articles 91 and 154 of the constitution, and therefore the review was dismissed. The principle argument bought before the court was that the proposed law was not compatible to article 8 and third

[114] *Privacy Act 1988*, s 6.

[115] Walters, R. Trakman, L. Zeller, B, (2019) *Data Protection LawA Comparative Analysis of Asia-Pacific and European Approaches*, Springer.

[116] Article 9, Charter of Fundamental Rights of the European Union, Official Journal of the European Union, 2007, C 303/01.

[117] Council Directive 2003/86/EC on the right to family reunification, Official Journal of the European Union 251/12.

[118] Article 53, The Constitution of the Republic of Slovenia, Official Gazette Republic of Slovenia Nos. 33/91-I, 42/97, 66/2000, 24/03, 69/04, 68/06, and 47/13.

[119] *Schalk and Kopf v Austria*, Application No. 30141/04, ECtHR, 10.

[120] UI -55/15, Official Gazette of the Republic of Slovenia, 15–10.

paragraph of Article 53 of the SC, and article 16 of the 1948 Declaration of Human Rights (being the right to marry). In Australia, the right to marry is not a constitutional right but the constitution provides the power for the commonwealth parliament[121] to legislate for marriage.[122] There has been community debate in relation to marriage between transsexuals. In Australia, where the person has had a sex change they can after that sex change get married. Despite the law in Australia, the Family Court[123] looked to Europe for guidance and referred to article 12 of the ECoHR, confirming countries across Europe recognize transsexual marriages. In Australia the marriage laws do not recognize same sex marriage, however, in Slovenia they do.

Establishing a family is an important part of the fabric of society.[124] The AC does not expressly recognize the right to establish a family, however the AC has gone further than the SC by describing what laws can be established to assist the family. These include support for widows, child endowment, unemployment, pharmaceuticals, sickness, hospital, medical treatment and students.[125] It is not suggested that Slovenia would or should adopt the same principles as Australia by expressing them in the Slovenian constitution, however Slovenia could consider whether it is plausible to do so.

8.4.2.5 Freedom of Thought, Conscience and Religion

Freedom of thought and conscience[126] are not constitutionally expressed in Australia. The legal concepts are well entrenched in western democratic states. However, s116 disallows the government from making laws that will restrict the practice of religion. Religion constitutes the belief in a supernatural being, and the acceptance of canons of conduct in order to give effect to that belief.[127] The Australian High Court in the *Jehovah's Witness Case* stated that due to the number of religions in the world it would be near impossible to define what religion is and means, but it is protected.[128] However, later, the High Court has construed the meaning of section 116 to have a number of elements. One the religion was based on two object criteria, 'belief

[121] Sections 51 (xxi) & (xxii), Australian Constitution Act 1901.

[122] *Marriage Act 1961* s7.

[123] *Re Kevin (Validity of Marriage of Transsexual)* (2001) FamCA 1074, 194, http://www.wallbanks.com/PDF/Re%20Kevin_ChisholmDecision.pdf

[124] Article 9, European Charter of Fundamental Rights 2000, Official Journal of the European Communities C 364/1.

[125] Australian Constitution, s51 (xxiiiA).

[126] Article 10, Charter of Fundamental Rights of the European Union, Official Journal of the European Union 2007, C 303/01. Australian Government, Attorney General's Department, Right of thought, conscience and religion or belief, http://www.ag.gov.au/RightsAndProtections/HumanRights/PublicSectorGuidanceSheets/Pages/Righttofreedomofthoughtconscienceandreligionorbelief.aspx

[127] *Church of the New Faith v Commissioner of Pay-roll Tax* (1983) 154 CLR 120.

[128] *Adelaide Company of Jehovah's Witness Inc v Commonwealth* (1943) 67 CLR 116, 123.

in supernatural Being, Thing or Principle and second the acceptance of cannons of conduct in order to give effect to that belief.[129] The Australian constitution provides four prohibitions where the commonwealth is not to make laws for establishing a religion, imposing religion, prohibiting religion or no religious test shall be required as a qualification for any office or public trust under the commonwealth.[130] An individual's religious belief is protected from discrimination.[131] Furthermore, the Australian Human Rights Commission has the power to ensure citizens are protected from religious discrimination in accordance with the ICCPR.[132] A prime example, could be where a person has their employment terminated because of their religious belief.[133] In Slovenia the SC[134] and the European Union[135] have followed a similar path to Australia. The European Court of Human Rights in *Hasan & Chauch v Bulgaria*, ruled that one's religion is protected under Article 9 of the 1950 European Convention on Human Rights and Fundamental Freedoms.[136] Slovenia considers the right to freedom of religion as a personal action and decision[137] that must be protected at all times. Furthermore, the Slovenian Religious Freedom Act[138] reinforces the position of the ECoHR, and ruled that religious freedom is guaranteed, and is one of the foundations of a democratic society.[139] Both Australia and Slovenia are democratic. Democracy is one of the key principles Slovenia used to establish their independence. Democracy is a component of Slovenia and Australia's national identity.

8.4.2.6 Conscientious Objection

Conscientious objection[140] is a fundamental right that is closely connected to the freedom of thought and religion that has been provided for in accordance with article 18 of the 1948 Declaration of Human Rights, and, article 18 of the

---

[129] *Church of the New Faith v Commissioner of Payrol Tax* (1983) 154 CLR 120.

[130] Australian Constitution, section 116. George Williams and David Hume, *Human Rights under Australian Constitution*, 2nd edit, Oxford University Press, 2013, 256.

[131] *Racial Discrimination Act 1975*, s18C, while no direct reference to religion is made, it has been implied it is unlawful to insult, humiliate or intimidate another person or group of people.

[132] Human Rights and Equal Opportunity Commission Act 1986, ss3, 8, 11.

[133] *Work Place Relations Act 1996* (Cth), section 695.

[134] Article 63, The Constitution of the Republic of Slovenia, Official Gazette Republic of Slovenia Nos. 33/91-I, 42/97, 66/2000, 24/03, 69/04, 68/06, and 47/13.

[135] Article 11, Council Directive 2000/78/EC, discrimination based on religion or belief, Official Journal of the European Union L 303.

[136] *Hasan & Chaush v Bulgaria*, Application No. 30985/96, ECHR, 62.

[137] U-I-92/07, Official Gazette of the Republic of Slovenia 46/2010, OdIUS XIX.

[138] Official Gazette of the Republic of Slovenia 14/07.

[139] *Kokkinakis v. Greece*, App. No. 14307/88, 260 Eur. Ct. H.R., 31 (1993).

[140] Article 10.2, Charter of Fundamental Rights of the European Union, Official Journal of the European Union, C 83/393.

ICCPR. Citizens of Slovenia and Australia can choose to serve their respective national armed forced, when their respective states are involved in conflict or war. The European Court of Human Rights in *Bayatyan*[141] found that Armenia violated the right to conscientious objection where a citizen who was a practicing Jehovah Witness was convicted for refusing to undertake military duties. The court went onto to say that a person's deeply held religious belief, constituted a conviction or belief of sufficient cogency, seriousness, cohesion and importance to attract a guaranteed protection, and, that pluralism, tolerance and broad mindedness are all hallmarks of a democratic society.[142]

Both Slovenian and Australian citizens have been involved in wars and conflict during the past century. Most notably for Slovenes, was the breakup of former Yugoslavia. For Australian citizens the conflicts in Iraq and Afghanistan have seen many Australians killed in those conflicts. Both states have at different time's invoked conscription of their citizens to undertake military service. Today, both Australia and Slovenia do not require their citizens to be conscripted. Those laws have been long abolished. For Slovenia the abolition of conscription only occurred in 2002,[143] and for Australia, this has been the case since 1973.[144] However, the issue of conscientious objection to military service by those individual citizens currently serving their respective armed forces as professional service men and women, may be able to use this right to seek discharge from military service.

Today, the right exists in both states. Slovenia, has guaranteed the right in accordance with article 46 of the constitution. Additionally, article 123 (2) of the Slovenian constitution states that 'citizens who for their religious, philosophical or humanitarian convictions are not willing to perform military duties, must be given the opportunity to participate in national defence in some other manner.[145] The right to conscientious objection to military service is not guaranteed by the Australian constitution, but rather, has been expressed in *Defence Act 1903*. Section 61A of the Act allows an Australian citizen to be exempt from military service where their conscientious beliefs do not allow them to participate in war. A Tribunal will determine what will, and, will not constitute a citizens conscientious belief.[146] Slovenia has guaranteed their citizens under the principle of conscientious objection from military service on grounds of religion, philosophical or humanitarian conviction. It is argued national identity straddles both the right to conscientious objection and the right of the citizen to partake in military service. As discussed in chapter two,

---

[141] *Bayatyan v Armenia*, no. 23459/03, ECHR, 7

[142] Ibid.

[143] Stolwijk, M, (2005) *The Right to Conscientious Objection in Europe: A Review of the Current Situation*, Quaker Council of European Affairs, 65.

[144] Brown, G, (1999) *Military Conscription: Issues for Australia, Foreign Affairs*, Defence and Trade Group, Parliament of Australia, http://www.aph.gov.au/About_Parliament/Parliamentary_Departments/Parliamentary_Library/Publications_Archive/CIB/cib9900/2000CIB07

[145] Articles 46 and 123, The Constitution of the Republic of Slovenia, Official Gazette Republic of Slovenia Nos. 33/91-I, 42/97, 66/2000, 24/03, 69/04, 68/06, and 47/13.

[146] *Defence Act 1903*, s61CA.

Australia's national identity has been influenced by the participation of its military, more so than Slovenia.

8.4.2.7 Freedom of Expression

Every Slovene citizen has the right to expression and information[147] in accordance with article 39 of the Slovenian Constitution. This freedom is also closely related to free speech and in Australia is an implied right that allows for free political communication.[148] According to Zimmerman and Finally free speech is a fundamental human right, and one that is a foundational requirement for the full realization of other human rights.[149] Brennan J in referring to AV Dicey in *Nationwide News Pty Ltd v Wills* noted that the right to free expression of opinion is a fundamental doctrine of English law,[150] which Australia's common law is derived. The freedom of expression is closely associated with many other freedoms such as the freedom of religion and information (media) and political communication. Australia has looked to Europe in determining the importance of the right to politically communicate. Mason J in *Australian Capital Television*[151] pointed out the freedom of political communication had been recognized by the European Court of Human Rights.[152] The ECoHR also recognized this freedom as being an important part of society and to the citizens of a state.

The expression of one's National Affiliation[153] has been provided to those citizens of other former nationalities (minorities) that are citizens of, and, reside in Slovenia. This is particularly the case for those national minorities such as Austrian, Italian or Hungarian who have the right to use their culture, language and script. There is no express equivalent in the AC. The right for other minority groups in Australia to maintain their culture and language is protected by the freedom of expression, association, assembly and discrimination legislation. Article 19 of the ICCPR states that 'everyone has the right to expression and includes the ability for individuals to seek, receive and impart information and ideas regardless of whether this is undertaken orally or in writing through such medians as the media'. However, as many states restrict the right to expression, article 2 of the ICCPR provides that the right is subject to certain restrictions, providing states with the ability to develop

---

[147] Article 11, Charter of Fundamental Rights of the European Union, 2000, Official Journal of the European, 2007 C 303/01.

[148] *Australian Capital Television Pty Ltd v Commonwealth* (1992) 177 CLR 106, 146.

[149] Augusto Zimmermann and Lorraine Finlay, *A Forgotten Freedom: Protecting Freedom of Speech in an Age of Political Correctness*, Macquarie Law Journal, Vol 14, 2014, 187.

[150] *Nationwide News Pty Ltd v Wills* (1992) 177 CLR, 46.

[151] *Australian Capital Television Pty Ltd v Commonwealth* (1992) 177 CLR 106.

[152] *Handyside v United Kingdom* (1976) 1 E.H.R.R 737.

[153] Article 61, The Constitution of the Republic of Slovenia, Official Gazette Republic of Slovenia No. 33/91-I, 42/97, 66/2000, 24/03, 69/04, 68/06, and 47/13.

national laws to regulate this area. Thus, the international law recognizes the right as an important right but allows it to individual states to decide it is regulated.

8.4.2.8 Access to Information

Citizens of both Slovenia and Australia have the right to access information from government. Freedom of Information legislation exists throughout Australian,[154] and is not a constitutional right. In Slovenia, the Access to Public Information Act[155] came into effect in 2003 and allows citizens to access information from government.[156] Access to information can also be undertaken by citizens to better understand the national identity. A prime example is the national archives[157] that provide information on the history, culture and citizens of the state.[158] The historical stories of Slovenia and Australia show very different paths it is this history and story that form the national identity. It is argued that an archive is a repository in which materials of historical interest are stored and is a place of the collective memory of the state and its citizens. The history of Australia's first citizenship laws has been documented by the Australian national archives.[159] The first Australian Immigration Minister Arthur Calwell held a ceremony for new citizens, including former Yugoslavia citizens that had migrated to Australia after WW II. Mr. Calwell stated that a Czech, a Spaniard, a Frenchman, a Yugoslav, Norwegian and a Greek will take the oath of allegiance and receive their naturalization certificates under the new legislation.[160] Without having access to this historical information citizens of Australia would not know or understand how the states citizenry and identity was formed.

The importance of this moment in Australia's history is encapsulated by Calwell's comment that 'this is the first time such a ceremony has been held, and it is important that on such an occasion we should pause for just a few moments to consider

[154] *Freedom of Information Act 1982.*

[155] Official Gazette of the Republic of Slovenia 24/2003.

[156] Official Journal of the European Union L 42, 14/2003.

[157] Australian Government, National Archives of Australia, Your Story, our history, www.naa.gov.au, accessed 27 June 2014. Republic of Slovenia, Ministry of Culture, Archives of the Republic of Slovenia, http://www.arhiv.gov.si/en/use_of_archival_records/use_of_the_records

[158] Legislation from Slovenia and Australia that regulates the establishment and access to archival information, Regulation on Administrative Authorities within Ministries (Official Gazette of the RS, 58/2003, 45/2004, 86/2004, 138/2004, 52/2005, 82/2005, 17/2006, 76/2006 in 132/2006, 41/2007), Regulation on administrative operations (Official Gazette of the RS, 20/2005), Access to Public Information Act (Official Gazette of the Republic of Slovenia, 24/2003)] Archives and Archival Institutions Act, Official Gazette of the Republic of Slovenia, 321,997, *Archives Act 1983, Freedom of Information Act 1982, Australian Information Commissioner Act 2010.*

[159] Australian Government, National Archives of Australia, First naturalisation ceremony under 1948 Nationality and Citizefrom ABC broadcast 3 February 1949, http://vrroom.naa.gov.au/print/?ID=25355, accessed 27 June 2014.

[160] Ibid.

what it is we do'.[161] It is with those words that new migrants from other states including the former YU, became Australian citizens for the first time, and began their contribution to the state and its growing identity. The former Yugoslav archives are located in Beograd (*English: Belgrade*), and are open to all citizens of the former Yugoslav Republics to gain an understanding of the operation and identity of Yugoslavia, Slovenia and the other former Republics.[162] Today, Slovenia has its own archives that document its history for its citizens, and of particular importance are records of the confiscation of property during German occupation in 1944, which affected many Slovenes.[163] The archival information also records and informs citizens of Slovenia, the importance castles have in Slovenia's cultural heritage and identity, and which can still be seen today.

8.4.2.9 Arts and Sciences

Arts and science form part of any nation's culture, history and identity,[164] and can be closely associated with the right to education. Arts and science in most states including Slovenia and Australia form part of the national curriculum. Australia has neither expressed the right to arts, science or education within the constitution, but rather, legislates these activities at the national level. Article 57 of the SC guarantees the right to education and article 59 ensures the freedom of one's individual scientific and artistic endeavors. In addition, the right to arts and science is associated with the right of expression. The right to education[165] is a fundamental part of the economic principles of growth and democracy that enables a nation state to build an educated, knowledgeable and informed society (citizenry). Across the European member states, children of a member state who is or has been employed in the territory of another Member State shall be admitted to that State's general educational courses[166] under the same conditions as the nationals of that State.[167] Slovenia recognises the importance of education and similar to Australia has national legislation

---

[161] Ibid.

[162] Yugoslavia Archives, http://www.arhivyu.gov.rs/active/en/home/glavna_navigacija/o_arhivu/delatnost_arhiva.html

[163] Republic of Slovenia, Ministry of Culture, Inventory of Expropriated Castles, http://www.arhiv.gov.si/en/areas_of_work/exhibitions/archivalia_of_the_month/archivalia_of_the_month_december_2012

[164] Article 13. Charter of Fundamental Rights of the European Union, 2000, Official Journal of the European, 2007, C 303/01.

[165] Ibid, article 14.

[166] Case – 413/99 *Baumbast and R v Secretary of State for the Home Department*, European Court Reports I-07091, 61,999 J0413, 1.

[167] Article 12 Council Regulation No 1612/68, on freedom of movement of workers within the community, Official Journal of the European Union L 257/19.

in place to regulate this state activity.[168] Education in Slovenia[169] and Australia is compulsory, however, the SC does not describe an age limit, unlike Australian[170] legislation.[171] The right to education can also be found in article 5 of the International Convention on the Elimination of All Forms of Discrimination 1969 and was discussed by the court in relation to the exclusion of a student of Romanian national origin and neither a citizen or having permanent residence in Australia.[172] The Australian court distinguished between discrimination of a class of person and the concept of citizenship. The court ruled that completing high school was not predicated on whether the person had citizenship or permanent residence, but the fact the person resided in Australia indefinitely. Residence becomes important in chapter five and six when discussing the private acts of citizens between Australia and Slovenia.

8.4.2.10 Association

The 2000 European Charter of Fundamental Rights enables all forms of association whether political, trade union or civil matters. On the other hand, the SC[173] is narrow and only provides for the peaceful assembly and public meetings. The European Court of Human Rights, stated the freedom of association is particularly important for persons belonging to minorities, as laid down in the preamble to the Council of Europe Framework Convention.[174] In Australia, the right has been connected with the implied right[175] of free movement.[176] Due to the broad and diverse area the freedom of association covers this section will focus on how Slovenia and Australia adopted the principle in relation trade unions. The Australian *Fair Work Act 2009* protects citizens and workers right to association in the workplace by allowing individuals to become members of unions. This right is also protected under the *Australian Human Rights Commission Regulations 1989* by protecting people from discrimination in employment based on one's membership or activity within a trade union. In U-I-249/10[177] the Slovenian Constitutional Court ruled that the 'autonomy of collective bargaining, which is also the international standard of a constitutional

[168] Ibid.

[169] Article 57 (2), The Constitution of the Republic of Slovenia, Official Gazette Republic of Slovenia No. 33/91-I, 42/97, 66/2000, 24/03, 69/04, 68/06, and 47/13.

[170] Higher Education Funding Act 1988, School Attendance Act 2008, Disability Discrimination Act 1992.

[171] Ibid.

[172] *AB v State of New South Wales* (2005) FMCA 1113, 16.

[173] Article 12 and 42, The Constitution of the Republic of Slovenia, Official Gazette Republic of Slovenia No. 33/91-I, 42/97, 66/2000, 24/03, 69/04, 68/06, and 47/13.

[174] *Gorzelik and Others v Poland* (Application No. 44158/98), Judgement 2004, ECoHR, 93.

[175] *Kruger v Commonwealth (Stolen Generation Case)* (1997) 190 CLR 1, 115.

[176] *Australian Capital Television Pty Ltd v Commonwealth* (1992) 177 CLR 106, 212.

[177] Official Gazette of the Republic of Slovenia 27/2012.

right that is derived from the freedom of association and enshrined in article 76 of the Slovenian Constitution', is protected. The Slovenian Constitutional Court in UI-57/95[178] ruled that the freedom association extends to citizens joining a union and that everyone has the right to peaceful assembly and association. A similar position has been taken by the Australian Federal Court in *Belandra*[179] where North J highlighted that collective bargaining is an integral and primary function of association, and citizens associating with one another. Notwithstanding the right to association between citizens from both states in relation to employment, they are also allowed to assemble.[180] However, any assembly must be peaceful and according to national laws.

Assembly is a guaranteed constitutional right in Slovenia, but not in Australia. The assembly of citizens can include protests against workplace relations laws. Both states have laws to restrict the coming together of citizens and non-citizens, in public, to protest.[181] The Slovenian Act on Public Assembly[182] allows citizens of Slovenia to organise a public gathering, to express ones opinion on questions of public and common importance. In 2014, in the state of Victoria, Australia, the state government amended legislation to provide the authority (police) with greater power to manage protester activities such as entry to buildings, disrupting traffic and further protecting other citizens in the event the protest becomes violent.[183] These laws extended to those who gather, assemble and associate in public protests that could include protests against workplace laws. Thus, states are looking at ways of restricting the extent and use of the right to association. These rights are core democratic principles of Australia and Slovenia, which form part of the overall rights framework that contribute to national identity.

8.4.2.11 Occupation

The freedom for a citizen to choose their occupation whether being employed by an employer, or undertaking their own business, assists in creating entrepreneurs across the European Union.[184] However, forced labour[185] is prohibited under the SC, consistent with international law. The *Fair Work Act* provides for international labour

[178] Official Gazette of the Republic of Slovenia, 13/98.

[179] *Australian Meat Industry Employees' Union v Belandra Pty Ltd* [2003] FCA 910.

[180] Article 42, The Constitution of the Republic of Slovenia, Official Gazette Republic of Slovenia No. 33/91-I, 42/97, 66/2000, 24/03, 69/04, 68/06, and 47/13.

[181] Australian state and territory laws regulate assembly and the peaceful protest.

[182] Article 2, *The Act on Public Assembly*, Official Gazette of the Republic of Slovenia 90/05.

[183] *Summary Offences Act 1996*, and Sentencing Act 1991, Victoria, Australia.

[184] Article 15 and 16, Charter of Fundamental Rights of the European Union, 2000, Official Journal of the European, 2007 C 303/01.

[185] Article 49, The Constitution of the Republic of Slovenia, Official Gazette Republic of Slovenia No. 33/91-I, 42/97, 66/2000, 24/03, 69/04, 68/06, and 47/13.

protections for Australian citizens.[186] The right for citizens and others to choose their occupation (employment) is not an inherent expressed right in Australia, but is seen as a societal norm in accordance with article 23 of the 1948 Declaration on Human Rights. The freedom to conduct business[187] was established to ensure all citizens of member states across the European Union have the ability to undertake and conduct business activities when trading with other nation states. This right is closely associated with the 'single market' policy if the European Union, ensuring there are minimal restrictions to economic activity. The ECJ[188] stated it is a general principle of European Law, and is closely associated with the right of free movement being recognized as the right to establishment under the TFEU.[189]

Nevertheless, and while there is no direct expression of the freedom to conduct business in the SC, the right in accordance with article 49 ensures that work is guaranteed,[190] and that a citizen is able to choose their employment. Doing business in Australia is not a right that has been expressed formally within the constitution. However, there can be links to section 92 (trade and commerce) and section 51(i) of the constitution that provides the Commonwealth the power to make laws. That is, the *Corporations Act 2001* and *Competition and Consumer Act 2012 Act* have been established to regulate corporations and business activity across Australia.

8.4.2.12 Property

The right to property[191] is an accepted principle of European Union law,[192] and is also acceptable under national constitutional law.[193] Article 33 of the SC guarantees a citizen to the right to property in Slovenia.[194] However, the state may limit the right to acquire and retain property on public policy grounds such as major infrastructure development and to expand the economic development of the state.[195] The right to

---

[186] Fair Work Act Australia 2009, s3.

[187] Article 16, Charter of Fundamental Rights of the European Union, 2000, Official Journal of the European, (2007/C 303/01).

[188] Case 70/10 *Scarlet Extended SA v Societe belge des auteurs, compositeurs et editeurs SCRL* (SABAM), Third Chamber, (2011) ECJ, 49.

[189] Case – *1/11Interseroh Scrap and Metals Trading GmbH v Sonderbfall-Management-Gesellschaft Rheinland-Pfalz mbH* (SAM), Fourth Chamber, 2012, 43.

[190] Article 49(1), Slovenian Constitution, Official Gazette Republic of Slovenia No. 33/91-I, 42/97, 66/2000, 24/03, 69/04, 68/06, and 47/13.

[191] Article 1, Protocol, Paris, 20, III, 1952, European Convention on Human Rights, Council of Europe, Rome, 4.XI. 1950.

[192] Case – *1/11Interseroh Scrap and Metals Trading GmbH v Sonderbfall-Management-Gesellschaft Rheinland-Pfalz mbH* (SAM), Fourth Chamber, 2012, 43.

[193] Case 44/79 *Hauer v Land Rheinland-Pfalz* ECR 3727 (1980), CMLR 42 (1979).

[194] Article 67, The Constitution of the Republic of Slovenia, Official Gazette Republic of Slovenia No. 33/91-I, 42/97, 66/2000, 24/03, 69/04, 68/06, and 47/13.

[195] Article 69, The Constitution of the Republic of Slovenia, Official Gazette Republic of Slovenia No. 33/91-I, 42/97, 66/2000, 24/03, 69/04, 68/06, and 47/13. Law of Property Code (SPZ; Official

property, not only ensures a citizen has a right to land, but also, has protection of intellectual property.[196] Property can include many things from land, dwelling as well as moveable property such as investments, incorporated interests,[197] intellectual property,[198] and contents of personal possessions. This section will only discuss immovable property (land) in both states.

In Australia, property rights in regards to land have been subject to political debate and decisions by the Australian High Court, in relation to indigenous peoples. The AC while not directly providing a right to property, the constitution does allow the commonwealth to make laws in relation to the acquisition of property 'on just terms'.[199] Property rights in Australia pertaining to the aboriginal people is closely associated with discrimination. Moreover, both Slovenia and Australia are consistent with article 17 of the 1948 Declaration on Human Rights, which provides that everyone has the right to own property. The right to purchase property by citizens is the private act and extends to private international law.

8.4.2.13 Right to Asylum

The European Union,[200] Slovenia[201] and Australia all apply the right to asylum consistently and in accordance with the 1951 Refugee Convention and 1967 Protocol. There is no constitutional right of asylum in Australia but rather section 51(xix) and (xxvii) of the constitution provides the parliament with the power to make laws in relation to aliens. Furthermore, Australia has looked to the European Court of Human Rights and borrowed the courts' standard in relation to a state's obligations to protect applicants in accordance with the Refugee Convention and Protocol.[202] However, the application of refugee, asylum and human rights law is in direct conflict with a state or supranational polity policy of exercising their right to exclude individuals from entering the territory. As discussed in chapter five, the recent

---

Gazette of RS, No. 87/2002, 18/2007) Building Act (Official Gazette RS, No. 110/2002, 102/2004-UPB1 (14/2005 revised), 126/2007 – ZGO-1). Australian legislation that may limit property rights include amongst others, Building Act 1993 and Planning and Environment Act 1987.

[196] Case – 275 *Promusicae v Telefonica* (2008) ECR I-271.

[197] *Newcrest Minning* (1997) 190 CLR 513.

[198] *Attorney- General (NT) v Chaffey* (2007) 213 CLR 651, 664.

[199] *Australian Constitution 1901*, s51(xxxi).

[200] Article 18, European Charter of Fundamental Rights 2000, Official Journal of the European, (2007/C 303/01). Council Directive 2005/85/EC on minimum standards on procedures in Member States for granting and withdrawing refugee status, Official Journal of the European Union L 326/13.

[201] Article 48, The Constitution of the Republic of Slovenia, Official Gazette Republic of Slovenia Nos. 33/91-I, 42/97, 66/2000, 24/03, 69/04, 68/06, and 47/13.

[202] *VRAW v Minister for Immigration & Multicultural & Indigenous Affairs* [2004] FCA 113, *NAIS V Minister for Immigration and Multicultural and Indigenous Affairs* (2005) 228 CLR 470. *Koniug v Federal Republic of Germany* (1978) 2 EHRR 170, *Osman v United Kingdom* (1998) 29 E.H.R.R. 245.

Syrian convict has seen a large number of people being displaced. Many of these people are now descending on and arriving in Europe and Slovenia. Even though both states had committed to accepting refugees from Syria, both Australia and Slovenia have to balance their sovereign needs to protect the state and their citizens, while protecting the rights of the refugee that are on the territory. Both Australia and the European Union (Slovenia) have strong border controls. It is argued immigration including those individuals that are declared refugees can obtain citizenship of Slovenia or Australia. The act of regulating immigration enables Australia and Slovenia to protect the state and their citizens. It also enables both states to choose who will and who will not be accepted into their territory, and ultimately who will become a citizen. It is argued this act of regulating migration and choosing who can enter the territory is a component of national identity. Notwithstanding the above, the rights and freedoms discussed thus far are an expression of both Australia and Slovenia's democratic society. They contribute to national identity by directing their respective citizens to behave in a certain way. Furthermore, the rights and freedoms allow citizens to protect themselves from each other and from the state.

8.5 Equality

Equality as a legal principle is important to all citizens (men, women and children of all ages). Equality is a legal norm that is synonymous with democratic states. In a globalized world that is continually having to cater for multiculturalism, equality ensures participation in public life and protection no matter the person's gender, ethnic or cultural background. Equality also forms part of the national identity that all people are equal being part of a community of citizens. Equality ensures states and citizens maintain their identity and enhance their respective integration programs. This legal principle has been included into the European Charter of Fundamental Rights and the Slovenian Constitution, but not, the Australian Constitution.[203]

The European Court of Justice affirmed the principle of equality is a legal rule of the highest order.[204] This was also reinforced by the Slovenian Constitutional Court, whereby, the court ruled the legislature has responsibility for prohibition against discrimination, including equality between men and women in relation to the right to access social security.[205] The court went onto say 'in Slovenia, as in the framework

[203] Article 20, Equality before the law, Charter of Fundamental Rights of the European Union, 2000, Official Journal of the European, 2007 C 303/01. Article 14(2), The Constitution of the Republic of Slovenia, Official Gazette Republic of Slovenia No. 33/91-I, 42/97, 66/2000, 24/03, 69/04, 68/06, and 47/13.

[204] Cases 261 and 262/78 *INTERQUELL STARKE-CHEMIE GMBH & Co. KG, Grossaitingen (Federal Republic of Germany) and DIAMALTAG, Munich (Federal Republic of Germany v The European Economic Community* (1979) ECR, 4(b).

[205] U-I-298/96, Official Gazette RS, No 98/99.

of the European Union and elsewhere in the world, the goal of enforcing the principle of equal treatment of men and women is universally accepted.[206] Thus, equality before the law is also considered to be an important legal principle in Australia law, whereby, discrimination arises from not treating individuals (men and women) as equals.[207] This legal principle has been discussed by the courts and is enshrined in legislation such as the *Racial Discrimination Act 1975*.[208] In *Leeth v Commonwealth*[209] Deane J and Toohey J stated there is an implied doctrine of equality between citizens, exists in Australia.

Equality also has enabled the European Union to give effect to the international conventions on the Rights of the Child[210] and is closely associated with persons (children) with disabilities.[211] These two legal principles have also been replicated in the SC respectively, that ensure children are properly protected and cared for economically and socially so as children across the EU[212] and in Slovenia are not wrongfully abused.[213] The Slovenian Constitutional Court, discussed at length, the Convention on the Right of the Child when challenging the Law on Marriage and Family Relations. The Slovenian Constitutional Court ruled the convention was signed by countries to ensure children grow up in a family environment ensuring the child's interest is the foremost consideration and not the parents.[214] The Federal Court of Australia recognized the importance of the Declaration of the Rights of the Child, and, International Covenant on Economic, Social and Cultural Rights in relation to parental responsibility of a child's education.[215] The court ruled the right includes whether the child has a disability or not.

---

[206] Ibid. the court referred further the Council Directive 79/7/EEC that established the gradual introduction of the principles of equal treatment of men and women in relation to social security, Official Journal of the European Union L 6.

[207] *Waters v Public Transport Corporation* (1991) 173 CLR 349, 402.

[208] Equality before the law as a legal principle can also be found in the *Sex Discrimination Act 1984, Disability Discrimination Act 1992 and Age Discrimination Act 2004.*

[209] *Leeth v Commonwealth* (1992) 174 CLR 455, 486.

[210] Article 24, Equality before the law, Charter of Fundamental Rights of the European Union, 2000, Official Journal of the European, 2007/ C 303/01. Article 56 The Constitution of the Republic of Slovenia, Official Gazette Republic of Slovenia No. 33/91-I, 42/97, 66/2000, 24/03, 69/04, 68/06, and 47/13.

[211] Article 26, Equality before the law, Charter of Fundamental Rights of the European Union, 2000, Official Journal of the European, 2007 C 303/01.

[212] Article 3 Treaty on European Union. Council Regulation 2201/2003/EC judgments in matrimonial matters and parental responsibility. Council Directive 2011/95/EC standards on international protection of third country nationals and stateless persons ensuring the best interests of the child. Council Directive 2011/92/EU combating sexual abuse and exploitation of children.

[213] Article 56 and 52, The Constitution of the Republic of Slovenia, Official Gazette Republic of Slovenia No. 33/91-I, 42/97, 66/2000, 24/03, 69/04, 68/06, and 47/13.

[214] U-I-53/93, Official Gazette of the Republic of Slovenia, No. 20/95, the convention regulates the rights of the child concerning the personal status, inalienable rights, civil and political rights as well as economic, social and cultural rights.

[215] *McBain v Victoria* (2000) FCA, 8–11.

The prohibition of discrimination under article 63 of the SC and article 20 of the European Charter of Fundamental Rights focuses on racial and religious discrimination. Discrimination[216] is a broad legal principle that covers physical and mental disabilities, and is closely associated with the right to religion, expression and association. For example, being dismissed from work on religious or gender grounds. In this section, it will be demonstrated how discrimination on the grounds of a disability has been defined by both states. In U-I-146/07[217] the Slovenian Constitutional Court stated the Slovenian legal system provides no single definition of disability and is consistent with the second paragraph of article 1 of the Convention on the Rights of Persons with Disabilities[218] (CRPD) in the same way the Australian *Disability Discrimination Act 1992* (DDA).[219] However, the DDA expands on the definition provided by the CRDP, and focuses on the disability at the personal level (physically or mentally [malfunction, illness or disease]). Both the TEU and TFEU have made discrimination one of the fundamental legal principles across the European Union to combat social exclusion, amongst European citizens, while promoting social justice.[220] To enhance the understanding, awareness and practice of equality a number of regulations and directives have been established. The European law in this area assist citizens to move freely, enjoy employment and an occupation irrespective of the individual's racial or ethnic origin.[221] For the European Union, discrimination is considered important because it ensures not only equality but stability across the Union and assists in integrating member states.

Across Slovenia, the European Union and within Australia the diversity in cultural, religious beliefs and languages have become varied.[222] This diversity can be seen through the recognition of minorities, particularly under Slovenian Constitution. Membership of a national minority is another important right because across the European Union there are minorities that exists in most MS. Slovenia for example, with its complex history has recognized under article 64 of the SC special rights of Italian and Hungarian national communities. In addition, article 65 has been put in

---

[216] Article 1 Protocol No. 12, and Article 14, European Convention on Human Rights, Council of Europe, Rome, 4.XI. 1950.

[217] U-I-146/07, Official Gazette of the Republic of Slovenia, No. 111/2008.

[218] Convention on the Rights of Persons with Disabilities, Treaty Series, vol. 2515, p.3.

[219] Disability Discrimination Act 1992, s4.

[220] Article 10, Treaty on the Functioning of the European Union, Official Journal of the European Union, C 83/94.

[221] Council Directive 2000/43/EC implementing the principle of equal treatment between persons no matter their racial or ethnic origin, Official Journal of the European Union L180. Council Directive 2000/78/EC establishing a general framework for equal treatment in employment and occupation, Official Journal of the European Union L 303. Council Regulation 492/2011 free movement of workers. Council Regulation 181/2011 rights of passengers in bus and coach transport, Official Journal of the European Union L 141/1. Council Regulation 1177/2012 passengers travelling by sea and inland waterway, Official Journal of the European Union L 334/1.

[222] Article 22, Charter of Fundamental Rights of the European Union, 2000, Official Journal of the European, 2007, C 303/01). Article 10 Treaty on the Functioning of the European Union, Official Journal of the European Union, C 83/94.

place to ensure special rights of the Roma community that reside within the Slovene territory. Australia does not provide for minority rights within the constitution, except the race power that has allowed the Australian Parliament to pass laws to protect people and citizens of any race.[223] This power has been used by consecutive governments to establish laws to protect indigenous peoples from discrimination. However, the constitution of Australia could be amended to not only recognize the rights of indigenous citizens, but also other minority groups, their language, culture and customs.

8.5.1 *Solidarity*

The analysis highlights that of the 12 articles within the European Charter of Fundamental Rights 2000 under solidarity, only three have been duplicated or expressed in the Slovenian Constitution. None are expressed or implied under the Australian Constitution such as collective bargaining,[224] the right to information[225] and consultation,[226] access to placement services,[227] fair work conditions,[228] and the protection from unjustified dismissal.[229] Across the European Union (EU), it is recognized that human relations among persons, groups and peoples of a state, and a moral expression of major religious and cultural groups treat others as you would like to be treated. This accords with Bosniak's position that citizenship is multicultural.[230] That is, the European Charter of Fundamental Rights has established the minimum requirements to protect all citizens no matter what member state they are employed. The same has been achieved in Australia by the Commonwealth

---

[223] Australian Constitution, s51 (xxvi).

[224] Article 28, Charter of Fundamental Rights of the European Union, 2000, Official Journal of the European, 2007 C 303/01. Articles 151, 153, 155, 156, Treaty on the Functioning of the European Union.

[225] *Kevin Denly v Commissioner of Taxation* (2012) FCA 1434, 40, the right to information was discussed in relation to tax related matters in relation to obtaining criminal records of the defendant.

[226] Article 27, Charter of Fundamental Rights of the European Union, 2000, Official Journal of the European, 2007 C 303/01. Article 151, 153 and 154 Treaty on the Functioning of the European Union, Official Journal of the European Union, C 83/94. Council Directive 91/533/EEC obligation to inform employees of conditions to contract or employment relationship, Official Journal of the European Union L 288. Council Directive 98/59/EC laws relating to member states collective redundancies, Official Journal of the European Union L 255. Council Directive 2001/23/EC safeguarding employees rights in the event of transfers of undertakings, business or parts of undertakings or businesses, Official Journal of the Union L 82.

[227] Ibid, article 29.

[228] Ibid, article 31.

[229] Ibid, article 30.

[230] Soysal, Y, (1994) *Limits of Citizenship: Migrant and Postnational Membership in Europe*, Chicago University Press, 1–15.

Parliament establishing legislation that regulates work places and employment throughout the country.

The principle of solidarity provides for a common set of employment rights throughout the EU such as the ability for collective action that can be taken by trade unions when entering into collective bargaining and agreements for workers as a fundamental right.[231] Rather than discussing each of these rights individually, the discussion will focus on collective bargaining because the other rights could be captured as part of the bargaining process. National legislation ensures employees and employers can consult as part of the bargaining process in order to determine the working conditions and grounds for dismissal of citizens. The Federal Court of Australia[232] stated it the federal legislation enabled individuals to exercise their right to collectively bargain.[233] Article 76 of the Slovenian Constitution ensures citizens have the right to join a trade union and guarantees collective bargaining in accordance with 2006 Collective Agreements Act.[234] Collective bargaining is closely associated with the ability for a citizen to join a union and the right to expression, association, assembly and discrimination. Article 156 of the TFEU allows the European Union to provide a consistent framework for labour law, working conditions, collective bargaining across all member states. The Community Charter of the Fundamental Social Rights of Workers[235] establishes the minimum principles for European labour law and protection of workers, employment, remuneration and collective bargaining in accordance with article 151 of the TFEU. This also supports the rights set out in the European Charter of Fundamental Rights 2000. Furthermore, articles 11 to 14 reaffirms the ability for individuals to associate and collectively bargain as part of their employment.

The following principles that have been expressed under the SC is the prohibition of child labour[236] and protection of young people at work,[237] social security,[238] health care.[239] The international Convention on the Rights of the Child[240] was the

[231] Case 438/05 *International Transport Workers' Federation and Finnish Seaman's Union v Viking Line ABP and OU Viking Line Eesti*, (2007), 47–55.

[232] *Automotive, Food, Metals, Engineering, Printed and Kindred Industries Union v Wesfarmers Premier Coal Limited* (2005) AIRC 873 – PR963714 (C2005/1044).

[233] *Fair Work Act 2009* establishes the framework for collective bargaining between employees, employers and nominated representatives.

[234] The Collective Agreements Act, Official Gazette of the Republic of Slovenia 001–22-52/05.

[235] The Community Charter of the Fundamental Social Rights of Workers http://www.eurofound.europa.eu/areas/industrialrelations/dictionary/definitions/communitycharterofthefundamentalsocialrightsofworkers.htm

[236] Chapter IV Solidarity, Charter of Fundamental Rights of the European Union, 2000, Official Journal of the European, (2007/C 303/01).

[237] Ibid, article 32.

[238] Ibid, article 34.

[239] Ibid, article 35.

[240] Convention on the Rights of the Child United Nations, Treaty Series, vol. 1577, p. 3. Australian and Slovenia have both ratified this convention in 1990 and 1992 respectively.

first international legal instrument developed to protect children's social, economic and political rights. The protection of children from being exploited through employment is closely associated with the protection against slavery (discussed earlier in this chapter). A child born to parents who are either Slovenian or Australia citizens themselves, or born on the territory of either state, can be citizens of these states. Australia ratified the Convention on the Rights of the Child in 1990, Slovenia did so in 1992. Article 32 of the convention stated that the right of the child is to be protected from economic exploitation when performing work that could have an impact in that individual's education and health. The convention does not determine the minimum age for a child to work, however, the Convention on the Minimum Age for Admission to Employment[241] provides the basis for states to describe the minimum legal age for employment. Article 2 specifies the minimum age of 15 years old for completing compulsory education and following consultation with employees and other organizations the minimum work age is 14 years. However, Australia has not ratified this minimum age convention, whereas, Slovenia did in 1992. Australia should ratify and implement this convention. The Australian Refugee Review Tribunal reinforces the above point that the international law surrounding child labour is important part of the social fabric of society and should be implemented by states.[242] The state of Victoria, in Australia, allows children 13 years old and above to be employed for a maximum time of 3 h a day and not more than 12 h per week.[243] Whereas, Slovenia described a minimum age of 15 years of age before a child can work, which is consistent with the European Union standard.[244] Article 1 of the Directive 94/33/EC requires member states to protect children to the age of 15 years of age. This applies to children when pursuing employment that is given effect by the Slovenian Employment Relationship Act 2002, the Rules on the Protection of Health at Work of Children, Adolescents and Young People, and the Rules on Permits for Work of Children Under the Age of 15 regulations.[245] There is a difference in protecting the age of when children can undertake employment in Slovenia and Australia.

[241] Convention No. 138 on the Minimum Age for Admission to Employment 1973. Adoption: Geneva, 58th ILC session (26 Jun 1973).

[242] *SZNP & Anor v Minister for Immigration & Anor* (2009) FMCA 738, 6–15.

[243] *Child Employment Act* 2003.

[244] Council Directive 94/33/EC on the protection of young people at work, Official Journal of the European Communities, L 216/12.

[245] Employment Relations Act, Official Gazette of the Republic of Slovenian 42-2006/02, Rules on the Protection of Health at Work of Children, Adolescents and Young People, Official Gazette 82-3920/03, Rules on Permits for Work of Children Under the Age 15, Official Gazette of the Republic of Slovenia 60–2760/04.

Social security and health care have been established by democratic states to protect the welfare of all citizens. Australia[246] and Slovenia[247] have established bilateral agreements in this area for when a Slovene citizen is present in Australia and vice versa. Nevertheless, both states have national laws and policy programs to provide their citizens social security and health care. Section 51 (xxiii) of the Australian constitution enables the Australian Parliament to make laws in relation to social security, however this provision is limited to only invalid (citizens with a disability) and citizens that are determined to be old age. Slovenia has gone further than Australia to express the right to social security is a guaranteed constitutional right to ensure the special protection of its citizens (unemployment, aged care and disability).[248] Health care as a right in Australia has been dealt with through a Charter that ensure citizens are provided the highest possible care.[249] The Grand Chamber in *Servet*[250] stated that when determining social security, social assistance and social protection must be in accordance with the principle of equal treatment must comply with the rights set out in the 2000 European Charter of Fundamental Rights. It is argued social security and health are a small component of national identity, as they provide a citizen with a level of protection, by the state.

In a globalized world protecting consumers[251] (protecting all citizens), access to services,[252] and more broadly the environment[253] has also become important. As a regional economic and social bloc, the Union and its citizens have greater consumer power than before the internal borders were extinguished. The improvements in technology with the ability for individuals to purchase consumer goods on the internet has risen significantly over the past decade. The dismantling of borders has also allowed citizens from Slovenia to more easily have access to services in not only

---

[246] *Social Security Act 1991, National Health Act 1953, National Health Amendment (Pharmaceutical Benefits Scheme) Act 2012, National Health Reform Act 2011, National Health Security Act 2007*, amongst others.

[247] *Pension and Disability Insurance Act*, Official Gazette of the Republic of Slovenia 72/05. Health Care and *Health Insurance Act*, Official Gazette of the Republic of Slovenia 76/05.

[248] Article 50, The Constitution of the Republic of Slovenia, Official Gazette Republic of Slovenia No. 33/91-I, 42/97, 66/2000, 24/03, 69/04, 68/06, and 47/13.

[249] Australian Charter of Health Care Rights, http://www.safetyandquality.gov.au/our-work/national-perspectives/charter-of-healthcare-rights

[250] Case 571/*10 Servet Kamberaj v Istituto per l'Edilizia sociale della Provincia autonoma di Bolzano* (IPES) [2012] ECR.

[251] Article 38, Chapter IV Solidarity, Charter of Fundamental Rights of the European Union, 2000, Official Journal of the European, (2007/C 303/01).

[252] Ibid, article 36.

[253] Ibid, article 37. Article 3 and 21 Treaty on European Union, Official Journal of the European Union C 191. Articles 4, 11, 191 and 192 Treaty on the Functioning of the European Union, Official Journal of the European Union, C 83/94. Regulation 614/2007/EC Financial Instrument for the Environment, Official Journal of the European Union L 149. Regulation 401/2009/EC European Environment Agency and the European Environment Information and Observation Network, Official Journal of the European Union L 126/13. At a national level in Australia the *Environment Protection and Biodiversity Act 1999* along with state legislation provide similar.

neighboring states such as Austria, Italy and Hungary but also the other member states. At the national level citizens in both states have access to services equally and consumer protection laws provide that citizens are protected from business by the *Consumer Protection Act, Official Gazette of the Republic of Slovenia 86/2009* and the *Competition and Consumer Act 2010 as well as the Trades Practices Act 1974*.

The European Union aims to protect the environment for all its citizens and to the highest standards for current and future generations. While there is no express protection stated in either the Slovenian or Australian constitutions, article 72 of the SC provides that every citizen and non-citizen has the right to a healthy living environment. Both states have implemented national law to meet their international environmental obligations and ensure the respective states and their citizens have a healthy living environment. In Slovenia, one of the principal acts is the *Environment Protection Act 1993*,[254] and in Australia the equivalent is the *Environment and Biodiversity Conservation Act 1999*. The objectives of the national laws from either state is to protect the natural environment, ecosystems (flora and fauna) including natural resources such as water and aquatic biota.

The analysis shows that Australia and Slovenia have very different constitutionally expressed rights and freedoms for citizens and non- citizens. Australia has taken the common law approach by providing for most rights in national legislation. Slovenia on the other hand provides greater legal certainty of their rights and freedoms being expressed in the constitution. The right, freedoms and protections discussed all form part of the respective states legal frameworks, and considered an important part of their respective democratic principles that form part of the foundation of both states. It is argued, the above rights, freedoms and protections, even in a small way, contribute to national identity.

8.6 Citizen's Rights [Political]

The rights of citizens are different from the rights of others in Slovenia and Australia. As discussed in chapter one, citizenship is the 'right to have rights'. Firstly, the notion of political rights enables citizens to fully participate as part of the political community. Barrington when describing a citizen as being an official (active) member of the state, or in the case of the European Union a member of a supranational polity, are afforded certain rights over and above non-citizens that enable access to European Union institutions.[255] This is an important point because, a dual citizen of

[254] Environment Protection Act, Official Gazette of the Republic of Slovenia 32/93.

[255] Articles 20 and 223, Treaty on the Functioning of the European Union, Official Journal of the European Union, C 83/94. Council Directive 93/109/EC laying down detailed arrangements for the exercise of the right to vote and stand as a candidate in elections to the European Parliament for citizens of the Union residing in a Member State of which they are not national, Official Journal of the European Union L 329.

Slovenia and Australia who is resident in Slovenia has the ability to participate not only in Australia and Slovenia's political community, but also the European Union. A dual citizen can vote and stand for elections in both Slovenia and the European Parliament.

The right to vote and stand for election[256] is a guaranteed and is crucial to maintaining the foundations of an effective democracy established by a constitution. The right to vote and stand for election strengthens national identity, through citizens being active participants in the political community. The analysis highlights that jurisdictions have ensured citizens have a right to participate in their respective community and political process.[257] However, all citizens across the EU are afforded these rights to enable them participation in the European Union and its institutions. This is an exclusive right only afforded to EU citizens. The right to vote and stand for elections also includes municipal elections in accordance with article 40 of the European Charter of Fundamental Rights 2000 and articles 20 and 22 of the TEFU, and Council Directives 96/30/EC.[258] Slovenes have the right to vote and stand for elections to the European Parliament, and municipal elections.[259] The right to vote in Australia, in federal elections, is regulated under the *Electoral Act 1918*. The SC states the right exists provided the citizens wanting to vote is 18 years of age.[260] Whereas, the AC under section 24 refers to the House of Representatives that the representatives can be chosen by the people (citizens) of the commonwealth. Section 25 allows individual states within Australia to exclude any race from voting at elections. Furthermore, section 41 provides an express right of electors of states, whereby no adult person who has or acquires the right to vote at elections for more numerous House of the Parliament of a State shall, while the right continues be prevented by a law of the commonwealth. However, section 44 for the Australian constitution restricts candidates from Federal Parliament, whereby, a person who has allegiance, obedience or adherence to a foreign power or is a citizen who has obtained rights and privileges of a foreign power cannot be chosen or sit as a senator or member of the House of Representatives. Therefore, a dual citizen of Slovenia and Australia is not treated equally by either state, or the EU. The dual citizen can stand for election and vote in and across the EU and Slovenia, although restricted. However, in Australia the dual citizens cannot stand for election at the national level. Australia should consider amending the constitution to allow certain country citizens such as Slovenia Australians to stand for election in the national parliament.

---

[256] *Scoppola v Italy* (No.3) (Application No 126/05), 2012, 81–82.

[257] Article 3, Paris, 20.III. 1952, European Convention on Human Rights, Council of Europe, Rome, 4.XI. 1950.

[258] Outlining the arrangements for the exercise of the right to vote and to stand as a candidate in municipal elections by citizens of the Union.

[259] Article 39, 40 & 43 Charter of Fundamental Rights of the European Union, 2000, Official Journal of the European, 2007 C 303/01.

[260] Article 43, The Constitution of the Republic of Slovenia, Official Gazette Republic of Slovenia Nos. 33/91-I, 42/97, 66/2000, 24/03, 69/04, 68/06, and 47/13.

Good administration[261] provides that citizen's affairs are handled impartially and fairly by the institutions of the EU. A democratic society ensures its institutions work on behalf of the citizens,[262] and they can be accessed by all citizens.[263] A similar approach allows citizens in Australia access to government[264] institutions, however it is not an expressed constitutional right. Article 42 of the European Charter of Fundamental Rights 2000 enables any citizen of the Union the right to access documents[265] of EU institutions, bodies, offices and agencies.[266] Council Regulation 1049/2001/EC and Council Directive 2003/4/EC assist in facilitating access by citizens to the European Parliament, European Council and European Commission documents. Citizens of the Union can refer matters to the European Ombudsman.[267] Australian national law enables citizens to refer matters such as immigration detention to the Commonwealth Ombudsman.[268] An Ombudsman was appointed for Slovene citizens through the *Human Rights Ombudsman Act 1993*.[269] Slovene citizens may petition the European Parliament.[270] The right to petition is not absolute in Australia and a citizen may petition the House of Representatives for any issue under the responsibility of the constitution such as citizenship and immigration.[271] The notable difference between Australia and Slovenia is Slovene citizens have access to a supranational polity, whereas Australian citizens do not. Access to these institutions ensures that a state, in accordance with the democratic principles of good governance, allows its citizens to have access to open, transparent and accountable government institutions.

---

[261] Article 41, Charter of Fundamental Rights of the European Union, 2000, Official Journal of the European, 2007 C 303/01.

[262] Ibid, article 11.

[263] Articles 15, 24 and 228, Treaty on the Functioning of the European Union, Official Journal of the European Union, C 83/94.

[264] *Freedom of Information Act 1982*, Section 11A.

[265] Article 15 (3), Treaty on the Functioning of the European Union, Official Journal of the European Union, C 83/94.

[266] Article 39, The Constitution of the Republic of Slovenia, Official Gazette Republic of Slovenia No. 33/91-I, 42/97, 66/2000, 24/03, 69/04, 68/06, and 47/13.

[267] Articles 20, 24 and 28, Treaty on the Functioning of the European Union, Official Journal of the European Union, C 83/94.

[268] *Ombudsman Act 1976.*

[269] Official Gazette of the Republic of Slovenia 71/93. 15/94 and 109/12. Article 159, The Constitution of the Republic of Slovenia, Official Gazette Republic of Slovenia No. 33/91-I, 42/97, 66/2000, 24/03, 69/04, 68/06, and 47/13.

[270] Article 44, Charter of Fundamental Rights of the European Union, 2000, Official Journal of the European, 2007, C 303/01. Article 45, The Constitution of the Republic of Slovenia, Official Gazette Republic of Slovenia Nos. 33/91-I, 42/97, 66/2000, 24/03, 69/04, 68/06, and 47/13. Articles 20, 24, 227 Treaty on the Functioning of the European Union, Official Journal of the European Union, C 83/94.

[271] House of Representatives, Amnesty for immigrants and refugees, 22 November 2010, http://aphnew.aph.gov.au/Parliamentary_Business/Committees/House_of_Representatives_Committees?url=petitions/presented.htm

The right of citizens to freely move and reside anywhere in the EU and Slovenia is well established.[272] While not an expressed right in the AC, section 92 provides an implied right to free movement allowing the free movement of goods, services and people throughout Australia. Australia could strengthen its constitution to resemble Slovenia's and clearly state that citizens have the right to enter and exit the territory. At the commonwealth level, rather than guarantee the right; the parliament has opted to restrict the right for example under division 104 of the *Criminal Code Act 1995* and the *Defence Act 1903*.[273] However, this restriction only pertains to criminal matters and not trade. Thus, Australia similar to the EU has developed a common single market that allows free movement and trade between states and territories. In *Cole v Whitfield*[274] the Australian High Court ruled that section 92 creates a free trade area throughout the Commonwealth enabling the free movement of people, goods and communications. The High Court of Australia went further stating 'a constitutional guarantee of freedom of interstate intercourse, if it is to have substantial content, extends to a guarantee of personal freedom to pass to and from States without burden, hindrance or restriction'.[275]

8.7 Justice

In building and establishing any democratic state including the EU, the rule of law and access to justice ensures every citizen has the right to an effective remedy to a fair trial.[276] Section 80 of the AC guarantees a right to trial for those offences stated under commonwealth law only. This does not apply to state or territory law (Victoria, New South Wales, Queensland, Tasmania, Western Australia, South Australia, Northern Territory and Australian Capital Territory). The difference between the SC and AC is that Slovenia expresses the right to a 'fair' trial, whereas, the AC is specific to only refer to a 'trial by jury'.[277]

The Slovenian Constitutional Court in U-I-204/99,[278] stated that article 29 of the Slovene constitution determined that anyone charged with a criminal offence must be guaranteed, in addition to absolute equality and the right to legal representation. Additionally, the Slovenian Constitutional Court in this case ruled that the free

[272] Article 45, Charter of Fundamental Rights of the European Union 2000, Official Journal of the European Union 2007, C 303/01. Article 32, The Constitution of the Republic of Slovenia, Official Gazette Republic of Slovenia No. 33/91-I, 42/97, 66/2000, 24/03, 69/04, 68/06, and 47/13.

[273] Part IIIAAA Defence Act 1903, the freedom of movement may be restricted when orders have been established enabling the Defence Force to exercise certain powers.

[274] *Cole v Whitfield (*1988) CLR 360, 391.

[275] Ibid.

[276] Article 47, Charter of Fundamental Rights of the European Union, 2000, Official Journal of the European, 2007 C 303/01.

[277] *Kingswell v The Queen* (1985) 159 CLR 264.

[278] Official Gazette of the Republic of Slovenia, No. 3/2003.

choice of a legal representative, as is explicitly provided in article 19 of the constitution, is to be understood as an element of the general right to defence determined in article 29 of the constitution. The court went further ruling that article 14 of the ICCPR allows an individual citizen to choose who may represent them in criminal proceedings.

The High Court of Australia in *Dietrich*[279] stated the right to a fair trial while not being an express constitutional right is to be granted a fair trial according to the law. The court also stated the right is a fundamental element of our (Australia's) justice system. Not only did the court emphasize the importance of this right, but also, referred to the article 6 of the European Convention for the Protection of Human Rights and Fundamental Freedoms 1950, whereby, everyone is entitled to a fair hearing. The court also stated that the obligations of the right to for a person to choose their own defence council can be found in article 14(3) of the ICCPR whereby, everyone shall be entitled to the minimum guarantees in full equality, and in defending themselves the person is able to choose their own legal assistance. Australia also having ratified the ICCPR, has given effect to this right by the *Human Rights and Equal Opportunity Commission Act 1986*.

Citizens are presumed innocent[280] until proven guilty and have a right of defence in accordance with the principle of proportionality[281] of criminal offence and penalties both in Slovenia and Australia. However, the rights are expressed differently in case law and legislation. The presumption of innocence[282] and proportionality are fundamental principles of common law. The High Court in *Momcilivic*[283] stated it is a right to be presumed innocent until proven guilty according the law'. In addition, a person cannot be punished twice[284] in criminal proceedings for the same criminal offence. Not having such a principle reflected in EU law would allow a person to be found guilty in two member states for the same offence. That is, a citizen punished in Slovenia and then later punished for the same offence in Austria or Italy. The Australian constitution does not express this right. Furthermore, in Up-383/11[285] the Slovenian courts recognize that the respect for final decisions is an important

[279] *Dietrich v R* [1992] HCA 57; (1992) 177 CLR 292.

[280] Article 48, Charter of Fundamental Rights of the European Union, 2000, Official Journal of the European, 2007 C 303/01. Article 27, The Constitution of the Republic of Slovenia, Official Gazette Republic of Slovenia No. 33/91-I, 42/97, 66/2000, 24/03, 69/04, 68/06, and 47/13. In Australia this is not an expressed right within the Constitution, but nevertheless, is Commonwealth Criminal Code Act 1995 established proof provisions from criminal offences under commonwealth law.

[281] *Veen v The Queen* (No2) (1988) CLR 164 CLR 465, the High Court made it clear that proportionality is the key consideration to take into account in sentencing.

[282] Article 14(2) International Covenant on Civil and Political Rights, Article 6(2) European Convention for the Protection of Human Rights and Fundamental Freedoms, Article 11 Universal Declaration of Human Rights 1948.

[283] *Momcilovic v The Queen* (2011) HCA 34, 2–22.

[284] Article 4, Protocol No. 7, Convention for the Protection of Human Rights and Fundamental Freedoms, Council of Europe, Rome, 4.XI. 1950.

[285] Official Gazette of the Republic of Slovenia, No. 85/2013.

constitutional value and is fundamental to the rule of law providing stability of legal relationships that is aimed at protecting the holders of rights and obligations. The court when referring to divorce of Slovene citizens and who should be granted custody is closely associated to the rights and best interest of the child, and therefore, the final decision.

Similarly, the High Court of Australia is the court of last resort and final appeal in a similar way to the Slovenian Constitutional Court. However, as stated earlier, Slovenes can take human rights matters to the European Court of Human Rights. One of the core legal principles associated with democratic states and in the common law in Australia, allows every citizen to be presumed innocent, until the contrary it proved by a court of law.[286] An expansion of the presumption of innocence in that no person is to be punished for something that has not been declared by law to be an offence.[287] Court hearings are to be public, and the final judgement or judgements are to be made public,[288] unless the state expresses otherwise. It is argued this is not so much an individual citizen's right. Rather a community right, enabling access to court information in relation to a particular individual or group of citizens. Even so, any citizen charged with a criminal offence has the right of adequate time and facilities to prepare for the defence; be present at trial and conduct their own defence or be defended; the right to represent evidence and not to incriminate themselves.[289] This was expressed by the Slovenian Constitutional Court in U-I-345/98, whereby, articles 22 and 23 of the SC define the basic right to a fair trial, and that this right is closely linked to the right to obtain legal representation under article 19 of the SC.[290] Furthermore, where a person has been wrongly convicted[291] they are able to be rehabilitated and seek compensation from the state.[292] No citizen shall be convicted or punished for the same criminal offence twice.

The state of Slovenia guarantees the equal protection of rights in any proceeding before a court,[293] while having the right to judicial protection. A judge appointed by the relevant court can hand down a decision to the individual citizen.[294] The protection is closely related to equality before the law. Citizens in their pursuit of free establishment (undertaking business) can fall into financial difficulties and be subject to a states bankruptcy and liquidation laws. In Up-328/04, U-I-186/04[295] the

[286] Article 27, The Constitution of the Republic of Slovenia, Official Gazette Republic of Slovenia No. 33/91-I, 42/97, 66/2000, 24/03, 69/04, 68/06, and 47/13.

[287] Ibid, article 28.

[288] Ibid, article 24.

[289] Ibid, article 29.

[290] Official Gazette of the Republic of Slovenia, No. 63/94.

[291] Article 3, Protocol No. 7, European Convention on Human Rights, Council of Europe, Rome, 4.XI. 1950.

[292] Article 30 and 31, Official Gazette of the Republic of Slovenia, No. 63/94.

[293] Article 22, The Constitution of the Republic of Slovenia, Official Gazette Republic of Slovenia No. 33/91-I, 42/97, 66/2000, 24/03, 69/04, 68/06, and 47/13.

[294] Ibid, article 23.

[295] OdIUSXIII, 82.

Slovenian Constitutional Court had to consider whether article 22 of the SC had been violated in connection with the Maribor District Court Rulings on the Bankruptcy and Liquidation Act.[296] The court stated that while there was no violation of this right, the requirement that the equal protection of rights be guaranteed in proceedings before the court and other state authorities, does not mean a domestic court should apply the procedural law of the state which a foreign legal entity is from.[297] The court was referring to how the German courts had dealt with the equal protection of rights in insolvency proceedings. The protection also ensures discrimination of a person's race, sex, religion or cultural should not be a factor in court proceedings, as stated above the relevant state protections.

Equality before the law is closely associated with the right to legal remedies such as the ability to appeal[298] against the decision of the court or state authorities.[299] The court[300] ruled where authorities in performing their duties, do so, by exceeding their powers, a citizen has the right to compensation. Furthermore, equality before the law also encompasses the protection against discrimination, and the Australian High Court stated in *Walters*[301] that 'discrimination can arise just as readily from an act which treats those as equals to those who are different as it can from an act which treats differently persons whose circumstances are not materially different'. That is, the national discrimination laws discussed in this chapter both in Slovenia and Australia, including the EU direct and indirect discrimination. The Slovenian Constitutional Court in U-I-284/94[302] stated the principles of equality does not determine equality before law only for citizens of Slovenia but applies to all persons. The court went onto rule that Slovenia as the future state obliged itself in its acts concerning independence that it would guarantee the protection of human rights to all persons in the territory of Slovenia regardless of their nationality, and without any discrimination.

The comparison demonstrates the recognition of rights afforded to citizens by the European Charter of Fundamental Rights 2000 and the Slovenian constitution are significantly more advanced in expressing rights and freedoms to citizens and non-citizen, than the constitution of Australia. Citizenship is the right to have rights that have been provided for in national, supranational and international law. Human rights are central to the ongoing relationship between the citizen, citizens and the state. Human rights assist a state in demonstrating to the world their democratic values and principles, by ensuring equality for all citizens and non-citizens. They also protect citizens and non-citizens from each other and from the state. However,

[296] Official Gazette RS 52/99.

[297] OdIUSXIII, 82.

[298] Article 2, Protocol No. 7, Official Gazette of the Republic of Slovenia, No. 63/94.

[299] Article 25, The Constitution of the Republic of Slovenia, Official Gazette Republic of Slovenia No. 33/91-I, 42/97, 66/2000, 24/03, 69/04, 68/06, and 47/13.

[300] Official Gazette of the Republic of Slovenia, No. 103/2009.

[301] *Walters v Public Transport Corporation* [1991] HCA 49 [10]; 173 CLR 349, 402.

[302] Official Gazette of Republic of Slovenia, No. 14/99.

citizens are afforded additional rights to non-citizens, whereby, they are able to participate in the political community by voting and standing for election. With the continued expansion of globalization states more than ever are wanting to retain their identity, one way to achieve this is following Slovenia's example of providing expressed rights within a state's constitution. The European Union has ensured member states achieve this through their respective institutional structures and constitutions. Slovenia has maintained its identity through constitutional recognition of rights. Thus, it is well documented that Australia's constitution is in need of reform. Australia can learn a lot from the Slovenia and the European Union is further developing constitutional rights. Australia could amend its constitution, develop a commonwealth Human Rights Charter or express the rights within the citizenship act. Doing so, will advance the national identity of Australia with its citizens and residents.

Nonetheless, Slovenia is at an advantage compared to Australia in having access to and being part of a supranational legal framework and institutions. The rights and protections afforded to Slovenian citizens are easily located and clear within the current constitution and national laws. In Australia, many of the rights are spread across a large body of national law, even though both jurisdictions are signatories to the United Nations rights law. Australia having similar democratic principles and law to Slovenia and the European Union could enhance its legal framework by borrowing from Slovenia to change its constitution.

8.8 Conclusion

The international and regionalization of rights has benefited the state and its citizens by protecting citizens from each other and the state. However, states have to grapple with the concept of human rights for all of humanity, human rights for their citizens and the management of the country. For instance, the right to asylum enables a person to seek asylum in accordance with international law. The right protects those individuals from persecution from a state. However, Australia, Slovenia and the European Union do not automatically grant this right and have a strictly controlled border policy. It is argued that such a policy approach enhances national identity because Australia and Slovenia are indirectly communicating to the world they will choose who will enter their territory and stay. The rights and responsibilities expressed by the EU, Slovenia and Australia, all have a special place in the identity of each jurisdictions. For the EU, they pride themselves on how they have a comprehensive legal and policy framework that supports human rights, like no other. In other words, there has been no state that has a comparable framework that, comes close to the EU. That said, it is argued the rights identified in this chapter are and important expression of identity and cohesion.

This chapter has identified areas that Australia and Slovenia could adopt to improve their respective laws. At issues is how the Slovenian constitution states that 'citizenship is regulated by the law', and that Australia's constitution does not, and could be amended to resemble Slovenia's constitution. Furthermore, Australia's official language is English, however this has not been codified in the same way as Slovenia. Australia could investigate whether the English language should be recognized in the constitution in the same way as article 11 of the Slovenian constitution has recognized the Slovenian language. However, there is likely to be strong opposition to such a proposal by many in the community. It is argued that Australia has considerable work to do in the area of constitutional reform. While the rights of citizens and non-citizens in Australia have been reflected in a number of Acts, it is time for those rights to be better and more clearly reflected in either (1) the Constitution, (2) a Charter or (3) the Citizenship Act. This third option may not be considered viable. Constitutional reform is needed in Australia and could resemble Slovenia's modern day constitution.

Notwithstanding the above, further work by Australia is needed to recognize minorities in the state. Australia can look to Slovenia and the EU, to resemble their legal framework law, as Slovenia has been able to achieve with the national communities and the Rom community. This is particularly relevant to Australia, who need to do a lot more to respect Aboriginal rights. It is time that the Australian Government undertakes to provide the Indigenous community far greater recognition and a voice both nationally and locally. Apart from formal recognition within the Australian constitution, there are other policy and legal mechanism that, Australia should adopt to be more inclusive of the First Australians. Some of these mechanisms include, a Treaty/Convention (state and commonwealth), Charter, Bill of Rights, Act, Regulations, amongst others. They should be afforded a permanent voice within the Australian polity, whether they are elected as a member of parliament or not. While these are ambitious and aspirational, it is not out of Australia's ability and capacity to achieve this over the next decade.

Arguably, one of the most significant rights challenges facing the EU, Slovenia and Australia is their ability to reconcile the balance between the trade in personal data, while maintaining a level of privacy over the Internet. This disruption this potentially has to identity and cohesion cannot be underestimated. The world has seen how the Internet is being used to galvanize citizens to undertake acts against other citizens and the state. The three jurisdictions have established data protection laws. Slovenia has been required to follow the EU GDPR, which is heavy weighted towards protecting the privacy of citizens over the Internet. Yet, Australia, has taken a slightly different approach under the Privacy Act.

References

Brennan, S. (2003). *Native title in the High Court of Australia a decade after Mabo*. Tobin Centre of Public Law, Faculty of Law, University of New South Wales, 14 PLR 209, 209–201.

Brown, R., & Davis-Brown, B. (1998). The making of memory: The politics of archives, libraries and museums in the construction of consciousness. *History of the Human Sciences, 11*, 17–32.

Donelly, J, (2009) *Human dignity and human rights*. Geneva Academy of International Humanitarian Law and Human Rights in the framework of the Swiss Initiative to Commemorate the 60th Anniversary of the Universal Declaration of Human Rights, University of Denver, 10.

Irving, H. (2001). Australia's constitutional identity: A conundrum for the 21st century. In Not known (Eds.), *Unity and diversity: a national conversation*: Barton lectures (pp. 194–221). Sydney: ABC Books.

Jacobsohn, G. (2012). *Constitutional identity*, Harvard University Press, 21(3), 132–134.

Lipott, S. (2013). The Hungarian National Minority in Slovenia: Assessment of protection and integration after the EU accession. *Romanian Journal of European Affairs, 13*(3), 65–70.

Marshall, T. (1998). *Citizenship and social class and other essays*. Cambridge: Cambridge University Press. 1950.

Matt Harvey, M. (2001). Australia and the European Union: Some similar constitutional dilemmas. *Deakin Law Review, 6*, 312.

Mavčič, A. (1998). Slovenia, *International encyclopedia of laws*, Constitutional law, suppl. 27, 28. The Hague; London; Boston; Kluwer Law International, *44*(302), 250–258.

Mavčič, A. (2008). *Constitutional values in practice with a special reference to the Slovenian System outline*, The Analysis and International Cooperation Department, Constitutional Court of the Republic of Slovenia, 1–18.

Novak, M. (2010). Three models of balancing (in constitutional review). *Ratio Juris, 1*, 101–112.

O'neil, C., & Watts, T. (2015). *Two future: Australia at a critical moment* (pp. 200–205). Melbourne: The Text Publishing Swann House.

Soysal, Y. (1994). *Limits of citizenship: Migrant and postnational membership in Europe* (pp. 1–15). Chicago: Chicago University Press.

Stolwijk, M. (2005). *The right to conscientious objection in Europe: A review of the current situation* (Vol. 65). Brussels: Quaker Council of European Affairs.

Walters, R., Trakman, L., & Zeller, B. (2019). *Data protection law: A comparative analysis of Asia-Pacific and European approaches*. Singapore: Springer.

Williams, G., & Hume, D. (2013). *Human rights under the Australian constitution* (pp. 112–113). Oxford: Oxford University Press.

Zimmermann, A. (2006). What is wrong with a charter of rights? *Original Law Review, 1*, 29.

Chapter 9
Naturalization Through Immigration

Abstract Migration is a pathway to citizenship. It supports and contributes to a state's identity. On the one hand it can also support social cohesion. On the one hand, it also can divide and fragment societal cohesion. Immigration law is naturally exclusionary because it allows a state to restrict who can enter, stay and take out citizenship. Moreover, immigration policy and law challenges the very notion of social cohesion, because it opens the state to welcoming people from anywhere within the world. However, this is controlled under a tight regulatory framework, which enables state to choose who can enter. Today, the policy approach, particularly in Australia takes a stronger economic approach to immigration, under its skilled and business migration program. On the other hand, being a much smaller state, Slovenia (EU) has a very limited economic migration program. This is a reflection of their respective identity, and to a lesser extent social cohesion. The immigration laws discussed in this chapter are for the period of 2014 and 2017. This chapter has been divided into two parts. Part one discusses why people migrate and the respective policy approaches adopted by the respective jurisdictions. Part two, discusses some of the visas and residency issues associated with immigration.

Keywords Deportation · Detention · Immigration · Migration · Residency · Visa

9.1 Part One: Immigration

Immigration is a pathway to citizenship. There is nothing natural about a person becoming a citizen of a state through the naturalisation process.[1] The naturalisation process of Slovenia and Australia are different. It is only when a non-citizen meets the respective states naturalisation requirements such as length of stay in the state,

[1] Goodman Wallace, S, (2010) *Naturalisation Policies in Europe: Exploring Patterns of Inclusion and Exclusion*, EUDO Citizenship Observatory, Robert Schuman Centre for Advanced Studies in collaboration with Edinburgh University Law School, 1–10.

R. Walters, *National Identity and Social Cohesion in a Time of Geopolitical and Economic Tension: Australia – European Union – Slovenia*,
https://doi.org/10.1007/978-981-15-2164-5_9

can the person apply for and obtain citizenship. However, and as discussed in Chaps. 2 and 3 a person can obtain citizenship by birth or descent, which allows the person to obtain the necessary documents from the state to enable them to obtain a passport.

Immigration challenges and in some cases reaffirms the notion of national identity, sovereignty and state control.[2] By regulating immigration Australia and Slovenia reinforce their respective national identities by protecting their sovereignty and choosing who will enter and stay, and may become a citizen. With the increased mobility of people across the world, the expansion of globalisation and the influx of various ethnic groups taking up residence and citizenship, it could be argued that the national identity is being diluted. More recently, the world has experienced an increase in terrorism, which has resulted in states strengthening their national identity through the law. Claire O'neil and Tim Watts[3] argue it is important for states to build an inclusive national identity that requires the government to expand its actions to ensure a sense of inclusiveness. It is argued that an inclusive national identity can only be realised provided the Slovenian and Australian governments have a sound legislative framework. This legal framework must include citizenship and immigration law, along with the other laws discussed in throughout the research.

Immigration is a complex balance between sovereignty and rights[4] and is highly politicised.[5] Apart from a state overseeing immigration, they also monitor emigration. Within Australia emigration is common between states and territories. The same is the case in Slovenia where people may emigrate from Maribor to Kranj. Furthermore, with the dismantling of internal borders across Europe and the right to move and reside in another member state, emigration also occurs. However, this chapter does not discuss the breadth or depth of emigration in both jurisdictions.

Migration theory involves two aspects. The first is how a state regulates immigration, and the second is the personal decision of an individual to migrate from one state to another. The 'management of immigration by states is not easy'[6] and is both economic and humanitarian. Economic migration is those individuals who enter a state to contribute to the national economy through, for example, business, education, employment and tourism. Humanitarian migration is those non-citizens fleeing conflict in their state of origin. Douglas Massey and others view 'migration as a household decision taken to minimise the risk to family income, or, to overcome capital constraints on family production activities'.[7] This has also been reinforced

---

[2] Irene Bloemraad, Anna Korteweg, Gokce Yurdakul, *Citizenship and Immigration: Multiculturalism, Assimilation, and Challenges to the Nation-State*, Annu, Rev., Sociol, 2008, 153–179.

[3] Claire O'neil, Tim Watts, *Two Future: Australia at a Critical Moment*, The Text Publishing Swann House, 2015, 200–205.

[4] Crock, M., Saul, B., Dastyari, A, (2006) *Future Seekers II, Refugees and Irregular Migration in Australia*, The Federation Press 23.

[5] Castles, S., Miller, M, (1998) *The Age of Migration*, London, Macmillan Press.

[6] Crock, M, (2007) *Defining Strangers: Human Rights, Immigrants and the Foundations of a Just Society*, Melbourne Law Review 39, 1–14.

[7] Massey, D., Arango, J., Hugo, G., Kouaouci, A., Pellegrino A., Taylor, E, (1993) *Theories of International Migration: A Review and Appraisal*, Population and Development Review, Vol 19, No. 3, 431–466.

by Roel Jennissen[8] who believes labour migration at a personal level involves a person wanting to improve their economic situation. This is particularly noticeable when states are competing for highly skilled individuals to contribute to their economy. Apart from the personal economic benefits of migrating, migrants are able to establish new networks. Jennissen argues that the 'network theory' becomes important when relatives and friends of the migrant encourage others to migrate by providing financial or other assistance.[9] Having close networks in a state helps to inform individuals wanting to migrate to that state[10] of the opportunities that might be available such as employment, and the ability to take out citizenship, and assists with settling in.

Migration enhances the host state by becoming more socially and culturally diverse.[11] However, immigration can also result in tension, insecurity and anxiety. This has certainly been the case in Australia over the past two decades, as discussed in chapter three. Kymlicka[12] highlights that migration brings with it different cultures, food, music, clothing, values and practices that when integrated and accepted by a state, form part of the national identity. This has certainly been the case in Australia, which has become a state that consists of an amalgam of ethnic groups. Slovenia has been and currently is open to immigration.

The Organisation for Economic Co-operation and Development (OECD)[13] estimated that approximately 221,000 people entered Australia[14] permanently in 2011 and about 27,400 for the same period in Slovenia.[15] Putting these figures into context, Australia had a population estimated at 22.62 million in 2012,[16] while Slovenia's population for the same period was estimated at 2.052 million.[17] This is an important point. Australia having a much larger land mass and population is able to accommodate more immigrants than Slovenia. The total land area for Slovenia is about 20, 151 square kilometers[18] whereas Australia's land mass is approximately

[8] Jennissen, R, (2007) *Causality Chains in the International Migration Systems Approach*, Population, Research and Policy Review, Vol 26, 411–436.

[9] Ibid.

[10] Stary, O., Taylor, E, (2007) *Relative Deprivation and international migration*, Demography, 1989, in Roel Jennissen, *Causality Chains in the International Migration Systems Approach*, Population, Research and Policy Review, Vol 26, 411–436.

[11] Laurie Ferguson, Warren Gardner, Fostering *Australian Citizenship in a Changing World*, in Glenn Patmore, Gary Jungwirth, The Vocal Citizen, Fitzroy Vic, (2004),163.

[12] Kymlicka, W, (2006) *Multiculturalism: Success, Failure, and The Future*, Migration Policy Institute, 4.

[13] Organisation for Economic Co-operation and Development, *International Migration Outlook*, SOPEMI, 2011, 30.

[14] Ibid, 41.

[15] Ibid, 41.

[16] The World Bank, Data Indicators, Australia, 2012, http://data.worldbank.org/country/australia

[17] Ibid.

[18] Slovenia, History, Geography, Government and Culture, www.infoplease.com/ipa/A0107971.html

7,692,030 square kilometers, some 32 times larger than the United Kingdom.[19] Even so, much of Australia is considered to be uninhabitable. In 2012 and 2013, more than 28,000 people immigrated to Slovenia,[20] from outside of the European Union. That is, this figure does not account for emigration from other member states within the Union. However, for 2014 it was estimated there was more than 16,000 people had immigrated to Slovenia from other European member states.[21] In comparison immigration to Australia for 2013–2014 was estimated to be 212,000.[22] Interestingly, for the size of the Slovenian state compared to Australia and their population, on a per capita basis, there has been a higher level of immigration than in Australia.

The 2006 census found that close to three million immigrants living in Australia had taken out citizenship. This indicated a take up rate of about 68 per cent of 4.4 million migrants at the time.[23] Immigrants taking out citizenship in Australia from 2001 to 2010 was been estimated at 368,000.[24] Slovenia for the same period recorded 3.2 people for every 1000 who immigrated to the country took out citizenship. However, since 2006 there has been a steady decline with the most recent figures being available from the 2011 indicating 1.8 for every 1000 person.[25] Migration today has resulted in many citizens leaving their home state to take up permanent residence or citizenship in another state, forming part of the diaspora community. Rainer Bauböck[26] argues that engaging the diapsora is becoming increasingly important to states.[27] Slovenia has implemented specific laws to assist the state's engagement with their Slovene diaspora.

In 2011, it was estimated there were more than 228, 000 residents in Slovenia that were born in another nation state, of whom 198,000 hailing from the former Yugoslav Republics (Croatia, Bosnia and Herzegovina, Montenegro, Kosovo, Macedonia and Serbia).[28] The number who migrated to Slovenia from Oceania

---

[19] Australian Facts and Figures, www.australiatravelsearch.com/trc/facts.htm

[20] Eurostat, Immigration, European Commission, Code: tps00176.

[21] Slovenian Statistical Office, http://pxweb.stat.si/pxweb/Dialog/Saveshow.asp

[22] Australian Bureau of Statistics, Immigration, 3412.

[23] Smith, D., Wykes, J., Jayarajah, S., Fabijanic, T, *Citizenship in Australia*, Department of Immigration and Citizenship, 2010, http://www.immi.gov.au/media/publications/research/_pdf/citizenship-in-australia-2011.pdf

[24] Ibid.

[25] European Commission Eurostat, Acquisition of citizenship statistics, http://epp.eurostat.ec.europa.eu/statistics_explained/index.php/Acquisition_of_citizenship_statistics. This data represents the number of individuals taking out citizenship of a MS, including Slovenia.

[26] Bauböck, R, (1994) *Transnational Citizenship: Membership and Rights in International Migration*, Aldershot: Edward Elgar.

[27] Bauböck, R, (2003) *Reinventing urban citizenship*, Citizenship Studies, Taylor Francis Group, 139–160.

[28] Migration, Slovenia, 1 January 2011-final data, Statistical Office of the Republic of Slovenia, http://www.stat.si/eng/novica_prikazi.aspx?id=4430

(including Australia) was 458.[29] In the same year, it was estimated there were more than 800,000 non-citizens residents in Australia.[30] The number of people from the former Yugoslav Republics resident in Australia was estimated to be 25,000 from Bosnia and Herzegovina, 48, 828 from Croatia, 40,222 from the Former Yugoslav Republic of Macedonia and 20,167 people from Serbia.[31] For the same period, Slovenia recorded the least number of people resident in Australia at 4955, with more than 17,000 individuals recording Slovenian ancestry.[32]

At the time of concluding this research the mass movement of refugees from Syria to the European Union begun unfolding. According to the European Commission, the Syrian conflict has resulted in the world's largest humanitarian crisis since WW II.[33] Of the estimated 4.5 million people who have fled Syria, more than 600,000 had entered the European Union.[34] Slovenia has been viewed by the refugees as a transit country to Austria and Germany, however, during October 2015 it was reported that more than 100,000 asylum seekers had arrived in Slovenia.[35] The huge influx of refugees has to date had such an impact on European member states that the issues is beginning to have wider legal ramifications that could see the European project being diluted. The evidence has confirmed that most of the people arriving in the European Union are from Syria. Syria is a very different country to the member states of the European Union. Firstly, the Syrian's speak a very different language. Secondly, they have very different religious beliefs and customs. Thirdly, those beliefs and customs may not align to the values, beliefs and customs of member states and more generally the European Union. The large influx of people not only has an economic burden to member states including Slovenia, but also, has the potential to create tensions and xenophobic behavior amongst citizens. This would impact national identity by the community potentially forcing government to implement strong exclusionary measures so as entry to the territory is difficult. For instance, some member states have begun to close their borders, which could result in the entire Schengen legal framework and common immigration policy and law being reviewed. At its extreme, member states and the European Union could

[29] Ibid.

[30] Andrew Markus, *Australian Population and Immigration Statistics*, Scanlon Foundation Social Cohesion Research Program, Faculty of Arts, Monash University, http://www.arts.monash.edu.au/mapping-population/%2D%2Ddocuments/statistics-tables.pdf. However, the figures only show New Zealand citizens, individuals on 457 long stay business visas, and 417 and 462 working holiday maker.

[31] Australian Bureau of Statistics, 2011 Census, http://www.censusdata.abs.gov.au/census_services/getproduct/census/2011/quickstat/3202_0

[32] Australian Government, Department of Immigration and Citizenship, Community Information Summary, Slovenia born, http://www.immi.gov.au/media/publications/statistics/comm-summ/_pdf/slovenia.pdf

[33] Syria Crisis, European Commission, Humanitarian Aid and Civil Protection, http://ec.europa.eu/echo/files/aid/countries/factsheets/syria_en.pdf

[34] Ibid.

[35] The Guardian, Still the refugees are coming, but in Europe the barriers are rising, http://www.theguardian.com/world/2015/oct/31/austria-fence-slovenia-wire-europe-refugees

dismantle the Schengen and immigration framework, which would see a return to a closed Europe that was evident during the mid 1900s.

Reinstating the historical closed border policy across European Union member states would have a significant economic and social impact. This would delay the movement of goods and services. The resultant effect could see member states restrict and tighten their citizenship laws so as refugees cannot apply for or obtain citizenship. Further restrictions may also be applied to short and longer term residency permits and dual nationals. Australia agreed to increase its humanitarian intake of people from Syria by 12,000, in 2015.

9.1.1 Psychological Migration

Citizenship provides a sense of belonging and identification to a national community (values, history and culture), through a collective identity. Apart from the decision to migrate which could be to improve a person's economic conditions or to flee conflict or for love, the psychology to migrate commences long before the person is on a boat or in a car or truck.[36] The psychology of migration along with citizenship and immigration law is also multidimensional. It can involve a person's expectations of what their life will be, the people, culture, security, foods, values and individual rights. Migrating can have a positive or negative impact on people. The person may or may not be able to adjust to the local environment (weather, food, culture), or they may be able to assimilate and embrace their new environment. For Briton's coming to Australia, there is a lot of commonality that is connected through history such as place names, food, sport (such as cricket, rugby, cycling amongst others) and legal system.[37] Following WWII, there were large numbers of people who arrived in Australia from the former Yugoslavia. This also occurred following the conflict and disintegration of Yugoslavia between 1990 and 1995.

Unlike their British counterparts who migrated to Australia without being subject to war, conflict or the disintegration of a state, people from Yugoslavia experienced massive change. Firstly, the legal system was and is different from the former socialist state, and the foods, customs and values were also different. Secondly, the climate, depending on where the person settled in Australia is very different to the climate across the former Yugoslavia. Slovenia has significantly cooler weather in the winter and cooler more temperate summers compared to Australia. The housing and infrastructure of a state can vary greatly.

Today, there are greater similarities between Slovenia and Australia. Since 1990 similar democratic values appear within the legal and policy discourse of both states. Slovenians migrating to Australia are at an advantage as they have a large

[36] Tabor, A., Milfont, T, (2011) *Migration change model: Exploring the process of migration on a psychological level*, International; Journal of Intercultural Relations, 818–820.

[37] Ibid.

diaspora community to call upon. Even though the language is different, many Slovenians speak English. In a period of increasing globalisation, the decision to migrate can be enhanced through the personality of an individual. Aidan Tabor and Taciano Milfont argue that students who are high achievers and value their personal life and employment more than their family are likely to decide to migrate and undertake study in another country. The resulting effect is to enhance their employment prospects.[38] Nevertheless, whatever the choice for a person to migrate from Slovenia to Australia or vice versa, the immigration laws and policy of both states play a part in that process.

9.2 National Immigration Policy

Slovenia and Australia's immigration policies account for economic and international (humanitarian) protection. This section examines the respective policy approaches adopted in either territory.

9.2.1 Slovenia

It was nearly 10 years after becoming an independent state that an immigration policy was finally established which saw the recognition of, and progression towards multiculturalism.[39] In the early period following independence Slovenia did not welcome migrants. Slovenia had many challenges in the early years of independence, which resulted in former Yugoslav citizens being excluded from the state. With the implementation of the Slovenian Aliens Act and the 2002 Slovenian Resolution on Migration Policy[40] the country's legislation was developed to be consistent with European Union law.

The current day Slovenian immigration policy is based on the principle of solidarity being responsible to Slovenia and its citizens (and includes the long term macro-economic and equality, freedom and mutual cooperation).[41] In 2010, the

[38] Ibid.

[39] CoMide – Initiative for Migration and Development, Report/Slovenia, Peace Institute, Institute for Contemporary Social and Political Studies, January 2012, 3–7.

[40] Resolution on Migration Policy of the Republic of Slovenia, Official Gazette of the Republic of Slovenia No. 106/2002.

[41] Resolution on Migration Policy of the Republic of Slovenia, Official Gazette of the Republic of Slovenia No. 106/2002, in CoMide – Initiative for Migration and Development, Report/Slovenia, Peace Institute, Institute for Contemporary Social and Political Studies, January 2012, 3–7. The immigration policy ensures the protection and free migration to refugees, while controlling admission of migrants to meet demands of Slovene's labour and capital markets.

'Economic Migration Strategy from 2010 to 2020'[42] was released identifying its future migration and population needs. Slovenia like many other countries is facing labour shortages, and the management of migration has become one of the principal political and economic priorities for the state.[43] Since joining the European Union, Slovenia has been required to transpose European Union immigration law into its national laws.[44] By doing so, Slovenia fulfils its obligation to implement the common immigration policy of the European Union. Comparatively, the Slovenian immigration policy resembles that of Australia, with both considering economic and social immigration. However, Slovenia's immigration policy is largely determined by the European Union, whereas Australia's immigration policy is stand alone. The next section outlines the European Union law Slovenia has transposed into national law.

9.2.2 *European Union Law Transposed into Slovenia Immigration Law*

European Union law provides a consistent approach[45] to entry, stay and the types of grounds on which a permit or visa will be issued by member states. Arguably, the EU imposing this obligation on member states such as Slovenia and others is exerting a level of a collaborative and united identity in the area of immigration law and policy. Thus, Slovenia has implemented European law through the Aliens Act and Law on International Protection.

9.2.2.1 Aliens Act [AA]

Slovenia has transposed[46] a total of 18 European Union legal instruments (Directives, Decisions and Regulations).[47] One of the most important inclusions in Slovenian law has been implementing the Schengen Agreement,[48] enabling the facilitation of unauthorised entry, transit and residence.[49] With the ability of individuals to take up

---

[42] Slovenia, Strategy of Economic Migration 2010–2020, European Website on Integration, Slovenia, http://ec.europa.eu/ewsi/en/info_sheet.cfm?ID_CSHEET=63

[43] Ibid.

[44] European Commission, Home Affairs, *Schengen Area*, http://ec.europa.eu/dgs/home-affairs/what-we-do/policies/borders-and-visas/schengen

[45] Article 78 and 79, Lisbon Treaty, Official Journal of the European Union, C 83/171.

[46] Ibid.

[47] Article 1, *Aliens Act 2011*, Official Gazette Republic of Slovenia, No 50/2011.

[48] Article 1, Council Directive 2001/51/EC, supplementing the provisions of Article 26 of the Convention implementing the Schengen Agreement, official Journal of the European Union L 187.

[49] Council Directive 2002/90/EC, defining the facilitation of unauthorised entry, transit and residence, Official Journal of the European Union L 328/17.

employment in another member state, they may wish to take their family.[50] The Slovenian Constitutional Court in 2011,[51] stated that member states are obliged to implement the common market principle across the European Union.[52] In other words, it is mandatory for member states to implement European Union law.

Many of the regulations and directives established by the European Union while not all directly related to economic activity, do assist the Union in protecting the economy from the influx of unauthorised non-citizens. Additionally, Union law provides a coherent approach to international protection. For instance, illegal entrants and overstays (people that over stay their permits) can take jobs from local citizens, as they can be operating on the black market of the economy. Thus, there can be situations where individuals[53] must be removed.[54]

Long term residents in the European Union enjoy residence in a member state for a continuous period of 5 years.[55] However, this does not include those individuals that are declared refugees. Furthermore, the European Union has established laws for residence permits issued to non-citizens who are victims[56] of the black economy (such as prostitution). Education forms and important part of member states economic activity and that of the Union. Harmonisation of training and education law boosts economic activity and enables students to travel,[57] work and reside in other member states where their qualifications[58] will be recognised.[59]

Notwithstanding the above, the Union immigration law protects and facilitates economic activity across member states. For instance, a non-citizen[60] requires travel

---

[50] Ibid, Council Directive 2003/86/EC, on the right to family reunification, Official Journal of the European Union L 251/12. Council Directive 2004/38/EC on the right of citizens of the Union and their family members to move freely and reside within the territory of the Member States L 158/77.

[51] Official Gazette of the Republic of Slovenia, 98/2011.

[52] Ibid.

[53] Council Directive 2003/109/EC, concerning the status of third-country nationals who are long-term residents L 16.

[54] Council Directive 2003/110/EC, on assistance in cases of transit for the purposes of removal by air L 321/26.

[55] Council Directive 2003/109/EC concerning the status of third country national who are long term residents, Official Journal of the European Union L 16/44.

[56] Article 1, Aliens Act 2011, Official Gazette Republic of Slovenia, No 50/2011, Council Directive 2004/81/EC OJL 261, 6.8.2004.

[57] Ibid, Council Decision 94/795/JHA, on a joint action adopted by the Council on the basis of Article K.3.2.b of the Treaty on European Union concerning travel facilities for school pupils from third countries resident in a Member State Official Journal of the European Union L 327.

[58] Council Directive 2005/71/EC, on a specific procedure for admitting third-country nationals for the purposes of scientific research Official Journal of the European Union L 289/15. Council Directive 2009/50/EC, on the conditions of entry and residence of third-country nationals for the purposes of highly qualified employment Official Journal of the European Union L 155/17.

[59] Council Directive 2004/114/EC, on conditions of admission of third-country nationals for the purposes of studies, pupil exchange, unremunerated training or voluntary service Official Journal of the European Union L 375/12.

[60] Regulation 380/2008, amending Regulation (EC) No 1030/2002 laying down a uniform format for residence permits for third-country nationals Official Journal of the European Union L 115/1.

documents[61]; a visa[62] to enter[63] the Union[64]; who decide to stay long-term.[65] The other Union law that applies includes the Stockholm Program[66]; Eurodac (Dublin Convention)[67]; displaced persons,[68]reception of asylum seekers,[69] and granting and withdrawing refugee status.[70]

9.2.2.2 Law on International Protection [LIP]

Slovenia has implemented programs to meet their international and regional obligations to refugees and asylum seekers. The policy programs that commenced outside of the treaty process for refugees and asylum include the European Union Tampere Program, later replaced by the Hague Program that was superseded by the Stockholm Program.[71] In addition, Council Regulation (EC) No 2725/2000 was implemented to enable the establishment of Eurodac that allows for fingerprints of non-citizens to be compared between member states.[72]

---

[61] Regulation 2252/2004 on standards for security features and biometrics in passports and travel documents issued by Member States Official Journal of the European Union L 385.

[62] Regulation 810/2009 establishing a Community Code on Visas, Official Journal of the European Union L 243/1.

[63] Ibid, Regulation 539/2001 listing the third countries whose nationals must be in possession of visas when crossing the external borders and those whose nationals are exempt from that requirement Official Journal of the European Union L 81/1.

[64] Regulation 562/2006 establishing a Community Code on the rules governing the movement of persons across borders (Schengen Borders Code) Official Journal L 105/1.

[65] Regulation 265/2012, implementing Article 8a(1) of Regulation (EC) No 765/2006 concerning restrictive measures in respect of Belarus Official Journal of the European Union L 85.

[66] The Stockholm Programme – An Open and Secure Europe Serving and Protecting Citizens, Official Journal of the European Union C 115/01.

[67] Council Directive (EC) No 343/2003, establishing the criteria and mechanisms for determining the Member State responsible for examining an asylum application lodged in one of the Member States by a third-country national, Official Journal of the European Union L 50/1.

[68] Council Directive 2001/55/EC, on minimum standards for giving temporary protection in the event of a mass influx of displaced persons and on measures promoting a balance of efforts between Member States in receiving such persons and bearing the consequences thereof, Official Journal of the European Union, L 12/2012.

[69] Council Directive 2003/9/EC, laying down minimum standards for the reception of asylum seekers, Official Journal of the European Union L 31/18.

[70] Council Directive 2005/85/EC, on minimum standards on procedures in Member States for granting and withdrawing refugee status, Official Journal of the European Union, L326/13.

[71] The Stockholm Programme – An Open and Secure Europe Serving and Protecting Citizens, Official Journal of the European Union C 115/01.

[72] Council Directive (EC) No 343/2003, establishing the criteria and mechanisms for determining the Member State responsible for examining an asylum application lodged in one of the Member States by a third-country national, Official Journal of the European Union L 50/1.

In 2001, minimum standards for giving temporary protection to displaced persons were established.[73] While this directive is not formally recognised within the LIP, it is nevertheless, European Union law that Slovenia is obliged to implement. In 2003, Council Directive laying down the minimum standards for the reception and housing of asylum seekers,[74] and the granting or withdrawing refugee status,[75] was established and later reinforced by the Slovenian Constitutional Court.[76] In the same year, the European Union extended the criteria for family,[77] and the mechanisms for determining the member state that would be responsible for examining asylum applications.[78] A year later in 2004, minimum standards were established for the qualification and status of non-citizens or stateless persons as refugees that require international protection by MS including Slovenia.[79] Furthermore, article 16b of the LIP was determined by the Slovenian Constitutional Court to be inconsistent with the Slovenia constitution. The Constitutional Court ruled that the authority may under exceptional circumstances consider a family member to also be a relative who has refugee status.[80] Article 16b did not originally apply to this situation.

The Slovenian Constitutional Court[81] had to determine whether articles 60, 61 and 63 of the LIP were consistent with Directive 2005/85/EC.[82] This Directive narrows the guarantee of non-refoulment under the principles set out in the Geneva Convention. The court ruled that the procedural Directive should allow member states to regulate their own way of determining a safe third country. However, the Slovenian government disagreed because the directive is clear that a third country is to have an asylum procedure and the concept of protection is consistent with the international convention. As a result, the court decided that article 61 of the Law on

[73] Council Directive 2001/55/EC, on minimum standards for giving temporary protection in the event of a mass influx of displaced persons and on measures promoting a balance of efforts between Member States in receiving such persons and bearing the consequences thereof, Official Journal of the European Union, L 12/2012

[74] Council Directive 2003/9/EC, laying down minimum standards for the reception of asylum seekers, Official Journal of the European Union L 31/18.

[75] Council Directive 2005/85/EC, on minimum standards on procedures in Member States for granting and withdrawing refugee status, Official Journal of the European Union, L326/13.

[76] U-I-295/12, Official Gazette of the Republic of Slovenia, 47/2013.

[77] Council Directive 2003/86/EC, on the right to family reunification, Official Journal of the European Union, L 251/12.

[78] Council Regulation No 343/2003, establishing the criteria and mechanisms for determining the Member State responsible for examining an asylum application lodged in one of the Member States by a third-country national, Official Journal of the European Union, L 50/1.

[79] Council Directive 2004/83/EC, on minimum standards for the qualification and status of third country nationals or stateless persons as refugees or as persons who otherwise need international protection and the content of the protection granted Official Journal European Union, L 304.

[80] U-I-309, Up-381, Official Gazette of the Republic of Slovenia, No. 6/2015.

[81] Official Gazette of the Republic of Slovenia, No. 114/2013.

[82] Council Directive 2005/85/EC, on minimum standards on procedures in Member States for granting and withdrawing refugee status, Official Journal of the European Union, L326/13.

International Protection was not inconsistent with the Slovenian Constitution. Articles 60 and the first paragraph of article 62 were to be repealed, while article 63 was determined to be inconsistent with the Slovenian Constitution.

Despite the obligation for Slovenia to implement the European Union's immigration legal framework, there are an estimated 23 European Union Directives and Regulations that have been established to regulate the entry and stay of citizens and non-citizens. Therefore, the European Union could undertake a review of this legislation in accordance with the smart regulation program to determine what legislation could be consolidated to simplify and reduce their number. This could reduce the regulatory burden to business and individuals. A starting point could be determining where duplication exists, for example, having a single Regulation or Directive that deals with all international protection matters. In conclusion, Slovenia's immigration policy, legal framework and implementation of the law is constrained by the common policy and law of the European Union. On the other hand, Australia is not constrained by any other state or regional supernational polity in its development or implementation of immigration law. This is an important point because Slovenia, while having full autonomy in the development of its citizenship laws, the immigration laws are predominantly imposed by the European Union. However, it is argued that even though the immigration policy and law of Slovenia must conform to the European Union, it in no way reduces Slovenia's national identity. Rather, the European Union immigration law not only ensures consistency across all member states, but also enables member states to determine who will enter, stay and become a citizen.

9.2.3 Australia

The current immigration policy approach taken by the Australian Government has a strong focus on border protection, particularly at sea, by deterring and stopping boats entering Australian territorial waters. It sends a clear message to those involved in getting people to Australia and the illegal arrivals that Australia will intercept them and send them back to their country of origin. Australia's projected population[83] could be 35 million by 2050,[84] and will have impacts for economic growth,[85] urban and environmental amenity as well as social and cultural outcomes.[86] This is an important point because both Slovenia and Australia are grappling with immigration and the potential impact this will have economically and socially on their states. Since federation and immigration being constitutionalised in Australia, it has

[83] Productivity Commission, *Population and Migration: Understanding the Numbers*, Research Paper, Australian Government, 2010, 1–10.

[84] Ibid, 1.

[85] Productivity Commission, *A Sustainable Population – Key Policies Issues*, Roundtable Proceedings, Australian Government, 2011.

[86] Ibid.

evolved into a complex area of policy and law for Australia. Consecutive immigration policies of Australia since WWII have been closely intertwined with the state's citizenship policy, and creating[87] the nation state.

Furthermore, like citizenship, the evolution of immigration in Australia can be summarised as being closely related to world and regional events. There were many people displaced in the former Yugoslavia who migrated to Australia. Furthermore, post WWII and the Vietnam conflict saw the influx of migrants from Indo-China. Secondly, the fall of Dili in East Timor resulted in large numbers of Timorese people escaping to Australia in 1975. The next major influx was students from China as a result of the Tiananmen Square uprising in 1989. Shortly after, people would begin to arrive from the breakup of Yugoslavia. In the last 15 years there have been arrivals as a result of conflict in Afghanistan, Iraq and more recently Syria. As discussed above the Syrian conflict is not only seeing large numbers of refugees arriving in Europe, but Australia is also playing a role in receiving refugees from this country.

The mass influx of ethnic groups into Australia has challenged the notion of the traditional concept of the Australian identity.[88] The influence immigration has had on citizenship policy, has seen citizenship evolve into what Stephen Castle[89] would describe as multicultural. Multicultural citizenship is where everyone is equal and consideration of everyone's different needs[90] is taken into account. Australia, the European Union as a whole and to a lesser extent Slovenia are having to balance the high influx of legal and illegal immigrants and the rising xenophobic behaviour of different ethnic groups. As discussed in chapter three, xenophobic behaviour has been overtly evident in Australia. Today, across the European Union including Slovenia, xenophobic behaviour is also overtly present with the large scale influx of refugees from the Middle East and North Africa.

A notable absence from the immigration policies of Australia, Slovenia, and the European Union is the reference and linkages of immigration to citizenship. Both states, including the European Union could improve this area within their respective immigration policy, to encourage new immigrants to take out citizenship. Furthermore, the immigration policy of each jurisdiction could be expanded to identify how and what level of testing should be undertaken of immigrants that will not take out citizenship but reside in the state. The testing could be similar to citizenship testing and be required every 5 years to ensure immigrants understand and practice the values and identity of the state. This will allow both states to promote their national identities and assist in unifying citizens and residents. However, this proposal comes with its own dangers. Testing of long term residents could be viewed

[87] Crock, M, (2001) *Contract or Compact: Skilled Migration and the Dictates of Policies and Ideology*, Georgetown Immigration Law Journal, Vol 16, Issue 1, 133–154.

[88] Hage, G, (2003) *Against Paranoid Nationalism: Searching for Hope in a Shrinking Society*, Pluto Press Australia.

[89] Castles, S, (2005) *Migration and Community Formation Under Conditions of Globalisation*, International Migration Review, 1143–1166.

[90] Ibid.

(by scholars, government, and immigration specialists) as a threat to multiculturalism. This proposal could also be viewed as contradicting (the focus of this research in supporting) postnational citizenship. Nevertheless, this must be viewed in the context of states such as Slovenia and Australia continuing to retain and even strengthen their national identities. Thus, if a person fails the test, the state would need to decide whether the person has to undertake the test again until they pass, or develop a program where the individual is to attend schooling or undertake community.

9.3 Part Two: Migration Legislation

Immigration in Slovenia is regulated by the Aliens Act (AA) and the Law on International Protection (LIP). In Australia the equivalent legislation is the *Migration Act 1958*. The AA does not apply to those people seeking international protection.[91] This is regulated by the LIP.[92] The AA has no more than 100 pages consisting of about 152 articles. The LIP is about 70 pages comprising of 142 articles. In contrast, Australia's *Migration Act 1958* (MA) and *Regulations* are more than 800 pages in length, and consist of 507 provisions dealing with both economic and humanitarian (international protection) migration. The current migration laws of Australia and Slovenia assist both states to reinforce their respective national identity, by enabling a state to choose who will enter, stay and apply for citizenship. The extent of Australia's legislative framework for migration is long overdue for a review. Consideration needs to be given by Australia to simplify the migration legislative framework and adopt a similar framework to Slovenia.

9.3.1 Entry to Slovenia and Australia

The AA and MA regulate the entry and exit, of lawful and unlawful non-citizens in either state.[93] Article 6 of the AA stipulates that entry can only be undertaken through the designated external borders that have been established under the European Union legal framework in accordance with the Schengen rules. Chapter II of the AA regulates the entry of non-citizens into and their departure from the Republic of Slovenia. Articles 10 and 11 assist in implementing elements of the Schengen Borders Code pertaining to the movement of persons, their vehicles, and items in their possession (when entering and exiting the state). Information may be verified in accordance with the Schengen SIS data base, which provides all member

[91] Article 3(4), *Aliens Act*, Official Gazette Republic of Slovenia, No 50/2011.

[92] Article 3, *Law on International Protection*, Official Gazette Republic of Slovenia 2011/11.

[93] *Migration Act 1958*, sections 13 and 14.

states with the ability to track and record information on individuals of concern (those that may be involved in criminal activity).

Australia being an island continent, can only be entered by air or sea.[94] Slovenia can be entered by land, sea or air. Generally, a non-citizen cannot enter Australia without a valid visa and passport.[95] There are specific provisions for people who are crews on shipping vessels that allow entry under a temporary visa arrangement.[96] Australia's migration zone includes the States, Territories and Australian resources and sea installations such as piers, and ports along with land to the mean low water mark.[97] Furthermore, there are areas the Australian Government can declare to be parts of the Australian territory and form part of the overall migration zone such as Ashmore Reef, Keeling Islands or Christmas Island.[98] This addition has been included so that the government can manage illegal entrants offshore. In contrast, the territory of Slovenia has been incorporated into the wider immigration and border area defined by the Schengen arrangements of the European Union.

The states that make up the Schengen area include Austria, Belgium, Czech Republic, Denmark, Estonia, Finland, France, Germany, Greece, Hungary, Iceland, Italy, Latvia, Liechtenstein, Lithuania, Luxembourg, Malta, The Netherlands, Norway, Poland, Portugal, Slovakia, Slovenia, Spain, Sweden and Switzerland. Secondly, Slovenia unlike Australia has borders with other nation states that include Austria, Italy, Hungary and Croatia. Slovenian borders of Italy, Austria and Hungry were open and free without any border controls. Croatia which only become a full member of the European Union in 2013, has not yet implemented the Schengen Borders Code and security program. Thus, at 30 June 2015, the southern border of Slovenia with Croatia remained one of the external Schengen borders. An Australian or Slovenian 'citizen' who enters and exits their state of origin, is also subject to immigration clearances. But, instead of having a visa or residence permit, they are only required to hold a passport.[99] To enter Slovenia a non-citizen will need to be in possession of a valid permit[100] to enter the Schengen area.[101] Immigration clearance requires the person to provide a valid passport, visa or permit at the border control. However, a dual citizen of Slovenia and Australia who has entered the European Union through Munich, Germany may not be required to produce their Slovenian passport upon entering the Ljubljana airport (as they are deemed to have entered the Schengen area by entering through Germany).

---

[94] Ibid, s42.

[95] Ibid, Division 3, section 29.

[96] Ibid, s38B,

[97] Ibid, s5.

[98] *Migration Amendment (Excision from Migration Zone) Act 2001.*

[99] *Australian Passports Act 2005*, section 7 an Australian citizen is entitled to be issued an Australian passport. *Law on passports of citizens of the Republic of Slovenia,* Official Gazette 65/00, article 3 states a citizen has the right to leave and return to the country with a valid travel document.

[100] Article 8, *Aliens Act 2011*, Official Gazette Republic of Slovenia, No 50/2011.

[101] Ibid, article 8(1), party to the Schengen Agreement 1985.

9.4 Visas

A non-citizen entering either Australia[102] or Slovenia[103] is required to be in possession of a valid travel document (visa or permit) and passport.[104] A visa or permit provides the non-citizen with the authorisation to enter and stay within Australia or Slovenia. Australia refers to the term – visa, whereas Slovenia and the European Union use the term-permit. However, both the visa and permit authorise the same activity. The Australian visa framework consists of visa classes and their subclasses.[105] The Slovenian Aliens Act along with the Community Code[106] (Schengen Borders Code[107]) sets out the conditions for non-citizen[108] to enter Slovenia or the European Union, and includes[109]:

- Being in possession of a valid travel document or documents, authorising them to cross the border (the acceptance of travel documents for this purpose remains within the domain of the member states).[110]
- Those non-citizen possessing a valid visa (if required) or a valid residence permit.[111]
- Third-country nationals who are the holders of a residence title of a Schengen state may freely enter into and stay in any other Schengen state for a period of up to 3 months.[112]

---

[102] *Migration Act 1958*, s30 (1) & (2)

[103] Article 8, *Aliens Act,* Official Gazette of the Republic of Slovenia 50/2011.

[104] Ibid, article 7(1) & (2).

[105] *Migration Act 1958* s31,

[106] Council Regulation 810/2009, OJL No. 243. Articles 61 and 251, Consolidated version of the Treaty Establishing the European Community, security, public health or international relations threat, http://eur-lex.europa.eu/en/treaties/dat/12002E/htm/C_2002325EN.003301.html, accessed 26 January 2015.

[107] *Schengen Borders Code*, Official Journal of the European Union L 105. Regulation 562/2006 requires that non-citizen must have a valid travel document being a visa and passport in order to enter Slovenia, official Journal of the European Union L 81/1. Council Regulation 539/2001, listing the third countries whose nationals must be in possession of a visa when crossing the external borders and those whose nationals are exempt from that, Official Journal of the European Union, L 81/1.

[108] Article 19 of the *Schengen II* Agreement for third-country nationals requiring a visa; Article 20 of the *Schengen II* Agreement for third-country nationals who do not require such visa.

[109] Article 5 of the Schengen Borders Code – Regulation (EC) No 562/2006, also Article 4, Council Regulation No 539/2001.

[110] Article 6 of Consolidated version of the Council Regulation (EC) No 539/2001, listing the third countries whose nationals must be in possession of visas when crossing the external borders and those whose nationals are exempt from that requirement.

[111] Regulation No 562/2006, establishing a Community Code on the rules governing the movement of persons across borders (Schengen Borders Code).

[112] Article 21, of the Schengen Agreement.

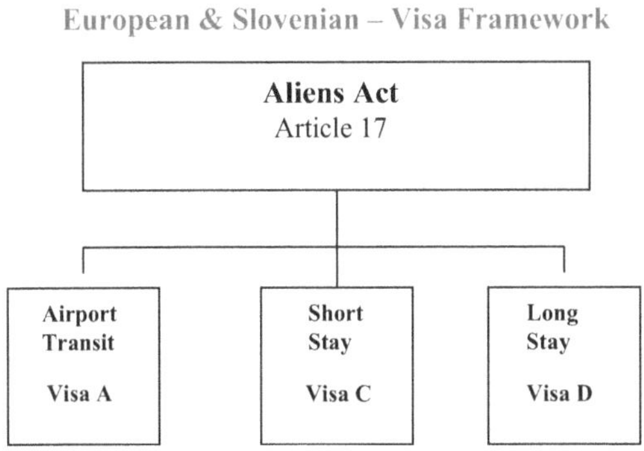

- **Visa A [Schengen visa]**[113] – only for airport transit (not entering the country) for a short list of countries such as Afghanistan, and Iraq, or humanitarian reasons; or
- **Visa C [Schengen visa]**[114] – (used also for transit, but transit only for a very specific reasons. For example, a diplomatic passport holder of Pakistan does not need a visa for Germany and Austria, but needs a visa for Slovenia). Generally issued for short term stays, valid for all Schengen states. This visa can be issued for so called LTV (limited territorial validity) for Slovenia only or for a number of Schengen states only; or
- **Long stay (visa D)**[115] – issued for long term stays, there is no restriction of 90 days in 6 months and they are usually issued for up to 1 year but not shorter than 3 months. Residence permits are issued for work or employment (residence permit that is either temporary or long stay)[116]; work or research in higher education[117]; study[118]; seasonal work, trans-border employment and posted workers[119];

[113] Article 17, *Aliens Act*, Official Gazette of the Republic of Slovenia, 50/2011.

[114] Visa C, Short stay, Article 17, Aliens Act, Official Gazette of the Republic of Slovenia, 50/2011, ADS tourism (specific for China only), Events in partner cities, Family member of EU citizen, Humanitarian reasons, Seminar/symposium/congress, Short term education, Culture, Journalism, Funeral, Professional driver, Business, Research, Rehabilitation ITF (specific rehabilitation treatments in Slovenia for land mine victims), Sport, Transit, Tourism, Official delegation, Private visit, Health treatment

[115] Article 17, Aliens Act, Official Gazette of the Republic of Slovenia, 50/2011, D – visa and include; BCASMM (specific for Canada only), BNZPDP (specific for New Zealand only), Accreditation of foreign diplomats who will serve in Slovenia, Economic interest (specific reason that the person is important for Slovenia), Humanitarian activity, Education, Journalism – accreditation, Sport – employment in Slovenia, Religious activity, Family reunion, Science interest (specific reason that the person is important for Slovenia) Other reasons.

[116] Article 37, *Aliens Act 2011*, Official Gazette Republic of Slovenia, No 50/2011.

[117] Ibid, article 38.

[118] Ibid, article 44.

[119] Ibid, article 45.

daily work migrants[120]; family reunion[121]; residents in other EU countries, family members or foreigners of Slovenian origin[122]; children of aliens born in Slovenia[123]; victims of human trafficking and illegal employment[124]; and other justified reasons.[125]

Australian - Visa Framework

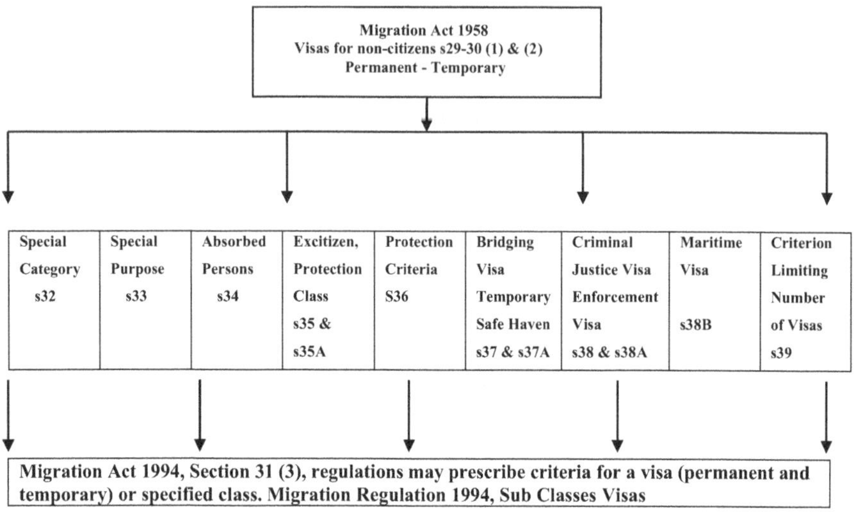

Comparatively, Australia has ten (10) classes of visa and more than 100 subclass visas (see Appendix One). Slovenia on the other hand has a total of three permits. Australia should borrow from Slovenia and Europe and consider reforming its visa framework by reducing their number. A starting point would be to commence with business visa classes and subclasses, reducing the administrative burden to business and government. Reducing the number of visas types could also reduce the cost to business.

The visa frameworks of Slovenia and Australia reinforce that states concurrently include and exclude non-citizens from the state. Both states through their respective visa and permit programs extend the postnational, civic and universal citizenship to include economic and humanitarian entrants. The visa and permit programs along with various other provisions of migration law enable a states citizenry to be mobile and participate globally (by entering and exiting the state). The visa framework assists the state to implement its immigration and citizenship policy. The Australian

[120] Ibid, article 46.
[121] Ibid, article 47.
[122] Ibid, article 48.
[123] Ibid, article 49.
[124] Ibid, article 50.
[125] Ibid, article 50.

framework has enabled the state to establish a cottage industry (creating business and jobs such as migration agents). Slovenia's model is not as advanced. However, promoting legal harmonisation, and reducing the number of visas available in Australia, may not be accepted by industry or government. It is argued that the respective visa and permit systems, are at the front line of a state's national identity. That is, an individual requires a visa or permit to enter and stay.

The economic benefits of establishing a regional model requires further research. Australia and Slovenia could develop a pilot project to take to other countries and test whether they would be interested in harmonising their visa or permit framework. The benefits would not only extend economically to the individual and the state, but also to the state's diaspora, making it easier for them to exit and return to their original state, in the same way as dual citizenship. The visa and permit framework established by both states, along with the visas and permits discussed in this chapter all make a contribution to the national identity.

However, governments continue to look at areas of services that should be provided at full cost recovery. Thus, Australia may not want to reduce the cost or number of visas, as this provides a revenue stream for the government agency responsible for administering immigration. Due to the large number of visas under Australian law, the next section only compares the Highly Qualified Employment (Skilled), Family Reunification, Student (Education), Permanent Residence and Refugee visa types. The challenge for both states and the EU will be the changing economic activity. On other words, it is predicted that with the emergence of artificial intelligence and quantum, it could result in less jobs. Should this be realized, there will be a fundamental shift required towards immigration policy.

9.4.1 Highly Qualified Employment (Skilled)

In 2009, the European Union (EU) implemented the Blue Card (BC)[126] to boost competitiveness and address labour shortages across European member states.[127] To qualify for a BC a valid contract must have been established such as a binding job offer.[128] A member state can refuse an application when there is a severe recession.[129] The Blue Card can be withdrawn where fraud has been identified or where the card holder does not meet the conditions of residence.[130] The individual who obtains a BC is subject to the same working conditions including pay, dismissal,

[126] Council Directive 2009/50/EC, conditions of entry and residence of third country nationals for the purposes of highly qualified employment, Official Journal of the European Union L155/17.

[127] Ibid, Preamble (7).

[128] Ibid, article 5.

[129] Ibid, article 8.

[130] Ibid, article 9.

health and safety as the citizens of that member state.[131] However, the BC does not guarantee family reunion once the person is physically in a member state.[132] Article 16 is an important provision providing that residence periods may accumulate where there has been residence in different member state across the Union (for a period up to 5 years).[133] For example, where a person has obtained the BC to work in Slovenia then through that employment has moved to The Netherlands the time of residence in The Netherlands will be included along with the time of residence in Slovenia. Even so, periods of absence from the European Union can be undertaken provided they are shorter than 12 months and do not exceed 18 months. Provided the person meets these restrictions, their cumulative calculation of residence will not be affected.[134] However, for the person which has been issued the BC to move from one member state and reside in another, they can only do so provided they have resided in the member state who issued the card for a period of at least 18 months.[135]

Moreover, and provided the conditions of residence have been met[136] a long term residence permit can be issued by Slovenia, and the individual could if they choose to do so, apply for, and obtain, citizenship. Nonetheless, the Blue Card Directive has simplified the conditions of entry and residence for highly skilled employees across the European Union. While Australians have access to the APEC card (discussed below), a similar approach could be developed and established between Australia and ASEAN member states.

Comparatively, the employer nominated visa[137] assists Australian employers to recruit and obtain highly skilled individuals. However, an individual is subject to the points test.[138] The points test is based on age, level of competence in the use of English (in accordance with the international English Language Testing System) and length of skilled employment. That is, the longer the stay in Australia, the more points will be earned. A person who has a doctoral degree would gain 20 points.

---

[131] Ibid, article 14.

[132] Ibid, article 15.

[133] Ibid, article 16.

[134] Ibid, article 16 (3).

[135] Ibid, article 18.

[136] Ibid, article 17.

[137] Schedule 2, *Migration Regulations 1994*, Statutory Rules No. 268, Employer Nomination AN, subclass 119 regional sponsored migration scheme, subclass 121 employer nominated scheme, Employer Nomination Residence BW, subclass 856 employer nomination scheme, subclass 857 regional sponsored migration scheme.

[138] *Migration Act 1958,* sections 92 to 95, Visas, Immigration and Refugees, Professional and other Skilled Migrants, The Points Test, Department of Immigration and Citizenship, http://www.immi.gov.au/skilled/general-skilled-migration/points-test.htm. The following General Skilled Migration (GSM) visas are subject to a points test assessment Skilled (Migrant) (Class VE) Independent subclass 175 visas, Skilled (Migrant) (Class VE) Sponsored subclass 176 visas, Skilled (Provisional) (Class VC) Regional – Sponsored subclass 487 visas, Skilled (Provisional) (Class VF) Regional – Sponsored subclass 475 visas, Skilled (Residence) (Class VB) Independent subclass 885 visas, Skilled (Residence) (Class VB) Sponsored subclass 886 visas.

Furthermore, a person can also earn points for studying in Australia and points will be afforded where the individual undertakes that study in a regional centre. In addition, more points can be earned where the individual has a recognised community language or their partner has specific skills that make a contribution to the local community.

Niether the European Union, nor Slovenia has a points system, and they could benefit significantly from implementing a similar system to Australia. The United Kingdom, also a member of the European Union has a similar points system to Australia. The benefit for member states and the broader Union, is that the points system enables the state to better understand and direct where migrants (skills) are required in the economy. The European Union and Slovenia could consider adopting a Directive that is based on the points system that has been established in Australia. This consideration is for the European Union and Slovenia to attract skilled labour from third countries and not from within the Union.

A person can also be nominated by an Australian State Government in accordance with the relevant state migration plan to enter and stay under the skilled migration program.[139] A number of business visas are available that include business skills[140] (provisional, owner, investor, senior executive, state and territory sponsored business owner, executive, talent).[141] A regional (state) program has been established by Australia whereby an individual can gain entry and residence in Australia, but only in the state of Victoria or the nominated state. The requirements are linked to the Victorian Government's State Nomination Occupation list.[142] This list also reflects the skills that have been outlined in the national skills list. Slovenia has established Administrative Units (AU) throughout the state. These Units have delegated responsibility from the Ministry of Interior to assist in the administration of visas (excluding analysis of local business and skills required). The AU's role could be extended to have a greater focus on local business and skilled shortages, in a similar way to Australia and its states.

It is noteworthy that there has been controversy in Australia in relation to the use of 457 visas that allow a non-citizen to enter Australia and take up employment. To do so, there has to be an agreement in place where a business is sponsoring the individual. The business is located in Australia and has the appropriate processes and practices established to ensure the individual is safe. Similar measures and

[139] Points Test for Certain Skilled Migration Visas, Department of Immigration and Citizenship, http://www.immi.gov.au/skilled/general-skilled-migration/pdf/points-test.pdf

[140] Schedule 2, Migration Regulations 1994, Statutory Rules No. 268, Subclass visas 160, 161, 162, 163, 164.

[141] Ibid, Business talent 132, established business in Australia 845, state/territory sponsored regional establishment business in Australia 846, Business owner 890, investor 891, state/territory sponsored business owner 892, state-territory sponsored investor 893.

[142] Victorian Government, State Nomination Occupation List for Graduates in Victoria 2012 & 2013, www.LiveInVictoria.vic.gov.au/graduates. The list outlined groups of occupations that Biotechnology and Science, Health, PhD Graduates, Engineering and Building, Financial Services and Human Resource Management, Information and Communications Technology, Tourism and Hospitality, Education and Trades.

protections apply across member states of the European Union. Thus, individuals working under this visa are subject to the same safety standards as local citizens. Additionally, the 417 visa enables a person to come to Australia and undertake temporary work, similar to the guest worker program across the European Union and Slovenia.

The Asia Pacific Economic Cooperation (APEC)[143] card is the equivalent in Australia[144] and allows a person to enter any of the APEC member states for 60–90 days. In addition to the above, there are also short stay sponsored,[145] medical practitioner,[146] work and holiday,[147] domestic worker,[148] cultural and social,[149] education,[150] student,[151] retirement,[152] and medical treatment (visitor),[153] visas,[154] made available by Australia. The other remaining skilled visa categories have been established under labour agreements[155] or been defined as distinguished talent visas.[156] Labour agreements, are those agreements where the Minister for Immigration or the Minister responsible for employment has developed an agreement with other nation states. These consist of the Regional Headquarter Agreement (Invest in Australia Supported Skills Agreement) that have been developed to enhance Australia's research and investment by companies that want to establish their head office within the state. As discussed above, Australia could explore adopting a similar 'Blue Card' model between Australia and ASEAN member states. Doing so, will not only be symbolic diplomatically and politically, but it would also

---

[143] Asia Pacific Economic Cooperation (APEC), Members Australia, Brunei Darussalam, Canada, Chile, The Hong Kong Special Administrative Region of the People's Republic of China, Republic of Indonesia, Japan, Korea, Malaysia, Mexico, Papua New Guinea, China, Peru, Philippines, Russia, Singapore, Taiwan, Thailand, United Stated of America, Vietnam. http://www.immi.gov.au/skilled/business/apec/

[144] Schedule 2, *Migration Regulations 1994*, Statutory Rules No. 268, Temporary Business Entry UC, subclass 456 business short stay and 457 business long stay.

[145] Schedule 2, *Migration Regulations 1994*, Statutory Rules No. 268, class UL.

[146] Ibid, class UE.

[147] Ibid, class US.

[148] Ibid, class TG.

[149] Ibid, class TE

[150] Ibid, class TH.

[151] Ibid, subclass 571 independent sector, 571 schools sector, 572 vocational education and training sector, 573 higher education sector, 574 post graduate research, 575 non-award sector, 576 AusAid or defence sector, 580 student guardian.

[152] Ibid, TQ.

[153] Ibid, UB.

[154] Jennissen, R, (2007) *Causality Chains in the International Migration Systems Approach*, Population, Research and Policy Review, Vol 26, 411–436.

[155] Schedule 2, *Migration Regulations 1994*, Statutory Rules No. 268, Labour Migrant AU, subclass 120 labour agreement, Labour Agreement BV, subclass 855 labour agreement.

[156] Ibid, Distinguished Talent Migrant AL, subclass 124 distinguished talent, Distinguished Talent Residence BX, subclass 858 distinguished talent.

provide a pathway to greater integration and social acceptance throughout increased trade.

9.4.2 Investment Visas and Permits

Australia has recently extended its visa system to include investment visas. The current investment visa in Australia is valued at $1.5 million for a 4 year period.[157] The national Government wants to expand the current residency permits to fast track the entry and stay of investors from the United States of America who have $15 million or more.[158] The Significant Investor Visa allows a person who has more than $5 million to invest into Australia[159] to fast track their permanent residency and citizenship. In June 2015, the Victorian State Government of Australia assisted in fast tracking residency visas for individuals from China who agreed to invest $2.1 million, directly into the Victorian state.[160] Furthermore, a recent study undertaken by the Australian Productivity Commission on Migrant Intake into Australia, proposed that a fee be imposed to cover the full administrative cost of processing a visa. The proposal is to charge the migrant a fee which could be made up front or the Australian Government provide a loan.[161] The then Australian Prime Minister Tony Abbott stated in 2015 that the proposal by the Productivity Commission was not the policy of the Australian Government.[162] In addition, the Australian government is considering the idea of also charging a fee for refugee visas[163] (as discussed later in this chapter).

However, the above is not limited to Australia. Greece and the United Kingdom provide resident permits to individuals from third countries that make investments to member states.[164] For example, in Greece[165] the individuals must have €250,000, and the United Kingdom requires £1,000,000. States such as Hungary, France,

[157] Migration Law, The Australian Significant Investor Visa and Premium Investor Visa, http://aussiemigrationlaw.com.au/the-significant-investor-visa/

[158] Mark Dunn, *Chinese migrants pay billions to settle here, Wealthy buying visas*, HeraldSun, 1 July 2015.

[159] Australian Government, Significant Investor Visa, https://www.immi.gov.au/faqs/Pages/What-is-the-significant-investor-visa.aspx

[160] Ibid.

[161] Productivity Commission, *Migrant Intake into Australia* Australian Government, Issues Paper, 2015, 31.

[162] Citizenship for cash is not our policy: Tony Abbott – The Sydney Morning Herald, 4 May 2015.

[163] Government Plan to fast-track refugees in exchange for potential $19,000 fee, http://www.msn.com/en-au/news/australia/government-plan-to-fast-track-refugees-in-exchange-for-potential-dollar19000-fee/ar-BBlh0sR?ocid=SKY2DHP

[164] European Parliamentary Research Service, http://epthinktank.eu/2014/01/15/eu-citizenship-and-residence-permits-for-sale/

[165] European Parliamentary Research Service, http://epthinktank.eu/2014/01/15/eu-citizenship-and-residence-permits-for-sale/

Spain, Latvia, Portugal and Ireland also have investor programs.[166] The issue has been debated in the United Kingdom to the extent that a radical approach has been proposed to charge $50, 000 [US] for a permit to enter and stay in the state. Gary Becker argues that by charging such an extensive fee it would ensure that only those individuals who have a commitment to the state would apply.[167] Cyprus has developed a similar investment scheme where a person can invest €5000.000 however the individual must have a permanent privately-owned residence in Cyprus. However, one argument could be that citizenship or permanent residence should be limited to those individuals who have the financial resources available to pay. Even so, the earlier postnational concept did not have such a hefty fee attached to a guest worker permit, but rather enabled Europe to fill labour requirements (usually unskilled). The issue has been identified as an area for future research to better understand the positives and negatives to a state and prospective resident (citizen). It could be argued that investment visas and the ability for people to purchase their way into citizenship, is exclusionary. While not opposing the policy objective (s) for establishing these visa types, they can, in part, contribute to division rather than social cohesion.

9.4.3 *Student (Education)*

To obtain a student visa the applicant needs to be able to fulfil the financial, language proficiency[168] health and national security requirements.[169] Moreover, there needs to be evidence of accommodation and welfare arrangements with whom the person will reside. This includes evidence of family or other arrangements provided through the educational institution.[170] A student from a third country in Europe will not need a visa to enter and stay in another member state provided:

- The student travels as a member of a group studying at a general education institution; or
- The group is accompanied by a teacher from the institution who is able to present a list of the children they are accompanying; or
- The pupil presents a valid passport or other entry document specified in an international agreement or decision issued by the Slovenian government.

---

[166] Sumption, M., Hooper, K, (2014) *Selling Visas and Citizenship: Policy Question for the Global Boom in Investor Immigration*, Migration Policy Institute.

[167] Gary Becker, G, (2011) *The Challenge of Immigration – a Radical Solution*, The Institute of Economic Affairs, 1–5.

[168] Schedule 5A, *Migration Regulation 1994.*

[169] PAM3, Generic Guidelines, Student visas – application & related procedures, Australian Immigration Law

[170] Ibid, 12.

This process was established in 1994 by Council Decision 94/795/JHA. The European Council decided on the basis of article K.3.2.b of the TEU that travel arrangements for students from third countries could be liberalised for those students resident in a MS.[171] A non-citizen that has entered Australia under a student visa[172] can travel and reside anywhere. There are a significant number of subclass visas prescribed by the 1994 MR[173] that will not be discussed. Nevertheless, both states provide for short and long term visas or permits[174] to enable a person to enter and stay for the purposes of education that could then lead to the individual obtaining permanent residency, and, applying for and obtaining citizenship. Education is important to Australia and in 2011 the education economy contributed $16 billion to the state.[175] Slovenia is encouraged to look at Australia's education system, which has attracted a steady inflow of international students and made a significant economic a contribution to the economy. Adopting a similar approach would allow Slovenia to not only benefit economically, but also make citizens of other states more aware of what and who Slovenia and Slovenia are. Adopting a similar approach would also assist Slovenians in identifying future talented citizens that could make a significant contribution to the state. It is argued that this would also translate to Slovenia spreading its identity regionally and to the rest of the world.

9.4.4 Family Reunification

Family migration allows the family to reunify through sponsorship (temporary and permanent). The ability for citizens to create and maintain basic family relationships is a defining aspect of a free, democratic society. Both Slovenia and Australia are founded on democratic principles such as the rule of law. The discussion here is narrow and only focuses on marriage and international adoption. Marriage and international adoption are those personal activities undertaken by citizens within a

---

[171] European Council, Official Journal of the European L 327, 19/12/1991 P. 0001–0003.

[172] Australian Government student visa types, The Student (Temporary) (Class TU) visa comprises 8 subclasses. Subclasses 570–576 are based on the education sector of your main course.

[173] Schedule 1, *Migration Regulations 1994*, ppermanent business visas are also able to be obtained under class Business skills – Business Talent EA and subclass; Business talent – 132; Business skills – Established business residence – BH; Established business in Australia – 845'State territory sponsored regional established business in Australia – 846; Business Skills residence DF; Business owner – 890; Investor – 891; State territory Sponsored Business Owner – 892; State Territory Sponsored Investor – 893.

[174] Temporary visas can be issued for such things as work, education, study, seasonal work, daily work, family reunion, residents in other MS, family members or foreigner of Slovenian origin, children of aliens born in Slovenia, victims of human trafficking and illegal employment amongst other reasons article 37 to 51 Aliens Act 2011.

[175] Australian Bureau of Statistics, Australian Social Trends 2011, http://www.ausstats.abs.gov.au/ausstats/subscriber.nsf/LookupAttach/4102.0Publication14.12.113/$File/41020_International_Dec2011.pdf

nation state or transcend international borders under the legal framework of private international law. Furthermore, family migration has served Australia well by providing a competitive advantage for countries seeking to attract highly skilled immigrants.[176]

A sponsor for a family visa must be an Australia citizen or permanent resident. People do migrate to a state where they have family networks. Networks extend to relatives and friends of the migrant by providing financial or some other assistance such as accommodation, job opportunities and transport. Stark and Taylor point out that having an awareness of family members who have migrated to improve their living standard, is the most important factor for others in the family when deciding to migrate.[177] It is the knowledge and experience from this network that is used by an individual when migrating to another state. The family class visa includes partner, child, adoption, parent, aged dependent relative, remaining relative, orphaned relative, designated parent and contributory parent.[178] Family reunification is considered a right across the EU[179] in accordance with article 8 of the European Convention for the Protection of Human Rights and Fundamental Freedoms, and the Charter of Fundamental Rights. Family reunification can be achieved under both Slovenian and Australian law, although under slightly different banners. In Australia this is undertaken similar to the EU directive and Slovenian legislation under the principle of a 'sponsor',[180] including a spouse and children, and can include (family) relatives under certain conditions.

The child migrant class AH adoption subclass 102 visa allows children from overseas who have either been, or about to be adopted to be provided a permanent visa. However, the child must be under the age of 18 years. This visa allows the child to reside in Australia permanently with their adoptive parents.[181] Inter-country adoption has become more common over the past two decades and Australia is a signatory to the Convention on the Protection of Children and Cooperation in Respect of Inter-country Adoption 1993. Slovenia is also a signatory to the convention. There are two ways an inter-country adopted child can become an Australian citizen. Firstly, citizenship will be granted automatically provided at least one of the parents is an Australian citizen. Secondly, where the child has been adopted overseas they may apply for citizenship by conferral.[182] Citizenship by conferral in

[176] Ibid.

[177] Stark, O., Taylor, E, (2007) *Relative Deprivation and international migration*, Demography, 1989, in Roel Jennissen, Causality Chains in the International Migration Systems Approach, Population, Research and Policy Review, Vol 26, 411–436.

[178] Schedule 2, *Migration Regulations 1994*, Statutory Rules No. 268.

[179] Council Directive 2003/86/EC on the right to family reunification, Official Journal of the European Union L 251/12.

[180] *Migration Act 1958*, Division 3A.

[181] *Migration Regulations 1994*, Schedule 1, Child Migrant, Adoption subclass visa 102.

[182] Hague Conference on Private International Law, *Country Profile for Inter-country Adoption, Australia*, 2005, 1–25.

Australia is subject to a number of conditions under section 19G of the ACA.[183] These requirements have been outlined in chapter three.

Notwithstanding the general requirement of family reunification, other ways a non-citizen can enter either state is as a partner[184] or, prospective marriage.[185] Both states provide for family reunification, yet the European Union considers this to be a fundamental right, whereas Australia does not. Nevertheless, this could include getting married to a foreigner and bringing them back to Australia. In the case of an Australian marrying a Slovene in Slovenia and deciding to relocate to Australia, a spousal visa can be obtained. However, the couple will be subject to the requirements to prove they are actually in a relationship. This test includes demonstrating they have joint ownership of real estate or other assets, joint liabilities, financial resources, care of children, living arrangements and sharing day to day living expenses.[186]

Similar arrangements are in place in Slovenia, with one of the deciding factors in either state that the spouse will not be a financial or other burden on the state. The Australian court in *Asif*[187] refused a spousal visa because it was not being convinced the marriage was genuine as the applicant lied to the department about the history of the marriage. Migrants who have taken citizenship of the destination state can, under the family reunification policies of Slovenia and Australia, get their family to accompany them, thus allowing these new family members to enter and stay. Upon meeting the residency requirements, these individuals are eligible to apply for and obtain citizenship. Australia has reduced its family immigration program over the past three decades. However, it is argued that this is an area of migration policy that should be strengthened because, generally, most people that follow their family to a new state are likely to embrace and integrate into that country – a lot quicker. Thus, the process for social cohesion is strengthened and enhanced, and results in less intervention by the state. There needs to be greater alignment of skilled and economic migration policy with family migration policy.

9.5 Permanent (Long Term) Residence Visa

The alternative to citizenship, particularly in Australia is the opportunity for a person to obtain a permanent residence visa.[188] Long term or permanent residency, along with other visas and permits is a pathway to citizenship, however, individuals

---

[183] *Citizenship Act 2007*, Section 19G.

[184] Subclass 100 and 309, Partner (Provisional) and Partner, Schedule 2, *Migration Regulations 1994*.

[185] Subclass 300 Prospective Marriage, Schedule 2, Migration Regulations 1994. In Slovenia, this would be issued under the Long stay visa.

[186] *Migration Regulations 1994*, 1.09A, 1.15A.

[187] *Asif v MIMA* (2000) 60 ALD 145.

[188] *Migration Regulation 1994*.

may not wish to apply for citizenship but remain in the state. It allows a person to reside in the state, where that person cannot or doesn't want to take out citizenship.

In Australia permanent residency comes in a limited form compared to Slovenia. Permanent residence includes family based (partners, fiancé, children or dependent relatives) and work based (employer sponsor, general skilled, and select skilled).[189] Additionally, skilled workers can also obtain sponsorship for permanent residence. A permanent resident who has been residing in another state, can apply for a Resident Return Visa, and also applies to a former permanent resident whose last permanent resident visa was cancelled, or a former Australian citizen who has lost or renounced his or her Australian citizenship. In Slovenia a person obtains a Long Term Stay permit,[190] then issued a Residence permit issued depending on the situation, work or employment; work or research in higher education; study; seasonal work, trans-border employment and posted workers; daily work migrants; family reunion, residents in other EU countries, family members or foreigners of Slovenian origin, children of aliens born in Slovenia.

9.5.1 Deportation or Expulsion

Comparatively, both states have the ability to remove or deport non-citizens who are resident. Slovenia, however is subject to the deportation and removal requirements set out by the European Union. In Australia sections 201 and 501 of the Migration Act 1958, allow for long term residents to be either removed or deported. However, there are separate processes that apply, whereby, section 501 allows for the cancellation of a visa on grounds of character. Upon cancellation the person is automatically removed from the territory. Section 201, allows for a non-citizen to be deported who have been in Australia less than 10 years, and have committed a serious criminal offence, which resulted in imprisonment for 1 year or more. However, in accordance with section 201, the person is immune from deportation after the 10-year period as expired. That is, a person who has been in the country 11 years, is immune from deportation. This has provided government with a foot in each camp. Where they cannot use one provision to force a person out of the state, they can use the other. Thus, the opportunity is there for the government to deport residents even after the period of immunity comes into effect (after 10 years).

There have been numerous decisions by the judiciary in Australia regarding the deportation and removal of residents. In *Shaw*, the deportation of British nationals who had been resident in Australia since 1949 could occur, even though the person clearly exceeded the 10 year requirement for residency.[191] However, the ruling in

[189] *Migration Regulation 1994*, Subclass 820, 801, 101, 130, 189, 190, 489, 186.

[190] Article 17, Aliens Act, Official Gazette of the Republic of Slovenia, 50/2011.

[191] *Shaw v Minister for Immigration and Multicultural Affairs* [2003] HCA 72.

Shaw was an example of how the court 2 years earlier stated that such non-citizens could not be removed.[192] This had significant ramifications for all non-citizens who had migrated to Australia and only took out permanent residency. Nevertheless, in *Nystrom*[193] the court ruled that the administration of section 501 had lost its way. The court went onto rule that the bona fide use of this section to cancel the permanent absorbed person's visa who is 30 years old and spent all their life in Australia, has family in Australia, and deported for a criminal offence, should not be used to circumvent section 201.

The case of Robert Jovicic (originally from Serbia) who was deported to Serbia by the Australian government in 2004. The case raises the notion of who is "morally" a citizen of a state. The notion that a person has membership of a state due to the length of stay Jovicic had been in Australia resembles times when states in transition from one ruler to the next would grant citizenship automatically based on *jus domicili*. Jovicic, Yugoslav born, was a non-citizen of Australia who had been living in Australia for 36 years before being deported due to criminal convictions for drug use. To further complicate the matter, he was only granted a 7-day visa in Serbia which did not allow him to work, and furthermore, he had not met the citizenship application requirements, and thus was declared stateless. He would later return to Australia after much publicity,[194] and would be granted a permanent residency visa in 2008 by the Minister for Immigration and Citizenship.[195] Today Mr. Jovicic is still not a citizen of either Serbia or Australia.

The issue of deportation and removal of long term residents[196] is also a concern across European member states. Similar to Australia European Union member states including Slovenia have requirements that relates to a non-citizen's criminal records and financial situation as an assessment of good character. The European Union has largely applied general rules for member states to manage the removal of non-citizens. However, the law and procedures is at two level. One third of country nationals (migrants) are resident in a member state. Secondly, a European citizen residing on another member state. The test for migrants (non-European citizens) where they may be expelled is on public policy grounds, such as public security or a conviction of a serious criminal offence.[197] There is a subtle difference, as the European citizen would need to pose a genuine and present serious threat affecting the interests of society, and must be exclusively the persons own conduct. Whereas, the migrant (third country national) has no explicit requirement that it must be

---

[192] *Re Patterson; Ex parte Taylor* (2001) 207 CLR 391.

[193] *Nystrom v Minister for Immigration and Multicultural and Indigenous Affairs* [2005] FCAFC 121.

[194] Julian Burnside QC, *Citizens rights and the rule of law in civil society: not just yet*, 2008, 1–12, www.valuesineducation.org.au/pdf/burnside080310.pdf

[195] Chris Bowen, Minister for Immigration and Citizenship, Permanent Visa granted to Robert Jovicic, http://www.minister.immi.gov.au/media/media-releases/2008/ce08018.htm

[196] Council Directive 2003/109/EC concerning the status of third country national who are long term residents, Official Journal of the European Union L 16/44.

[197] Ibid, article 12.

exclusively their conduct, as such it could be similar to Australia where a person has an association with a criminal.

Both European citizens and migrants are afforded similar 10-year period where the individual has resided in the host state. However, the European Union has placed a higher level of oversight by aligning deportation (expulsion) to equal rights. Generally, European citizens will be assessed in the same way as migrants. Thus, the principles set out for the assessment include length of stay, family and employment arrangements. Deportation is viewed as interference to the right of 'private life and family'.[198] The rules established by the European Union appears to be more certain that Australia. The notable difference is European law automatically allows a person the right of access to judicial and, where appropriate, administrative redress procedures by the host member state.[199] This has been reaffirmed by the European Court of Justice that ruled a member state could not execute a deportation order without giving the migrant the chance to avail themselves of the right to remedy.[200]

The fragility of permanent residence in Australia cannot be underestimated. Even though the judiciary and government committees have identified a problem exists with sections 201 and 501 of the migration laws, there appears to be little appetite for a change in the law. Moreover, Australia by continuing to adopt such an approach could be breaching international human rights law.[201] Across the European Union there doesn't appear to be the same concerns as in Australia, because no matter whether an individual is a citizen of the Union or a migrant they are afforded the same rights to protect themselves against deportation. Australia should change its migration laws to fix this tension and provide certainty. Additionally, Australia could promote citizenship better as the option to long term residency, so as people would not be subject to in appropriate application of the law.

9.5.2 Residence Versus Citizenship: Benefits

Citizenship today is symbolic when compared to those individuals that are permanent or long term residents.[202] However, citizenship is much more important in that it provides a greater sense of belonging. It is argued that citizenship, by providing a

[198] Morano-Foadi, S., Andreadakis, S, (2001) *The Convergence of the European Legal System in the Treatment of Third Country Nationals in Europe: The ECJ and the ECtHR Jurisprudence*, The European Journal of International Law, Vol. 22 no. 4, 1071–1088.

[199] Council Directive 2004/38/EC, the right of citizens of the Union and their family members to move freely and reside freely within the territory of the MS, Official Journal of the European Union L 158/77.

[200] Case 48/75, *Royer* http://eur-lex.europa.eu

[201] Australia could be breaching the provisions of the International Covenant on Civil and Political Rights 1966.

[202] BettS, K., Birrell, B, (2007) *Making Australian Citizenship Mean More*, People and Place, Vol 15, No 1, 44–55.

greater sense of belonging also provides a greater level of social coherence. Citizenship allows a person to participate in the political process through voting and standing for elections. Citizenship is not only important to an individual, but also the state. It also enables people to identify with the national identity of the state, by embracing the values, rights and responsibilities, of the state. The benefits of Australian citizenship enable a person to apply for certain jobs in the national civil service. A citizen is entitled to a passport that allows them to travel (exit and enter the state), and receive assistance from (Australia's) consular offices while abroad. Furthermore, in the case of deportation or removal in Australia, citizenship provides greater certainty.

9.5.3 Testing Permanent Residents

Permanent residency appears to be a well-entrenched feature of both Australia and Slovenia's legal framework. In the same way as prospective citizens are obliged to undergo testing to obtain citizenship in Australia, the same process should be exploring for long term residents. Nevertheless, states should consider imposing testing (language, history and culture) requirements for permanent residents every 5 years. The testing of permanent residents is new, and could be similar or an advanced model to that of citizenship testing. The benefits could translate to greater and improved assimilation and understanding of the state and its identity. In other words, this translates to a greater level of social coherence. However, it is acknowledged that encouraging people to take out citizenship may force them to lose their citizenship of the other state. Thus, Australia and Slovenia should take a leadership role and work with those states that they deem to be friends and allies to encourage law reform and provide for dual citizenship.

9.6 Special Category Visa

Citizens from New Zealand can reside and work permanently within Australia under a Special category visa[203] that applies to New Zealand visitors. To become an Australian citizen they need to apply in accordance with the naturalization process. It is asserted that this could be the start of a wider regional based citizenship, similar to the European Union. Even though this visa category is restricted to New Zealand citizens. Further research is required to explore this concept. Australia has acknowledged closer ties with one neighbouring state, and could explore a similar framework with ASEAN member states.

[203] *Migration Act 1958*, s32

9.6.1 *Bridging Visas*

The bridging visa has no direct effect on whether citizenship is granted by a state. A bridging visa[204] is issued to non-citizens who have entered into Australia on another visa (for example, a student visa) and have applied for permanent residency.[205] This visa can also apply where a person has been detained after arriving within the territory illegally.[206] The visa allows a person to remain in the Australian territory for a specified period until a decision has been made by the authorities as to whether permanent residency is granted, or a visa is re-issued. Slovenia does not have a bridging visa. However, if an individual is within the territory of Slovenia, and has submitted an application for extension, a visa is issued.

A similar process applies in Australia, where the person's visa is about to expire and they have made an application for residency. This allows the person to stay within the territory while the application is processed. An example, of when an extension would be provided is where the individual is injured and unable to leave hospital. Not only are bridging visas used in Australia and Slovenia where a person's original visa has expired, but also, used to avoid the arrest and detention of a person of unlawful status. This visa type have been established to help facilitate the individual's current immigration status, which could include business, skilled, education, family reunification or refugee. Australia has seven bridging visa types whereas, Slovenia and the European Union only have one. The above visas and permits vary across both states. It is argued that the framework are an important part of Slovenia and Australia's ability to control who stays within the territory and obtains citizenship. The visa and permits system provide one of the elements within the immigration laws that form the pathway to citizenship.

9.7 General Requirements

The general requirements for obtaining a visa includes the public interest test, health check[207]; and character test.[208] The discussion in this section will only focus on the general requirements of health. Failure to meet the health requirement will result in the person not being able to enter the state. A non-citizen will require health

---

[204] Bridging visa types from A, B, C, D, E, F, R, are granted for different situations, but, generally allow individual to be in Australia whether in detention or in the community, travel overseas, and those waiting for another visa type to be processed or their current visa extended, such as for permanent residence, or, full citizenship.

[205] *Migration Act 1958*, s73.

[206] Ibid, s75.

[207] *Migration Act 1958*, ss60, 496, 505, and *Migration Regulations 1994*, regulation 13 interpretation of community services; 225A referral to a Medical Officer of the Commonwealth; 5.41 fees, and Schedule 4, 405,4006A and 4007.

[208] *Migration Act 1958*, ss501–503, *Migration Regulations 1994*, regulation 1.03, 2.25 and 2.53.

insurance.[209] Similarly, in Australia[210] a non-citizen will need to obtain a medical certificate confirming whether they have HIV or hepatitis B.[211] Generally, the health examination will be determined by the departmental medical officer and is an important aspect of public policy[212] in keeping the Australian community and its citizens safe.[213]

Apart from the general character and health checks, individuals may be required, depending on the visa type they are applying for, may be required to provide financial and information in relation to family members. Moreover, as the economy and jobs become even tougher to obtain, it is likely that individuals will be required to show evidence or the level of education attained, and any business they may have been involved in. In addition, individuals will also be required to provide personal information in regards to being subject to bankruptcy, or even having citizenship of another country.

9.8 Conclusion

This chapter has confirmed that immigration is a pathway to citizenship. Putting the law on immigration to one side, it is a complex policy area. Australia has a very different policy approach to that of the EU and Slovenia. While all jurisdictions do adopt a liberal approach. They all restrict the approach through various mechanisms such as the law and population policy, along with business, investment (purchasing citizenship), skilled and international protection, migration.

Arguably, immigration supports citizenship. It is further argued that immigration helps to define, strengthen and develop a national identity. On the other hand, it can also dilute national identity, along with social cohesion. While jurisdictions, due to size approach immigration differently, the fundamentals of the law are the same. They both provide visas or permits from entry and stay. However, the number of visas in Australia is complex and cumbersome. Even though it has developed a cottage industry, Australia should look to the EU, to reduce the number of visas. More

---

[209] Article 6 Council Directive 2004/114/EC, Official Journal of the European Union L 375/18.

[210] *Migration Act 1958*, section 5 (1) relates to the application for the visa, or the members of the family unit of that applicant for a prescribed disease, physical or mental condition, prescribed examination and treatment.

[211] Vrahnas, J., Bagarič, M., Dimopoulos, P., Pathinayake, A, (2012) *Migration and Refugee Law*, Principles and Practices in Australia, third edition, Cambridge University Press, 152–158.

[212] *Robinson v Minister for Immigration and Multicultural and Indigenous Affairs* [2005] FCA 1626, in John Vrahnas, Mirko Bagarič, Penny Dimopoulos and Athula Pathinayake, *Migration and Refugee Law*, Principles and Practices in Australia, third edition, Cambridge University Press, 2012, 152–158.

[213] *Migration Act 1958, Migration Regulations 1994*, PAM3. Aliens Act 2011, Official Gazette Republic of Slovenia, No 50/2011.

problematic is the emerging practice that people can buy their way into a state not only to obtain citizenship, but also, a business visa.

On the backdrop of the above, is the ability to effectively migrate and take out permanent residency. This is good for the person who does not want to give up their citizenship, from their state of origin that, only provides for single citizenship. While this chapter has not examined the effects of permanent residence on identity or social cohesion, it is argued that more should be done for this practice to be limited. Chapter 10 discusses residency. Doing so, will go some way to ensuring identity and cohesion are not diluted.

References

Betts, K., & Birrell, B. (2007). Making Australian citizenship mean more. *People and Place, 15*(1), 44–55.

Bloemraad, I., Korteweg, A., & Yurdakul, G. (2008). Citizenship and immigration: Multiculturalism, assimilation, and challenges to the nation-state. *Annual Review of Sociology, 34*, 153–179.

Castles, S. (2005). Migration and community formation under conditions of globalisation. *International Migration Review, 36*, 1143–1166.

Castles, S., & Miller, M. (1998). *The age of migration*. London: Macmillan Press.

Crock, M., & Berg, L. (2011). *Immigration refugees and forced immigration, law, policy and practices in Australia* (p. 149). Sydney: The Federation Press.

Crock, M., Saul, B., & Dastyari, A. (2006). *Future seekers II, refugees and irregular migration in Australia* (p. 23). Sydney: The Federation Press.

Hage, G. (2003). *Against paranoid nationalism: Searching for hope in a shrinking society*. Annandale: Pluto Press.

Jennissen, R. (2007). Causality chains in the international migration systems approach. *Population, Research and Policy Review, 26*, 411–436.

O'neil, C., & Watts, T. (2015). *Two future: Australia at a critical moment* (pp. 200–205). Melbourne: The Text Publishing Swann House.

Stary, O., & Taylor, E. (2007). Relative Deprivation and international migration. *Demography*, 1989. In Jennissen, R. (ed) *Causality chains in the international migration systems approach*. Population, Research and Policy Review, *26*, 411–436.

Tabor, A., & Milfont, T. (2011). Migration change model: Exploring the process of migration on a psychological level. *International Journal of Intercultural Relations, 35*, 818–820.

Wallace, S. G. (2010). *Naturalisation policies in Europe: Exploring patterns of inclusion and exclusion* (pp. 1–10). Florence: EUDO Citizenship Observatory, Robert Schuman Centre for Advanced Studies in collaboration with Edinburgh University Law School.

Chapter 10
International Protection

Abstract International protection is an important part of the migration policies of Australia, Slovenia and the EU. Today, more than any other time in history, large numbers of individuals are fleeing their country of origin due to war, poverty, persecution or a natural disaster. However, only a small number of people that fall within this category, ever obtain refugee status. Moreover, since WWII, the next mass exodus from the European continent was the violent dissolution of Yugoslavia. The resulting effect lead to the largest refugee crisis in Europe. Many individuals found their way to Australia. Recently, there has been a rise in people being displaced across North Africa and the Middle East reached its height from 2014 to 2017. Many of these people found their way into the EU, and placed a lot of pressure of member states, particularly those smaller states such as Slovenia. Even though Slovenia was considered a transit state, people did apply for asylum. This chapter explores the challenging area of international protection law across the EU, Slovenia and Australia. Thus, this chapter will demonstrate how the respective jurisdictions have established a legal framework that enable these people to obtain citizenship. Finally, it highlights the differences between the jurisdictions in relation to residency requirements and bilateral arrangement that have been established between the states.

Keywords International protection · Humanitarian visa · Refugee · Xenophobia

R. Walters, *National Identity and Social Cohesion in a Time of Geopolitical and Economic Tension: Australia – European Union – Slovenia*,
https://doi.org/10.1007/978-981-15-2164-5_10

10.1 Introduction

Individuals flee their country of origin due to war,[1] poverty,[2] persecution or a natural disaster.[3] Only some people are considered refugees. A refugee has been defined as; 'Any person who owing to a well-founded fear of being persecuted for reasons of race, nationality, membership in a particular social group or political opinion, is outside the country of his nationality and is unable to, or owing to such fear, is unwilling to avail himself of the protection of that country'.[4] Australia, Slovenia and the EU[5] all define 'refugee' in accordance with the Geneva Convention. Australia ratified the 1951 Convention and 1967 Protocol in 1973 Slovenia[6] automatically assumed responsibility for its implementation, upon independence.[7]

The European Union has taken a broader role in regulating elements of refugee law, ensuring a consistent approach by member states.[8] The harmonization of laws across the Union has extended to managing the reception of asylum seekers,[9] refugees,[10] fingerprints[11] applications,[12] and establishing a minimum standard for temporary protection.[13] Mary Crock argues that the continued influx of illegal

---

[1] Walzer, M, (1983) *Spheres of Justice: A Defense of Pluralism and Equity, Oxford:* Martin Robinson, 25–40.

[2] Carens, J (1992) *Migration and Morality: A Liberal Egalitarian Perspective*, in Brian Barry and Robert Goodin (eds), Free Movement: Ethical Issues in the Transnational Migration of People and Money, New York, Havester Wheatsheaf, 1992, 25–47.

[3] Wolfe, A, (1991) *Whose Keeper: Social science and moral obligation*, Berkley and Los Angeles: University of California Press, 1–23.

[4] Article 2, Convention relating to the Status of Refugees 1951, adopted by the United Nations Conference of Plenipotentiaries on the Status of Refugees and Stateless Person, Geneva, 2 to 25 July 1951, entry into force 22 April 1954, Treaty Series, vol. 189, p. 137. Protocol Relating to the status of Refugees 1967, noted by the UN General Assembly, in resolution 2198 (XXI), 2 to 16 December 1966, Treaty Series, vol. 606, p. 267.

[5] Joint Position 96/196/JHA of March 1996 defined by the Council on the basis of article K.3 of the Treaty on European Union on the harmonised application of the definition of the term 'refugee' in article 1 of the Geneva Convention of 28 July 1951, Official Journal of the European Union L 63.

[6] Up-1136/11-24, Official Gazette of the Republic of Slovenia 26/2012.

[7] Notification of succession in respect of United Nations Conventions and conventions adopted by IAEA.

[8] Article 62, Lisbon Treaty 2007, Official Journal of the European Union C 306/1.

[9] Council Directive 2003/9/EC, laying down minimum standards for the reception of asylum seekers, Official Journal of the European Union, L 31/18.

[10] Council Directive 2005/85/EC, on minimum standards on procedures in Member States for granting and withdrawing refugee status Official Journal of the European Union, L 326/13.

[11] Council Regulation No 2725/2000, Official Journal of the European Union, L 316/1.

[12] Council Regulation No 343/2003, establishing the criteria and mechanisms for determining the Member State responsible for examining an asylum application lodged in one of the Member States by a third-country national Official Journal of the European Union, L 50/1.

[13] European Union: Council of the European Union, Council Directive 2001/55/EC of 20 July 2001 on Minimum Standards for Giving Temporary Protection in the Event of a Mass Influx of Displaced Persons and on Measures Promoting a Balance of Efforts Between Member States in Receiving

immigrants seeking international protection has created a fear of xenophobia in Australia.[14] The same can be seen in Europe with immigrants from North Africa and Syria arriving in Spain, Southern Italy, Greece and transiting through Slovenia.[15] More recently, in 2015, there has been huge numbers of migrants from Syria and other countries entering, Slovenia, the European Union and (Schengen area) and Australia. Refugees who enter a state's territory illegally in some cases are subject to racism, prejudice and xenophobia[16] as opposed to those individuals arriving legally and over staying their visas. Arguably, people arriving illegally are a lot more visible than those that have already arrived legally and have begun integrating into the community. As discussed in chapter three, xenophobic behaviour (violence) exists in Australia, Slovenia and across the Union. The increase in illegal arrivals at the border of the European Union (Schengen area) and Australia from the conflict in the Middle East did result in an increase in this type of behaviour by states and their citizens. Any further discussion on this matter is outside the scope of this book, but it is suffice to say that the crisis in Syria and the rise of Islamic State has also posed a significant challenge to Australia's multicultural identity.

10.2 Humanitarian Visas

Those declared refugees[17] or asylum seekers are issued a visa,[18] (or temporary safe haven visas).[19] Slovenia provides temporary stay that is valid for a period of 6 months, although this may be extended. Australia on the other hand, has established seven offshore and three onshore visas. Onshore visas allow the person to stay in the territory upon arriving in Australia without a visa or without a valid visa. These individuals are usually placed in detention until it has been determined if they warrant refugee protection. Australian offshore visas consist of seven types (1) refugee and humanitarian class XB; (2) refugee; (3) inter-country special humanitarian;

such Persons and Bearing the Consequences Thereof, 7 August 2001, Official Journal of the European Union L 212–223 7.8.2001, http://www.unhcr.org/refworld/docid/3ddcee2e4.html

[14] Crock, M, (2000) *A sanctuary under review: where to from here for Australia's Refugee and Humanitarian Program*? University New South Wales, Law Journal, 246–250.

[15] Flood of desperate refugees test Spaniards tolerance, April 2015, http://www.npr.org/sections/parallels/2015/04/25/402035778/flood-of-desperate-refugees-tests-spaniards-tolerance

[16] International Migration, *Racism, Discrimination and Xenophobia*, International Labour Office, Office of the United Nationals High Commissioner for Human Rights, International Organisation for Migration, 2011.

[17] Articles 30, 31, 32, 33, 34, 35, 39a, 41, 46, 47, 48, 49, 55, 56, 57. 58, 119, *Law on International Protection*, Official Gazette Republic of Slovenia 2011/11. The *Migration Act 1958* allows a person who provides incorrect or false information in their application to be refused. Similarly, for Australia a visa will be granted or refused in accordance with the *Migration Act 1958*, whether outside or inside the migration zone provided they meet the refugee status.

[18] *Migration Act 1958*, s36.

[19] Ibid, s37A.

(4) global special humanitarian; (5) emergency rescue; (6) women at risk; and (7) secondary movement relocation.[20] These are used where the individual has been detected, for example, on a boat outside of the Australian territory, intercepted by authorities and sent to an offshore detention centre. The policy response can vary depending on the government of the day. Successive governments over the past decade have continued with both the onshore and offshore detention of individuals. Additionally, there is the territorial asylum visa that enables an individual to be declared as an asylum seeker.[21]

There are a number of other visas provided in Australia however they will not be discussed here (for example, special visas for permanent or temporary stay). Nevertheless, to be eligible for a refugee visa[22] the individual must be assessed and approved by the United Nations High Commissioner for Refugees. In Slovenia, a refugee passport can be issued for a period of 10 years,[23] however such a passport will not be issued to an individual who has been granted subsidiary protection[24] Australia does not have a similar passport.

It has been documented that climate change will potentially be a future threat causing displacement of people.[25] States may need to take a closer look at their current legislative framework to ensure they are able to adapt to people being displaced as a result of climate change. The former Australian Senator Kerry Nettle from the Australian Greens Party in 2007 proposed to amend the Migration Act in 2007 in an attempt to create a new visa category to accept individuals displaced by environmental disasters.[26] However, by the conclusion of Parliament in 2008, the Bill had lapsed and there was no amendment to the Migration Act. No such proposal has been put to the Slovenian Parliament on the same issue.

Australia and Slovenia, as well as the EU could consider expanding their current legislation to include and allow for environmental refugees. The international protection visas and permits discussed in this chapter ensure both states continue to implement their immigration policies. Additionally, they allow the state to determine the number of people to whom they provide a visa or permit. In the case of Australia this is about 15,000 to 20,000 people annually, depending on government

[20] Schedule 2, *Migration Regulations 1994*, Statutory Rules No. 268, Class XA, subclass 866, subclass 851, class XB, subclass 200, subclass 2012, subclass 202, subclass 203, subclass 204, subclass 451.

[21] Schedule 2, *Migration Regulations* 1994, Statutory Rules No. 268, subclass 800.

[22] *Migration Regulations 1994*, schedule 2. Department of Parliamentary Services, Parliamentary Library, United Nations High Commissioner for Refugees, Frequently asked Questions about resettlement, 2011, 1–29, www.aph.gov.au/library/pubs/bn/law/RefugeeResettlement.pdf

[23] Article 115, *Law on International Protection*, Official Gazette Republic of Slovenia 2011/11.

[24] Ibid, article 116.

[25] Perkiss, S., Bowrey, G., Gill, N., *Environmental Refugees: An accountability Perspective*, University of Wollongong, http://ro.uow.edu.au/cgi/viewcontent.cgi?article=1990&context=commpapers

[26] The Parliament of the Commonwealth of Australia, The Senate, Migrations (Climate Refugees) Amendment Bill 2007, Explanatory Memorandum, 1–3.

policy. Nonetheless, this process reinforces the right of states to implement laws that control this activity while meeting their international obligations, thus, retaining and strengthening their national identities.

10.3 Purchasing a Refugee Visa

The Australian Government recently considered the idea of charging $19,000 to fast-track refugee applications.[27] The proposal has not progressed. Such a proposal could raise serious questions in relation to a nation state's meeting its international obligations to provide a safe place for all people who are classified as refugees. By charging a fee, an argument could be formulated that there is little difference between people smugglers (charging a fee) and the government charging a fee, in order for a person to escape their country of origin due to war or persecution. The only difference is that the government would be guaranteeing that the person obtains a refugee visa and is able to enter Australia whereas a charge (or sum of money) paid to people smugglers does not guarantee the person will enter Australia, or obtain refugee status. The proposal to charge a fee for a refugee visa, further reinforces Australia's right to choose who enters and stays. It has the potential to exclude many people who are experiencing serious harm and persecution. Such a proposal should not be supported in Australia or Slovenia. It is argued that a proposal such as this may have a negative impact to the national identity, by sending a message to the world community that Australia will take the highest bidder. No such proposal has been discussed in Slovenia.

10.4 Refugee Status Terminated, Excluded or Withdraw

At any time, the refugee status can be terminated, excluded or withdrawn. Upon termination[28] or withdrawal by the state, the individual would no longer be eligible to apply for and obtain citizenship. This can be achieved in Slovenia[29] even though it is left up to member states[30] to examine the application.[31] However, the state is

[27] Government plan to fast-track refugees in exchange for potential $19,000 fee, http://www.msn.com/en-au/news/australia/government-plan-to-fast-track-refugees-in-exchange-for-potential-dollar19000-fee/ar-BBlh0sR?ocid=SKY2DHP

[28] Ibid, article 4.

[29] Council Directive 2005/85/EC, minimum standards for granting and withdrawing refugee status, Official Journal of the European Union, L 326/13.

[30] Council Directive 2004/83/EC, on minimum standards for the qualification and status of third country nationals or stateless persons as refugees or as persons who otherwise need international protection and the content of the protection granted, Official Journal of the European L 304.

[31] Ibid, article 19.

obliged to ensure the individual is not subject to persecution or harm upon return to their state of origin. The termination of refugee status can be undertaken where a refugee voluntarily takes protection or has re-acquired citizenship from their country of origin.[32] Australia has the same process. Termination will also take place where, for example, a stateless person returns to the state of former residence.[33] Furthermore, protection ceases when refugee status is terminated or expires.[34]

Withdrawal of international protection[35] and refugee status will occur in Slovenia where the individual has misrepresented or omitted relevant facts or made false documents.[36] This also extends to where the person has been determined to be a threat to Slovenia or has been convicted of a crime against humanity.[37] The states use different language when referring to cancellation (termination) and withdraw of refugee status. In Australia, rather than terminate the refugee status of a person, it is a single step to terminating the individual's visa. A visa can be cancelled at any time where it is determined the person has provided incorrect information, or completed the relevant forms incorrectly.[38] Additionally, where the individual has been cleared by immigration and later found to have provided incorrect information, a notice may be issued cancelled the visa, thus, withdrawing international protection.[39] For example, a person who has claimed refugee status by providing information they have been subject to persecution which did not actually exist, but was using refugee status to gain entry, stay and citizenship in either state, could have that status withdrawn or cancelled.

10.5 Undocumented (Irregular – Human Trafficking) Migration

The issues underlying irregular migration are complex. While asylum policies have been discussed, irregular migration is otherwise outside the scope of this research. The problem varies widely depending on the region of the world being discussed. Over the past decade, both the European Union and Australia have experienced criminal activity involving people smuggling.[40] A prime example is where people are trafficked into the sex industry. The International Labour Organisation estimated

---

[32] Article 4, *Law on International Protection*, Official Gazette Republic of Slovenia 2011/11.

[33] Ibid, article 4.

[34] Ibid, article 4 (2).

[35] Ibid, article 108.

[36] Ibid, article 6.

[37] Ibid, article 6.

[38] *Migration Act 1958*, sections 97 to 107.

[39] Ibid, s107.

[40] *Migration Act 1958*, Division 12, Offences in relation to entry into, and remaining in Australia, subdivision A – People Smuggling and related offences.

in 2014 that the private economy generates $150 billion in illegal profit annually, with an estimated $99 billion estimated to come from sexual exploitation.[41] The remaining $51 billion includes domestic workers, agriculture and other economic activity.[42] Slovenia has been considered to be both a transit and destination country, and to a lesser extent a source country for women who are subjected to sex trafficking. Illegal prostitution in Germany and Italy alone is estimated at more than €50–60 million.[43]

Labour exploitation in Slovenia has been documented with people coming from the Ukraine, Romania, Serbia and Bosnia and Herzegovina.[44] For Australia, it were estimated in 2013–2014 that there was between 50,000 and 100,000 people working illegally[45] across the state. But this figure does not provide an accurate assessment of the total number of people who are subject to forced labour, in the sex industry. It has been reported that people from Thailand, Malaysia, South Korea and the Philippines have been forced into migrating to Australia and into the illegal sex industry.[46] Between 2009 and 2011 it was reported at least 110 people entered Australia and were subjected to sexual exploitation.[47] Unlike Slovenia, Australia is seen as a destination state, rather than a transit state. Both Slovenia and Australia have criminalised trafficking of human beings.[48] Permits are issued to people subject to human trafficking.[49] Australia takes a slightly different approach and has the ability to issues four visa types for human trafficking.[50] Individuals who have been subjected to human trafficking can apply for citizenship.

[41] International Labour Organisation, Strengthening action to end forced labour, SAP-FL Newsletter, 2014, 1–6.

[42] Ibid.

[43] Ibid.

[44] Ibid.

[45] Border Crossing Observatory, Trafficking in Persons, Newsletter, Monash University, 2014, http://artsonline.monash.edu.au/thebordercrossingobservatory/files/2014/02/BOb-News-Issue-7-Feburary-2014_Trafficking-in-Persons.pdf

[46] Australian Institute of Criminology, *People Trafficking in Australia*, Trends & Issues in Crime and Criminal Justice no. 441, http://www.aic.gov.au/publications/current%20series/tandi/441-460/tandi441.html

[47] Joudo Larsen, J., Renshaw, L, Australian Institute of Criminology, *People trafficking in Australia*, Trends & issues in crime and criminal justice no. 441, http://www.aic.gov.au/publications/current%20series/tandi/441-460/tandi441.html

[48] *Criminal Code Act 1995, Criminal Code*, Official Gazette of the Republic of Slovenia 55/2008. Slovenia has transposed the EU Directive 2011/36/EU into the Criminal Code along with Council Directive 2004/81/EC that allows the state to issue a residence permit to those individuals that are subject to and victims of trafficking.

[49] Article 50, *Aliens Act*, Official Gazette Republic of Slovenia, No 50/2011.

[50] Bridging visa F (provided for 45 days for those will to assist police in investigations), Criminal Justice visa (issued to assist police ion their investigations), however, the principal visas issued for trafficking victims are the Witness Protection visa (permanent or temporary).

10.6 Detention

Immigration law extends to the detention of non-citizens who enter a state illegally. Moreover, people who have over stayed their visa or permit may be detained before being deported. Detaining non-citizens entering Australia has been the approach taken by government since the 1990s. Detention in Australia can be onshore or off-shore. The government has had a general approach to detaining illegal boat arrivals offshore in third countries. Onshore there is a combination of detention centres and community based detention. A similar approach is taken in the European Union and Slovenia with detentions centres and community (housing detention). Slovenia and the European Union largely deal with detention within the border of the Union.

As discussed in chapter four, in article 18 of the European Charter of Fundamental Rights 2000 provides the right to asylum is guaranteed, across the Union including Slovenia in accordance with rule of the Geneva Convention 1951 and 1967 Protocol. This right is not guaranteed in Australia, although Australia has ratified the international Geneva Convention 1951 and 1967 Protocol and assumed responsibility for managing asylum seekers, including detention. However, the detention of children and women for extended periods can pose significant challenges to government and the individuals involved. The mental and physical impact that long term detention has on refugees can be detrimental to their overall well-being. This is an area for further research, comparing Australia, Slovenia and the European Union.

Detention in Australia works against the interest of asylum seekers.[51] It does not allow the person to assimilate and begin to understand, practice and embrace the values of the state. The negative impacts on the wellbeing of the individual from detention can be physical or psychological or both. The detention of non citizens allows a state to verify whether the individual should be classified as a refugee. Upon release from detention they are provided with a humanitarian visa or permit to stay in the state. Individuals seeking asylum who have entered the Australian or Slovenian[52] territory illegally can be detained and placed in immigration detention[53] (either a detention centre onshore or off shore, or home placed accommodation).[54]

The grounds for detention are similar in both states and enable relevant authorities to ascertain the identity of the person and ensure they pose no health or security threat to the state.[55] Detention extends to adults and children, but, the respective

---

[51] Crock, M, (2000) *A sanctuary under review: where to from here for Australia's Refugee and Humanitarian Program*? University New South Wales, Law Journal, Vol 23(3), 246–250.

[52] Council Directive 2003/343/EC establishes the criteria for determining the MS responsible for assessing an asylum application, Official Journal of the European Union, L 50. Council Directive 2008/767/EC regarding the exchange of data between member states, Official Journal of the European Union, L 218. Council Directive 2000/2725/Establishing Eurodac for comparing fingerprints, Official Journal of the European Union, L 316.

[53] *Migration Act 1958*, Division 6.

[54] Ibid, Subdivision B.

[55] *Migration Act 1958*, s18. Article 51, Law on International Protection, Official Gazette of the Republic of Slovenia, 2011/11.

legislation does not provide for a minimum age. Both states have established different periods of time for the detention of asylum seekers. Article 51 of the Slovenian Law on International Protection provides that detention may be effective for no longer than 3 months and can be extended for a further 1 month. An applicant who is being removed from Australia or being granted a visa will cease being detained.[56] However, in practice, the detention of illegal entrants in both states and across the European Union can be for extended periods. The European Court of Justice in *Kadzoev*[57] confirmed that the 18 months is the maximum time for a person to be in detention, and must not be exceeded. The case also reaffirmed that the European Union's policy on detention considers the rights of individual being detained, whereby, a person's liberty cannot be denied. Upon release from detention a person may be granted a visa or permit to remain in the state. The visa or permit will allow the person, once eligible, to apply for citizenship. To be eligible, the individual will need to fulfill the residency requirements set out in accordance with the respective state's citizenship la). The detention and granting or a visa or permit enables Slovenia and Australia to determine who enters and stays in their respective territories. The legal framework that enables either state to regulate this area, contributes to their national identity. Thus, it is well settled that immigration laws is a pathway to citizenship and they play a small but important role in national identity.

10.7 Administration

In Slovenia, migration policy and legislation matters are the responsibility of the Ministry of Interior.[58] In Australia the equivalent is the Department of Immigration and Border Protection. The administration of the law is an important part of a state's sovereignty. These central agencies are responsible for the legislation and policy for immigration (on shore), and their respective Ministries for Foreign Affairs and Department of Foreign Affairs and Trade are delegated administrative functions and power to issue visas and permits from and in third countries.

Once an individual is granted a visa or permit and is present within the respective states, both ministries have sub offices. In Australia, the department has sub offices in each of the states such as Victoria. This allows the individual holding the visa to apply for citizenship. The Commonwealth ministry still determines the process for eligibility for either another visa, extending the visa or application for citizenship. In Slovenia, a similar role is delegated to the local Administrative Units. There are 58 Administrative Units spread across Slovenia. These Administrative Units are separate to the central Ministry of government. While Australia is a larger nation in

[56] *Migration Act 1958*, ss178, 181, 182 and 189.

[57] Case 357/09 *Kadzoev* [2009] ECR I-11189.

[58] Ministry of Interior Organisational Structure September 2013, http://www.mnz.gov.si/fileadmin/mnz.gov.si/pageuploads/SOJ/Organigrami/ORG._MNZ_1.9.2013_ang.pdf

size and population having a single focused department has ensured effective and efficient administration of immigration, naturalisation and citizenship law and policy.

The major difference is that the Australian model has a single ministry responsible for immigration, citizenship and naturalization policy and legislation. That is, the Department of Immigration and Border Protection's sole focus is on these policy areas. However, the Slovenian Ministry of Interior has a larger portfolio that is also responsible for immigration and naturalization, public sector administration and policing.[59] Slovenia is a smaller state but a single focus could benefit Slovenia rather than having the administration coupled with other government responsibilities, and, the administration delegated to Administrative Units. Therefore, it is suggested that the future administration of citizenship, immigration and naturalization of law and policy in Slovenia could come under a single Immigration or Citizenship Authority, Commission or Ministry. This recommendation has been confirmed in an interview with staff from the Slovenian Ministry of Foreign Affairs in July 2013. It is argued that, while being a very small part of national identity, is still important. Having a single Ministry responsible for citizenship and immigrations ensure effective administration and oversight of future policy and legislative development in these area. It could enable the state to better inform and enhance national identity.

10.8 Residency

Migration enables a non-citizen to enter and stay in Slovenia and Australia but does not guarantee that the person will obtain citizenship. This section will not discuss the application process for citizenship, but rather focus on the residency requirements to obtain citizenship.

An individual who has been granted a residency permit in Slovenia or in the case of Australia, permanent residence can apply for citizenship. However, the person must be 18 years of age and have been in Australia for a period of 4 years and not absent for more than 12 months. Where an individual has been resident for 12 months and has not been absent from the state for more than 90 days, they can also apply for citizenship.[60] The notable difference between Australia and Slovenia is apart from having the same age requirement the individuals must have resided for a longer period in Slovenia. That period constitutes 10 years and 5 years prior to making application must have been uninterrupted.[61] In both states, there is a requirement to have a level of proficiency in language. Apart from the requirements of having to prove good character (criminal record), financial status, health and public interest test (not a threat to the state), in Australia an individual must demonstrate their

---

[59] Ibid.

[60] *Australian Citizenship Act 2007*, sections 21 and 22.

[61] Article 10, *Law on Citizenship*, Official Gazette of the Republic of Slovenia 24/2007.

knowledge of the responsibilities and privileges that come with having citizenship.[62]

Nevertheless, there are different requirements for skilled migration. If an applicant has a scientific, economic (skilled) or cultural benefit to Slovenia, the residency requirement is significantly reduced to 1 year.[63] Australia has a longer period of 2 years during a period of 4 years for the same benefits to the state. However, the individual must have been a permanent resident for 12 months before making an application.[64]

Education is also an integral part of a nation's economic and social development, and therefore individuals who wish to obtain citizenship in Slovenia can do so by naturalization, and having resided in the territory for 7 years.[65] The residency requirement associated with education is 3 years less than the general 10 year requirement stated above. Furthermore, for those individuals that would suffer significant hardship, disadvantage, or are a spouse, defacto partner of an Australian citizen there is the ability for the Minister to treat the time period no matter the length as being permanently resident.[66] The residency requirement can also be altered where there is a person undertaking activities in Australia that are beneficial to the state. This includes sport, employment within an agency of the Commonwealth, medical research a PhD in a specialty field of research, or a person who is a writer engaged in the Arts.[67]

Once the application for citizenship has been lodged in Slovenia, Maša Kovič Dine argues that a 'decision to grant citizenship is made at two levels in Slovenia, with the initial decision made by the administrative unit of the applicants place of residence'.[68] Secondly, the decision will then go to the Interior Ministry for finalization.[69] The Australian Department of Immigration and Border Protection has responsibility for making the decision to grant or refuse citizenship. Upon approval the individual would be notified and would take the oath in Slovenia, and in the case of Australia the pledge and attend a citizenship ceremony. This separation in administrative function reinforces, as argued above, the need for a single agency in Slovenia

[62] *Australian Citizenship Act 2007*, section 21.

[63] Article 13, *Law on Citizenship*, Official Gazette of the Republic of Slovenia 24/2007.

[64] *Australian Citizenship Act 2007*, section 22B, the further requirements attached to section 22B include being present for a total of 480 days during the 4 year period, being present for 120 days in the period of 12 months, being resident in Australia throughout the 4 year before applying and was not present in Australia unlawfully.

[65] Article 12, *Law on Citizenship*, Official Gazette of the Republic of Slovenia 24/2007.

[66] *Australian Citizenship Act 2007*, section 22 (6) (9).

[67] Explanatory Statement, *Australian Citizenship Act 2007*, Special Residence Requirement – Legislative Instrument.

[68] Kovič Dine, M, *Naturalisation Procedures for Immigrants Slovenia*, EUDO Citizenship Observatory European University Institute, http://eudo-citizenship.eu/admin/?p=file&appl=countryProfiles&f=33-Slovenia.pdf

[69] The decision process allows an applicant to be heard and require information in accordance with the *Administrative Act*, Official Gazette of the Republic of Slovenia, No. 8/2010.

to not only administer both immigration and citizenship. The residency requirements imposed by both states are exclusionary policy measures that go some way to strengthening a state's national identity.

10.9 Bilateral Arrangements

To assist citizens moving between Slovenia and Australia, the states have established bilateral agreements in the areas of health care and social security. Moreover, the introduction of bilateral agreements strengthens the role of postnational citizenship, as citizens from both states are able to take certain benefits with them to another state. The establishment of bilateral agreements has confirmed the ongoing relationship Slovenia and Australia have had for many years. It also supports the purpose of this research to compare their respective citizenship, immigration, rights and private international laws. It is argued by states establishing these types of agreements enhances national identity, through the engagement and exchange of ideas between citizens. These agreements enhance cross border private activities such as migration and marriage.

10.9.1 Health Care

Slovenia and Australia have established an agreement for medical protection of their citizens should they be injured in either state.[70] However, the agreement is limited to certain visa types. For instance, a Slovenian citizen (Y) travelling to Australia under a 405 or 410 retirement visa is covered for health insurance,[71] however they cannot reside in Australia for more than 6 months in a 12 month period.[72] This extends to free treatment in a public hospital, subsidized medication, and out of hospital care. This will also be extended to the child who will study in Australia on a student visa from Slovenia, provided they have taken out Overseas Student Health Cover. X, (an Australian citizen) travelling to Slovenia under these arrangements, will also have access to Slovenia's health care system that includes hospital, medical, pharmaceutical, dental and ambulance services. Australia and Slovenia should investigate the opportunity to expand this agreement to also include other visa and permit types. It could be limited to only dual Slovenia and Australian citizens or those individuals

---

[70] Australian Government, Department of Immigration and Citizenship, http://www.immi.gov.au/visitors/retirement/410/

[71] *Health Care and Health Insurance Act 1992*, Official Gazette of the Republic of Slovenia 99.

[72] Australian-Slovenia Reciprocal Health Care Agreement, Australian Government, Department of Human Services, http://www.humanservices.gov.au/customer/enablers/medicare/reciprocal-health-care-agreements/slovenia. For proof the individual needs a current Slovenian Passport, evidence of eligibility of health insurance in Slovenia and European Health Insurance Card.

who have a connection to the state. Additionally, the agreement could be extended but limited to business and others who are making a valuable contribution to the state.

10.9.2 Social Security

Australia and Slovenia[73] have established a social security agreement[74] that allows the states to manage portable social security between their citizens.[75] For these arrangements to be effective, individuals must be citizens of either state and they must have been resident in either state.[76] For instance a person having dual citizenship[77] and having worked in Australia for 30 years,[78] is able to claim an age or disability pension.[79] These reciprocal arrangements enable a Slovenian[80] citizen to receive those payments in Australia.[81]

10.9.3 Tax

With the constant movement of people across international borders for work (skilled migration), states have developed tax arrangements to ensure their citizens do not pay income tax twice.[82] Slovenia and Australia do not have a double tax treaty. The European Australian Business Council[83] has recognized the twenty seven (27) MS making up the European Union as part of the strategic alliance for business between the European Union, its member states and Australia. Slovenia forms part of that alliance. As part of enhancing the economic activity between Slovenia and Australia, while small, and part of the broader objective of business relationships with the European Union and Australia, consideration should be provided to establishing a tax treaty.

---

[73] Agreement on Social Security between the Government of the Republic of Slovenia and the Government of Australia, Official Gazette of the Republic of Slovenia, No 36/2003.

[74] *Social Security (International Agreements) Act 1999*, Schedule 17.

[75] Agreement on Social Security between the Government of Australia and the Government of the Republic of Slovenia, 2002, www.aph.gov.au/.../House_of_Representatives_Committees?.../slove

[76] Article 5, Social Security Act, Official Gazette of the Republic of Slovenia, No. 105/06.

[77] *Social Security (International Agreements) Act 1999*, s19.

[78] Ibid, s23, Residence Factor is calculated at 300 months.

[79] *Social Security (International Agreements) Act 1999*, Schedule 2.

[80] Social Security Act, Official Gazette of the Republic of Slovenia, No. 105/06.

[81] Social Security (International Agreements) Act 1999, section 5, schedule 2.

[82] Slovenia: Double Tax Treaties, LowTax, Global Tax and Business Portal, http://www.lowtax.net/lowtax/html/slovenia/slovenia_double_tax_treaties.asp

[83] European Australian Business Council, http://www.eabc.com.au/

10.10 Conclusion

Despite immigration providing a pathway to citizenship, immigration along with citizenship is multidimensional. This chapter has confirmed a number of differences in the way the respective provide for international protection. Even though they maintain an open door, and liberal policy approach, the level of international protection available fluctuates significant. It is highly political and has over time polarized the community, whether in the EU, Slovenia and Australia. One of the major threats the world is facing is climate change, and it is arguably a matter of time before there is possibly large scale displacement of people. This will result in further mass migration.

Thus, environmental refugees will not only be a problem for Australia, but also the European Union and Slovenia, whether directly impacted or becoming destination countries for refugees. Former Australian Senator Kerry Nettle from the Australian Greens Party in 2007 put forward the Migration (Climate Refugees) Amendment Bill 2007, to create a new visa category so the government can recognise and accept those individuals displaced by environmental disasters due to climate change. Australia, Slovenia, and the European Union should expand their current legislation to allow for environmental refugees. Australia and Slovenia could include this proposal as a category under the current humanitarian visa.

Moreover, it is argued that immigration and the notion of the nation state and identity creates not only a sense of security, it also creates a sense of insecurity. The insecurity comes about as a result of the politicisation by the political elites of how immigration is to be managed. When borders are and were established following Westphalia, as by product of the development of the nation states was a defined border. It is the identity of the defined border that, goes some way to establishing insecurity about migrants entering a territory legally or illegally.

Streamlining the regulatory framework has many benefits, politically and economically. There are up to 23 European legal instruments transposed into Slovenian national immigration law. Slovenia could take a lead role and propose to the European Union to explore consolidating and simplifying the large number of Regulations, Directives and Decisions pertaining to migration (entry and stay) in member states. This would include all legislative instruments pertaining to economic and humanitarian entry and stay. Finally, the bilateral agreements between Australia and Slovenia, and while listing those agreements between Australia and the EU, do provide a symbolic relationship that, can support identity and cohesion.

References

Carens, J. (1992). Migration and morality: A liberal egalitarian perspective. In B. Barry & R. Goodin (Eds.), *Free movement: Ethical issues in the transnational migration of people and money* (pp. 25–47). New York: Havester Wheatsheaf.

Crock, M. (2000). A sanctuary under review: Where to from here for Australia's refugee and humanitarian program? *University New South Wales Law Journal, 23*, 246–250.

Crock, M., & Ghezelbash, M. (2010). Do loose lips bring ships? The role of policy, politics and human rights in managing unauthorised boat arrivals. *Griffith Law Review, 19*(2), 239.
Walzer, M. (1983). *Spheres of justice: A defense of pluralism and equity* (pp. 25–40). Oxford: Martin Robinson.
Wolfe, A. (1991). *Whose keeper: Social science and moral obligation* (pp. 1–23). Berkley/Los Angeles: University of California Press.

Chapter 11
Private International Law

Abstract The ability of a Slovene citizen to migrate from Slovenia to Australia or vice versa and engage with citizens in private activities is regulated by both states. Private International Law helps facilitate those private activities of a citizen such as marriage and divorce across international borders. This chapter demonstrates that citizenship is not the deciding factor when determining the choice of law and jurisdiction in private activities. It will also demonstrate how both jurisdictions have applied the legal principles of citizenship, residence and location (country) in private international law (marriage, divorce, paternity or maternity, maintenance, parental responsibility, international adoption, matrimonial property [immovable and common assets], inheritance and superannuation). Slovenia's *Private International Law and Procedures Act* (PIL Act) provides the basis for determining the choice of laws and jurisdiction in private activities. Australia does not have equivalent legislation and that responsibility rests with the judiciary. This chapter does not examine the procedural laws or the dispositive and indicative (Dispositive laws describe the rules of law which determine the rules (national or domestic) that are applied in a matter. The indicative rules identify the legal system, and in this case it could be either the civil law or common law of either Slovenia or Australia) rules to ascertain the governing law.

Keywords Divorce · Marriage · Maintenance · Parental responsibility · Matrimonial property · Inheritance · Superannuation · Tax

R. Walters, *National Identity and Social Cohesion in a Time of Geopolitical and Economic Tension: Australia – European Union – Slovenia*,
https://doi.org/10.1007/978-981-15-2164-5_11

11.1 Introduction

Laws established by states assist in the 'process by which citizens forge and sustain multi-stranded social relations that link them to societies of origin and settlement'.[1] Citizens being transnational[2] is not new but today states such as Slovenia and Australia have established laws to facilitate cross border private engagements. Private international law (PIL) can be traced back over many centuries to the civil law of Rome, when it was applied in disputes between citizens,[3] across international jurisdictions.[4] Karen Knop reinforces this view and argues that 'private international law is the private side of citizenship' and is triggered by travel and cross border engagements between citizens from different states.[5] As stated throughout this book citizenship is multidimensional and has been used to provide a legal status and unify a state's populations amongst others. The state has control over a territory and the people of the state are joined by citizenship. Having citizenship enables a person to move between states and encounter the foreign. This is the private act of the citizen. Furthermore, the private act of citizens constitutes an individual's decision to marry a foreigner, divorce, buy property and have a family. The state does not intervene in a citizen's private activities, other than providing the legal framework to enable this cross border private engagement. These concepts of citizenship enable citizens to participate in a globalized and regionalized world. However, PIL doesn't confirm the legal status of a citizen within a state, but rather, in the cosmopolitan[6] sphere of globalization enhances a citizen's individual freedom.

The international legal instruments established by the Hague Conference on PIL cover those private activities across international borders and include civil procedure, residence, divorce, and maintenance of children[7] and assist and guide states in PIL matters. Australia and Slovenia have a private legal framework that allows citizens from both states to take up residence and citizenship. Citizenship and residence form part of the connecting factors when determining which law will apply in private international law. However, as discussed later in this chapter citizenship only

---

[1] Koopmans, R., Statham, P, (2001) *How national citizenship shapes transnationalism*. A comparative analysis of migrants Claims-making in Germany, Great Britain and the Netherlands, Revue Eurohernna des Migrations Internationals, REMI, 63–100.

[2] Vetovec, S, (2001) *Transnationalism and Identity, Journal of Ethnic and Migration Studies*, Vol. 27, No. 4.

[3] Mortensen, R., Garnett, R., Keyes, M, (2011) *Private International Law in Australia*, 2nd Edition, LexisNexis Butterworths, 8.

[4] Stone, P, (2010) *EU Private International Law*, Second Edition, Elgar European Law, 3.

[5] Knop, K, (2008) *Citizenship Public and Private*, Law and Contemporary Problems, Vol. 71:309, 309–340.

[6] Kant, I (2003) *To Perpetual Peace: A Philosophical sketch*, in Ted Humphrey, Hackett Publishing, para 358.

[7] Hague Conference on Private International Law, http://www.hcch.net/index_en.php?act=text.display&tid=26

plays a minor role in determining the connecting factors in PIL matters. The connecting factors include residence, intention, family and employment.

11.2 Private International Law

Slovenia and Australia have taken a very different approach to the administration and regulation of private international law. A key feature of Australia's common law system is the responsibility of the judiciary to determine the choice of law. Australia, when compared to Slovenia has limited legislation specific to PIL. Slovenia on the other hand relies on legislation that codifies the legal principles. The next section discusses the approaches taken by Slovenia and Australia.

11.2.1 Slovenia

Slovenia has implemented the *Private International Law and Procedures Act* (PIL Act) of 1999. The PIL Act provides the basis for determining the law to be used in personal, family, property and other civil relations with an international element.[8] Kreso Puharič[9] states that Slovenia upon independence tried to maintain legislative continuity from the former Yugoslavia. However, this did not extend to all aspects of PIL, and did not account for European PIL.[10] Furthermore, Puharič highlights that the initial draft of the PIL Act considered private international law from Austria, Germany, and Switzerland, and retained some elements from the former Yugoslavia PIL. Today, the PIL Act reflects the modern day independent state of Slovenia within the European Union.[11]

The PIL Act operates between Slovenia and third countries such as Australia. The PIL Act determines where citizenship or residence, or both will apply in cross border personal activities such as marriage,[12] divorce,[13] matrimonial property,[14]

[8] Article 1, *The Private International Law and Procedure Act*, Official Gazette of the Republic of Slovenia No. 56/99.

[9] Puharič, K, (2003) *Private International Law in Slovenia*, in Yearbook of Private International Law, Kluwer Law International & Swiss Institute of Comparative Law, Vol 5, 155–157.

[10] Ibid.

[11] Ibid.

[12] Article 34, *The Private International Law and Procedures Act*, Official Gazette of the Republic of Slovenia, 56/99.

[13] Article 37, *The Private International Law and Procedures Act*, Offcial Gazette of the Republic of Slovenia, 56/99.

[14] Ibid, article 38.

relations between children and parents,[15] paternity or maternity,[16] maintenance,[17] international adoption,[18] wills[19] probate affairs,[20] personal names,[21] and guardianship.[22] The PIL Act also describes where residence will apply such as dual citizenship,[23] stateless persons,[24] or a person having temporary residence.[25] The PIL Act describes where the place or location (state law) will apply to such issues such as contracts with employees,[26] contracts for matrimonial property,[27] and personal injury while employed. Not only does the PIL Act provide certainty for Slovenian citizens, the legislation also assists the citizen and state by providing clarity of when citizenship, residence and location will be applied.

11.2.2 Australia

Australia has adopted a minimalist approach to developing legislation that specifically deals with PIL matters. Australia relies on the judiciary to determine whether residence or citizenship applies in private international law matters. Alex Mills argues that PIL has assisted states in retaining and strengthening their sovereignty, nationalism and identity.[28] Australia could consider whether adopting similar PIL legislation to that of Slovenia, would benefit the state and its citizens.

The benefit of legislative rules as Federick Hayek argues is that legislation is supposed to provide a greater level of legal certainty[29] and minimises the gaps in the law. Providing clarity in the law and its text allows the law to be easily understood by all its recipients. It is this legal certainty that could be improved in Australia and would close the gaps in the law. Australia could look to Slovenia's private international legal framework to assist.

---

[15] Ibid, article 42.

[16] Ibid, article 43.

[17] Article 44.

[18] Article 46.

[19] Article 33.

[20] Article 32.

[21] Article 14.

[22] Article 15.

[23] Article 10.

[24] Ibid, article 11.

[25] Ibid, article 11.

[26] Ibid, article 21.

[27] Ibid, article 39.

[28] Mills, A, (2009) *The Confluence of Public and Private International Law: Justice, Pluralism and Subsidiarity in the International ordering of Private Law*, Cambridge, 66.

[29] Hayek, F, (1973) *Law, Legislation and Liberty: A New Statement of Liberal Principles of Justice and Political Economy*, Routledge & Kegan Paul, Vol 1, 116–118.

Australia has adopted the common law principle of domicile via the *Domicile Act 1982*[30] *(The DA) (Cth).* Australia moved away from domicile of legitimacy, to domicile of residence.[31] In *Henderson*,[32] the court determined that domicile is the legal relationship between the citizen and the country where that person is able to invoke the country's laws as their own. Section 8 provides that a person has independent domicile at the age of 18. Children have the domicile of their parents or, in the case of adoption, domicile becomes that of the adoptive parents.[33]

An individual's domicile (of choice) is the country with which the individual has their closest connection.[34] The intention of a person to choose their domicile becomes important when determining the subtle differences between the common law principle of domicile and the civil law concept of habitual residence (residence). However, the domicile legislation of Australia does not extend to those cross border activities that have been provided for by the Slovenian PIL Act. The *Domicile Act* applies to domicile in or outside the area that constitutes Australia only[35] and clarifies the intention of a person to acquire domicile of choice.[36]

11.3 Domicile and Habitual Residence

Domicile and residence form part of the legal process to allow a person to acquire citizenship in time of state succession.[37] The common law of Australia has traditionally relied on domicile, whereas Slovenia (the EU) relies on residence or habitual residence. Nonetheless, the Hague Convention relating to the settlement of the conflicts between the law of nationality and the law of domicile was established in 1955 to overcome the conflict between the law of nationality and residence. The convention reinforces the principle that domicile rather than citizenship or nationality is applicable in PIL matters. However, the convention does not define or discuss the differences between domicile and habitual residence.[38] Despite this international convention being established in 1955,[39] it has only been signed by five countries

[30] *Domicile Act 1982*, Commonwealth, http://www.comlaw.gov.au/Details/C2008C00386

[31] Dirkis, M, (2013) *Nowhere man sitting in his nowhere land: The continuing saga of cross border arbitrage*, Revenue Law Journal, Vol 21, Issue 1, 5, 179.

[32] *Henderson v Henderson* [1965] 1 All E.R.

[33] *Domicile Act 1982*, s 9.

[34] Ibid, s10.

[35] Ibid, s3.

[36] Ibid, s10.

[37] The Saint-Germain – en-Laye Peace Treaty 1920. Treaty of Trianon 1921.

[38] Articles 4 & 5, Convention relating to the settlement of the conflicts between the law of nationality and the law of domicile was established in 1955, Hague Conference on Private International Law, http://www.hcch.net/index_en.php?act=conventions.text&cid=35

[39] Ibid.

with two countries fully ratifying the instrument. The legal instrument today may not be relevant, but neither Australia nor Slovenia has ratified the convention.[40]

According to Cavers the American courts have 'had to decide whether 'residence was intended as a synonym for domicile'.[41] Cavers argues that "habitual residence is not a half-way house between domicile and residence, but rather a connection between a person and a territory. This is distinct from the notion of a legal headquarters and can be freed from the constraining rules of the function of domicile.[42] Habitual residence concludes when the resident no longer continues to use the residence habitually.[43] Cavers further highlights that a person may not have residence anywhere, particularly if they are constantly mobile. Therefore, it will come down to the state of mind (the individual's intention) of where their residence is located. Additionally, it will be the connecting factors that are determined by a jurisdiction that will ultimately decide where a person habitually resides (resides).[44]

There are arguments for and against both principles, but in a global transient world the connecting factors provide greater certainty of where an individual is located. In other words, a person could have a base in Melbourne, Australia (property, family and investments), but spends four out of 5 years working and living in Jakarta, Indonesia. The concept of domicile is not uniform throughout the world and to a civil lawyer it means habitual residence.[45] Conversely, at common law it is regarded as an individual's permanent home. Although, increasingly, common law states such as Britain are applying habitual residence to matrimonial jurisdiction, recognition of foreign divorces and succession matters.[46] Habitual residence appears to be the most appropriate concept to use in meeting the demands of a modern day society.[47] Habitual residence (residence) provides greater flexibility and is more relevant today. This also demonstrates that Britain, like Australia and Slovenia has borrowed from civil law to modernize, where appropriate, its application of the law in private international legal matters.

Habitual residence has been defined to include 'the state in which the person or persons is concerned to be habitually residing and where the habitual center of their interests is located.[48] This is an important point, because the center of the individuals interests also becomes one of the most important tests to determining where the

---

[40] Hague Conference on Private International Law, Status Table, http://www.hcch.net/index_en.php?act=conventions.status&cid=35, Belgium, France, Luxembourg, Netherlands and Spain.

[41] Cavers, D, (1972) *Habitual Residence: A Useful Concept*, The American University Law Review, Vol 21, 480–483.

[42] Ibid.

[43] Ibid.

[44] Ibid.

[45] Fawcett, F., Carruthers, J., North, P, (2008) *Cheshire, North and Fawcett, Private International Law*, fourth edition, Oxford University Press, 154–195.

[46] The Law Reform Commission, Domicile and Habitual Residence http://www.lawreform.ie/_fileupload/consultation%20papers/wpHabitualResidence.htm

[47] Ibid.

[48] Ibid.

person habitually resides. In considering the center of the individuals interests, the courts may consider a number of things such as employment and family situation,[49] and the length and continuity of residence.[50] Both domicile and habitual residence as legal principles are also used in accordance with European law - Brussels I Regulation.[51] Brussels I and European PIL operates where the defendant is domiciled in one of the member states, other than their state of origin.[52] Brussels I repeatedly refers to both domicile and habitual residence in civil and commercial matters where a court is required to determine the applicable laws in private matters, except revenue, customs or administration.[53] Brussels I,[54] as Peter Stone puts it, is the most important legal instrument in the sphere of PIL within the European Union.[55] It extends to natural persons, marriage, bankruptcy, wills and succession as well as social security. The European Court of Justice[56] has interpreted 'residence' as 'habitual' or 'normal residence', pointing to an underlying attachment with a state. The PIL law espoused by the EU further contributes to the overall, but, limited identity the Union has created since the end of WW II.

For matrimonial proceedings and parental responsibility for children located in the European Union - Brussels II was introduced.[57] It applies to civil matters in relation to divorce, legal separation or marriage annulment, but does not extend to grounds for divorce or property consequences of the marriage.[58] In *Marinos v Marinos*[59] the court had to decide on what constituted habitual residence. The case related to a Greek man and an English woman who married, had children and, for a period worked and resided in England. The court calculated the time spent in Greece and the United Kingdom, in addition to other connecting factors (center of their interests) such as employment and family. This demonstrates that there are many considerations a court will take into account when determining habitual residence. The court ruled that habitual residence in a member state will be where the

[49] Case 90/97, *Swaddling v Adjudication Officer* [1999] ECR I-1075, 29. The case also referred to Case 76/76 *Di Paolo v Officer of National de l'Emploi* [1997] ECR 315 paragraphs 17 to 20.

[50] Case 90/97, *Swaddling v Adjudication Officer* [1999] ECR I-1075, 29. The case also referred to Case 76/76 *Di Paolo v Officer of National de l'Emploi* [1997] ECR 315 paragraphs 17 to 20.

[51] Article 2, Council Regulation (EC) No 44/2001, on jurisdiction and the recognition and enforcement of judgments in civil and commercial matters, Official Journal of the European Union L 12/1.

[52] Ibid, article 2.

[53] Ibid.

[54] Council Regulation (EC) 44/2001, on jurisdiction and the recognition and enforcement of judgments in Civil and Commercial matters, Official Journal of the European Union L 12.

[55] Stone, P, (2010) *EU Private International Law*, second Edit, Elgar European Law, 6.

[56] Wouters, J, (2010) *Residence of Individuals in EU law*, Institute for International Law, Katholieke Universiteit Leuven, Working Paper No. 148.

[57] Council Regulation 2201/2003 concerning jurisdiction and he recognition and enforcement of judgments in matrimonial matters and the matters of parental responsibility, Official Journal of the European Union L 338.

[58] Ibid.

[59] *Marinos v Marinos* [2007] EWHC 2047 (Fam).

matrimonial home (the family home) is located.[60] The court also ruled the connecting factors were based on the central 'interests' such as employment, education, children, land (state) of birth, time spent in the state, and the state and emotional attachment, including a commitment that was retained by individuals to these connecting factors.[61]

Similar to domicile (of origin and choice), habitual residence can be categorized as the ordinary residence and the voluntariness of residence.[62] A person may lose their residence: for example, a Slovenian who has permanent residency in Australia could lose that residency where they have committed a crime against the state. Nevertheless, there is an overlap between the meaning of ordinary residence and habitual residence, whereby ordinary residence means that the person must be habitually and normally resident, in a particular place.[63] That includes the partial or temporary absences from that residence such as a citizen being on holidays, or employed to work in another state for a short period.

In *Bank of Dubai v Abbas*[64] the court, rather than refer to habitual residence, stated that 'residence' requires a settled place of abode with a substantial degree of performance or continuity. Additionally, the presumption of a substantial connection from 3 months' residence provides no guidance as to whether the person was, or has become, a resident. While this case related to international trade, it nevertheless, demonstrates the different permutations the courts have defined to be residence, habitual residence or domicile. Nonetheless, there is a key theme running through residence, habitual residence and domicile. In other words, the connecting factors will in most circumstances include the period of time, intention of the person, nature and circumstances of the individual's or parties' residence. However, being a concept of common law, domicile is defined by a person always having a domicile but a person can only have one domicile at any one time.[65] Furthermore, it can be defined as 'a person's domicile that connects him with a system of law for the purposes of determining a range of matters principally related to status of property (immovable).[66] David Cavers argues there has been a shift away from domicile to habitual residence as the connecting factors in private international law. This has come about because of the increasingly mobile population and the introduction of dual citizenship.[67] However, and even though there has been a shift from domicile to habitual residence, it is argued that domicile is a rigid concept when compared to habitual residence.

---

[60] Ibid.

[61] Ibid.

[62] *Nessa v The Chief Adjudication Officer and Another* [1999] UKHL 41; [1999] 4 All ER 677; [1999] 1 WLR 1937.

[63] Ibid.

[64] *Bank of Dubai v Abbas* [1997] ILPr 308.

[65] *V v V* [2011] EWHC 1190 (Fam).

[66] Hong Kong Law Reform Commission and the Consultation Paper on Rules for Determining Domicile, HKLRCCP, 12004, PARA 1.2.

[67] Cavers, D, (1971) *Habitual Residence: A Useful Concept?*, The American University Law Review, 476.

In *Korkein hallinto-oikeus*[68] it was stated that habitual residence must be distinguished from mere presence, and normally be for a certain period of duration. It was also determined that in family law disputes, determining habitual residence of a child, further contributing factors needed to be understood such as the age of the child, leisure activities, schooling, friends, command of the local language, and contact with other family members including relatives.[69] What the court is saying is that one test will not fit all circumstances and must be evaluated on its merits.[70] However, under common law, habitual residence has been more problematic. The High Court of Australia in *LK v Director General, Department of Community Services*[71] stated there was a lack of uniformity in determining habitual residence, and that the settled intention was necessary to understand what constituted the principle. Moreover, in Australia, in matters concerning tax, the expression 'permanent place of abode' is also used to determine whether a person has permanent residence or the residency requirement of 183 days is met in order for tax to be paid. In *Applegate*[72] the expression 'place of abode' was qualified as being the physical surroundings in which the person lives. Therefore, similarities between the use of the word and domicile exist, as they both refer to where the person lives. In other words, where the person permanently resides. European law in accordance with Council Regulation 2201/2003 has accommodated both habitual residences for most member states of the European Union, and for the United Kingdom and Ireland, domicile can be used.[73] Thus, there is clear recognition by the European Union that domicile, being a common law principle still, operates within those MS that use common law.

It is difficult to distinguish between domicile and habitual residence. Even so, and while, the differences are subtle, domicile is arguably more rigid. It is further argued that domicile is the legal registration of a citizen to a state where that citizen has their permanent home. On the other hand, habitual residence is where a citizen is resident, no matter in what state they reside. Therefore, a citizen may not be habitually resident in the state in which they were domiciled or where they have citizenship. It is further argued that the connecting factors including employment, family, birth, property, investments and the intention of the person will provide guidance to the courts in determining what law will apply. Slovenia, unlike Australia, provides greater clarity under article 10 of the PIL Act that states where a persons' residence cannot be determined, no matter where that person holds citizenship, the 'closest ties' will be the determining factor of what laws will apply. Domicile con-

[68] Case – 523/07 *Korkein hallinto-oikeus* [2009], http://eur-lex.europa.eu/LexUriServ/LexUriServ.do?uri=CELEX:62007CJ0523:EN:HTML

[69] Ibid.

[70] Ibid.

[71] *LK v Director-General, Department of Community Services* [2008] FamCAFC 81 INCADAT HC/E/AU 995.

[72] *Applegate v Federal Commissioner of Taxation* (1979) 9 ATR 899, 910–11, 79ATC 4307, 4317.

[73] Council Regulation (EC) 2201/2003, concerning the jurisdiction and the recognition and enforcement of judgements in international matters and the matters or parental responsibility, Official Journal of the European Union L 338.

tinues to be a common law principle applicable to PIL and habitual residence originated by the civil law. Even though it is difficult to separate the two principles, it will be the connecting factors and center of interest, which ultimately determines the jurisdictional laws that apply.

11.4 Private Activities Across International Borders

The table below outlines how citizenship, residence and location applies in private international law matters between Slovenia and Australia (Table 11.1).

Comparatively, there are many similarities associated with the application of citizenship, residence and location in private international law between the two jurisdictions. Furthermore, the similarities confirm that the universality of legal principles both states have adopted, resulting in the rules pertaining to private activities, are close to being the same. Therefore, it is argued that even though there are many similarities between Slovenia and Australia, the rules reflect the national identities of both states. Firstly, Slovenia has implemented the PIL Act that has provided clear, concise and easy to follow rules in PIL matters. Australia has PIL rules throughout the common law (the judiciary). Despite the similarities, marriage is based on citizenship law of where the marriage was registered.[74] However, there are many variables between both states legal frameworks in the area of cross border private

Table 11.1 Table outlining where citizenship applies in transnational private activities

Private activities (across international borders)	Residence		Citizenship/ nationality		Location
	Australia	Slovenia	Australia	Slovenia	Slovenia/ Australia
Marriage	X	X	X	X	
Divorce	X	X	X	X	
Paternity or maternity	X	X	X	X	
Child maintenance	X	X	X	X	
Parental responsibility	X	X	X		
International adoption			X	X	
Matrimonial property (purchase of immovable)					X
Matrimonial property (common assets)	X	X	X	X	
Inheritance (succession)					X
Will probate			X[a]		X
Superannuation	X	X			

[a]Citizenship at the time of death

[74]Article 35 & 36, *The Private International Law and Procedures Act*, Official Gazette of the Republic of Slovenia 56/99.

activities such as marriage and divorce. Below outline examples of the complex nature of choice laws that apply in private (cross border) activities. It will also be confirmed that citizenship has little relevance in marriage, divorce, parental responsibility, child maintenance, purchasing property, inheritance and personal income tax.

11.4.1 Marriage

The registration of the marriage in Australia can occur after the marriage has been finalised in Slovenia. That is, the marriage in Slovenia will be deemed to be valid when the marriage certificate has been issued and the registration concluded in Slovenia.[75] Despite this process in Slovenia, a (foreign) marriage in Slovenia (between a Slovenian and an Australian) will be recognized under Part VA of the Australian *Marriage Act 1961*.[76] The marriage of a Slovene and an Australian citizen in Australia will be valid in Slovenia, provided the marriage was valid under Australian law.[77] The minimum age for marriage in either state is generally the age of 18. However, section 12 of the Australian *Marriage Act 1961* enables a person between the age of 16 and 18 to be married provided the courts approve. With special permission from a Social Work Centre, individuals under the age of 18 can be married in Slovenia. However, and unlike Australian law, Slovenia does not specify a minimum age.[78]

Pre-marital contracts exist in both Australia[79] and Slovenia.[80] These can be established between spouses in relation to matrimonial property and used at the time of divorce to manage the settlement of property and assets.[81] The general principle will be dividing the assets equally between the parties.[82] During a marriage the parties can establish a contract in order to divide the property between them.[83] Similar to the process in Australia, in Slovenia a marriage contract can be arranged (in

[75] *Marriage Act 1961*, Part VA – Recognition of foreign marriages,

[76] Ibid.

[77] Article 36 and 82, *The Private International Law and Procedure Act*, Official Gazette of the Republic of Slovenia 56/99.

[78] Article 23, *Law on Marriage and Family Relations*, Official Gazette of the Republic of Slovenia 69/2004.

[79] *Family Law Act 1975*, sections 90B, 90D, 90UB, 90UC, 90UD,

[80] Tratnik, M *Unexpected Circumstances*, Slovenian Report, University Maribor, www.unexpected-circumstances.org/Slovenian%20report.doc

[81] Article 39, *The Private International Law and Procedures Act*, Official Gazette of the Republic of Slovenia 56/99.

[82] Ibid, article 59.

[83] Ibid, article 58.

Slovenia) between the parties but the technical arrangements for recognition are slightly different as there is a requirement for notarial recording.[84]

11.4.2 Divorce

Divorce in both states is based on citizenship and residence.[85] The grounds for divorce in Slovenia constitutes that the marriage is unbearable.[86] In the case of Australia the marriage must have been broken for not less than 12 months before the application for divorce.[87] The order should not be made where it is likely the couple will continue to reside together.[88] A major difference is that the Australian legislation goes further than the marriage laws of Slovenia, by specifying a 12 month period of separation. The divorce between an Australian and Slovenian will be recognized by Slovenia when undertaken in Australia.[89] However, should the divorce not be able to be achieved in Australia, article 37 (3) of the PIL Act would allow the laws of Slovenia to be used. This is provided that one of the partners to the marriage is permanently residing in Slovenia. There is further flexibility provided for Slovene citizens to divorce. Should the partners to the marriage are not permanently residing in Slovenia, and the law of Australia cannot be used, the couple can opt to use Slovenian law to dissolve the marriage.[90]

A divorce undertaken in Slovenia will be recognized by Australia where the applicant has their ordinary residence in Slovenia. However, residence must have continued for not less than 1 year, or, the last place of cohabitation.[91] The Slovenia PIL Act specifies that the divorce will be recognised on the basis of permanent residence. The *Family Law Act 1975* defines 'ordinary residence to mean the couple are 'habitually resident'. Therefore, the divorce of a Slovenian and Australian (couple) can be undertaken in either state. Australia is a signatory to the Hague Convention on the Recognition of Divorces and Legal Separation 1970. However, according to the Hague Conference on International Law August 2013, Slovenia has not ratified this convention, and therefore, it should ratify this international legal instrument. Moreover, Slovenia has determined that where individuals are from different states it could be the cumulative laws of those states that apply.[92] For instance, in a divorce

[84] Article 129, *Notaries Act*, Official Gazette of the Republic of Slovenia, No. 2/2007.

[85] *Family Law Act 1975*, Section 39 (3). Article 37 *The Private International Law and Procedures Act*, Official Gazette of the Republic of Slovenia 56/99.

[86] Article 65, *Marriage and Family Relations*, Official Gazette of the Republic of Slovenia, 69/2004.

[87] *Family Law Act 1975*, s48.

[88] Ibid.

[89] Ibid, article 37.

[90] Ibid.

[91] *Family Law Act 1975*, s104 (3).

[92] Article 37 *The Private International Law and Procedures Act*, Official Gazette of the Republic of Slovenia 56/99.

that is in dispute under Australian law, the law of Slovenia may be used provided the spouses (citizens) are from either state. Divorce in Slovenia will be recognized under Australian law.[93] This will apply where the individual is resident in Slovenia for more than 1 year, and the last cohabitation or their residence was in Slovenia.[94]

11.4.3 Parental Responsibility

Parental responsibility and child maintenance are closely linked. The laws pertaining to access and custody are based on residence. In other words, a person (parent) upon divorce will have responsibility for the custody for a child or children, more than the other parent. The Australian *Family Law Act 1975* (Cth) enables the Australian Family Court to decide on matters relating to a child's custody, guardianship and access. In Slovenia, the Marriage and Family Relations Act is the relevant legislation.[95] The Slovenian constitution[96] (also) provides that parents have a duty to maintain, educate and raise their children. Article 42 provides that where the parents and child are citizens of different nation states, and do not have permanent residence in the same state, the law that will apply, is the state where the child is a citizen.[97] Nevertheless, both states have ensured parents maintain an obligation to care for their children. Where the marriage between an Australian and Slovene citizen has broken down, and divorce has been settled, with the Australian citizen returning to Australia, there could be disagreement on custody arrangements. As the couple prior to separation resided in Slovenia, (in accordance with article 104 of the Law on Marriage and Family Relations)[98] a Slovene court could determine that the agreement between the parents was in the best interests of the child. That is, where there is agreement that the child would visit Australia every 2 years to ensure the child has access to other parent, the court is likely to ensure this agreement is fulfilled.

However, upon return to Australia the former husband (X) wanted to revise the agreement and have the child permanently migrate to Australia in order for X to raise the child. Thus, when back in Australia, X filed with the Australian courts a new agreement to have permanent custody. The original order issued in Slovenia had been registered in Australia, and as such, has the same effect as being an order made by a court in Australia.[99] An Australian court that is aware of the order cannot

[93] *Family Law Act 1975*, s104, captures private international law regarding recognition of overseas decrees.

[94] Ibid.

[95] Marriage and Family Relations Act, Official Gazette of the Republic of Slovenia, No. 15/76.

[96] Article 54, The Constitution of the Republic of Slovenia, Official Gazette Republic of Slovenia Nos. 33/91-I, 42/97, 66/2000, 24/03, 69/04, 68/06, and 47/13.

[97] Article 42, Marriage and Family Relations Act, Official Gazette of the Republic of Slovenia, No. 15/76.

[98] Official Gazette of the Republic of Slovenia, No. 15/76.

[99] Family Law Act 1975, ss70G and 70H.

exercise jurisdiction over the order unless it is relation to the child and not the parents, to ensure the welfare of the child is not adversely impacted.[100] Therefore, at all time, the interest of the child is put at the forefront. Additionally, an Australian court has no jurisdiction in cancel the Slovenian order.[101] This process has been reaffirmed by article 73 of the Slovenian PIL Act. Thus, where there is a dispute between the parents and because X has returned to Australia and no longer permanently resident in Slovenia, the order remains in force[102] Furthermore, where the mother and child have maintained their residence in Slovenia, and, both being Slovene citizens, jurisdiction will continue to be Slovenia.

11.4.4 Child Maintenance

Maintenance is based on common nationality and residence. A Slovenian court can have jurisdiction to establish or contest paternity or maternity, when the defendant is not permanently resident in Slovenia.[103] The court of Slovenia may also have jurisdiction when the parties are Australian citizens and one of the individuals has permanent residence in Slovenia.[104] X (an Australian citizen) has remained in Australia, and is obliged to continue to pay their maintenance obligations for child and spouse.[105] A maintenance assessment is undertaken to ensure there is agent reimbursement or arrears of payments made under a court order from Slovenia requiring the Australian citizen to pay maintenance.[106] Slovenia is listed in schedule 2[107] that has been identified by Australian legislation as a reciprocating jurisdiction. An assessment is undertaken of both parents to determine the level of support[108] necessary for the child.[109] The child must be an Australian citizen or resident in Australia when the application was made to the Registrar.[110]

Maintenance liability will remain valid while both individuals remain resident in Australia and the other in Slovenia.[111] However, this liability will cease on the day

[100] Ibid, s70J.

[101] Ibid, 70k.

[102] Article 73, *The Private International Law and Procedures Act*, Official Gazette of the Republic of Slovenia 56/99.

[103] Article 71, *The Private International Law and Procedures Act*, Official Gazette of the Republic of Slovenia 56/99.

[104] Ibid, article 72.

[105] Schedule 2 *Child Support (Registration and Collection) Regulations* 1988.

[106] Sections 4 and 18A *Registration and Collection Act 1989*, Regulation 4A *Registration and Collection Regulations 1988*.

[107] Child Support (Assessment) Act 1989, section 25A.

[108] Child Support (Assessment) Act 1989, section 25A.

[109] Ibid, Part 5.

[110] Ibid, s24.

[111] Registration and Collection Act 1989, section 4.

both individuals are no longer resident in Australia, or, one of the individuals is no longer resident in Slovenia, or, a reciprocating nation state.[112] Similar arrangements apply where a child[113] and spouse[114] can obtain maintenance under Slovenian law.[115] The Convention on the International Recovery of Child Support and other Forms of Family Maintenance 2007 has been established to assist cross jurisdictional issues surrounding divorce and child maintenance. The European Union has signed this convention. Australia has neither signed nor ratified the convention. Therefore, it is recommended that Australia sign and ratify this legal instrument (Slovenia does not have to sign or ratify this legal instrument).[116] The international legal instrument aims to improve co-operation between nation states for the international recovery of child and family maintenance.

Nevertheless, The United Nations Convention on the Recovery Abroad of Maintenance 1956 of which Australia[117] and Slovenia are signatories can be found in respective legislation from either jurisdiction.[118] The Convention on the Recovery Abroad of Maintenance has been in place since 1956,[119] and is given effect by section 111 of the Australian *Family Law Act 1975* and Regulations 40–56 of the *Family Law Regulations 1984* (Cth). Slovenia under succession of the former Yugoslavia signed and ratified the convention on 31 December 1956.[120] The principles of the 1956 convention were used and updated in the modern day text of the 2007 Convention on the Recovery of Child Support and Other Forms of Family Maintenance. Child maintenance that has been established by a Slovenian court will cease when the Australian Child Support Agency (ACSA) registers a subsequent overseas maintenance liability in accordance with regulation 30AA(1)[121] or, accepts and application for a child support assessment, or, both parties cease to be residents in Australia or Slovenia.[122] However, where there is a dispute over maintenance, a Slovenian court could have jurisdiction where the individual (defendant) does not

[112] Schedule 2 Child Support (Registration and Collection) Regulations 1988.

[113] Article 103 and 123 Marriage and Family Relations Act, Official Gazette of the Republic of Slovenia 69/2004.

[114] Article 50 and 81 Marriage and Family Relations Act, Official Gazette of the Republic of Slovenia 69/2004.

[115] Marriage and Family Relations Act, Official Gazette of the Republic of Slovenia 69/2004.

[116] The Hague Conference on Private International Law, http://www.hcch.net/index_en.php?act=conventions.status&cid=131

[117] Child Support (Assessment) Act 1989, Child Support (Assessment) Regulations 1989, Child Support (Registration and Collection) Regulations *1988*.

[118] Section 111, Family Law Act 1975 and Regulations 40 to 56 Family Law Regulations 1984. Marriage and Family Relations Act, Official Gazette of the Republic of Slovenia 69/2004.

[119] Convention on the Recovery Abroad of Maintenance, United Nations, Treaty Series, vol. 268, p. 3, and vol. 649, p. 330.

[120] The Hague Conference on Private International Law, http://hcch.cloudapp.net/smartlets/sfjsp?interviewID=hcchcp2012&t_lang=en

[121] Child Support (Registration & Collection) Act 1988.

[122] Child Support (Registration & Collection) Act 1988, ss152(2) and 4(1),

have permanent residence in Slovenia and the child permanently resides in Slovenia. A Slovenia court will have jurisdiction where both parents are Slovene citizens residing in Slovenia, or where individual is a minor and a Slovenia citizen.[123]

An Australian citizen who is not resident in Slovenia, but, the mother being a Slovene citizen resides in Ljubljana a Slovene court can have jurisdictions. This will also apply where the parent's last joint permanent residence was in Slovenia and the mother continues to reside in Slovenia during the court proceedings.[124] Maintenance payments will usually conclude when the child reaches the age of 18.[125] However, both states have extended the law to allow for further maintenance support beyond the age of 18, although somewhat under different arrangements. In Australia a person over 18 years of age may obtain continued support for ongoing schooling, illness, or the individual has a physical or mental disability.[126] Article 118 of the Marriage and Family Relations Act of Slovenia provides that a child over the age of 18 who has a physical or mental handicap can still be supported through maintenance payments. Article 118 does not extend to those children who are undertaking schooling. Even so, it could be argued a court in Slovenia may decide that ongoing support for the child beyond 18 years is required where they are continuing schooling. This would only be attainable where an extension of parental rights has not been lodged in time. Thus, the courts can step in and make a decision.

11.4.5 Property Purchase

Citizenship and residence are not the deciding factors in relation to property purchase. The status of ownership will be the place where the immovable is located (*lex rei sitae*).[127] A married couple from Slovenia and Australia can take ownership of property in either state. Foreigners are able to own property in Slovenia,[128] and Australia[129] without being a citizen of either state. However, unlike Slovenia foreign ownership of property in Australia is not a constitutional right. Article 68 of the Slovenian constitution, states that aliens may acquire ownership rights to real estate that allows a foreigner to own property in Slovenia. Whereas, the Australian constitution in accordance with s51 xxxi provides that acquisition of property on just

[123] Article 74, *The Private Internal Law and Procedure Act*, Official Gazette of the Republic of Slovenia 56/99.

[124] Ibid.

[125] Child Support (Registration and Collection) Act 1988, Child Support (Assessment) Act 1989, Law on Marriage and Family Relations, Official Gazette of the Republic of Slovenia, 69/2004.

[126] Child Support (Assessment) Act 1989, s151B.

[127] Article 18, *The Private International Law and Procedures Act*, Official Gazette of the Republic of Slovenia 56/99.

[128] Article 68, The Constitution of the Republic of Slovenia, Official Gazette Republic of Slovenia Nos. 33/91-I, 42/97, 66/2000, 24/03, 69/04, 68/06, and 47/13.

[129] Foreign Investment Board, http://www.firb.gov.au/content/real_estate/real_estate.asp

terms by the Commonwealth or any State, or, a person for any purpose in respect of which the Parliament has power to make laws. At the constitutional level, Australia focuses on property rights and the acquisition of that property by the State. Nevertheless, depending on where the property is acquired in Australia, for example, property acquired by the state in Victoria (just terms through compensation[130]), will be subject to that state's legislation,[131] unlike the national laws of Slovenia. The process for the purchase of property by citizens is similar in both Slovenia and Australia.

The purchase and ownership of property is undertaken under two different systems of law in Australia and Slovenia. Australia, adopting the Torrens Title system that can also been found in the United Kingdom, Ireland, Malaysia, Singapore, Iran, Canada and Madagascar, operates by land titles register detailing the information of the land (size and location and other interests) in a title. That title deed ensures the citizen or foreigner has a registered interest in that land, which is protected by government (in the state of Victoria Australia this is undertaken through the Transfer of Land Act 1958).[132] Under the common law, a landowner must be able to prove they have ownership of that land, and protects the citizen if challenged. The court in *Breskar*[133] stated that the Torrens system is not a system of registration, but rather, a system of title 'by' registration.

Purchasing of property in Slovenia is undertaken under a different legal framework to Australia. Real estate, land and rights *in rem* is registered, however the obligatory rights need not need to be registered. Unlike Australia's systems where the land is registered and recorded accurately, in Slovenia, registration of land is undertaken in 'good faith' and is based on the land registry being accurate, with no guarantee of a title deed.[134] Citizens of other EU MS can purchase property unrestricted in Slovenia. The purchase of property can be undertaken, unless the law of the state has restricted the purchase of property to Slovenes. A Slovenian citizen purchasing property in Australia is subject to the restrictions set out by the Foreign Investment Review Board (FIRB).[135] The Australian Government, Foreign Investment Board has established rules and policy principles that regulate the foreign acquisition of property (residential, commercial, shares and other business) such as dwellings throughout Australia. The restrictions on a Slovenian citizen will be dependent of their residency status, whether a non-resident, or, permanent

---

[130] Legislation allows the government to acquire property such as for building roads and infrastructure.

[131] Victorian Legislation for the purchase and sale of property includes the *Property Law Act 1958, Sale of Land Act 1962, Sale of Land Regulations 1962, Transfer of Land Act 1958, Transfer of Land (General) Regulations 2004, Trustees Act 1958.*

[132] Transfer of Land Act 1958 (Victoria, Australia), s42.

[133] *Breskar v Wall* (1971) 126 CLR 376, 381.

[134] Law on Land Registry, Official Gazette of the Republic of Slovenia, 33/95. Law on Land Cadastre, Official Gazette of the Social Republic of Slovenia 16/74 and 42/86.

[135] *Foreign Acquisitions and Takeovers Act 1975, Foreign Acquisitions and Takeovers regulations 1989, Foreign Takeovers Notices) Regulations 1975.*

resident.[136] For example, where a Slovenian who does not reside in Australia, while being able to invest in real estate in Australia, they can only do so, where this will add to the housing stock.

11.4.6 Inheritance

The laws related to inheritance are based on where the property is located. In determining the jurisdiction and laws to apply, movable (*lex domicile*) and immovable property (*lex situs*) is to be dealt with separately. This distinction was discussed in *Lewis v Balshaw*[137] whereby, the forum of choice will be the jurisdiction where the deceased was domiciled at the time of death unless the representative is disqualified under the law of the forum.[138] This was reaffirmed in *Pipon v Pipon*[139] where the court stated movable property should be governed by the law of the place where the deceased was resident at the time of death. The Australian law will apply where a will with an appointed executor[140] has been determined.[141] However, where there is no will, contract or other agreement, the assets located in Slovenia, will be subject to the Slovenia law. The law of the place of where the testator was resident at the time the will was made[142] applies. The probate affairs and will, is based on the country of citizenship at the time of death.[143] The court has exclusive jurisdiction to announce the death of a Slovene citizens in Slovenia.[144] In situations where the citizenship of the person cannot be determined, Article 81 of the PIL Act provides the Slovenian courts have exclusive jurisdiction.[145] The jurisdiction of the court is also

[136] Australian Government, Foreign Review Board, Guidance Note 3, Australia's Foreign Investment Policy Residential Real Estates, http://www.firb.gov.au/content/guidance/downloads/gn3_jan2012.pdf

[137] *Lewis v Balshaw* (1935) 54 CLR 188 in Reid Mortensen, Richard Garnett, Mary Keyes, *Private International Law in Australia*, 2nd Edition, LexisNexis Butterworths, 2011, 520.

[138] Ibid.

[139] *Pipon v Pipon* (1744) Amb 25; 27 ER 14, in Reid Mortensen, Richard Garnett, Mary Keyes, *Private International Law in Australia*, 2nd Edition, LexisNexis Butterworths, 2011, 270–275.

[140] Section 18 *Administration and Probate Act 1958*. It is encouraged two executors are appointed in the event one dies. *Wills Act 1997*.

[141] *Bremer v Freeman* (1857) 10 Moo PC 306; 14 ER 508.

[142] Article 33, *The Private International Law and Procedures Act*, Official Gazette of the Republic of Slovenia 56/99.

[143] Article 32 & 33, *The Private International Law and Procedures Act*, Official Gazette of the Republic of Slovenia 56/99.

[144] Article 78, *The Private International Law and Procedures Act*, Official Gazette of the Republic of Slovenia 56/99.

[145] Article 81, *The Private International Law and Procedures Act*, Official Gazette of the Republic of Slovenia 56/99.

based on the principle of domicile where the deceased had their permanent or temporary residence.[146]

Moreover, the testamentary capacity and the form of a will is covered under sections 32 and 33 PIL. In 1989, the Hague Conference on Private International Law established the Convention on the Law Applicable to Succession to Estates of Deceased Persons; however, neither the EU, nor any member state of the EU including Slovenia, nor Australia are contracting parties.[147] This convention assists states and their citizens in determining the applicable law to succession of estates of deceased person. However, it does not apply to property upon death, disposing of property upon death, matrimonial property, pension or insurance plans.[148] Therefore, it is recommended that Slovenia and Australia sign the convention. However, the UNIDROIT Convention providing a Uniform Law on the Form of an International Will 1973,[149] came into force in Slovenia as a successor to the former Yugoslavia. In Victoria, Australia the UNIDROIT Convention providing a Uniform Law on the Form of an International Will 1973, was only recently included into domestic legislation. The convention deals with personal capacity of the testator or witness relating to the revocation, destruction or modification of wills. This legal instrument ensures a consistent approach between states. Slovenia ratified the convention in 1992. Slovenia and Australia are both signatories to the Hague Convention on the Conflict of Laws relating to the Form of Testamentary Dispositions 1961.[150] The convention provides the basis for confirming the place where a testator was made, nationality possessed by the testator, place where the testator was domiciled or had habitual residence at the time of death.[151] Therefore, reaffirming an earlier point that both domicile and habitual residence are used to determine jurisdiction of private international legal matters.

[146] Article 177, Inheritance Act, Official Gazette of the Republic of the Socialist Republic of Slovenia, No. 15/76,

[147] The Hague Conference on Private International Law, http://www.hcch.net/index_en.php?act=conventions.status&cid=62

[148] Article 1, Convention on the Law Applicable to Succession to Estates of Deceased Persons 1989,

[149] *Wills Amendment (International Wills) Bill 2011*, Explanatory Memorandum. The convention also came into force in Slovenia as a successor to the former YU. Slovenia and Australia are both signatories to The Hague Convention on the Conflict of Laws relating to the Form of Testamentary Dispositions 1961. Convention Providing a Uniform Law on the Form of International Will 1978. Note: dates of notification of succession to the Convention by former states of Yugoslavia including Slovenia, deposited and instrument of accession to the Convention on 9 August 1977.

[150] Australia and Slovenia have both ratified the Hague Convention on the Conflict of Laws relating to the Form of Testamentary Dispositions 1961.

[151] Ibid, article 1.

11.4.7 Personal Income Tax

Personal income tax law in Australia and Slovenia[152] is based on residence and length of stay and not citizenship. The length of time resident in Australia[153] and Slovenia[154] for personal income tax purposes is continuous presence of 183 days without interruption. The 183 day rule is common throughout the world. Annually, citizens of Slovenia[155] and Australia[156] are required to submit personal income tax returns. For example, an Australian citizen working in Slovenia on contract for an Australian company for 300 days, and maintains banking, family and other private activities in Australia, the residence rule of 183 days will not apply and the person will pay tax in Australia.[157] The notable differences are the current personal income tax rates. For an Australia citizen, or, individual on a skilled migration visa and is employed, the personal income tax rate includes; from $18,201.00 to $37,000.00; 32.5% from $37,001.00 to $80,001.00; 37% from $80,001.00 to $180,000.00; 45% from $180,000.00.[158] For a Slovenia citizen, or, an Australian citizen resident in

---

[152]Article 35, Law on Personal Income, Official Gazette of the Republic of Slovenia 151/2006, income from employment is considered income received on the basis of past or current employment.

[153]Income Tax Assessment Act 1936, section 6, resident of Australia means a person who resides in Australia, a person whose domicile is in Australia unless determined by the Commissioner not to be, who as been in Australia continuously or intermittently, during more than one-half of the year of income. The Australian Tax Office (ATO) and courts have further expanded on this definition recognising specific principles that will apply to determining what constitutes residence being physical presence, family, employment or business ties, maintenance of a place of abode and assets, frequency, regulatory and duration of visit, habits and mode of life. However, the position is not clear in relation to where a person has been present in Australia for more than 6 months and a resident for the 183 day tests S19 85 ATC 225, in Paul Kenny, *Australian Tax 2013*, LexisNexis Butterworths, 2013, 88–99. Note: the scenario does not account for part stay and leaving the Australian territory, as certain other rules will apply.

[154]Article 6, Law on Personal Income, Official Gazette of the Republic of Slovenia No 151/2006, residency means officially registered permanent residence in Slovenia, resides outside of Slovenia for employment in diplomatic mission, consulate, international mission, permanent representation to the European Union, was resident in Slovenia during any period in the previous year and resides outside Slovenia for employment, has habitual residence or the centre of their personal and economic interests is in Slovenia, or time spent during the tax year is present in Slovenia for a total of more than 183 days.

[155]Ministry of Finance, Republic of Slovenia, Submission of tax returns, http://www.durs.gov.si/si/angleske_strani/faq/individuals/. Personal income tax returns are automatically generated and would be sent out by 15 June in any 1 year, these individuals have 15 days upon receipt to lodge a complain if they disagree with the data on their individual calculation.

[156]Australian Government, Australian Taxation Office, tax returns are lodged between 30 June and 31 October of each year, http://www.ato.gov.au/Individuals/International-tax-for-individuals/Coming-to-Australia/Paying-tax-and-lodging-a-tax-return

[157]*Pillay v Commissioner of Taxation* [2013] AATA 447.

[158]Australia Rates of Income Tax as from 1 July 2012, personal income tax rates include 19% income from $18,201.00 to $37,000.00; 32.5% from $37,001.00 to $80,001.00; 37% from $80,001.00 to $180,000.00; 45% from $180,000.00 and over. However, there is a 30% taxable rate

Slovenia employed beyond the 183 requirement will be subject to the following tax rates; 16% up to €7814.04, 27% €18,534, 41% €69,312.96, 50% exceeding €69,312.96.[159] However, note that these rates are likely to change annually.

The examples outlined above highlight how an Australian and Slovenian citizen can be engaged in private activities that transcend both states. This section reinforces the point that the private side of citizenship is just as important as the public side, in the modern world.

11.5 Conclusion

The rise of the nation state has seen the development of laws to control the movement of citizens and non-citizens across international borders. It is well understood that PIL facilitates the regulation of the cross-border private activities of citizens. To assist Slovenes and Slovenia, the state has implemented specific laws - the Private International Law and Procedures Act. Australia does not have similar legislation and deals with those issues in common law. The legislative framework established by Slovenia provides a greater level of legal certainty and minimizes the gaps in the law. It is this legal certainty that could be improved in Australia and would close the legislative gaps.

Moreover, it has been confirmed that there are limited PIL matters that directly relate to citizenship. However, both residence and citizenship can be the connecting factors used to determine the appropriate jurisdiction and laws that will apply. PIL adds to a state's ability to direct its citizens to behave according to the defined rules that have been established. Finally, Slovenia unlike Australia has a single Private International Law Act (PIL). The PIL Act provides the basis for determining the law to be used in international personal, family, social labour, property and other civil matters. Australia should take advantage of the work that has been undertaken by Slovenia and establish a single Act outlining the high level principles associated with private international legal matters. According to the Hague Conference on International Law, Slovenia has not ratified he Hague Convention on the Recognition of Divorces and Legal Separation 1970. Slovenia should consider ratifying this international legal instrument. The Convention on the International Recovery of Child Support and other Forms of Family Maintenance 2007 has been established to assist cross jurisdictional issues surrounding divorce and child maintenance. The European Union has signed this convention. Slovenia being a member state of the

---

for dividends unless they have been franked, http://www.lowtax.net/lowtax/html/australia/australia_personal_taxation.asp

[159] Deloitte International Tax, Slovenia 2013 personal income tax rates, 16% up to €7814.04, 27% €18,534, 41% €69,312.96, 50% exceeding €69,312.96, http://www.deloitte.com/assets/Dcom-Global/Local%20Assets/Documents/Tax/Taxation%20and%20Investment%20Guides/2013/dttl_tax_highlight_2013_Slovenia.pdf. The rule change where other income has been sourced within or outside the state.

European Union does not have to sign this convention. Australia has neither signed, nor ratified the convention.

Finally, it is argued that while PIL has very little to do with national identity and cohesion, PIL does provide a subtle level of support to the concepts. It enables citizens to take their values and, in small part, introduce them to other citizens they interact with in other states. The interaction alone can, over time, influence and may result in change of the policy direction and the law to strengthen identity and cohesion. For instance, the movement of people from environment displacement and displacement from war and conflict.

References

Cavers, C. (1972). Habitual residence: A useful concept. *The American University Law Review, 21*, 480–483.

Dirkis, M. (2013). Nowhere man sitting in his nowhere land: The continuing saga of cross border arbitrage. *Revenue Law Journal, 21*(1), 5, 179.

Fawcett, J., Carruthers, J., & North, P. (2008). *Cheshire, North and Fawcett, private international law* (4th ed., pp. 154–195). Oxford: Oxford University Press.

Hayek, F. (1973). *Law, legislation and liberty: A new statement of Liberal principles of justice and political economy* (Vol. 1, pp. 116–118). London: Routledge & Kegan Paul.

Kant, E. (2003). *To perpetual peace: A philosophical sketch* (T. Humphrey, Ed.). Indianapolis: Hackett Publishing,. para 358.

Kenny, P. (2013). *Australian tax 2013* (pp. 88–99). Chatswood: LexisNexis Butterworths.

Knop, K. (2008). Citizenship public and private. *Law and Contemporary Problems, 71*(309), 309–340.

Koopmans, R., & Statham, P. (2001). *How national citizenship shapes transnationalism. A comparative analysis of migrants Claims-making in Germany, Great Britain and the Netherlands*. Revue Eurohernna des Migrations Internationals, REMI, pp. 63–100.

Mills, A. (2009). *The confluence of public and private international law: Justice, pluralism and subsidiarity in the international ordering of private law* (p. 66). Cambridge: Cambridge University Press.

Mortensen, R., Garnett, R., & Keyes, M. (2011). *Private international law in Australia* (2nd ed., p. 8). Chatswood: LexisNexis Butterworths.

Puharič, K. (2003). Private International Law in Slovenia, in yearbook of Private International Law. *Kluwer Law International & Swiss Institute of Comparative Law, 5*, 155–157.

Stone, P. (2010). *EU Private International Law* (2nd ed.). Edward Elgar.

Vetovec, S. (2001). Transnationalism and identity. *Journal of Ethnic and Migration Studies, 27*(4), 2001.

Wouters, J. (2010). *Residence of individuals in EU law*. Institute for International Law, Katholieke Universiteit Leuven, Working Paper No. 148.

Chapter 12
A Pathway Forward

Abstract This chapter highlights some of the policy drivers that will influence the development and retention of national identity and social cohesion in the future. More pervasively, the impact on national identity and social cohesion will be influenced by world population growth and migration. Tensions are appearing between generations and among various population groups. Australia, Slovenia and the EU are facing a structural slowdown of global economic growth, and therefore, increasing the growth of productivity which is necessary and needs to be sustained. With the fourth industrial revolution well underway, the digital economy (robotics, trade in data and artificial intelligence), is creating new models of business, work and jobs which demands the development of new knowledge and skills and adaptation in numerous areas of the economy, society and the environment. Thus, the polarization of economic and political power increases pressures, while new forms of social conflict are created which are reflected in citizens' increasing distrust of institutions. Citizenship, immigration, rights and PIL while settled legal and policy concepts are likely to be impacted from this change. If so, the resulting effect for states and the EU may require a rethink and either tightening or relaxing of these laws.

Keywords Citizenship · Migration · National identity · Population growth · Social cohesion

12.1 Introduction

Globalization, the development of regionalization (supranational polity and regional associations), ethnic and geopolitical tensions, demands for group recognition and group rights, and the restructuring or retrenchment of the welfare state, are all placing pressure on national identity. Along with the rise in terrorism, the resulting effect has seen nation states take a greater focus on citizenship, immigration, rights law and policy.

R. Walters, *National Identity and Social Cohesion in a Time of Geopolitical and Economic Tension: Australia – European Union – Slovenia*,
https://doi.org/10.1007/978-981-15-2164-5_12

The understanding of national identity, citizenship, migration, human rights and private international law has made for a fascinating, but at times a very complex study. This book has confirmed that three forms of identity have emerged from the examination of these laws. Firstly, Australia has been developing and refining its identity for more than a century. Secondly, Slovenia has for more than two centuries has been working hard to develop and now retain its identity. Thirdly, the EU not being more than 75 years old has, through its laws, institutions and judiciary developed a limited (supranational) identity, when compared to Australia and Slovenia. However, the identity established by the EU is having far reaching effects that transcend the Union border to influence third countries such as Australia. There is no better example than in the area of human rights law and more recently data protection law. Thus, this book has established that not only does a national identity become important to a state, the establishment of a supranational identity plays an important role to a nation (member) states identity.

Such is the complex nature of national identity, it is not only influenced by the law (s) and policy discussed in this book, but, when aligned with social coherence, the multilayered approach (economically, socially and environmental) is vast and formidable. However, the notion of social cohesion has not gone unnoticed by some states, outside the ones that form part of this book. Social cohesion as a concept supports identity. In 2012, the OECD noted:

> The world has changed markedly since the beginning of the new millennium. "Shifting Wealth" describes a phenomenon in which the centre of economic gravity of the world has progressively shifted from West to East and from North to South, resulting in a new geography of growth. The new scenario presents some major opportunities and challenges for the creation of socially cohesive societies. A cohesive society works towards the well-being of all its members, fights exclusion and marginalisation, creates a sense of belonging, promotes trust, and offers its members the opportunity of upward mobility.[1]

The OECD reinforce the formidable task that lies ahead for nation states to retain and strengthen social coherence. While not specifically referring to citizenship, they go onto say that migration, both internal and external, must be considered as part of any future policy in relation to social coherence and national identity. That is, and while they refer to international migration as being urbanization of developing countries, this still occurs in developed countries such as Australia and Slovenia, where the population continues to gravitate towards major centers for education and employment opportunities. However, Australia, is beginning to reverse this trend by forcing new arrivals to regional centers. Australia, over the past decade has also forced new arrivals to understand and embrace the Australian way, through citizenship testing and other policy programs. This has significant benefits to community cohesion. The OECD argue that international migration is having a major impact on social coherence because of the:

[1] Organisation for Economic Development, Perspective on Global Development 2012: Social Cohesion in A Shifting World. OECD Publishing. https://doi.org/10.1787/persp_glob_dev-2012-en

> Shifting wealth is characterized by growing South-South trade and factor movement. Migratory flows are no exception to this pattern: migration between developing countries has significantly increased over the last two decades. Moreover, South-South migration flows are likely to rise relatively faster in the future, in part because migration policies in developed economies are increasingly restrictive, but also because the fast- growing economies of the South are new magnets for potential migrants.[2]

What the OECD are saying, is that:

> the South is geographically diverse and emigrants face very different challenges according to whether they settle in Africa, Asia, or in Latin America. There is also great political diversity and host countries can just as easily be autocratic regimes as democracies, although the latter obviously offer greater opportunities for integration. Although emigrants (particularly refugees) are more likely to head for politically stable countries, unstable ones also attract them. This is particularly true of some resource-rich countries, where immigration coexists with civil unrest and low levels of freedom.[3]

This is an important point, because ongoing immigration places economic, social and environmental impacts on, and too, the host state. Thus, Australia, the EU and Slovenia are directly affected by these challenges. Australia, being geographically located in the Asia Pacific, continues to be a destination state for many from across Asia. On the other hand, and as highlighted earlier, Slovenia and the EU, are and continue to be impacted by waves of people migrating out of North Africa and the Middle East. Moreover, the wider perceived impact from migration to social cohesion in many developing countries, is that, local populations do not always view the arrival of newcomers (e.g. foreign workers) favorably. Thus, states including in the EU need to maintain and have an ongoing vigilance in addressing those issues to promote inclusiveness that, will result in greater social cohesion. For instance, there are a number of cross-cutting policy issues, which states implement that will strengthen inclusiveness of new arrivals. Therefore, the question arises, what and how can citizenship, rights, immigration and private international law underpin and contribute to social coherence? The further question is what level of social coherence can be provided by these laws? The short answer is Yes. However, this is a lot more complex than simply stating yes. A more pervasive question is whether the current laws are adequately, to achieving social coherence? The OECD highlights that the social problems faced today by most immigration host countries are the result of a lack of long-term strategy. Migration-related social cohesion must indeed rely on a coherent policy framework that goes beyond anti-discrimination measures. A smooth integration process should incorporate a comprehensive set of social, employment, education and housing measures. Efforts also need to be made to improve native-born citizens' perceptions of immigrants.[4]

On the backdrop of the above and the issues raised by the OECD, in part, the laws discussed in this book go some way to addressing the ongoing issues and needs of deepening and expanding social cohesion. However, beginning with the EU, ele-

[2] Ibid.

[3] Ibid.

[4] Ibid.

ments of member states' national identities are challenged by regionalist or minority nationalist identities. For instance, across Germany and Austria there has been the rise of racial tensions between nationalists seeking to curb the number of migrants entering the country.[5]

Over the past decade there has also been the region of Catalonia, whereby the Catalan, Basque and Galician autonomy or independence from Spain, which has placed considerable strain on social cohesion. In addition, and even though there is a push for the United Kingdom to leave the EU, and at the time of writing this book Ireland/Irish do not want to leave. The resulting effect has seen the Scottish, Welsh and Irish identities provide the basis for nationalist challenges to the unitary United Kingdom state. Thus, what can be seen is those other policy drivers that are impacting on the social cohesion of a state. Furthermore, and even though these groups are pushing a particular nationalist agenda, every time there is a change in territory or rule, the identity and social cohesion is likely to also change.

Nonetheless, for Slovenia and the Slovenes this is nothing new. They have experienced these challenges for more than a century. The people and the state continue to be challenged by external forces, such as the rise of nationalism in neighboring states such as Austria and Hungry. Thus, it is argued that even with these policy and societal tension that are localized, the laws in this book go some way to ensuring the retention of the national identity and social cohesion. As discussed earlier, citizenship is more than a policy or legal concept that enables an individual to have a connection with a nation state. Citizenship provides for a formal membership and a legal status of, and to, a state, even though, as in the case of Slovenia, it has been the basis for strengthening their homogenous society. On the other hand, it has provided the basis for Australia to build a multicultural community. As a legal concept, citizenship affords individuals with rights and responsibilities. It provides a sense of belonging and more importantly – certainty. Those individuals who lack these elements find themselves in the unfortunate position of not attaining the full benefits of citizenship. Therefore, and arguably, according individuals a set of rights and responsibilities, while essential, may not be sufficient.

Providing people with an identification with an imagined community underpins citizenship, by allowing them to be active participants in society, and more importantly the polity. This, participation, while varied from individual to individual, provides a level of social cohesion. However, that level, is very difficult to measure. Nonetheless, it is arguable that being an active participant through citizenship provides a higher level of social cohesion and identity than permanent residence. It also enables individuals to have a common identity with others who were either born on the territory, or had migrated there. Citizens will be more likely to contribute to society in a variety of ways and to participate in its political processes if they have an emotional identification with the wider community, developed through cultural affiliation.

[5] Ibid.

12.1.1 *Australia*

Australia's narrative in relation to national identity and social cohesion, is like no other. The historical identity and cohesion of Australia can, in part, be summarized as being exclusionary, disconnected, elitist, white, discriminatory, defamatory, and lacking a clarity. There has been no better example than that of the First Australians. Australia's Indigenous people became "citizens without rights" in their own country. It is well understood that their treatment was doubly invidious because they were Australian citizens, formally subjects of the Queen, who were denied basic citizenship rights and privileges.[6] This was achieved by successive Commonwealth and State governments, parliaments, and officials maintaining discriminatory legislation and administrative practices. These practices continue today to varying levels and degrees across the country.

More recently, Australia has been undertaking social cohesion projects across the country. The Australian Human Rights Commission reports that for Australia, social cohesion has been successful. They stated that:

> Social cohesion refers to positive social relationships – it is the bond or 'glue' that binds people. A socially cohesive society is one which works towards the wellbeing of all its members, fights exclusion and marginalization, creates a sense of belonging, promotes trust and offers its members the opportunity of upward mobility. Compared to other countries, Australia has a remarkable degree of social cohesion given its diversity. However, maintaining this cohesion can be a challenge. Rapid social change, particularly in growth areas, can result in disharmony between newly arrived groups and established communities. Social tensions in the wider community can also play out at the local level. Local governments are at the center of this ever-changing environment. They know and understand their communities better than any other level of government. They deliver economic, environmental and social outcomes across a range of areas which affect community cohesion. As such, they are well placed to implement initiatives to reap the benefits of stronger, more resilient and productive communities.[7]

While not mentioning citizenship, social cohesion neither commences nor concludes with the conception of rights. It is one concept that goes partway to building social cohesion and identity in the state. Moreover, for more than a decade, the Scanlon Foundation has play a pivotal role in the study of social cohesion.[8] Its report highlights how more than 24,000 people were interviewed in relation to their views on immigration, multiculturalism, trust in government, discrimination and belonging. Their view on citizenship has been summarized in the Australian context that, as a concept that consists of more than a person's legal status. It is at least as much about behavior and identity. That is, an individual citizen, or group of citizens consider their behavior in terms of the duties, obligations and functions of

---

[6] Galligan, B. (2017) *Australian Citizenship in a Changing Nation and World*, https://link-springer-com.wallaby.vu.edu.au:4433/content/pdf/10.1007%2F978-3-319-53529-6_4.pdf

[7] Ibid.

[8] Scanlon Foundation, Citizenship Discussion 2015, https://scanlonfoundation.org.au/wp-content/uploads/2018/12/Citizenship.pdf

citizenship. A community of people think about their commitments to social values and national ideals.[9] They further note that, Australia has experienced significant population growth over the past decade. Since 2001, Australia's population has increased by more than four million people. During the 2012–2013 period alone, the population increased by 400,000 people, which 60% accounted came from overseas migration.[10] This is an important point, because people deal feel that the demographic in Australia is changing. In the recent 2019 election, while immigration was not front and center of the political debate, it was raised by minor parties as having an impact to Australia in a number of ways. That is, similar to the Howard government period, political parties were asserting nationalist thoughts and practice by demanding a reduction in immigration numbers of Australia.

Therein lies a major dichotomy for Australia. On the one hand, it needs constant immigration for economic benefits. On the other hand, too much immigration creates disquiet and disconnection from the broader Australian community. However, it must be noted that this is not the view of everyone, and is limited to a few. This dichotomy is unlikely to change any time soon. Furthermore, Australia continues to be a destination state for people, particularly from Central and East Asia, for people who want to improve their economic and social standing. The Scanlon Foundation argue that now more than any other time in Australia's history does citizenship play an important role in social cohesion and identity, as providing a broader sense of belonging. The Scanlon Foundations most important findings in a time of constant volatility was that:

> Many Australians are fearful of external threats and this has led some to a false belief that the formal citizenship process is a protection against violent extremism.[11]

This is an important point because, it is the citizen that identifies with the way in which the state establishes formal legal and policy drivers to support immigration, rights, citizenship. It is also the state that uses these drivers to create and enhance the identity of the state. However, a more pervasive issue has arisen, and that is the role of technology. Liberal democracies to date have taken a hands off approach. Other states however, have controlled their citizens access to technology and the Internet. Therefore, the unknown is how citizenship, cohesion and identity are being challenged through technology. Nevertheless, it is somewhat of a circular argument, because the state uses technology to promote social cohesions and identity; yet, it is also used to challenge these very concepts. The balance is where the information and access to information on technology informs the community, while maintaining the core values of the state. This may never be achieved, because even politicians have expressed their concerns over the misuse of technology and the creation of fake news. Thus, while these principles and concepts are well grounded in Australian society and its legal policy framework, they are fluid, political, socially contestable and far from settled.

---

[9] Ibid.

[10] Ibid.

[11] Ibid.

12.1.2 European Union [EU]

The identity of the EU can be best described as a movable feast that is grounded in legal norms predominantly economic and social that have been applied to integrate member states. The EU identity is like no other, and it is considered complex to understand and even identify. Following WWII, the European community has come together to establish a community of nation states, which apply comparable human rights and economic values, within their respective national frameworks. They are based on democratic values of the West. However, and as highlighted earlier in this book, the development of the EU through a treaty and convention process, its legal framework, along with the expansion and possible contraction of EU membership, is shaping the future identity of the supranational polity. Today, the supranational polity has been able to exert its influence around the world. While all the elements, concepts and norms that make up the identity of the EU, is outside the scope of this book, democracy has its own inherent problems in relation to identity and cohesion. It could be argued that there is a democratic deficit due to a lack of transparency and accountability within the current democratic framework. This argument can, in part, apply to Australia, EU and Slovenia, because the citizens do not have full access to government. However, it is arguable in determining which framework is best, and how important is establishing identity and cohesion as policy tools by which a state manages its population.

The common identity of the EU, in the early period was identified by Smith[12] as looking to reference points such as a common language, cultural geography and territorial symbolism, historical memories, myths and traditions, religion, ethnicity or outsider groups. However, the EU and its member states have very few of these underlying reference points. While there is no commonly agreed definition or conceptualization of European identity, there is broad consensus that the presence of an "other" is an indispensable part of the identity concept.[13] Just as out-groups are central to identification in social identity theory, classic texts on nationalism and territorial identities have long been concerned with notions of 'othering'.[14]

Notwithstanding the above, the identity of the EU had taken some time to form. During the early period following WWII, the identity of the EU began to take shape. Karl Deutsch adopted the 'transnationalism' theory to describe the political integration of the Union. He pointed out how the attainment of a "sense of community" among the public in terms of mutual loyalties and "we-feelings" was conceived to be a critical precondition for European and international integration in "security

[12] Smith, A. (1992) *National Identity and the Idea of European Unity,* International Affairs, vol 61 (1), 55–76.

[13] Mendez, C. Bachtler, J. *European Identity and Citizen Attitudes to Cohesion Policy: What do we know?* http://www.cohesify.eu/downloads/Cohesify_Research_Paper1.pdf

[14] Ibid.

communities" in the post-war era.[15] Key to strengthening this sense of community, according to Deutsch, was the need to intensify communication through personal contacts and social interactions among citizens across different countries. The neo-functionalist theory of European integration espoused by Ernst Haas[16] took a top-down approach, whereby the formation of a collective European identity was conceived to be an outcome of European integration. Haas defined integration as a 'shift' in 'loyalties' from nation-states to the European level of decision-making, although the empirical focus of his work was primarily on political actors (governments, parties and interest groups) rather than societal actors (citizens).[17]

Over the past 75 years the European community, which began from an initial membership of 6 nations, today, in 2019, has 28 member states. The identity of the EU, is and can be summarized as very different to that of any national identity, even though it is based on similar policy and legal concepts. Arguably national identity is complex, and as the book has demonstrated, it is multilayered. However, the EU identity is just as complex and multilayered. It is argued that the one of the major platforms that has underpinned the evolution of the EU identity, has been the push for 'common policy' approach to many areas of society and governance. This includes, but is not limited to, citizenship, immigration, economic, rights and responsibility, trade, finance and technology. Rather than enshrine an identity and cohesion into a constitution, even though there has been an attempt to do so, the EU has opted to, in part, retain its treaty and convention framework. In other words, the EU has, according to Articles 9 and 10 of the Treaty of the European Union (TEU), provided the basis for a supranational identity. While high level, that has established a baseline for all member states to adopt the democratic (open and transparent) approach to governance.[18]

Member States are represented in the European Council by their Heads of State or Government and in the Council by their governments, themselves democratically accountable either to their national Parliaments, or to their citizens. Every citizen shall have the right to participate in the democratic life of the Union. That is, they take a bottom up approach, on certain policy issues that encourages citizens to be involved in the decision making process. Political parties at the European level contribute to forming European political awareness and to expressing the will of citizens of the Union.[19] In addition to the above, the robust legal framework on human

---

[15] Deutsch, K., Burrell, S., Kann, R., Lee Jr., M., Lichterman, M., Lindgren, R., Loewenheim, F,. and Van Wagenen, R., (1957) *Political Community and the North Atlantic Area: International Organization in the Light of Historical Experience,* Princeton, NJ: Princeton University Press, 30–38.

[16] Haas, E. (1958) *The Uniting of Europe: Political, Economic and Social Forces, 1950–1957,* London: Steven & Sons.

[17] Ibid.

[18] Consolidated Version of the Treaty on European Union, Official Journal of the European Union C 115/13.

[19] Ibid. Article 9 states that in all its activities, the Union shall observe the principle of the equality of its citizens, who shall receive equal attention from its institutions, bodies, offices and agencies.

rights, undoubtedly adds to strengthening the identity of the EU. More importantly, the human rights framework, which was confirmed by the Lisbon Treaty in 2007, making the 2000 EU Charter on Human Rights binding all member states. While not widely reported, its contribution to identity and social cohesion cannot be underestimated. The ability for citizens of the EU to bring human rights issues before the EU courts, does, in part, provide a level of cohesion. By identifying as a citizen of the Union, the individual can also identify with the EU institutions that have been established to enhance and protect their standing within the Union, itself.

Nonetheless, and on the backdrop of the well-established legal framework of the EU, in 2017, Donald Tusk, President to the European Parliament stated:

> We continue to look for the best way towards a Europe that is united, solidary and sovereign. Our quest must be accompanied by a constant and profound reflection on the essence of our community. Firstly, we are a territorial community, which means that we have a common territory and common external borders. Our duty is to protect them. The migration crisis has made us aware, with full force, of the need to rebuild effective control of our external borders, while the aggressive behaviour of certain third countries, and the destabilisation around Europe, has made us aware of the need to defend our territory. Secondly, we are a cultural community, which doesn't mean that we are better or worse – we are simply different from the outside world. Our openness and tolerance cannot mean walking away from protecting our heritage. We have the right and obligation to care for what distinguishes us from other cultures – not in order to be against someone, but to be ourselves. Thirdly, we are a political community. It is high time we renewed our vows in the name of our political values enshrined in article 2 of the Treaty on the European Union. Let me quote: The Union is founded on the values of respect for human dignity, freedom, democracy, equality, the rule of law and respect for human rights, including the rights of persons belonging to minorities. These values are common to the Member States in a society in which pluralism, non-discrimination, tolerance, justice, solidarity and equality between women and men prevail.[20]

The importance of what Tusk states highlights that, in accordance with the EU legal framework, the EU has identified core concepts that underpin the supranational polity. By basing continued integration on the concepts of a united, solidarity and sovereign, territorial community, cultural community and political community only serves to strengthen the democratic values if the EU. The focus remains, as it has been for more than 50 years, to strengthen the European community, within a single Union. This alone, is what sets the identity of the EU apart from its current 28 member states, but also, from Australia. For Slovenia, as a new member of the EU with only membership for 15 years, acquiring these attributes of identification is an ongoing process.

Every national of a Member State shall be a citizen of the Union. Citizenship of the Union shall be additional to national citizenship and shall not replace it. Article 10 goes further by establishing the fundamental democractic values of the EU. It states: The functioning of the Union shall be founded on representative democracy. Citizens are directly represented at Union level in the European Parliament.

[20] Report by President Donald Tusk to the European Parliament on October European Council meetings and presentation of the Leaders' Agenda, Council of the European Union, https://www.consilium.europa.eu/en/press/press-releases/2017/10/24/tusk-report-european-parliament-strasbourg/pdf

Even so, there is the possibility of a contraction of that membership. At the time of writing this book, there has been, and impending exit of the United Kingdom (UK). While BREXIT may not result in a substantial change to the overall values of the EU, the impending exit of the UK to likely to have a significant impact to the way in which the law is considered across the EU. The UK, being the only current member of the EU that has for centuries practiced under the common law model, has to a large extent integrated itself into the EU civil law system. The EU, in turn, has accommodated the UK common law within its law-making structure. BREXIT could see the EU not having to consider common law principles when deciding on cases within European courts. More pervasively, the current economic conflict between the EU and Switzerland will have a wider impact on EU cohesion and there may be further lessons in integration and cohesion arising from BREXT.[21]

As highlighted in an earlier, EU citizenship consists of a package of rights. The Treaty on European Union (Maastricht Treaty) was enacted in 1992 and came into force in November 1993 provides a list of such rights. Jo Shaw summarizes EU citizenship as a concept in which this catalogue of citizenship rights is exceedingly limited and rather specific, and hardly comparable with domestic (generic) conceptions of citizenship. In fact, she argues that, one of the key concessions made to Danish sensibilities after the first referendum, which narrowly rejected the Treaty of Maastricht, was a declaratory confirmation by the European Council that nothing in the provisions of the Treaty of Maastricht in any way displaces national citizenship. Furthermore, Shaw points out that, it is not an 'independent' status of membership: EU citizenship attaches to those with the nationality of the Member States, and it is prima facie the Member States who determine – as sovereign states under international law – who are their nationals.[22]

Another layer to EU identity that supports citizenship is immigration. Since then the EU has developed a comprehensive common policy in immigration that, member states have had to implement. The contribution to the overall identity of the EU cannot be underestimated. Apart from providing a coherent and consistent approach, it indirectly provides for social cohesion, by forcing member states to adopt a single economic and international protection approach to who can and cannot enter the EU.

However, and similar to other regions and countries, the identity of the EU, while underpinned by a sound framework, is also being challenged. In other words, the revival of populism and extremism is a strong symptom of the identity crisis that is affecting many of the European Union's Member States.[23] From Denmark to Italy, Austria, France and the Netherlands, various national elections are confirming the strength of populism and the parties on the far right who are imposing their discourse

---

[21] Will London be berned like Switzerland? Finacial Times (July 2019), https://www.ft.com/content/fe903f9b-926d-36c8-b950-f2f56e014cff

[22] Shaw, J *'Individual Rights and Citizenship: A Dynamic Interaction'* (Centre for the Study of Law in Europe, Univ. of Leeds, UK) (1998).

[23] Schuman, R, *The research and Study Center of Europe, Europe and the identity challenge: who are "we"?,* https://www.robert-schuman.eu/en/european-issues/0466-europe-and-the-identity-challenge-who-are-we

upon public debate, the heart of which comprises economic and cultural protectionism, as well as that of identity. The question of identity also seems to be a point shared by many populist and far right parties in Europe. All set the following question: what links societies that are challenged by the crisis and the process of globalization?[24] While, the European Union is not necessarily a condition for the existence of the different types of populism in Europe, it is however exacerbating the themes that such populism fosters and amplifies anxiety about identity. Added to that anxiety is tension between an "open and a "closed" society,[25] both of which can be identified with the same country.

More recently, the identity of the EU has been summarized by the citizens of the member states as being "European". The research and policy discourse of the EU, has over the past decade, taken a more concerted effort to better understand what and how EU identity is viewed across the Union. Mendez and Bachtler have identified three areas in which EU citizens identify with social cohesion. First, a majority of citizens identify themselves as European to some extent, compared to a minority that consider themselves exclusively national. However, this majority consider themselves national first and then European, which has been termed 'inclusive nationalism' or European 'identity lite'.[26] Few citizens consider themselves European first and then national, and fewer still view themselves as being exclusively European. Second, levels of dual (national and European) identity overall do not vary dramatically over time. However, they go onto say that, it is striking that following a dip after the crisis in 2007/8, the level of European identity overall recovered to pre-crisis levels in 2010; and that it reached an historical high in 2015 when more than half of EU citizens (52 percent) felt national and European for the very first time.[27] Political support for the EU in terms of positive perceptions of membership and associated benefits has also increased in recent years, although citizens' trust in the EU remains significantly below pre-crisis levels. Third, the authors identify that there are significant variations in European identity across Member States. Historically, citizens of the founding Member States and Southern European Member States had greater levels of European identity than citizens in Scandinavian countries or the in UK.[28] The UK has the lowest level of European identity historically. This is consistent with the impending BREXIT. Levels of identity in the new member states are also generally lower than in the older member states.[29] The most recent Eurobarometer data reveals marked increases in European identity from 2010 to 2015 in many countries (notably in Germany, Belgium,

[24] Ibid.

[25] Ibid.

[26] Mendez, C. Bachtler, J. *European Identity and Citizen Attitudes to Cohesion Policy: What do we know?* http://www.cohesify.eu/downloads/Cohesify_Research_Paper1.pdf

[27] Ibid.

[28] Ibid.

[29] Ibid.

Finland, France, Ireland, Netherlands and Sweden), while only Cyprus has witnessed a significant fall.

On the backdrop of this most recent analysis demonstrates how citizenship goes some way to support and underpin identification with the Union, and more importantly, social coherence. More importantly, the EU has identified the importance of social coherence, and have recently released its "Cohesion Policy is the EU's main investment policy: targets all regions and cities in the European Union in order to support job creation, business competitiveness, economic growth, sustainable development, and improve citizens' quality of life".[30] While largely a funding policy to enhance economic development in the EU through education, jobs, amongst others, one of the key aims from this initiative is to build social inclusion. Working with member states, it is a cross-cutting policy program that aims to strive for positive economic, education, social and environmental outcomes for the citizens of the Europe Union. Similar policies also apply in Slovenia and Australia. For Slovenia, they are required to demonstrate that, how and what they are doing to achieves the aims of the cohesion Policy.

Moreover, and while somewhat separated from citizenship and immigration, the Cohesion Policy impacts, directly on current and future citizens of the EU. Thus, in reinforcing the concept of identity and social cohesion through citizenship and immigration, is complex and multilayered. Adopting the high level economic, social and environmental policy approach to social cohesion and identity through citizenship and immigration alone, it can be demonstrated that they are all intertwined and influence each other. Put simply, it is a circular legal and policy argument. There is no definite end point, because society, and the economic, social and environmental issues will never be fully addressed. Thus, identity and social cohesion will not only continue to evolve, it will also continue to be challenged. Adopting this position in the EU context, arguably adds a further layer of complexity. That is, the geopolitical challenges the EU faces with member states coming in and potentially leaving, could have a profound impact on it further developing its identity, into the future.

12.1.3 Slovenia

The role of citizenship in Slovenia's national identity and social coherence has taken a very different path to that of Australia and the EU. Social cohesion and identity for Slovenes has been developing over a long period of time. In the opinion of Božo Repe, the Slovenes formed both their country and their national identity during the Austria-Hungarian era.[31] Until the end of the nineteenth century, they perceived themselves mainly as residents of historical provinces whose formation

[30] European Commission, European Cohesion Policy, 20124-202, https://ec.europa.eu/regional_policy/sources/docgener/informat/basic/basic_2014_en.pdf

[31] Božo Repe, *Regional Differences, Slovene National Identity, And The Foundation of The Slovene State*, https://journals.lib.washington.edu/index.php/ssj/article/viewFile/14774/12383

can be traced back to the Middle Ages (i.e., as Carniolans, Styrians, Carinthians, or Istrians), and at the supranational level, as loyal subjects of the Habsburg Monarchy. He believes the national program was created in 1848 did not extend beyond demands for Slovene autonomy and the use of their own language. However, the national program can be traced to this period. Slovenes have, as a people and community struggled for many years to fully express their identity, up until they obtained independence in 1990–1991. Even under the former Yugoslavia, in which they were defining their identify under a federal structure, WWII would set them back many years.

One of the most important elements retained and strengthened by the Slovenes has been their language. Repe argues that, by preserving their language and cultural autonomy, and their Austrian (or Habsburg) identity was not wholly replaced with a Yugoslav identity. Under communist-authoritarian Yugoslavia, the status of the Slovenes actually improved: they were granted the constitutional right to self-determination, including the right to secession. Arguably citizenship, immigration, their ability to embrace the democratic principles of the EU, joining the EU club in 2004, and also making human rights a core pillar within their policy and legal discourse, has contributed to their national identity and cohesion.

However, it must be noted that, while they have a clear national identity, not unlike Australia, and other member states of the EU, within Slovenia there are sub identities. This is not unlike Australia citizens who identify as being a Victorian or Queenslander (or with one of the other states or territories). Repe argues that within Slovenia today, there are still strong regional identities. He goes onto say that Prekmurje is believed to be the most distinctive, partially because the people in this region were secluded in the Hungarian part of the monarchy for centuries. Repe argues that there are possible head winds for Slovenia to face going forward.

He argues that:

> self-satisfied Slovene politicians believe that the Slovenes reached the peak of their history by attaining independence and forming a state, and that growth in gross national income (which, by the way, is less a result of innovativeness than of service and similar activities) indicates that Slovenes are on an upward path. However, critical intellectuals caution that the way backwards, from citizen of an independent state to a mere provincial man, is an equally realistic option if Slovenes continue to persist in today's prevailing traditionalism, seclusion, and prejudices and do not manage to activate sufficient intellectual power (cultural, educational, and scholarly) to carry out the modernization processes that they have been unable to catch up with for over one hundred years.[32]

What Repe is saying is that, while it is understood that the Slovenes have, from a small base, undertaken and achieved something that is quite remarkable. There are not many other nation states with small populations that can espouse the same level of identity or autonomy. A comparable nation would be Singapore, located in South East Asia. Moreover, it could be argued that Slovenes have enjoyed expressing their national identity for nearly 20 years. During this period, they have, through the respective citizenship and immigration laws, expressed and retained their

[32] Ibid.

homogenous society. Arguably, they continue to retain a high level of homogeneity such as in the Slovenes appearing to be reluctant to accept too many foreigners. While this is in part due to the size of the country, Slovenes have largely restricted immigrants unless they have a connection with Slovenia.

Even as a member of the EU club, Slovenia did not see a mass exodus, but rather, and while some of the younger generation have exited, most have remained. That retention, arguably is a result of many different factors. Nonetheless, it can be argued that, as the people and the state has moved away from its past and into the EU, Slovenes saw greater freedoms and, social and economic opportunities. Arguably, these new found opportunities have made a significant contribution to retaining and strengthening their Slovene identity, along with building a strong platform for social cohesion. These are now, in my view, underpinned and reinforced by the legal framework, which in part, citizenship, immigration, rights and PIL. However, Slovenia, in seeking to preserve its identify, cannot relax. Slovenia must be vigilant, but also balance that vigilance with the opportunity to allow others into the country, provided the new arrivals embrace the Slovene identity, values and social discourse.

12.2 Future Policy Settings

The multilayered approach required to maintain national identity and social cohesion is a formidable one. Citizenship, immigration, rights and to a lesser extent private international law that all support and strengthen the identity of a state, its people, or a supranational polity is not a new concept. However, with significant head winds (geopolitical, economic and environmental) on the horizon, the question is what are the challenges ahead? What can be demonstrated is the need for constant vigilance.

The OECD call for states to do more by setting a social cohesion agenda that seeks to leverage different sector policies so that they promote social inclusion, build trust and civic participation, and foster social mobility. Taking these three dimensions as the pillars of a social cohesion agenda goes beyond the traditional "pro-poor-growth" approach that has been extensively discussed in the last 5 years.[33] They go onto to say that to promote social cohesion is not to promote an apolitical vision of the challenges facing a society. Fostering it as an overarching objective can only be realized if the main stakeholders of a society – the authorities, business organizations, and civil society groups – are involved and actively work together to jointly address collective action.[34] The transition process that many converging countries are now undergoing is likely to be turbulent and prone to conflict. Arguably

[33] Organisation for Economic Development, Perspective on Global Development 2012: Social Cohesion In A Shifting World, OECD Publishing. https://doi.org/10.1787/persp_glob_dev-2012-en

[34] Ibid.

what the OECD is saying is the need for states, including the EU, to create an environment in which citizens can participate more fully in government activities.

The position taken by the OECD, largely applies in Western democratic jurisdictions that have embraced t traditional western democratic principles and concepts. However, the question is whether this approach would be adopted by states that do not fully adopt and apply comparable democratic principles adopted by Australia, the EU or Slovenia? This is questionable. Yet, those states still retain a strong identity and social cohesion. In other words, it is well understood that states, which adopt an authoritarian or totalitarian form of governance do achieve a level of social coherence. Arguably, the EU and Slovenia for the last 15 years, has sought to s to foster the involvement of citizens through the Council of Europe's "Social Cohesion Plan". That Plan defines priorities and responsibilities by promoting the principle of shared social responsibility in order to channel the knowledge and resource of individual and collective players, strong and weak alike, to attain jointly agreed objectives. However, the OECD plan/policy is set to conclude in 2020 and needs to be upgraded. Australia, could look to the EU to develop a more comprehensive policy approach to identity and social cohesion grounded in shared objectives.

Liberal foundations that have been embraced by all three jurisdictions by adopting individual liberty and equality, assume the mantle of a nation defining its values. Thus, democratic political leaders instinctively revert to civic values and political institutions when pressed to define the core values of their nation. This can be seen across Australia, the EU and Slovenia, that have embraced Western neo-liberal democratic thought.

Moreover, in 2017, Australia through the *Multicultural Australia: United, Strong, Successful*,[35] stated the importance of 'inclusion', 'inclusiveness' or 'a sense of belonging' no less than 11 times. In this respect, the current policy's approach is a long overdue correction. One of the issues that emerged was how to approach cultural liberty and respect, and access and equity that have always been integral to Australian multiculturalism. The cultural liberty approach places all the onus on individuals and, especially, on migrants. It reinforces the values and customs of the state, and ensures new migrants integrate into the community. However, the outcome of how this impact on national identity or social cohesion is yet to be fully understood.

For Australia, they are grappling with similar macro policy issues to that of the EU and Slovenia. One such challenge relates to discrimination against migrants. In the EU, some states such as Germany and Austria, discrimination exists and is more overt than in Slovenia. The Australian Human Rights Commission note that a recent survey of 10,000 respondents by Andrew Markus, supplementing the annual Scanlon Foundation social cohesion survey, found a number of groups that experienced significantly higher levels of discrimination compared to the general population. For example, 51% of Muslim Australians born in Australia reported experiencing dis-

[35]Australian Government 2017, *Multicultural Australia: United, Strong, Successful*. Canberra: https://www.homeaffairs.gov.au/LifeinAustralia/Documents/MulticulturalAffairs/english-multicultural-statement.pdf

crimination over the past 12 months.[36] According to Markus, who conducted extensive focus group research in addition to quantitative surveys, 'Muslim respondents indicated concern at what they saw as deterioration in relations, linked to the actions of politicians who they saw as inciting division within the community, and at much of the Australian media which was seen as biased and ill-informed in much of its coverage'. It is concerning that there is a small minority within the Muslim Australian population that does not appear to be positive in outlook towards Australia, or who identify with it. While close to 75% of Muslim Australians indicated they had a sense of belonging in Australia to a 'great' or 'moderate' extent, 14% indicated they did not know or declined to answer. This recent research found a strikingly high level of discrimination experienced by those of African backgrounds.[37] For example, 77% of those born in South Sudan, 75% of those born in Zimbabwe, 67% of those born in Kenya and 60% of those born in Ethiopia reported they had experienced discrimination over the last 12 months.[38] The research also indicated that those born in South Sudan had reported markedly higher levels of discrimination in areas including employment, property damage and physical attack. For Australia, apart from national security, economic and technological imperatives, it is located in a region in which geopolitical influence and power is slowly being challenged, if not shifting. Australia still grapples with discrimination, not only of the indigenous community, but also many other ethnic groups.

Europe has home grown challenges. Across the EU, they are experiencing social anxiety and cultural fear can be clearly detected. In Austria, there will be a re-run of its presidential election, which in May almost saw the far-right Freedom Party candidate, Gerhart Holzinger, claim victory.[39] In Germany, for much of this year, the far-right Alternative for Germany party has been polling well above 15%. In the Netherlands, Geert Wilders' Party for Freedom is leading the polls, and is pledging to ban all Islamic symbols and mosques. Across Scandinavia, anti-immigrant far-right parties have been growing in popularity, and are even partners in coalition governments. The identity and social cohesion project across the EU have been an important part of the objective to promote integration in all member states. Similar to Singapore, and to lesser extent Australia, and Slovenia, the EU is considered developing a framework for cohesion and a sense of identity. Josef Janning believes that to be European is that:

> Europe's history is shaped by the peculiar proximity of difference, and proximity is more than just a geographical term. Europe's many languages are mostly, but not exclusively, derived from two linguistic sources: the Romance and Germanic languages. Indeed, European ethics too are mostly, but not exclusively, shaped by Judeo-Christian religious

---

[36] Australian Human Rights Commission, The Challenge of Social Coherence, https://www.humanrights.gov.au/about/news/speeches/challenge-social-cohesion

[37] Ibid.

[38] Ibid.

[39] Ibid.

> norms and beliefs. The proximity of difference has given birth to a high level of pan-national engagement.[40]

Janny further highlights that Europeans have traditionally interacted across borders, not just commercially, but in the arts and sciences as well. He goes onto to say that movements in music, visual arts, literature, and architecture are also deeply interwoven across Europe. However, and despite their interaction with each other on so many developments in the arts and sciences, Janny notes that Europeans have fought endlessly against each other, over territory and people, over resources and trade-routes, over power and religion. This has been well documented over the past century. Janny goes onto point out that the EU Cohesion Monitor illustrates how cohesion is affected by changing attitudes and political and economic events over a given period of time – in this case, the 7 years between 2007 and 2014.[41] The data shows that the glue between European societies consistently helps to deal with disruption and conflict, and apparently acts as a buffer to political frustrations. Combines with EU citizenship and the EU identity is enhanced. The Global Financial Crisis in 2008 had a significant impact across the EU. More importantly, the impact of the mass migration of people through 2015–16 resulted in a crisis of the Schengen system, leading, among other things, to the reintroduction of border controls between Denmark and Sweden, Germany and Denmark, and Austria and Germany. These border controls serve as an early warning of how daily life could change if the system guaranteeing free movement in Europe were to fall apart. In this sense, the refugee crisis in Europe has, in fact, raised awareness of the density of interaction across Europe, on both macro and micro levels. These new border controls remain in place.

More pervasively, BREXIT is creating an environment of instability that, could be seen by other member states to follow the same path. While BREXIT has not been implemented at the time of writing the book, an impending decision is not far away. Janny notes that this is one of the major challenges to identity and cohesion. He states that, while interdependence and interaction on economic issues and among citizens deepens, constraints to cohesion also seem to be growing, mostly driven by anti-EU political rhetoric. He further highlights that in most EU countries, a political discourse has developed, rejecting the notion of integration in response to interdependence. Furthermore, perceived social imbalances in one's own country can stand in the way of European solidarity.

The British debate about "in-work benefits" is a case in point. However, the phenomenon of social imbalance restricting EU cohesion is wider.[42] More importantly, Janny argues that political divergence between EU countries and the EU poses more complex challenges. Many EU countries have engaged in considerable political

[40] Janny, J, *Making Sense of Europe's Cohesion Challenge*, European Council on Foreign Relations, https://www.ecfr.eu/page/-/ECFR171_-_MAKING_SENSE_OF_EUROPE%2527S_COHESION_CHALLENGE_%28WEB%29.pdf

[41] Ibid.

[42] Ibid.

ring-fencing to defend the national status quo against an intrusive Europe. The reason behind this reflex stems from the effects of deep integration: the single currency and the single space of mobility have eliminated the principle of non-interference in domestic affairs. Now, political narratives and political organizations from individual member states impact others, and are impacted by others. Janny further highlights that one of the most complex issues facing EU identity and cohesion is the rise in nationalism. For Slovenia, it is argued that since independence they have largely held their nationalist program.

However, the new populist nationalists in Europe (particularly Austria-Germany and others) have one common view: that the pooling of sovereignty is a key problem for Europe's nation states. That which was once the essence of integration to its founding generation has now become the arch-nemesis of many Eurosceptic politicians. To return sovereignty to the nation state and to national parliaments is the principal goal for all of these new political parties and movements. Janny's concerns, if realized, will result in an unwillingness to cooperate. Should this prevail, it would destroy European cohesion. The connectivity among Europeans would be significantly diluted in favour of a national identity that has been set up in opposition to European integration. To overcome these hurdles will be complex politically for the EU. Not getting it right, could result in member states finding ways to exert their nationalist ideology. The EU needs to continue to work with member states to retain the EU current policy approach. EU member states need to ensure they exert their rights and single market credentials, to ensure nationalism does not rise, where the EU continues to fracture, and member states leave the Union. Roberta Capello call for greater work in the development and implementation of Cohesion policies.[43]

Apart from the general economic and social concepts and principles that other states, such as Australia adopt to support and enhance national identity and cohesion, Slovenia focuses far more on culture and language. As highlighted throughout the book, Slovenia and Slovenes have placed possibly the highest value on language as the single denominator that binds the community. In 2017, the Slovenia government released the 2030 Development Strategy[44] (the strategy), in conjunction with the European Cohesion Policy. The strategy notes that:

> we are facing numerous challenges and long-term trends with significant consequences. Conditions at home, in the EU and around the world have changed dramatically. We are experiencing increased uncertainty and unpredictability and are searching for new development paradigms which take our planet's capacities into account. In addition to dangers, these development challenges also bring numerous opportunities. In order to become a society that understands how to deal with change, uncertainty and challenges, we want to create the conditions for and establish a systemic approach to sustainable development.[45]

---

[43] Capello, R, (2017) *Cohesion Policies and the Creation of a European Identity: The Role of Territorial Identity*, Journal of Common Market Studies.

[44] Slovenian development strategy 2030, edited by Timotej Šooš ... [et al.]; translated by Polona Vrabec; photography Archives of the Government Office for Development and European Cohesion Policy, http://www.vlada.si/fileadmin/dokumenti/si/projekti/2017/srs2030/en/Slovenia_2030.pdf

[45] Ibid.

This statement put out by Slovenia, reinforces the current concerns, not only raised by the EU, but also by the OECD. More pervasively, Slovenia understands that the speed of technological progress has completely changed societal expectations, and at the same time is quickly exceeding society's capacity to adapt to it. Therefore, the paradox of global social progress is becoming increasingly significant, as it brings new opportunities and increased development potential, but simultaneously also constitutes a threat and creates numerous challenges.[46]

The Development Strategy goes onto say that, for Slovenia, culture and language are the most important attributes of national identity. In the eyes of Slovenia, culture is a reflection of the conditions, dialogue and relations in society, that together inform and reflect the national identity. It contributes to the recognition of our uniqueness and the openness of our society, to the development of creativity, innovativeness and collaboration, and is an important factor in economic and regional development.[47] Slovenia is characterized by the historical tradition[48] and the local segmentation of the fundamental cultural diversity, with standard literary Slovene serving as the foundation and framework for cultural Slovene [ness] and the most visible bearer of the collective identity.[49] Slovenia's cultural sphere also includes indigenous national communities and the Roma community, which contributes significantly to the reduction of all forms of intolerance.[50] This also sets Slovenia and the EU policy discourse apart from that of Australia. As highlighted earlier, Australia's lack of legal and policy recognition of indigenous peoples is well documented. At least Slovenia has recognized these people in its constitution. Australia could do so even though the Australian Constitution is much older (more than 90 years older than Slovenia). Access to the Slovene language and culture and the growth in the creative fields is also supported by digitalization. Slovenia's rich cultural heritage, as a reflection of its values, beliefs, knowledge and traditions, represents a significant development potential. It will also be important to strengthen connections with Slovenes in neighboring countries and around the world within a global network. The entire Slovenian cultural sphere should be connected in order

---

[46] Ibid.

[47] Ibid.

[48] Ibid.

[49] Ibid. Slovenia aim achieve the cultural and language goal by: a) developing and preserving the Slovene language and culture, and the cultural and natural heritage; b) strengthening the national identity and protecting cultural diversity; c) promoting sound management of the cultural heritage based on collaboration among all stakeholders; d) promoting cultural activities and through digitalisation, which makes it possible to preserve, provide access to and promote cultural materials; e) providing open access to language tools and resources and cultural materials to all, particularly to disabled persons and people with various forms of functional disabilities; f) strengthening cooperation between the business and cultural spheres, and promoting creativity and the creative industries and research sciences as a synergy between science and art; g) promoting international cultural collaboration, promoting Slovenian culture and sports internationally, making connections with Slovenes across the border and around the world, and developing an effective public diplomacy system in order to increase Slovenia's recognition and reputation around the world.

[50] Ibid.

to enable the utilization of all cultural, political and economic capacities. We would like to develop the national culture and the Slovene language as determinants of identity, recognition and economic progress.

Another unique factor that Australia does not need to consider is Slovenia's place in the EU. It is well understood that Slovenia must transpose the laws of the EU into national laws. Nonetheless, the population policy of Slovenia, while not complex due to the size of the state, is that the territory can only retain and allow so many people into the country. The strategy highlights that are facing demographic changes which will have a significant impact on the development of society and the quality of life there in the future. This is indicated by an increase in the number of people older than 65, the low birth rate and the shrinking of the population aged 20–64, which is the current definition of the working-age population. The projections relating to the population indicate that its aging process will continue to accelerate, and the share of the population over 65 will go from around 19% in 2017 to approximately 30% in 2060.[51] This poses a significant challenge for Slovenia, particularly its identity. That is, should the Slovenia population decline from the natural reproduction of its citizens, the impact to its identity could be enormous. It could, even though it is unlikely, to result in a loss of language and culture. Slovenia, while identifying this as a long term issue need to maintain vigilance.

Consistent with the policy direction of the EU, Slovenia continues to place human rights as a key strategic outcome to achieve a stronger national identity and community cohesion. The strategy highlights how Slovenia's respect:

> for human rights and fundamental freedoms and legal certainty and the rule of law are among the key factors of the quality of a democracy and social development. In order to increase trust in the legal system, it will be necessary to ensure the independence of the judiciary and strengthen the integrity and authority of judicial bodies, which can be created and established only through high-quality and timely judicial decisions. Ensuring the uniformity of judicial practice and ensuring the impartiality and objectivity of the operation of the judiciary will be crucial, whereby it will be essential to prevent potential abuses and to impose zero tolerance for corruption. The important factors for achieving this are a transparent legislative process, clear regulations and enforcement, and effective and high-quality judicial protection. Therefore, it will be necessary to strive for a legal system that creates a high-quality and effective legal framework. It will be necessary to ensure the transparency and clarity of regulations and monitor their effectiveness. Satisfaction with the judicial system in Slovenia is relatively low in comparison with OECD member states.[52]

Interestingly, for Slovenia as a democratic state, this becomes a strategic action and outcome to be achieved. In contrast, in Australia it is argued that trust is the legal system is most likely taken for granted. Thus, Slovenia and other member states of the EU can be best described, even with the recent mass migration from

[51] Ibid. The size of the younger population is increasing primarily in the vicinity of urban areas, while it is decreasing in remote and border areas. Without appropriate measures this trend will continue, which will also result in the reduction of the workforce in remote areas, the abandonment of farming, increased reforestation and security issues, and in cities to increased demand for housing and adjustments to service networks.

[52] Ibid.

Syria and other countries, as having a higher level of homogeny than Australia. On the other hand, Australia has become a melting pot of different ethnic and religious groups. Moreover, for Slovenes located in the border regions, it remains not only constant vigilance, but also ongoing work for Slovenia to ensure their identity is not lost and coherence continues.

The most complex overlay that will not only influence, but also, direct how states and the EU respond to citizenship, immigration, rights, PIL is; national identity and social cohesion. However, they alone have many variables. These include but are not limited to technology, population, rise of authoritarian states, recessions or depressions, and the displacement of people from other countries. It will also be influenced by national, regional and international security. A further influence will be the rise of the East, and diminished rights (legal, religious, political), along with religion. There will be no single silver bullet or policy issue that will address or even retain a strong sense of national identity and social cohesion because of the multi-level and multidimensional layers of policy discourse involved. Moreover, the legal principles of citizenship are well grounded, such as in birth, descent and naturalization (immigration), rights and PIL. What is not grounded are those policy and political overlays that are discussed above.

However, it is not enough to only consider what these jurisdictions are doing in the policy area. Singapore is a good example and comparison to discuss briefly. Singapore has a similar land mass to that of Slovenia. Singapore is part of ASEAN, even though it is not a supranational polity with the same institutional framework as the EU. However, Singapore is also similar to Australia. It is very multicultural and has had to grapple with national identity (create an identity following separation from Malaysia more than half a century ago). In the early period of Singapore establishing itself as a nation state, it is well documented as to their plight and challenges between the Malays and Chinese, and over time many other ethnic groups. In 2019, Singapore had a national conference and discussion in relation to social coherence. It faces similar challenges to Australia, Slovenia and the EU. However, a notable difference is that Singapore's open borders mean that international and regional geopolitical developments have the potential to affect social cohesion. Singapore has welcomed foreigners for a number of years, which has strengthened its economic position in the region. They have, however, been very strategic largely welcoming foreign talent that can make a contribution to the state. Tan and Teng are of the view that the pace of technological change has transformed how Singaporeans consume information and interact with one another.[53] Digital communities are forming alongside physical ones. On one hand, this creates more opportunities to bring people together, but on the other hand, people tend to only talk to those who share similar views, leading to echo chambers. The authors note that:

[53] Desmond Tan and Eugene Teng *Fostering Social Cohesion in 21st Century Singapore* in C.-H. Leong and L.-C. Malone-Lee (eds.), *Building Resilient Neighbourhoods in Singapore*, Advances in 21st Century Human Settlements, https://doi.org/10.1007/978-981-13-7048-9_2

> The texture of Singaporean society is evolving in many ways. First, our demographic makeup is changing. We face an ageing population, with the old-age support ratio likely to change rapidly from 4.2 in 2018 to 2.0 in 2040. This means that there is a greater role for PA to play in keeping seniors socially engaged and physically active. Second, whereas in the past social integration was focused on the different racial groups, there is now an additional dimension of integrating new immigrants with native-born citizens. This is given the current pace of immigration as well as the rise in transnational marriages among Singaporeans. Integrating new citizens within the Singaporean social fabric can be challenging. Third, new social cleavages may be emerging. In addition to the traditional cleavages of race and religion, a recent study by the Institute of Policy Studies found that most Singaporeans' social networks are bounded by their housing type and educational level.[54]

Thus, the question arises, can the other jurisdictions learn anything from Singapore? Apart from continuing to focus on the economic, social and environmental needs of the states, Singapore is moving in a different direction to other states. While citizenship and immigration are not widely mentioned, Singapore is focusing on its citizens. Tan and Teng highlight how, being able to trust one's neighbors and feel a sense of belonging to Singapore and the immediate community, is important for building resilience at the grassroots. Trust enables people to demonstrate civic responsibilities even when they disagree and provides a ballast against influences that threaten to sow discord amongst people. Similarly, a sense of belonging creates a shared identity among otherwise disparate peoples. It also helps residents feel they have a stake in their community and be more willing to contribute to enhancing its wellbeing. It must be noted that this approach for Singapore is a valid approach because of the high density living. However, the other jurisdictions can look to Singapore to consider the grass roots and 'trust' approach. Australia, has through its various government agencies, provide funding for community programs to build community inclusiveness and reliance.

Internationally work continues to be undertaken through the United Nations. The 2016, the United Nations' New Urban Agenda in 2016.[55] Singapore has adopted this UN Agenda. It aims to foster social cohesion, inclusion and safety in peaceful and pluralistic societies. The Agenda promotes the commitment of states to embrace diversity in cities and human settlements, to strengthen social cohesion, intercultural dialogue and understanding, tolerance, mutual respect, gender equality, innovation, entrepreneurship, inclusion, identity and safety, and the dignity of all people, as well as to foster livability and a vibrant urban economy. Most notably, the Agenda encourages cultural infrastructures and sites, museums, indigenous cultures and languages, as well as traditional knowledge and the arts, highlighting the role that these play in rehabilitating and revitalizing urban areas and in strengthening social participation and the exercise of citizenship. While not mentioning national identity, the Agenda provides for consideration of the identity, safety, and dignity of all people. By doing so, the indirect effect will be citizenship, immigration, rights and

---

[54] Ibid.

[55] United Nations' New Urban Agenda in 2016, http://habitat3.org/wp-content/uploads/NUA-English.pdf

PIL. Australia, to a lesser extent, has considered the Agenda, when compared to Singapore and the EU.

The current patchwork approach, only confirms that more work is required. Apart from relying on citizenship, immigration, rights and to a lesser extent PIIL, more work is needed for Cohesion policies and programs to be established. Additionally, Australia and Slovenia, along with the EU, could consider the proposals outlined at the conclusion of each of the chapters in this book. These proposals, while not exhaustive, go some way to providing valuable tools for these jurisdictions to strengthen their identities and subsequently provide a higher level of social cohesion. They will not only underpin the identity of the jurisdiction, but also go some way to support citizenship and immigration.

12.3 Conclusion

The historical paths of both Slovenia and Australia have been very different but share some similar features. The path to the development of the EU has travelled on a very different pathway to that of Australia and Slovenia. This research is new, and has compared two very different legal frameworks. No other research has compared Australia, Slovenia's and the EU's citizenship, immigration, rights and private international laws and their contribution to identity – as a collective.

Modern day Slovenia had been under the rule of the Roman Empire, the Habsburg Monarchy, the Austrian Empire, the Austro-Hungarian Empire, the Kingdom of Serbs, Croats and Slovenes (later renamed the Kingdom of Yugoslavia), Democratic Federal Yugoslavia, the Federal People's Republic of Yugoslavia. The Federal People's Republic of Yugoslavia would later become the Socialist Federal Republic of Yugoslavia and in 1990 the Republic of Slovenia was born. Throughout this long history, citizenship had evolved by adopting exclusionary and inclusionary measures. Upon membership of the EU, Slovenia and Slovene's have not only assumed citizenship of the Union, but also, elements of its limited identity.

Australia's relationship with Slovenia began in 1855, with the first Slovenia arriving on the Australian territory. Australia had been occupied by the indigenous aboriginal people, and settled by the British who imposed their governance and legal framework over the people and the territory. Australian citizenship had evolved from the British Empire and allegiance to the King, and later to an independent legal status.

WWI commenced, and a new Kingdom was born. The Kingdom of Serbs Croats and Slovenes would form, and in 1928 the new citizenship laws were introduced to unify the citizens. The early period benefitted women who were included in the political discourse across the Kingdom. However, this lasted a decade and they found themselves again excluded from political participation. The Federation of Australia commenced in 1901, and the inhabitants were defined as British subjects. Australia had adopted a very restrictive policy that excluded anyone that was not deemed to be white. Not only did the immigration laws require persons to undertake a dictation test, the constitution was silent on citizenship. Australia had excluded the indigenous aboriginal people from citizenship, the polity and community.

WWII had a profound impact on the Slovenian territory. German and Hungarian citizenship laws were imposed over the territory. WWII concluded; and in Yugoslavia dual citizenship would emerge at the Federal and Republic level. Australia would become a destination country for many Slovenes fleeing the war. In 1948, the first citizenship laws of Australia were implemented, defining who its citizen would be. A decade later the *Migration Act 1958* was introduced that began to change how migration was managed. A visa system was established, and non-citizens would have to have a visa to enter and stay in the country. British subjects and Irish nationals were absorbed into the migration laws to ensure all non-citizens were equal according to the law. They along with other non-citizen's resident in the state could be deported upon conviction of a criminal activity.

In 1967, the Australian Constitution was amended to recognize the Indigenous people, and by the mid- 1970s Australia had opened its doors to different ethnic group. Multiculturalism was alive and the citizenship laws were welcoming. Australia had adopted a welcoming policy that would see the influx of large numbers of migrants from various different ethnic backgrounds, over the next three decades.

The Yugoslav experiment was complex, and during the time of Josip Broz Tito the long time leadership, the state and its people experienced another form of governance (totalitarianism). The direction of Yugoslavia and its Republics would change significantly. Slovenia, along with the other Republics, demanded greater autonomy and the economy of Yugoslavia began to decline. The loans from the IMF placed a heavy burden on the state. Worker strikes were increasing, and while uniting the people in the early stages, was turned into the happenings of the people. In other words, the political elites were able to manipulate the narrative and turn the issue from the collective (working in solidarity) to fragmenting and causing dysfunction and trust between minority groups that resulted in them turning on each other. Nevertheless, the citizenship laws remained unchanged. However, this would not be enough to hold the Federal state together.

As the 1980s drew to a close, a defining moment for Australia was in 1987 when finally, the term British subject was removed from the citizenship legislation. By 1986, Australia was embracing migrants from across the world to participate in building the nation, and accepted the fact that some citizens would hold dual citizenship. The citizenship laws continued to restrict an Australian citizen from taking out citizenship of another country.

The collapse of communism across Europe would see the collapse of Yugoslavia. In 1990 and 1991 a new legal framework would be established across Slovenia. This new legal framework provided the basis of a new identity that today is known as Slovenian. This includes, but not limited to, geography, political institutions, language and the rule of law-citizenship. Citizenship of the new Slovenia in 1990 not only confirmed the legal status of individual's residence in the territory. Slovenia's new citizenship laws were based on a number of principles including (1) continuity and transition of the previous Republic level citizenship upon state succession,[56] (2) membership based on civic conception and participation in the political community,[57] (3) evolving statehood, and (4) the opportunity to define an independent national identity. In 1991, Slovenia established its migration laws – the Aliens Act, which were the beginnings of the new state being able to include foreigners and excluded individuals from the state. Slovenia would, in the same way as Australia, implement a permit (Australia: visa) system, however very different in nature. Doing so strengthened national identity allowing both states to choose who entered and stayed.

The early period of independence was complicated as Slovenia used its new citizenship laws to exclude former Yugoslav residents on the territory. The Slovene diaspora became an important extension to Slovenia and its citizenship framework. It was the diaspora that pushed the government to establish a more liberal approach to citizenship and allow descendants of Slovenes to obtain citizenship.

In 1996, Australia entered a period of xenophobia and the Australian Government responded by encouraging tolerance, but acknowledged that the country remained confused about its identity. This same behavior would also play out in parts of Europe and to a lesser extent Slovenia as a result of the mass migration of people in 2015/16 from Syria and other parts of North Africa. Exclusive measures were introduced into the law to deport long term residents by having the ability to cancel their visas. Multicultural citizenship was embraced and dual citizenship was introduced in both states, although to varying degrees. Slovenia decided to restrict dual citizenship to those who could demonstrate a connection with the state.

The decade of 2000 to 2010 was a busy period for Slovenia, as it prepared for accession to the European Union and in 2004 obtained full membership. Australia was one of the first countries outside of the EU to recognize their independence. Slovenia was obliged to implement European law and major amendments to the Aliens Act to ensure their migrations laws were consistent with other member states. Slovenia had inherited a European external border with Croatia. All Slovenian citizens automatically assumed European citizens, and a new found set of rights. The concept of a person being able to buy their citizenship emerged in Malta, which added a new dimension to citizenship. Many states around the world, including Australia have also adopted similar concepts.

Between 2001 and 2018, the world saw the rise of terrorism, and with it, states responded by invoking restrictive (exclusionary) measures as part of their migration and citizenship laws. Australia introduced citizenship testing and the residency requirements were extended. Slovenia continued to push its nationalist agenda and only allows people that could show a direct line to Slovenia, to obtain dual citizenship. Additionally, Slovenia continued to use its language has a clear point of

[56] Medved, F, *Unified Slovenian Nation: Slovenian Citizenship Policy towards Slovenians Abroad*, in Gyõzõ Cholnoky, Zoltán Kántor, András Ludányi and Eszter Herner-Kovács, Minority Studies Special issue Trends and Directions of Kin-State Policies in Europe and Across the Globe, Lucidus Kiadó, 2014, 153–184.

[57] Medved, F, (2010) *Country Report: Slovenia*, EUDO Citizenship Observatory, European University Institute, Italy, 23.

reference and restriction, ensuring future citizens would have the knowledge and ability to use the language in their daily interactions. Even though Australia was fully embracing the idea of multiculturalism, there were national security concerns about non-citizens and citizens engaging in terrorist activities. Australia responded and introduced legislation to place restrictions on their citizen's activities when abroad. To date, Slovenia has not adopted the same approach. This extension of government power over its citizens may continue to expand into the future, as the world becomes more global. However, during this 15-year period this was where Australia and Slovenia had developed similar law reforms to citizenship. Arguably, this was on the back of Slovenia becoming a member of the European Union and having to implement European Union law.

More problematic is the ability for individuals to purchase both citizenship and long term residence, recently introduced. This exclusionary policy approach will likely divide the community, rather than build cohesion. It is clearly directed at those individuals who have the financial resources to buy their way into a state. From an economic perspective, this approach serves governments well, as there is less financial burden to the state and its citizens. On the other hand, it is by definition sending a message to the rest of the world that to enter and stay, you need to be part of a select club.

Today, citizenship in the private sphere is just as important as states regulating citizenship and citizens in the public sphere. Both states allow non-citizens to obtain long term resident permits. In the case of Australia, the evolution of residency has resulted in long term residents being deported, and in some cases the migration laws have been applied inappropriately by government to achieve this objective. The rights afforded to long term residents and citizens are subtly different, and it can be argued that residency has diluted the strength that citizenship provided to the state and individual. Long term residents are afforded all rights by the state's (education, social security, passport, health care) except voting and standing for election. It is citizenship that allows a person to be full participant of a polity. However, more can be done by both states to inform and appraise long term residents of the benefits associated with citizenship. It is also argued that citizenship, while being fragile, has not been diluted to the extent that some may think. Thus, there appears to be a circular argument regarding citizenship and residency.

There are considerable differences between Slovenia and Australia's constitutions. Australia could learn a lot from Slovenia in the area of constitutional human rights. Slovenia upon independence had the opportunity to establish what could be considered a modern day constitution. Australia should reform its constitution. It has been highlighted how Australia has looked to the European Court of Human Rights, European Union and European Commission for guidance regarding the interpretation and application of human rights law.

Citizenship has contributed to national identity and social cohesion in a number of ways. Citizenship evolved from allegiance to a master, excluding women from having legal status. It has been used to unify an Empire, Kingdom or states' inhabitants. It has also been used to assist Empires to colonize a territory, and provide continuity to inhabitants of territory when rulers have changed. Both Slovenia and

Australia have used citizenship to exclude residents on the territory, and impose restrictive rules that make it difficult for a non-citizen to enter the state and become a citizen. The early exclusionary and discriminatory approach Australia took to the indigenous Australians slowly dissipated and they were integrated into society, however there is still a long way to go. These measures have allowed both states to continue to shape their respective identities. More importantly, the evolution of citizenship combined with long term residence has exposed potential ongoing issues for Australia's residents, and the ability to be deported from the state with relative ease. Nevertheless, what has emerged from this book is how both states have used citizenship to enhance their respective nationalist values and position in the world. However, this nationalist approach has had to be balanced against the need for both states, including the EU to build and strengthen social integration and cohesion.

What sets Australia, Slovenia and the EU apart are the concepts and principles that sit outside the legal framework for citizenship, immigration, rights and PIL. That is, in my view, Slovenia holds culture and more so language as two of the most important components of their national identity and cohesion. For the EU it is the single market (economy) and human rights in recognition of the different cultures and languages. While EU citizenship does provide a level of what it is to be European. It does not rely on language in the same way as Slovenia. On the other hand, for Australia language is far from the most important component of its identity. Even though it is the official working language of the state, it was imposed over the territory at colonization. It is the view of the author that, Australia's identity, as reinforced by Ma Crock, remains confused. While it is based on democratic values, that in itself is where the similarities between Slovenia, Australia and the EU conclude. Even then, the implementation of democratic concepts and principles differ. For instance, the recognition, legal framework, judiciary and institutions that support human rights in the EU and Slovenia are very different to Australia. In part, this is because their legal families differ. However, as highlighted earlier, Australia's legal framework and jurisprudence arguably sits a long way away from the EU and Slovenia.

The road ahead for national identity and social cohesion in not going to be smooth. Rather, it is going to be a formidable task for states and the EU to combat the many competing forces facing identity and cohesion. In the likelihood that Western democracy is diminished as a result of geopolitical changes, states and the EU are possibly going to have to revisit their citizenship, immigration, rights and PIL to ensure the identity is retained so as social cohesion continues to be retained, if not strengthened.

Finally, and as highlighted earlier in Chap. 1, this book has been written by an Australian with historical connection to Slovenia. They are both remarkable countries, within their own right and have a great story to tell the world. In writing this book, the author does not in any way intend to challenge, influence or discredit other scholar's views or thoughts in relation to Slovenia's or Europe's story. The positive story of each jurisdiction come from, being in a special position to enjoy the benefits of globalisation and liberal democracy that, has enabled the author to obtain citizenship of two countries, which has also provided for European citizenship.

References

Capello, R. (2017). Cohesion policies and the creation of a European identity: The role of territorial identity. *Journal of Common Market Studies, 49*(5), 1089–1111.

Chesterman, J., & Galligan, B. (1997). *Citizens without rights: Aborigines and Australian citizenship*. Cambridge: Cambridge University Press.

Chesterman, J., & Galligan, B. (1999). *Defining Australian citizenship: Selected documents*. Melbourne: University of Melbourne Press.

Deutsch, K., Burrell, S., Kann, R., Lee, M., Jr., Lichterman, M., Lindgren, R., Loewenheim, F., & Van Wagenen, R. (1957). *Political community and the North Atlantic area: International organization in the light of historical experience* (pp. 30–38). Princeton: Princeton University Press.

Haas, E. (1958). *The uniting of Europe: Political, economic and social forces, 1950–1957*. London: Steven & Sons.

Medved, F. (2010). *Country report: Slovenia*, EUDO Citizenship Observatory, European University Institute, Italy, p. 23.

Medved, F. (2014). Unified Slovenian nation: Slovenian citizenship policy towards Slovenians abroad. In G. Cholnoky, Z. Kántor, A. Ludányi, & E. Herner-Kovács (Eds.), *Minority studies special issue trends and directions of kin-state policies in Europe and across the globe* (pp. 153–184). Budapest: Lucidus Kiadó.

Shaw, J. (1998). *Individual rights and citizenship: A dynamic interaction*. Leeds: Centre for the Study of Law in Europe, University of Leeds.

Smith, A. (1992). National identity and the idea of European Unity. *International Affairs, 61*(1), 55–76.

Appendix

The table below details the number of subclass visas available to non-citizens wanting to enter Australia in accordance with the Migration Regulations 1994, at 2016/7.

Business Skills – Business Talent (Permanent) (Class EA)	Partner (Residence) (Class BS)	Extended Eligibility (Temporary) (Class TK)	Work and Holiday (Temporary) (Class US)
132 (Business Talent)	Subclasses	445 (Dependent Child)	417 (Working Holiday)
Business Skills (Permanent) (Class EC)	100 (Spouse) visa;	Investor Retirement (Class UY)	462 (Work and Holiday)
888 (Business Innovation and Investment (Permanent))	100 (Partner) visa;	405 (Investor Retirement)	Working Holiday (Temporary) (Class TZ)
Business Skills (Residence) (Class DF)	110 (Interdependency) visa;	Medical Treatment (Visitor) (Class UB)	417 (Working Holiday)
890 (Business Owner)	309 (Spouse (Provisional)) visa;	602 (Medical Treatment)	Maritime Crew (Temporary) (Class ZM)
891 (Investor)	309 (Partner (Provisional)) visa;	New Zealand Citizen Family Relationship (Temporary) (Class UP)	988 (Maritime Crew)
892 (State/ Territory Sponsored Business Owner)	310 (Interdependency (Provisional)) visa;	461 New Zealand Citizen Family Relationship (Temporary))	Superyacht Crew (Temporary) (Class UW)

R. Walters, *National Identity and Social Cohesion in a Time of Geopolitical and Economic Tension: Australia – European Union – Slovenia*,
https://doi.org/10.1007/978-981-15-2164-5

893 (State/ Territory Sponsored Investor)	801 (Spouse) visa;	Partner (Temporary) (Class UK)	488 (Superyacht Crew)
1108. Child (Migrant) (Class AH)	801 (Partner) visa;	820 (Partner)	Skilled (Provisional) (Class VF)
101 (Child)	814 (Interdependency) visa;	Prospective Marriage (Temporary) (Class TO)	476 (Skilled – Recognised Graduate)
102 (Adoption)	820 (Spouse) visa;	300 (Prospective Marriage)	Skilled (Provisional) (Class VC)
117 (Orphan Relative)	820 (Partner) visa;	Resident Return (Temporary) (Class TP)	485 (Temporary Graduate)
Child (Residence) (Class BT)	826 (Interdependency) visa.	159 (Provisional Resident Return)	487 (Skilled – Regional Sponsored)
802 (Child)	Resolution of Status (Class CD)	Resolution of Status (Temporary) (Class UH)	570 (Independent ELICOS Sector) visa;
837 (Orphan Relative)	Return (Residence) (Class BB)	450 (Resolution of Status – Family Member (Temporary))	485 (Skilled – Graduate)
Confirmatory (Residence) (Class AK)	155 (Five Year Resident Return)	850 (Resolution of Status (Temporary))	Skilled – Regional Sponsored (Provisional) (Class SP)
808 (Confirmatory)	157 (Three Month Resident Return)	Retirement (Temporary) (Class TQ)	489 (Skilled – Regional (Provisional)
Designated Parent (Migrant) (Class BY)	Partner (Migrant) (Class BC)	410 (Retirement)	400 (Temporary Work (Short Stay Activity))
118 (Designated Parent)	100 (Partner)	Tourist (Class TR)	Temporary Work (Long Stay Activity) (Class GB)
Designated Parent (Residence) (Class BZ)	Contributory Parent (Migrant) (Class CA)	676 (Tourist)	401 (Temporary Work (Long Stay Activity)
859 (Designated Parent)	162 (Investor (Provisional)	Visitor (Class TV)	Training and Research (Class GC)
Distinguished Talent (Migrant) (Class AL)	163 (State/Territory Sponsored Business Owner (Provisional)	651 (eVisitor)	402 (Training and Research)
124 (Distinguished Talent)	164 (State/Territory Sponsored Senior Executive (Provisional)	Special Category (Temporary) (Class TY)	Temporary Work (International Relations) (Class GD)

Distinguished Talent (Residence) (Class BX)	165 (State/Territory Sponsored Investor (Provisional)	444 (Special Category)	403 (Temporary Work (International Relations)
858 (Distinguished Talent)	Business Skills (Provisional) (Class EB)	Partner (Provisional) (Class UF)	Temporary Work (Entertainment) (Class GE)
Nomination (Permanent) (Class RN)	188 (Business Innovation and Investment (Provisional)	309 (Partner (Provisional)	420 (Temporary Work (Entertainment))
187 (Regional Sponsored Migration Scheme)	Special Program (Temporary) (Class TE)	Contributory Parent (Temporary) (Class UT)	Visitor (Class FA)
Special Eligibility (Class CB)	416 (Special Program)	(Contributory Parent (Temporary)	600 (Visitor)
151 (Former Resident)	Diplomatic (Temporary) (Class TF)	Contributory Aged Parent (Temporary) (Class UU)	Bridging A (Class WA)
Norfolk Island Permanent Resident (Residence) (Class AW)	995 (Diplomatic (Temporary)	884 (Contributory Aged Parent (Temporary))	010 (Bridging A)
834 (Permanent Resident of Norfolk Island)	Electronic Travel Authority (Class UD)	Student (Temporary) (Class TU)	Bridging B (Class WB)
Other Family (Migrant) (Class BO)	601 (Electronic Travel Authority)	570 Independent ELICOS Sector	020 (Bridging B)
114 (Aged Dependant Relative)	Emergency (Temporary) (Class TI)	571 Schools Sector	Bridging C (Class WC)
115 (Remaining Relative)	302 (Emergency (Permanent Visa Applicant)	572 Vocational Education and Training	030 (Bridging C)
116 (Carer)	303 (Emergency (Temporary Visa Applicant)	573 Higher Education Sector	Bridging D (Class WD)
Other Family (Residence) (Class BU)	Bridging F (Class WF)	574 Postgraduate Research Sector	040 (Bridging (Prospective Applicant)
835 (Remaining Relative)	60 (Bridging F)	575 Non-Award Sector	041 (Bridging (Non-applicant)
836 (Carer)	070 (Bridging (Removal Pending)	576 AusAID or Defence Sector	Bridging E (Class WE)
838 (Aged Dependent Relative)		580 Student Guardian	050 (Bridging (General)
Parent (Migrant) (Class AX)		Temporary Business Entry (Class UC)	051 (Bridging (Protection Visa Applicant)

Aged Parent (Residence) (Class BP)		457 (Temporary Work (Skilled)	
804 (Aged Parent)		Temporary Safe Haven (Class UJ)	
Protection (Class XA)		448 (Kosovar Safe Haven (Temporary))	
866 (Protection)		449 (Humanitarian Stay (Temporary)	
Refugee and Humanitarian (Class XB)		Temporary (Humanitarian Concern) (Class UO)	
200 (Refugee)		(Temporary (Humanitarian Concern)	
201 (In-country Special Humanitarian)		Transit (Temporary) (Class TX)	
202 (Global Special Humanitarian)		771 (Transit)	
203 (Emergency Rescue)			
204 (Woman at Risk)			

Index

R. Walters, *National Identity and Social Cohesion in a Time of Geopolitical and Economic Tension: Australia – European Union – Slovenia*,
https://doi.org/10.1007/978-981-15-2164-5